THE SACRED TREE OF THE SEPHIROTH

THE HOLY KABBALAH

By A. E. Waite

With an Introduction by Kenneth Rexroth

*A Study of the Secret Tradition in Israel
as unfolded by Sons of the Doctrine
for the Benefit and Consolation
of the Elect dispersed through
the Lands and Ages of
The Greater
Exile*

ISBN: 978-1-63923-098-3

All Rights reserved. No part of this book maybe
reproduced without written permission from the publishers, except by a reviewer who may quote brief passages in a review to be printed in a newspaper or magazine.

Printed:

Cover Art By: Paul Amid

Published and Distributed By:
Lushena Books
607 Country Club Drive, Unit E
Bensenville, IL 60106
www.lushenabks.com

ISBN: 978-1-63923-098-3

Printed in the United States of America

THE HOLY KABBALAH

By A. E. Waite

With an Introduction by Kenneth Rexroth

*A Study of the Secret Tradition in Israel
as unfolded by Sons of the Doctrine
for the Benefit and Consolation
of the Elect dispersed through
the Lands and Ages of
The Greater
Exile*

UNIVERSITY BOOKS　　New Hyde Park, New York

1960

COPYRIGHT © NEW MATERIAL
BY UNIVERSITY BOOKS, INC., NEW HYDE PARK, NEW YORK

Originally Published by
Williams and Norgate, London, 1929

THE
HOLY
KABBALAH

INTRODUCTION

by KENNETH REXROTH

There is singularly little on Jewish mysticism of any sort to be found in English. Furthermore, most of it is not very rewarding. Much of it is definitely antagonistic. However Routledge published long ago, 1910 in fact, a book, *Aspects of the Hebrew Genius*, edited by Leon Simon, a collection of essays once given as lectures in the North London Jewish Literary Union. There is a chapter on Jewish mysticism by H. Sperling, and in the very first paragraph he says these tremendous words: "They (the vague mystical yearnings of man) can, however, fitly be compared to that invisible chain that binds husband to wife, parents to children, relation to relation, friend to friend, social unit to social unit. Without these lesser mysticisms society would dissolve into its first atoms; without the larger mysticism man would break away from his Maker and be flung into nothingness." On these words hang all the Law and the Prophets. This is the essence of Judaism. It is also the essence of Jewish mysticism, whether the speculations of Hellenistic Neo-Platonists. Medieval Kabbalists, Polish or Levantine Hasidim, or the sophisticated and fashionable philosophy of Martin Buber.

Kabbalism and Hasidism seem, to a Christian taught in his own religion to view Gnostic and theosophic tendencies as the source of all heresy, to be a kind of Jewish heterodoxy. They are not. Jewish orthodoxy is not defined by the correctness of the answers it gives to metaphysical and cosmological questions. The Torah, the Rites of Passage, the Ceremonies of the Holidays, the poetic and narrative books of the Bible, philosophy and fantasy, from Maimonides to Isaak Singer — the consensus of faith is never broken. Kabbalism is nothing but a transcendental way of looking at the "purely formal" rites of Circumcision, Marriage, Confirmation. There is no

"Kabbalistic Mystery," however profound, that cannot be found, clearly and simply exemplified in the ceremonies of Succoth, the Feast of Tabernacles.

Under the influence of millenia of legalistic interpretation of the Law, and guided by the extreme rationalism of Maimonides and other Jewish scholastics, Judaism has come to seem, at least to the outsider, a "religion of the Book" in the most extreme sense, a code, rather than living faith. This is illusory. All the Talmuds in the world cannot make a religion. Religion is what people do—act and contemplation. Whitehead said it was what man does with his aloneness—a very Protestant, in fact, Lutheran statement, and the expression of a theory rather than of actuality. Even the most extreme neo-Lutheran, Kierkegaard, spent much of his time and energy struggling with the community of the Church of Denmark. The casuistry of rabbis, the exhortations of prophets—we must never forget that these take place in the context of a people, held together in a rite. That, after all is their only significance—to insure the integrity of the people and the continuity of the rite.

Someone back in the nineteenth century said that religion is what humanity uses to fill in the gap between technology and the physical environment. Historically this was certainly true. But it is a kind of inverse and diminishing definition. Ideally, religion is what would be left after man *knew* everything. Kabbalism, like all other Gnosticisms, does concern itself very much with knowing, with cosmology and cosmogony, the nature and process of the Universe. "You shall know and the knowledge shall make you free." Free for what? Today we are inclined to forget how trapped man was by the recalcitrance of his environment, by puzzling vagaries of the universe. Before the universe could be given significance— "valued" as we say nowadays—it had to be given coherence. Gnosticism has been accused by its opponents, from Plotinus to the present, of equating coherence and significance, structure and value. This may be true where Gnostic movements have been heretical—split off and isolated from the main body of religious development. Kabbalism is not heterodox. It is a symbolic and aesthetic elaboration of the actual cult of Israel, with which it never loses contact. The Jewish *Prayerbook* as we have it today is essentially a Kabbalistic

INTRODUCTION

document.* "*Credere est orare, orare est cognoscere,*" said the great Roman Catholic modernist, Father Tyrell, "To believe is to pray, to pray is to know."

When man cannot understand nature, and insofar as he cannot understand it at any point, he is confronted with an actual vacuum, and into this he projects himself. What is sought in Alchemy or the Hermetic Books or the Memphite Theology, or irrational fads like flying saucers, is the basic pattern of the human mind in symbolic garb, as it presents itself in the individual believer, and behind that, in the enduring structures of the human organism itself. As the speculative constructions of religion fall away as explanations of "reality" they assume the character of symbolic masks of states of the soul. If they persist in the practices of a cult, we say they have been etherealized. It is precisely their irrationality which keeps dogma and ritual alive. If they can be reduced to "common sense" explanations or denials they die away. Only the mysteries survive, because they correspond to the processes of man's internal life, outward visible signs of inner spiritual realities.

To go back to the beginning, Kabbalism dates back into the most obscure past of Judaism. What are the distinguishing ideas of Kabbalism? It is first of all a theory of emanations ("degenerative monism" it is called philosophically). The inscrutable Godhead fills and contains the universe. To become active and creative God emanated ten *sephiroth* or intelligences. A special prominence is given to one of these emanations, who functions as a female principle in the Deity, a demiurge and a term to creation. This is the final emanation, Malkuth the Queen, the physical manifestation of Deity in the universe. She is thought of as a Divine Woman, the Bride of God (like the Shakti of Shiva). Finally, the "innermost secrets" of the Kabbalah are what are "occult" in all occultism, erotic mysticism and a group of practices of the sort we call yoga—autonomic nervous system gymnastics. For the Kabbalist the ultimate sacrament is the sexual act, carefully organized and sustained as the most perfect mystical trance. Over the marriage bed hovers the Shekinah. Kabbalism

*This Prayerbook—*Siddur*—is not something relegated to Sabbath service in the Synagogue. Both man and woman use it day and night. What the Bible was to the Protestant in the great days of Dissent, this grimoire of Kabbalah is to the orthodox Jew and his wife.

also includes, of course, a group of divinatory and magical practices, manipulations of the alphabet and the text of the Pentateuch, magic spells and rites. All of these elements go back to very early days—to the beginnings of Israel in Palestine, and it is these beginnings which shed most light on both scholarly Kabbalism and popular Hasidism, and, in addition, go far to illuminate the real—the abiding spiritual meaning—of Judaism in all times and places.

By and large the special details of Kabbalism which distinguish it from the mainstreams of Jewish thought are what is "occult" in occultism everywhere, and most of the world's religions can be reinterpreted in these terms. They give Kabbalism its fascination but they do not give it its substance. As A. E. Waite so well points out—beneath the glittering and mysterious superstructure of the Kabbalah, which purports to be occult Judaism, lies—Judaism.

Kabbalism is probably the only religious movement of the Gnostic type to come full circle in this fashion, to create mysteries and explain them, to hide secrets and discover them, and come at last back to the greater mystery from which it started, but with deeper insights and wider knowledge. Insight and knowledge of what? In the last analysis of the human soul, of man within himself, united with another in marriage, united with his fellows in love. I suppose certain tendencies and individuals in Catholicism have done the same thing. Bonaventura is a sort of enraptured, orthodox Gnostic. There is the Protestant, Jacob Boehme. In modern times there have been all sorts of rationalizing, philosophizing, psychologizing movements which have in fact accomplished similar ends, from the Theosophists and A. E. Waite himself to Martin Buber and Carl Jung. These are different—either eccentric individuals or modern sophisticated cults. Whoever wrote or gathered and edited the tracts of the *Zohar*, Kabbalism shows all the signs of being a perfectly natural, Near Eastern Gnostic movement, evolved directly from the local soil, the "clerkly lore" of an "anthropological religion."

It might be wise to note some of these sources. Emanationism is found in the socalled "Memphite Theology," a text dating back to the beginnings of Egyptian civilization. Four pairs of gods emanate from Ptah in a hierarchy of power, and the creative process is described in language which still echoes

INTRODUCTION

in the Gospel of John. The very word "Isis" means "throne" and many of her attributes survive in the terms applied to the Shekinah, to Malkuth, to the personified Wisdom of Proverbs and finally, in the titles of the Litany of the Blessed Virgin. Pre-Hebraic Palestine is full of Els (Elohim) and Ba'als (Adonai, the Lord) and they all have consorts, at once wives, daughters and mothers—Asherah, Anat, Astarte, Ashtaroth. In Egypt they were identified with Isis, with Hathor, and with Sekmet, wife and daughter of Ptah, the ultimate creator. In the fifth century we discover Anat in an Aramaic Elephantine papyrus specifically described as the consort of Yahweh.

Asherah survives in the Scriptures as a term for the phallic pillars, *mazzeboth*, which stood beside the altars and in the holy places until the fall of the Temple. But she also survives in person and the story of Elijah is the tale of a bitter struggle with Jezebel, a regal priestess of Ba'al-Asherah. Temples of Asherah and Yahweh stood side by side in ninth century Mizpah. In the seventh century Jeremiah found children in the streets of Jerusalem gathering wood and the fathers kindling the fire and the women kneading the dough to make cakes for the Queen of Heaven. The sacred prostitutes and sodomites of the Goddess appear again and again in the Scriptures. The First Isaiah begets a son with a *zonah*—called a "prophetess" in the King James Version, Jephthah is the son of a *zonah*, Hosea's description of his relations with a sacred prostitute are amongst the most cryptic in the Bible and as late as the mid seventh century, under Manasseh, the cult was flourishing. With the Assyrian and later Babylonian and then Persian conquests, Ishtar was substituted for Ashteroth, and, as has been pointed out time and again, the *Book of Esther* (simply another English transliteration of Ishtar) is an elaborate euhemerization of the Spring New Year fertility rites and the *heirosgamos*, the sacred marriage—as the folk rites of Purim are paralleled all over the world at the season.

The most likely interpretation of the *Song of Songs* is that it is a collection of songs for group marriage rites, focused in the *heirosgamos* of priestking and priestess, which accompanied the opening of the irrigation channels from the main ditches into the dry fields. In fact, a book which casts great light on the Song of Songs is Granet's *Festivals and Songs of*

Ancient China, an interpretation of the erotic songs of the ancient Chinese collection, the *Shi Ching.* Do not misunderstand, this parallelism does not "prove" diffusion from some imagined prehistoric religious center. It shows the fundamental identity of man's response to the great rhythms of life. Nothing is more illuminating than to look up "Shekinah" or "Succoth" or "Wisdom" or "Power" or for that matter any of the other epithets of the *Sephiroth* in a good Biblical Concordance, and ponder on the mysterious sentences. Do they just seem mysterious because our attention, with minds full of presuppositions, has been directed to them? I think not. These words are keys which unlock some of the oldest material in the Scriptures, and they survive because of their traditional sanctity. The post-Esdras editors, working over the old documents, might disguise them, but they did not dare omit them, any more than they dared wipe out the memory of the sacred groves and the pillar circles and the high places. At last the Samaritan Gnostic, Simon Magus, with his consort, the Mystic Helen, a temple prostitute out of Ephesus of the great Mother, comes to meet and struggle with the earliest Christians.

Now, we must understand that we have come to view "orthodoxy" after millenia of narrowing definition. To some extent the prophets, some of them, were "orthodox" in this way, or at least they were so represented after the Persian period. But the people knew nothing about these questions. Religion for them was the whole body of cult *acts*, it was what they *did*. We think of such conflicts in terms of Athanasius vs. Arrius, Dominicans vs. Albigensians, Calvin vs. Servetus, Massachusetts vs. the Quakers and witches, and the deliberations of Senator McCarthy's Committee. They were nothing of the sort. True, the prophetic movement in Judaism and later the Rabbinical schools, represent the slow evolution of such sharpening distinctions and the purging of old practices. But the average inhabitant of Palestine went right on practicing religion as he found it in place—there—in the cult of his ancestors, and even the evolution of Yahvistic monotheism was an enormously drawn out process. The ancient folk ways have never vanished from Judaism, even at its most reformed, and today—the day I am actually writing this—Purim, C. E. 1960—customs whose broken relics we find at the very bottom of mounds of ruins in the Holy Land linger on in the parlors of the thoroughly assimilated and Americanized "High Society" of San Francisco where I live.

Last night I went to a celebration of the hundredth anniversary of one of the city's most fashionable Congregations — an oratorio — a *Purimspiel* — *Queen Esther,* given to a packed Opera House, with a very Nordic looking Esther. At the reception afterwards the President of the Congregation said, opening his speech, "This is the happiest day of my life," and the Rabbi interrupted, "How about your marriage?" This was a joke, a wisecrack as American as anything on television — and it brought as much laughter from the audience. But it was something more, and it somehow elicited a slightly different kind of stir — an undercurrent that wouldn't have been there with a Gentile audience. That spontaneous joke had touched one of the great nerve centers of Jewry, the Sacrament of Israel, watched over and nourished under the wings of the Shekinah, that gesture, the physical embodiment of the turn in the creative process, the moment at which all being, having reached its last term, begins its long return to the inscrutable and holy center from which it came. On the buffet, along with champagne and caviar were *hamanohren.*

A. E. Waite was an odd fish out of an odder barrel. He was not only one of the few persons in modern times, Jew or Gentile, to write a sensible and sound book on Kabbalah. He was a genuine scholar of occultism who himself came out of the welter of occult sects and movements of the end of the last century. He lived in the world of Eliphas Levi, Stanislas de Guaita, "Papus," Sar Peladan, Mme. Blavatsky, A. P. Sinnett, Macgregor Mathers, Wynn Westcott, Annie Besant, and "Archbishop" Leadbeater, and more American oddities and rascals than you could shake a stick at. Some of these people are genuine literary curiosities and still make fascinating reading. Others are unbelievably fraudulent and silly. But, to a man, they are mines of misinformation, rash hypotheses and unsupportable conclusions. They are as far from being scholars as could well be imagined. It is a pity that they all, the whole movement, have never become the subjects of scholarship on a large and really serious scale, because they certainly do represent, like the Marxists or the Neo-Catholics, a significant mass movement of the human mind in its long march out of folly. The subjects they were all interested in are amongst the most interesting subjects for scholarship that exist, but they produced only two scholars, A. E. Waite and G. R. S. Mead. Mead was a Theosophist, and hence suspect in the halls of scholarship, but his is still the only readable translation of the Hermetic literature in English, he edited a Gnostic tractate, the *Pistis Sophia*, and he wrote an estimable book on Gnosticism, *Fragments of a Faith Forgotten*. There is nothing specially odd or cultish about any of these books. In contrast, the acceptably academic translation of the Hermetica, by Scott, is the work of a Higher Critic, and is a violent, shameless, distortion of the text.

Waite *was* odd, cultish and eccentric. He wrote the most dreadful prose conceivable, an awful mixture of Walter Pater, Cardinal Newman, Arthur Machen and plain vulgar pretentiousness. It is the last survival of the last spasms of literary PreRaphaelitism. Fortunately, though it was common in its day there is nothing left around to compare it with except Sebastian Evan's *High History of the Holy Grail* still to be found on shelves of out of print Everyman's Library, and William Morris' slightly lunatic translation of the Icelandic Sagas into a kind of PreRaphaelite studio code, today utterly unreadable. Waite, however, is not unreadable. You have to read between the balderdash, but it is easy to get used to. Soon you no longer notice it, and he does have, almost always, something very interesting to say. At last the absurd rituals he uses to say the simplest things come to endear him to you, like the wen on grandma's nose.

In his autobiography, Waite gives the impression that his books all came more or less by accident, as assignments from publishers. I rather doubt that, because throughout his life he seems to have followed a definite program. Eventually, and it certainly seems, systematically, he came to cover all the main aspects or traditions or myths of occultism. His works include: *The Secret Tradition in Alchemy, The Brotherhood of the Rosy Cross, The Secret Tradition in Freemasonry, The Hidden Church of the Holy Grail, The Pictorial Key to the Tarot, Raymund Lull, Louis Saint Martin*, and careful editions of the works of Eliphas Levi and the greatest of the English mystical alchemists, Thomas Vaughan, whose works are mysteriously missing from the bibliographies of Dr. Jung's many books on this subject. Besides all this he wrote a lot of dreadful poetry full of Mystic Veils and Clinking Thuribles, and a couple of general statements of his own philosophy — as well as a rather cobwebby autobiography. Self-evidently this is a program, a carefully planned work of a lifetime. The remarkable thing about it is that, coming although it does from an era of windy nonsense and smoky pretence, there is nothing seriously wrong with it. They are all books of wide, painstaking scholarship. Waite went to all the sources he could find, in itself a Herculean labor, and he exposed all the errors of quotation and interpretation in the secondary sources that he could uncover. He is almost always right. Not only is he right, but he never loses, however dear to his heart may be the misty mid-regions of Weir in which he wanders, the true scientific scholar's scepticism. In fact, since he was himself the leader of a "Mystic Circle of Seekers for Illumination," who took his somewhat absurd vows very seriously, he uses this very scholars' scepticism as a mask and a refuge. On the question of the very existence of "Spiritual Alchemy," let alone on the sexual yoga, so plainly illustrated in Chinese works on the subject, for which most alchemy is just a kind of double talk, Waite is non-committal. He leads you to the sources, quotes and analyzes them for you, and leaves you to draw your own conclusions. So likewise with the Grail legend, so with Rosicrucianism, so with occult Freemasonry, so with that *I Ching* of the Western World, the Tarot cards — he strips away the nonsense, exposes the facts, and leaves you to draw your own conclusions. With charlatans he is merciless. Although he is in a sense a product of the school of Eliphas Levi, he never misses a chance to expose the pretensions of that most fascinating of mountebanks. With St. Martin or Lull he is careful, even reverent, although he does an excellent job of taking apart the complicated Lull legend.

The Holy Kabbalah is his greatest work. Although he was a kind of Christian, even a sort of Liberal Catholic, Kabbalah is, out of all the past, the closest thing to his own philosophy. He wrote three books on the subject, each later one incorporating and correcting its predecessors. He seems to have read everything he could find on the subject in every language he knew, and meditated on it deeply and long. It has been said that he did not read Hebrew, but I doubt this. There is much in *The Holy Kabbalah* which he could not have found in Knorr von Rosenroth's *Kabbalah Desnudata*, or in the very unsatisfactory French translation of the *Zohar*, the only comprehensive expositions of the Kabbalah itself available to him in any other language than Hebrew. No other Gentile writer on Kabbalism can even remotely be compared to him, and no modern Jewish writers are any better. We have to go back to the great *zaddikim* of Hassidism to find such a thorough Kabbalist, and they, alas, present altogether too many problems of their own to be readily assimilated by anyone in the twentieth century. Kabbalism is the great poem of Judaism, a tree of symbolic jewels showing forth the doctrine of the universe as the vesture of Deity, of the community as the embodiment of Deity, and of love as the acting of God in man. Nobody knew this better than A. E. Waite.

ANALYSIS OF CONTENTS

PREFACE

The Kabbalah as Esoteric Philosophy—Origin in Christian Centuries—Importance and Connections—Design of the present work—Its precursors in England—Kabbalistic MSS. purchased by Picus de Mirandula—Their identity with the chief text of the Secret Tradition in Israel—SEPHER HA ZOHAR—The Christian construction which he sought to place upon them—The SEPHER YETZIRAH and its translation by William Postel—The Kabbalah and Cornelius Agrippa—John Reuchlin and Messianic Doctrine in Kabbalism—Petrus Galatinus on the same subject—Paulus Riccius on the Law of Moses and the Law of Christ—How these writers sought to prove from Kabbalism that the Christ had come—Motive of the study which follows—The students to whom it appeals—The question of Secret Tradition—A Secret Doctrine of Religion—Vestiges of a Great Spiritual Experiment—Records of a Theosophical School in Jewry—A Preliminary Statement on the Age of the Records.

BOOK I
POST-CHRISTIAN LITERATURE OF THE JEWS
ARGUMENT

The literature of Kabbalism is mainly of historical interest for ordinary students of philosophy, while students of Scriptural exegesis will find therein a field of research only into very curious extravagances of the human mind. It has a living interest only for two classes, and firstly for those who believe (*a*) that a Secret Religious Tradition has been perpetuated from the past; (*b*) that the literature in question has served as one of its vehicles. It is customary to describe such persons as esoteric or occult students, because in most cases they are so denominated by themselves. One purpose among others of this initial book is to shew that their equipment in respect of textual and other knowledge is not only insufficient to maintain the claim but is of a kind which exposes it to ridicule in respect of the particular alleged vehicle in the sense that their claim implies. Kabbalism, however, by its hypothesis is a Doctrine of Religion transmitted in secret, though it does not contribute evidence for a Universal Religious Tradition, and so far as it is concerned therefore the actuality or otherwise of the latter remains an open question. The second class for whom Kabbalism possesses a living interest is those who are concerned, for what reason soever, with the records of mystical experience in the union of the soul with God and believe that the literature is a part of these records. The main object of the present inquiry is to determine whether they are right.

		PAGE
I.	THE HIDDEN CHURCH OF ISRAEL	3
II.	FOLLIES OF OCCULT EXEGESIS	21
III.	THE KABBALAH AND THE TALMUD	26
IV.	DIVISIONS OF THE KABBALAH	33

BOOK II

SOURCE AND AUTHORITY OF THE KABBALAH AND THE AGE OF THE CHIEF TEXTS

ARGUMENT

The two chief cycles of Kabbalistic literature, in spite of destructive criticism, are referable to Talmudic or early post-Talmudic times, as regards sources and inspiration. There seems indeed no reason why the BOOK OF FORMATION should not derive from R. Akiba, as tradition affirms. There is no real evidence in support of the theory that R. Moses de Leon wrote the ZOHAR or BOOK OF SPLENDOUR towards the end of the thirteenth century. At the same time the opinion of a few students, not too well accredited and not adequately equipped, that these works are of great antiquity or at least pre-Christian must be set aside decisively. The attempts which refer the Kabbalah in any direct manner to some prior theosophical system must be rejected also: it has antecedents everywhere, but its analogies with other systems are explained mainly by natural likeness between independent views on fundamental problems of being. Antecedent Jewish influence through Aristobulus and Philo must not be overlooked, but also it must not be exaggerated. The Kabbalah is *sui generis*. It has many accidental connections, but fundamentally it is of and from within a school of thought in Jewry. If there be any preponderance in a given direction, the records suggest that its wider sphere of influence has been on Christian rather than on Jewish minds.

		PAGE
I.	DATE OF THE BOOK OF FORMATION	41
II.	MODERN CRITICISM OF THE BOOK OF SPLENDOUR	45
III.	THE DATE AND AUTHORSHIP OF THE BOOK OF SPLENDOUR	51
IV.	THE AGE OF ZOHARIC TRADITION	59
V.	ALLEGED SOURCES OF KABBALISTIC DOCTRINE	64
VI.	ISLAMIC CONNECTIONS OF THE KABBALAH	75
VII.	INFLUENCE OF THE KABBALAH ON JEWRY	80

BOOK III

THE WRITTEN WORD OF KABBALISM: FIRST PERIOD

ARGUMENT

The subject-matters of Kabbalistic literature outside the SEPHER YETZIRAH, and prior to the appearance of the ZOHAR, are surveyed briefly, to indicate that there was a growth of the Tradition and to correct exaggerated notions concerning it. There are various old tracts which connect with Kabbalism but are not regarded by some modern scholarship as Kabbalistic in the technical sense. This is the case with the SEPHER YETZIRAH itself; but there is no doubt that all such works laid claim upon oral knowledge transmitted from the past, or that it was the elements of such Oral Tradition which received developments subsequently from the commentators on SEPHER YETZIRAH, as well as from the ZOHAR, and, at a much later period, from expositors of Zoharic teaching. The attention of early Kabbalists was concentrated on the BOOK OF FORMA-

TION, and several elucidations of that work appeared between the eleventh and thirteenth centuries, under notable names.

		PAGE
I.	EARLY KABBALISTIC LITERATURE	87
II.	THE BOOK OF FORMATION	98
III.	CONNECTIONS AND DEPENDENCIES OF THE BOOK OF FORMATION	103

BOOK IV

THE WRITTEN WORD OF KABBALISM: SECOND PERIOD

ARGUMENT

The text-proper of the ZOHAR and its numerous connections are examined in successive sections, in order to furnish a comprehensive notion of the materials incorporated by this composite work, prior to the study of its Doctrines at a later stage in detail. A certain prominence is given to their intimations from a mystical or theosophical point of view.

		PAGE
I.	THE BOOK OF SPLENDOUR: ITS CONTENT AND DIVISIONS	115
II.	THE BOOK OF CONCEALMENT	134
III.	THE GREATER HOLY SYNOD	139
IV.	THE LESSER HOLY SYNOD	146
V.	THE DISCOURSE OF THE AGED MAN	147
VI.	THE LUMINOUS BOOK	150
VII.	THE FAITHFUL SHEPHERD	157
VIII.	HIDDEN THINGS OF THE LAW	163
IX.	THE SECRET COMMENTARY	167
X.	MINOR TRACTS OF THE ZOHAR	169
	A. The Omissions	169
	B. The Additions	170
	C. Repetitions	172
	D. The Secret of Secrets	173
	E. The Discourse of the Young Man	174
	F. The Mansions or Abodes	175
	G. The Commentary on Ruth	177
XI.	THE ANCIENT AND LATER SUPPLEMENTS	179

BOOK V

THE DOCTRINAL CONTENT OF THE KABBALAH IN RESPECT OF GOD AND THE UNIVERSE

ARGUMENT

The Fundamental Doctrines of the Kabbalah are shewn to be (1) A Philosophy of the Absolute; (2) The evolution of the universe in part by way of emanation and in part by creative acts; (3) The distinction of the evolution into four worlds, the last of which was brought into being by a process of making. The subsidiary Theosophies connected with these subjects are (1) The contrast between God in Himself and God as revealed to His people, that is, to finite intelligence; (2) The sacramental nature of the conventional symbols in which the human Logos is formulated; (3) The way of attainment in respect of human knowledge and wisdom in Divine Things.

		PAGE
I.	THE MAJESTY OF GOD IN KABBALISM	185
II.	THE TEN SEPHIROTH	191
III.	THE DOCTRINE OF THE FOUR WORLDS	196
IV.	THE PATHS OF WISDOM AND GATES OF UNDERSTANDING	213
V.	THE DOCTRINE OF COSMOLOGY	219

BOOK VI

HIERARCHIES OF SPIRITUAL BEING

ARGUMENT

The Doctrine concerning the soul of man is of great importance in Kabbalism, for man in reality is the centre about which the whole Tradition revolves. We must have recourse to the great text of the ZOHAR for all vital intimations on the parts, divisions or states of the human soul, its pre-existence and its destiny. The developments thereof and the commentaries arising therefrom may be useful for occasional tabulations, but they add nothing of living consequence. It is otherwise concerning the Choirs of Angels and Kabbalistic Demonology: in the main they are of and belonging to that Third Period of the Written Word which will be dealt with in Book IX. The ZOHAR is casual and inchoate on these subjects, except regarding the Fall of the Angels, which will be considered in a section apart. The later Kabbalists drew materials from the TALMUDS to build up their formulated scheme of Celestial and Infernal Hierarchies.

		PAGE
I.	THE SOUL IN KABBALISM	235
II.	ANGELS AND DEMONS	253

BOOK VII

WAYS OF GOD WITH MAN

ARGUMENT

It is shewn that the Biblical Mythos concerning the Earthly Paradise is a Mystery of Sex in the mind of the Secret Tradition. The Fall of the Angels connects indirectly enough with this obscure subject, but it was responsible, *ex hypothesi*, for all uncleanness subsequently on earth and in man. It comes about in this manner that the Fall of Man belongs to the same Mystery, is developed as such at great length and with numerous variations. The wickedness which was " great upon the earth," which broke up " the fountains of the great deep " and opened " the windows of heaven " in the Deluge Legend was an iniquity of sex aberration; and even the subsequent sacrifice of Noah, " a sweet savour " to the Lord, was sanctified and acceptable because of its high intent respecting the Supreme Mystery. There is little need to dwell upon the Covenant with Abraham in this connection; but the foundation of the whole subject is said to abide therein. It is obvious also that the Law promulgated on Sinai was not apart therefrom; but the history of Moses is itself a history of spiritual espousals. When the time came for a House of the Lord to be built in Zion the Great Mystery in its transcendence was illustrated by the presence of Shekinah in the Holy of Holies, as a Bride in the abode of her Spouse. Finally, the Advent of Messiah, the Divine Son of the Secret Tradition, the letter VAU in the Sacred Name of Four Letters, is to raise up her who is His Bride in exile and to prepare for the Sabbath of creation, which is a period of true bridals.

		PAGE
I.	THE MYTH OF THE EARTHLY PARADISE	261
II.	THE SERPENT, SON OF THE MORNING, AND FALL OF THE ANGELS	269
III.	THE FALL OF MAN	277
IV.	THE LEGEND OF THE DELUGE	290
V.	THE COVENANT WITH ABRAHAM	296
VI.	OF MOSES, THE MASTER OF THE LAW	303
VII.	THE TEMPLES IN JERUSALEM	312
VIII.	THE COMING OF MESSIAH	316
IX.	THE DOCTRINE CONCERNING SHEOL	324
X.	CONCERNING RESURRECTION	332

BOOK VIII
THE HIGHER SECRET DOCTRINE

ARGUMENT

The Secret Doctrine of the ZOHAR concerning the Holy Shekinah is the Mystery of Sex at its highest and she herself is the Mystery of the Oral Law. It is intimated that behind this Mystery there appears to be an authentic doctrine of Knowledge, based on experience. We are led on in this manner to a more particular study of the Mystery of Sex in the light of the Secret Tradition, and there is a sense in which it is still a study of Shekinah. It is suggested that there is or may be a Mystery of Human Nuptials behind it which has not been conceived by the heart of man in ordinary ways of life.

		PAGE
I.	THE MYSTERY OF SHEKINAH	341
II.	THE MYSTERY OF SEX	377

BOOK IX
THE WRITTEN WORD OF KABBALISM: THIRD PERIOD

ARGUMENT

The growth of Kabbalistic literature is sketched in certain expository works or commentaries on the ZOHAR and in some independent tracts which connect with the general Tradition. Two other works are chosen for separate consideration, being one on the Mysteries of Love, because of its general diffusion, and one on the application of Kabbalistic Apparatus to Alchemy, because of the credit which it has obtained in the modern school of Hermetic students.

		PAGE
I.	EXPOSITORS OF THE ZOHAR	409
	A. Moses of Cordova	410
	B. Isaac de Loria	412
	C. Napthali Hirtz	420
	D. Abraham Cohen Irira	422
	E. Issachar ben Napthali	423

		PAGE
II.	THE BOOK OF PURIFYING FIRE	424
III.	THE MYSTERIES OF LOVE	428
IV.	MINOR LITERATURE OF KABBALISM	432

BOOK X

SOME CHRISTIAN STUDENTS OF THE KABBALAH

ARGUMENT

The opinion of certain modern writers—chiefly of Victorian days—that the Kabbalah is a vehicle of a Secret Doctrine concerning Absolute Religion was never held in the past, more especially as it proves on examination not only to be utterly distinct from the claim of Israel in respect of its Secret Tradition but a spurious Liberal Religion or qualified Natural Theology. Even those who ascribed the Kabbalah of old to a Divine Source were actuated chiefly by the notion that it was a disguised Christianity, and in several cases their real concern was the conversion of Jewry by its presentation from this standpoint. The chief Christian students of the subjects are reviewed in succession to establish these facts. Some minor misconceptions are corrected and some extrinsic points of interest are developed in the course of the sketches.

		PAGE
I.	INTRODUCTORY	437
II.	RAYMUND LULLY	438
III.	PICUS DE MIRANDULA	442
IV.	CORNELIUS AGRIPPA	452
V.	PARACELSUS	455
VI.	JOHN REUCHLIN	458
VII.	WILLIAM POSTEL	461
VIII.	THE ROSICRUCIANS	465
IX.	ROBERT FLUDD	467
X.	HENRY MORE	470
XI.	THOMAS VAUGHAN	473
XII.	KNORR VON ROSENROTH	476
XIII.	RALPH CUDWORTH	480
XIV.	THOMAS BURNET	482
XV.	SAINT-MARTIN	486
XVI.	ÉLIPHAS LÉVI	487
XVII.	TWO ACADEMICAL CRITICS	494
XVIII.	THE MODERN SCHOOL OF FRENCH KABBALISM	498
	A. Papus	500
	B. Stanislas de Guaita	503
	C. Léon Meurin, S.J.	505
XIX.	THE KABBALAH AND ESOTERIC CHRISTIANITY	507
XX.	THE KABBALAH AND MODERN THEOSOPHY	510

BOOK XI

THE KABBALAH AND OTHER CHANNELS OF SECRET TRADITION

ARGUMENT

Modern speculations on the part of believers have represented the alleged Secret Sciences as vehicles of a Great Occult Tradition; but the question lies beyond the limits of the present inquiry, which can estimate only the quality and extent of the influence exercised by Kabbalism on other departments of "esoteric thought" in the West. It is found that this influence has been magnified. In the case of Ceremonial Magic it has been unquestionably large, but very small in that of Alchemy and Astrology. Freemasonry has been regarded also as a channel of Secret Tradition, but its connection with Kabbalism is at once adventitious and slight. Among arts of divination, the claims of certain picture-symbols, known as Tarot cards, have been presented as a Key to Kabbalistic Doctrine and Tradition; but they are dismissed for specific reasons. As a conclusion to the subject of other Channels of Secret Tradition, the Doctrine of Pure Mysticism is contrasted with that of Kabbalism, and the points reached by the investigation are brought into a single focus.

		PAGE
I.	THE KABBALAH AND MAGIC	517
II.	THE KABBALAH AND ALCHEMY	534
III.	THE KABBALAH AND ASTROLOGY	542
IV.	THE KABBALAH AND FREEMASONRY	548
V.	THE KABBALAH AND THE TAROT	554
VI.	THE KABBALAH AND MYSTICISM	557

BOOK XII

FINAL CONSIDERATIONS

ARGUMENT

A brief recurrence to developments of later Kabbalism introduces a study of recent contributions to the scholarship of the whole subject and a word on its chief findings. The question of Christian elements imbedded in the ZOHAR as in a doctrinal system is considered at some length and dismissed. There arises in fine the living question whether and in what manner the Secret Doctrine of Israel can be held to affect mystics at the present day. It is surveyed in respect of that branch which deals with the Mystery of Sex, but afterwards in that of the Doctrine that the soul comes forth from God and that to God the soul returns. The conclusion is that Zoharic Kabbalism, under the veils of its proper symbolism, offers a living message to those whom it concerns.

		PAGE
I.	DEVELOPMENTS OF LATER KABBALISM	563
II.	THE ALLEGED CHRISTIAN ELEMENTS	574
III.	CONCLUSION ON JEWISH THEOSOPHY	588

APPENDIX I

SEPHIROTIC DEVELOPMENTS 605

XXIV ANALYSIS OF CONTENTS

PAGE

APPENDIX II

THE FOUR WORLDS IN LATER KABBALISM 610

APPENDIX III

THE INSTRUMENTS OF CREATION 612

APPENDIX IV

DIVINE NAMES 617

APPENDIX V

PHASES OF THE SOUL 619

INDEX 621

PREFACE

FEW educated persons, and certainly none belonging to the class of students for which this work is designed more especially, will require to be told that the Kabbalah is a form of Esoteric Philosophy, that it makes for itself a high claim, or that this claim has been admitted, from time to time, by persons who are entitled to our consideration. Nor will it be needful to state that the literature called Kabbalistic rose up among the Jews during the Christian centuries which succeeded their dispersal and the destruction of their Holy City. It offers a strong contrast to the sacred scriptures of Israel, which are direct, beautiful and simple, while Kabbalism is involved, obscure and even repellent occasionally, as regards its outward form. The Bible is in focus with humanity; the Kabbalah is distorted out of all correspondence with the simple senses, and we must grind our intellectual lenses with exceeding care if we would bring it into perspective.

From whatever point of view it may be approached, the Kabbalah is, however, of importance: it connects with other literatures which are included like itself under the general denomination of mystical, and there is a sense in which it has been thought, in its highest development, to stand at the head of all. It is part of the history of philosophy, and as such it entered once into the thought of Europe. It is responsible in its degeneration for all that strange tissue of symbolism and procedure which made up the Ceremonial and Philosophical Magic of the fourteenth to the seventeenth centuries; at a comparatively late period it entered into the story of Alchemy; it tinctured many of those conventional practices and beliefs which are called superstitious in our loose fashion of words, and the guise in which we know them is very often a Kabbalistic guise. Were it possible to suppose for a moment that behind Magic, behind Alchemy and Astrology there were any mystery of real knowledge, then it would be entitled to peculiar respect, at least by the hypothesis of some of its defenders, because it is through this seemingly impassable literature that—in their view—the road to the secret lies. It is, however, on the theosophical side and as a contribution to the thought of the past on problems of life and mind that its appeal—if any—will be found at the present day.

A comprehensive account of the Kabbalah, on the surface expository and historical, but seeking to establish its connections with other forms of alleged Secret Tradition, to determine its influence and importance from more than one standpoint, and to shew forth its contribution to the sacred science of the soul, are the design of the present work, in which regard has been paid also to the limitations and requirements of English readers—in other words, of those unacquainted with the languages, dead and living, in which Kabbalistic literature has been, with few exceptions, available heretofore. The subject has been classed as abstruse and was presented by early expositors after a highly technical fashion: in this case there is no antecedent knowledge assumed in the reader. It is to be understood otherwise that this work has been written by a Christian Mystic and chiefly for the use of mystics; in offering materials for their judgment, it indicates also the lines of those conclusions to which the writer leans, and seeks to enforce some of them. It has been preceded in England by only two books dealing directly with the subject; one is the slight but not inconsiderable essay of Dr. Ginsburg,[1] which is critical rather than descriptive, and is, on the whole, hostile in its tendency. The second is by S. L. MacGregor Mathers,[2] but is mainly translation and commentary from Latin sources, and, in addition to other limitations, embraces only a minute portion of an extensive literature. The present comprehensive account fulfils a distinct purpose and, it is hoped, may be held to occupy a vacant place from which there is a wide prospect, by no means deficient in consequence for those even who are not mystics, for the student of philosophy and history, and for the curious in paths of literature which the elder D'Israeli, despite the bias of his birthright, forebore to enter.

---

[1] THE KABBALAH. By C. D. Ginsburg. London, 1865.
[2] THE KABBALAH UNVEILED, containing the following books of the Zohar: 1. THE BOOK OF CONCEALED MYSTERY; 2. THE GREATER HOLY ASSEMBLY; 3. THE LESSER HOLY ASSEMBLY, Translated into English from the Latin version of Knorr von Rosenroth, and collated with the original Chaldee and Hebrew Text. By S. L. MacGregor Mathers, London, 1887. The Commentary is partly that of Rosenroth, and partly the work of the translator. A new impression was published in 1926. I believe also that the essay of Dr. Ginsburg has been reissued in America.

The rumour of a great literature which had subsisted—*ex hypothesi*—from time immemorial in Jewry may not have been heard of first through a signal piece of good fortune which befell Picus de Mirandula in the fifteenth century, when he purchased, from an unknown Israelite, certain strange codices in manuscript; but nothing which came into his hands and proved to be a treasure of the past was likely to lie unnoticed on his own part; while this artist of the schools was a trumpet of fame for anything announced by his voice during the brilliant, too few years that he carried the quest of learning and the proof of his attainments from place to place in Europe. He was himself the pupil in Jewish Theosophy of Elias del Medigo, who filled a chair at Padua and wrote two treatises at the instance of Picus, one being on the Intellect and on Prophecy, in 1481–82, which seems to have remained unprinted and was written in Hebrew, like its companion DE SUBSTANTIA ORBIS, the work of 1485; but this appeared at Basle in 1629. It was edited also with a commentary by Isaac Reggio and so republished at Vienna in 1833.

Picus de Mirandula was in some sense a critic of his day, for he wrote upon the vanity of Astrology; but it was by no means a period which debated the authenticity of works referred to antiquity either by repute or by the simple audacity of claim, while it was still less concerned with polemics on questions of authorship. I believe that I have mentioned elsewhere how perilous it would have seemed then to have entered such a field of research. To deny in the particular case that, e.g., the ZOHAR—which is pre-eminently the chief text of Kabbalism—embodies the actual discourses of Rabbi Simeon ben Yohai might have been a prologue to impeaching the authorship of the Pentateuch—by which I mean that it would have opened such a vast speculative horizon that one might have suggested the other.

There came a time, and it was not far away, when the treasure of Picus was questioned, when people began to distinguish between a false and a true ZOHAR, the first as the work of one Moses de Leon, belonging to the late 13th century, and the second as something undemonstrable in respect of age and value. The distinction remains at a high point in the world of speculation, because no one has met with the second; and it might not be worth while to mention it in the present place, but it gives an opportunity of stating that the manuscripts purchased by Picus represented the identical work which has been known for six centuries and over under the name of SEPHER HA ZOHAR. An index of the codices acquired by him was published in 1651 by the French bibliographer Gaffarel,[1] and in the only full translation of the ZOHAR into a living language [2] its instalments are appended to the various sections. There are innumerable mistaken references, but the index reflects the text; what is missing in items referred to one section may be found sometimes in another; and though the pains of Gaffarel can in no wise be called representative as an attempted summary—it is not even the shadow—there is no question that the treasures of Picus are those which we know under the distinctive name of ZOHAR. There is no alternative text, and the differentiation given above is a supposition which can deceive no one.[3]

The contribution of Picus de Mirandula to the knowledge of the ZOHAR in Europe does not exceed to any considerable extent the simple fact of its existence. His Latin thesis on the subject cannot be termed representative, nor can anything else from his pen. It remains that he was the first Christian into whose hands the work came in any guise whatsoever, and it seems to have been that authoritative form which was represented later on by the Cremona and Mantua editions.[4] We may never know under what circumstances these were produced at their several dates,[5] and so far as I and others have been able to trace the bibliography of Kabbalism, it does

---

[1] Jacobus Gaffarel: CODICUM CABBALISTA EORUM MANUSCRIPTORUM QUIBUS EST USUS Joannes Picus, Comes Mirandulanus, INDEX, 1651.

[2] SEPHER HA ZOHAR (*Le Livre de la Splendeur*) *Doctrine Ésotérique des Israélites. Traduit pour la première fois sur le texte chaldaique.* ... par Jean de Pauly, 6 vols., 1906–1911.

[3] Curiously enough, the report has reached us through Richard Simon, the well-known author of HIST. CRITIQUE DU VIEUX TESTAMENT. See G. C. Sommer: SPECIMEN THEOLOGIÆ SOHARICÆ. It is of course within possibility that the statement mentioned above does not question the claims of the work published long after at Mantua and Cremona, but indicates that there was a false ZOHAR circulated by Moses de Leon and presumably now unknown.

[4] The edition of Mantua appeared in 1558 and that of Cremona almost coincidentally—1558–60. The latter is called bibliographically the GREAT ZOHAR because it contains certain tracts and fragments which are not found in the Mantua edition, whence the latter has been named the LITTLE ZOHAR. Other editions are those of Dublin, 1623; Amsterdam, 1714 and 1805; Constantinople, 1736; and Venice, with the date of which I am unacquainted.

[5] The Mantua edition appeared under the auspices of R. Meir ben Ephraim de Patavio and R. Jacob ben Napthali de Gazulo. See Julius Bartolocci: MAGNA BIBLIOTHECA RABBINICA, vol. iv, p. 416, col. 2, published at Rome in 1693. They were, however, the printers merely. See *Ib.*, p. 15, col. 2.

not appear that there is any earlier codex in manuscript. As he was the first to see the volumes, so Picus was the first to discern in the ZOHAR that it incorporated various elements which have been held capable of a Christian construction—whatever its value.[1] I shall deal with them at the close of the present study, when there will be something to say on the fact that the Christian predisposition of which Mirandula may be called the prototype became—almost without exception—the predisposition, the dedication indeed, of the *literati* who followed him, up to and including those who have translated and edited the French text. Picus passed away in his youth [2] or there are indications which lend colour to the possible realisation of his great dream that the Latin Pontificate itself, in the person of Pope Julius, might have lent an ear to his eloquence and done something to approach Israel from the standpoint of Christianity in Kabbalism.[3]

Well, it was after this manner that the work began to be known in Europe, and there passed something like a century away, after which the next name to our purpose is that of William Postel. It was he who translated the SEPHER YETZIRAH—or BOOK OF FORMATION—for the first time into Latin, and thus introduced to the curious and learned of Europe the root of all Kabbalism concerning the doctrine of the SEPHIROTH, the powers and virtues of the twenty-two Hebrew letters and the mystery which resides in numbers. I must not say that THE BOOK OF FORMATION is like that legendary grain of mustard which grows into a vast tree, because the ZOHAR is in no sense its development, except in so far as letters and numerations are concerned; but it ranks as the primitive text of accepted Kabbalistic doctrine in Israel, and the contribution of Postel to our knowledge—minute as it is—seems much more to our purpose than the detached and almost sporadic CONCLUSIONES KABBALISTICÆ of

---

[1] See his HEPTAPLUM, a sevenfold exposition concerning the six days of Genesis.—OPERA, 1572.

[2] He died at Florence in 1492.

[3] The points of correspondence observed by Picus de Mirandula led him to infer that the ZOHAR contains: (1) The Doctrine of the Holy Trinity, (2) The Fall of the Angels, (3) Original sin, understood as the Fall of Man, (4) The necessity of redemption, (5) The Incarnation of the Divine Word. With certain reserves in respect of the Trinity, and what is to be understood by redemption, these doctrines are not only to be found in the text, but are of continued recurrence therein, and yet the most surprising thing about the work, having regard to its period of origin, is the comparatively slight tincture that it has received from the Christianity in the midst of which it originated and developed.

Picus. Postel is credited by tradition with a translation of the SEPHER HA ZOHAR which would be a rare treasure, had it ever come into existence or been maintained therein.[1] I do not know how or with whom the attractive story arose, but twenty years since it took a very strong hold on the mind of French students and there was a great research after it, terminating as might have been expected. There is, however, rather more basis for the quest than mere legend, as it is impossible to read Postel's most memorable work, called CLAVIS ABSCONDITORUM, without inferring that he must have been acquainted with the text, and might therefore, by bare possibility, have undertaken such a task.[2] It speaks of the Soul of the Mediator as the first creature of God and the Law, the Reconciler of the universe, referred to the SEPHIRA BINAH, which titles and which local habitation are those of Shekinah, according to the ZOHAR.[3] This is by no means the only direction in which Postel connects with the chief text of the Secret Tradition in Israel, but it is sufficient at this point to have established the fact without enlarging thereon.

Between the period of Mirandula and that of William Postel there are, as we shall see, the names of Cornelius Agrippa and Paracelsus; but the first connects more especially with the practical Kabbalah so called, with powers of Divine Names, mysteries of numbers, doctrines of angels and demons, drawn for the most part from sources other than the ZOHAR; while in respect of the second his use of the word Kabbalah has no connection with any monopoly of Jewry.

Contemporary with Postel there was John Reuchlin or Cadmion, who dedicated his three books entitled DE ARTE CABALISTICA to Leo X. His work may be best described as a study of Messianic doctrine, the object of which was to shew that He who was expected by Israel had already come. I am not actually certain, but I believe that he was the first to affirm that the Hebrew name of Jesus was formed of the

---

[1] Picus de Mirandula also is said to have caused the ZOHAR to be translated into Latin, or alternatively a Latin version was one of the manuscripts which came into his possession by purchase from the unknown Jew.

[2] The legend of a Latin version is recurrent. A French gentleman of Lyons is supposed to have purchased a copy in 1890, paying many thousands of francs, and a translation is also ascribed to Gui de Viterbi. There is nothing improbable in the notion that the text may have been so rendered, and may be in hiding somewhere, though I do not set much value on the Lyons story.

[3] Later Kabbalism regarded ADAM KADMON, the Lesser Countenance of Zoharic symbolism, as the pre-existent soul of Messiah. It was also the Word in CHOKMAH.

consonants of Jehovah = יהוה with the addition of the sacred letter SHIN = יהשוה—*i.e.* Jeheshuah.[1] He quotes a large number of Zoharic writers on Kabbalism, but does not mention the ZOHAR, at least by name.[2] Reuchlin wrote also DE VERBO MIRIFICO. Belonging to the same period as Reuchlin there was Petrus Galatinus, an Italian convert from Jewry, the author of DE ARCANIS CATHOLICÆ VERITATIS,[3] drawn from the texts of Kabbalism into twelve great books in the form of a debate between himself, a certain Hogostratin —of whom I know nothing otherwise—and Reuchlin. It is a work of much greater extent and more considerable learning than the books of the last writer and it does mention the ZOHAR, but without shewing much first-hand acquaintance. This also is a study of Messianic doctrine and is masterly after its own kind.

A third name of importance is Paulus Riccius who was another Jewish convert to Christianity, but his work on CELESTIAL AGRICULTURE[4] did not exercise any considerable influence. He wrote also STATERA PRUDENTUM on the Law of Moses, Christ and the Gospel, but the work was condemned, and a number of other treatises, including one on the doings of the Kabbalists, which appeared at Nuremberg in 1523.

The purpose so far of these prefatory words has been to indicate briefly the circumstances under which the chief text of Kabbalism came to be known in Europe, and at a later

---

[1] It should be observed that the Hebrew spelling is ישוע.

[2] There are several editions of both these works, and they are included in the collection of Pistorius entitled, ARTIS CABALISTICÆ SCRIPTORES, *Tomus Primus*, but the second volume—if that was the limit intended—never appeared. This publication belongs to the year 1587.

[3] Petri Galatini: DE ARCANIS CATHOLICÆ VERITATIS, LIBRI XII, 1672. The text in this edition is followed by Reuchlin: DE ARTE CABALISTICA. It is of course a reprint, the work itself having been completed in 1516, according to its colophon. An intermediate edition appeared in 1602. Those who can suffer its prolixity will not be unrepaid by its reading, even at this day. The analysis of contents in respect of the twelve books is worth giving: (1) Treats of the TALMUD; (2) The Trinity of Divine Persons; (3) The Incarnation of the Son of God; (4) The First Advent of Messiah; (5) The Jewish Argument that the Messiah has not come is confuted; (6) The Redemption of Mankind; (7) The Blessed Virgin; (8) Mysteries concerning the Messiah; (9) Rejection of the Jews and Call of the Gentiles; (10) The Institution of the New Law; (11) The Passing of the Old Law; (12) The Second Advent. Galatinus is supposed to have possessed a copy of the lost TARGUM of Jonathan Ben Uzziel to the hagiographical books of the Old Testament—*i.e.* prophets, *op. cit.*, Book I., c. 3.

[4] This is the first text given in the collection of Pistorius: ARTIS CABALISTICÆ, hoc est, Reconditæ Theologiæ et Philosophiæ Scriptorum TOMUS I. Basle, 1587. It is known usually as ARTIS CABALISTICÆ SCRIPTORES.

stage the Christian students and exponents of the subject will be considered in particular monographs. It is sufficient at the moment to have established the fact that there was a succession of Kabbalistic scholarship from the beginning, outside Jewry, and that its early concern was to unfold the Christian elements which it discovered in the Secret Doctrine of Israel, above all in the ZOHAR and in the Jewish literature which arose therefrom.

To those who may approach the present work from a philosophical and historical standpoint the presence of its leading motive and its more especial appeal to a single class of students will require some explanation. It was once, I believe, suggested that since the first appearance of Dr. Ginsburg's destructive criticism there has been no attention paid among English scholars to the subject of the Kabbalah. Within the region of research which has only a scholastic horizon—whether metaphysical or historical—there was no interest that calls for special mention at the period which preceded that work immediately, and it is quite true that there has been as little subsequently to its publication, but not on account of Dr. Ginsburg's criticism. There has been always or, speaking exactly, since the days of Robert Fludd and Thomas Vaughan, of Cudworth and the Cambridge Platonists, a certain class of students for whom the claims made by and on behalf of the Kabbalah have possessed importance, and this class is possibly larger now than at any date prior to 1865. It forms also intellectually a more considerable body than the academical reader might be disposed to imagine in the absence of particular acquaintance with the literature by which it is represented. One is obliged to speak of these students and thinkers under the designation of theosophical or esoteric groups, though the phrase is inexact and has been used to describe persons who have little title to consideration. A proscribed mode of thought is here, as in other cases, identified with the lesser capacities that follow it, and what was once an unpopular subject has been classed according to the waste and drift which has collected about it. But the class to which I have adverted does not in itself deserve either ridicule or contempt: it is that which believes in the perpetuation of a secret religious or more correctly mystical Tradition from an early period of human history, and this is not manifestly an absurd or unwarrantable consequence to draw from the study of religions undertaken in a comparative sense. It is a question of evidence and should be left to establish its values. Now, the Kabbalah is not only, as I have said, the Secret Theosophy of Jewry, but it has been represented further to be the channel of such a Tradition as I have just mentioned. It is therefore not merely reasonable to suppose, but it is true as a fact, that to theosophists and mystics, more than all, if not unto these exclusively, an inquiry like the present must appeal. Other interests are accidental; their interest is vital. To determine the claims of the Kabbalah as a department and perhaps inspiring centre of Secret Doctrine is to determine that which is of most real moment regarding it.

It is for this reason that I have been led to consider the Kabbalah, not only as a mystic in the accepted sense, but from the mystical standpoint, and to recur with a certain frequency to the belief in a Secret Doctrine of Religion, as well as to some other connected questions which need reconsideration at the hands of those who hold them. If I have had in the course of the inquiry to reduce various illusions to their proper place in the realm of the fantastic, and have contracted the sphere of what is called Mysticism within its proper dimensions, I shall be justified, so far as regards my intention, by those whom I have sought to disabuse. It remains to say that from its nature the foundation of Mysticism cannot be in so-called occult science or in occult philosophy, while it is on the historical side alone that it connects with any traditions of the past, popular or acroamatic.[1]

Now, it is to be understood above all that these volumes are not addressed to members of the Religion of Israel and—at least in any primary sense—that they are not planned as a contribution to scholarship, though it happens in the accident of things that they are the first extended memorial of Kabbalistic literature which has appeared in this country. They are part of a scheme proposed long since to myself for an exploration of the Secret Tradition in Christian Times and the determination of that one question which matters about Secret Tradition, as indeed about all other subjects of human

---

[1] The reason is indicated by Schopenhauer, when he remarks on the astonishing unanimity of mystics in all ages, unlike in everything except those principles which constitute Mysticism, and yet not holding such principles as a sect clings to its tenets, for they are not and can never be a sect.

thought and inquiry. The question is whether on its surface or somewhere down in its deeps, and even below the deeps, there is any vestige of that great spiritual experiment which—awaiting a more adequate or exact mode of definition—must be called the Science of the Soul in God. Within historical times it has been always in the world; it is in the West as well as in the East; but it has been overlaid everywhere by heavy veils of doctrine and practice which are particular to places and times, to the psychological characteristics of different races and peoples. It is of all things simple and single, which notwithstanding it emerges everywhere in the mode of a particular complex on account of these accretions. Thus an universal subject which does not belong to learning, in the formal sense of this term, has become a matter of expert research on the one hand, while on the other it has been represented as impossible of examination in a living and plenary sense, except by ascetics, and, among these, usually by those who are leading some kind of monastic or conventual life, isolated from the world and its activities. That which has been planned and attempted in my several studies of Mysticism is a liberation of the subject from these old trammels, while the variations of its outward forms have been considered in volumes devoted to the Secret Tradition, that which is offered here to students of THEOSOPHIA MAGNA being a final revision and digest of my old books and monographs on MYSTERIUM RECEPTIONIS in the mind of Jewry.

It is delivered to the keeping of that scattered and unincorporated brotherhood which is of my kindred in the spirit, as a memorial of its understanding according to the light of an individual Christian mystic and not that of Israel, supposing that at this day of the world there were any real concern of Israel in these its records of the past, unless it be in a few synagogues or ghettos of Croatia and Dalmatia. The doctrine of TSURE and the Mystery of Shekinah are the root of my concern in Kabbalism. They are not of my concern solely for that which they signified in a Theosophical School of Jewry but for whatever may belong therein to the life of Catholic Mysticism here and now. It is shewn that at their best and highest the old Sons of the Doctrine were on a quest which is also ours and that the experience which at rare moments is felt in our deep of heart is no other than is shadowed forth—sometimes a little dimly—in their obscure records. The part of us which abides in God and communicates the sense of the Eternal is that which in their own veridic dream belongs to ATZILUTH, the Supernal World, and never leaves the Supernals. I think also that as some of us, within our own measures, do now "know in part," awaiting "that which is perfect," so also they—or some of them—were not without an inward realisation of a great reality which they expressed outwardly as the "Bond of Union."

It remains to say that while the age of the records is of large consequence on the historical side and so has been considered at length, the antiquity of Kabbalistic Tradition cannot be an essence of the consideration, having regard to the purpose set forth in these prefatory words. The implications of one's own standpoint must be acknowledged in the logic of things, and the message of the texts at their highest is all in all for me and not their date or authorship. The plays passing under the name of Shakespeare would be no less immortal plays and greatness of greatness in the world of literature, were it proved beyond challenge to-morrow that they were written by Bacon or a stableman of the Globe Tavern. So also if SEPHER HA ZOHAR is not of time immemorial but belongs to the 13th century, which almost certainly it does not in the root-matter, my investigation is not stultified. There remains the question of values, the question of life and essence. If the Tradition has warrants herein, seven hundred years will suffice for its age at need. But if it has none, it can be a matter of curious research only, supposing that it is seven thousand years old. The myths of Babylon remain Babylonian myths even if they are older than Genesis; and if the strange Tale of a Garden, with which Genesis opens, holds something within it which belongs to the spiritual deep, to the authentic legends of the soul, it signifies little enough if the figurative myth concerning the Fall of Man is a century or an age later than the BOOK OF THE DEAD.

A. E. WAITE.

BOOK I

POST-CHRISTIAN LITERATURE OF THE JEWS, INCLUDING THE TALMUD

BOOK I

POST-CHRISTIAN LITERATURE OF THE JEWS

I.—THE HIDDEN CHURCH OF ISRAEL

THE construction of the Exile placed by the "Princes of the Exile" upon the Sacred Oracles of ancient Israel cannot be dismissed as unimportant. From the period of the dispersal of the Jews after the destruction of Jerusalem by Vespasian down to our own times—the productive activities of which lie far beyond the scope of this reference—Hebrew literature has developed in many of the chief centres of Europe; but outside the scattered remnant of the Children of the Covenant it has remained largely unknown. Many persons, not otherwise ill-informed, might be astonished to discover that so far back as the end of the seventeenth century there were nearly four thousand works [1] written in the Hebrew tongue which were known individually and quoted by one authority on rabbinical bibliography, namely, Julius Bartolocci, of the Reformed Order of St. Bernard.[2] Almost every conceivable department of human learning and intellectual activity is represented in this literature,[3] which, in things secular as in things sacred, has the seal of the sanctity of Israel upon all its leaves. On the purely religious side, it is otherwise an extremely curious and in some respects a profound literature, which translation has done little to make known, which is represented incompletely enough even in

---

[1] It is perhaps unnecessary to say that they were for the most part in manuscript.
[2] BIBLIOTHECA MAGNA RABBINICA: *De scriptoribus et scriptis rabbinicis, ordine alphabetico Hebraice et Latine digestis,* auctore D. Julio Bartoloccio de Cellerio, folio, 4 vols. Roma, 1678-1692. The work is paged from left to right, after the Hebrew manner.
[3] For one of the accessible collections which give some idea of its variety, see the CATALOGUE OF HEBRAICA AND JUDAICA in the Library of the Corporation of the City of London. With a Subject-Index by the Rev. A. Löwy. London, 1891.

the great and authoritative text-books of Jewish history. There is no need to add that its extent and its difficulties make it a formidable subject of approach. It is, indeed, an undiscovered country, still awaiting its Columbus,[1] a land full of wealth and mystery, of strange shrines and sanctuaries shining weirdly far away, through the darkness of our ignorance, with a light which might recall the traditional radiance of Shekinah, so foreign does it seem to that which enlightens most men who are born into the modern world.

Within this literature there is, so to speak, another and stranger literature included, the report of which has been amongst us for several centuries, and in a certain way and measure it must be admitted that it is known to some, but chiefly because it has been made available by the fathers of bibliographical erudition, the Latin-writing scholars of the past. This storehouse of Hebrew Theosophy, for such it is, has exercised a peculiar fascination on many great minds of Christendom, and its Gentile students were at one time as keen, if not as numerous as its Jewish disciples. It is called the Kabbalah, of which term there has been more than one explanation suggested in the credulous past by the makers of ridiculous romance in etymology, and it seems worth while to mention two of them in passing, as examples of the follies which have encompassed the subject of research. The word has been derived from the name of the Hindoo teacher Kapila,[2] to whom a Philosophy of Numbers is ascribed, seemingly on the slender ground that one branch of Kabbalistic literature is connected with this subject. Another fantastic suggestion makes the term an analogue of Cybele,[3]

---

[1] The work of Dr. Moritz Steinschneider, the German bibliographer of rabbinical literature, is the most important contribution to our knowledge which has been made during comparatively recent years.

[2] C. W. Heckethorn made himself responsible for this view in an enlarged edition of his very unequal and indeed negligible work on SECRET SOCIETIES OF ALL AGES. See vol. i. p. 83.

[3] The responsibility in this case rests with the late Edward Vaughan Kenealy, whose anonymous BOOK OF GOD and its sequels were quoted once upon a time by a certain class of writers as if they carried seals of authority. Its philology is of the period of Godfrey Higgins, of the author of NIMROD and of Bryant's ANCIENT MYTHOLOGY. See Kenealy's INTRODUCTION TO THE APOCALYPSE OF ADAM-OANNES, p. 613. If writers of this calibre, so-called occult "authorities" and old works belonging to the field of research are mentioned here and there in these notes, the explanation is that I know those whom I address. The student at large of things which are called mystical may have sound titles to consideration in respect of sincerity and zeal, but he is like the Victorian student of secret arts and sciences, with a fatal tendency to accept bad evidence and rely on exploded writers. It is desirable therefore to indicate, as occasion

the mythological Queen of Heaven, who is thus connected with the Jewish personification of Wisdom under a female aspect. As to the true derivation there is no room for uncertainty, and it possesses that simplicity which is so often a warrant of truth in things of language as it has been said to be in those of Nature and Art. The word comes from a Hebrew root which signifies to receive. Kabbalah equals reception.[1] The knowledge embodied in the literature which passes under this title purports to have been transmitted orally from generation to generation. The literature as it exists is the Tradition put into writing, and in this form it has been supposed by some other dreamers to be veiled—that is to say, the meaning which appears on the surface is not the true sense.[2]

The Kabbalah in any case claims to be the light of a Secret Traditional Knowledge[3] preserved among the "chosen people,"[4] and the subjects with which it is concerned, as might be expected, are Sacred and Divine Subjects: they include the most profound Mysteries of God and the Emanations of Deity; the celestial economy; the process of creation; the scheme of Providence in regard to man; the communications of God in revelation and to the just in his Church; the offices and ministries of good and evil angels; the nature and preexistence of the soul, its union with matter and its metempsychosis; the mystery of sin and its penalties; the Messiah, His kingdom and His glory to be revealed; the state of the soul after death and the resurrection of the dead, with occasional, too rare but pregnant intimations on the union of the soul and God. Hereof is the aspect and this the part which was conceived and unfolded *sub specie æternitatis*. Here also,

---

arises, that such sources are wrong. Were my work addressed only to scholarship, it is obvious that a different procedure would be followed herein.

[1] In Hebrew it is קבלה. The ENCYCLOPÆDIA PERTHENSIS observes that the word is written also as Gabella, which is, of course, a nonsensical corruption, and would not be worth noting if it were not true in fact that it occurs in this form among a few old writers on Magic. See ENCYC. PERTH. iv. 543, 544.

[2] We shall see afterwards that this view is not so much to be received with caution as to be rejected utterly.

[3] One of the titles ascribed to it was חכמה נסתרה = Secret Wisdom; the initials of these words gave another title, signifying Grace = חן. See Kitto: CYCLOPÆDIA OF BIBLICAL LITERATURE, *s.v.* Kabbalah. (Third edition, London, 1864.)

[4] The recipients of this knowledge were termed MEKKUBALIM, a name which will be familiar to the readers of the astrologer Gaffarel. On this point see the worthless article, *s.v.* Kabbalah, in T. H. Blunt's DICTIONARY OF DOCTRINAL AND HISTORICAL THEOLOGY. London, 1872.

if anywhere, is the abiding part, rooted in everlasting values, and the one voice among many voices of old Tradition which bears a message from the past to the modern world.

It is needless to say that by a literature so considerable in its capacity there are many other subjects embraced, but these are the heads of an instruction, as I find them set forth in an excerpt from a Latin epistle in the collection of Baron von Rosenroth.[1] The Kabbalah, in a word, is the hidden thought of Israel upon doctrines of Jewish Religion, which are in many cases Christian doctrines, and upon the proper understanding of that Written Word which is referred to a Divine Origin both in Christendom and Jewry. It is obvious therefore that in a general sense it might be expected to cast light of a certain kind upon the problems of Christian faith; but some of its expounders have held that it does this also in a more special way; that the New Testament and the writings of the early Fathers of the Church did not only derive from the inspired memorials of the First Covenant, but from the construction placed on those memorials by this Esoteric Tradition.[2]

It may be said at once, and possibly for the relief of some for whom this work is intended, that the question here outlined is not of my concern. There is no proposition to elucidate official Christian doctrine, whether by the help of Kabbalism or otherwise, nor to explore the Gospels and early Patristic literature in the hope of discovering alleged vestiges of Secret Jewish Theosophy. It has been suggested also that Christ Himself testified to the existence of a Tradition [3] in Israel and gave His judgment on its value; but if so—and

---

[1] KABBALA DENUDATA, *seu Doctrina Hebræorum Transcendentalis et Metaphysica*, vol. i. *Apparatus in Librum Sohar, pars secunda*, pp. 3-5. It should be said that the last clause has been added by myself.

[2] "It is apparent from the many similarities in this Kabbalistic philosophy to the doctrines in the New Testament and early Patristic literature that both of the latter most probably have had a common germ and origin in the esoteric teachings of the Israelites, as well as in the more open and exoteric teachings of the Hebrew Holy Writings." Isaac Myer: THE PHILOSOPHICAL WRITINGS OF SOLOMON BEN YEHUDAH IBN GEBIROL, Philadelphia, 1888, 8vo, p. 7. This is cited as a point of view at its value, for which no brief is held. The letter of St. Jerome to Marcella, which dwells consecutively upon mysteries contained in the books of the Old and New Testaments, has been regarded sometimes as a case in point. All that can be said, however, is that it enumerates "ten Names by which God is known among the Hebrews," and the sole Kabbalistic connection resides in the fact that ten Divine Names—not identical throughout with those cited by St. Jerome—are allocated to the ten SEPHIROTH which constitute the Tree of Life in Kabbalism.

[3] "Thus have ye made the commandment of God of none effect by your tradition."—S. Matt., xv. 6.

for me it is more than doubtful—the purpose of the research to come is by no means to determine whether the later literature of Reception is to be included in the condemnation of the Divine Rabbi. But these assurances lead up to the point in view, and it is by this also that they are justified. A study of the Secret Doctrine or of Theosophy in Israel, as it is embodied in the Great Book of the ZOHAR and in other texts of Kabbalism, might be made assuredly on one or other of several plans; but as there can be no object in particularising further those which it is not intended to adopt, it shall be explained only that I have approached the subject from that point of view which is important to my own mind and in the one way that is possible, having regard to the nature of the work proposed. I have taken it as it is essentially, namely, a store-house of affirmed Secret Doctrine, and for the use of students of Secret Doctrine I design to present it, so to speak, at first hand—in all its important aspects—for the purpose of ascertaining—as already mentioned—whether it must remain with us merely as an historical landmark, or whether it conveys an understanding of things which, when considered in their true light, is of moment to us as mystics here and now. To complete the circle of these preliminary remarks, I will add that the plan thus outlined will be found in the outcome to include all that is of importance in any alternative scheme, for by the nature of the case there is no paramount doctrine under the ægis of the Old Covenant, no vital phase of Scriptural Tradition and no large event in the history of Israel about which we shall not learn in due course, and fully, the mind of Kabbalistic Theosophy.

There is one thing more which it may seem well to make clear as a point of fact: it is not of my design to produce a kind of *prolegomenon* which is intended to facilitate research when readers have recourse to the texts themselves and their developments. After due allowance has been made for the predilection and enthusiasms of a mystic who has taken the business of the Secret Tradition into his heart of hearts, I shall be glad if those whom I address will be content to believe on my testimony that the ZOHAR—being the text in chief—is one of the great books of the world, one also which stands alone and is comparable to nothing save itself; but I have no intention of recommending it to their particular and earnest consideration at full length. In the French translation—

whatever the value thereof [1]—it contains, roughly speaking, about 1,250,000 words, distributed throughout six very large volumes, and in the absence of a special dedication it will prove frankly unreadable. I am embodying an account of its essence on the great subjects of its concern—things which a careful collation has lifted out of the mass of material. Beyond these there is all the drift and scattermeal of rabbinical speculations, like a vast waste beyond the garden of the wise, arid as a field of quest, arbitrary beyond words as exegesis, out of all reason as thesis and ridiculous at every turn and corner of the streets of thought. I am confusing images or mixing metaphors rather of set purpose, to produce the kind of effect which is fitting to the kind of subject. If the ZOHAR may be likened otherwise to a temple of learning, then for ordinary critical minds the words inscribed on its porch are: " Abandon hope, all ye who enter here."

In attempting to educe from the body-general of the records that root-matter of Secret Doctrine which they claim to embody, we are brought quickly to a pause by the fact not merely of many inconsistencies characteristic of the text-major at large in a variety of lesser respects, but of the obvious manner in which the great ingarnering seems continually at issue with itself over matters of prime importance. It is easy to allow for those cases—and they are comparatively few—in which the doctors correct one another, whether or not they reach an agreement subsequently in the course of their long debates; but we are confronted with irremediable variation over clear issues in the fontal source itself, while to establish those which distinguish this source from its subsequent

---

[1] It should be said that the value has been challenged and the translator himself placed in a lurid light, from the standpoint of Israel, by certain Jewish critics. It will be sufficient for most of my readers to consult the strictures and references of Dr. Robert Eisler in THE QUEST quarterly review, vol. xxiv.; but there may be mentioned also the hostile judgment of Dr. Gerhard Scholem, who is reader in Talmudic and Kabbalah at the Jewish University in Jerusalem. The translator of the ZOHAR was a Jew who turned Christian and the consequent bias may have coloured the rendering of certain passages and exaggerated their Christian aspects; but the question is whether the version at large—all faults, wilful and otherwise, notwithstanding—is or is not sufficiently representative of its original—if even by way of paraphrase—and that it is, or appears to be, seems indicated by the fact that it is quoted at need even by those whose voice has been raised against it, e.g., by Paul Vulliaud, LA KABBALE JUIVE, 2 vols., 1923. Like these, " we must even be content with what we have," until a better is offered. The ZOHAR is a most obscure text, and no translation is likely to escape criticism. For an historical example we may remember the animadversions of German scholarship on Adolphe Franck's rendering of certain Zoharic excerpts. In 1913 Dr. Abelson said that De Pauly's translation was indispensable, as the only complete one yet attempted: JEWISH MYSTICISM, p. 179. That is the exact position.

developments in the mind of later Kabbalism would demand the research of years. I mention these points only to indicate my intention to find—as we move forward—a middle way, wherever possible, between statements that exclude one another, even if in the last resource we must recognise that the Secret Doctrine issues in a mystery in all directions because there is no place at which it enters into expression fully, so that the adequate materials are never in our hands. When things appear mutually or commonly exclusive, it will be little to our purpose if we decide that one of them seems to have a preferential claim; but we may get to our term if we can find a point of coincidence between the things which they tend to intimate, though they are scarcely expressed by any.[1]

According to the form of another school of symbolism, I will proceed now to open the Lodge of Research by affirming that I am approaching the Holy Kabbalah from a standpoint heretofore unattempted in the history of all its criticism, so that I am as usual without precedents, while I am also without any specific intention of creating them.[2] The remark is in a sense helpful, because those who are in favour of established ways and notions can take their proper warning before they go further. And again, in so far as it is possible, I should wish to exclude from the auditorium those who understand *Scientia Kabbalistica* as an art of making, consecrating and using talismans and amulets, as a magical mystery concerning the power of Divine Names, or as source and authentication of Grimoires and Ceremonial Rituals of Evocation. I can tell them at least that they will be saved from disappointment if they go elsewhere for enlightenment: here is no guide to the perplexed in the paths of occult arts. I mention this matter because there is a debased Kabbalism, improperly so called, which deals in these putative mysteries and claims some roots in the past, as if it belonged to the authentic Tradition of

---

[1] To give almost a frivolous example of disparities which arise in this way, the ZOHAR proper everywhere condemns Astrology, but the FAITHFUL SHEPHERD, a tract inserted at different points of the text, acknowledges one of its root principles.—Z., Pt. II, fol. 42a; III, 191. It should be observed that throughout these notes the reference which follows immediately on the Part and Folio of the ZOHAR is always and only to the French translation, its particular volume and page. The ZOHAR reference is also to the codex used by the translator, De Pauly, unless stated otherwise.

[2] I do not refer here to what is sometimes called the Practical Kabbalah, in which are included the artificial methods of GEMATRIA, NOTARIKON and TEMURA, which are principles of exegetical interpretation. The reader may consult W. Wynn Westcott: AN INTRODUCTION TO THE KABBALAH, 1910. These methods are old: about the Magical Kabbalah, the antiquity must be left unsettled; regarding its folly and iniquity there is no question.

Israel when it is not even a reflection. The mind of the ZOHAR on the subject of pretended occult sciences will be shewn towards the end of this study, so that there may be no mistake hereon at the term of quest. I mention it at this initial stage, so that there may be no mistake now.

I have termed the present chapter THE HIDDEN CHURCH OF ISRAEL, but it is not in the sense of suggesting that there was any formal incorporation,[1] much less that there were Secret Religious Rites and Ceremonies in use among a company of adepts; it was an entirely inward, spiritual and mystic Church, for all purposes of which the official forms of the external Holy Assembly would have been held to be of sufficient efficacy, had the Temple, during the period when the records came into existence, stood at Jerusalem, as it did in the days of old. One reason is [2] that the Secret Doctrine was judged to be inseparable from the literal or written word; it was developed to deepen its meaning and extend its office, but never to make it void within its own measures or in the place to which it belonged.[3] Our first task is therefore to ascertain what is established in the great texts concerning the fact of Secret Doctrine; and at some later stage subsequently we must take in succession the chief points of intimation on doctrine and religion in Jewry, so as to elicit the sense of that Tradition respecting each and all. Lastly, we must find—if this indeed be possible [4]—whether the Tradition has a central root from which the great tree of the concealed knowledge has grown up; whether also—as I have said—and how far we are concerned or perhaps even are integrated therein as

---

[1] At the same time we do meet with a number of occasional instances, the suggestion of which is almost as if the colleagues formed a College of Initiates. Sometimes it even looks as if there were almost a ceremonial manner of imparting Mysteries. See, for example, Z., Pt. I, fol. 133a; II, 124. Again, it is said that the Mysteries are guarded secretly in the hearts of those who possess them and communicated secretly to each other. *Ib.*, fol. 96b; I, 55c. For further allusions, see *ib.*, fol. 133a; II, 124; *ib.*, fol. 155b; II, 212, shewing that what was known by one of the adepts was not always familiar to another; *ib.*, Pt. II, fol. 8b; III, 6b; *ib.*, 14a; III, 61; *ib.*, fol. 168a; IV, 116; *ib.*, Pt. III, fol. 187a; V, 489.

[2] In illustration of this, there is one similitude which says that the Written Doctrine is the candle or lamp, while the flame is the Oral Law.—Z., Pt. II, fol. 166a; IV, 112.

[3] The thesis was that the written word of Scripture, in every passage and syllable, was the word of the Living God. The meanings, however, were many, but they are usually reduced to three: (1) the historical sense, which corresponds to the Court of the Temple; (2) the moral sense, which answers to the Holy Place; and (3) the mystical sense, which is in analogy with the Holy of Holies.

[4] It is perhaps just to myself if I add in this place that, since I am not concerned with compilations as such, there would have been no excuse for the present work if I had not satisfied myself: (1) that such a root exists, and (2) that its nature can be set forth clearly. This has been implied already in several places.

mystics at this day. I should add that while the last point is obviously the most important and vital, it can be reached only by the mediation of the two others.

The question is therefore as to the fact of the Secret Doctrine and under what terms it is mentioned in the records. It is of course, broadly and generally, a method of interpreting Scripture,[1] but so far as this expression is to be understood in an ordinary sense—as an actual and logical construction of the letter—the interpretation, as I have indicated already, is of no value—for the most part, at least. It is to be taken or left in the sense of its own motive, which is to establish, at any and all cost, a Secret Doctrine on the foundation of the Old Testament; and in the light of this it signified little that the Doctrine, in respect of exegesis, was arbitrary to the last degree: one would scarcely expect it to be otherwise, having regard to the Rabbinical mind. The point in chief for ourselves is that the mills of those lesser gods who are called Sons of the Doctrine produced and polished great things in their processes—pure and precious jewels of the spirit—as well as much dust and scoria from the matter which they passed through their hands. It is only as if casually that the word interpretation [2] can be held to apply in any solid sense: the Secret Doctrine is rather the sense below the sense which is found in the literal word—as if one story were written on the obverse side of the parchment and another on the reverse side. This is not an exact comparison, but it gives my meaning clearly enough for the purpose. There are hard things said from time to time about the outward sense and they must not be taken too seriously, for the letter was always precious, if only as a vesture; but the difference between that which was

---

[1] The symbolism of the Secret Doctrine is extracted also from Scriptural words and phrases which antecedently seem far from the mark. The word "waters," as it is used sometimes in the TALMUD, is said to signify the Secret Doctrine, and when David cried: "Create in me a clean heart, O God, and renew a right spirit within me" (Ps. li, 10), he was praying for his heart to be opened by the study of Divine Mysteries. So also it is said: "Let the waters under the heaven be gathered together into one place" (Gen. i, 9). The waters refer to the Secret Doctrine, and the one place designates Israel, whose soul depends from that region to which Scripture alludes in the words: "Blessed be the glory of the Lord from His place" (Ezek. iii, 12). The "Glory of the Lord" signifies the Shekinah below and "from His place" signifies the Shekinah above. From this point of view, Shekinah is the Doctrine itself personified.

[2] The canon of interpretation is often exceedingly simple: for example, any reference to vegetation coming up out of the ground is explicable by symbolical vegetation, the one and the other being confused together, and either taken to explain the other. In Ps. lxxxv, 11, it is said that "truth shall spring out of the earth," and literal grass is held therefore to signify truth.

within and without is well illustrated [1] by a similitude which says that those who interpret Scripture according to the literal sense set the Sacred King and His Bride upon an ass, while those who understand it according to the mystic sense mount them nobly on a horse.[2] This notwithstanding, the two belong to one another, because the Written Law is completed by that which is traditional,[3] and the latter issues from the former as woman was brought forth from man: it can exist only in union with the Written Law, and this it serves to enlighten—by the hypothesis at least. We shall see at the proper time that chief among the root-doctrines is that Jehovah is one with Elohim in a sense which is very far from the theological understanding of Scripture; but it is held also that the Written Law is the image of Jehovah, as the Oral Law is of Elohim, meaning the Holy Shekinah, from which it would follow that at heart they are two aspects of one and the same Law. That which is oral is called the voice of the turtle,[4] and it comes from the side of mercy; it is also the green wood, while the literal Law is the dry,[5] coming from the side of judgment. But as a further instance of the unity in both it is laid down that there are three things which are at once hidden and revealed —being God, the Law and Israel itself. The vulgar man sees only the material side, but the initiate discerns also that which is imbedded within it. In virtue of this bond of union, we meet with intimations occasionally in which terms are applied to the one that seem referable rather [6] to the other. It is said, for example, that the written Law is above and that which is oral below, as also that the former penetrates and fructifies the latter.[7] That which is without seems, however, to be clearly a manifestation

---

[1] The ZOHAR gives another illustration when it says that the Oral Law enlightens the Written Law. Z., Pt. III, fol. 23a; V, 61.

[2] Z., Pt. III, 275b; VI, 47.

[3] The Written Law is designated in another place under the name of heaven, while the Oral Law is called earth. On the surface this appears somewhat against the more obvious sense and intention, but what is signified may be an obscure counterchange in virtue of correspondences between things above and below, and this is a recurring Zoharic doctrine.—*Ib.*, Pt. I, fol. 247b; II, 578.

[4] Z., Pt. III, fol. 4b; V, 9.

[5] *Ib.*, fol. 27b, and V, 76.

[6] According to the rabbi in Longfellow's GOLDEN LEGEND, all Bible lore is water and MISHNA is a strong wine; but according to the ZOHAR, it is the Written Law which is wine; the Oral, however, is not water but milk. I conclude that the one is the lesser, the other is the greater salvation, according to the voice of the Doctrine. See Z., Pt. I, fol. 240a; II, 549.

[7] Z., Pt. II, fol. 200a; IV, 200; also Z., Pt. II, fol. 206a and IV, 208.

of that which is within, though there is a sense also in which the Law was regarded as written on high; but this I should understand to signify that the Oral Law passes into expression here and into realisation there. To conclude upon these analogies: the manifested part bears no comparison with that which is contained within; that which is essential is called the Soul of Scripture; the commandments are its body and the tales are the garments thereof. This is in the world below, while in that which is above the Ancient of Days is the Soul of soul in the Law; the soul is that mystery which is called the Beauty of Israel; the body is the Community of the Elect; while the vesture is heaven and its region. Cursed be he, says the text,[1] who pretends that the recitals of Scripture have no other meaning than that which appears on the surface. Scripture, if this were the case, would not be the Law of Truth, the Holy Law and the Perfect Witness, more precious than gold and jewels. If it contained only simple stories and such vulgar elements—as of Esau, Hagar, Laban and Balaam's ass—it might be possible to produce something better, apart from all inspiration, after the manner of profane books; but the truth is that every word of Scripture enshrines a Supreme Mystery, and is capable of sixty methods of interpretation.[2] This is a characteristic extravagance, but every one who has followed the quest of the mystic sense knows how manifold it is, and for this reason no doubt it has been testified that the original ZOHAR was at least a camel's load. That is like St. John saying: "I suppose that even the world itself could not contain the books that should be written," if all the acts of Jesus were reduced into a complete memorial.[3] I am very sure that the beloved disciple was guilty herein of no extravagant utterance, because Christ has been always in the world; and I am not less certain that the extent of the ZOHAR has been understated, for the variations of inward meanings are numberless as the Sons of the Doctrine, and all may be true analogically, though some of them are brighter jewels, while the pearls of greatest price may be few enough. Whatever

---

[1] Z., Pt. III, 149b; V, 386, 387.
[2] *Ib.*, Pt. I, fol. 26a; I, 161. It is said otherwise that there are sixty sections, which are the sixty queens of the SONG OF SOLOMON. The "young maids" without number are the HALAKHOTH, otherwise, things belonging to the outward, ceremonial Law, its customs and enactments—*Ib.*, Pt. III, fol. 216a; V, 548. Another statement concerns seventy modes of interpreting Scripture, all of which are true in their results. *Ib.*, Pt. I, fol. 54a; I, 310.
[3] St. John xxi, 25.

belongs to man at his highest belongs also to Christ: so too the Divine Sayings are like the Divine Acts, and from the first time of manifestation until that moment when God shall be All in all, there is no end to either.

Now, it is said that the inner sense of the Law is not less concealed than the world from which it emanates,[1] wherefore the Mysteries known to the Sons of the Doctrine are guarded secretly in their hearts. Those who apply themselves to its study receive as their inheritance the World to Come, as well as that of Jacob, for it is the path of the Life Beyond.[2] He who is so dedicated and so consecrated is accounted as if he had received its sweet and heavenly words on Mount Sinai itself.[3] It is the way of the Garden of the Sacred King and the way of the King Himself.[4] A certain price has to be paid however, for it is said hyperbolically that the study of the Law succeeds only in the case of him who kills himself for the Law, meaning that it is a path of poverty and a poor man is considered as one who is dead.[5]

I have dealt so far with preliminaries, and if the next question be how did the Secret Doctrine originate, the answer seems that it was before the world was with God. The sense of this must be that it was implied in Elohim, whose image it is, as we have seen. Another explanation is that it is on the side of mercy, and by mercy the world was made: it is the *beneplacitum termino carens*. We find, moreover, that God created the world by joining thereto the Secret Doctrine.

---

[1] Z., Pt. I, fol. 156b; II, 215.

[2] *Ib.*, fol. 158a; II, 220. I should mention here that consecration to the study of the Secret Doctrine brings down what is called the Supplementary Soul which Zoharic Kabbalism attributes frequently to all pious Children of Israel who observe the Sabbath in the plenary sense. It remains with them during that day and returns thereafter whence it came. But it would seem that true Sons of the Doctrine are in permanent enjoyment of this added part. He who does not cultivate the mystic science is therefore in a state of deprivation. The Soul is brought down by the voice of him who studies the Secret Doctrine and it comes from the Land of the Living, making him whom it overshadows equal to the angels. When it is said in Ps. ciii, 20, " Bless the Lord, ye His angels," the reference is to those who study the Doctrine and are called God's angels on earth. In the world to come they will have wings like those of the eagle.

[3] *Ib.*, Pt. III, fol. 179b; V, 471.

[4] *Ib.*, I, 224b; II, 485.

[5] *Ib.*, Pt. II, fol. 158b; IV, 95. But against this, he who is dedicated to the study of the Law opens the 50 gates of BINAH, corresponding to the letter YOD multiplied by the letter HE.—*Ib.*, III, fol. 216a; V, 548. Now, YOD is the Sign of the Covenant and therefore of the male principle, while HE—the letter of Shekinah—is that of the female principle, which produces fruit to the male through intercourse; and the multiplication here in question alludes to the generations of mind as the fruit of study— that is to say, of Divine Research. The Study of the Doctrine is not a barren study, but brings forth " the eternal brood of glory excellent."

The world was founded thereon, and it is added that so long as Israel is consecrated to its research, so long will the world be stable. When the lovers of truth [1] rise for its study at midnight [2] the Holy One and all the just who are with Him in the Garden of Eden listen to their voices.[3] The versicle appertaining hereto is: "Thou that dwellest in the gardens, the companions hearken to thy voice: come out to hear it." [4] We may understand by this that those who work below are really listening to the Voice which is above and that when they hear it, it is the Mystery of Doctrine which they hear. There is no need to add that the Voice is speaking in the heart. The word BERESHITH, with which Genesis opens and which has been rendered sometimes "in wisdom," not "in the beginning," is said to signify the Secret Doctrine and its part in the work of creation. The Scriptural allusion is: "The Lord possessed me in the beginning of His way, before His works of old. I was set up from everlasting, from the beginning, or ever the earth was." [5] It will be observed that this is personified Wisdom testifying on her own part, and the application of the text by the ZOHAR in connection with the beginning of things is, under the circumstances, rather subtle. It goes on to affirm that this was the kind of beginning in which God created the heaven and earth, the basis of which is His Covenant. Hence it is said also: "If the Covenant which I have made existed not, there would be neither day nor night, neither heaven nor earth." [6] All accepted renderings of this passage from the Vulgate downward are quite different; but the point to be remembered is the allusion made to the Covenant in the particular connection, for we shall find at a much later stage that it is the

---

[1] Z., Pt. I, fol. 77b; I, 455.
[2] I may mention at its value that the annotator of the French version—M. Lafuma-Giraud—distinguishes between that which the ZOHAR designates Mysteries of Doctrine and that which it calls Mysteries of Tradition. The first is the spiritual sense of Scripture and the second that of Tradition.
[3] The study of the Doctrine is held to call for adornment of body as well as attention of mind. It was needful for the doctors who rose at midnight to clothe themselves for the purpose of study, out of respect to Shekinah, who accompanies Students of the Doctrine. Moreover, the study calls for serenity of mind, and it was held difficult to ensure this in a reclining posture.—Z., Pt. I, fol. 72a; I, 426.
[4] SONG OF SOLOMON, viii, 13. Z., Pt. I, fol. 77b; I, 455.
[5] Prov. viii, 22, 23. Z., Pt. I, fol. 24b; I, 153.
[6] This is Pauly's rendering of the ZOHAR, but the Authorised Version reads: "If my covenant be not with day and night, and if I have not appointed the ordinances of heaven and earth; then I will cast away the seed of Jacob, and David my servant," &c. Jer. xxxiii, 25, 26. Compare the Vulgate: *Si pactum meum inter diem et noctem, et leges cæli et terræ non posui, equidem et semen Jacob et David, servi mei, projiciam*, &c.

sign manual or visible of one of the Divine Hypostases and it is also one of the keys to the whole Mystery of the ZOHAR. We are not, however, dealing with the question of creation at this point of our debate, and it has been mentioned only to indicate the seemingly eternal pre-existence of the Secret Doctrine.[1] After what manner was it brought down to earth, so that it came to the knowledge of the elect? The thesis of possession and successive custody depends from a legend of Paradise, and this in its turn arises from the Scriptural reference to a BOOK OF THE GENERATIONS OF ADAM.[2] It is supposed by the ZOHAR to signify that there was a Secret and Supreme Book, the source of all, including the Hebrew letters[3]—presumably in that form under which they are manifested below. It expounded the Holy Mystery of Wisdom and the efficiency resident in the Divine Name of seventy-two letters.[4] It was sent down from heaven by the hands of the angel Raziel[5] and Adam was entrusted therewith. Raziel is said to be the angel of the secret regions and chief of Supreme Mysteries. The gift placed Adam in a superior position to that of any celestial being—possibly with the exception of the messenger, though indeed he may have carried that which he was not permitted to understand. Adam was made acquainted in this manner with Supernal Wisdom,[6] and the Celestial Choirs came down to be present when he read the book. He was cautioned, however, to conceal it, and he seems therefore to have studied it in silence, with recollection of the heart. The book proved later on to

---

[1] See Book V, § 5, *passim*.
[2] Gen. v, 1.
[3] Z., Pt. I, fol. 37a *et seq.*; I, 231—233.
[4] The Mysteries of this Name and the mode of its formation will be considered in their proper place. There are said to be three books which are opened in heaven on the first day of the year. The first is that which was transmitted to Adam, and this is the book of the just who are perfect. The second has a part in heaven and a part on earth, but it is not otherwise described. The third is the Written Law, which was designed for the first man and was presumably known of the heart, for it is not said that it was manifested at that time on earth.—*Ib.*
[5] Z., Pt. I, fol. 55b; I, 319, 320. There is a legend of an old MIDRASH called the BOOK OF RAZIEL: it is said to have been developed by Eleazar of Worms and to have been reproduced in various debased forms by late Kabbalism. There is also an imposture of Ceremonial Magic which passes under the name. Compare E. V. Kenealy's notice of a Book of the Wisdom of Adam, received in an ecstasy and "full of mysteries and signs expressive of profound knowledge." See THE BOOK OF GOD, pp. 243 and also *ibid.*, pp. 273 *et seq.*, for a rabbinical account of a staff given to Adam and supposed to signify the support of Secret Knowledge.
[6] The Sacred Name of 72 letters was explained in the GENESIS OF MAN by means of the 670 mysteries which it contains. The Mystery of CHOKMAH discovered the 1500 keys which are not entrusted to any celestial being.

be like the LIBER GRADALIS or fundamental record concerning the Holy Graal, for it took unto itself wings at need, when Adam—his advantages notwithstanding—fell ultimately into sin. It was clasped in his hands when he was driven out of the Garden of Eden, but thereafter it vanished, and for long and long he lamented the loss of his treasure. Ultimately it was given back to him in answer to his tears and prayers,[1] by the angel Raphael: he returned to its study and bequeathed it to his son Seth, who entrusted it to later messengers, so that the Secret Doctrine might be spread through the world.[2] It became known as the BOOK OF ENOCH after passing through the hands of that patriarch,[3] and it is said that Abraham penetrated the glory of his Master by means of its mysteries. Moses, however, was the first man who attained perfection in its fullness,[4] and perhaps on this account it is not suggested that he derived his knowledge from a book, so that after Abraham we hear nothing of the secret text: it was a treasure of the patriarchal age. The External Law and the Secret Doctrine were both revealed on Mount Sinai, and as Moses transmitted the one to his nation at large so he communicated the other to certain elders, by whom it was handed on. But there are two remarkable passages designed to shew that the whole secret knowledge came down to the Zoharic period under the darkening of successive clouds. It is said that at the death of Moses the sun was eclipsed and that the Written Law lost its splendour. At the hour of King David's death

---

[1] The variant account in fol. 55b says that he smote his forehead when the work vanished and plunged up to his neck in the river GIHON, being the second river which flowed out from the "garden eastward in Eden." Gen. ii, 13. The result was that all his body was covered with wrinkles, so that he was no longer recognisable.

[2] A genealogy of this kind will recall the fabulous origins once ascribed to institutions like Freemasonry, the appeal made by alchemists to sages of antiquity and other fictions which deserve to be classed as monstrous. We must beware, however, of fixing wilful imposture on an archaic literature because its attribution is mythical: it should be remembered that we are dealing by the hypothesis with a body of Secret Doctrine, and an Oral Tradition is liable to the exaggeration of its antiquity: we must distinguish therefore between the possible fact of its existence at a more or less distant period and the growth of legend about it.

[3] There are several Enochian legends which offer curious points in themselves, but seldom connect with our subject. According to one account, Enoch became the great archangel Metatron; according to another, he was exalted to the high heavens and made guardian of their treasures, including the 45 keys to the combinations of graven letters.—Z., Pt. I, fol. 56b: I, 326. An apocalyptic BOOK OF ENOCH, believed to be a Hebrew text in its original state and belonging as such to the beginning of the Christian era, has been known in an Ethiopic translation since the year 1778, when a manuscript copy was brought from Abyssinia by J. Bruce.

[4] This is one of the theses, but we shall see that there was a certain Gate of Understanding which he failed to open.

the light of the moon diminished and the radiance of the Oral Law was tarnished. The consequence was that discussions and controversies began among the sages of the MISHNA, so that joy in the study of the Law has ceased for all future generations.[1] It was pursued previously in clear and full light, and there was that unanimity which comes from certitude among the Sons of the Doctrine; but afterwards it was followed from afar in a state of doubt and separation, amidst wrangling of the schools, who saw only as in a glass and darkly. This state of things is sometimes symbolised by a division in the Divine Name, by the loss of the true method of pronouncing the Tetragram in conformity with its proper vowels, and so forth. Occasionally there are intimations of a new breaking of light, as when it is said that Ezekiel was less faithful than Moses, for he divulged all the measures of the king[2]; but apparently those measures were not displayed before doctors who—whatever their zeal and sincerity—were unable to value them in understanding at their proper worth. It was otherwise in the days of Rabbi Simeon, for the glory of the mystic light was at its zenith in him, according to the ZOHAR, which, considering that he was the revealer in chief of its doctrines, exalts that master of wisdom above all the stars of heaven. It is added that from the day when Rabbi Simeon came out of his cavern[3] the Mysteries were secrets no longer for the colleagues, because the Hidden Doctrine had become no less familiar to them than it was to their precursors when it was revealed on Mount Sinai. But the time came for this great sun to set in the hour of the master's death; and when afterwards his disciples and successors sought to reproduce the words which they heard from his lips, the attempt proved a failure.[4] The withdrawal of the Secret Doctrine is mentioned also, but with a suggestion of vestiges remaining over: these are to be consulted, notwithstanding

---

[1] Z., Pt. II, fol. 156a, b; IV, 88.
[2] Ib., Pt. II, fol. 5a; III, 19.
[3] The reference is to the TRACT. SABBATH, which contains the history of Rabbi Simeon, the reasons which led him to find refuge in a cave for twelve years and the circumstances under which he came out. See Michael Rodkinson: BABYLONIAN TALMUD, vol. i, c. 2. I cite this translation, which was done in America, because it is available to the English reader; but its method of condensation has been a subject of hostile criticism, and the unexcised German rendering of L. Goldschmidt, begun in 1898, is preferred reasonably by scholars.
[4] This disposes of the ridiculous tradition that R. Simeon wrote anything in the cavern where he found a refuge from Roman imperial persecution.

their incompleteness, because the Doctrine is incorruptible gold, and even its shards are priceless.[1]

The next point which calls for our consideration here is whether the general references to the Secret Doctrine as a whole, apart from its various branches, offer any ground of presumption concerning its radical nature. Now, it is said that the Supreme Mystery is concealed in the Law,[2] that it is the Secret of the Law, meaning the Secret of the King—*Sacramentum Regis quod abscondere bonum est*—revealed only to those who fear sin, and that as to its nature, this is bodied forth by the Sacred Covenant concerning circumcision.[3] In other words, it is a Mystery of Sex. It was on account of this that Rabbi Simeon consecrated to the study of the Secret Doctrine the entire night in which the Heavenly Bride is united to her Heavenly Spouse, being the night of that day when the Law was revealed to the Israelites and the Covenant contracted between God and His people. The reason was that the Mystic Knowledge constitutes the jewels of the Heavenly Bride. We can understand this only on the hypothesis that the science in question is concerned at some stage or under some aspect with a most holy Mystery of Sex, as if some unknown path of splendour and path to the height can and may open therefrom. It is said that "the King's Daughter is all glorious within," and the ZOHAR explains that there is glory and glory, a glory of the male and a glory of the female principle.[4] It is said also, as if in connection with the pursuit of this path, that whosoever follows in the train of the Heavenly Bride on the night of union [5] shall be preserved from all evil for ever, in heaven and on earth—as if death and the second death had no power. He will enjoy celestial peace to the end of time. The counsel in this respect is : "Taste and see that the Lord is good." [6]

If the study of the doctrine adorns the Bride of Heaven with

---

[1] Z., Pt. I, fol. 216b, 217a; II, 453–455. See also *Ib.*, fol. 9a; I, 50, from which it follows that the Secret Doctrine is the explanation and unfoldment of all. This is founded on Ps. xix, 6: "There is nothing hid from the heat thereof." But this was the Doctrine in its fullness.
[2] *Ib.*, fol. 236b; II, 533.
[3] Z., Pt. I, fol. 237; II, 535. Cf. *ante* concerning a "Sign manual," p. 16.
[4] This is based on Ps. xlv. 13: "The King's daughter is all glorious within," which the Zohar renders: "All the glory of the daughter of the King is within"; and the Vulgate: *Omnis gloria ejus filiæ regis ab intus*. The words are held to designate the Community of Israel.
[5] Z., I, 9a; I, 51.
[6] Ps. xxxiv, 8.

jewels, as we have just seen, it seems that it adorns also the souls of its students with all manner of graces and sanctities. When the ZOHAR affirms that their desert is far above anything which follows on mere works, there is no doubt that it gives expression to a great truth, though it may be one that is reserved only for the understanding of the elect. But in the ordinary sense the explanation is that it enables good works to be fulfilled with knowledge, under the operation of Divine Will. Those who study the Doctrine are set free from fear, whether of things in heaven or things on earth, whether of evils which may overwhelm mankind, because such students are grafted on the Tree of Life and are taught daily thereby. As regards things in heaven, the meaning is that the fear of God, which is the beginning of wisdom, has been absorbed by the love of God, which is wisdom in realisation, and the Divine Doctrine cannot be studied without imparting love for the Divine. To walk in the path of the Doctrine is therefore to follow the path of love: it is said otherwise to lead into the way of truth, so that we learn how the soul may return to its Master. It is not the work of a certain day or of a certain hour, but one of the day and the night. We come to understand in this manner that the study is a question of life, of living with the face towards Jerusalem, having the awareness of God in the heart, and herein is the *moyen de parvenir*, the counsel of real being. We shall understand also why it is added that he who neglects or forsakes the study of the Doctrine is not less guilty than if he separated himself from the Tree of Life, for he is leading the life of separation.[1]

The last considerations follow, as it seems to me, the ordinary course of thought in the direction to which they belong; but the extracts out of which they arise are a counsel to those who would study the Secret Doctrine that there is needed a conscious union by intention, contemplation and the art of finding in the heart, so that the heart and mind of the student may concur in an ineffable union which is said to be consummated above. As to its nature we know enough to be certain that the night thereof is not of a festival below but of the eternal oneness in that Divine Darkness which is called otherwise in the records AIN-SOPH AOUR, the limitless and undifferentiated light. The festival of the Paschal Lamb

---

[1] Z., Pt. I, fol. 11a; I, 62.

in the Calendar of Jewry is only a specific memorial on earth, so that what it is held to signify may be kept in the soul of Israel; and this is not really an act of unreason: on the contrary, the intention is so to proceed here as if that which is remembered below is in particular remembrance above; yet the union there is in the still rest and the changeless simplicity, being infinite and eternal therein. Lastly, the extracts out of which these things arise would be worse than idle words if the quest concerning their meaning could be carried no further.

It will be seen as we move forward on the strange path of our research that the Sons of the Doctrine were only from time to time, and as if by accident, concerned with reserving any common, or indeed any merely remote and arbitrary understanding of the Written Word in Israel; that in short there was something, on the contrary, which—at least from their point of view—imposed a reasonable and even a zealous reserve, because it was pre-eminently one of those matters which the unprepared and sensual mind would wrest to its own destruction.

It has been necessary at this initial stage to establish the root fact of an alleged Secret Doctrine, in order to justify the long research which follows. An examination of the Doctrine itself and of its message to us, if any, belongs to a much later stage. Between these vital matters and the simple point of fact there intervenes all that belongs to the apparatus of the texts, including their external and critical history.

II.—FOLLIES OF OCCULT EXEGESIS [1]

As the Kabbalah claims to be a Tradition long received in secret by one generation from another and reduced at length into writing, so one of its legends informs us,[2] because of the bad state of the affairs of Israel—that is to say, after the destruction of Jerusalem—it is to be expected that its literary

---

[1] When it was found by experience that the Kabbalah had no office for the propagation of the Christian Gospel in Jewry, the subject at large fell almost unconditionally into the hands of occult students and schools. It comes about in this manner that, much against my own will, their views and pretensions will obtrude for consideration in brief at different stages of my research, so that they can be reduced to their proper value.

[2] It is an explanation offered by a commentator on the SEPHER YETZIRAH or BOOK OF FORMATION.

methods will offer difficulties to the ordinary student.[1] It has, indeed, proved so unintelligible upon the surface in some of its developments that, on the one hand, it has been considered merely meaningless jargon, while a few—like the late Macgregor Mathers—who claim that they have penetrated to its real sense have, on the other, found pleasure in believing that it is sealed to uninitiated persons, for whom it must ever remain a matter of curious and unrewarded research, though not perhaps wanting some gleams of unexpected suggestion. The first view suggests that more patience and greater pains were needed; the second, that the faculty for painstaking is a kind of peculiar election which is possible only to the few, and this appears unwarranted. As a fact, it is a pretence brought forward by expositors of Kabbalism belonging to occult schools of the last century, and it carries no other warrant than is characteristic of those schools.

Specialists in cryptography assure us, and we have even higher warrant in the testimony of reason itself, that no cipher writing devised by human ingenuity is incapable of solution, also by human ingenuity; but the assumption, of course, supposes good faith in the cipher: it must follow a certain method and conceal a definite sense. There is further no system of symbolism and no form of philosophical speculation, however complex, which will not surrender its secrets to the searchlight of analysis, provided always that the symbolism is systematic and that the speculation is methodised, however curious in its involutions. There are cryptic philosophies and concealed metaphysics, even as there is cryptic writing; but if they possess a meaning, it cannot escape ultimately the penetration of competent criticism, subject, however, to the distinction which must subsist of necessity between the sense of a cipher—which is unmistakable from the moment that it is disengaged—and the construction of a debate in jargon which in its minor issues may be open always to debate.[2]

There are, however, two considerations which arrest

---

[1] Obscurities, complexities and confusions do not point, however, to the existence of a double sense.

[2] The best example of a really cryptic literature is that concerned with Alchemy, and yet it is not cryptic in the sense of cipher-writing. It has a perfectly simple surface meaning; the concealment is the significance of certain conventional words and recipes. This also is its great difficulty. While cryptography must disclose its secret to skill and patience, it is nearly impossible to say what the word Vitriol, for example, may represent to any writer, if it be not the ordinary substance passing under that name.

attention on the surface of this debate. The first is whether cryptic philosophies are not inherently unmeaning, and unable therefore to disclose what, in fact, they do not possess; or alternately, in the case that they are methodised after some manner, whether the mystery which they cover is not out of all proportion to the intellectual cost of unravelling it. Of these two points one at least must be determined according to individual predilection. For my own part, after spending many years among strange pathways of human ingenuity, I know certainly that Kabbalistic Theosophy does constitute a methodised system which is curiously inwrought, at least in its later development, and since *la science est une noblesse qui oblige*, I must bear testimony to this fact, which leaves the question of values over, even though an imaginative reader may transfigure the statement and interpret too liberally the narrow concession which I have made here to sincerity. About the second point it is extremely difficult to indicate even a personal opinion on esoteric philosophies at large. So far as knowledge is its own reward, I suppose that it may be worth the cost; but if any department of research should be ruled out of the sphere of operation possessed by this truism, it is that of so-called occult science and philosophy. The labour involved by their study can repay those who undertake it only in a few cases. In the pursuit of its hidden "knowledge" Campaspe is never finished. But it is precisely for this reason that an inquiry like the present may be held to deserve a welcome, because it offers all those who may be disposed to concern themselves with one important department of esoteric philosophy an intelligible statement of the issues and their central point of value which will save such persons the need of first-hand research. It is to be observed further and finally as a clearance of all the issues that in so far as the Secret Tradition of Israel, and in so far as the cryptic metaphysics and Theosophies of other schools and nations, offer grave difficulties, they are not those of a sense within the sense, but of the one and only meaning which should and can be attached to the *chaos embrouillée* of what I have termed their jargon language.

The importance of the Written Tradition of Kabbalism can be regarded only from two standpoints. There is that which it may possess for the Sacred Scriptures of the Jewish and Christian Religions and for the exoteric doctrines which more or less derive from these.[1] Under this first head may be included its significance, if any, for the science of Comparative Theology and for the history of human thought.[2] Besides such obvious and unquestioned grounds upon which it is entitled to consideration, there is another warrant in the interest which it possesses for a sincere and informed seeker after the authentic vestiges—if any—of hidden knowledge in the past. And here it is necessary to determine what is meant and involved by such knowledge, whether real or alleged. The study of the large literature which incorporates the secret pseudo-sciences and the occult philosophies is pursued by many persons from many motives, but few of these can, in the proper sense of the term, be regarded as esoteric and much less as mystical students. Nor, indeed, does the attempted practice of one or other of the "secret sciences" in any sense constitute a claim to that title. In a very large number of cases such occupations suggest titular distinctions which are not of a flattering kind. As I understand him, the true student of THEOSOPHIA in its widest meaning is seeking evidence for the existence of a knowledge—which in effect is hidden science—handed down from remote ages,[3] which knowledge

---

[1] From the conventional occult standpoint this is of more consequence than from that of ordinary exegesis. Adolphe Bertet, in his APOCALYPSE DU BIENHEUREUX JEAN . . . DÉVOILÉE (Paris, 1861, p. 51), gives the position very clearly in respect of its arbitrary assumptions. "We find on every page of the five books of Moses Kabbalistic expressions which proclaim that everything must be taken in a figurative sense, yet in none of these books do we possess a complete treatise of initiation, whence it follows that prior to Moses oral tradition was alone charged with transmitting the secret of initiation." Bertet owed his inspiration and frequently his language to Éliphas Lévi. His dogmatic assertions are, moreover, of like value as those of his master. The Kabbalistic sense of the Pentateuch had to be invented before it could be found, and it happens that the "oral tradition" transmitted its "secrets" long ages after the books supposed to contain it had been reduced to writing.

[2] It is to be understood that this aspect of the Secret Tradition in Israel is beyond the field covered by my present undertaking, which is concerned with an examination of the literature to ascertain its mystical value.

[3] The chief aspects of this belief are, as might be expected, quite modern; it cannot be shewn to have existed prior to the end of the eighteenth century, and even then it had taken no definite shape. One of its presentations was attempted by M. de Brière, who in his ESSAI SUR LE SYMBOLISME ANTIQUE DE L'ORIENT, *principalement sur le symbolisme Égyptien* (Paris, 1847), maintained: (*a*) A common origin for all religions; (*b*) The existence of sacerdotal sciences as an exclusive patrimony of the priesthood; (*c*) The existence among all eastern priests of a common idiom of high antiquity, which passed as a theurgic, magical and efficacious language; (*d*) The reproduction of this language by hieroglyphics, which were also theurgic and magical; (*e*) A dual sacerdotal method of expressing the principles of priestly sciences, and chiefly of Theology: (1) Imitation of words = hieroglyphs of the texts; (2) Imitation of thoughts = images, idols, emblematic figures of gods; (*f*) The existence of the sacred language and hieroglyphic writing among all peoples possessing sacerdotal sciences, the Phœnicians and Chaldeans for example. This speculation may be called suggestive; but it has come to pass that after all the phantoms and all the oracles of dream we have heard the voice of Egyptology.

concerns, in Saint-Martin's language, an exposition of the relations between God, man and the universe, or the way of union between man and God. It has, according to its legend, assumed, for various reasons, the disguise of many veils; it is not confined to one country or people, nor is it the interior sense of any single religion or of any single cycle in literature to the exclusion of all others. There are alleged traces of its existence in far-off times, among many nations, through all the chief religions : [1] it has been held even to lie behind the conventional occultism of Magic and the transcendental physics of Alchemy; among Secret Traditions, Kabbalistic literature has been regarded sometimes as one of its most important vehicles.

From this standpoint the true message of the Kabbalah is not exegetical or historical; it is not of systems, schools, or interpretations; it is of a living and spiritual kind. Here is, indeed, the only vital point of view from which the subject can be regarded, and it redeems the whole circle of my present inquiry from the charge of vanity. It explains also why the research has been undertaken and why its results are offered at full length to those whom they concern.

Given this standpoint, Kabbalistic literature is indescribably momentous; but so far, unfortunately, it has been maintained and unfolded, either on the warrant of alleged knowledge which cannot be made public,[2] and is therefore idle to proclaim, or on that of evidence which is without much title —if any—to consideration. If we take, for example, the expository literature of Kabbalism which has been written from the occult standpoint in any modern language, there is not a single work which does not break down at once in the hands of the most temperate criticism. Mathers, in England, translated many years since a small portion of the ZOHAR from a printed Latin version, and prefixed an introduction which takes the whole claim for granted, while he leaves on the mind of his readers an indistinct impression that Dr. Ginsburg, who errs on the side of hostility, is not only one of its supporters, but gives credit to the most fabulous side of Kab-

---

[1] As regards the Christian religion, see Eckartshausen concerning " a more advanced school," or " invisible celestial Church," to which the " deposition of all science has been confided." THE CLOUD UPON THE SANCTUARY, Letter I. Translated by Isabel de Steiger and introduced by myself. 3rd edition, 1919.

[2] I refer to the pretensions of certain societies which worked under pledges of secrecy, here and in Paris, towards the close of the nineteenth century.

balistic Legend.¹ In America, Isaac Myer, whose learning—undigested as it is—entitles him to respect, is forced on crucial points to assume many things that are required for his hypothesis.² In France the real questions at issue are scarcely skirted in the tabulation attempted by Papus.³ In Germany, which exhausts everything, I do not know that in any true sense of the term the position has found a single defender. I propose on my own part to determine, by the testimony of its texts themselves, whether there is ground for believing that the Kabbalah has been a channel of old Tradition, and if this view must be abandoned, to place those who are willing to follow me in possession of a method of regarding it which will make its existence at least intelligible without taking anything for granted and without appealing to any source of knowledge which is not fully in evidence—the latter for the best of reasons, namely, that there is no such source.

III.—THE KABBALAH AND THE TALMUD

The post-Christian literature which is of authority in Israel must be distinguished, of course, from the multifarious productions of its scholars and *literati* which it was the object of rabbinical bibliographies, like those of Bartolocci and Wolf,⁴ to resume in brief. In order to understand the place occupied by the Kabbalah it is necessary to say something of that great and authoritative collection which is known to everyone as the TALMUD. The latter is a large as it is also an ancient growth. Its starting-point has been placed by a moderate criticism shortly before the birth of Christ,⁵ and, to use a

---

¹ It is significant also that in THE KABBALAH UNVEILED Mathers classes THE HOUSE OF GOD or of the Elohim and THE BOOK OF THE REVOLUTIONS OF SOULS—which are late developments and commentaries—among the most important sections of the ZOHAR.

² He assumes in fact the existence, antiquity and general but concealed diffusion of a Wisdom Religion, a term borrowed from Modern Theosophy, and one which, in the last analysis, is not entirely satisfactory to the mystic.

³ LA KABBALE. *Tradition Secrète de l'Occident. Résumé Méthodique.* Paris, 1892, 8vo. There was a second edition, revised and enlarged, which I have not seen, the first being conclusive as to the qualifications of the writer.

⁴ The work of Bartolocci has been cited and Wolf's title is as follows : BIBLIOTHECA HEBRÆA, *sive notitia tum auctorum Hebraicorum cujuscumque ætatis, tum scriptorum, quæ vel Hebraice primum exarata, vel ab aliis conversa sunt, ad nostram ætatem deducta.* 4 vols., Leipsic and Hamburg, 1715, 4to.

⁵ There are writers outside esoteric circles who ascribe a similar antiquity to the Kabbalah, as, for example, the author of the article *s.v. Cabale* in the GRAND DICTIONNAIRE UNIVERSEL DU XIXᵉ SIÈCLE (Pierre Larousse), t. iii. Paris, 1867. " In reality

somewhat conventional phrase, its two canons were said to have been less or more fixed in the fourth and sixth centuries, A.D.,[1] at which periods, although there are certain traces of a more esoteric doctrine, it cannot be shewn that Kabbalistic literature, according to the restricted sense in which the term is here applied, had as yet come into existence.[2] Put shortly, the sources of the TALMUD are said to be " the customs and regulations practised by the authorities in their administration of religious and civil affairs."[3] It is claimed that this source goes back to the period of Esdras, but the most that can be admitted is that materials embodied in the literature are older than their earliest collected forms. These materials were certain MISHNAYOTH, a term signifying repetitions—namely, notes of academical teachings, which received many subsequent additions.[4] Prior to the year 220, A.D., a considerable proportion of these was engarnered by Rabbi Judah the Prince,[5] by whom they were methodised carefully, short comments of his own being also added occasionally.[6] It follows that the collection received the impression of his peculiar views, from which other authorities differed. He endeavoured to destroy all rival MISHNAYOTH, but some of

---

the Kabbalah originated among the Jews five centuries before our era. Formed of the mixture of oriental ideas and Mosaism at the epoch of the captivity, it was elaborated silently, and in the main among the sect of the Karaites, but did not attain its definite development till the period of Philo and the schools of Alexandria." The inspiration here is Franck, but it must be added that the evidence is wanting. Philo, for example, cannot be cited as an indubitable witness to a Secret Tradition in Jewry.

[1] There may be mentioned, however, at its value a thesis in the JEWISH MESSENGER, July, 1837, according to which (1) the TALMUD has never been declared closed, (2) the MISHNA is an incomplete work, and (3) so also is the GEMARA.

[2] It is indeed obvious that nothing had come into writing. Professor Schiller-Szinessey testifies to a root-matter connected with the name of Rabbi Simeon and regarded as his in its source, but he offers no view as to the epoch when it began to assume a written form.

[3] THE BABYLONIAN TALMUD. English Translation. By Michael L. Rodkinson. Vol. i. New York, 1896, 8vo, pp. xv., xvi.

[4] In the HALAKOT OLAM it is said that Jewish teachers had little schedules or scrolls of parchment, in which they set down all the traditions, sentences, statutes, decisions and so forth which they learned from their masters, and that these scrolls were called the volumes of things secret. The work in question, i.e., עילובות עולם—see Habacuc iii, 6—is an introduction to Talmudic dialectic and formulæ. The author was R. Jescivah ben Joseph Hallevi, a Castilian who flourished before and after 1467. It was printed originally at Constantinople in 1510.

[5] He was the third patriarch of the Western Jews, and a legend says that, having converted the Emperor Marcus Aurelius, he compiled the MISHNA at the command of that Prince. See E. H. Palmer: HISTORY OF THE JEWISH NATION, London, 1883, pp. 204, 205. He has been called " redactor of the MISHNA." His birth is referred to circa 135, and he died in or near 220.

[6] For an old account of this labour, see David Ganz: GERMEN DAVIDIS, sive Chronologia Sacra et Prophana. Leyden, 1644.

them were preserved in secret and came to light after his death. In this way we have—

(*a*) The MISHNA, or repetition, being the methodised selection of Rabbi Judah.

(*b*) The TOSEPHTOTH, or additions, called also BARAITHOTH,[1] outsiders, or secondary matter, terms applied by the followers of Rabbi Judah to the rival MISHNAYOTH, by which the original collection is said in the course of time to have been almost extinguished. Their competitive claims were harmonised ultimately by later rabbis, and thus arose

(*c*) The GEMARA—*i.e.*, conclusion or completion.[2]

The union of the GEMARA and the MISHNA forms the TALMUD,[3] or instruction—from a word signifying "to teach" —of which there are two versions, the MISHNA being the same in each. The GEMARA collected by Jerusalem rabbis, representing the school of Tiberias and R. Johanon Ben Eliezer—*ob*. A.D. 279—with the MISHNA, forms the JERUSALEM TALMUD, and belongs to the end of the fourth century. The GEMARA collected by Babylonian rabbis, and especially by Rabina—*ob. circa* A.D. 420—R. Ashi—A.D. 353–427—and R. José, with the MISHNA, forms the TALMUD OF BABYLON, four times larger than that of Jerusalem.[4] It was begun in the fifth and completed in the sixth century, but even subsequently to this period much additional material was gathered into it.

It is exceedingly important that we should understand the position which is occupied by the great collections of the TALMUD in respect of the literature which is termed technically the Kabbalah. In the first place, this name, technical or conventional, as I have said, has suggested many errors of comparison. By the hypothesis of both literatures the TALMUD is Kabbalah even as the ZOHAR is Kabbalah, because both are matters of reception by tradition.[5] But to say that the

---

[1] And extravagances, in the sense of things extraneous.

[2] Simeon ben Yohai is represented as asserting that the study of the GEMARA was more meritorious than that of the MISHNA or the sacred Scriptures. But here a later predilection has sheltered itself under an earlier name. It may be noted that the term GEMARA came into use also as a description of the TALMUD.

[3] Strictly speaking, the term TALMUD applies only to the GEMARA, but it has obtained the wider application because the GEMARA is always accompanied by the MISHNA, the text being essential to the note.

[4] The proportion of the Babylonian GEMARA to the original MISHNA is about eleven to one.

[5] "In older Jewish literature, the name (Kabbalah) is applied to the whole body of received religious doctrine with the exception of the Pentateuch, thus including the

TALMUD is Kabbalistic in the sense of the ZOHAR is extremely misleading. The cycles are distinct and indeed divergent. There is no question as to the age and great authority of the one,[1] while some centuries of inquiry have not as yet determined the claims of the other. Moreover, could we assume the equal antiquity of both, the nature of the Tradition would be still generically different. The TALMUD is not in any sense of the term a Theosophical system:[2] it is law and commentary; it is the construction placed by authority on the jurisprudence, ecclesiastical and political, of old Israel.[3] It is sociology, not metaphysics, even if it has admitted metaphysics and has accretions which might be termed mystical.[4] To place it by the arbitrary use of a conventional term in the same category as the literature which discusses the Mysteries of the Supreme Crown, the evolution of withdrawn "Divine Subsistence," so-called, into positive being, the emanation or forthcoming of the SEPHIROTH and the origin, metempsychosis and destiny of souls, is to make a foolish and deceiving classification. M. Isidore Loëb[5] offers us the equivalent of an admirable distinction between the two literatures in his observations upon the comparative position of the French and Spanish Jews at the period of the promulgation of the ZOHAR. Talmudic Israel was, he tells us, circumscribed by the circle of the Law: it had no horizon and no future; it had no place in the life of philosophy.[6]

---

prophets and HAGIOGRAPHA, as well as the oral traditions ultimately embodied in the MISHNA."—AMERICAN ENCYCLOPÆDIA, iii., pp. 521, 522.

[1] I do not mean that there has never been a question, for the French ecclesiastic Morin, proceeding on the principle that the Jews cannot be believed in anything relating to the age of their literature, endeavoured to refer the MISHNA to the beginning of the sixth century and the GEMARAS to some two hundred years later.—EXERCITATIONES BIBLICÆ, Paris, 1660.

[2] Hence the conspicuous philosophical doctrines of the Kabbalah have no place therein. For example, the Sephirotic system, with which we shall be concerned later on, and the theory of emanation which it may suggest, cannot be traced in the TALMUD. Consult Edersheim : HISTORY OF THE JEWISH NATION, third edition, p. 406.

[3] It has been described as "a corpus juris in which the law has not yet been differentiated from morality and religion." See F. W. Farrar: LIFE OF CHRIST, illustrated edition, n.d., p. 758.

[4] It is possible to institute a comparison between the TALMUD and the Kabbalah as between Freemasonry and late Western Occultism. The TALMUD is not Mysticism, but it became the asylum of some mystical traditions. Freemasonry is not an occult teaching, but under the standard of the Craft all occult arts of the eighteenth century found not only a refuge, but a field of work and of development. The way of entrance in the one case was the Haggadic morality: in the other it was the High Grades.

[5] LA GRANDE ENCYCLOPÉDIE, Paris, 4to, s.v. CABBALE, vol. viii.

[6] "In the immense collections which have come down to us from the fifth or sixth centuries of the Christian era, in the TALMUD as in the allegorical interpretations of the Bible, there is no trace of philosophical speculations. If we find reminiscences of the

The ZOHAR gave to Israel the splendid impulsion of the ideal; it gave philosophy; it created a wide horizon; it brought the exiled Jew into correspondence with the thought of the world: it communicated the Eternal.

The first result of the confusion in question is to place a wrong construction upon Talmudic literature, to suggest that, as believed by some of the Kabbalah proper, it possesses a double meaning, and that we are to look below its literal sense.[1] It has been pointed out appositely that it would be as reasonable to admit a metaphysical construction in the Common Law of England, the deliberations of a Holy Synod in the collections of State Trials, and a theory of transmutation in Conveyancing. Yet this is what has been done actually in the case of the TALMUD by the one Kabbalistic expositor whose influence with certain groups of students in France and England was once so paramount as to have been considered almost beyond appeal. To Éliphas Lévi, who, as a fact, misstated so much and knew so little of post-Christian Jewish literature, we owe a grandiose presentation of the Talmudic system which does grave outrage to fact.[2] He lays down that the first TALMUD, the only truly Kabbalistic one, was collected during the second century of the Christian era by " Rabbi Jehudah Hakadosh Hanassi—that is, Judah the most holy and the prince "—who " composed his book according to all

---

Kabbalah, they concern, so to speak, the exoteric portion, or angelology; the existence of the speculative part is shewn in these books solely by the reference to Mysteries contained in BERESHITH, or the first chapter of Genesis, and in the MERCAVAH, or Vision of Ezekiel."—S. Munk: LA PHILOSOPHIE CHEZ LES JUIFS, Paris, 1848, p. 8. The author was an informed and accomplished defender of the existence of Kabbalistic Tradition in Talmudic times. It should be added that the Talmudic references to the Work of Creation and the Work of the Chariot would, if collated, do something to excuse the opinion that such a Tradition was known as regards the fact of its existence; but it was referred to only enigmatically, and its real nature does not transpire. While the TALMUD records occasionally that there were conversations between the doctors of Israel thereon, it does not report the utterances.

[1] Edersheim divides Talmudic traditionalism into two portions: HALAKHA = the legislative enactments of the Fathers; and HAGGADA = free interpretation.—HISTORY OF THE JEWISH NATION, p. 136. Some of the Haggadic legends may possess an inner meaning, that is, they may be allegorical stories: the history of the salting of Leviathan is so absurd in its literal sense that one is driven out of mere generosity to suppose that it meant something which does not appear on its surface. Compare ISRAEL AMONG THE NATIONS, by Anatole Leroy-Beaulieu, p. 24. As HALAKHA is rule, *norma*, so HAGGADA is legend, saga, " a collection of miscellaneous utterances touching on every possible subject." The HALAKHA alone is law.

[2] LA CLEF DES GRANDS MYSTÈRES. Paris, 1861, 8vo, p. 351, *et seq.* See also Waite: MYSTERIES OF MAGIC. Second edition, London, 1897, 8vo, pp. 112-120. It is to be noted that the ZOHAR describes the HALAKHA, MISHNA and GEMARA as heavy and involved casuistry, the MISHNA in particular being likened to a hard rock.—Part I., fol. 27b, and Part III., fol. 279.

the rules of supreme initiation." He "wrote it within and without, as Ezekiel and St. John have it, and he indicated its transcendental sense by the sacred letters and numbers corresponding to the BERESHITH of the first six SEPHIROTH"[1] of Kabbalistic Theosophy, the subject-general of which belongs to a later stage. This asserted Sephirotic correspondence has no place in reality. The MISHNA comprises six sections,[2] of which the first concerns tithes, the beasts which it is unlawful to pair, the seeds which must not be sown together in the earth, the threads which must not be interwoven, the fruits which must not be gathered till the trees have passed their third year, and so forth. It is by no means chiefly, much less exclusively, agricultural, as Lévi, who had obviously not read it, represents. Nor has it any correspondence with KETHER, except on the fantastic ground that "in the notion of the Supreme Crown is contained that of the fructifying principle and of universal production." Any attribution could be accredited after this fashion.

The second book concerns the festivals of Israel, the meats which are prohibited on these, the days of fasting and so forth. Lévi makes no attempt to justify the attribution which connects it with CHOKMAH. The third book deals with marriage and divorce, or, in the words of Lévi, "it is consecrated more particularly to women and the fundamental basis of the family." It is allocated by Lévi to BINAH, the third SEPHIRA. The fourth book embodies a consideration of civil contracts, general jurisdiction, civil and criminal actions, penalties, &c. Eliphas Lévi says that it is superior to any code of the Middle Ages and accounts for the preservation of Israel through all its persecutions. According to the natural order of the SEPHIROTH, it corresponds with CHESED or Mercy; but as it looks better under the attribution of Justice, the Sephirotic

---

[1] I should note that, long prior to Éliphas Lévi, Adrianus Relandus (ANALECTA RABBINICA, 1702) and Galatinus (DE ARCANIS CATHOLICÆ VERITATIS, 1656) supposed a second sense in the TALMUD. It was not, however, metaphysical or mystical, but was a concealment prompted by the necessities of a persecuting time. This supposition is not less idle than the other, for the first thing which prudence would have suggested would be to hide the real feelings of Talmudic Jews towards Christians, and these are not dissembled in the TALMUD. It embodies a number of stories which must not be construed literally, but, as in the case cited previously, they belong at most to the domain of allegory.

[2] The fifth section is missing from the PALESTINIAN TALMUD and it has fragments only of the sixth. See THE JEWISH ENCYCLOPÆDIA, vol. xii, s.v. TALMUD, and also for Mishnaic treatises which are wanting in the Babylonian collection.

system is reversed accordingly, and it is attributed therefore to GEBURAH. The fifth book, which is allotted to Mercy by this transposition, is concerned, according to the French transcendentalist, with consoling beliefs and things holy, which creates a completely false impression concerning it. As a matter of fact, it is dedicated to votive offerings. The sixth book treats of purifications, which Lévi terms " the most hidden secrets of life and the morality which directs it." [1] It belongs by his hypothesis to the SEPHIRA called TIPHERETH, which signifies Beauty.

It is procedures of this kind which have made occult criticism deservedly a byword among scholars.[2] The TALMUD has its correspondences with the Kabbalah, but they are of method rather than material. It is highly desirable to remember it in connection with the ZOHAR, but it is a consummate act of ignorance to confound and to regard them as written upon the same principle and with the same objects.

Another writer, who has been quoted previously and is governed by different sentiments of scholarship, the late Isaac Myer, makes an exceedingly proper distinction when he affirms that the Kabbalah and the ZOHAR " allow a great margin to speculative thought "—meaning that they are purely speculative, metaphysical and theosophical—while the TALMUD " deals with everyday life and humanity under the Law; " that the one " starts from a spiritual point of view, contemplating a spiritual finality as regards the Law and its explanation," but that the other is " eminently practical in both its starting-point and end, having, in the face of ignorance, want of perception and natural waywardness of the

---

[1] The exegesis thus inaugurated loses nothing in the hands of later occult writers. For example, an occult *opusculum* observes that the key which alone will open the revelations of the Christian Scriptures and manifest their interior sense, " exists in a book proscribed by the Christian Church—the JEWISH TALMUD." See THE ASTRAL LIGHT, by Nizida. Second edition, London, 1892, pp. 50, 51. It is just to add that this work was not regarded as of consequence by the circle to which it appealed.

[2] Some criticism which is not the work of occultists deserves the same condemnation. C. W. Heckethorn, author of the SECRET SOCIETIES OF ALL AGES AND COUNTRIES (new edition, 2 vols., 1897), presumed to treat the subject of the Kabbalah in the absence of elementary knowledge. Thus, he tells us that the literal Kabbalah is called the MISHNA (vol. I. p. 85), which, as we have seen, is traditional commentary on the legislative part of the Mosaic THORAH. So also Walton, in his eighth prolegomenon to the POLYGLOT BIBLE, observes that the terms KABBALAH and MASSORAH are applied to one science by the Jews. Richard Simon draws attention to this error, saying that the MASSORAH is the criticism of the Hebrew text.—HISTOIRE CRITIQUE DU VIEUX TESTAMENT, p. 498. Amsterdam, 1685.

masses, nothing but the strict observance of the Law in all its details in view."¹

IV.—DIVISIONS OF THE KABBALAH

Before we can proceed with our subject it will be necessary to remove some further false impressions which, unlike the esoteric aspect attributed to the TALMUD, are not errors which characterise occult pretence and ignorance, and have consequently a wider sphere of operation. They concern the nature and applications of the Tradition which is supposed to have been perpetuated in Israel. For most popular writers, for most encyclopædias of the past which have not had recourse to a specialist, the Kabbalistic Art is simply the use of Sacred Names in the evocation of spirits,² or it is that at least above all and more than all.³ We find it in sources of reference like the great dictionary of Calmet,⁴ while it obtains to this day in many slipshod accounts which pass from book to book, without any attempt at verification on the part of those who reproduce them. It illustrates the importance which is attributed everywhere to Magic, for in the last analysis all pretended occult science and all its oral traditions are resolved by the popular mind into a commerce with supposed denizens of the unseen world. I have done full justice elsewhere ⁵ to the enormous influence exercised by the belief in this commerce, so that the vulgar instinct is not entirely at fault. In a higher sense than that of Ceremonial Magic the ends of all hidden science, as of all occult arts, are assuredly in the unseen, and as to the processes of evocation I have said already that they are largely Kabbalistic processes.⁶

---

¹ PHILOSOPHY OF IBN GEBIROL, p. 35. Compare W. B. Greene: THE BLAZING STAR, 1872, 12mo. "The MASSORAH is in every respect the converse of the KABBALAH. The MASSORAH is that which was openly delivered by the Rabbi; the KABBALAH is that which was secretly and mysteriously received by the disciple," p. 29. It will be observed that this comparison appears to identify the MASSORAH and the TALMUD.
² Compare Frinellan: LE TRIPLE VOCABULAIRE INFERNAL (Paris, n.d.), p. 30: "What is termed the Kabbalah is the art of commercing with elementary spirits."
³ Sometimes, however, it is closely united with Astrology, and to speak of this occult art is considered equivalent to speaking of Kabbalistic matters. Such, apparently, was the notion of Démeunier, in L'ESPRIT DES USAGES ET DES COUTUMES DES DIFFÉRENS PEUPLES, tom. ii. lib. xi. London, 1776.
⁴ DICTIONARY OF THE BIBLE. For convenience of reference, consult C. Taylor's translation, London, 1823, vol. i. s.v. Cabbala.
⁵ THE BOOK OF CEREMONIAL MAGIC, i.e., THE SECRET TRADITION IN GOËTIA, part i. c. i. p. 3 et seq. London, 1911, 4to. It must be admitted that the term Kabbalah was applied early in its history to some forms of mediæval magical practice.
⁶ Refer to preface.

They are, however, either late and corrupt derivatives which are not the Esoteric Tradition, but applications, and hence accidents thereof; or, if we must admit that there were magical practices involving a conventional procedure and a formal Ritual prevalent among the Hebrews at a remote period,[1] which also were handed down, and are therefore entitled to be classed, in a sense, as Kabbalah, then that reception must be distinguished very carefully from the Kabbalah with which we are concerned here.[2] The Tradition of the BOOK OF FORMATION and the BOOK OF SPLENDOUR is not of Magic but of Theosophy. It has been described with enthusiasm by an almost unknown writer, in the following terms: "The Kabbalah claims to be that spontaneous philosophy which man, quoad man, naturally affirms now, always has affirmed, and always will affirm as long as man is man. The worlds confessed by the Kabbalah are worlds known to man, worlds upon which man has set the seal of his own nature, worlds related to man and of which man is the authentic form. There is nothing in the Kabbalah which is not found also in the nature of man."[3]

As we have proved it expedient to set aside the Kabbalah of the TALMUD in order to clear the issues, so also, or at least till a further stage of our inquiry, we must ignore the Kabbalah of Magic. We are dealing in part with an attempted explanation of the universe, but above all of the origin, nature and destiny of the human soul, which things are entirely distinct from processes of evocation and the art of dealing with spirits. The theurgic and talismanic use of Divine Names and the doctrine of efficacious words belong to a distinct category, and are liable to be encountered everywhere in Jewish Theosophy. As will be seen later on, there is no

---

[1] It is to these practices that I suppose Richard Simon alludes, when he says that "the ancient Jewish doctors brought many superstitious sciences from Chaldea," p. 93. This author can be hardly regarded as an authority on Kabbalistic questions; indeed, he seems to confess (*op. cit.*, pp. 116, 117) that he had not thought it worth while to expend time over "the ancient allegorical books of the Jews," such as the ZOHAR and the BAHIR.

[2] The opposite is held by an American writer, T. K. Hosmer, who says: "From this source all Jewry was overrun with demonology, thaumaturgy, and other strange fancies."—THE JEWS IN ANCIENT, MEDIÆVAL AND MODERN TIMES, London, 1890, pp. 222, 223. Speaking generally, it is most in consonance with the facts to regard the Magic which Europe received at Jewish hands as a debased application of Kabbalism.

[3] W. B. Greene: THE BLAZING STAR, p. 57. I am not endorsing the statement; but it follows from the specific teaching of the chief storehouse of Kabbalism, the ZOHAR, that apart from the human form, permanence and organisation are impossible to finite existences, whence, also, it is the form in which God communicates Himself.

question as to the antiquity of these notions, but they do not concern us now.

In virtue of another error the subject-matter of the Secret Tradition is confused with certain exegetical methods by which a scriptural authority is found for it. These methods obtained very widely, and there is no doubt that many of their most curious results contributed to swell the volume of Tradition; but the method which deals with material, and occasionally may even supply it, must be held distinct therefrom. They were, however, a matter of reception, and as such are Kabbalah; but they are not the doctrinal Kabbalah, and in the attempt to methodise our subject these also must be held as embodying things distinct.[1]

It follows from the above discriminations that there are, broadly speaking, four separate groups or species of Tradition in Israel which, by virtue of the meaning of words, are entitled to rank as Kabbalah :[2]

1. The Administrative Tradition of the TALMUD, the authoritative regulations as to the laws, customs, ceremonies and civil life of the Jewish nation. The literature of this Tradition is of great historical value, but it has no place in philosophy.

2. The Magical Tradition of the Hebrews, very important to the sources of occult arts, very obscure in its history, very much exaggerated by those who write about it, possessing little literature prior to the fourteenth century of the Christian era, by which time some speculations affirm that it had lost most of its antique elements.[3]

---

[1] P. J. Hershon divides the Kabbalah into two parts, symbolical and real. The first teaches the secret sense of Scripture and the thirteen rules by which the observance of the Law is expounded Kabbalistically, *i.e.*, GEMATRIA, NOTARICON, THEMURAH, &c. The real Kabbalah he subdivides into theoretical and practical : the one is concerned with the Emanations and Worlds of Kabbalism, the Nature and Names of God, the Celestial Hierarchy and its influence on the lower world, the Mysteries of Creation and so forth ; the other deals with the mystical properties of Divine and Angelic Names and the wonders performed with these.—TALMUDIC MISCELLANY, London, 1880. The essence of Zoharic Theosophy escapes in this division.

[2] Wynn Westcott, in a work on NUMBERS, THEIR OCCULT POWER AND MYSTIC VIRTUE, observes (p. 11) that the word Kabbalah " includes the Hebrew Doctrines of Cosmogony and Theology as well as the Science of Numbers." The first he terms the Dogmatic and the second the Literal Kabbalah. The Kabbalistic Science of numbers is included in GEMATRIA. There is, however, no such Science ; there is only a curious and unprofitable art.

[3] The indefectible title of Magic to a place in Jewish Kabbalah is enforced by all modern occultists, who have helped very much to confuse the issues in question. So far back as the end of the seventeenth century the distinction between the magical Tradition and the philosophical or doctrinal was recognised by R. Simon (HISTOIRE

3. Certain exegetical and other traditional methods by which a secret sense was extracted from the letter of Holy Scripture. Very curious results were sometimes obtained by these solemn follies, which appear so childish and ridiculous at the present day.[1] They comprise:

(*a*) GEMATRIA, a cryptographical system, by which the letters of a word were converted into numbers, and the arithmetical value was used to explain its internal sense.

(*b*) NOTARIKON, from *Notaricum*, described as a system of shorthand, by which each letter of a word was taken as the initial of another word, or, conversely, the initial letters of an entire sentence were combined to form a word, which word was held to throw light on the sentence.

(*c*) THEMURAH or Exchange, that is, the transposition of letters in a given word or sentence.

It is obvious that the field of these methods is not confined to one language or one literature; their application to the plays of Shakespeare might produce results which would exceed even the pretensions of any GREAT CRYPTOGRAM. It is a little humiliating to find an important subject and a fascinating literature connected with such diversions; but we shall see later on that the peculiar views of the Hebrews upon the divine character of their language invested them with a certain speciousness, while, for the rest, our inquiry is fortunately not concerned with them. These methods are sometimes termed the Artificial or Practical Kabbalah.[2] Their antiquity, like that of the Hebrew vowel-points, is a debated question. By some critics their traces have been discerned

---

CRITIQUE DU VIEUX TESTAMENT. Amsterdam, 1685, 4to), who said: "There is another sort of Kabbalah which is more dangerous and forms part of that which is commonly called Magic. It is mere illusion, the prepossession of certain persons who believe that they can perform miracles by means of it." (p. 374).

[1] The Kabbalistic method of interpreting Scripture, "which reduces the sense of the sacred books to vain and ridiculous subtleties, the mysteries contained in letters, in numbers, and in the dismemberment of certain words," was supposed by Simon to have passed from the school of Platonism to that of the Jews, chiefly in Europe. There seems no ground for this view. He adds (*op. cit.*, p. 374) that this "speculative Kabbalah" was, in his own day, still highly esteemed by the Jews of the Levant.

[2] They assumed sometimes the most extravagant forms. For example, the middle letter of any sacred book was written in an unusual position or of an unusual size, and was regarded as possessing a deep spiritual meaning. See THE BIBLE HANDBOOK, by Joseph Angus, D.D., 1860, p. 499. "The modes by which the Kabbalah educes the secret meaning veiled under the words of the Hebrew scriptures are manifold, extending to every peculiarity of the text. Even in what we should regard as critical marks or as errors or fancies of some transcriber, as when a letter is written too large or too small, is inverted or in any way distinguished, an occult intent was presumed." *American Encyclopædia*, iii. 521, 522.

even in Holy Scripture.¹   One point, however, which should be noted especially is that recourse to such devices is met with comparatively seldom in the ZOHAR.

4. The Philosophical Tradition, embodied in the SEPHER YETZIRAH and the ZOHAR cycles. To this only, in the interests of clearness, should the conventional term Kabbalah be applied, and it is this also which is signified by every informed writer who uses it. It is divided by Kabbalists themselves into

(*a*) The Doctrine of Creation,
(*b*) The Doctrine of the Throne or Chariot—*i.e.*, the Chariot of Ezekiel's vision.²

These divisions are concerned respectively with the natural and the metaphysical world, and are sometimes termed collectively the Theoretical Kabbalah. There is a broad and rough sense in which it may be said that SEPHER YETZIRAH embodies the Doctrine of Creation, while that of the Chariot is to be sought in SEPHER HA ZOHAR. But we shall find that the latter is full of creation myths, while, although it is our chief source of Tradition on Chariot Theosophy, the doctrine is only imbedded therein, its methodical extraction and development being the task of later Kabbalists. The so-called theoretical Kabbalah is that which gave to Israel—at least in respect of opportunity—the intellectual horizon which was impossible to the Talmudic Jew, and it is this also which gave the Children of the Exile a place in western philosophy. When we hear that the Kabbalah once fascinated some of the great minds of Christendom, it is to this only that the statement can be applied.³ It is this, finally, which it is the purpose of the present inquiry to elucidate.⁴ It should be added that

---

¹ The TARGUM to the Prophets, called the official TARGUM, which passes traditionally under the name of Jonathan ben Uzziel, a disciple of Hillel the Great, in the days of King Herod, has recourse occasionally to a species of transliteration when dealing with certain obscure scriptural names. It has been referred to the third century.

² Both these divisions are mentioned in the MISHNA by name (CHAGIGA, xi. 2), and are said to be Secret Doctrine, but the MAASEH BERESHITH and the MAASEH MERKABAH there referred to are not a written tradition, nor does that of the written Kabbalah necessarily represent it. The ZOHAR identifies MERCABAH with the SEPHIROTH or Ten Emanations, which will be examined at a further stage.

³ Drach distinguishes three uses of the term Kabbalah for which authority can be cited : (1) It is applied frequently by the TALMUD to the books of the Old Testament, outside the Pentateuch ; (2) The rabbins apply it to the Legal or Talmudic Tradition ; (3) It signifies especially the " mystic, esoteric, acroamatic portion of the Oral Tradition."—DE L'HARMONIE ENTRE L'ÉGLISE ET LA SYNAGOGUE. *Par le* Chevalier P. L. B. Drach, 2 vols., Paris, 1844, Vol. II., pp. xv-xxxvi.

⁴ Some readers may think it desirable to include the division of the Kabbalah proposed by Papus in one of his publications, though it is, critically speaking, fantastic.

outside the cycle of the ZOHAR there is a considerable Jewish theosophical and mystical literature, of which the SEPHER YETZIRAH is an instance. It was this which led up to the ZOHAR, and was embraced thereby. But whether it was Kabbalistic in the sense of the latter is one of the disputes of scholarship.

The Kabbalah, in his opinion, was attributable to Moses, and the written word of Scripture is therefore naturally a part of the Tradition. We have thus : (*a*) The written word ; (*b*) The oral word ; (*c*) An intermediate portion, being rules insuring the preservation of the text, *i.e.* MASSORAH. The last is the body of the Oral Tradition ; the MISHNA and GEMARA are its life ; the SEPHER YETZIRAH and the ZOHAR are its spirit. Unfortunately Papus did nothing to elucidate and nothing to justify his thesis, and assumed, as he did too often, the most important points at issue. Moreover, the Massoretic annotations are not comprehended by the explanation offered. See TRAITÉ ÉLÉMENTAIRE DE SCIENCE OCCULTE, 5ᵉ édition, Paris, 1898.

BOOK II

SOURCE AND AUTHORITY OF THE KABBALAH AND THE AGE OF THE CHIEF TEXTS

BOOK II

SOURCE AND AUTHORITY OF THE KABBALAH

I.—DATE OF THE BOOK OF FORMATION

HAVING sought to distinguish the subjects proper of the Secret Tradition in Israel from certain side issues and a mass of overgrowth, we have to ascertain in the next place whether and how far we are warranted by evidence in regarding the texts which embody it as authentic memorials and its doctrines as part of a Tradition perpetuated in Israel from early times.[1] For this purpose it will be convenient to accept the literature as divisible into four classes—(1) The BOOK OF FORMATION; (2) The commentaries on that work which preceded the public appearance of the ZOHAR; (3) The ZOHAR itself; (4) The writings subsequent thereto.[2]

The report of an Esoteric Tradition in Israel did not begin to circulate through Christendom till the fourteenth century, and this, as we shall see later on, is explained by the fact that the chief collection of its archives was unknown, at least generally, in Jewry itself till about 1290, A.D. This collection is that which is termed by Kabbalists the Work of the Chariot, represented by the ZOHAR. The Work of Creation—to

---

[1] It is pertinent to recall at this point what has been said in my prefatory words on the question of antiquity. The subject is approached here with that reservation in view, its determination being essential on what may be called the historical side. We must know under what circumstances the Tradition comes before us, whatever the final values.

[2] Solomon Munk, who still ranks high among French authorities on Kabbalism, tabulates the following classification in the DICTIONNAIRE DE LA CONVERSATION, *s.v.* KABBALE. (1) A symbolical portion, namely, mystical calculations, *i.e.*, THEMURAH, GEMATRIA, NOTARICON, on which refer to Book I. § 4; (2) A dogmatic or positive part, which is, in fact, concerned with the hypothesis of spiritual essences, *i.e.*, angels, demons, human souls and their transmigration; (3) A speculative and metaphysical part, namely, Sephirotic Doctrine and so forth. It is not an exhaustive classification, but there is no need to criticise it here. The Secret Tradition on its Theosophical side is not represented by a bare allusion to Sephirotic Doctrine.

which the SEPHER YETZIRAH[1] corresponds—was known, as we have some ground for believing, to at least one Christian student so far back as the middle of the ninth century, but there was no consequence attached to it for Christendom.[2] The SEPHER YETZIRAH is supposed to embody a Tradition handed down from the time of Abraham, and there is no doubt that the uncritical spirit of several centuries represented the patriarch as its author. This does not seem, however, as some modern criticism has supposed loosely,[3] to have been the view adopted universally by the Jewish learning which accepted the document. That he received and he transmitted it was held undoubtedly, but the work itself is not pretended to have been reduced to writing till after the destruction of Jerusalem, and tradition has ascribed its formal authorship to Rabbi Akiba ben Joseph,[4] the pupil of R. Joshua ben Hananiah,[5] who was himself the successor, as he was also once the opponent, of Rabban Gamaliel.[6] There is nothing flagrantly improbable in this attribution, though it reaches us late in history. Akiba was a speculator with whose notions the scheme of the SEPHER YETZIRAH was in complete accordance, and he is the reputed author of another work dealing with the mysteries of the Hebrew Alphabet.[7] In his interpre-

---

[1] See THE BOOK OF FORMATION (SEPHER YETZIRAH). Translated from the Hebrew, with Annotations, by Knut Stenring, 1923. The bibliography of the text is treated at some length in an introduction prefixed by myself.

[2] Maimonides explains in his GUIDE OF THE PERPLEXED that MAASEH BERESHITH corresponds to physical and MAASEH MERKABAH to metaphysical science. They have been termed otherwise the History of Creation and the History of the Divine Throne.

[3] Dr. Edersheim, HISTORY OF THE JEWISH NATION, observes that it is properly "a monologue on the part of Abraham, in which, by the contemplation of all that is around him, he ultimately arrives at the conviction of the unity of God." 3rd ed. p. 407. So also Ginsburg says that it professes to be a monologue of the patriarch. It does nothing of the sort; but the fifth chapter mentions "Abraham our father." Of course, the legend of patriarchal derivation became stereotyped quickly. In the twelfth century, R. Judah Ha Levi speaks of "the Book of the Creation which belongs to our father Abraham."

[4] He is said to have perished in the Bar Cochba rebellion, A.D. 120, but this is wrong, and the evidence points to his martyrdom twelve years later for transgressing the edict of Hadrian against the practice of the Jewish religion. He was born A.D. 50.

[5] He was the leading Tanna of the period which followed immediately on the destruction of the Temple. The Tanna was a Teacher of the Oral Law.

[6] He was the head of Palestinian Jews at the close of the first century and in the opening years of the second.

[7] It is called the ALPHABET of R. Akiba, being the letters allegorically explained. It was printed at Cracovia in 1597, with a *Commentarius Prolixus*. See Buxtorf's BIBLIOTHECA HEBRÆA RABBINICA. Basilia, 1618-19, 4 vols. fol. An earlier edition of the Alphabet appeared at Venice in 1546. See Bartolocci, iv. 274. Karppe suggests that it was originally a method of teaching children to read. ÉTUDES SUR LES ORIGINES ET LA NATURE DU ZOHAR, pp. 108, 109. Compare the analogous proposition that SEPHER YETZIRAH was meant to serve as a Hebrew Grammar.

tation of Scripture he followed and exaggerated the principles of Hillel the Great and Nahum of Giso.¹ He promulgated, or at least gave the weight of his authority to the doctrine that "every sentence, word and particle in the Bible has its use and meaning."² His literary labours were also very great, for to him is attributed the arrangement and redaction of the HALAKHA. Subsequent generations were so impressed by his marvellous knowledge of divine things that he was asserted to have discovered much of which even Moses was ignorant, which, in the sense not intended, is indubitably true. If we admit the existence of a Secret Tradition in Israel, we shall not need to question that Akiba was initiated therein; if we admit the existence of the SEPHER YETZIRAH in the second century, we can imagine no more probable author for that work.³ Nor is the date essentially disagreeable to a moderate criticism⁴; it is merely unestablished for want of overt evidence,⁵ which begins only with the ninth century, when there is barely tolerable reason to infer that it may have been known by St. Agobard.⁶ It is not possible from any internal testimony to fix the work as belonging to the later period, for obviously any book may be much older than the date of its first quotation, while the fact, if established, that it was known in France in or about the year 850 ⁷ would create a

---

¹ Hillel was of high authority among the Scribes and Pharisees in the days of King Herod, and is said to have been familiar with the whole Traditional Law. Nahum was the instructor of Akiba.

² Edersheim, HISTORY OF THE JEWISH NATION.

³ Curiously enough, M. Nicolas admits the date necessary but not the authorship it suggests, on the ground that Akiba was a rigid and head-strong doctor of the Law and not likely to indulge in speculative lucubrations. This estimate, with which it is difficult to agree, has also the authority of Franck, on the ground that the TALMUD reproaches Akiba for his incommensurate notions of God; but Franck is possibly more influenced by his belief in the earlier origin of the work.—LA KABBALE, p. 87 *et seq.* Whether Yetziratic notions of Deity are not inadequate also is another question.

⁴ It has been argued that the language of the SEPHER YETZIRAH is a Hebrew wholly analogous to that of the MISHNA.

⁵ Dr. Schiller-Szinessy says expressly that the book no doubt belongs to Akiba, "both in substance and form."—ENCYCLOPÆDIA BRITANNICA, 9th ed., *s.v.* MIDRASHIM, a term derived from a root signifying to seek out or to question. Munk also takes this view in the article *s.v.* KABBALE, contributed to the ninth volume of the DICTIONNAIRE DE LA CONVERSATION ET DE LA LECTURE, Paris, 1833.

⁶ The English reader may consult Taylor's translation of Basnage's HISTORY OF THE JEWS, p. 590 *et seq.* London. 1708. Agobard was Archbishop of Lyons, and wrote against trials by ordeal and other superstitions of his period. See the Abbé Migne: DICTIONNAIRE DES SCIENCES OCCULTES, vol. i. col. 32. Despite this apparent enlightenment he figures among the persecutors of Jewry. See Basnage: HISTOIRE DES JUIFS, t. v. pp. 1493, 1494.

⁷ The evidence falls far short of demonstration, and is confined to two short passages in the EPISTOLA S. AGOBARDI . . . DE JUDAICIS SUPERSTITIONIBUS. In the first, the Jews are branded for their gross notions of the Deity, on the ground that they believe

presumption that it was in existence much earlier, since literature travelled slowly in those days. We must remember also that a SEPHER YETZIRAH is mentioned in both TALMUDS, in connection with the doctrine that heaven and earth were created by a mysterious combination of letters, and that Franck characterises the attempt of some modern scholarship to distinguish two works under an identical title as founded in gross ignorance.[1] If, however, we do not place the work in Talmudic times, we may concede that it came into existence within a measurable distance of the stormy period in which the great Talmudic canons reached their term.

We have to distinguish in the next place between the date which may be surmised for the treatise and that which must perhaps be attributed to the notions embodied therein. Have we any ground for believing that the doctrine of the SEPHER YETZIRAH is older than the Egyptian captivity, as its legend affirms? This question must be answered by an emphatic negative. The doctrine under notice gives prominence to the sacred and divine character of the Hebrew alphabet, and we have no warrant for supposing that the art of writing was possessed by Abraham; every probability is against it and every authority is agreed on this point. But the SEPHER YETZIRAH contains, by implication at least, the doctrine of an occult power and sanctity inherent in certain Divine Names,[2] and we know that this belief is very old in humanity, that it is found at an early period in Chaldea, Akkadia and so forth. It is ridiculous for modern intelligence, but it is of great antiquity, and as it belongs to those countries with which Israel was in contact, there is reason to

---

Him to be possessed of a bodily form, having distinct members and lineaments, including organs of seeing, hearing, speaking and so forth; also that they note only one difference between the body of God and that of man who is in His image, namely, that the fingers are inflexible, because God effects nothing with his hands. It seems certain that St. Agobard draws here from the DESCRIPTION OF THE BODY OF GOD. In the second passage it is said: "Further, they believe the letters of their alphabet to have existed from everlasting, and before the beginning of the world to have received diverse offices, in virtue of which they should preside over created things."—S. AGOBARDI, LUGDUNENSIS EPISCOPI, OPERA OMNIA. *Patrologiæ Cursus Completus : . . accurante* J. P. Migne. Paris, 1851, p. 78 *et seq.* This appears to indicate an acquaintance with SEPHER YETZIRAH, though obviously misconstruing its meaning, or is alternatively a reference to Akiba's ALPHABET, the date of which in its two extant versions seems highly conjectural. The TALMUDS are also a possible source of the statement. Karppe (*op. cit.*, p. 129) affirms that St. Agobard quotes almost verbatim from the ALPHABET.

[1] On this fact Franck insists very strongly, maintaining that these references demonstrate the existence of a work reserved to a few and that this work is identical with the SEPHER YETZIRAH as we now have it.—LA KABBALE, Paris, 1843, p. 75 *et seq.*

[2] See Appendix IV.

think that it may have become part of the religious baggage of the Hebrew people long before any Master in Israel dreamed of the SEPHER YETZIRAH, the ALPHABET of Akiba, or even the MISHNA itself. Purveyors of occult reverie have attached themselves naturally and inevitably to this doctrine,[1] and we must allow that the most ancient document of Kabbalism[2] does embody in this subject something of Tradition from the past, perhaps even from the period of the Babylonian captivity, as the TALMUD itself indicates. On the other hand, we have no evidence to shew that the doctrine of the Instruments of Creation is much prior to the date of the treatise which develops it; it has no history previously, and can be placed therefore at most in Talmudic—*i.e.*, in post-Christian—times. It should be added that the SEPHER YETZIRAH is part of a considerable literature of an occult or cryptic complexion covering the period between the Talmudic Age and the first report of the ZOHAR.[3]

II.—MODERN CRITICISM OF THE BOOK OF SPLENDOUR

The commentaries on the SEPHER YETZIRAH which preceded the publication of the Zohar make no claim on antiquity, and may be reserved for consideration in their proper place later on. The alleged traces of Kabbalism in writers of known dates also prior to that event may be left in like manner till we deal with the documents consecutively. We can proceed therefore at once to the several problems connected with the BOOK OF SPLENDOUR. Chief among these

---

[1] And so also, it would seem, has one elementary form of modern Christian Mysticism. See, for example, the collection entitled LETTERS FROM A MYSTIC OF THE PRESENT DAY, by an anonymous writer. Second edition, London, 1889, pp. 205-207. "We seem to have to learn the *various* names of God before we can grasp *the* Name. *The* Name grasps us, while the others are various outer courts through which we come into the Sanctuary or Name of God; in that name we find pasture wherever our outer life may take us." Compare Saint-Martin: L'ESPRIT DES CHOSES, tom. ii. 65 *et seq.*

[2] I ought not, perhaps, to omit that Mayer Lambert, one of the French editors of the SEPHER YETZIRAH, affirms that it has nothing in common with the Kabbalah, by which he understands a mysterious explanation of the Bible drawn from the letters of the text and a metaphysical theory which connects God with the world through a series of emanations of Divinity. As regards its date, he agrees that it is one of the numerous MIDRASHIM produced by the Talmudic period. It should be added that this definition of Kabbalism does not answer to the ZOHAR in any adequate or tolerable sense.

[3] See Phineas Mordell—in the JEWISH QUARTERLY REVIEW, 1913—on the tradition that SEPHER YETZIRAH was written by Joseph ben Uzziel towards the end of the fifth century.

are the questions: (1) Whether some modern criticism is right in ascribing the ZOHAR to the thirteenth century as its period, and to R. Moses Shem Tob de Leon as its author. (2) Whether we have evidence that part at least of its doctrine was in existence at a much earlier period, or, as its legend states, at the time of the Roman Emperor Antoninus.

We shall get very little help from the insight of contemporary Israel as to either point. The SEPHER YETZIRAH was known and accepted before documentary criticism can be said to have been conceived or born; and so also when the ZOHAR was promulgated it was among a mixed audience who either took or rejected it on *à priori* grounds. Those who loathed the yoke of Aristotle, which Abraham ben David Ha Levi (*ob. circa* A.D. 1126), Abraham ben Meïr Ibn Ezra (*circa* 1092–1167), and Moses Maimonides (1131–1201) would have placed on the neck of Jewry, accorded it a glad welcome.[1] All that great section of Jewry which was addicted to Astrology and Magic took it into their heart of hearts: it was neither Magic nor Astrology, but it harmonised with their peculiar aspirations. On the other hand, it was hated by the Aristotelians because it did not consort with their methods.[2] It is not till recent times that we have any intelligent defence on the part of Jewish thinkers—Konitz in 1815,[3] Franck in 1843, David Luria in 1857,[4] Munk in 1859; or, on the other hand, a strong and informed hostility, as that of Graetz[5] in Germany, to quote only one instance.

---

[1] The contrariety of the two systems is best shewn by this fact. Myer says: "Its opponents were almost universally Jewish Aristotelians, who opposed the ancient secret learning of the Israelites because it was more in accord with the philosophy of Plato and Pythagoras, and indeed most likely emanated from the same sources, the Aryan and Chaldean esoteric doctrine."—PHILOSOPHY OF IBN GEBIROL, p. 12. It is the fact only which is of value: Myer's explanation may be read in the light of Book ii. § 5.

[2] "When the Saracens became the patrons of philosophy . . ., the attention paid both by Arabians and Christians to the writings of Aristotle excited the emulation of the Jews, who, notwithstanding the ancient curse pronounced on all Jews who should instruct their sons in the Grecian learning, . . . continued in their philosophical course reading Aristotle in Hebrew translations made from the inaccurate Arabic, for Greek was at this period little understood."—Gould: HISTORY OF FREEMASONRY, London, 1885, ii. 66, 67; see also 69, 70.

[3] See Isaac Myer, *op. cit.*, pp. 20 *et seq*.

[4] See his KADMOOTH HA ZOHAR, which appeared at Johannesburg at or about the date in question. It maintained that the completion of the ZOHAR was much prior to that of the BABYLONIAN TALMUD and that some of its doctrines were cited by Babylonian Geonim on the authority of a MIDRASH YERUSHALMI, which was in fact the ZOHAR.

[5] Perhaps it is more strong than it is well informed. I see no trace in Graetz of any real acquaintance with the Kabbalah, about which he writes savagely and with the indiscrimination which we connect with a savage. Thus, he terms the ZOHAR "a notorious forgery," whereas the chief notoriety concerning it is that after nearly seven

In estimating the influence exercised by the Kabbalah upon certain minds of Christendom, the SEPHER YETZIRAH must be distinguished from the ZOHAR. The former has had no influence; it was indeed introduced to our knowledge by a monk of exalted erudition and of eccentricity equally great, but it was not till the sixteenth century, and it found no sphere of operation. Some of its Sephirotic developments, the commentaries of Rabbi Abraham and Rabbi Azriel, met with a certain audience among a few men of learning; but they can bear no comparison with the appeal made by the larger cycle. For Christian students the Kabbalah was either the ZOHAR itself or it was developments therefrom, and, as we shall see subsequently, the office attributed to it was almost exclusively evangelical: that is to say, the discovery that there had existed in Israel, from time immemorial, as it was alleged, a Secret Doctrine which appeared to contain analogies and even identities with fundamental dogmas of Christianity, put the Jews so clearly in the wrong, by their own shewing, that their conversion was deemed inevitable.[1] Thus, the antiquity of the Tradition was not at that time challenged in Christendom, and again it was not a period when documentary criticism was pursued with any keenness. The fourteenth century made the grave, but yet excusable, mistake of supposing that most people wrote the books attributed to them. They accepted the claim of the ZOHAR for much the same reason that they were persuaded of the antiquity of Homer. In the existing state of scholarship to have challenged one might have opened an abyss beneath the other, and could well have included all ancient literature in a common uncertainty. Of course, as time went on and the evangelical instrument proved to be of no effect, its validity began to be challenged, but even then it was scarcely on critical grounds. So also even at the inception of the enthusiasm, some sceptical voices

---

centuries of criticism scarcely two authorities can be found to agree in their estimate. Throughout this part of his history we encounter things uncertain described in the language of certitude, and things for which there is little evidence as if there were overwhelming testimony.

[1] " Some Christians have also esteemed them (*i.e.*, the Kabbalistic books and their connections) because they found them more favourable to the Christian religion than recent commentaries of the Rabbins. But they failed to consider that these same allegorical books are filled with an infinitude of ridiculous fables, and that Jewish superstition is much more clearly proved from them than are the Mysteries of our Religion. William Postel has imposed on several theologians in this matter, having pretended to find Christianity in the books of the ZOHAR."—Richard Simon: HISTOIRE CRITIQUE DU VIEUX TESTAMENT, p. 371.

were raised, but again from uncritical and predetermined motives.[1] The Christians who rejected the Zohar were like the Jews who rejected it—the latter because they were Aristotelians, the former because they were Christians, who saw no good in the Ghetto, and only the final impenitence of the lost thief in the erudition of Toledo.[2]

The credulity, or at least the disability, of early students has been atoned for amply in the spirit which has governed later critics of the Kabbalah. I must confess that in some cases they seem, after their own manner, to have prejudged the question much as that laborious bibliographer Julius Bartolocci prejudged it in the seventeenth century. It was offensive to the dignity of the Latin Church to suppose that there was a rival Tradition, full of illumination and wisdom, preserved unknown to the Church in the rejected House of Israel. By a similar sentiment it has seemed intolerable to modern notions that any cryptic literature should possess a real claim on attention. It is therefore said out of hand that the Kabbalah, represented by the ZOHAR, is a forgery of the thirteenth century. We must endeavour to comprehend precisely what is involved in this standpoint.

There are some literary fabrications which do not need a high degree of scholarship to expose them, for they may be said to betray themselves, often at every point. In the department of *belles lettres* it is sufficient to mention the so-called Rowley poems. These, as everybody is aware, were forgeries pure and simple, and their disguise is so entirely spurious that it can be peeled off without any difficulty. It is not necessary to add that they possessed their believers, and not further back than the days of the Bell edition of Chatterton, the race of Rowleyites had still a few survivals, for we find the editor describing their characteristics in terms which have a wider application than he was concerned with at the moment. A true Rowleyite, he says, is not open to

---

[1] Among writers who did not permit themselves to be deceived by the alleged instrument of conversion, a high place must be accorded to Petrus Galatinus and his DE ARCANIS CATHOLICÆ VERITATIS *contra Judæorum perfidiam*, first published in 1518.

[2] The connection between Christianity and the ZOHAR once found an occasional expositor in French occult circles. Consult Stanislas de Guaita : ESSAIS DES SCIENCES MAUDITES. I. *Au Seuil du Mystère. Nouvelle édition, corrigée.* Paris. 1890. "The ZOHAR has wedded the Gospel ; the spirit has fructified the soul ; and immortal works have been the fruits of this union. The Kabbalah became Catholic in the school of St. John," &c. A romantic criticism, inspired by Éliphas Lévi and utterly devoid of warrant.

conviction, and the statement obtains in the case of all pertinacious defenders of spurious literary productions. The position of the Rowley MSS. is fairly paralleled by that of many occult documents, among which, as typical instances, we may select the handboks of Ceremonial Magic. There are no works which betray themselves more transparently and abundantly than certain versions of the KEY OF SOLOMON and its connections, or the SACRED MAGIC OF ABRAMELIN THE MAGE, and yet they possessed their believers in England only some decades ago, enthusiasts for the good faith of their claims to a high antiquity or a Hebrew origin, as the case might be.

There are again some fabrications which possess a certain basis in fact, over which a mass of forgery has been arranged. One ready instance in point is found in the poems of Ossian, for which there was indubitably a nucleus of floating Gaelic tradition, and it was wrought into his production by MacPherson. The result may deceive for a moment even sound scholarship, but its full exposure is only a matter of time. In this case the epic of WALLACE was fatal to the possibility of Fingal. The Latin alchemical writings attributed to Geber might be regarded as typical instances in occult literature of this form of fraud, if we could accept Berthelot's view that they have scarcely any resemblance to the Arabic originals, for such originals exist.[1]

Finally, there are certain works which may or may not be fabrications, but either they incorporate so much genuine material belonging to the department of literature which they pretend to represent, or else are constructed so skilfully that the balance of probability is poised pretty equally concerning them, and it is almost impossible to arrive, by impartial methods, at the determination of their claims. I do not know whether there is any good instance in *belles lettres* of this kind of alleged fabrication. Hogg's JACOBITE RELICS OF SCOTLAND is perhaps the nearest approach to a parallel. That collection contains undoubtedly a large proportion of genuine material, but it is suspected that the Ettrick Shepherd supplied a proportion of the memorable garner by his own skill in

---

[1] See my SECRET TRADITION IN ALCHEMY, 1926, p. 117, for a note on Djaber texts which have come to light since Berthelot wrote. There is ground for believing that they—and not the texts edited by the French chemist—are the originals of the Latin Geber.

verse-craft, and criticism, though it has not concerned itself seriously, is perhaps divided fairly on the question. In so-called occult literature we have several signal examples of such suspected writing which has not been found out to the satisfaction of the impartial mind. For example, a few of the Hermetic books, which are classed by scholars as productions of the Alexandrian period, and therefore as post-Christian, are held by others to represent traditions of considerable antiquity, and I do not know that the case has been decided for all time as regards one or two of these works. But the most renowned of all the instances is that with which we are here concerned—the Kabbalah itself. Destructive criticism has maintained that its foremost work was forged by a single writer, of indifferent claims to our intellectual consideration, at the end of the thirteenth century. There is, as we shall see, no positive evidence on this point which is worth naming, and the presumptive evidence is not at all strong. There is very good proof of late writing, but the theory of the fabrication of the ZOHAR by Moses de Leon puts an almost impossible burden on the shoulders of that questionable personage, and is generally the work of writers who have not paid sufficient regard to the possible existence of much of the traditional doctrine which is summarised in the ZOHAR at a period preceding its appearance, perhaps even by some centuries.

It must be recognised therefore that Kabbalistic literature belongs to a suspected class, but how we are to regard its impeachment is a different question. In respect of material and usually as regards its motive, spurious literature belongs to the most accountable class. It falls into line readily. Where there are complex workings of the human mind, as in the ZOHAR, there sincerity is usually present. The Kabbalah is much too singular in its mechanism, and far too piecemeal in its numerous texts, to be referable to a solitary author. So far as there is evidence on the subject, that evidence tends to shew that it grew, and that in its final state it was neither wholly old nor entirely new, but doctrine more or less familiar or following from familiar doctrine.[1] These facts are in

---

[1] This is very nearly the position of Solomon Munk, who maintained that the ZOHAR and its connections, that is, the various tracts and fragments which enter into the compilation, are not the inventions of an impostor, but that ancient documents were used by the editor, including MIDRASHIM which are not now extant.—MÉLANGES DE PHILOSOPHIE, JUIVE ET ARABE. Paris. 1859, p. 275 *et seq.* In spite of this,

course of open recognition in the academic circles which rule general opinion. Of this Dr. Schiller-Szinessy offered perhaps in his day the best evidence when he observed that " almost all that the latest critics have said concerning the age of the various TARGUMIM and MIDRASHIM," including the ZOHAR, " will have to be unsaid." [1]

III.—THE DATE AND AUTHORSHIP OF THE BOOK OF SPLENDOUR

The theory which accounts for the ZOHAR on the ground that it was written by Moses de Leon in the latter half of the thirteenth century does not depend merely on internal evidence: it is not exclusively an inference made by modern criticism from allusions to late events found here and there in the work; it is not a presumption arising only from an alleged fact that the Spanish Jew who is suspected of the splendid imposture lived by transcribing copies of it; [2] that it had never been heard of previously; or that the original MS. from which R. Moses claimed to have drawn has never come to light. It is based upon supposed evidence which claims to be contemporary, or thereabouts, with the appearance of the ZOHAR itself. It may be highly probable that in the absence of such testimony, if it could pass muster, the same point would have been reached independently; but the fact remains that, supposing the evidence has been construed rightly, then the chief charge against the ZOHAR is not a discovery of modern criticism at all; it transpired without being sought for, and hence the case against the work is based both on external and internal grounds. It is not therefore at

---

Munk did not consider that the ZOHAR, at least in its present form, was anterior to the seventh century, but rather that the Kabbalistic developments which it represents took place in the thirteenth century, and were either influenced by Gebirol (1021–1070) or by sources common to both.—*Ibid.* pp. 276, 277.

[1] See the article on MIDRASHIM in the ninth edition of ENCYCLOPÆDIA BRITANNICA, already cited.

[2] It is accepted as such by all critics who depend on the account of the ZOHAR given in the SEPHER YUHASIN, but it seems to me that the statement has an air of fable. The ZOHAR is a very large work, and Moses de Leon must have employed a staff of copyists in order to transcribe it frequently. There is no evidence, however, that he employed any one; but if he worked single-handed, he could not have " made large sums," as alleged, by so slow a process. It has been suggested alternatively that he profited much by the patronage of wealthy Jews, to whom he dedicated his books; but as to this there is no conclusive evidence. It is merely an inference from the fact that he addressed several other works to co-religionists who were, *ex hypothesi*, his patrons.

first sight a weak case and must be sketched fully and frankly, that I may not be accused of any bias in the matter. At the same time it is my purpose to shew that the indictment breaks down altogether.

Let us dispose first of all of the alleged external evidence. In the year 1566 there appeared in Hebrew at Constantinople a work entitled SEPHER YUHASIN, or BOOK OF GENEALOGIES, by R. Moses Abraham ben Samuel Zakut, who belongs to the second half of the fifteenth century.[1] Its point of view with regard to the ZOHAR is that the splendour of that work is truly an illumination of the world; that it contains deep secrets of the Law and of concealed Tradition in Israel; that it is conformed to the truth as regards both Written and Oral Law; that it embodies the sayings of R. Simeon ben Yohai, of the period of the Emperor Antoninus, under whose name it appears, but is really the work of his disciples; and that, finally, it did not become public till after the death of Nahmanides, namely, the second half of the thirteenth century.[2] It is therefore obvious that R. Moses Abraham must not be classed among those who opposed the ZOHAR, as some modern critics have attempted to shew.

It will seem almost incredible that in this work, which so defends the ZOHAR, a narrative should be found which appears to represent it as an imposture devised from mercenary motives by Moses de Leon, otherwise, Moses ben Shem-Tob; yet such at first sight is the case, and as such it has been accepted by those who impeach the work. The explanation is in reality simple; the narrative in question is a fragment, and the proof that its missing conclusion is really to the credit of the ZOHAR, and exculpatory as to the transcriber of that work, resides in the fact that the person whose adventures it relates became assured subsequently that the ZOHAR was not a splendid forgery, seeing that he embodied some of its principles in one of his own treatises. The most biassed of modern critics, Dr. Graetz, admits the force of this fact.

---

[1] That is to say, to the reign of Ferdinand and Isabella. He was a Jew of Salamanca, but he taught at Saragossa. When the edict of expulsion was published he retired into Portugal and was appointed Royal Historiographer by King Emanuel. The YUHASIN embraces the entire period between the creation of the world and the year 1500 A.D. It was in great repute among Latin bibliographers of Kabbalism and is cited continually by Bartolocci.

[2] Moses ben Nahman Gerondi, the Spanish Talmudist of Gerona, called also Ramban and Nahmanides, died in Palestine, *circa* 1270.

ANTIQUITY OF THE ZOHAR

The narrative is concerned with the adventures of Isaac de Acco [1]—a disciple of Nahmanides—who laid claim to the performance of miracles by a transposition of Hebrew letters according to a system which he pretended that he had learned from the angels. It will be seen that he was therefore a visionary, unless a rougher criticism be held to apply. In any case, he was at Novara, in Italy, about 1293, when he heard that a Spanish Rabbin was in possession of the original ZOHAR MS., and, being very anxious to see it, he made a journey into Spain. He learned there by report that the erudite Moses Nahmanides was said to have transmitted the book to his son in Catalonia from Palestine,[2] but that the ship which bore it was driven by wind to Aragonia [3] or to Catalonia, and the precious volume came into the hands of Moses de Leon. At Valladolid Isaac de Acco made the acquaintance of the latter, who declared upon oath that he was in possession of the MS. and that it was at his home in Avila, where he would exhibit it to Isaac. They undertook a journey together with this object, but Moses de Leon died at Arevolo on the way.[4] His companion proceeded to Avila, and there prosecuted his inquiries among the relatives of the deceased. By one of these, namely, by David Rafon of Corfu, he was informed that Moses de Leon had been a spendthrift who derived great profit from his writings,[5] but neglected his wife and daughter,[6] while as for the ZOHAR he had made it up out of his own head. How far Isaac was impressed by this testimony does not appear explicitly; but he next had recourse to a wealthy Rabbin of Avila, named Joseph, who communicated with the widow and daughter of Moses, offering for the maiden the hand of his son and a substantial dowry if they would produce the original MS. of the ZOHAR. The women had been left in poor circumstances, and there was every reason to suppose that they would comply gladly. They concurred, however,

---

[1] I.e., Acre, besieged by the Sultan of Egypt in 1291. Isaac was one of the Jewish refugees from that city, and seems to have suffered imprisonment for a time.

[2] It is curious that the disciple should first learn that his master was in possession of such a treasure by a floating rumour from a great distance.

[3] The reference is probably to Alicante, as Arragon has no seaboard.

[4] So far the account represents Moses de Leon as acting with sincerity in the matter.

[5] It is obvious that the statement has no evidential character.

[6] There is evidence, on the contrary, (1) that when elected Rabbi of the Synagogue at Avila, his poverty was such that he could not defray the expenses of the journey, and (2) that his emoluments in that position did not enable him to support his family.—See SEPHARDIM, or the *History of the Jews in Spain and Portugal*, by JAMES FINN, 1841, pp. 303, 304.

in affirming that there was no such MS., that the dead man had composed the work out of his own head and written it with his own hand.[1] His quest having thus failed, Isaac de Acco left Avila and proceeded to Talavera, where he met with R. Joseph ben Todros, and Jacob, a pupil of Moses, both of whom, in reply to his inquiries, affirmed that the genuine ZOHAR was in the hands of Moses de Leon, as they had proved conclusively. The nature of the proof does not appear, and the account of Isaac breaks off abruptly in the middle of a sentence describing some testimony which he received at Toledo as to an ancient Rabbin, named Jacob, who had "testified by heaven and earth that the book ZOHAR, of which R. Simeon ben Yohai is the author * * *."

I have passed over purposely in this brief account several minor details which have awakened suspicion as to the honesty of the narrative, for it is unnecessary to confuse the issues. The point is that it closes with a solemn testimony to the authenticity of the ZOHAR, and by the course which he took subsequently Isaac de Acco must have concluded to abide by this. Assuming that the narrative is authentic, the evidence which was set aside as insufficient by the one person who has recorded it cannot be accepted by impartial criticism unenforced by other considerations. So far therefore as the account in the SEPHER YUHASIN is concerned, it is not proved that Moses de Leon wrote the ZOHAR " out of his own head."[2] R. Moses Abraham himself mentions an opinion that he did produce it under the guidance of the Writing Name, *i.e.*, by angelic revelation; but I do not conceive that it is necessary to discuss this possibility.

The state of the case as it stands is confused, and most persons who have taken part in the controversy have been led into more or less contradiction. Those who have regarded

---

[1] Hence he did not employ transcribers, and whatever price he may have obtained for copies of the work he could not have multiplied many. If assiduous, he could have had no time for squandering; if idle, no money to spend. Moreover, he must have had a copy of his invention from which to make his transcripts and there would have been that at least in the house, to be shewn and seen.

[2] Outside this document there is, moreover, no proof, so far as I am aware, that he was even connected with it as transcriber. If, however, he did act in this capacity, and as its editor, codifier, or what not, it is desirable to point out that the antiquity of the ZOHAR is not certified for this reason. Finally, speaking still under correction, the YUHASIN is the one authority by which we can fix so important a date as the death of Moses de Leon. Who was the Rabbi of this name and place, for whom Samuel, son of Isaac, transcribed a copy of the MOREH, anno 1452, which copy is still preserved in the Günglung Library, Paris? It is numbered 771, according to Friedlander's preface to the third volume of his version of Maimonides, p. xiv.

Moses de Leon as nothing more than a transcriber have had to reckon as they could with certain damaging references to late events which are found in the ZOHAR, and their explanations are often quite worthless; those who regard the transcriber as the concealed author have had to meet as they might the extreme difficulty of supposing that such a collection was the production of one individual, and that individual Moses de Leon. Their explanations also are of little value and are for the most part ingenious or other assumptions.

The internal evidence against the ZOHAR may be reduced under the following heads:

(1) It refers to the vowel points which are alleged to have been invented in post-Talmudic times.[1] (2) It quotes or borrows from a book entitled the DUTIES OF THE HEART, written by a Jew of Saragossa,[2] about the middle of the eleventh century. (3) It mentions two kinds of Phylacteries, or Tephilin, which fact is supposed to prove the late origin of the entire work.[3] (4) It quotes authorities posterior to its alleged period. (5) It is written in Aramaic, whereas at the period to which it is ascribed—meaning presumably that of R. Simeon—Aramaic was the vernacular, while Hebrew was made use of in religious writings.

These difficulties are met by defenders of the ZOHAR in the following way:

(1) The vowel points are not the invention of times posterior to the TALMUD; the proof is that they are mentioned in the TALMUD, and there is no question that this work is long anterior to the thirteenth century, being the period of Moses de Leon. In the TALMUD they are said to have been a rule given to Moses the Prophet on Mount Sinai.[4] The pre-

---

[1] Elias Levita, a German Jew of the sixteenth century, was one of the first to affirm the late institution of the points, which he ascribed to the Jews of Tiberias about the beginning of the sixth century. In reply to this it has been advanced that at the period the schools of Judæa had been closed, and that Jewish learning was then centred at Babylon (see David Levi: LINGUA SACRA, part i. c. iii. § 1, London, 1785). Ginsburg, however, adopts the theory of Levita, subject to the modification that they were introduced by the Karaite, R. Mocha, at the end of the sixth century. David Levi, on the other hand, makes their reception by the Karaite Jews a proof of their antiquity, because they were "professed enemies to tradition and innovation." Unfortunately, there are no pointed Hebrew MSS. prior to the tenth century.

[2] R. Behai ben Joseph Ibn Bakoda.

[3] For a general description of the TEPHILIN, see Basnage: HISTOIRE DES JUIFS, tom. iii. pp. 752 et seq. Any dictionary will tell the unversed reader that the Phylactery was a strip of parchment inscribed with certain passages from the Pentateuch. It was worn on the forehead, otherwise on forehead and arm, during prayer.

[4] Treatise NEDAREEM, also BAB. MEGILLAH, BAB. BEROCOTH, and BAB. ERUBIN.

Christian existence of the point system, with the exception of a very few cases occurring in the Pentateuch, which, moreover, are not vowel-points, this is one thing, and must be left to those who affirm it; its existence in early post-Talmudic times [1] is another, and all that is required in the present case to destroy the validity of this objection to the reasonable antiquity, as affirmed, of the ZOHAR.[2]

(2) The treatise on the DUTIES OF THE HEART is certainly a work of the eleventh century, but it is advanced that its author himself borrowed from the ZOHAR in an early form, the existence of which is traceable, from Talmudic references, under the name of MIDRASH of Rabbi Simeon ben Yohai.[3] It is said also that the author was a contemporary of Rabbi Abraham, who wrote a commentary of repute upon the BOOK OF FORMATION, but this personage, identified by some dreamers as the pretended instructor of Nicholas Flamel in the secrets of Alchemy, died at the close of the twelfth century. We may choose as we please between the alternatives offered, but the fact remains that the ZOHAR contains matter which is found in a work belonging to the eleventh century.

(3) The existence of two kinds of Phylacteries arose through a difference of rabbinical opinion as to the Scriptural passages to be used on them. The question is whether this difference of opinion occurred in the eleventh century and later, or whether it originated in earlier Talmudic times. Certain statements and inferences therefrom are set forth by defenders of the ZOHAR in support of the second view; but the use of two kinds of Phylacteries before the tenth century has not been demonstrated.

This at its value is, moreover, the testimony of the ZOHAR, obviously reproducing current legend, or borrowing from the traditional storehouse of the TALMUD.

[1] See David Levi, *op. cit.*, who says that in several places of the BABYLONIAN TALMUD mention is made of "the distinction of the accents, and, in particular, of the accents of the law, which might be shewn and pointed at by the hand, consequently they must be visible marks or figures, and are to be understood both of the vowel points and accents." Though belonging to an early period of the controversy, Levi's defence is still worth reading. Basnage, tom. ii. p. 763, refers the invention to the eleventh century.

[2] The commentary of St. Jerome on Jeremiah has been regarded as positive proof that the vowel signs were not in existence at his day. A critical dissertation on their antiquity will be found in MÉMOIRES DE LITTÉRATURE DE L'ACADÉMIE DES INSCRIPTIONS ET BELLES LETTRES, *Tome* xx., pp. 22 *et seq.* It tends to prove that vowel-points existed in the middle of the third century A.D.

[3] According to Jellinek the great classic of the Kabbalah has passed under three names: (a) MIDRASH of Rabbi Simeon ben Yohai; (b) MIDRASH: Let there be Light! (c) ZOHAR, *i.e.*, Splendour or Light, after Daniel xii. 3.—DIE KABBALA, *oder die Religions philosophie der Hebraei von Franck*. Leipsic, 1844. The MIDRASH is a symbolical narrative or account.

(4) The citation by the ZOHAR of late authorities belonging to the Amoraim school is met by representing it in its extant form as the growth of several centuries, which is true of much early Hebrew literature, canonical or not. The indirect strength of this view is considerable; but it is weakened by its supporters when they attempt to argue that had the ZOHAR been forged by Moses de Leon he would have avoided the citation of later authorities. The history of literary impostures points wholly in the opposite direction, and the objection demonstrates quite clearly that the work as we have it is later than its latest authority. For it to be otherwise is impossible. How the late authorities came to be included is a distinct matter.

(5) When Isaac de Acco set out on his quest for the original MS. of the ZOHAR, he is recorded to have said: "If it be written in the Jerusalem idiom it is genuine, but if in Hebrew it is not." The value of an objection to the ZOHAR founded on its use of Aramaic is here exhibited by the express statement of a Jewish witness referred to the thirteenth century.[1] It is argued furthermore, by its defenders: (*a*) That Aramaic is the language of the Targums, which are mystical; (*b*) That the uncanonical language is used to increase the symbolism, but this may be regarded as a subtlety; (*c*) That supposing the antiquity of the ZOHAR, the scribe of R. Simeon ben Yohai was undoubtedly the Rabbi Abbah whom it mentions, and he as a Babylonian must have been thoroughly conversant with Aramaic;[2] (*d*) That supposing the ZOHAR to be a forgery produced by Moses de Leon, he was more likely to have written it in Hebrew, which is the language of his other books.[3]

---

[1] Compare the article *s.v.* MIDRASHIM in the ninth edition of the ENCYCLOPÆDIA BRITANNICA, by Dr. Schiller-Szinessy, Reader in Talmudic at Cambridge. "The ZOHAR was begun in Palestine late in the second or early in the third century, A.D., and finished at the latest in the sixth or the seventh century. It is impossible that it should have been composed after that time and before the Renaissance, as both language and contents clearly shew."

[2] There is no evidence for the editorship of R. Abbah, but if anything Zoharic was committed to writing in the second century there might be ground for accepting the express statement of the LESSER HOLY SYNOD that the recorder was the son of R. Simeon, obviously and of course in respect only of that particular text.

[3] On the entire question compare Munk: MÉLANGES DE PHILOSOPHIE, JUIVE ET ARABE, pp. 280, 281. "The Aramean dialect of the ZOHAR is not that of Daniel and Ezra, of the Chaldaic Paraphrase of Onkelos and Jonathan, of the Targums, the Talmuds, the MIDRASHIM or the *Gueonûm*, but an incorrect and most corrupt mixture of all." Munk also sees traces in the ZOHAR of unfamiliarity with the language used. By this a double and altogether intolerable burden seems placed on the shoulders of its reputed forger. The question raised by Franck in 1843 remains still pertinent and still

From these objections and these answers the general conclusion must be that the internal evidence for the late origin of the bulk of the ZOHAR as it stands is not of any real force. The two tabulations have by no means exhausted the difficulties or the counter-evidence, as to which, even at the present day, Franck is in many cases the best and certainly the most lucid expositor.[1] Putting aside the alleged absence of Christian influence, if not of all reference to Christianity, his remarks on the absence of Aristotelian influence, and some points of the argument from the dialect in which the work is written, seem to possess as much force as they did originally in 1843. But the strength of the case in favour of the ZOHAR is also the strength of the chief objection against it. It does quote later authorities, but this may exhibit that it grew like the Talmudic writings and several of the canonical Hebrew books. It has been well urged that if contemporary with the TALMUD, the latter ought to have mentioned it, and it is replied that it does, not, however, under the catchword of its late name, but by the title of the Secret Learning, and by other titles which have been mentioned in this section. It would exceed my province to pursue the subject further. The minute considerations are of course highly technical, and there are some on both sides which it is wise to abstain from pressing. One of these is the argument that Moses de Leon was an unlikely person to have written such a work as the ZOHAR, because he was intellectually and morally unfit.[2] I have noted that he was unlikely, but possibilities of this kind can only be determined by the event. Many great books

---

unanswered :—How could Moses de Leon at the beginning of the fourteenth century treat matters of the most elevated order in an idiom which the most distinguished scholars had been for so long content merely to understand and which, on this hypothesis, had not produced a single work capable of serving him as a model ?—LA KABBALE, p. 104.

[1] On the opposing side there is negative force at its value in one contention of Karppe (*op. cit.*, pp. 307, 308). He cites Juda Hadessi and his ESHKOL HAKOFER, written in 1148 and exhibiting vast knowledge of Jewish religious and philosophical tendencies. It inveighs bitterly against the anthropomorphisms of the Talmudists and cites everything of this nature in rabbinical literature, but it says no word about the ZOHAR, the inference being that if this great and occasionally most anthropomorphic collection had been in existence at his period Juda Hadessi must have known and could not have failed to cite it.

[2] Dr. Schiller-Szinessy shews that he was proud of the authorship of his books, and hence unlikely to conceal his hand in the composition of any; but this argument also must not be pressed too far. The same writer terms him an inferior Kabbalist, and it seems admitted on all sides that his original books are poor in quality. From these works Jellinek has extracted passages which are parallel to others in the ZOHAR and some critics have thence concluded an identity of authorship. In any other branch of research such parallels would be held to prove nothing.

have been produced by those who were antecedently improbable, and after all, at the best, we know Moses de Leon only through his other writings and the alleged testimony of a hostile relative. There is no doubt that the ZOHAR was to some extent sprung upon the Jewish people at the period of its appearance. The manner of its reception was not unmixed; it received the kind of welcome which would be given to a work which may have been old as regards its materials, though unfamiliar—less or more—in its form, and this is sufficient to account for any silence of previous authorities, while in the shaping of those materials and the impressing of that form the individual who is supposed to have multiplied copies may have had a hand.[1]

IV.—THE AGE OF ZOHARIC TRADITION

It must not be supposed that the field of criticism is occupied entirely by a hypothesis of unmixed fraud, or that this hypothesis has fastened always upon the same person.[2] The most favoured delinquent is, of course, Moses de Leon, because he is reported to have circulated the ZOHAR, but occasionally he appears as the tool of other conspirators. Thus, Samuel Cahen maintained that the Zoharic writings were composed by a convocation of converted Rabbins, assembled for the purpose in a Spanish monastery, employing Moses as their publisher, and hence the Church itself might almost figure as

---

[1] And by those who accept this view it is considered that he interfered only to disfigure it. The view itself is not to be regarded as advanced altogether on my own behalf, for I have done little more than summarise and deduce from intimations on the part of apologetic writers, without feeling that it can be satisfactory to either side. A long debate is possible on the nature of alleged materials which were or might be old; while if admitted as of fact, it does not follow that they give evidence of a Secret Tradition corresponding to that of the ZOHAR and perpetuated by reception from an early period. Some things were obviously familiar, including Yetziratic notions, and developments therefrom would have been welcome to certain rabbinical minds. It may be noted that the JEWISH ENCYCLOPÆDIA, s.v. ZOHAR, concludes that the text originated among Persian Jews of the eighth and following centuries. But the same epoch-marking work has a yet longer study, s.v. CABALA, from which it may be gathered (1) that the testimony of Joseph ben Judah in the second half of the second century seems to indicate the existence of an esoteric doctrine at that time in the world of Jewry and its connection with the name of Johanan ben Zakkai, who lived before and after the destruction of Jerusalem; (2) that the apocalyptic literature " belonging to the second and first pre-Christian centuries contained the chief elements of the Kabbalah "; (3) that one thousand years before the supposed date of SEPHER YETZIRAH the BOOK OF JUBILEES offers a cosmogony based like that on the letters of the Hebrew Alphabet.

[2] Basnage is inclined to refer the original ZOHAR to the tenth century, and, following Bartolocci (BIBLIOTHECA RABBINICA, t. iv. p. 82), represents Moses de Leon as in possession of several exemplars, which he amplified.—HISTOIRE DES JUIFS, t. ii. 781; t. v. 1775, 1776.

an accomplice.[1] Others, like M. H. Landauer,[2] argue that the true author was Abraham ben Samuel Abulafia,[3] while the voice of Graetz was raised in favour of the school of Abraham ben David of Posquière—who belonged to the twelfth century.[4] Isaac the Blind of Narbonne [5]—*ob. circa* 1219—is also a favoured name, and to him it seems indubitable, in any case, that Kabbalism owed something of development and of impulse. Meanwhile this extreme opinion in all its varieties is balanced by counterviews which also denaturalise the literature. It may be suspected therefore with reason that on both sides there is an error of enthusiasm: there are the children of intelligence who look to find the Secret Doctrine of Judea a mere transcript from that of Egypt, or whatever land is for them the well-spring of all truth and all truly sacred knowledge. These remember, for example, that Abraham was in Egypt, and, accepting at once the fairy-tale attribution of the BOOK OF FORMATION to the patriarch, conclude that this document is older than the RITUAL OF THE DEAD. It is useless to reason with those whose confidence is not shaken in the face of impossibilities, whose imagination can bridge all gulfs in evidence by fantastic suppositions. On the other hand, there is the crass criticism which rules off a literature by a single stroke of the pen into the region of forgery and imposture, as it rules off all psychical phenomena into that of imposture or hallucination. It does not matter that this criticism is always in disgrace. It proved Troy town to be solar mythos till Troy town was excavated; it undermined, as it believed, the Book of Daniel till fresh archæo-

---

[1] At the opposite extreme was Christianus Schœttgenius in his considerable work, HORÆ HEBRAICÆ ET TALMUDICÆ *in Theologiam Judæorum Dogmaticam antiquam et orthodoxam de Messia impensæ*, 2 vols., Dresden and Leipsic, 1733, 1742. See vol. ii. *Rabbinicorum Lectionum Liber Secundus*, c. ii., *docens R. Simeonem filium Jochai, auctorem Libri Sohar, Religionem fuisse Christianam*. There are eight heads to the argument, the most important being that the ZOHAR contains the precise, orthodox doctrine concerning the Messiah and His divine and human nature, and this not in one place or mysteriously, but in many and openly. As regards Samuel Cahen, I know his fantastic story at second hand only and have failed to trace its source, but it is buried somewhere in what is called his "Great French Bible."

[2] He maintained the apocryphal nature of the Isaac de Acco story and that the ZOHAR did not come into general knowledge till a much later period. See ORIENT LIT., vi, 710–713, 1845–46.

[3] A prophet and Messiah of his period, A.D. 1240–1291, who is said to have termed his system "a prophetical Kabbalah."

[4] He has been described as the chief Talmudic authority of his period in Southern France, but most of his works are lost.

[5] That is, Isaac ben Abraham, referred also to Posquière. He has been termed "father of the Kabbalah," and is supposed to have conferred on the Ten SEPHIROTH those names by which they are known.

logical discoveries cast it into the pit which it had dug. It is truly not less stupid, and it is far less engaging, than the opposed excess.¹

The antiquity of the Zohar does not depend so much upon the date of its documents as on that which may belong to its Tradition.² It is clear that the speculations, for example, of mediæval Rabbins, referred backward in virtue of a fabulous claim to the dawn of the Christian era, are in a worse position than the HIERARCHIES of pseudo-Dionysius, and that their importance, if any, will differ in kind rather than degree from that which must attach to a Tradition which interlinks with the far past.³ We are therefore more concerned in ascertaining the state in which modern criticism has left the content of the ZOHAR than the form in which it is presented to us. The early students of the work, who accepted and defended its antiquity, did not make this saving distinction, and in many instances modern hostility does not make it either. Upon the surface of the history of Kabbalistic criticism the first presumption is, of course, unfavourable to any hypothesis of antiquity, because this would seem to have been admitted in days when scholarship was equipped insufficiently for the determination of such a question. In the light of fuller knowledge it will be thought that the claim has lapsed, or remains only as a pious belief prevailing among an uncritical minority, a few persons being always found whose mental bias predisposes them to the defence of exploded views. It happens, however, in the present case that an indiscriminate rejection is not much less superficial than an overcredulous acquiescence in a non-proven claim. Moreover, the history of debated questions of this kind teaches another lesson, and the closest approximation to truth is found usually in the mean of extreme views. Now, in the history of Zoharic criticism we find that the old students not only accepted the claim of the Tradition to antiquity, and were disposed to understand the

---

¹ In Kabbalistic criticism its typical representative is Graetz, and one can scarcely conjecture by what principle he was guided in his estimate of Moses de Leon. It is the height of exaggeration, the account in the YUHASIN transcendentalised till it almost exceeds recognition.

² According to Edersheim in his JEWISH SOCIETY AT THE TIME OF JESUS CHRIST, "there existed indubitably" at this epoch "a mass of doctrines and speculations which was concealed carefully from the multitude" and even, he adds, from ordinary scholars. He says also that it bore then, as it bears now, the name of Kabbalah.

³ It should be added, however, that their importance and validity might be so great and unchallengable that the question of their date would pass into the background.

genealogy more or less literally, but that further they regarded the books which contain both as belonging to certain dates and produced by certain writers without much suspicion, on the simple authority of the literature.[1] Later scholars, on the other hand, having found something to countenance the modern origin of the documents, have overlooked frequently the possible antiquity of their Tradition. The question of this antiquity as something which calls to be surveyed apart from the date of publication will explain what I mean by possible moderate and middle views in which the truth should be sought. If we fail entirely here we may regard the case as closed, it being understood that essential values in respect of *Theosophia Mystica* remain over.

I believe that a careful and unbiassed comparison of all the evidence will lead us to conclude that there are elements of old doctrine in the ZOHAR: their exact antiquity is, in part, highly speculative, but it is quite sufficient to invest them with considerable interest, from this point of view only. Like the SEPHER YETZIRAH, some of it may be even referable to a comparatively remote period. I refer here to Yetziratic notions concerning the virtue of Divine Names, for this also is found in the ZOHAR, as it is found abundantly in the TALMUD: a residuum of its teaching concerning angels and demons may be also an inheritance from Babylon. All this, however, is the negligible part of the ZOHAR, as it is the negligible, if curious, part of Talmudic literature. With regard to the Scriptural exegesis which constitutes so large a portion of it, we shall not offend possibility by supposing that some of it may be an obscure transmission from Talmudic times.[2] If we take the hints and references found in the Talmuds to the existence of a Mystical Tradition, and follow them through the large mystical literature which intervened

---

[1] Some modern ecclesiastical historians, for no solid reason, incline to this view. Thus, we have in Dean Hook's compilation, A CHURCH DICTIONARY. (fourteenth edition, London, 1887), the statement that the chief Kabbalistic author was Simeon ben Yohai, and also that most of the heretics in the primitive Christian Church fell into the vain conceits of the Kabbalah, particularly the Gnostics, Valentinians and Basilidians. There is perhaps no more warrant for the second than the first view, but it has been advanced warmly, as readers of Matter's HISTOIRE DU GNOSTICISME and of King's GNOSTICS will not need to be told. It is understood, however, that the day of these works, in so far as the second can be said to have had a day, has some time ceased to be.

[2] In other words, we may follow the learned author of the article on the MIDRASHIM in the ENCYCLOPÆDIA BRITANNICA, who says that the nucleus of the work is of Mishnic times and that R. Simeon was its author in the same sense that R. Johanan was of the PALESTINE TALMUD, namely, that he gave the first impulse to its composition.

between those works and the ZOHAR as we now have it, we shall be led not to the conclusion of the mere occultist and dreamer, that there was a great body of Secret Doctrine which became revealed gradually, but that there was a kernel of Tradition which was planted in the secret heart of Israel, which many watered and fostered, till the growth at length put forth, not without something of transformation and of suddenness, the strange flower of the ZOHAR. As regards form its most ancient part is probably the BOOK OF CONCEALMENT, but it is entirely improbable that any conspicuous portion could have existed in writing till after the sixth century, while the growth of most of it is probably much later and subsequent to the latest date which can be ascribed to SEPHER YETZIRAH.[1] It is advanced, as we have seen, by its defenders that the ZOHAR is a subject of reference in several texts both of the BABYLONIAN and JERUSALEM TALMUD under the name of the MIDRASH of Simeon ben Yohai, and the parallels between Talmudic sayings attributed to this Rabbi have been compared with the extant work in order to exhibit their identity. The existence of a text entitled MYSTERIES OF SIMEON BEN YOHAI before the middle of the eleventh century and possibly much earlier, is acknowledged by Dr. Graetz. It is reasonable therefore to conclude that early written and oral materials entered into the composition of the ZOHAR as we now possess it.[2] This is the most that can be urged, and this is sufficient to prove that no one person wrote it out of his own head.[3]

It must be confessed, on the other hand, that the legend

---

[1] I put forward this hypothesis because Dr. Schiller-Szinessy has not stated his reasons why it is impossible that it should have been later than the seventh century, and subject to the conclusiveness of those reasons. We may speculate what Dr. Szinessy would have thought of Israel Zangwill, had he read the epilogue to the CHILDREN OF THE GHETTO, in which it is remarked casually that the ZOHAR was "forged by a Spanish Jew in the thirteenth century." By the way, are copies of the ZOHAR likely to be found in a small room, used as a synagogue, outside Jerusalem and so poor that it is bare even of seats?

[2] An interesting article by M. Nicolas in Lichtenberger's ENCYCLOPÉDIE DES SCIENCES RELIGIEUSES, t. xi. s.v. CABALE (Paris, 1877), regards it as certain that the philosophical speculations which compose the Kabbalah generally began to form during the century which preceded the Christian era; but they were oral, imparted to a few only, and under the seal of secrecy. Unfortunately, the article is not trustworthy, representing, as it does, the AIN SOPH doctrine to be part of the SEPHER YETZIRAH.

[3] Compare Blunt's DICTIONARY OF DOCTRINAL AND HISTORICAL THEOLOGY, which argues that the variety of style and the disjointed character of its contents shew that the ZOHAR is the growth of ages. But Blunt's work indicates no real acquaintance with the Kabbalah and its criticism.

which attributes its origin to R. Simeon ben Yohai seems to have made an unfortunate choice, for this great authority of the TALMUD represents a reaction against the tendencies attributed—rightly or not—to R. Akiba, and there is some evidence for believing that he did not investigate the hidden meaning of Scripture, but rather its rational principles. He is described by a modern writer as cold, exclusive and stoical. At the same time, if we accept the existence of a genuine Tradition which became incorporated in the ZOHAR, it is difficult to reject its leading and central figure.[1]

If we turn now for a moment to the unequipped standpoint of so-called modern occultism we shall see that so far we have no warrant for connecting the chief cycle of Kabbalistic literature with the high antiquity to which occultists incline.[2] While we leave them once more in full possession of the alleged virtue inherent in Divine Names, and perhaps with some elements of legend concerning angels and demons, we are forced to take all that remains a considerable distance into the Christian era. But the ZOHAR, although it embodies the entire content of Kabbalistic doctrine, is not the sole nor the earliest storehouse of that doctrine, and we have next to consider whether the antiquity of the metaphysical Tradition is to be inferred from its points of contact and correspondence with other theosophical systems which have prevailed in the past.

V.—ALLEGED SOURCES OF KABBALISTIC DOCTRINE

On the basis of considerations so far enumerated, it would appear that we are warranted in regarding some part at least of the materials incorporated by the ZOHAR as earlier than

---

[1] The author of the article CABALA in Herzog's REAL ENCYCKLOPÄDIE takes a middle view, namely, that the ZOHAR is not the work of Moses de Leon, nor is it of R. Simeon's period, though its doctrines are referable to him. It was completed in the eighth century. The evidence adduced for this view seems inconclusive, so far as the article is concerned.

[2] Take, for example, the following typical instance of the exaggerations which have found currency on this subject. "The origin of the Kabbalah is lost in the night of time. Is it of India or of Egypt? We do not know; but it is certain that to Egyptians and Indians it was alike known. Pythagoras returned with it into Greece after his travels in the East, then the region of the light. One asks vainly whether its first revelation was divine or the product of inspiration."—Desbarrolles: LES MYSTÈRES DE LA MAIN, 14me édition, Paris, n.d. Desbarrolles knew nothing of the Kabbalah, but he reflected his friend Éliphas Lévi, who claimed knowledge but wrote frequently in the same distracted strain.

the period of their promulgation. We cannot say whether the SEPHER YETZIRAH is much anterior to the ninth century.[1] But both works are in connection with Talmudic times and, within the limits of the Christian centuries, there seems therefore to have been an esoteric tradition in Israel.[2] Whether it existed prior to Christianity itself is the next concern of our inquiry. At this point the difficulties begin to multiply, because the range of research is exceedingly large, and it has been covered in every direction by successive generations of hardy speculators. We must proceed step by step and shall do well to begin first of all by a general survey of the subject.

The doctrines of the Kabbalah have been referred for their origin to almost every philosophic and religious system of antiquity, and its points of alleged correspondence with each have been tabulated with some care. They have been derived from Akkadia, from India, from China, from ancient Egypt,[3] from Platonism and Neo-Platonism, from the categories of Aristotle, from early Christian Gnosticism.[4] The most reasonable conclusion which can be drawn, I think, from all this rival evidence—in so far as it can claim the term—is that it is not derived from any one of these sources specifically and exclusively, but rather that the human mind, when engaged on certain fundamental and perhaps insoluble problems of the universe, tends independently to reach conclusions that are similar and may even wear sometimes an aspect of literal identity; that the Kabbalah is largely an outcome of such

---

[1] But we can say that one of the most pronounced opponents of Jewish Theosophy assigns it to early Gnostic times.—See Grätz: GESCHICHTE DER JUDEN, 11 vols., 1853-1870.

[2] One of the most credulous and also most pretentious exponents of the English school of Kabbalism in a debased occult interest states that, according to Hebrew Tradition, the doctrines of the oldest portions of the ZOHAR are antecedent to the Second Temple.—W. Wynn Westcott, SEPHER YETZIRAH. Translated from the Hebrew. Second edition. London, 1893. A third edition has been published recently, since the decease of the author.

[3] This is the view which obtained most widely among French occultists. " It is in Egyptian science," says Stanislas de Guaita, " carried from Mitzraïm by Moses at the exodus of the Sons of Israel, that we must discern the source of that Sacred Tradition transmitted among the Jews from generation to generation, by the oral way, down to the disciples of Simeon ben Yohai, who wrote, at the dictation of this master, about the second century of the Christian era, the GREAT BOOK OF THE LIGHT (ZOHAR)."—AU SEUIL DU MYSTÈRE, pp. 183, 184. The last statement is, of course, merely an assumption of the vital point at issue, and the speculations of the French Marquis are worth as much and as little as the rest of the rubbish-heap which used to pass in Paris for occult learning and criticism. It will be noted that R. Simeon is referred to the second instead of the first century.

[4] Even the so-called " Symbols of Pythagoras " have been approximated to Kabbalistic teaching. See COLLECTANEA HERMETICA, edited by W. Wynn Westcott, vol. v. id est, SOMNIUM SCIPIONIS, &c., London, 1894.

unaided research; that its results are in the main *sui generis*, but that they offer points of contact with other attempts of the kind in all ages and nations; and that they owe something to other traditions and memorials of the past, in part by filtration therefrom, but in part also because they belong thereto and were born among them. We must, of course, distinguish the fundamental part of the Kabbalah from its developments. Included in the first class are the doctrine of the Ten Emanations, that of AIN SOPH, of the MACROPROSOPUS and MICROPROSOPUS, some of which may go far back in the history of post-Christian Jewish literature, indeed almost to Talmudic times. They are mentioned of necessity here, but must be unfolded and explained later. The subsequent developments possess a complexion reflected from many sources, not excluding the scholastic philosophy of Christian Europe during the Middle Ages.[1] AIN SOPH is that final concept of the Deity which is reached by all true metaphysics; it is not necessary to suppose that it was derived from Babylonian initiations during the exile of seventy years, or from Greek speculation at Alexandria: it may be regarded more probably as a product of the unfinished exile of Christian centuries, a fruit of first-hand reflection by the theosophical mind of Jewry on problems present to the mind, but not altogether untinctured by the debates which encompassed it at different centres of culture. It is the ultimate point of theosophical speculation possible to the human mind, at which the mind tends always to arrive. The doctrine of the SEPHIROTH is, in its turn, an intelligible form of another widespread device of old-world thought when it sought to bridge the gulf between finite and infinite, between absolute purity and that material world which, in one or other way, seems to have been regarded always as unclean. The MACROPROSOPUS and MICROPROSOPUS, whether late or early in Jewish literature, are late at least in the history of human speculation. They are an attempt to distinguish between God as He is in Himself and in His relation with His children. As might be expected, they are the most characteristic of Jewry and, as such, offer the least connection with any external system. Yet they have some points of contact. As regards each and all, given the times and the circumstances, the people and their places, they

---

[1] I refer here to the Kabbalistic schools of Isaac de Loria and Moses of Cordova.

are the kind of speculative doctrine which one might have expected *à priori*. The peculiar conventional forms under which they are conveyed were characteristic of the rabbinical mind, its own and no other's throughout. We shall find that some of them are crude and monstrous; but it happens that the Secret Tradition at its highest can be separated from its extravagant and materialistic developments.

When we remember the persistence of Tradition which has characterised the most persistent of all races, when we remember that the Jew of the Christian Dispensation may be said to have lived in the remembrance of his glory passed away, we can believe that he was encompassed by an atmosphere of legend on which his fervid mind was at work continually, out of which he never stepped, and it would be unreasonable to suppose that all his literature, like all his thought, was not tinctured profoundly by this his intellectual environment. But it is a wide and an unwarrantable step from the belief in such a natural and inevitable operation to a belief that Jewish Tradition must or may be referred to one distinctive source in the past, from which it was perpetuated by some conventional transmission, as occult writers suppose, and some others also who have no such bias towards the mysterious to intervene in apology for their opinion. We have no ground for affirming with Basnage[1] that old Egypt is the true nursery of the Kabbalah, though it is quite possible that Israel brought something from the Nile valley which does not appear in the Pentateuch. Nor are we justified in agreeing with a quondam Grand Master of the Ancient and Accepted Rite of Freemasonry, United States Southern Jurisdiction, when he suggests a direct communication of doctrine from the religion of Zoroaster[2] to Kabbalism which must be referred to the period of the exile.[3] That the Jews may have derived something from Babylon I have noted already, and amidst their chequered experience under Persian domination, after their final scattering, possibly the great body

---

[1] L. iii. c. xiv.
[2] For some tables indicating " the harmony and identity of the Chaldean philosophy with the Hebrew Kabbalah," see CHALDEAN ORACLES OF ZOROASTER, edited by *Sapere Aude*, London, 1895, pp. 8-11. The true value of such parallels is shewn by such frenzied developments as Archbishop Meurin's SYNAGOGUE DE SATAN, which will be noticed in Book X. § 18. *Sapere Aude* was a pseudonym adopted by Wynn Westcott in some English occult circles.
[3] MORALS AND DOGMA, Charleston, A.M. 5641, pp. 266, 267, and elsewhere throughout the compilation. Compare Matter: HISTOIRE CRITIQUE DU GNOSTICISME. It refers the Gnostic systems to the ZENDAVESTA and Kabbalah.

of Haggada may have received increment and colouring. More fantastic theorists have imagined that not only is there a Chinese Kabbalah, but that it is the source of that which was in Israel. That the great unknown empire, in which all things from Alchemy to the art of printing are said to have germinated, possessed and still possesses a body of traditional lore, of so-called secret teaching,[1] is mere commonplace on which there is no call to insist, and if some persons will be so foolish as to term this Kabbalah, as if in the sense of Israel, it is idle to dispute with them about the improper and confusing use of a mere word. That the book called YI-KING,[2] or MUTATION, contains an Esoteric Religious Tradition which has, as it is affirmed, some analogies with Kabbalistic doctrine, is neither surprising nor significant of anything except the irresistible tendency of the human mind to reflect after much the same manner, in all lands and times, upon mysteries that are everywhere the same, ever urgent, ever recurring. Such analogies do not prove, as dreamers would have us believe, the existence of a conventional Wisdom-Religion, unfolded through ages of initiation. In the natural order, the truly fundamental religion is the common ground of all, which stands in need of no formal perpetuation, as it is inborn in the heart and mind of humanity.[3] And yet the undoubted existence of the Mongolian race in Mesopotamia almost at the dawn of history may suggest that the Semite drew something from Mongolian Chaldea even in the days of Abraham,[4] as afterwards the Jew of Babylon may have had a certain contact with Confucianism in its earliest form. We may admit, readily and reasonably, that the Jew received everywhere and always retained the reception, provided that we leave him

---

[1] In conformity with which Bryant's ANALYSIS OF ANCIENT MYTHOLOGY (vol. i. p. 94) and Oliver's HISTORY OF INITIATION (pp. 79 *et seq.*) would have us believe that there were Mysteries in China " similar to those of India," which again were more or less the same as those that flourished subsequently in Greece.

[2] For some information concerning this work and its Kabbalistic analogies, see L'INITIATION, *revue philosophique des Hautes Études*, tom. xxxvii. No. 3, Dec., 1897. Paris. *S.v. Yi-King, Tao-see, Tao-te-King et la Numération*, pp. 266 *et seq.* Also Eugène Nus: A LA RECHERCHE DES DESTINÉS. Paris, 1892.

[3] I refer here to sacramental and not to natural religion so-called.

[4] " The power of the Mongol rulers of Chaldea, about the time of Abraham, was far more extensive than that of the contemporary rulers of Thebes and of the Delta, and the victories of the great eighteenth dynasty in Egypt, extending over some three centuries at most, form only a passing episode in the story of Asiatic civilisation, which dates back probably earlier than the time of the Pyramids, which was native and original, and from which Egypt borrowed much in the days of its greatest rulers."— BABYLONIAN DISCOVERIES, EDINBURGH REVIEW, April, 1898.

everywhere his own intellectual initiative, and bear in mind that the process was everywhere natural and informal, not arbitrary and conventional.

Passing over the regions of wild surmise in which Odin the Norse God becomes identified with the Kabbalistic ABBA, the Supernal Father; Frea with AIMA, who is the Mother in transcendence; Thor with ARIK ANPIN, the Lesser Countenance; and the Supreme Being discerned behind the northern mythology with AIN SOPH; passing over also certain alleged Druidic correspondences into which it would be folly to enter,[1] we may take much the same view as before regarding the alleged Gnostic connections of the Kabbalah. We may concur with King when he argues that whatever the date of the ZOHAR in its present form, some of its traditions are similar to those taught in the schools of Babylon and Tiberias.[2] They are the same and they are also different, and the difference represents the growth of the intellectual thought of Israel, its proper native development under the various impulsions which it received between the period of Gnosticism and the period of the promulgation of the ZOHAR. We may acknowledge also that Marcus, as "a born Jew," transmitted something of his national heritage to the system which he produced. Yet Gnosticism is not Kabbalism, though there are occasional analogies between them, and something of common source may be attributable to both. M. Amélineau is nearer the truth when he speaks of a coincident development of the two systems.[3] There are analogies in nature and appearance between glass and rock-crystal, but glass is glass and a pebble is a pebble.[4]

---

[1] Pike, following his usual unacknowledged authority, affirms that the Druids were true children of the Magi, whose initiation came from Egypt and Chaldea, "that is to say, from the true sources of the primitive Kabbalah."—MORALS AND DOGMA, p. 103. The inspiration is Éliphas Lévi, who uses substantially the same terms.

[2] THE GNOSTICS AND THEIR REMAINS. Second edition. London, 1897.

[3] ESSAI SUR LE GNOSTICISME EGYPTIEN, ses développements et son origine Egyptienne. Par M. E. Amélineau, published in Annales du Musée Guimet, tom. xiv. Paris, 1887, but written so far back as 1882, the date affixed to the preface. Compare Edersheim, who believed that "Gnosticism, like later Jewish Mysticism, sprang from the contact of Judaism with the religious speculations of the farther East." Compare also the JEWISH ENCYCLOPÆDIA, which is disposed to recognise in the ZOHAR an influence referable to Vedanta Schools of Hindu Philosophy through Persian channels of Mohammedan Mysticism in the eighth century and later.

[4] The PISTIS SOPHIA has been considered the most valuable document for analogies between Gnosticism and the Kabbalah, but it is easy to exaggerate its evidence. King says that the doctrines are identical, and that it exhibits the leading principles of the Kabbalah; but he does not seem to speak with any first-hand knowledge of Jewish Theosophy. The Gnostic text has been edited since his day by Mr. G. R. S. Mead, who neither establishes nor alludes to the alleged correspondences.

It is unphilosophical because unneedful to go far back and far off when the explanation of given facts lies near in time and place. "That is best which lies the nearest," says the poet, and, artists or dreamers, makers of verse or Kabbalistic commentators, we should shape our work of art or interpretation without drawing needlessly from things remote. The prototype of Yetziratic and Zoharic Theosophy is close to our hand in Jewry. The fusion of all systems which is a characteristic of the present day, has its parallel in that epoch of the past which witnessed the rise of Christianity. "At the time when John the Baptist made his appearance in the desert, near the shores of the Dead Sea, all the old philosophical and religious systems were approximating toward each other. A general lassitude inclined the minds of all toward the quietude of that amalgamation of doctrines for which the expeditions of Alexander and the more peaceful occurrences that followed, with the establishment in Asia and Africa of many Grecian colonies, had prepared the way. After the intermingling of different nations, which resulted from the wars of Alexander in three-quarters of the globe, the doctrines of Greece, of Egypt, of Persia, and of India met and intermingled everywhere. Many barriers that formerly had kept the nations apart were at last thrown down; and while the people of the West readily connected their faiths with those of the East, the latter hastened to learn the traditions of Rome and Athens. . . . The Jews and Egyptians, then the most exclusive of all peoples, yielded to that eclecticism which prevailed among their masters, the Greeks and Romans." [1] National ambition, however, rather than eclecticism influenced the Jews, and though it was impossible, having regard to their environment, that they should not be tinctured largely, it was their object to tinge other systems and not to modify their own, to shew that the ethnic philosophers owed everything to the Divine Doctrine of Palestine. Philo the Greek of Alexandria to some extent Hellenised the Hebrew religion that he might the better Judaise the philosophy of Hellas.[2] From this fusion there arose the nearest approach, if not in time and place at least in form and subject, to Kabbalistic Theosophy as regards its source in Jewry. There is no need in the present study, which

---

[1] MORALS AND DOGMA, p. 247.
[2] For an illuminating study of Philo's eclecticism, in the higher sense of this term, see H. A. A. Kennedy: PHILO'S CONTRIBUTION TO RELIGION, 1919.

is intended to simplify and not to enlarge the issues, that I should do more than cite Aristobulus, who a century before had exercised a similar vocation. Philo, and the movement and mode of thought which he represents, cannot have been without an effect upon the literature of later ages in Jewry,[1] though the history of that influence and the mode of its transmission cannot be traced conclusively. We must not fall, however, into the error of supposing that the Kabbalah is Platonism derived through Philo and the Jewish school of Alexandria, or that it is Jewish Tradition modified by Philoism. When we find in the SEPHER YETZIRAH the alphabetical symbols of the Logos made use of by God in the formation of the universe, it is very easy to set it down to Greek influence, but the fact remains that the BOOK OF FORMATION is essentially and characteristically Hebrew, and this fact lifts it altogether out of the category of Platonic succession. Yet we know where to look for the explanation of certain points of contact. As regards the doctrine developed by commentators on the SEPHER YETZIRAH prior to the appearance of the ZOHAR, as regards the literature which makes contact with these, and as regards the ZOHAR itself, saying nothing of the later literature, which had recourse consciously and openly to Greek sources, the case is much stronger.[2] Philo insists on the antithesis between God and the material world, the infinite and the finite; so, let us say, does the ZOHAR, which may be taken to stand for the literature. Philo affirms the absolute transcendency of God; so does Zoharic doctrine. Philo regards

---

[1] I should observe here that Arthur Lillie, who once argued a process in the Buddhistic origin of Christianity, discovered in the ZOHAR not only the Trinity of Philo, but the Trinity of Buddhism, and he held that the Kabbalah " was one of the secret books of the Essenes."—MODERN MYSTICS AND MODERN MAGIC, p. 14. He testified also that it was " written down from tradition by one Moses de Leon," thus shewing that he was not aware of the existence of Kabbalistic books outside the ZOHAR. —*Ibid.*, p. 13. Finally, he affirmed that it is " a book of Magic."—MADAME BLAVATSKY AND HER THEOSOPHY, p. 194. After this we shall not be surprised to find that St. Paul was a Kabbalist.—*Ibid.* So also was Jacob Böhme, whose Three Principles, one of which was the " Kingdom of Hell," have something to do with the three supernal SEPHIROTH. For similar worthless speculations, see Lillie's BUDDHISM IN CHRISTENDOM.

[2] For example, the PORTA CŒLORUM of R. Abraham Cohen Irira, which forms the third part of Rosenroth's APPARATUS IN LIBRUM SOHAR, was written expressly to exhibit the correspondences between Kabbalistic dogmas and the Platonic Philosophy. Later on the same theme was taken up by Christian writers, some of whom connect the Kabbalah with Aristotle, and so we have works like Burgondo's PODROMUS SCIENTIARUM ARTIUMVE LIBERALIUM *ad ipsos Peripatetica Scholæ et Kabbalisticæ doctrinæ purissimos fontes revocatus*, Venice, 1651. So also at an earlier period Thomas Campanella in his DE SENSU RERUM ET MAGIA, Frankfort, 1620, joined Neoplatonism and Kabbalism in his attempt to explain the universe.

the Divine Nature as in Itself escaping definition and in Itself without quality; Kabbalism denounces those who would attempt to describe God as He is in Himself even by the attributes which He manifests. Philo's descriptions of God are all negative: compare the LATENS DEITAS of the Kabbalah. Philo says that no name can be given Him; all Kabbalism agrees,[1] though its unfolded reveries confer many Names on the Deity and explain their powers and meanings Philo regards the Scriptural God as anthropomorphic, and allegorises upon all the descriptions, attributions and manifestations of Deity in the Old Testament: compare the doctrine of the Two Countenances, designed—as some have supposed—to explain the same anthropomorphisms by their exaggeration to a *ne plus ultra* degree. Philo regards the letter of Scripture as a veil: so does the ZOHAR. Philo interprets it literally or mystically according to his purpose: so does Kabbalistic exegesis. Philo regards the visible world as the gate of the world unseen; he believes in the possibility of an immediate contemplation of God, in the existence of an archetypal world, and that things seen are a counterpart of things unseen,[2] in all of which we are enumerating express points of Kabbalistic doctrine. These analogies are too numerous, too close, too consecutive, to leave any room for doubt that the heads of Kabbalistic teaching pre-existed in Israel, and we have further the explicit testimony of Philo as to the fact of a Jewish mystic doctrine. Spontaneity, initiation, subsequent influences, all remain unimpeded and all are necessary to explain the existence of the ZOHAR and its connections, but its source is not Philo of necessity, much less Philo exclusively: it is that which produced Philo. And more than all, it is hardy, independent speculation, wearing tradition like a veil which does not conceal its essential individuality, and much nearer to ourselves at times in its spirit than we should ever suspect from its form. Yet we may suspect it on philosophical grounds, for however concealed

---

[1] It is to be understood also that the ZOHAR affirms a Divine Mode, wherein God was alone with His Name; but there was an antecedent and nameless state.

[2] There is a twofold correspondence in Kabbalism between superior and inferior things: one transcendental, being that of phenomena with their archetypes in the noumenal world, and one natural in the narrower sense of the term, being that which is summed up in the axiom: "There is no herb on earth to which a certain star does not correspond in the heaven." See Kircher: MUNDUS SUBTERRANEUS, ii. 401*b*. The whole theory of Natural Magic is imbedded in this maxim. Compare ZOHAR, one might say, *passim*, for it is a recurring doctrine.

SOURCES OF KABBALISTIC DOCTRINE

behind the veil of symbolism, however distorted in strange glasses of vision, the sentiments and aspirations of humanity have ever a common root, and through the vehicle of Kabbalistic apparatus, under many covers and tinctured by many fantastic colourings of art and artifice, we see that our own yearnings and longings find expression, after their own manner, in this book of the words of the exile. We acknowledge therefore with the poet how truly all the lore and the legend is

> "A part
> Of the hunger and thirst of the heart,
> The frenzy and fire of the brain,
> Which yearns for the fruitage forbidden,
> The golden pomegranates of Eden,
> To quiet its fever and pain."

When the FAITHFUL SHEPHERD of the ZOHAR puts these words into the mouth of the Father of universal Israel: "In this world my Name is written YHVH and read ADONAI, but in the world to come the same will be read as it is written, so that Mercy shall be from all sides," [1] we see that here and now, at this point of the twentieth century, we might express differently the longing, the hope, the faith, for which this symbol stands, but the old symbolism stands in its own way for that which we all desire to express, and, furthermore, I do not know that our modern terms would represent it better. Herein is the justification of the ways of God to man and herein the pious conviction of the believing heart that in the great day of the Lord there shall be no scandal to His children; that in spite of the darkness of our ways we have held rightly that He is light; that though we write Mercy in our hearts but read Law and its inflexible order in all around us, we shall one day know that it is Mercy on every side, the highest expression of the Law, or that Law is that order under which Divine Love is manifested. It is in messages like this that the abiding beauty and significance of the Kabbalah are contained, not in the beard of MICROPROSOPUS or in the number of worlds suspended from the hair on the cranium of ARIKH ANPIN. GEMATRIA and METATHESIS may be pastimes fit only for ultra-serious children, but the voice of the Rabbis of the ZOHAR expressing the language of the heart of Israel needs

---

[1] Cremona edition, part ii. fol. 106a.

no TEMURAH to expound its meaning; and it is by the ring of such utterances that the true believer of to-day is made conscious electrically that the Holy Synods were composed of men who are our brethren.

As this view disposes implicitly of any claim on a divine authorship, and places the theory of aboriginal Tradition among fables, so also it forbids us to suppose that Kabbalistic doctrines are the work of a single mind.

One feels instinctively, without any necessity of evidence, that these things are not and cannot be the unaided creation of Moses de Leon. They are a growth and a result. As, however, the ZOHAR assumed its present shape at a late period admittedly, it may by possibility have taken part of it at the hands of this Spanish Jew. That his other works are inferior is no argument. Cervantes produced many worthless romances before and after the sum of all chivalry. The GALATEA did not make DON QUIXOTE impossible. So also Beroalde de Verville wrote books on Alchemy which are despised even by alchemists, but he wrote also the MOYEN DE PARVENIR. Every *magnum opus* is antecedently improbable, and the intellectual distance between the SORROWS OF WERTHER and the second part of FAUST is like the void between AIN SOPH and MALKUTH, which it was the purpose of the SEPHIROTH to fill.

But if all masterpieces are antecedently improbable, it is true also that they are impossible without antecedents. There are certain dull old histories known to *literati* which were necessary to the plays of Shakespeare. So the formulation of the ZOHAR must have been preceded by much raw material, both oral and written, parts of which were no doubt incorporated without any change in their formulation. For example, the BOOK OF OCCULTATION bears all the marks of antiquity, no less considerable than that of the BOOK OF FORMATION.

There is, of course, a point beyond which the reasonable critic will not pass. So far as it goes we are on tolerably safe ground with the meagre testimony of St. Agobard—supposing that it is allocated correctly; with R. Simeon Ben Yohai we are on purely traditional ground, and it is not to be supposed for a moment that more authenticity resides in the *dramati personæ* of the Holy Synod than in those of the TURBA PHILOSOPHORUM. I do not mean that such names are entirely pretexts, for they may possess an honest basis in legend, but they are not literal or historical. They occupy a middle position between the script of a shorthand reporter and imaginary conversations like those of W. S. Landor.

VI.—ISLAMIC CONNECTIONS OF THE KABBALAH

When the Jew of the Exile sought a consolation in Theosophy, and thus produced the higher part of Kabbalism, compounded of his traditions, his speculations, his external receptions, his longings, the memories of his election and its glory, we must bear in mind that all exotics adjust themselves to their environment, not without certain changes even in the most persistent types. Now, the Jew is an anthropological exotic in all countries of the world, and just because his persistence is so enormous that it is explained by a special law of Providence, we find that in all countries he has been modified sufficiently to guarantee his survival. As in things physical, as in matters of daily life, so in the intellectual order, he lost nothing but he assumed much. The Jew of Salerno differed from that of France, and the Jew of Spain offered contrasts to both. Without attempting to add another hypothesis to the scores extant as to the origin of Kabbalism, I propose to indicate that this literature is naturally, if partially, elucidated by the place in which it grew up, if it did not in part originate.

Having made a reasonable allowance for spontaneity in Jewish thought, and having noted its observed connections and correspondences in distant times and places, it seems fitting that we should look now to that which lay the nearest. Without disputing or defending the opinion that Israel may have possessed a Tradition handed down by the oral way from comparatively early times, of which there may be barely sufficient evidence to warrant a presumption that it existed but not enough to determine what it was, let us begin by considering where the Kabbalistic books first began to circulate. That was in Spain. Now, what was the environment of Jews in the Peninsula at the period in question—let us say, from the ninth century and onward? It differed considerably from that which surrounded them in other countries of Western Europe. Spain was for Israel not indeed a Garden of Paradise, but a species of oasis in the great wilderness of the Exile,[1] for the simple reason that much of it was not then under Christian rule.[2] The Jew of Spain enjoyed comparative immunity; he possessed even political influence; he rose occasionally to high political power. It is not surprising therefore that Spain became a centre of Jewish literature and philosophy. Thence Jewish treatises passed into France and Italy under the Arabian equivalents of their authors' names, and were accepted as speculations or teachings of the learned among the Moslems. Avicebron is a case in point. There can be no doubt whatever that the learning of Mohammedanism exercised an influence on the Rabbins,[3] who reacted in their turn on the Moslem doctors.[4] The questions of priority and preponderance may be passed over, because they are of no importance here.

We have concluded already that the ZOHAR presents the theosophical thought of preceding centuries in Israel under a certain aspect of transformation. The traditional knowledge, of which we have evidence as to its existence in Talmudic times, had received many developments from many sources and under the influence of many minds. There is ground for supposing that the nucleus in Christian times is first heard of in Palestine, which indeed follows from its connection, once admitted, with R. Simeon ben Yohai. But despite the legend which represents the ZOHAR as sent from Palestine by Nahmanides, everything points to Spain and the South of France as the chief scenes in which the literature developed, and it is not unreasonable to suppose that it has been affected by the prevailing tone of mystical thought in one or both of these places. There is evidence to shew that such influence was at work outside the ZOHAR and prior perhaps to its existence in the form that it now possesses. In post-Zoharic Mysticism, and in the commentaries on the ZOHAR which are the work of Spanish Jews, it may be traced more fully and plainly. In no case does it justify the now exploded criticism which would

---

[1] See Finn's SEPHARDIM, already cited, c. xi., and especially pp. 142, 143.

[2] So also the necessities of Christian princes in Spain till the thirteenth century led them usually to protect the Jews.

[3] The translation of the TALMUD into Arabic by R. Joseph, disciple of Moses the sack-clothed, during the reign of Al-Hakim, Caliph of Cordova, in the tenth century, would be the best evidence which could be cited on this point, but the undertaking is no longer extant, if indeed it came into being.

[4] Islamic Mysticism is almost coincident with the mission of the great Islamic prophet. For example, the Ghoolat sect, famous for the "extravagance" of its doctrines, is referred to the time of Ali. See SECRET SOCIETIES OF THE MIDDLE AGES, London, 1846, pp. 29, 31.

make the ZOHAR merely a reproduction or echo of Arabian Theosophy, or would regard all Kabbalism as referable to Islamic Mysticism for its sole source, *plus* the Greek influence at work in Islam. This was the hypothesis of Tholuck. We are concerned only with a question of complexion and of tincture, and have other criteria by which to judge the true significance of the points of doctrinal resemblance between Sufi and Kabbalist concerning the hidden state of Deity, the operation of the Divine Will at the beginning of creation, the emanation of the world, &c. The analogies are interesting enough and the Orientalist who first specified them had everything to justify him at his period.[1] As it may not be uninteresting to cite a few cases in point derived from other sources, let us take a fact, one of many concerning which we possess impregnable testimony. About the middle of the fifteenth century, or, more exactly, from 1414 to 1492, there flourished a Sufi poet named Nuruddin Abdurrahmann, known as Jami of Herat, among whose works the SEVEN THRONES is most famous. One of the poems in this collection is entitled SALOMON AND ABSAL, a mystical story of earthly and heavenly love. In the epilogue to this poem, where the author unfolds his meaning, the following lines occur:

> The Incomprehensible Creator, when this world
> He did create, created first of all
> The First Intelligence, First of a chain
> Of Ten Intelligences, of which the last
> Sole agent is in this our Universe,
> Active Intelligence so called.

It may be admitted at once that if we are to accept the method and admit the quality of evidence which has satisfied heretofore the several authorities who have referred Kabbalism to definite sources in philosophy and religion, we may feel at liberty to infer from this passage that somewhere about the year 1450 a Sufic poet, so far away from Spain as Herat, was adapting, with slight variations of a verbal kind, the Sephirotic Doctrine of the Kabbalah [2] a century before the BOOK OF FORMATION and the ZOHAR came into circulation through the medium of print. I have chosen this instance because it proves nothing of itself on account of its lateness, but it gives a point of

---
[1] See F. A. D. Tholuck: SUFISMUS, *sive* THEOSOPHIA PERSARUM PANTHEISTICA, Berlin, 1851, c.v. *passim*. Also DE ORTU CABBALÆ, Hamburg, 1837.
[2] See Book V., § 2.

departure backward for tracing a possible connection between the mystical sects of Mohammedanism and the mystical sects of Israel.

With this let us compare for a moment the doctrine developed in the CELESTIAL DESATIR, which has been described as "a very early attempt on the part of the ancient Persians to form a cosmological theory."[1] The DESATIR, it should be observed, is a revelation addressed to the great prophet Abad, who has been identified incautiously with Abraham. "The nature of God cannot be known. Who can dare to know it but He (Himself)? The entity and the oneness and the personality are 'His very nature and nothing beside Him.'" From this Being proceeded by free creation "him whose name is BAHNAM, called Prime Intellect and First Reason," and through him "ASHAM, the second intellect," who created in turn the intellect of the next lower heaven named "FAMESHAM." From these proceeded the "Intellect of the heaven of KANIAN," or Saturn; of HARMUZD, or Jupiter; of BAHRAM, or Mars; of KHURSHAD, or the Sun; of NAHID, or Venus; of ZIR, or Mercury; and of MAH, or the Moon.

Here, again, we have the production of ten primary intelligencies, recalling the Sephirotic emanations, which themselves have planetary attributions.

Let us now take another step. At the beginning of the twelfth century, or actually in the year 1100 A.D., Abū Bakr Ibn Al-Tufail, a noted Arabian physician, poet, mathematician and Sufi philosopher, was born at Guadix in Spain, and he died at Morocco in 1186. His chief work is a species of philosophical romance called THE LIFE OF HAI EBN YOKDAN, *the self-taught Philosopher*. In this curious narrative we find Ibn Al-Tufail using a form of comparison which occurs almost verbatim in the Kabbalistic books. "The Divine Essence is like the rays of the material sun, which expand over opaque bodies and appear to proceed from the eye, though they are only reflected from its surface." We find also substantially: (*a*) The AIN SOPH of the Kabbalists under the name of that One True One; (*b*) the reflection of this Being, dwelling "in the highest sphere, in and beyond which there is no body, a Being free from matter, which was not the Being of that One True One, nor the sphere itself, nor yet anything

---

[1] My knowledge is confined to the translation by Mirza Mohamed Hadi which appeared in successive issues of THE PLATONIST, vols. iii. and iv.

different from them both; but was like the image of the sun as it appears in a well-polished mirror, which is neither one nor the other, and yet not distinct from them"; (c) the immaterial essence of the sphere of the fixed stars; (d) the sphere of Saturn—and so with the rest, in harmony with the scheme of the DESATIR, ending at this world, which is subject to generation and corruption, and comprehending all that is contained within the sphere of the Moon. None of the material essences were identical and yet none were different, either as regards the rest or in comparison with the One True One.[1]

The doctrine of Divine Absorption is the very essence of Sufism and Sufism is contemporary with Mohammedanism itself. It is also mainly pantheistic,[2] as may be gathered from its proposed object. Some refer it to India, others to a Gnostic origin, but the question does not concern us, for the significant fact is that this form of Islamic Mysticism was one of the environments of the Kabbalistic Jews to whom we are indebted for part at least of the ZOHAR. The influence of such environment was felt outside the Kabbalists, and was confessed even by the most inflexible of the sects in Jewry— that of the Kairites, or Literalists, who rejected all innovations in the primeval doctrine of Israel, who set no store by Tradition, and were thus as much opposed to the TALMUD as to Zoharic writings. The proof is their analogies, indeed one might say their fusion, with the Motozales, a sect of scholastic Arabs.[3] A Kairite Jew of the period allows that his brethren followed the doctrines of this sect, and they even assumed its name.

The purpose of the present section should not be misconstrued. Once more, it is by no means designed to indicate that the mystical sects of Mohammedanism are responsible for the peculiar scheme of the Kabbalah, or that the Sufi drew only from the rabbin. Such devices belong to a scheme of criticism which has passed fittingly away. If we know anything concerning the early connections of Sufism it is that they are Neoplatonic, and that the Gnostics of the early Shiite

---

[1] See the Improvement of Human Reason exhibited in the LIFE OF HAI EBN YOKDHAN. "Written in Arabick above 500 years ago, by Abu Jaafar Ebn Tophail." ... *Newly translated from the original Arabick* by Simon Ockley, A.M. London, 1711.
[2] See, on this subject and generally, Professor Reynold A. Nicholson's STUDIES IN ISLAMIC MYSTICISM, 1921, especially Chapter II.
[3] Munk: LA PHILOSOPHIE CHEZ LES JUIFS, p. 10.

sects were attracted to it because of these connections.¹ But to name Neoplatonism and Gnosticism is to cite analogies of Kabbalism, however remote. To say that Sufism has been referred to a woman who died at Jerusalem in the first century of the Hegira is to say that Sufism began to live and move in an atmosphere of Jewish Tradition. To say that Spain was the forcing-house of the Kabbalists is to say that the theosophical doctors of Jewry brushed arms with those of Islam, and to deny that there was any consequence of such contact is to deny Nature. Sufism was pantheistic and emanationist; Kabbalistic emanationism was saved from pure pantheism by the doctrine of Divine Immanence, and their literatures have no real likeness; but between the metaphysics of Divine Love and the mystical absorption of Islam, and between the Kabbalistic return of the soul to God, or its union with the transcendent principle which never departs from ATZILUTH, and the theory of ecstasy in Islam, it seems possible to suppose that there was not only the connecting link of analogy between all mystics but a bond even in history.²

VII.—INFLUENCE OF THE KABBALAH ON JEWRY

There is perhaps no one at the present day, certainly no Christian student of the subject, who is in a position to define precisely what kind of profit accrued to the mind of Jewry from the promulgation, let us say, of the ZOHAR—notwithstanding the statement, already cited, that it gave to Israel the splendid propulsion of the ideal.

So far as it is possible to ascertain, the Kabbalah has exercised only a very subsidiary influence upon the Children

---

¹ On this point the reader may consult with advantage an admirable account of Islâmic Mysticism in A YEAR AMONG THE PERSIANS, by E. G. Browne. London, 1893. It makes no references to Kabbalism, with which the author seems unacquainted, but it may be gathered from what it tells us of Sufic commentaries on the KORAN that these, although pantheistic, have many points of contact with later Kabbalism. We find not only the unmanifest state of Deity, but the attempt to explain why the contingent world (compare LIBER DRUSHIM) was evolved from "the silent depths of the non-existent," the use of which term is so typical of AIN SOPH doctrine. See p. 129 for Browne's opinion that the early schools of Mohammedan philosophy in Persia were adaptations either of Aristotle or Plato, and were also the scholasticism of Islam.

² Dr. Abelson speaks of a comparatively recent theory—or newer at least than are theories of Neoplatonic and Gnostic sources—which "finds echoes of Persian Sufism in the ZOHAR," but unfortunately he gives no references.—JEWISH MYSTICISM, p. 119.

of the Exile—those excepted obviously for whom it was a path of devotion, a path of life in sanctity for the attainment of the Good and the One. We can point to certain enthusiasms for which it is partially responsible, among the crowd of Ghetto believers who understood only its aberrations, and they are those precisely which did their best to wreck Jewry and of which Jewry is now ashamed. The history of Abraham Abulafia, of Sabbataï Zevi and the founder of the Hassidim,[1] are typical cases in point which warrant us in saying that the Kabbalah gave spurious Messiahs to Israel.[2] It was perhaps the last instance of its open activity before it ceased to exercise any powerful influence, and with this also it would have begun if we cared to believe that Rabbi Akiba was the author of the BOOK OF FORMATION, and that he was connected with the bogus or at least the frenzied mission of Bar Cochba. We have seen that there is no truth in the story; but this notwithstanding it has, I fear, to be admitted that if a literature may be judged by its influence, that of the Kabbalah has been small on the external side, while it has encouraged false enthusiasm, and has been the warrant for direct imposture.[3]

So far as its operation was intellectual, there is tolerable ground for thinking that its field was the Christian rather than the Jewish mind.[4] And having established one useful point there is an opportunity here of making another. Kabbalistic influence on Christendom has been of two kinds, but it has

---

[1] *I.e.*, the new Order of the mysterious Baal Shem, which is said to have had its representatives even at the close of the nineteenth century in a number of Jewish communities and to have held the ZOHAR in high esteem.—ISRAEL AMONG THE NATIONS, pp. 61, 40, 345. The sect had its chief hold among Russian and Galician Jews: the name signifies " pious ones." In the time of Judas Maccabæus, it meant the strict party among the Jews.—Edersheim, HISTORY OF THE JEWISH NATION. Compare Scaliger's Order of Knights of the Temple, with which the sect has been identified. There is a long contemplation by Paul Vulliaud on Sabbataï Zevi and the Hassidim in LA KABBALE JUIVE, Vol. II., pp. 139 *et seq.* The accounts of the original HASSIDIM are full of mythical elements.

[2] Zangwill in his DREAMERS OF THE GHETTO was perhaps the first who brought this notion to the knowledge of the external and popular world.

[3] It has given also a few obscure sects to Jewry. A knowledge of Kabbalistic Mysteries was alleged to have imparted superhuman power to Löbele, chief Rabbi of Prague in his day; to Jacob Franck, the Polish distiller, of whose followers the so-called Christian Jews of Poland represented a small survival; and to his contemporary, Israel of Podolia, who established the New Saints and had a recipe for miracles by means of the name TETRAGRAMMATON.

[4] Zangwill is not of this opinion. Referring to the period which antedated immediately the mission of Sabbataï Zevi, he says: " The ZOHAR—the Book of Illumination, composed in the thirteenth century—printed now for the first time, shed its dazzling rays further and further over every ghetto." But perhaps he follows here the principle that he has borrowed from Spinoza, " to see things *sub specie æternitatis.*" I wish the same principle had inspired him to lay less stress on the exact date of the ZOHAR.

been much more of one kind than another. It has been an influence exercised by a peculiar theosophical claim upon the students and the acceptors of such. But it has been much more the influence of possible missionary material on the missionary enterprise of the Christian Church. To begin at a late date—What gave the Kabbalah of the ZOHAR to the Latin-reading scholars of Europe? The *magnum opus* of Rosenroth—or more at least than all. What impelled Rosenroth? The "splendid spectrum" of the conversion of Jewry *en masse*. And now, if we sweep backward to the very beginning of the Christian interest in Kabbalism, almost coincident, in fact, with the appearance of the ZOHAR, and suppose that Raymund Lully was really, as it has been said that he was, the first Christian student of the Kabbalah, what was the life-long labour of that amazing seneschal of Majorca, and for what did he renounce the world? To wrest, as it has been said, from reluctant Nature the elusive Mastery of Nature, the Great Palingenesis of Alchemy? The Hermetic treatises ascribed to him may say Yes, but we know that they are ascribed falsely, and that this was by no means the ambition of Raymund Lully. But was it the attainment of a religion behind all religions? Nothing of the sort; that is modern fantasy. The work of Raymund Lully was apostolical and missionary, and it closed with martyrdom at Bugia, in a feverish attempt to evangelise "Mahound." What prompted the fiery energy of Picus de Mirandula, that he filled the Papal Court with the rumour and the wonder of Secret Jewish Tradition? The fact that he also regarded it as a way, revealed against all expectation and as if on the part of Divine Providence, by which the Princes of the Exile might be brought to the gates of the Eternal City and the Ghetto might be transformed into a Baptistry. Suppose, lastly, that Nicholas Flamel was really initiated by the BOOK OF ABRAHAM THE JEW,"[1] so that Kabbalism connects integrally with Alchemy, what prompted the unostentatious scrivener of old Paris to make precious metals by occult arts when his wants were few and his trade sufficient for a modest man? Why, he also had the missionary spirit—witness his bequests, actual or fabulous, for the conversion of the heathen.

The inference is that the Kabbalah was imported out of

---

[1] See my SECRET TRADITION IN ALCHEMY, c. x.

Jewry to prove that Jewry might be Christianised if it were handled wisely according to the lights given in the Holy Synods.[1]

Now, I do not need to say that there are very few students of cryptic literatures at this late day of the world who would take any interest in the Kabbalah, regarded from this point of view. They are not, as a class, inspired by missionary zeal for any form of official religion, and their memorials, as they stand, do not manifest more than a distant respect for the great orthodoxies of Christendom. On the other hand, it is only in virtue of some immense misapprehension that the Esoteric Tradition of the Jews can be supposed to offer them the religion behind all religions. What it does offer them on the surface falls almost infinitely short. At its highest a bizarre but strenuous attempt to unriddle the universe, the most unaided of all metaphysics, the *systema mundi* excogitated in a darkened synagogue with the praying-shawl drawn over the eyes. What darkness to be felt in the void! What strange lights flashing in the darkness! In such a state Spanish Jew or Spanish Mystic of the Latin Church, Moses de Leon, if you will, or St. John of the Cross, exile of Babylon or recluse of the Thebaid, may enjoy a certain communication of the Infinite. But to say more than this is frenzy. And at its lowest, that is to say, on that side upon which it makes contact no longer with the infinite, but with the occult as it was understood by occultism at its zenith—let us say, in Victorian days—finite of all things finite: what sombre trifling unredeemed by a saving sense of triviality; the physiognomy of the section YITHROH, the astrology of the processes of Gaffarel, the star messages of the Hebrew planisphere, the paper tubes of Éliphas Lévi;[2] or, again, NOTARIKON, METATHESIS, GEMATRIA,[3] the arcana of the Extended Name, the virtues of AGLA and ARARITA for conjuring heaven and earth. It is

---

[1] One writer in modern times has even gone so far as to maintain that "Christian doctrine, except the Trinity, which is Platonic, issues wholly, with all its details, from the TALMUD. Christianity is son and brother of the TALMUD."—Alexandre Weill: MOISE, LE TALMUD ET L'ÉVANGILE, ii. 92. The statement sounds perilous, but M. Weill is not to be taken seriously. Compare *ibid.* ii. 91: "The TALMUD is itself the most violent adversary of Moses," *i.e.*, the Moses of M. Weill. One paradox enables us to judge another.

[2] And the kind of Kabbalah which A. Lelièvre undertook to defend in his JUSTIFICATION DES SCIENCES DIVINATOIRES (Paris, 1847).

[3] Observe also the developments which these subjects received in works like the CABALLA ANAGRAMMATICA of Ranutius Longelus, *Placentiæ*, 1654—*ars mirabilis* indeed, as the author terms it.

here that occultism illustrates how it receives only what it can give and how it comes to pass that the interest of the occultist in the KABBALAH was less inspired by Zoharic Theosophy than by the magic garters of the KEY OF SOLOMON.[1] Hence writers like Papus in France found it necessary to include in their scheme of Kabbalism the sorry literature of the Grimoires.[2] And they and he had nothing to tell us of the ZOHAR. But we do not find the Grimoires in Picus de Mirandula, or in Raymund Lully; we do not find Mysteries of Magic in the KABBALA DENUDATA. The Lexicon of Rosenroth does not include the occult wonders of AGLA, nor does it tell us after what manner the Extended Name is compounded, by a child-craft of acrostics, out of three verses in Exodus. We do find all these in Agrippa, who wrote as a young man of things that he had heard and read, making a very dignified retractation of it all in his book of great excellence which unfolds their solemn vanity.

There remains, of course, the mystical side of Kabbalism, the return of the soul to God, and that path of ecstasy already mentioned, by which it was conceived that the soul might effect such reunion even in this life; but it is precisely this side of which we see no effect whatsoever in Jewry, and it is also this which has been neglected by later occultism. For example, the present work is the first published in England which has any reference to the highest principle of the human soul in Kabbalism and the Instrument of Unification with the Divine. But it is here and only here that we encounter what gave to Israel " the splendid propulsion of the ideal "; and it is here, as in all whatsoever of Zoharic Theosophy which led up and belongs thereto, that a justification shall be sought and found for an inquiry at large into a Secret Tradition in Israel and into the doctrine of the Holy Kabbalah.

---

[1] I am referring here to the past of the nineteenth century. It happens at the present time that the subject is dead in England and is almost extinct in France, not that French occultism has improved, but that it has varied the fashion of its follies.

[2] LA KABBALE, pp. 10, 16, 26, the last especially, where the reference to Molitor makes the author of the PHILOSOPHY OF TRADITION apparently responsible for the identification of the *clavicula* and "magical MSS." as a serious branch of Kabbalism.

BOOK III

THE WRITTEN WORD OF KABBALISM: FIRST OR YETZIRATIC PERIOD

BOOK III

THE WRITTEN WORD OF KABBALISM: FIRST PERIOD

I.—EARLY KABBALISTIC LITERATURE

It seems beyond controversy that there was a not inconsiderable mass of old theosophical speculation and doctrine once extant in Jewry, of which vestiges are to be found in the TALMUD, and that it is connected occasionally with brilliant and even with a few great names. It is this somewhat nebulous material which prepared a way for later developments, leading up in fine to the ZOHAR, and should scholarship forbid us to confer on its earlier stages the distinctive denomination of Kabbalism,[1] we must defer to scholarship, though with the mental reservation that if the question be more than of words it is at most one of stages of growth, for that which was of Mysticism in Israel between the period of the TALMUD and the period of the promulgation of the ZOHAR is that which in the course of its evolution became—as just intimated—the Kabbalah and ZOHAR.

The title of this section is obviously tentative or speculative, but the modest conclusions of the previous book are a sufficient warrant for supposing that there are evidences of Kabbalism, outside the SEPHER YETZIRAH, prior to the promulgation of the ZOHAR, and possessing in fact certain literary remains. It is indeed essential to the natural history of the later work that it should have had its antecedents and precursors in the world of texts. According to the most

---

[1] There can be, I think, little doubt that the Kabbalah was the " reception " of the BERESHITH and MERKABAH Mysteries mentioned in the TALMUD, or that this was the view always taken by Kabbalistic Jews. My readers should be referred at this point to an important study of the subject in THE JEWISH ENCYCLOPÆDIA, vol. iii., s.v. CABALA, under the names of Dr. Kaufmann Kohler, Rabbi of Temple Beth-El, New York, and of Dr. Louis Ginzberg, Professor of Talmud at the Jewish Theological Seminary of America, New York City.

acceptable view these were various MIDRASHIM which, in many cases, are no longer extant, and it is fair to suppose that such memorials must have exercised some influence.

So also the SEPHER YETZIRAH, whatever the date ascribed to it, was of high authority, and the respect in which it was held was of the kind which creates literature. We must beware, however, of assuming that there was an unbroken line of Kabbalists, maintaining and unfolding one and the same Tradition, from the second to the twelfth century, as some incautious writers have pretended. There was, however, "the mystical literature of the Geonic period." Whatever the date ascribed to SEPHIR YETZIRAH in its present form, we must regard as its prototype a work already mentioned under the title of the ALPHABET OF AKIBA,[1] while the predecessor of THE BOOK OF OCCULTATION, one of the most challengeable sections of the ZOHAR, must be sought in the anthropomorphic SHIUR KOMAH, *i.e.*, THE MEASURE OF THE HEIGHT, or MEASURE OF BEING, in other words, the DESCRIPTION OF THE BODY OF GOD, a development of the various Scriptural places in which divine members are mentioned. It survives only in two fragments which are held to be not later than the eighth century. The dates of both these works are, however, conjectural, but there can be no doubt, as indeed there is no question, of their comparative antiquity, in respect of rootmatter. Connected with them are the GREATER and the LESSER PALACE, known also as DELINEATION OF THE HEAVENLY TEMPLES,[2] which, in common with the others, is not regarded by some modern critics as Kabbalistic, though it is allowed that all were instrumental in calling the Kabbalah into existence.[3]

In accordance with the exigencies of his standpoint, Dr

---

[1] There are two versions, of which A is considered older by Jellinek, while Graetz takes the opposite view. A third MIDRASH, on the ornamentation of the letters, is also referred to Akiba.

[2] Not to be confused with a work mentioned by Bartolocci under the name of R. Eliezer and dealing with the measurements of the earthly temple. The PIRKE HAIKLUTH, otherwise PIRKE MERKABAH, is an account of Seven Heavenly Temples or Palaces which must be visited in succession by the elect before they can enter the region of the Sacred Chariot. They would appear to represent stages of rapture and vision. Compare the Palaces of the ZOHAR.

[3] "By the difficulty," says Ginsburg, "in which they placed the Jews in the South of France and in Catalonia, who believed in them almost as much as in the Bible, and who were driven to contrive this system whereby they could explain the gross descriptions of the Deity and of the plains of heaven, given in these Haggadic productions." It may be affirmed indeed that one spirit informed the chief works of Kabbalistic complexion which preceded the ZOHAR.

Graetz, who may be taken to represent at his period all that is most acrid and uncompromising in hostility to Jewish Mysticism, fixes the origin of Kabbalism, as to its date, in the tenth century, and thus by implication denies the claim of the SEPHER YETZIRAH to be included in its literature. He is followed, as we have seen, by Ginsburg,[1] but it is not open to question that the work is indispensable to the Kabbalah on its artificial and external side, though it contributes nothing to the heights and deeps of the HOLY ZOHAR. The tenth century is, however, an important period in Jewish history and Jewish letters, for at this epoch the quickening of the Arabian mind was followed by that of Israel[2] and was sometimes eclipsed thereby. There was for the moment a lull in persecution; the Academies in the East flourished, and in the West the internecine struggle of Christians and Moslems in Spain insured a breathing space to the Children of the Exile. Prior to that period, from the sixth century and onward, there was a hiatus in the literature of Israel. The canons of the Talmud were closed to all intents by the terror and peril of the time, and the history of Israel became one of bitter struggle for existence. A certain hazardous shelter was found under Persian dominion, and ultimately the intellectual lamp of Israel shone forth clearly and steadily during the Moslem domination of Spain, which country—from that period till the beginning of the thirteenth century—was like a second Palestine to the Jew, and this land of refuge, under the tolerant and enlightened sway of the Spanish Khalifs, became almost as dear to his heart as the Land of Promise. Montpellier in France and Salerno in Italy were famous for their Jewish Schools, but that of Seville was, perhaps, more illustrious than either. Spain also was a nursing-land of Kabbalistic literature, and the traces of an Esoteric Tradition between the epoch which produced the BOOK OF FORMATION[3] and that of the BOOK OF SPLENDOUR must be sought chiefly therein, though in the twelfth century something may be gleaned from Southern France and earlier still from Hay Gaon, who

---

[1] Kitto's CYCLOPÆDIA, third edition, 1864, s.v. KABBALAH.
[2] Basnage, HISTOIRE DES JUIFS, livre vii. c. 4, tom. v. pp. 1503 et seq.
[3] Outside the dates and authorship ascribed by old Kabbalists to the SEPHER YETZIRAH and the ZOHAR there are other treatises attributed to the early days of the Exile. Thus tradition regards Eliezer Hagabite, son of Jose, a contemporary of Simeon ben Yohai, as a Kabbalistic doctor and the author of a treatise on the thirty-two qualities of the Law.

flourished in the eleventh century, a Babylonian, on the borders of the Caspian Sea.[1]

There is neither space nor occasion here to produce a bibliographical list, and indeed the materials at our command cannot be regarded as extensive, serving mainly to correct false and highly coloured impressions regarding the claims of Kabbalistic Tradition. The chief names of the period with which we are concerned are :

I. Rabbi Eliezer ben Hyrcanus, whose supposed mystical system, as presented in his PIRKE = *Capitula*, connects on the one hand with SEPHER YETZIRAH, and on the other with Zoharic teaching.[2] We have, in the first place, God subsisting prior to the creation of the world, alone with his Ineffable Name ; next, the creation, prior to the visible world, of the THORAH or Law, together with the Throne of Glory, the Name of the Messiah, Paradise, Hell and the Temple of Jerusalem, *i.e.*, the archetype of the earthly temple ; subsequently, the creation of the world by means of ten words. With this work may be connected the ancient MIDRASH CONEN,[3] which represents the THORAH as the foundation of the universe and the gage of its stability. It is a matter of conjecture whether these works are slightly later or earlier than the SEPHER YETZIRAH.

II. The Gaon R. Saadiah ben Joseph, *nat. circa* 892, *ob.* 942, head of the Persian Academy of Sura, was the author of a commentary on the SEPHER YETZIRAH preserved in the Bodleian Library and only printed recently in France, as we shall see in the third section of this book.

III. R. Abn-Yussuf Chasdai, a Spanish physician who died at Cordova between 970 and 990 A.D., was a Prince of the Exile and temporal head of the Jews in that city. He was also a political minister under two Khalifs. For the rest, he is said to connect the school of Hay Gaon with that of Gebirol ; but the dates do not correspond.

IV. The Gaon R. Shereerah—otherwise Sherira b. Hanina—

---

[1] Hay Gaon is said to have died A.D. 1038. Gaon was a title given to the heads of two Jewish Academies at Babylon.

[2] The first edition was printed at Venice in 1544, and a Latin version appeared at Leyden precisely one hundred years later. The PIRKE is held to have been written soon after A.D. 833.

[3] MIDRASH CONEN = מדרש כונן = *Expositio Stabiliens*. See Prov. iii. 19. It was the first treatise in a collection entitled ARZE LEVANON = *Cedri Libani*. See Ps. civ. 16. It appeared at Venice in 1601.

head of the Academy of Pherruts Schibbur [1] in the neighbourhood of Babylon, was perhaps more distinguished for the violence with which he wrote against the Christians than for his Kabbalistic knowledge. But Nahmanides [2] has preserved his critical observations on the DELINEATION OF THE HEAVENLY TEMPLES,[3] or more correctly on the fragments which it embodies under the title of the PROPORTION OF THE HEIGHT, otherwise called the DESCRIPTION OF THE BODY OF GOD, which shew the Kabbalistic leanings of Shereerah and create that antithesis to the anthropomorphism of these early works which has been mentioned already as a keynote of the higher Kabbalism. "God forbid," he exclaims, "that man should speak of the Creator as if he had bodily members and dimensions!" This Rabbi was despoiled of his wealth and hanged by order of Cader, Khalif of the race of the Abassides.

V. The Gaon R. Hay, son and successor of Shereerah as the head of the Babylonian School of Schibbur, is also credited with a commentary on the SEPHER YETZIRAH, which will be dealt with in its proper place. The interpretation of dreams was one of the daily occupations of Jewish Academies, and the skill exhibited therein, or the credulity of the times, often purchased toleration and respect for the Rabbis at the hands of the Khalifs. To Rab Hay is attributed a treatise on this art, which was printed at Venice.[4] Outside his alleged commentary on the BOOK OF FORMATION his voluminous works have many Kabbalistic references, especially that entitled THE VOICE OF GOD IN ITS POWER. It will be sufficient to mention among these the doctrine of correspondences, of man as a microcosm and a peculiar theory of mystical contemplation. He possessed enormous influence and became subsequently the head of the Academy of Pumbaditha in the neighbourhood of Bagdad. He died in 1038.

VI. Solomon ben Yehudah Ibn Gebirol, the scholastic Avicebron and in all respects, Kabbalistic and otherwise, a focus of intellectual and literary interest, was a contemporary of the famous Nagrila.

---
[1] Or of Pumbaditha according to some authorities, including Graetz. He is supposed to have died at the age of one hundred years, *circa* A.D. 1000.
[2] In his commentary on the THORAH.
[3] Attributed to R. Ishmael, apparently the doctor of that name whose sentences are sometimes quoted in the TALMUD.
[4] Bartolocci: BIBLIOTHECA RABBINICA, ii. 387.

VII. R. Abraham ben David or Ben Dior Ha Levi, *ob. circa* 1180, the great orthodox apologist of the twelfth century, has been included in the chain of Kabbalism. He is described otherwise as a Spanish astronomer, historian and philosopher.

VIII. Moses Ibn Jacob ben Ezra,[1] one of the greatest Jews of his time, was of Granada, and flourished in the earlier part of the twelfth century. His work entitled the GARDEN OF AROMATICS shews traces of the doctrine of Gebirol, but it appears by his COMMENTARY ON ISAIAH that he was in disagreement with this doctor. Basnage says that he did not reject the Kabbalah, though he knew its weakness, because he did not wish to be embroiled with contemporary writers.[2] He wrote upon the Divine Name and the mystical attributes of numbers in connection therewith.

IX. The name of Juda Hallevi—*ob. post* 1140—who has some references to the SEPHER YETZIRAH in his work entitled KUSARI, of Jacob Nazir—referred to the second half of the twelfth century—of Solomon Jarki, of R. Abraham ben David, the younger, bring us to the thirteenth century and to the period of (*a*) Maimonides, who is reported, chiefly on the authority of R. Hayyim, to have turned Kabbalist at an advanced age but in any case connects with the subject, and was acquainted at least with the existence of the twofold Mystical Tradition, distinguished as that of the Creation and that of the Chariot; (*b*) R. Azriel, of Valladolid, a famous commentator on the SEPHER YETZIRAH; (*c*) Shem Tob Ibn Falaquera, a disciple of Maimonides, who connects with Gebirol; (*d*) R. Abraham Abulafia,[3] who wrote on the TETRAGRAMMATON, the mysticism of Letters and Numbers, and the Mysteries of the Law, but his works have not been published.[4] He endeavoured to combine the theoretical and practical schools, but he was a quixotic adventurer and a Messianic enthusiast, whose opinions it is unnecessary to

---

[1] See ESSAYS ON THE WRITINGS OF IBN EZRA, in the TRANSACTIONS OF THE SOCIETY OF HEBREW LITERATURE.

[2] Basnage quotes Skinner's letters and Usher in support of this view, but he and they are in some confusion as to important dates in Kabbalistic history and literature. Graetz has a good account of Ibn Ezra, but it is unnecessary to say that his analogies with Kabbalism are not mentioned.

[3] See Frankel: MONATSHRIFT FÜR GESCHICHTE UND WEISSENSCHAFT DES JUDENTHUMS, vol. v. p. 27, Leipsic, 1856. Graetz has also a long account of Abulafia, designed to ridicule the mental condition to which he refers the Kabbalah.

[4] They include also THE FOUNT OF LIVING WATERS, of which there is a Latin version in the Vatican. Graetz extends the number of his works to twenty; Bartolocci knew only of three.

determine. It may be noted also that he exhibits some Christian tendencies.

Those who maintain the authenticity of Kabbalistic Tradition find something to their purpose in all these writers and personalities; but they often proceed on a misconception. What, for example, is more likely to lead an unpractised student astray than the treatise of Abraham ben David Ha Levi—*ob. circa* 1150—by the mere fact of its title? It is called SEDER HA KABBALAH, the Order of the Tradition.[1] As a fact, it is the least mystical of all productions, and though I have termed its author a great orthodox apologist, he had a strong Aristotelian leaven. The occasion of his book was a Sadducean heresy prevalent in Castile and Leon, and represented by a work of Abu Alphrag, which maintained that the true synagogue was to be found among the Sadducees. The SEDER HA KABBALAH vindicates the authority of the orthodox claim under the two heads of succession and universality, or community of doctrine among all the synagogues. It embraces the entire history of the Jewish Church and the perpetuation of Mosaic doctrine, which is the tradition named in the title.[2] The work of Abraham ben David Ha Levi is perhaps greater than was the occasion which called it forth. The Jews were divided among themselves upon many questions, of which Saducean pretentions were certainly not the most important. The great distinction of the time for the purpose of our own inquiry was between the Jews who had adopted Aristotelian principles and the Jews who opposed the innovation. The enlightenment and culture were incontrovertibly on the side of the former; the fascination of bizarre thought, and its occasional flashes of a great mystical light, in a word, all that we connect with the ideal of rabbinical Israel, went, however, into the opposite scale. There were important names on both sides. For the rest, Rabbi Abraham and his SEPHER exercised a large influence: his contemporary, Maimonides, who survived him by almost a quarter of a century, was described by the enthusiasts of his period as " the elect of the human race," and by a play upon his name it was said of him

---

[1] It was the prototype of several later productions, such as that of Ghedalia on the CHAIN OF THE KABBALAH, the YUHASIN of Zakut, famous in connection with the ZOHAR, and finally TSEMACH DAVID = *Germen Davidis*, already quoted. The last was the work of R. David Ganz, a treatise on sacred and profane history from the beginning of the world.

[2] Bartolocci: MAGNA BIBLIOTHECA RABBINICA, i. pp. 18 *et seq.*

that "from Moses to Moses there was no one like unto Moses."

The rival school was to some extent represented by Avicebron, and some of those who assert that the ZOHAR incorporated Traditions belonging to preceding centuries are content to rest their case on the writings of this poet and philosopher. The evidence, however, is in a very confused state. On the one hand, the system of Avicebron has many Aristotelian traces; on the other hand, it has been asserted that Maimonides has much to connect him with Avicebron, though he was not acquainted with his works, while, further, the great masterpiece of the Talmudic Jew of Cordova, entitled THE GUIDE OF THE PERPLEXED, offers many indications of his sympathy with doctrines which are no other than those of the Speculative Kabbalah.[1] In a general sense, however, those who wished to introduce Aristotelian principles into Jewish philosophy belonged to that school which subsequently opposed the ZOHAR,[2] as, for example, Joseph ben Abraham Ibn Wakkar of Toledo, at the beginning of the fourteenth century,[3] while those who accepted the ZOHAR belonged to that school which connects with Avicebron, among whom was Rabbi Abraham ben David of Posquière, to whom one section of modern criticism attributes the invention of the Kabbalah, and Isaac the Blind—*ob. circa* 1219 —with his disciples Azriel and Ezra, whose supposed alternative claim is favoured by Ginsburg.[4] The Kabbalistic interests of this school are outside all debate; it prized the SEPHER YETZIRAH, and one of the most important commentaries on that treatise was produced within it.

When we investigate the claim made with regard to Avice-

---

[1] There does not seem, however, the slightest ground for supposing, with Isaac Myer, that Maimonides was acquainted with the ZOHAR. On the contrary, there is more perhaps to be said for the conjecture of S. Munk that the ZOHAR quotes, or rather borrows, from Maimonides. See MÉLANGES, &c., p. 278. Among the Kabbalistic correspondences of Maimonides are (1) His recognition of a secret sense in Scripture; (2) Of the inaccessible nature of God; (3) Of the universe as an organic whole. The student should consult also an interesting NOTICE SUR LA CABALE DES HÉBREUX, prefixed by the Chevalier Drach to the second volume of his work already cited on the HARMONY BETWEEN THE CHURCH AND THE SYNAGOGUE. He establishes (*a*) That where Buxtorf supposes the TALMUD (Tract ROSH HASHANAH) to allow the same authority to the Kabbalah as to the text of Moses, the reference is really to the spiritual power of the Synagogue; and (*b*) that the alleged mention of the mystical Kabbalah by Maimonides is a misconception (L'HARMONIE, ii. xvi. xvii. xviii.). It is certain, however, that Maimonides mentions a Lost Tradition.

[2] In which, however, Munk traces Aristotelian influences.—MÉLANGES, pp. 278, 279.
[3] See the English translation of Steinschneider's JEWISH LITERATURE, p. 114.
[4] Who follows Graetz literally.

bron, we must not be discouraged at finding that writers like Isaac Myer have much enhanced the extent and kind of his Kabbalistic connections. We meet, it is true, the doctrines of the Inaccessible God, of intermediaries between God and the universe, of the emanation of the world and even of the universal knowledge attributed to the pre-existent soul of man by most Jewish Mysticism. But what we should like to discover in a Theosophist of the eleventh century is some distinct trace of typical Zoharic doctrine, let us say, that of Shekinah, not mere Yetziratic references, Sephirotic correspondences and so forth. The two latter are to be expected at the period, and in this case the former is wanting. There remains, however, sufficient to concern us, perhaps even to warrant the inclusion of Gebirol among precursors of Zoharic Kabbalism, and a short account of this author may be appended as a conclusion to this section.

At that period when the influence of Arabian imagination was infused into the romantic literature of Western Europe, Scholastic Philosophy and Theology were imbued with the tincture of Arabian thought; but as, on the one hand, this tincture was received sometimes without much consciousness of its origin, so, on the other, influences were occasionally credited to Arabian sources which were in reality referable only to Spanish Jews living under the protection of the Khalifate during the Moslem domination of the Peninsula. A case in point was the once renowned Avicebron, whose identity with Solomon ben Yehudah Ibn Gebirol, a Jew of Cordova, was first demonstrated by Munk in the early part of the nineteenth century.[1] His chief treatise, entitled the FOUNTAIN OF LIFE, became widely diffused in a Latin version ascribed to the middle of the twelfth century. Albertus Magnus, St. Thomas of Aquin and Duns Scotus, all cited it; and it is said to sum the philosophy of the thirteenth century. According to Renan, Avicebron preceded the school of Arabian philosophy which arose in Spain. He wrote philosophy in Arabic and poetry in Hebrew; the Jews valued his poetry, but his speculations were not in repute among them; the Christian scholastics debated his metaphysical notions, and knew nothing whatever of his verses. By both classes of

---

[1] MÉLANGES DE PHILOSOPHIE JUIVE ET ARABE. The hostile school of Zoharic criticism has not done sufficient credit to Munk for his discovery, but he was not a *persona grata* among them on account of his theory that the ZOHAR was founded on genuine ancient MIDRASHIM. This school has almost passed away.

admirers he was celebrated respectively as the greatest philosopher and the greatest poet of his time. But the nominalists denounced him; realists like Duns Scotus entailed on him their own condemnation; while he is said to have exercised an influence upon mystics of the Middle Ages, he was proscribed by the University of Paris at the period of the publication of the ZOHAR on the ground that he favoured Aristotle. When the school of Averroes arose he was unknown among it; at a later period he was unknown to Maimonides; he was unknown also to the encyclopædic learning of Picus de Mirandula; and on the threshold of the Reformation his memory may be said almost to have perished at the pyre of Giordano Bruno.

Avicebron was born about the year 1021 at Malaga; he was educated in the University of Saragossa, and he died at Valencia in 1070. He was patronised by Nagdilah—*i.e.*, Samuel-ha-Levi ben Josef Ibn Nagréla—a Prince of the Exile, who was also Prime Minister of Spain under the Khalifate of Habus. Nagdilah was the centre and mainspring of Jewish learning in that country, and it has been proposed that through him the Sacred Tradition of the Hebrews was communicated to Avicebron at a period when the ZOHAR and its connections were still in course of formation. It seems certain, in any case, that some of the conceptions and the system incorporated in the literature may be found in his writings, more especially in the FOUNTAIN OF LIFE and the CROWN OF THE KINGDOM. The first is affirmed to be the earliest known exhibition of "the secrets of the Speculative Kabbalah."[1] The second, composed towards the end of his life, is a hymn " celebrating the only one and true God, and the marvels of His creation."

The existence of Zoharic tradition previously to the time of Moses de Leon, the reputed forger of the ZOHAR, has been rested, among other supports, on the writings of this Spanish Jew, and he seems to have been acquainted indubitably with the BOOK OF FORMATION. In the second book and twenty-second section of the FOUNTAIN OF LIFE this passage occurs: "Hence it hath been said that the construction of the world was accomplished by the inscription of numbers and letters

---

[1] There is some confusion here, as the SEPHER YETZIRAH is certainly speculative if contrasted with the so-called Practical Kabbalah, which was mainly the working of miracles by the use of Divine Names.

in the air," which is in obvious analogy with a fundamental notion of the Kabbalistic work in question. The table of the Thirty-Two Paths, which arises out of the BOOK OF FORMATION, was the theme of one of his poems. Whether the later Kabbalists derived from Avicebron or both from a common source cannot be determined conclusively, but having regard to the Jewish indifference for his philosophical writings, and to the probable existence of a vast mass of floating Esoteric Tradition, there can be no doubt as to the direction in which probability points.[1]

The connection between Avicebron and the Kabbalah is not sufficiently explicit upon the surface of the FOUNTAIN OF LIFE to have attracted the attention of scholars like Ernest Renan: while Kabbalistic critics refer the system which it develops to the ten SEPHIROTH, others suppose it to be based on the ten categories of Aristotle, a pantheism analogous to that of the early realists.[2] "On the one hand," says Renan, "his application of Peripatetic principles to Mosaic doctrine alarmed the theologians; on the other hand, his concessions to orthodoxy concerning the creation and the free will of the Creator did not satisfy the extreme Peripatetic Jews." Of his alleged Kabbalistic connections Renan was either unaware, as suggested already, or they were ignored by him.

An impartial examination of the FOUNTAIN OF LIFE makes the pantheism of Avicebron perhaps less apparent than his Kabbalistic correspondences. So far from identifying the universe with God, it establishes no uncertain contrast between them. In order to bridge the abyss, and to make it conceivable that one derived being from the other, he supposes nine intermediaries, *plus* the Divine Will, "through which the Absolutely Existing, Which is above number," is "attached to Its corporeal universe." The analogies that this conception offers to Sephirotic Doctrine are self-evident and do not need enforcing, even if an impartial judgment must pronounce the philosophy of Avicebron to be of Greek rather than Jewish complexion. It is clear at least that FONS VITÆ, which is a dialogue after the manner of Plato, is tinctured deeply by Hellenic thought.

---

[1] Graetz takes the opposite view, saying that the Kabbalah borrowed many principles from Ibn Gebirol. He offers, of course, no evidence on the subject.
[2] The nature and names of the SEPHIROTH will be explained fully in Book V, §§ 2 and 3. At the present stage, and in respect of a few further preliminary allusions, the reader is referred to the first three plates which illustrate this volume.

Modern scholarship has recognised three chief schools which led up to Zoharic Kabbalism: (*a*) that of Isaac the Blind, to which belongs Azriel, with his celebrated commentary on the SEPHER YETZIRAH; (*b*) that of Eliezar of Worms, which is largely of the theurgic order; and (*c*) that of Abulafia, which to some extent united the preceding two and made use of theurgic formulæ combined with contemplation to achieve union with God—that is to say, the exteriorisation of mental images for the attainment of an end which is of all things inward and apart from the forms of mind.

II.—THE BOOK OF FORMATION

The attribution of SEPHER YETZIRAH to the patriarch Abraham is imbedded in the text itself of that minute tract which is regarded by most scholars as the chief nucleus of all Kabbalism. Depending from this there arose inevitably the rabbinical legend which affirms that Abraham transmitted it orally to his sons, by whom it was perpetuated in turn till certain " sages of Jerusalem " committed it finally to writing, so that the Tradition might not perish, even when the chosen people seemed themselves on the eve of perishing. We are acquainted already with this story and are in a position to gauge its value, which lies indeed upon the surface. It is the claim on a Secret Tradition *ab origine Symboli*, personified, so to speak, and it is carried back further still by the ZOHAR. It belongs to the mythos of successive custodians for the transmission of that which was itself a myth, so far as the claim on antiquity is concerned.

At the period when we hear first of the existence of such a tract it may have been old already, and most old books have fables designed to explain them. Those who take the fables historically convert honest legend into something approaching farce. We must be content therefore to say that the first Christian reference to SEPHER YETZIRAH may belong to the ninth century; it has been held also that it is quoted in the TALMUD; but criticism has proposed an alternative text under the same title and that the subject of Talmudic reference is no longer extant.[1] However this may be, there is no question

---

[1] The treatise SANHEDRIM contains the following passage: " By means of combining the letters of the Ineffable Names as recorded in SPR ITsIRH "—meaning the Sealing Names enumerated in the first chapter, being permutations of IHV—" Rava once created

that the BOOK OF FORMATION may have antedated its first citation in literature by a generation, a century, or an age. It should be realised that we do not know, and that those who judge the question dogmatically on either side deserve to be classed as intemperate.

Let us look now a little more closely at the work itself. It is divided into six chapters, the first being concerned with the office of the SEPHIROTH in creation and the remaining five with what have been termed the Instruments—namely, the letters of the Hebrew Alphabet. It was after the revelation of these Mysteries to Abraham that he received the manifestation of God and that the Covenant was instituted. According to the expression of the original, God " bound the twenty-two letters " on the tongue of the patriarch and discovered to him His secret.[1]

There are two points which require to be noted at this preliminary stage of the Yetziratic myth. One is the absolute distinctness between God and the instruments of creation,[2] whether numbers or letters,[3] which is established by this early Kabbalistic work. Separated from all number and transcending all expression, He is represented as a Faithful King sojourning in eternity and ruling the SEPHIROTH for ever from His holy seat. The second point concerns the emanation of the SEPHIROTH, to which, in preference to their creation, later Kabbalism inclines. There is little on the face of the BOOK OF FORMATION to countenance this view, though the latest

---

a man and sent him to Rav Zeira. The man being unable to reply when spoken to, the Rabbi said to him, Thou art a creature of the company "—or those initiated in the Mysteries of Necromancy—" return to thy dust." It seems idle to suggest that this allusion is not to the tract which has been known for centuries and has been edited on so many occasions. As a fact, however, the reference is in reality to HILKOT YETZIRAH, a magical work belonging to the Talmudic period.

[1] SEPHER YETZIRAH, chap. vi.

[2] Hence C. G. Harrison was in error when he implied that pantheism is involved in the Sephirotic system, and when he proceeds to argue that " it takes no account of the element of illusion which is necessarily implied in the theophanic doctrine."— See THE TRANSCENDENTAL UNIVERSE, London, 1894, pp. 86, 87. Cf. Alexander Weill: LOIS ET MYSTÈRES DE LA CRÉATION CONFORMÉS À LA SCIENCE LA PLUS ABSOLUE. Paris, 1896. The writer refers to a work under a similar title which he issued forty years previously, purporting to be the translation of a Hebrew MS. by a master of Kabbalah. " This writing is distinguished from all rabbinical and philosophical treatises by proclaiming the identity of the Creator with His creatures, based on the text of Genesis itself." Weill was a fantasiast who pretended to separate the frauds and contradictions which Esdras and his assistants introduced into the Pentateuch from the real work of Moses. Cf. the same author's MOÏSE, LE TALMUD ET L'EVANGILE. Paris, 1875, tom. i. p. 99. According to Franck, the last word of the system developed by SEPHER YETZIRAH is the substitution of absolute unity for every species of dualism.— LA KABBALE, p. 159.

[3] See Appendix III.

translation makes use of the word "emanate" in one place only, *i.e. Cap.* I, v. 6. A literal rendering would be "go forth"; for they appear as the instruments and servants of the King of Ages, informed by Whose word they do actually go forth "and returning, fall prostrate in adoration before the Throne."[1] It is said, however, that their end is bound to their beginning, as the flame is bound to the firebrand, and perhaps the principle of emanation is contained implicitly in this statement. We have no reason for rejecting a construction which has been adopted invariably, but it is just to draw attention to the fact that the first work which mentions the SEPHIROTH leaves this point in obscurity, while it depicts God as the active Former, Artificer and Maker, Who graved, sculptured and builded. In Masonic terms, He became and was the Great Architect of the Universe; and anthropomorphism is postulated therefore at the very root of being.

The first SEPHIRA—classified therefore as ONE—is described as the Spirit of the Living Elohim, the Living God of Ages, eternal and for ever. It is said otherwise that the Spirit of the Holy One is Voice, Spirit and Word. Two is the Breathing of the Spirit, described otherwise as Air; the twenty-two letters depend herefrom and each one of them is Spirit. THREE is the moisture which comes from the Breath—otherwise, Water from Air: herewith God sculptured and engraved the first lifeless and void matter. He built TOHU, the line which circles snake-like about the world,[2] and BOHU, the concealed rocks imbedded in the abyss whence the waters issue. This triad of the Spirit, the Breath and the Water corresponds to the conception formed subsequently of the Atzilutic or Archetypal World.[3] FOUR is the Fire which comes forth from the Water: with this God sculptured the Throne of Honour, the SERAPHIM, the OPHANIM or Celestial Wheels, the Holy Animals—*i.e.*, the Four Living Creatures—and other Ministering Spirits. Within their dominion He established His habitation.

When this numeration is combined with those which follow immediately, namely, FIVE and SIX, there is formed a second triad, which comprises the conception of BRIAH, the

---

[1] SEPHER YETZIRAH, chap. i. See the BOOK OF FORMATION. Translated from the Hebrew, by Knut Stenring, already cited.

[2] Compare the "green line"—*linea viridis*—which encircles the world in the CONCLUSIONES KABBALISTICÆ of Picus de Mirandula: see p. 446 of the present work.

[3] On the Four Worlds of Kabbalism, see Book V, § 3.

archangelic world of late Kabbalism. It should be remembered, however, that the BOOK OF FORMATION is concerned only with the sphere of operation tabulated subsequently as the Third World of Kabbalism. As each SEPHIRA was supposed at a later period to contain all the SEPHIROTH, so there was a superincession of the Four Worlds, which were all contained in each. The arrangement of the SEPHER YETZIRAH does not conform with this and indeed excludes it; for the numerations from five to nine inclusive must be held to represent the Yetziratic World, while the tenth and last numeration corresponds to ASSIAH—otherwise, the World of Action. FIVE is the seal with which God sealed the Height when He contemplated it above Him. He sealed it with the name IHV. SIX is the seal with which He sealed the depth when He contemplated it beneath Him. He sealed it with the name IVH. SEVEN is the seal with which He sealed the East when He contemplated it before Him. He sealed it with the name HIV. EIGHT is the seal with which He sealed the West when He contemplated it behind Him. He sealed it with the name HVI. NINE is the seal with which He sealed the North when He contemplated it on His right. He sealed it with the name VIH. TEN is the seal with which He sealed the South when He contemplated it on His left. He sealed it with the name VHI. The ten numerations are classed finally together under the one title of "Ineffable Spirits of God." The Sealing Names are combinations of three letters, successively transposed, which enter into the name TETRAGRAMMATON.

The SEPHER YETZIRAH was published at Mantua in 1592, but the Latin translation of Postel had preceded it by ten years.[1] The Mantua edition was accompanied by five commentaries.[2] Another Latin version will be found in the collection of Pistorius; it is ascribed to Reuchlinus and Riccius. In 1642 a further edition was published at Amsterdam in Hebrew and Latin by Rittangelius. It was issued by

---

[1] The full title of this curious little volume is ABRAHAMI PATRIARCHÆ LIBER JEZIRAH, *sive Formationis Mundi, Patribus quidem Abrahami tempora præcedentibus revelatus, sed ab ipso etiam Abrahamo expositus Isaaco, et per Profetarum manus posteritati conservatus, ipsis autem 72 Mosis auditoribus in secundo divinæ veritatis loco, hoc est in ratione, quæ est posterior authoritate, habitus. Vertebat ex Hebræis et commentariis illustrabat 1551, ad Babylonis ruinam et corrupti mundi finem*, GULIELMUS POSTELLUS, *Restitutus. Parisiis*, 1552.

[2] It contained also two recensions of the text, the differences between which are regarded by some authorities as considerable and by others as unimportant variants. Karppe (*op. cit.*, p. 138) terms them *très divergents*.

Meyer at Leipsic in 1830, with a German translation and notes, and at Frankfort, 1849, with a German translation and commentary,[1] by L. Goldschmidt. In 1887 the Parisian occultist Papus made a French translation, to which he added the Thirty-two Paths of Wisdom and the Fifty Gates of Intelligence. With laudable sincerity he admitted later on that this was superseded by Mayer Lambert in 1891.[2]

There is a question at its value which remains over for consideration, and this is how we are to account for the importance attributed in certain circles to such a work as the SEPHER YETZIRAH. Did its defenders believe that the combination of ALEPH with all the other letters and all the rest with ALEPH, BETH with all the others and all the rest with BETH, &c., &c., actually produced the universe? That is an insupportable assumption for any class of persons except possibly occult fantasiasts in the ecstasy of aberration which seems to have been their normal mode during the second half of the nineteenth century. Did they regard the letters as symbols of forces and hold that SEPHER YETZIRAH teaches that the universe originated in their orderly combination? That is tolerable speculation for the same class in its lucid intervals, having regard to its equipment, though it does not demand the apparatus of a Secret Tradition to secure its transmission from Abraham to Eliphas Lévi and from Lévi to Westcott and Mathers. But did they consider that the letters represent occult powers of a fixed, determinable character, and that initiation into the real meaning of Kabbalistic Tradition would discover their nature, explaining thus the secret behind the arbitrary doctrine of a virtue inherent in words and letters? Having known most of the groups, personally and otherwise, I have never met with any maker of reveries who took such a view, or had anything to substantiate it if he did. In the absence of light on this point one can conclude only that it is the arbitrary doctrine in question which accounts for the interest taken in the SEPHER YETZIRAH, outside that which it represents for pure scholarship, about which something has been said in an introduction

---

[1] The AMERICAN ENCYCLOPÆDIA, iii. 521, 522, mentions the Amsterdam edition of 1642, with a Latin translation, but does not connect it with Rittangelius.

[2] Other translations are those of (1) Isidor Kalisch, New York, 1877; (2) Edersheim in an Appendix to his JEWISH MESSIAH, 1886; (3) Wynn Westcott, 1887 and 1893, which I have described as paraphrase; (4) Phineas Mordell, Philadelphia, 1914: it reduces the genuine text to twenty-four paragraphs; and (5) Rabbi A. B. Joseph, 1923.

prefixed by myself to the most recent English translation, being that of Mr. Knut Stenring, cited already in a note. I do not propose to retrace this ground and hence refer thereto. In conclusion, if the ZOHAR absorbed the SEPHER YETZIRAH as to its essence, it must be added that the older text brought nothing to the later which is part of its Theosophy at the highest.

III.—CONNECTIONS AND DEPENDENCIES OF THE BOOK OF FORMATION

Were there evidence to warrant us in believing that Moses de Leon did actually, as his hostile relative is reported to have affirmed, write the ZOHAR bodily " out of his own head," there would be substantial evidence still that the Kabbalistic system which it contains was not his invention at the root. The existence of the SEPHER YETZIRAH is part of this evidence, which appears, however, more fully and more strongly in the commentaries and developments of that work. We have seen already that when it came to be printed at Mantua, the BOOK OF FORMATION was accompanied by five such connections, which at the same time do not exhaust the list that might be given in a complete bibliography. The best known is unquestionably the SEPHER SEPHIROTH, or " Commentary on the Ten SEPHIROTH by way of Questions and Answers," the work of R. Azriel ben Menahem; that of Rabbi Abraham has been regarded as the most important from an esoteric standpoint, while the earliest in point of time is the work of Saadya Gaon [1] in the tenth century. Another, which has been attributed to Hay Gaon in the early part of the eleventh century, would rank next in antiquity, but it has been rejected usually as spurious in respect of date and attribution. Commentaries are ascribed also to R. Moses Botarel,[2] R. Moses ben Nahmann,[3] R. Abraham ben David Ha Levi the younger and R. Eleazar. Of these personalities the first and last are subse-

---

[1] That is, Saadiah Ben Joseph, Gaon of Sura. The JEWISH ENCYCLOPÆDIA suggests that Saadia is " an artificial Hebrew equivalent " of his Arabic name Sa'id. GAON is a title which distinguished the heads of the two Academies at Babylon, those of Sura and Pumbedita, as we have seen. It arose late in the sixth century. The plural is GEONIM.

[2] He describes the Kabbalah as a most pure and holy philosophy, but exhibits no acquaintance with the ZOHAR. He belonged to the fourteenth and fifteenth centuries, and was instructed in the Secret Tradition by Jacob Sefardi.

[3] Bartolocci, iv. 267.

quent to the period when Moses de Leon is supposed to have been at work on the ZOHAR, and the two others have been cited to shew that the novelty of that work " is of form rather than material."

The commentary of R. Saadya Gaon is one of those which was published in Hebrew at Mantua, together with the SEPHER YETZIRAH [1]; but it was written originally in Arabic, and a copy is preserved in the Bodleian Library. After remaining in MS. for over eight hundred years this Arabic original was at length printed at Paris, together with a French translation, in 1892. In the introduction prefixed to his version, M. Lambert observed that Saadya Gaon appears as a Theosophist in his commentary, which is almost equivalent to saying that the first expository treatise on the SEPHER YETZIRAH possesses a Kabbalistic complexion, though the author has been regarded as a purely rationalistic writer. It must be confessed, however, that Saadya offers little connection with Zoharic doctrine. We have noted that the SEPHIROTH of the SEPHER YETZIRAH shew scarcely any trace of an emanational system. For Saadya Gaon there is one intermediary between God and the world, but this is the physical air and not the transcendental numerations. In this air God is present everywhere, and it penetrates all bodies, even the most compact. Of the doctrine of AIN SOPH there is also no real trace. It is recognised however, on the one hand, that we cannot have an adequate notion of the Divinity or His correspondences with the world, but, on the other, that some approximate idea may be obtained as to the latter and that they may be shewn forth by means of figures and comparisons. One of these illustrations tells us that God is the life of the world as the soul is the life of the body, and as in man the soul is all-powerful, so God is omnipotent in the world. He is also its Supreme Reason, and as in man the rational faculty is the guide of life, so the Divine Power is directed by the Divine Reason. Above this elementary form of Natural Theology the commentary never soars, and we are warranted in saying that the work, as a whole, has little inherent interest, though it is valuable as a historical document.

Unlike the SEPHER YETZIRAH, which makes no reference to pneumatology, Saadya Gaon devotes a certain space to the

---

[1] See p. 90.

consideration of the soul in man; and here, in a sense, he connects with Zoharic Kabbalism, though he rejects metempsychosis utterly, for he recognises the soul's five aspects or divisions and calls them by their conventional names, which names, however, occur in the Talmud.[1] They will be tabulated at a later stage. Unfortunately, his classification is exceedingly clumsy, and he begins by following Plato in the recognition of three faculties—reason, concupiscence and anger. On account of reason the soul is called NESHAMAH; on account of concupiscence it is called NEPHESH; and on account of anger it is called RUAH. The two other names, HAÏA (living) and YEHIDAH (unique), refer to the vitality of the soul and to the fact that no other creature resembles it. We shall see that the Zohar knows nothing of such material attributions.

The doctrine concerning Divine and Angelic Names is also a subject of some references which are important to our inquiry because they establish the fact that Saadya Gaon did not ascribe to them any thaumaturgic virtues. The names of the angels vary according to the events which they are commissioned to accomplish, and in like manner those referred to the Deity are descriptive of His operations. In the Work of Creation He terms Himself ELOHIM; when ordaining the Covenant of Circumcision He is called EL SHADDAI; He is the I AM in connection with the wonders of the ten plagues; and He is JAH when producing the great miracle of the Red Sea.[2] As it is with the names of God and the angels, so is it with those of the stars, which vary according to their qualities —namely, their greater or lesser brilliance, their hot or cold natures, &c.

When explaining that the SEPHER YETZIRAH is concerned with created things and how they came into being, there is a

---

[1] Despite his hostility to reincarnation, as understood by the Kabbalah, he accepts the pre-existence of souls and teaches that the resurrection of the body will take place when all souls destined for earthly life have passed through it. Here is one example of Zoharic doctrine, pure and simple, but it has been reflected from the past into the later text.

[2] The ZOHAR teaches that the Divine Name AHIH, which signifies I AM, indicates the unification and concealment of all things in such a manner that no distinction can be established between them. The words ASHR AHIH, THAT I AM, represent God on the point of manifesting all things, including His Supreme Name. On the other hand the Name or Title AHIH ASHR AHIH, I AM THAT I AM, refers to the Deity, or is that Name assumed by Him, on the occasion of the manifestation of the Cosmos, when God is called JEHOVAH.—Zohar iii. 65b, Mantua. Compare the French translation, v. 179.

reference to the ten categories—namely, substance, quantity, quality, relation, place, time, powers, position, activity, passivity; and if these are to be regarded as referring to the numerations of the SEPHER YETZIRAH, it is clear that Saadya Gaon understood the latter as an Aristotelian philosopher. With these categories, the ten commandments are also forced to correspond in an arbitrary manner. For example, that against adultery answers to the category of position, for the act itself is a position and a contact.

Lastly, in his analysis of the Hebrew Alphabet, the commentator seeks to account for its sequence. ALEPH is the first sound pronounced—*i.e.*, it is vocalised at the back of the tongue. SHIN is vocalised in the middle of the mouth and MEM on the lips. Unfortunately for the analogy, MEM precedes SHIN in the alphabet, and indeed the design of the speculation seems past conjecture.

About the commentary ascribed to Hay Gaon there is considerable confusion, which Isaac Myer increases by representing that it deals with the BOOK OF CONCEALMENT, instead of that of FORMATION. There are no historical notices and no traces whatsoever of the former text before the appearance of the ZOHAR, in which it was first made known. The tract of Hay Gaon needs only to be mentioned in passing on account of its disputed authenticity. Other works attributed to him are not above suspicion, but it may be admitted in a general way that he had more distinct Kabbalistic connections than Saadya. The condemned commentary deals largely with the Mysteries of TETRAGRAMMATON and gives perhaps for the first time the curious quadrilateral method of writing it by means of letters and circles, to which so much importance has been attributed by modern occult writers.[1] The commentary of Abraham ben David Ha Levi,[2] the younger of that name and a contemporary of Maimonides, whom he attacked bitterly, is included also in the Mantua edition of the BOOK OF FORMATION, and was used largely by Rittangelius in that of Amsterdam, 1642.[3] The uttermost

---

[1] By Éliphas Lévi above all, who reproduces its diagram with additions which are merely fantastic (DOGME DE LA HAUTE MAGIE, section dealing with the Kabbalah), and elsewhere (LA SCIENCE DES ESPRITS) illustrates these additions by a Kabbalistic document which I think also is one of his specimens of invention.

[2] Bartolocci, i. 15. His birth is referred to *circa* 1110, and he is supposed to have suffered the death of a martyr in or near 1180.

[3] LIBER JESIRAH (Hebrew and Latin) *qui Abrahamo patriarchæ adscribitur, una cum commentario Rabbi Abraham F. D. (i.e., Ben Dior, i.e., Daur and also Rabad) super* 32

confusion prevails with regard to the personality of the author, who, on the one hand, is frequently identified with the writer of the SEDER HA KABBALAH, and is, on the other, the subject of many contradictory myths prevailing in occult circles. Éliphas Lévi, who cites a passage from his treatise as a proof of the authenticity and reality of his own "discovery" of the *Magnum Opus*,[1] makes a great deal of mystery concerning it and its rarity, but he has used evidently the edition of Rittangelius, which is perfectly well known and attainable in almost any national library.

We have recognised that the commentary of Saadya Gaon can scarcely be termed Kabbalistic; we have agreed to set aside another which abounds in Kabbalistic material because its date and attribution have been challenged; in the work of R. Abraham, however, there are Zoharic elements which admit of no question, and it is indeed to the school which he represents that Graetz and others have referred the authorship of the BOOK OF SPLENDOUR. There is the peculiar distinction between upper and lower SEPHIROTH which is not only characteristic of the Zoharic period, though it is not found in the ZOHAR, but offers a connecting link between R. Abraham and the late Kabbalism of Isaac de Loria.[2] Moreover, there is the doctrine of the Unknowable God, of "the Cause of Causes which is not apprehended by any one outside Itself," being void of all distinction and all mode of existence. The doctrine has not assumed that final shape in which it is presented by the ZOHAR, and its notion of the Divine Being appears to be, if possible, more concealed and latent than the conception of AIN SOPH, the NON ENS, which Itself is distinguished by R. Abraham from KETHER, the Crown of Creation, on the remarkable ground that "the accident is not

---

Semitas Sapientiæ . . . Translatus et Notis illustratus à Joanne Stephano Rittangelio . . . Amstelodami, 1642. The thirty-two Paths referred to at the beginning of the SEPHER YETZIRAH are given in Latin and Hebrew, each followed immediately by the commentary of R. Abraham, likewise in Latin and Hebrew. Then comes the explanation of Rittangelius, which sometimes extends to many pages, quoting various authorities, including the ZOHAR and its Supplements. After the Paths, we have the SEPHER YETZIRAH itself, in Latin and Hebrew, with the editor's commentary, also in both languages. It should be added that the entire commentary of R. Abraham is not given by Rittangelius, who is content with presenting that part only which is devoted to the Paths of Wisdom.

[1] RITUEL DE LA HAUTE MAGIE, c. 12, where the Hebrew passage cited is completely unintelligible. It has been rectified in my annotated translation, s.v. TRANSCENDENTAL MAGIC. *Cf.* LA CLEF DES GRANDS MYSTÈRES, pp. 233, 234.

[2] There is no doubt that the ten SEPHIROTH were an evolved system in the time of the Yetziratic commentator.

made from the essence, nor the RES from the NON RES or NON ENS," thus occasioning an insoluble difficulty as to the emanation of the manifest universe. This view offers a strong contrast to Zoharic Theosophy. Otherwise, the AIN SOPH of our commentator is described in terms which are almost identical with Zoharic teaching. "Neither unity nor plurality can be attributed to It, because unity cannot be ascribed to that which is incomprehensible in its essence," the reason being that number is an accident belonging to the world of extension, place and time.

Among minor Zoharic contrasts, it may be noted that a more peculiar importance is attributed to the letter ALEPH than to the BETH with which Genesis opens; it is the form of all the letters, and all the Paths of Wisdom are contained therein, but after an universal mode. There are traces also of the peculiar angelical system which was destined to receive so much elaborate extension from expositors of the BOOK OF SPLENDOUR.

Before dismissing this commentary we may note the alleged connection of its author with that Abraham the Jew [1] who belongs to the literature of Alchemy. The testament of this mysterious personage transformed the legendary Nicholas Flamel from a simple scrivener into a seeker after the Great Work—a search, moreover, which his story represents as crowned with high success. The memorial in question was addressed to the nation of Israel, dispersed by the wrath of God in France, by one who styled himself "Priest, Prince, Levite, Astrologer and Philosopher." The description which constitutes our sole knowledge concerning it is given in another testament, that of Nicholas Flamel, and I have shewn elsewhere that this memorial cannot be regarded as authentic.[2] Belonging as they do to Alchemy, there is no ground here to discuss their respective claims; but it is well to say that the attempt made by Éliphas Lévi to identify the Abraham of Flamel with the commentator on the SEPHER YETZIRAH not only institutes a connection between Alchemy and Kabbalism which is unwarrantable in itself but has no colourable evidence to cite in its own support, as there is no trace whatever of any alchemical meaning in the Hebrew commentator. Abraham

---

[1] This title is used by Bartolocci in his bibliography to describe numerous writers who cannot be identified more closely.
[2] See my SECRET TRADITION IN ALCHEMY, 1926, c. x., pp. 137 *et seq.*

the Kabbalist belongs, moreover, to the twelfth century, while Flamel was two hundred years later, and the book which he mentions could scarcely have existed in Jewry, even on the Lévi hypothesis, for such a space of time without something transpiring concerning it.

As a literary and philosophical work the first place among dependencies of the SEPHER YETZIRAH seems assigned correctly to the commentary of Azriel. Its author was born at Valladolid in or about the year 1160 and died in 1238. According to some authorities he was a pupil of Isaac the Blind,[1] but others say that his teacher was R. Jehuda, son of Rabad. He became in turn the instructor of R. Moses Nahmanides, who also belongs to the chain of Yetziratic tradition.[2]

Azriel is said to have travelled much in search of Secret Wisdom, but it was an age when men of learning were frequently wanderers, and it was perhaps less recondite motives which actuated him. He connects with the Kabbalistic system which was expounded by the school of Gerona, and there are no real grounds for supposing that he acquired knowledge elsewhere, but he added the result of his own reflections. Many works have been attributed to him, of which some are lost and some have remained in MS. THE EXPLANATION OF THE TEN SEPHIROTH *by way of Questions and Answers* must have helped to shape the metaphysical speculations of the Kabbalah and may well enough have originated more than it derived.

The teachings of Azriel aroused the opposition of the Aristotelian Jews, and it is thought by Isaac Myer that the logical form of his commentary was a concession to this school of thought. Whatever its motive, the fact, broadly taken, is of importance to our inquiry: it shews that the Sephirotic notion in its earliest development could not have been that of the categories, since it had to be conformed to the principles espoused by the disciples of Aristotle. The Jewish *literati* followed various schools, and the influence attributed to the Stagirite has been perhaps exaggerated. The votaries of the so-called Secret Wisdom were a small minority. Platonism, as it is needless to say, was very little known in the

---

[1] Was in evidence A.D. 1190 to *circa* 1210. He taught the doctrine of metempsychosis and a few fragments of his writings are still extant.

[2] And brought, as Graetz admits, the influence of his great reputation to bear upon its fortunes.

West at the period in question, though it appears in later Kabbalism.

As regards both matter and form, Azriel's commentary has been the subject of high praise. It contains the doctrine of AIN SOPH, which is not in the SEPHER YETZIRAH, and it has express views on the emanation of the SEPHIROTH, which are said to be contained in AIN SOPH and of no effect when separated. Their emanation was possible because it must be within the omnipotence of Deity to assume a limit. The essence and the real principle of all finite things is the Thought of the Supreme Being;[1] if that were withdrawn, they would be left as empty shells, and this is true not only of the visible world but of the intermediaries between God and the creation. With his philosophical speculations the Kabbalist mingles something from the fantastic region, attributing, for example, to the SEPHIROTH[2] certain symbolical colours. KETHER is "like the Concealed Light," or the light which is veiled in darkness, the comparison intended being probably that of a luminous mist. BINAH is sky-blue, because BINAH is the great sea of Kabbalism. CHOKMAH is yellow, CHESED white and GEBURAH red; TIPHERETH is white, red, or pink, NETZACH is whitish-red and HOD reddish-white. JESOD is a combination of the previous triad, while MALKUTH is like the light which reflects all colours. Azriel countenances also the Sephirotic division of the human body which is found in later Kabbalism.

Moses ben Nahman, or Nahmanides, was born in 1194 at Gironne. Before he made acquaintance with the Kabbalah he is said to have had a prejudice against it, but he was afterwards an enthusiastic student both of its speculative and practical parts, and by his writings and influence contributed much to its development. His Kabbalistic EXPLANATION OF THE LAW was completed in 1268, and among his many other works that called the GARDEN OF DELIGHT, and another on the SECRETS OF THE THORAH, are full of theosophical speculations.[3] He left his native land to settle in Palestine, where he

---

[1] Cf. ZOHAR, Pt. I. fol. 74a; I. 440.
[2] According to the ZOHAR the colour attributions are as follows: KETHER, black, white, or colourless; TIPHERETH, purple; MALKUTH, clear sapphire.
[3] His other works include an epistle on the use of matrimony in exercising the fear of God—no humorous suggestion being intended; a work on the nature of man, from the text of II. Samuel, vii. 19; a BOOK OF FAITH AND CONFIDENCE; another on Wars; and yet another on the Pomegranate. These are not professedly Kabbalistic,

died, apparently at a great age, but at what precise time is not known: it was *circa* 1270.

The commentary on the SEPHER YETZIRAH which passes under the name of R. Eliezer of Worms seems to have been the work of a German Jew of Germesheim,¹ one of the greatest Kabbalists of his period. That he was the instructor of Moses Nahmanides, as some authorities have stated, is, however, a mistake, as Basnage has indicated, for he belongs to a later date. His works, which are wholly Kabbalistc, are (1) THE VESTMENT OF THE LORD, but this has never been printed. (2) THE GUIDE OF SINNERS, exhorting them to repentance and amendment of life (Venice, 1543). (3) A TREATISE ON THE SOUL, cited by Mirandula in his thesis against astrologers. (4) An explanation of Psalm cxlv. (5) A commentary on SEPHER YETZIRAH, appended to the Mantua edition of that work. The author flourished before and after the middle of the fourteenth century. Commentaries on the SEPHER YETZIRAH are referable or ascribed —as the case may be—to R. Aaron the Great,² under the title of BOOK OF THE POINTS; R. Judas Ha Levi³; Sabbatai Donolo⁴; Judah ben Barzillai⁵; and Isaac the Blind. The Bodleian has a manuscript entitled MISHNAT, by Yosef ben Uzziel, which has been classed as a commentary on SEPHER YETZIRAH, but is said otherwise to be a supplement to the text itself. See JEWISH ENCYCLOPÆDIA, *s.v.* Joseph ben Uzziel.

---

like the TREASURE OF LIFE, the TREASURE OF THE LORD, the GARDEN OF DELIGHT (mentioned in the text above), or the mystical epistle on the thing desired. As regards the practical part of the Kabbalah, he treated it with grave consideration, including its arts of necromancy, the evocation of evil spirits and the methods of their control.

¹ Basnage: HISTOIRE DES JUIFS, c. vii. t. v. p. 1859. See also Bartolocci, i, 186, 187.
² Bartolocci, i. 15.
³ See his work entitled KUSARI.
⁴ Edited by M. Castelli. Florence, 1880. He was an Italian physician and astrologer, who was born in 913 and died subsequently to 982. He is known otherwise as Shabbethai b. Abraham b. Joel.
⁵ Edited by M. Halbertstamm. Berlin, 1885. The Judah in question was a Spanish Talmudist of Barcelona, who flourished at the end of the eleventh and early in the twelfth centuries.

BOOK IV

THE WRITTEN WORD OF KABBALISM: SECOND OR ZOHARIC PERIOD

BOOK IV

THE WRITTEN WORD OF KABBALISM: SECOND PERIOD

I.—THE BOOK OF SPLENDOUR: ITS CONTENT AND DIVISIONS

THE cycle of the SEPHER YETZIRAH lies within a small compass; the text is extant in several languages; and its most important dependencies will be found in Latin translations.[1] It has been available therefore to students and inquirers at large, even if they were unacquainted with Hebrew. The SEPHER HA ZOHAR, on the other hand, is not only large in itself but has considerable supplementary matter belonging to a later period and an extensive connected literature. Moreover, it is written—for the most part—in Aramaic, "the Jerusalem idiom" of Isaac de Acco; and only three short tracts imbedded in the general text are extant in Latin. Between the thirteenth and twentieth centuries it was therefore a sealed book for the great majority of scholars, till a full-length version appeared in French—as we have seen—within recent years.[2] Prior to this event great confusion had obtained in regard, firstly, to the content of the work and, secondly, to the comparative importance of its various divisions.[3] Part of this must be attributed to the ambitious design of Rosenroth's historical collection. The KABBALA

---

[1] The first printed edition appeared at Mantua in 1562 and contained two recensions, the second being longer and embodying important additions.

[2] The Italian reader may be referred also to an analysis of the Zohar by the Abbé de Rossi, which appeared in his DIZIONARIO STORICO DEGLI AUTORI EBREI. The writer follows Morin as to the late date of the work.

[3] The case of Basnage may be mentioned as that of a well-informed writer, whose history of the Jewish people from the time of Jesus Christ to his own date—the beginning of the eighteenth century—is memorable in several respects, yet whose knowledge of the ZOHAR does not even extend so far as it might have been taken by Rosenroth. He terms (*Livre* iii. p. 775) the BOOK OF CONCEALMENT the first part of the work, and seems to regard it as comprised simply in that and the two Synods. In a word, he had not read the preface to KABBALA DENUDATA, vol. ii.

DENUDATA, by attempting to cover much too wide a field, gives no adequate idea of the work which it is meant to elucidate. It attributes an exaggerated importance to three tracts introduced into the body of the ZOHAR and to late commentary on these; the apparatus in the form of a lexicon which fills most of the first volume, though it has a methodical appearance, is little more than a chaos, in which late and early expositors are bundled together after the uncritical manner of the period; in a subsequent section undue prominence is given to some personal discussions and correspondence between the Editor and Henry More, the English Platonist; finally, the second volume includes an enormous treatise on the doctrine of the Revolutions of Souls by a Kabbalist of the seventeenth century. With all its defects the KABBALA DENUDATA remains of prime value, but it would have been beyond all price had a clearer genius governed its arrangement. As it is, the class of persons who have proved to be most concerned with the subject have been content to follow the lead of Rosenroth, by accepting a little tract called the BOOK OF CONCEALMENT as the fundamental part of the whole ZOHAR, and the developments of that tract as entitled to the next highest consideration. There are, of course, several sources of information which might have corrected this false impression—the work of Franck in France and that of Ginsburg in England, to name two only—but it has endured notwithstanding, and a notable example to the point is found in an enlarged edition of a compilation by Dr. Papus. There a bibliographical appendix states that "the only complete translation" of the ZOHAR is the work of M. H. Chateau,[1] whereas the enterprise in question is confined only to the tracts rendered into Latin by Rosenroth, and these have been available for years in the English version of Mathers. The BOOK OF OCCULTATION—or CONCEALMENT—and its Zoharistic commentaries are only accidents of the ZOHAR, and they furnish no notion of the scope of that vast Theosophical Miscellany. I should add that from an esoteric standpoint the ZOHAR itself is only an accident of the Kabbalah—an

---

[1] LE ZOHAR, *Traduction française et Commentaire de* M. H. Chateau. The bibliographical annotation accredits the translator with *minutieuse érudition* and adds that he has carefully collated the Hebrew texts, the Latin and the other versions. The work is poorly produced, it bears no trace of the scholarship imputed to it and the commentary is of no real value. Moreover, the title itself deserves to be called fraudulent.

accident in the life of the alleged Tradition, much as, from the standpoint of Latin Christianity, the New Testament is not the exclusive foundation of the Church but an event in her development.

The ZOHAR proper, as stated in my preface, purports to be a commentary on the Pentateuch, and to indicate its scope, prior to any presentation of my own, I will vary my general rule of confining quotations from modern authors to footnotes and summarise an account of Ginsburg: " The ZOHAR does not (apparently) propound a regular Kabbalistic system, but dilates upon the diverse doctrines of this Theosophy, as indicated in the forms and ornaments of the Hebrew alphabet, in the vowel points and accents, in the Divine Names and the letters of which they are composed, in the narratives of the Bible and in the traditional and national stories. The long conversations between its author, R. Simeon ben Yohai, and Moses, which it records; the short and pathetic prayers inserted therein; the religious anecdotes; the attractive spiritual explanation of Scripture passages, appealing to the hearts and wants of men; the descriptions of the Deity and the SEPHIROTH under the tender forms of human relationship, comprehensible to the finite mind, such as father, mother, primeval man, matron, bride, white head, the great and small face, the luminous mirror, the higher heaven, the higher earth, &c., which it gives on every page, made the ZOHAR a welcome text-book for the students of the Kabbalah, who, by its vivid descriptions of Divine Love,[1] could lose themselves in rapturous embraces with the Deity."

We are placed by this quotation in a position to understand, firstly, after what manner the literature of Kabbalism affected the fervid imagination of the rabbinical Jew and the kind of influence which it had on him, well illustrated in one of its aspects by the fascinating and terrible histories of Messianic enthusiasm and illusion, as already noted, but in another by Zoharic Theosophy at its highest development. We can understand, secondly, how much there is to correct in the pretence of a French speculation which once fixed upon the ZOHAR as embodying traditional knowledge of a religion

---

[1] It is in this respect that the ZOHAR suggests analogies with Christian Mysticism as well as Arabian Sufism. For the rest, my readers must be dissuaded from supposing that Ginsburg's summary is adequately representative of the work, for it contains no reference to the Doctrine of Shekinah or the Zoharic Mystery of Sex.

behind all religions.¹ No system responds less readily to what is involved in such a conception. No person would be less disposed than the conventional occultist, present or past, to accept Kabbalistic notions of religion, were he really acquainted therewith, after due allowance has been made for Zoharic and other reveries which connect with occult beliefs, as these seem in their turn to connect magnetically with everything unsound in faith and unreasonable in doctrine. That God is immanent in the material world is a much simpler and more rational hypothesis than to establish intermediaries between finite and infinite, which create innumerable difficulties without resolving any, while on another side of the subject we have better means of excusing the anthropomorphisms of the Bible, than their *reductio ad absurdum*, which has been regarded as implied in the Kabbalistic Doctrine of the Two Countenances.

The ZOHAR proper—apart, that is to say, from all supplements and interpolations—is divided into five parts, corresponding to the five Scriptural Texts on which it is supposed to be a commentary, namely, Genesis, Exodus, Leviticus, Numbers and Deuteronomy. The first two are complete to all intents and purposes, the third and fourth have certain missing portions, while of Deuteronomy there is little more than fragments. The extant work, as printed, is in three parts only, of which the last comprises all that remains of the Commentary on the three later books of the Pentateuch. Each part is subdivided into various sections, separately entitled, *e.g.*, SECTIO BERESHITH, SECTIO TOLDOTH NOAH, and so forth. There is no call to enumerate them in this place. There are twelve sections of alleged interpretation in respect of Genesis, ten on Exodus, nine each on Leviticus and Numbers, and five only on Deuteronomy, manifestly imperfect as such. The Commentary on Genesis is followed by certain Appendices, being I, HASHMALOTH = OMISSIONS; II, TOSSEFTOTH = ADDITIONS; and *sub voce* Appendix III, two important Supplements, comprising extracts from MIDRASH HA NEELAM = SECRET MIDRASH, and SITHRE THORAH = SECRETS OF THE LAW. The following independent texts are introduced between certain sections of the Commentary on Exodus and sometimes within the sections themselves, namely: *post* § I,

---

¹ According to Éliphas Lévi, "all religions have issued from the Kabbalah and all return thereto."

Midrash Ha Neelam (continued); *post* § III, Raaiah Mehemnah = Faithful Shepherd; *post* § V, Sepher Ha Bahir = Luminous Book, and Sithre Thorah (continued); *post* § VI, Faithful Shepherd (continued), and Idra de Maschcana = Assembly of the Sanctuary; *post* § VII, Siphra Di Zenioutha = Book of Concealment. The Commentary on Exodus has also three Appendices, two embodying Additions and one containing an independent tract on Palaces. The sections of Exodus have, moreover, certain Mathnitin = Repetitions interpolated. Others follow § I of the Commentary on Leviticus, while §§ VII, VIII and IX are reinforced by further continuations of the Faithful Shepherd. The Commentary on Numbers has the following independent texts introduced between its sections: *post* § II, Faithful Shepherd (continued), and Idra Rabba Kadisha = Great Holy Assembly; *post* § III, Faithful Shepherd (continued); *post* § VII, Faithful Shepherd (continued), and certain Miscellanies. Among the fragments of Deuteronomy, § I is followed by a further instalment of the Faithful Shepherd, while portions of this work constitute the extant sections numbered III, V and VI. To § X is appended Idra Zouta Kadisha = Little Holy Assembly.

With this very simple and unpretentious collation there may be compared the analytical scheme of Rosenroth, which remains of bibliographical interest after the lapse of more than two centuries. The Zohar is divided thereby into internal and external parts, which are tabulated at length as follows.[1]

I. The internal parts are those which are collected together in one edition.[2] They are:

(*a*) The text of the Zohar, properly so called. Apart from all its additions this is not of unmanageable dimensions.

(*b*) Siphra Di Zenioutha, or Book of Concealment —otherwise, that of Modesty.

(*c*) The Idra Rabba, or Greater Synod.

---

[1] Kabbala Denudata, vol. ii. pp. 8 *et seq.*
[2] So far as it is possible to estimate the intention of this statement there is no correspondence with fact. The Book of Concealment and Idras are certainly not internal parts of any Commentary on the Pentateuch, and in the Zohar they are not combined with the text proper so as to form one scheme therewith. It may be said on the contrary that all interpolations are casual, while the Appendices to the part of Exodus might change places with those of Genesis, and so of the rest.

(d) The IDRA ZOUTA, or LESSER SYNOD.

(e) SABAH DI MISHPATIM, the *Discourse* or *Story of the Ancient One in section* MISHPATIM.

(f) MIDRASH RUTH, or COMMENTARY on the Scriptural book of that name. These are fragments only.

(g) SEPHER HA BAHIR, the RENOWNED or ILLUSTRIOUS BOOK, sometimes called BOOK OF BRIGHTNESS.

(h) TOSSEFTOTH = ADDENDA, or ADDITIONS.

(i) RAAIAH MEHEMNAH, or the FAITHFUL SHEPHERD.

(j) HAIKLUTH, *i.e.*, PALACES, MANSIONS, or ABODES.

(k) SITHRAI THORAH, or *Mysteries of the* THORAH, *i.e.*, the LAW.

(l) MIDRASH HA NEELAM, or SECRET COMMENTARY.

(m) RAZÉ DERAZIN, or SECRET OF SECRETS.

From this account are omitted the following tracts and fragments, because they do not appear in the Mantua edition of *circa* 1558, known as the LITTLE ZOHAR:[1]

(a) MIDRASH HAZEETH, or *Commentary on the Song of Solomon.*

(b) PEKOODAH, or *Explanation of the Thorah.*

(c) YENOOKAH, or the *Discourse of the Youth.*

(d) MAAMAR TO HAZEE, or the *Discourse* beginning, Come and See.

(e) HIBBOORAH KADMAÁ, or *Primary Assembly.*

(f) MATHNITIN, or Repetitions = *Traditional Receptions*, according to Rosenroth.

The ground on which these portions are set aside appears insufficient, as the sections *e*, *f*, *g*, *j*, and *m* in the first tabulation are also wanting in the Mantua edition. The GREAT ZOHAR, the Cremona edition (1558–60), contains all the treatises enumerated in both the above lists. I am not aware that any superior authority resides in the Mantua ZOHAR.[2]

II. As understood by Rosenroth, the external parts are those superadded to the earlier editions. These are:

(a) TIKKUNIM HA ZOHAR, or SUPPLEMENTS of the BOOK OF SPLENDOUR, called also the ANCIENT SUPPLE-

---

[1] The GREATER ZOHAR being that of Cremona. Blunt's DICTIONARY OF DOCTRINAL AND HISTORICAL THEOLOGY makes a ludicrous confusion over this point, representing the GREATER ZOHAR as the Commentary on Genesis and the Lesser as the BOOK OF CONCEALMENT.

[2] A Hebrew translation in MS. by Barachiel ben Korba is preserved—it is said—in the Public Library of Oppenheim.

THE BOOK OF SPLENDOUR

MENTS, to distinguish them from further and later additions.

(b) ZOHAR HADASH—the NEW ZOHAR, containing matters omitted in the printed editions. This has four parts.

(1) The text of the ZOHAR itself, scattered through which is the supplement of the tract MIDRASH HA NEELAM, part of which appears in the original work.

(2) TIKKUNIM HADASHIM, or *New Supplements*.

(3) ZOHAR SHIR HA SHIRIM, or EXPOSITION OF THE SONG OF SONGS, appertaining to the ZOHAR.

(4) ZOHAR AIKE, or *Exposition of Lamentations*, appertaining to the ZOHAR.

In the above tabulations are contained everything of the ZOHAR that has come down to us.[1] It may be thought that its authenticity did not increase with its bulk, but on this subject no canon of criticism can be said to have emerged.

For the better comprehension of the cycle Rosenroth recommends:

(a) SEPHER DEREK EMETH, that is, the *Way of Truth*, being various readings in the ZOHAR arranged according to the Mantua edition.

(b) BINAH IMRI, or *Words of Understanding*, being an elucidation of difficulties in Zoharistic vocabulary.

(c) ZOHAR CHAMAH, or SPLENDOUR OF THE SUN, a short commentary which follows the Mantua edition.

(d) PARDES RIMMONIM, or GARDEN OF POMEGRANATES, by R. Moses of Cordova, an explanation of numerous texts in the ZOHAR and TIKKUNIM.

(e) MEQUR CHOKMAH, or FOUNT OF WISDOM, forming a continuation or new part of the WAY OF TRUTH.

(f) MARAH KOHEN, or the VISION OF THE PRIEST, a synoptic work, the greater part of which appears in KABBALA DENUDATA, vol. ii. part i.

(g) ZER ZAHAB, or a CROWN OF GOLD, used largely in the apparatus of Rosenroth.

(h) PATHACH AINIM, or GATE OF THE EYES, for the Biblical quotations in the ZOHAR and TIKKUNIM.

Rosenroth also recommends and reproduces largely the manuscript treatises of Isaac de Loria, compiled by R. Hayyim

---

[1] KABBALA DENUDATA, ii. p. 9.

Vital, and further acknowledges his indebtedness to two other unprinted works, a Kabbalistic commentary on the whole Law and a treatise entitled CHESED ABRAHAM.

The ZOHAR proper, the conversations of Simeon ben Yohai with the prophets by whom he was visited, with the disciples by whom he was surrounded and of these, as we have seen, with each other, is not a work that is to be judged by the same standard as certain symbolical portions which have been incorporated therewith, and to which Christian students of Kabbalism have given so much prominence. There are extravagant speculations and wild exegesis, but it is uncontaminated by monstrous symbolism; it has occasionally a touch of Nature to indicate its kinship with humanity, and condescends even at times to a Rabelaisian episode.[1] Finally, it does not betray any trace of that secret meaning, otherwise double doctrine, that hypothetical sense withdrawn far down below any primary inward sense, which has been sometimes ascribed loosely to its entire content, by those who would and do likewise discern a latent transcendental philosophy in Pantagruelism.[2]

We have seen that in a certain manner—somewhat occasional and informal—the ZOHAR is a commentary on the Pentateuch, and it is to be understood and passed over that as such it is not only casual and occasional, that not only has it nothing in harmony with the simple sense of Scripture, but that for us in the western world and at this age of the world it opens abysses where dark clouds hang out and fire of madness flashes, more often than deeps of meaning which resound with pregnant messages. It would serve no purpose to enlarge upon this fact, which applies to so much of Kabbalistic interpretation. The governing principle affirmed is the existence of several senses in the written word. These are enumerated differently, and there seems no reason why they should not be extended; but they are reducible broadly under three heads, which are compared by the ZOHAR to the garment, the body which is within it and the soul which is within the body.[3] They are to be distinguished in all cases

---

[1] Many rabbinical histories, fables and apologues are narrated in it, sometimes elucidating a knotty point of Scripture, as, for example, whether the destruction of animal life at the Deluge may indicate that the beasts also sinned, sometimes recounting the death of a just man, sometimes describing visions and narrating tales of wonder.

[2] Following the lead of Éliphas Lévi, especially in LE SORCIER DE MEUDON.

[3] See *ante*, Book I, § 1, pp. 11-13. They do not emerge in the text.

from those speculations on hidden significance to which reference has been made above. The design of Theosophy in Israel was to magnify the election of Israel by exalting its title-deeds, but that of the expositors in question was to represent the Sons of the Doctrine as the custodians of a Liberal Theology which made all election void.

"There are those unwise," says the ZOHAR, "who behold how a man is vested in a comely garment, but see no farther, and take the garment for the body, whereas there is something more precious [than either], namely, the soul. The Law has also its body. Some of the commandments may be called the body of the Law, and the ordinary recitals mingled therein are the garments which clothe this body. Simple folk observe only these garments, *i.e.*, the narrations of the Law, perceiving not that which they hide. Others more instructed do not give heed to the vestment but to the body which it covers. And there are the Wise, the servants of the Great King, who dwell on the heights of Sinai and concern themselves only with the soul, which is the foundation of all and the true Law. These shall be ready in the coming time to contemplate the soul of that soul which breathes within the Law."[1]

This passage illustrates what is meant by an added depth and significance which the Kabbalah would read always into the Bible,[2] and does, moreover, at least from time to time. It offers, I think, also an instance of intellectual humility in the great rabbins of the Exile, who confessed on occasion to a sense in Scripture which exceeded their own loving penetration,[3] so that after all subtleties of exegesis, all the symposiums of synods, the Word of God issued in a mystery, and the key of this mystery was the reward of the just and wise man in the world to come.

The necessity of the manifold sense follows from the insufficiency of the letter. Simple recitals and common words suggest only the human lawgiver; if these were the sum of the THORAH, it would be possible to equal, perhaps even to excel it. Moreover, the sayings of Esau, Hagar, Laban, of

---

[1] Zohar, part iii. fol. 152*b*, Mantua edition. De Pauly, v. 391.
[2] I mean, of course, *ex hypothesi*. The extracted sense was too often a ridiculous illusion.
[3] Isaac Myer supposed that the higher soul of the THORAH signifies God Himself, but no doubt it is the Divine Sense of the Word which gives knowledge of the Word Itself.

Balaam and Balaam's ass, cannot be "the Law of Truth, the Perfect Law, the faithful witness of God."[1] And hence a hidden meaning, in which is the true Law, was supposed to save Israel from scepticism, and it may have postponed rationalistic criticism in Jewish circles for some centuries. It led of course into extravagance; the second sense became in its turn inadequate and one more concealed was inferred. So also, besides a general latent meaning, there was that more particular triple significance attributed to each several word. As the possibilities suggested by such a method are boundless, it is unnecessary to say that these senses were never methodised, or that the ZOHAR does not unfold in a consecutive form either the allegorical or mystical meaning. It gives glimpses only, and it may be for such reason that the original ZOHAR is said to have been a camel's load. That original was a latency in the minds of Kabbalistic rabbins, but it was never written with pen.

As the ZOHAR establishes the necessity of the concealed meaning on the insufficiency of the outward, and as the sense of such insufficiency is indubitably a late event in the history of sacred documents, we have full evidence for deciding the value of that claim which it makes elsewhere to a high antiquity for its interpretation. Had the Jew never come in contact with culture outside Judea he would never have conceived the "Tradition," and the kind of culture which helped him to the sense of insufficiency is not to be looked for in old Egypt or in Babylon, but in the Hellenised thought of the late Roman Empire at the international clearing-house of Alexandria.[2]

As the doctrinal, theosophical and mystical content of the ZOHAR will be the concern of several ensuing divisions of this study, it is obvious that the reference is to these on all important questions of subject-matter in the great text as well as its *additamenta*. That which remains over may be called accidental and casual, in the spirit of which description we may glance at the Commentaries in search of occasional sidelights. Summary is out of the question here, and so is also analysis: the office of these belongs to hypotheses on cosmo-

---

[1] Mantua edition, Part III. fol. 149*b*. De Pauly, V. 390. Compare *ante*, Book I, § 1, p. 13.
[2] It does not follow that the Kabbalah is Platonism or Neoplatonism. It was the consequence of a contact, but the growth and increase were fostered in the mind of Jewry.

logy, to myths of Paradise, Creation and the Fall of Man—to these and the sequence at large of those other matters which are to be treated at some length later on. The purpose of the present survey is therefore to offer gleanings and illustrative instances, drawn from there and here.

In the PRELIMINARIES attached to Genesis and the work of exposition thereon, a tradition is cited which says that whensoever just men undertake a journey together and discuss on their way subjects belonging to the Secret Doctrine they are favoured by visits of Holy Ones who dwell in the world beyond.[1] When Rabbi Eleazar and Rabbi Abba were travelling to call on Rabbi Yosse, they were accompanied by an unknown porter who carried their baggage. But when they began to commune one with another on things appertaining to the Mysteries of Law and Doctrine, it came about that he interposed between them, asking pregnant questions and preferring points of debate. It did not take long to discover that he was one endowed with knowledge; but when he spoke of the Sabbath and its keeping, of the day and the night thereof, of the Liturgy belonging to the Sabbath, of Divine Hypostases and the Seventy Names of God, they saw also that his science was greater than theirs. They came down from their saddles to embrace him, and would have mounted him on one of their horses, seeing that he rode upon an ass. He refused them, however, but resumed his discourse otherwise, opening deeps and heights in the hidden themes of Wisdom, explaining the secret influence exercised by names on the lives of men, telling strange things and new concerning the Temples at Jerusalem, but over and above all on the mystical union between Moses and her who is called Shekinah throughout the great record. It is said that they halted again and again dismounted, but this time it was to fall on their faces before him. When they looked up, however, it was to find that he had vanished from their eyes. Who was this Master in Israel and Keeper of Hidden Doctrine, to them unknown and clothed in weeds of service? They had asked many times, and he had answered nothing; but it was inferred or assumed at the end that he was Rab Hammenouna the Ancient, who had returned for their inspiration and enlightenment from the world beyond.

---

[1] Z., Pt. I, fol. 7a; I, 37.

I have cited this gracious story to shew that thus early in the BOOK OF SPLENDOUR it is about the great things of speculation, as if faring through a land filled with wells of refreshment and running with streams of light. I might indeed have begun earlier, as the ZOHAR itself begins, and told how a conference opens on page one of the mythos concerning the Rose of Sharon, and after what manner the deeply-imbedded meanings of the Song of Solomon are unfolded through its length and breadth. The Rose is the Community of Israel; but the Rose is red and white, and in the first of these States the elect people abide under the ministry of judgment, while in the second they are encompassed by thirteen ways of mercy.[1] For in another aspect the Rose is a Cup of Blessings, as it is also a Chalice of Redemption. Great doctors of the Christian Church have written many commentaries on the immortal Song, and it has been expounded by notable mystics down even to this day; but the ZOHAR on the Rose and the Lily—*flos campi et lilium convallium*—and the ZOHAR on CANTICUM CANTICORUM has not been known to any, howsoever late or early. A most amiable clergyman of the Church Catholic and Anglican has given us, not so long since, an extended thesis on the MYSTICAL WAY, and this is the Way of the Song.[2] It is all for our delectation, and in his agreeable company the path is travelled pleasantly; but it is a path of moonlight refreshed by draughts of water, while those who walk with the ZOHAR go forward in sunlight and strong wine is poured into their cups.

There is also a travellers' tale as the last story of all on matters appertaining to Genesis—after what manner must be left to those who are concerned. It tells how two other Masters were faring on the way to Cappadocia, intending to visit Rabbi Simeon, and they refer as they go to a Sacred Tradition by which man is directed to meditate on the glory of God before he begins to pray. They had learned already, it may be—as others before and since—that there is a prayer in the silence which dispenses with the prayer of words and is itself a contemplation in the heart. They knew otherwise, no doubt, that the study of the Secret Doctrine and communing one with another thereon constitute a prayer of

---

[1] Z., Pt. I, fol. 1a; I, 3.
[2] VIA MYSTICA: A Devotional Treatise on the Life of Prayer. By the Rev. Jesse Brett, 1925.

works; and we have seen how it lifts *ex hypothesi* the veil between two worlds. That which they confessed to each other was, however, of a diverse order, namely, that prayer is in place of sacrifice, the obvious—though unexpressed—reason being that true prayer is love. And seeing that it opens the fountains above and below, with the well-springs on every side, we find among the sayings of the time one perfect utterance at least. It affirms that the Holy One, blessed be He, drove Israel into exile among the Gentiles for the sole and only reason that the nations of mankind at large might be gladdened by the presence of the Chosen People which draws down blessings on the world below from that World of Benedictions which is above.[1] It follows in the radiant dream that Israel suffered crucifixion to aid in the salvation of the world.

Very early in the Commentary on Exodus we are delving again for treasure in the herb-sweet earth of the Song,[2] and that which is brought to the surface belongs to the Mystery of Union between the Voice and the Word. There have been intimations on the same subject much earlier in the ZOHAR, on thought as the origin of all things, on the inward contemplation of the Holy One before He made the worlds, on the uttering of the Voice, which brought forth or manifested the thought, and on creation as the Word expressed. The Commentary ends also on the Keynote of Thought in the Holy One, the mysterious joy thereof and the light which flows out therefrom. It drew together the forty-two letters comprehended by one of the extended Sacred Names, and out of the relation established in this manner it is affirmed that the world came forth. They fared to some purpose in those days, did the Doctors of Hidden Law, whether they went on horses or whether an ass bore them, for in these words, brief and plain as they are, is found at full length the Doctrine of Divine Immanence, the Presence of the Father Almighty—by and within the Word—in all that lives and is.

It is said in the first leaves of the Commentary on Leviticus that faith completes the Sacred Name, and a little further on that from the thought of the Holy One come forth those ways and paths which lead to a knowledge of the Name and

---

[1] Z., I, 244a; II, 566.
[2] Song of Solomon, iv. 8.

to perfection thereby and therein.¹ We are told also that it were better for a man never to have been born than to live without uniting the Sacred Name on earth.² The secret of such union belongs to the study of the Law,³ which is the work of men of faith, the reference being not to the Expounded Law delivered *coram populo* but to that of the Secret Doctrine, which in another place is identified with and affirmed indeed to constitute the Name of the Sacred King.⁴ But prayer and good works are said otherwise to promote unity in the Name of God,⁵ and this is the intention which should occupy the priest when he proceeds to the work of sacrifice.⁶ We shall see later on that there has been a division brought about between the four sacramental letters comprised in the Hebrew Name which we are accustomed to render Jehovah, and there is a very true sense in which it is the work of man to make an end of this separation. On the surface, however, the mythos develops its symbolism after a diverse manner, while so far as the Commentary on Leviticus is concerned, we are in the presence of another and highly figurative Mystery. The Complete Name is Jehovah Elohim, and the work which devolves on all Sons of the Doctrine is to make evident on earth that Jehovah is indeed Elohim, even as these Divine Hypostases are One in Heaven. We shall see, also later on, that the kind of union is that between male and female.⁷ It is affirmed elsewhere that the Glory of the Sacred Name must be the end of all our works ⁸; but this is the Glory of Union. A part in the Sacred Name is allotted to those who possess the Hidden Law, the reason being that they possess God therein. The meaning is that those who live the Doctrine are those alone who possess it, and God is the life of these. We shall realise therefore the sense in which it is defined presently, and shall not fail to understand that the Sacred Name is revealed by successive stages.⁹ It is revealed in proportion as it is lived and becomes alive within us—a

---

¹ Z., III, 4b; V. 9, and III, 5b, V. 13.
² *Ib.*, 7a; V. 18. Meaning of course by the mode and manner of life which is led here below.
³ *Ib.*, 12b; V. 37. It is to be understood that those who study the Law to a real purpose are those who live thereby.
⁴ *Ib.*, 21a; V. 56.
⁵ *Ib.*, 26a; V. 67.
⁶ *Ib.*, 32a; V. 86.
⁷ *Ib.*, 46b; V. 129.
⁸ *Ib.*, 51b; V. 139.
⁹ *Ib.*, 65b; V. 179.

simple question of growth, but very deep withal. We shall understand in like manner when it is affirmed further that the Name is hidden and revealed at once,[1] because there is ever " a deep below the deep and a height beyond the height " of its knowledge, while for ever they grow therein who study and exemplify that Doctrine which is both the Name and Law.[2] It is added in fine that those who practise charity do cry forth the Sacred Name daily. The explanation is not only that offices of love are channels of grace and power, which are also modes and aspects of the Name of God, but that the work of love is an uttering forth of the Name, and there is indeed no other way given unto man by which he shall express it on earth.

And now as to that veridic parable at large, the messages of which have been drawn from so many pages. In part at least only implied—since the Secret Doctrine emerges in sudden flashes through a mist of clouded light—but in part at least shadowed forth, there is a correspondence established in Zoharic Theosophy between the four letters of the Sacred Name—יהוה—and certain diverse parts or aspects of the soul in man about which we shall hear at full length at a proper point in the sequel. The letter י = YOD is in analogy with YEHIDAH, a spiritual state or mode in the ascending scale of inward being, and with all that is postulated above it, the human *singularitas*, the Christian apex of the soul and Divine Selfhood. The ה = HE primal answers to NESHAMAH, the sovereign reason within us, above material mind; the ו = VAU or VAV connects with RUA'H, which is normal intellectuality, the rational principle; and HE final with NEPHESH, the side on which humanity is related to the animal world. It is the lower *vitalitas*, and is not as such the physical body, which is, however, its vehicle. When a man lives in the light and law of his Higher Selfhood he has built up the Divine Name within him and has become it within the measures of his humanity. Here is theosophical symbolism which may seem at its highest, but it does not enlighten that of the Commentary on Leviticus, unless we are able to look below the surface and realise that there is a marriage of male and female proclaimed by the consonants which form the

---

[1] Z., III, 65b; V. 179.
[2] Ib., 71b; V. 195.

Sacred Name of Four Letters, יהוה, whence it follows that whosoever affirms Jehovah does affirm Elohim also; that he who completes the one within him completes the other, is a witness in his own person that Jehovah is Elohim and makes their union perfect. As our *Theosophia Magna* unfolds, we shall learn also that there is a supernal part of our nature which does not come down to earth, but abides in Heaven and God; that it is possible to be united therewith according to the Secret Doctrine; while if this is accomplished it will follow that what corresponds at the height of our being to the Divine Hypostasis Jehovah has entered into bonds of marriage with that which makes answer to the Divine Hypostasis Elohim. In the light of this hypothesis and its symbolism we shall understand what is meant by the Commentary on Leviticus when it speaks of the Divine Name being complete on earth as it is in Heaven and in Heaven also as on earth. The completion is accomplished below by a true Son of the Doctrine in his own being; but when it is fulfilled therein, for himself and for those about him, before whom his light shines forth, it is seen by the eyes of faith—as at a gate and threshold of knowledge—that the Name is indeed perfect on all planes of being.[1]

The Commentary on Numbers is full of occasional lights on great subjects. We know that the Israelites in the desert were fed by manna which God sent down from heaven; but a time came when that stiff-necked generation loathed the light food and cried for material fleshpots. The opportunity offered to parable is not lost on the ZOHAR in its consideration of Exodus; but it is in the present place that we hear more especially of a supersubstantial bread which on a day to come shall feed the elect and fill them.[2] The mystery of this *panis vivus et vitalis* is hidden in the Tree of Life, which is said to be above, while the Averse Mystery of the meat demanded by Israel is contained in the Tree of Death, and this is said to be below.[3]

We hear more than once in the ZOHAR that the Archangel Michael sacrifices the souls of the just on the Supernal Altar

---

[1] It is said elsewhere in the ZOHAR that the Sacred Name is peace.—Z., III, 176b; V. 459. It is understood that peace is union.
[2] Z., III, 156a; V. 399. Compare III, 208a; V. 530, which says that the manna sprang from the dew above which came down from the Hiddenness of all the Hidden Ones and was the food of higher angels.
[3] *Ib.*, III, 157a; V. 405. See also *ante et post*.

of Burnt Offerings; but once only in the text—and it happens to be in this Commentary—is it said that some souls go up, as of their free will and by their own high intent, to make a holocaust of themselves, amidst rejoicing in the Supreme Light which shines forth from the Holy King.[1] For us, at least, it reads like a parable of the union in its last and highest mode, when God becomes All in all for the individual soul. It was revealed to certain Masters in Israel by one who was unknown, who had asked and received water to quench his thirst. After such manner is the reward of the just unfailing and comes quickly, as a cloud of stories makes evident throughout the radiant pages. So also he who gives bread in God's Name on asking may receive a star. Hereof is the sweetness of the Law, about which it is declared a little later that its works are holy, heavenly and mild withal.[2] It is life and the blessing of life for those who are consecrated thereto, as if each had received it himself on Mount Sinai. He has indeed and certainly, because Sinai is also within. It is said elsewhere that the Hidden Law is the Tree of Life and that this Tree is Knowledge,[3] meaning that which is Science of Unity, not of divorce and separation like the Tree of Death. As there is a School of Doctrine on earth which cultivates this Knowledge, so is there a Heavenly School above which is in the state of science attained and is said therefore to be nourished by the Tree of Life. Of those enrolled therein we hear from time to time; but the Commentary on Numbers tells us that some children who die in tender years are admitted to its teaching, in one or other of the classes—for example, a son of R. Juda, whom two Pillars of the Doctrine brought into that Sacred Conclave and into the presence of its Chief.

In the fragments on Deuteronomy we hear more of the Heavenly Bread, which is Fruit of the Tree of Life, and learn that it is not alone eaten by those in the Heavenly School but by those of the School on earth,[4] meaning that *Summa Scientia* is not beyond attainment here and now. At the end of all, in the last of all the sections, we are brought back to that which is the subject-matter of discourse in the first leaves. I refer to the Mystical Rose and its connotations *ab origine symboli*.

---

[1] Z., III, 157b; V. 407.
[2] *Ib.*, III, 179b; V. 471.
[3] *Ib.*, III, 182a; V. 474.
[4] *Ib.*, III, 260a; VI. 5.

It is still the Community of Israel, which is likened to a Rose composed of six Petals. There is, however, one new and eloquent affirmation—that Israel is united with the Rose when it is united with the Supreme King. It is another way of saying that Jehovah is Elohim and that Jehovah Elohim is the Complete and Perfect Name. But more than all it is the proclamation of an unity possible on earth as it is actual and eternal above.

It will be understood that my extracts have been made with the object of shewing that there are strange lights and pregnant theses here and there in the ZOHAR proper, apart from anything that it may prove qualified to communicate on those subjects of formal doctrine which remain for our examination at a subsequent stage of this study. If it be said that the miscellany has been made to appear at its best, an adequate answer and one offered in sincerity would be that much more might have been quoted without invading the ground of later themes. For the rest, I have called it a medley, and after the manner of a medley the ZOHAR combines with things precious some others and many that are of little or no value, and not a few which to us, and to Jewry itself at this day, must appear indescribably foolish. They are in much the same position as its modes of scriptural interpretation, and as stated already, it would be idle to suppose that these can have the least exegetical importance. I speak of them obviously as a whole, and do not mean that they hold up no lamps which light up there and here some dark and doubtful path. It must be understood, moreover, by those who are addressed especially, that modes and scheme and purview are essentially Jewish, supposing the exclusive claim of Israel to Divine Election and therefore the last source to which any one so disposed could look for confirmation of the romantic notion that a transcendental doctrine of absolute religion has been handed down from the far past. That which is transmitted in the ZOHAR, but in fragments only, is a Secret Doctrine peculiar to Israel, and it makes contact with the deep things of universal religion, the religion behind religion of Max Müller, in so far as it offers vestiges of inward experience on the union of the soul and God, because the records of this experience are everywhere in the world, in all ages, in all the great religions, and it counts its living witnesses among us at this day.

Understood as it actually is, a thesaurus of Jewish Theosophy, Jewish visionary doctrines, Jewish yearning and aspirations, which, because Jewry is part of humanity, is in contact at a thousand points with the aspiration and yearning of the whole heart of the world, it is a priceless memorial; but it loses all significance in the attempt to misplace it. Because it is theosophical although Jewish, it has otherwise its points of connection with other theosophical systems, and not infrequently with matters which are beyond the range of that which is usually understood by this word, with the things of Mysticism, as, for example, in its transcendental speculations on the identity of subject and object in God and, as I have intimated above, in the mystical experience of the soul. It has other and obvious connections with past speculations and the systems into which they have been drawn. It enters, for example, into that strange doctrine of correspondences which we meet everywhere in the domain embraced by the higher understanding of the term Magia. It might be described indeed as the extended mystery of correspondence. "Whatsoever is found on earth," says the ZOHAR, "has its spiritual counterpart on high and is dependent on it. When the inferior part is influenced, that which is set over it in the upper world is affected also, because all are united." From this doctrine the art of Talismanic Magic must be called a logical consequence, and so far as that which passes under the denomination of occult philosophy is based on this postulated law, so far it belongs to Kabbalism in the kinship of descent. Elsewhere it is said: "That which is above is in the likeness of that which is below, and the likeness of that which is below is in the sea"—meaning that the sea reflects the inferior heaven—"but all is one."[1] This is, of course, identical with the pseudo-Hermetic maxim: *Quod superius est sicut quod inferius, et quod inferius est sicut quod superius, etc.* Apart from its context, this citation from the EMERALD TABLE might have been a Zoharic dogma. We know, however, that the law of correspondences is in Zosimus the Panopolite as well as in the Secret Tradition of Israel.

It may be added that the ZOHAR took the SEPHER YETZIRAH into its heart of hearts, dwelt upon it, extended, magnified, almost transformed its symbolism. The Hebrew letters

---

[1] ZOHAR, Cremona, Part II, fol. 9a. Cf. Part I, fol. 91a: "As it is in all things below, so is it above."

which figure in the earlier tract as the instruments of creation are for it the ciphers or vestures of the Written Law, the expression of the THORAH, and the THORAH is the archetype of all the worlds. Whether or not we are able to agree with Franck that the SEPHER YETZIRAH ends where the ZOHAR commences, and that they are exact complements of each other, it is certain that the instinct of those early students who singled out the BOOK OF FORMATION from the rest of pre-Zoharic MIDRASHIM was not at fault in regarding it as the head and source of Kabbalism.

But, in conclusion, as there was an occultism and Mysticism in Israel prior to the SEPHER RAZIEL and to the ZOHAR, so both were incorporated in the latter; both in the process underwent a species of transmutation, and as I venture to think the process, like that " sea-change " of the poet, produced something more strange and rich. There are, at least, flights of mystical thought and aspiration in this great book of Theosophy which are unknown to Ibn Gebirol and Ibn Ezra, and are more direct and strong in their appeal to the inner consciousness of man at this epoch of the twentieth century than anything in the famous commentary of Azriel or in the School of Isaac the Blind. And to confess this is to confess out of hand that the ZOHAR has still a message for the mystic. Perhaps all that is of value therein would be contained within a few leaves; but, as said of the choicest poems of Coleridge, they should be bound in pure gold.

II.—THE BOOK OF CONCEALMENT

Passing now from the Commentaries on the Pentateuch to the texts and fragments which are, so to speak, imbedded therein, or thereunto added, it seems reasonable in the first place to pass those in review which, owing to Latin translations, have represented the ZOHAR at large for most readers during a space of some two hundred and fifty years. They differ generically from the *corpus* of the great text and from the other additions or supplements because their subject-matter is " veiled in allegory and illustrated by symbols." For the time being, moreover, we have finished with things belonging to discussion and debate, and are entering a realm of revelation. The statement obtains throughout, though it happens that two of the tracts in question are expository of the third, which ranks therefore first in the sequence. But he who expounds is he also who reveals, that is to say, Rabbi Simeon ben Yohai, while the office of his auditors is to learn, mark and digest inwardly—not to question and dispute. I refer to SIPHRA DI ZENIOUTHA, with its sequels, the IDRA RABBA and IDRA ZOUTA. Their places have been indicated, from which it follows that the BOOK OF CONCEALMENT or of OCCULTATION,[1] to which so much prominence has been given from the days of Rosenroth, is not as some have supposed, the beginning of the great cycle entitled the ZOHAR, nor is it the most important part, or perhaps any part that is vital, at least from my own standpoint. In the Sulzbach edition, produced by Rosenroth, it begins at fol. 176b and ends at fol. 178b of the second volume. Several editions are either paged in correspondence with one another or refer readers to the pagination of previous codices. Among early printed texts that of Lublinensis follows the Cremona edition, which, though used by Rosenroth for his references, was regarded by him as inferior to the simultaneous or slightly prior edition of Mantua. The latter he terms invariably *Codex correctus*. From the silence of certain writers on the subject of the ZOHAR proper it might be judged that it was not regarded as of great exegetical or indeed any other importance; but there is a simpler explanation, which is not far to seek: it was known to them only by excerpts prior to 1906–1911. The BOOK OF CONCEALMENT, on the contrary, though small in its dimensions, was of the highest consequence, the presumed root and foundation of the ZOHAR,[2] and also the most ancient portion of that collection. The last view is not, on the whole, unlikely.[3] It has been said further that it is a theogony comprised in a few pages, but with developments more numerous than the TALMUD.[4] In a word, for occult dreamers of the past in France and England, the BOOK OF CONCEALMENT and the BOOK OF FORMATION are the fountain-heads of all Kabbalism. The Hebrew term which is rendered Mystery, Concealment, or Modesty by Isaac Myer, is given as Concealed

---

[1] A literal translation would be BOOK OF MODESTY—of course in the sense of concealment.
[2] Mathers: KABBALAH UNVEILED, p. 14. He was unfortunately not qualified to speak.
[3] Myers: QABBALAH, p. 118.
[4] Éliphas Lévi: LE LIVRE DES SPLENDEURS, preface, p. ii.; MYSTERIES OF MAGIC, 2nd ed., p. 97. The comparison of one who was unacquainted with both cycles of literature.

Mystery by Mathers, without affirming that the version is literal. For SIPHRA DI ZENIOUTHA Rosenroth renders LIBER OCCULTATIONIS.[1] The work is concerned, however, with the manifestation of the Divine Being, as the term of His concealment in the eternity which preceded manifestation. The first chapter deals with the development of what is termed the Vast Countenance, the image of the Father of all things, the MACROPROSOPUS, when equilibrium had been established in the universe of unbalanced forces. This Countenance, which is referred to KETHER, or the Crown—first of the ten SEPHIROTH—is compared to the tongue of a balance, *lingula examinis*. When equilibrium obtained, the Countenance was manifested, the Ancient of Days appeared, God issued from His concealment.[2] This symbolism of the balance depicting the harmony of the universal order is a key-note of the treatise, which, in its own words, is the book describing "the libration of the balance." The balance is suspended in the place which is no place, that is to say, in the abyss of Deity, and it is said to be the body of MACROPROSOPUS, referring to the SEPHIROTH Wisdom and Understanding,[3] which are the sides of the balance. The Countenance, of which no man knoweth, is secret in secret, and the hair of the head is like fine wool hanging in the equilibrium. The eyes are ever open, and the nostrils of the Ancient

---

[1] Rabbi Loria says that it refers to things which are secret and should be kept secretly, and compares Prov. xxv. 2, "The Glory of God is to conceal the word." But he supposes also an allusion to the circumstances under which the work is reported to have been composed—namely, during the concealment of R. Simeon for twelve years in a cave.

[2] See COMMENTARIUS GENERALIS METHODICUS . . . *è Libro Emek Hammelech* in KABBALA DENUDATA, vol. ii. pp. 47 *et seq.* of the second part. For casual and miscellaneous references to the Divine Head, see Z., Pt. I, fol. 65a; I, 381. *Ib.*, fol. 232a; II, 515. *Ib.*, fol. 251b; II, 591, 592. *Ib.*, Appendices, III, fol. 6a; II, 689. *Ib.*, Pt. II, fol. 192b; IV, 79, quoted from a BOOK OF ENOCH. *Ib.*, fol. 268b; IV, 302. *Ib.*, Pt. III, fol. 7b; V, 21. *Ib.*, fol. 10b; V, 30. *Ib.*, fol. 48b; V, 135. *Ib.*, fol. 66b; V, 183. *Ib.*, fol. 119b; V, 306. For the Doctrine of Countenances, see *Ib.*, Pt. II, fol. 61b; III, 271. *Ib.*, fol. 64a; III, 283. For the Great Adam, see *Ib.*, Pt. I, fol. 134b; II, 132. *Ib.*, Pt. III, fol. 48a; V, 132.

[3] "For Wisdom is on the right, upon the side of Benignity; Understanding is on the left, upon the side of Severity; and the Crown is the tongue in the centre which abideth above them."—K. D., II, p. 48. The meaning of the symbolism is that an equilibrium between Justice and Mercy must be assumed before the universe, having man for its object, could become possible, and the source of this notion must be sought in BERESHITH RABBAH—a Haggadic Commentary on Genesis, of historical and exegetical importance. It is ascribed by tradition to the third century, but modern scholarship is disposed to place it a little later than the TALMUD of Jerusalem. Compare also the teaching of the pre-Zoharic MIDRASH CONEN, according to which the Grace of God prevents the opposing forces out of which the world was created from mutual destruction.

One are as two doors whence the Spirit goes forth over all things. But the dignity of all dignities is the beard of the Countenance, which also is the ornament of all. It covers not only MACROPROSOPUS as with a vestment, but the SEPHIROTH Wisdom and Understanding, called here the Father and the Mother,[1] descending even unto MICROPROSOPUS—of whom we shall hear shortly—and it is divided into thirteen portions, flowing down as far as the heart, but leaving the lips free. Blessed is he, says the text, who receiveth their kisses! From the thirteen portions there descend as many drops of purest balm, and in the influence of all do all things exist and all are concealed.

In addition to the manifestation of MACROPROSOPUS, the BOOK OF CONCEALMENT shews how the Most Ancient One expanded into MICROPROSOPUS, to whom is referred the name TETRAGRAMMATON, whereas "I am" is that of the first Ancient.[2] The letter YOD, which is the first of TETRAGRAMMATON, corresponds to the SEPHIRA Wisdom, the supernal HE to Understanding, and the union of these twain brought forth MICROPROSOPUS, corresponding to the six SEPHIROTH from Mercy to the Foundation inclusive, and referred to the letter VAU.[3] It follows, according to this text, that the primal manifestation of Deity, which is connected with the conception of the Crown, has no other name than that which proclaims His self-existence, as if—according to a French commentator—the Hebrew Jehovah were in some sense a reflected God. MACROPROSOPUS, although manifesting in the Crown, is still regarded as ever hidden and concealed, by way of antithesis in respect of MICROPROSOPUS, who is both manifest and unmanifest. When the life-giving influx rushes forth from the Ancient One, amid the intolerable refulgence of that great light the likeness of a head appears. The distinction between the two Countenances is the distinction of the profile and the full face, for whereas the God Who comes forth is revealed in so doing, the Great Countenance is only declared partially, whence it is obviously inexact to speak of MICROPROSOPUS as a reflection[4]: He is rather a second manifestation, taking place in the archetypal world.

---

[1] *I.e.*, ABBA and AIMA.
[2] This is at issue on the surface with what may be called the ZOHAR proper, for which YAH = יה is the Divine Name of KETHER. The fact is that allocations vary in different texts of the medley.
[3] The HE final is referred to the tenth SEPHIRA, or MALKUTH.
[4] This is a device of Éliphas Lévi and connects with his method of interpretation.

From the sides of the Lesser Countenance depend black locks, flowing down to the ears; the eyes have a three-fold hue, resplendent with shining light; and a three-fold flame issues from the nostrils. The beard, considered in itself, has nine portions, but when that of MACROPROSOPUS sheds down its light and influence they are found to be thirteen. Though the Ineffable Name is referred to the Vast Countenance, it is said also that the manifestation of MICROPROSOPUS is represented by the ordinary letters of the Tetragam, his occultation by the transposition of the letters.

The BOOK OF CONCEALMENT is described in its closing words as the withdrawn and involved Mystery of the King, and as it is added that " blessed is he who cometh and goeth therein, knowing its paths and ways," there is urgent need for some explanation of its significance. This, as we shall see, was unfolded in rabbinical commentaries, which are confessedly posterior to the period of the public promulgation of the ZOHAR. There are, moreover, two works possessing the same authority as the BOOK OF CONCEALMENT, and they constitute extensions at large of that work, being also expository, though there is good reason to demand—like Byron, referring to Southey—that their explanations should be themselves explained. The first of these will be the subject of some consideration in the next section.

The SIPHRA DI ZENIOUTHA is preceded in the ZOHAR by a fragment entitled אידרא דמשכנא = IDRA DE MASCHANA, *i.e.*, ASSEMBLY OF THE SANCTUARY, introduced at an arbitrary point [1] and followed by a brief colloquy between Rabbi Eleazar and Rabbi Abba, who affirms (1) that he has recorded its Mysteries by command of the Sacred Lamp, otherwise R. Simeon, for the use of the Colleagues; (2) that the Mysteries will abide henceforth in concealment, the inference being that the Light of the Oral Law has passed away; (3) that R. Simeon appeared to him in a dream and communicated certain secret teaching concerning the Divine Son or VAU, begotten from the Father and the Mother, represented by the letters YOD and HE, as we have seen otherwise. It will be seen that the ASSEMBLY OF THE SANCTUARY is misplaced obviously in the IDRA sequence, being inserted prior to the text which the ASSEMBLIES are designed to expound. In the fragment itself

---

[1] Z., Pt. II, fols. 122b–123b; III, 471–477.

there is nothing to shew that it forms part of a colloquy or of any discourse whatever. It opens with a statement on the authority of an instruction drawn from a supposed treatise entitled MYSTERY OF MYSTERIES and is concerned more especially with the Face and Head of the Son, the Word which comes from His mouth and the sound of His voice. The brief colloquy by way of supplement may be the vestige of a third IDRA, not otherwise extant, and the ASSEMBLY OF THE SANCTUARY may be part of a text after the manner of SIPHRA DI ZENIOUTHA and dealing obviously with the same symbolism.

III.—THE GREATER HOLY SYNOD

The BOOK OF CONCEALMENT has been simplified to the utmost in the preceding account. It must be added that it stands almost alone in the great body of texts, an anonymous revelation, without antecedents or history; it quotes no rabbinical writers and has no references by which a clue to its date may be obtained. It has, however, two characteristics which give it the appearance of a much older document than those which follow it immediately, and are designed, as intimated already—outside its monstrous symbolism—to develop and expound it. These are its rudeness and the multitude of its obscurities—even for a Zoharic document. The first translator, Rosenroth, supplies explanations placed within brackets, but even with these it is in an exceedingly faulty state. The treatise now under consideration is in several respects different. It possesses almost a literary aspect, begins in narrative form, methodises the ensuing dialogues in a manner which is perfectly explicit and stands in need of few emendations. It exists, however, to unfold further the barbarous allegories of the preceding book, and were it possible to admit any alleged motive behind it as something more than the subtlety of a later interpreter, it would still be incumbent to recognise that it has no message for us at this day rather than to describe it as repellent to modern taste, a fact which has been noted by at least one sympathetic critic who was himself a suggestive writer.[1] The first point which calls for notice otherwise is that the GREATER SACRED SYNOD claims Rabbi Simeon Ben Yohai as the author of the BOOK OF CONCEALMENT, and itself contains the discourses of this

---
[1] Éliphas Lévi: LA CLEF DES GRANDS MYSTÈRES.

Master in Israel, delivered in a field beneath trees in the presence of his disciples, namely, Rabbi Eleazar, his son; Rabbi Abba; Rabbi Jehuda; Rabbi Jose, the son of Jacob; Rabbi Isaac; Rabbi Hiskiah, the son of Rav; Rabbi Hia; Rabbi Jose; and Rabbi Jesse. Some of these are historical names belonging to the period which succeeded the destruction of Jerusalem.

For an account of Rabbi Simeon himself we must have recourse to TRACT SABBATH of the TALMUD, Babylonian recension, which contains a narrative that may be reproduced here in substance:

"On a certain occasion R. Jehudah, R. Jose and R. Simeon were sitting together, and with them also was Jehudah, the son of proselytes. R. Jehudah opened the conversation, saying: 'How beautiful are the works of this nation (the Romans). They have established markets; they have built bridges; they have opened bathing-houses.' Whereupon R. Jose was silent. But R. Simeon ben Yohai answered, saying: 'All these things have they instituted for their own sake. Their markets are gathering-places for harlots; they have built baths for their own enjoyment, and bridges to collect tolls from those who cross them.' Jehudah, the son of proselytes, repeated this conversation, and it came to the ears of Cæsar, who proclaimed: 'Jehudah, who extols us, shall be extolled; Jose, who said nothing, shall be exiled to Saphoris (*i.e.*, Cyprus); Simeon, who has disparaged us, shall be put to death.' R. Simeon and his son then went out and hid themselves in the lecture-hall, but afterwards in a cave, where a miracle took place, a date-tree and a spring of water being raised up for them. They laid aside their garments and sat covered with sand up to their necks, studying the whole time, and assuming their vestures only at prayer-time, for fear that the same might wear out. In this wise they spent twelve years in the cave, when Elijah came to the opening, and said: 'Who will inform the son of Yohai that Cæsar is dead and his decree is annulled?' Hereupon they left the cave."[1] The secret wisdom embodied in the ZOHAR is supposed to have been the fruit of the long seclusion enforced upon R. Simeon by the Roman decree.

The TALMUD mentions expressly the learning obtained

---

[1] Rodkinson: BABYLONIAN TALMUD, vol. i. pp. 57-59.

during this period, but without specifying its kind. According to the tradition of Kabbalists, the BOOK OF CONCEALMENT was the first form in which it was reduced to writing. The discourses of the GREATER SACRED SYNOD were recorded by Rabbi Abba and so also in the case of the LESSER SYNOD. When exposition was about to begin a voice heard in the air revealed that the Supernal Assembly had gathered in heaven to hearken, and the commentators add that not only the souls of the just were marshalled round the speakers, coming from their rest in Paradise, but that the Holy Shekinah of the Divine Presence descended.

The explanations and developments concern the world in its void state before the manifestation of the Supreme Countenance, the conformations of that Countenance, or MACROPROSOPUS, as also of MICROPROSOPUS, the Lesser Countenance, and after what manner the inferior depends from the superior. It must be said that the expounding and the extension neither are nor assume to be explanatory in the sense that they unfold any real significance of the symbolism. As a fact, the treatise ends, like all treatises concerned—shall I say, at a venture?—with Mysteries of Initiation, by testifying that he is blessed who has known and beheld the concealed words and does not err therein. In an account like the present, which does not even pretend to be synoptic, it is impossible to attempt a tabulation of the typology with which the GREATER SYNOD is concerned, and it should be noted in this connection that a few modern writers on Kabbalism who have claimed to speak magisterially and as if from within a secret circle of knowledge, may have shewn us glimpses in one or two rare instances—and then according to their individual hypotheses—of the system on which the symbolism is constructed, but have done nothing to elucidate and therefore recommend it to our understanding. It must be added that while the text is hard to approach from the side of its literal sense, the alleged esoteric aspects are matters of curious speculation only.

The unbalanced forces of the universe, the world in its void state, are considered under the symbolism of the kings who reigned in Edom before a king was raised up to rule over the children of Israel, that is to say, before the emanation of MICROPROSOPUS.[1] At that time there was neither beginning

---

[1] The Kabbalah represents the present universe as preceded by others which passed away quickly. According to Basnage, this notion occurs also in the TALMUD, where

nor end, and the Edomite kings were without subsistence. According to Rosenroth this signifies the fall of creatures partly into a state of rest, such as that of matter, and partly into one of inordinate activity, such as that of the evil spirits, in which case we are dealing not so much with cosmology as with the legends of souls. So also when the GREATER SYNOD represents the Ancient of Ancients creating and producing the essence of light, the same interpreter, who speaks with the authority of knowledge as regards the literature of Kabbalism, observes that the reference is to the Law,[1] in other words, to the letters of the alphabet, by the transpositions of which the Law was recorded subsequently. For the rest, symbolism of this order is not simplified by its multiplication, and the record of Rabbi Simeon's discourses is only the BOOK OF CONCEALMENT dilated in a glass of vision. Compare, for example, the description of MACROPROSOPUS with the indications on the same subject contained in the previous section. "White are His garments as snow, and His aspect is as a face manifested. He is seated upon a throne of glittering brightness, that He may subdue. The whiteness of his bald head is extended into forty thousand worlds, and from the light of the whiteness thereof shall the just receive four hundred worlds in the world to come." The Vast Countenance itself is said to extend into three hundred and seventy myriads of worlds. The brain concealed within the skull is the Hidden Wisdom, and the influence of this Wisdom passes through a channel below and issues by two and thirty paths.[2] The hair of MACROPROSOPUS radiates into four hundred and ten worlds, which are known only to the Ancient One.[3] The parting of the hair is described as a path shining into two hundred and seventy worlds, and therefrom another path diffuses its light, and in this shall the just shine in the world to come. When the

---

it is said, with characteristic crassness, that when God was alone, in order to kill time, He diverted Himself by the formation of divers worlds which He destroyed forthwith. These were successive attempts at creation, by which Deity became experienced and at last produced the existing physical order.—HISTOIRE DES JUIFS, t. ii. p. 712. Compare also the PIRKÉ of R. Eliezer, according to which the basis of the existing universe is the repentance of God over His previous failures. We have seen that this work is referred to an early period of the ninth century. For other Zoharic references to the subject see ZOHAR ii. 20a, Mantua.

[1] Understood as the essence of the light.

[2] It is therefore the influx of KETHER descending through the Tree of Life even to MALKUTH, understood as the Kingdom of this world.

[3] An intimation of Divine Knowledge which is withdrawn in the hiddenness of Divine Being.

forehead of MACROPROSOPUS, which is the benevolence of all benevolence, is uncovered, the prayers of the Israelites are received, and the time of its uncovering is at the offering of evening prayer on the Sabbath. The forehead extends into two hundred and seventy thousand lights of lights abiding in the Supernal Eden. For there is an Eden which shines in Eden: it is withdrawn in concealment, and is unknown to all but the Ancient One. The eyes of the Vast Countenance differ from other eyes, having neither lids nor brows, because the Guardian of Supernal Israel knows no sleep. The two eyes shine as a single eye, and were that eye to close even for one moment the things which are could subsist no longer.[1] Hence it is called the open eye, ever smiling, ever glad. In the nose of MACROPROSOPUS one of the nostrils is life and the other is the life of life. With regard to the Beard of the Vast Countenance, called otherwise the decoration of all decorations, neither superiors nor inferiors, neither prophets nor saints, have beheld it, for it is the truth of all truths. Its thirteen forms are represented as powerful to subdue and to soften all stern decrees of the judgments. Thirteen chapters of the GREATER SYNOD are devoted to the consideration of this subject, including the number of the locks in each portion, the number of hairs in each lock and the number of worlds attributed to them. This ends the discourse concerning MACROPROSOPUS, and the treatise proceeds thence to the consideration of the Lesser Countenance. The conformations of MICROPROSOPUS are disposed from the forms of the Vast Countenance, and His components are expanded on either side under a human form. When the Lesser Countenance gazes on the Greater, all inferiors are restored in order, and the Lesser is vaster for the time being. There is an emanation from the Greater towards the skull of the Lesser, and thence to numberless lower skulls, and all together reflect the bril-

---

[1] Compare, in Southey's CURSE OF KEHAMA, Part X, the episode of Parvati placing her hands on the eyes of Seeva.

"Thereat the heart of the universe stood still;
The Elements ceas'd their influences; the Hours
Stopt on the eternal round; Motion and Breath,
Time, Change, and Life and Death,
In sudden trance opprest, forgot their powers,
A moment, and the dread eclipse was ended;
But, at the thought of Nature thus suspended,
  The sweat on Seeva's forehead stood,
And Ganges thence upon the World descended,
  The Holy River, the Redeeming Flood."

liance of the whiteness of this emanation towards the Ancient of Days. From the brain of MACROPROSOPUS an influence descends, from the hair an outpouring of splendour, from the forehead a benevolence, from the eyes a radiance, from the nostrils a spirit and the spirit of life, from the cheeks gladness, and all these fall upon the Lesser Countenance. From the brain of MICROPROSOPUS there are emanations of wisdom, emanations of understanding and emanations of knowledge; in each lock of the hair of MICROPROSOPUS there are a thousand utterances; his forehead is the inspection of inspection, and when it is uncovered sinners are visited with judgment. For the lesson of the GREATER SYNOD is that wrath may dwell with MICROPROSOPUS, but not in the Ancient of Days. So also the eyes of the Lesser Countenance possess lids: when the lids are closed judgments subdue the Israelites and the Gentiles have dominion over them. But the eyes, when they are open, are beautiful as those of the dove, for they are then illuminated by the good eye. With one of those pathetic touches which soften occasionally for a moment the unyielding lines of Kabbalistic symbolism, it is said that two tears dwell in the eyes of the Lesser Countenance, and the Holy of Holies, when He wills to have mercy on the Israelites, sends down these two tears to grow sweet in the great sea of wisdom, and they issue therefrom in mercy upon the chosen people. The special seat of severity in MICROPROSOPUS is the nose, and judgment goes forth therefrom, unless the forehead of the Vast Countenance is uncovered, when mercy is found in all things.

As in the case of the Ancient of Ancients, the discourse appertaining to the beard of MICROPROSOPUS fills many chapters, full of strange scholia on various passages of Scripture, and details minutely the conformations of its nine divisions, what it conceals of the Lesser Countenance, what it permits to be manifested, with observations on the descent of a holy and magnificent oil from the beard of MACROPROSOPUS and a general description of the correspondences and differences of the two adornments.

It should be observed that the body of MICROPROSOPUS is androgyne, and at this point the symbolism is concerned largely with the sexual organs. A modern symbologist has said that Nature is not ashamed of her emblems,[1] and there is

---

[1] Gerald Massey on phallic symbols, in a letter contributed to the SPIRITUALIST.

no doubt that for the Kabbalist the body of man was peculiarly sacred, whence for him there would be nothing repellent in dealing exhaustively with its typology. But it will be unnecessary in a descriptive summary to do more than allude to this. The student who desires to pursue the subject may be referred to the French version.

The sum of the whole treatise can be given in the words of the original. " The Ancient of Ancients is in Microprosopus; all things are one; He was all things; He is all things; He will be all things; He shall know no change; He knoweth no change; He hath known no change."[1] Thus God in manifestation is not really separable from God in concealment, and if the symbolism depict Him in the likeness of humanity, it is by way of similitude and analogy.

At the conclusion of the GREATER SYNOD, we are told that three of the company died during the deliberations, and that the survivors beheld their souls carried by angels behind the " veil expanded above."[2]

Amidst all its obscurity and uncouthness there are sublime touches in this treatise. The Kabbalah is perhaps the first of all books which appeared in the western world reciting with no uncertain voice that God is altogether without mutation and vicissitude—that wrath and judgment are of man alone, placing thus a new construction on the divine warning: " Judge not, lest ye be judged "; and shewing also the higher significance of the not less divine promise: " I will repay." Never for the true Kabbalist could this mean that God would repay the sinner in his own spirit, outrage for outrage, hate for hate. The repayment of God is the compensation of everlasting justice or the gift of everlasting bounty. In a sense the writers of the ZOHAR anticipated some liberal conclusions of modern eschatology.[3] Amidst the firebrands of the Papal Church, it promulgated for the first time the real meaning of the forgiveness of sins. It is in the sense of such intimations and not in its body of extravagant symbolism that

---

[1] IDRA RABBA, *seu Synodus Magna, sectio* xxxix. par. 920, in KABBALA DENUDATA, t. ii. Compare De Pauly's translation, Vol. V, p. 365 : " The Ancient of Ancients and the ' Little Figure,' these are one and the same ; it was and shall be all. It is not subject to transformation ; it has never changed and will not change for ever ; it is the centre of all perfection."

[2] *Ibid.*, § xlv. par. 1138.

[3] Franck summarises the position as follows :—Nothing is absolutely evil, nothing is accursed for ever, not even the archangel of evil, for a time will come when his name and angelic nature will be restored to him. LA KABBALE, p. 217.

the Holy Assembly of Rabbinical Israel may speak to us at this day.

IV.—THE LESSER HOLY SYNOD

Similar in its chief characteristics to the more extended discourse which precedes it, the LESSER HOLY SYNOD, or IDRA ZOUTA, is termed by Rosenroth the Swan's Song of Simeon ben Yohai, a supplement to the subjects not discussed exhaustively in the Greater Assembly. As the master's death is recorded at the end of the treatise, the translator's words must be understood of the instruction it contains and not of its setting. The SYNOD consists of the survivors from the former Conclave, with the addition of Rabbi Isaac. Simeon begins by affirming that it is a time of grace: he is conscious of his approaching end; he desires to enter without confusion into the world to come; and he designs to reveal those sacred things in the presence of Shekinah which have been kept secret hitherto. Rabbi Abba is appointed as scribe, and Simeon is the sole speaker. The discourse still concerns MACROPROSOPUS and MICROPROSOPUS, with the correspondences between them; but it sketches only the subject of Concealed Deity and deals at length with the manifestation of the Lower Countenance. In both cases, as indeed would be expected, it repeats, substantially and verbally, much of the preceding Synod; but it gives some additional imagery, as, for example, concerning the three heads of MACROPROSOPUS, "one within the other and the other above the other," and at a later stage a very considerable extension of symbolism regarding the first manifestation of the Ancient One under the form of male and female, which is, in fact, the emanation or " forming forth " of the supernal SEPHIROTH— CHOKMAH, or Wisdom, and BINAH, or Understanding. So also the instruction concerning MICROPROSOPUS, when it is not a close reflection of the GREATER SYNOD, deals with His androgyne nature and His union with the Bride, who cleaveth to the side of the male until she is separated, *et accedat ut copuletur cum eo*, face to face. Out of this comes the Kabbalistic doctrine of the sexes, so much in advance of its time, in whatever Christian century we may elect to place the literature, namely, that male and female separated are but an incomplete humanity, or, as the text expresses the idea, are but half the body;

that no blessing can rest on what is mutilated and defective; that no divided being can subsist for ever or receive an eternal dowry, "for the beauty of the female is completed by the beauty of the male." [1] The conjunction of the supernal male and female is said to be in the place called Zion and Jerusalem, which further on are explained to signify Mercy and Justice. "When the Bride is united to the King in the excellence of the Sabbath, then are all things made one body." And then the most Holy God sitteth on His throne, then all things enter and are integrated in the One Undivided, Perfect and Holy Name. "When the Mother is united to the King, the worlds receive a blessing and are found in the joy of the universe." [2]

About this point the discourse of Simeon ceases and Rabbi Abba, the scribe, still in the act of writing and expecting that more should follow, heard nothing. But afterwards a voice cried: "Length of Days and Years of Life"; and yet another: "He seeketh Life from Thee." A fire abode in the house the whole day: when it burned no longer, Rabbi Abba saw that the holy light, the holy of holy ones, had been wrapped away from the world: he lay upon his right side and a smile shone upon his face. Rabbi Eleazar, the son of Simeon, rose up and taking his hands, kissed them. "But I," says Abba, "licked the dust under his feet." It is added that during his obsequies the bier of the deceased saint was raised in the air, and fire shone about it, while a voice cried: "Enter in unto the nuptial joys of R. Simeon."

It will be seen that in spite of a monstrous symbolism the Kabbalistic narratives have at times the touch of Nature which gives them kinship with this world of ours. Whether it has pearls of great price to offer from the world within is another question, as to which we are now only at the beginning of our research.

V.—THE DISCOURSE OF THE AGED MAN

The prominence given by Rosenroth to the BOOK OF CONCEALMENT and its sequels was not without its warrant, as they are certainly the most arresting, I might almost say sensational, of the tracts imbedded in the ZOHAR. Those which remain

---

[1] IDRA ZOUTA, *seu Synodus Minor*, § viii. *passim*. The foundation of this mysticism concerning the nuptial state must be sought in Talmudic literature.
[2] *Ibid.*, § xxii. par. 746 *et seq*.

to be examined will be taken now in the order in which they are placed in KABBALA DENUDATA, and their more sober interest will appear by the short analyses which will accompany their tabulation. The first to be enumerated is that contained in Section MISHPATIM (*Historia de sene quodam in sectione* MISHPATIM). The term SABAH signifies ancient man and MISHPAT is judgment, referring to Exodus, from the beginning of c. xxi.—" Now these are the judgments "—to the conclusion of c. xxiv. The discourse occurs in the Cremona edition, pt. ii. fol. 43 ; in the Mantua, vol. ii. fol. 94 ; in the Sulzbach, vol. ii. 94*a*.[1] The Section MISHPATIM opens with a conference between Rabbi Simeon ben Yohai and a certain aged man, not otherwise identified, on the subject of the ordeals and metempsychosis of the soul, to which there are allusions at some length in the BERESHITH division of the ZOHAR—otherwise the first part. It breaks off, however, abruptly, giving place to another conference which takes place at an inn between the same or a second aged man and two Sons of the Doctrine who have met together by accident. It is described in a colophon as a recital relative to Rabbi Yebba the Ancient, who is moved to reveal at great length the Mystery of the Soul, its nature, modes or parts and the law which governs its transmigrations. It is the most important and elaborate study of these subjects in the extant text, and Isaac de Loria's yet more complex treatise on the REVOLUTIONS OF SOULS is a development of the Section MISHPATIM. But as there has been occasion to note previously, the study of the soul in Kabbalism belongs to a later stage of our research, and it must be sufficient to state here that in the discourse under consideration the psychic nature of man is regarded under a sevenfold aspect, whereas other theses reduce it to three and by one it is extended to ten. The facts are worth stating at the present point, not only as an illustration of the discourse out of which they arise, but because they suggest a working canon of criticism in the case of those writers in the past who speak of a concealed sense in the ZOHAR and other Kabbalistic texts. It is not to be supposed that when Rabbi Yebba and other doctors divide and subdivide the soul they mean anything else than to distinguish the successive states and modes which are possible therein and may become actual.

---

[1] In De Pauly's translation see Vol. III, pp. 377-441.

In a word, it means what it says, just as Modern Theosophy does when it affirms that there are seven principles in man. The concealed sense of the ZOHAR, as indicated heretofore, is the extraction of some method from its vast and confused mass, which at first sight may appear inextricable. If and when the discrepancy between the variously divided aspects of the soul in man have been harmonised, we shall have reached the concealed sense of the Commentary and its connections as regards our inward nature. We may attain it in this case by assuming that the involved discourse of Rabbi Yebba describes the development of mystical experience and the ascent of the soul in sanctity according to a tabulation of seven stages, ending—as it states literally—in the realisation of Divine Union. The text says that a flame of fire comes down from the Supernal World and is joined to the Community of Israel, " that union may be perfect." [1]

At an early stage of the conference we hear of a Hidden Palace which is called the Palace of Love, and it is affirmed that the Heavenly King kisses the holy souls who arrive therein.[2] " And Jacob kissed Rachel "[3] is a text which alludes hereto. Thereafter, the Holy One—blessed be He—raises them into exalted realms and there rejoices with them, as a father with his beloved daughter. It is obvious, however, that the Beatified Life of this Palace is not the life of union, though it may be called a vestibule. It is a place of beatitude in the Beloved Presence. The distinction is vital, though its significance is likely to escape those who are in the Court of the Mystical Temple but not in its Holy Place, who have conceived the Vision but not the Ineffable Union. It may be noted in this connection that, according to Rabbi Yebba, the Most High has hidden in each word of Scripture a Supreme Mystery which constitutes the soul of that word. But the profane man sees only the external body of the word, meaning the literal sense. On the other hand, for those who have eyes the external word is an envelope through which the soul is seen.[4] This is illustrated a little later on after another manner, when the inward meaning is likened to a beautiful virgin shut up in a palace, who contrives a little chink that

---

[1] Z., II, 114a; III, 440.
[2] Ib., 97a; III, 389.
[3] Ex., xxix, 11.
[4] Z., II, 98b; II, 397.

her lover when he passes may have a glimpse of her beauty. There are many who go to and fro, but he only who has the eyes of love can see her. It is the same with Holy Scripture, which reveals its hidden secrets only to those who love it: the uninitiated go by on the other side and observe nothing.[1]

Outside these deeper aspects and the subject-general of the text, there are occasional intimations which will carry their simple messages as directly at this day as when the ZOHAR first shed light on the greater exile of Jewry and all its thorny paths. We are told, for example, that penitence cancels everything, looses all that binds, annuls all decrees and breaks all chains.[2] It is said also that man's conduct here below forms a window in his brain, and if he lives in a state of grace the glass of that window remains polished and diaphanous, so that his intelligence is a faithful reflection of the Most Holy Intelligence which is above. But the man of evil life clouds his window.[3] Finally, as an example of notions that offer a strange contrast to all that obtained and was current about Theosophical Jewry when the ZOHAR emerged, there is that which is said on the place of children in the world to come, namely, that there is a sojourn reserved for them which is higher than that of the just made perfect.[4] It is added that children die young to become the defenders in heaven of those who remain on earth.

VI.—THE LUMINOUS BOOK

Excerpts of considerable length, purporting to come from a work entitled SEPHER HA' BAHIR, or LIBER ILLUSTRIS, are given in the Cremona edition of the ZOHAR at the places which here follow. Part I., col. 76, 79, 82, 86, 88, 104, 110, 112, 122, 125, 127, 130, 137, 138, 185, 241, 462. Part II., col. 145 and 259. Part III., col. 151, 176, 301 and 333. They are omitted in the so-called LITTLE ZOHAR of Mantua, but reappear in Rosenroth's Sulzbach edition and in those of later date which are based thereon. In 1651 these excerpts were brought together into a volume and published at Amsterdam, which was at that period a great stronghold of Jewry. A

---

[1] Z., II, 99a; III, 399.
[2] Ib., II, 106a; III, 422.
[3] Ib., II, 110a; III, 433.
[4] Ib., II, 113b; III, 439.

reprint of this volume appeared at Berlin in 1706.[1] Some interesting but complex questions are involved in the consideration of this work, which is thus known to us only by quotations. It is alleged on the one hand to be of higher antiquity than any Kabbalistic book and hence of superior importance to the SEPHER YETZIRAH itself; on the other it is affirmed to be a manifest forgery, included in the condemnation of the ZOHAR, and by implication also the fruit of the inventive faculty of Moses de Leon. Between these extreme views there is placed that which considers the extant extracts unauthentic but believes in the existence of an old Kabbalistic treatise, under the same title, which is now lost. An examination of the ascertainable facts does not, I think, prompt and much less impose agreement with any one of these opinions, and a more modest, indeterminate conclusion will be the safest to form. In other words, there is evidence that the SEPHER HA BAHIR was in existence prior to the promulgation of the ZOHAR,[2] but there is no evidence that it preceded it by a considerable period, and there are no means of knowing whether or not the extracts which occur in the ZOHAR represent the original work. In the absence of evidence to the contrary it must be assumed that they do.

It is to be regretted that most English and French students have passed over the fragments of the SEPHER HA BAHIR as they have passed over the ZOHAR proper, and for the same reason, namely, because they were not available by translation until comparatively recent years. It would have been interesting to know whether the Kabbalistic legend which has gone abroad concerning it would have remained acceptable, had such persons been in a position to improve their equipment over certain points of fact. Of that legend one aspect appears in the bibliography of their spokesman Papus. It indicates, however, no first-hand research, reproducing information of which Molitor is the avowed source. In his METHODISED SUMMARY OF THE KABBALAH the quondam President of all Martinism ascribes the SEPHER HA BAHIR,

---

[1] See BIBLIOTHECA HEBRÆA on Wolf, especially p. 906. It was a mere pamphlet in quarto, the BAHIR occupying 10 pp., followed by a tract on Wisdom which accounted for a further three.

[2] Because it was denounced as a forgery by Rabbi Meir ben Simon in the first half of the thirteenth century, thus antedating the period at which hostile criticism places the public appearance of the ZOHAR. Graetz ascribes the forgery to Rabbi Azriel, on what grounds may be gathered from the general warrant of his Kabbalistic criticism.

which he renders LIGHT IN THE DARKNESS, to R. Nehunya ben Ha-Kanah, the master of R. Ishmael ben Elisha, a high-priest, who flourished during the half-century preceding the birth of Christ. Each, however, was a Tanna of the first and second centuries.[1] Some notable sayings of his are preserved in Talmudic collections, but it is quite certain that he left nothing in writing. This notwithstanding, other works are also ascribed to him, namely:

(*a*) Letter on Mysteries or Secrets concerning the advent of Messiah, His Divinity, Incarnation and Resurrection. This epistle was addressed to his son, who is said to have embraced Christianity. It betrays the hand of a Christian, and there can be no question in any case that it is a late production. Paulus de Heredia Hispanus translated it into Latin and dedicated it to Henry of Mendoza, legate of the King of Spain.

(*b*) SEPHER HA-KANAH, the Book of the Fragments of the Temple, but this is attributed also to Ismael (Samuel) ben Eliezer. It deals with the generation of Christ, embodying apocryphal narratives taken from the Talmud, and the real author was Abigdor Kanah, who belongs to the fifteenth century.

(*c*) A Kabbalistic Prayer, to be recited by pupils on entering or leaving the gymnasium.

(*d*) SEPHER HA-PELIAH, which is also the work of Abigdor.

(*e*) SEPHER HA-MINHAD, concerning the Mystery of the Name of God, a work akin to the BAHIR; but I have met with no opinion as to its date or history.

An alternative aspect of Kabbalistic legend concerning the LUMINOUS BOOK may be used to colour the pretension that the Zoharistic quotations do not represent the original. It is affirmed to be of such profound occult significance that it has been preserved among the hidden treasures of Israel, *in manus Cabbalistorum Germanorum*, says Wolf,[2] quoting Shem Tob. Buxtorf,[3] Bartolocci,[4] and Buddæus[5] relate the same story, and not one of them challenges the excerpts found in the ZOHAR, receiving them explicitly as genuine, while all agree likewise that the BAHIR was regarded by Kabbalists as their

---

[1] Nehunya's name occurs in one of the BAHIR fragments, where, however, he is cited as an authority and by no means as responsible for the work itself.
[2] BIBLIOTHECA HEBRÆA.
[3] BIBLIOTHECA HEBRÆA RABBINICA.
[4] BIBLIOTHECA MAGNA RABBINICA.
[5] INTRODUCTIO AD HISTORIAM PHILOSOPHIÆ HEBRÆORUM.

oldest document. The question of authenticity was renewed in comparatively recent times by Simon, who, speaking of the book printed in Holland, observes: " It does not appear that this is the ancient BAHIR of the Jews, which is much more extended and has not yet been printed." [1] Obviously this is neither the language of criticism nor of knowledge; we may infer that Simon was unacquainted with the fact that the Amsterdam publication did little more than collect the Zoharic extracts, and that he might not have challenged the extracts had he been aware of that circumstance. Bartolocci mentions a general opinion that manuscript copies of the BAHIR were to be found in many Continental libraries and particularises one such codex as contained in the Vatican collection. Wolf bears witness to others, but as to their claims and content it would seem that they await examination to this day.

The impeachment of the Zoharic excerpts naturally became part of the general charge against the ZOHAR itself; the theory which ascribed that work to Moses de Leon was exceedingly comprehensive and made a clean sweep of everything included therein. It finds an almost exact parallel in the consistent application of those principles which are held to prove the Baconian authorship of the Shakespeare plays: serving equally well for Marlowe, Massinger and all Elizabethan literature, that literature directly or indirectly is attributed to Bacon. Legend says as we have seen, that the complete ZOHAR was originally a camel's load, and were the whole of it now extant no doubt the Jew of Leon would still have been its exclusive creator. Raymund Lully is credited with the authorship of five hundred separate treatises: a list may be seen in the first volume of an unfinished and impossible attempt to collect them into a folio edition, the editor supplying not only the precise years but the months in which they were composed. What Raymund did, as they say, could not have been impossible to R. Moses. But, as a fact, the *doctor illuminatus* wrote only a low percentage out of all that gorgeous range, and reasonable criticism regards the alleged spendthrift Israelite as a possible compiler and polisher who may have played a little at " writing out of his own head," and that is all, not, however, because it allocates the ZOHAR as the work

---

[1] HISTOIRE CRITIQUE DU VIEUX TESTAMENT.

of Simeon ben Yohai, or even of R. Abba, but because it regards R. Moses as human.

Graetz, the German historian of Jewry, whose distinctive views of Kabbalistic literature once obtained much vogue, lays down a principle of criticism which ought to be written in capitals at the head of most impeachments of the ZOHAR, namely that it is not compulsory for a hostile critic to be more careful in his arguments than those who plead in defence. Without seeking to determine what is compulsory in criticism, it may be observed that there is also no binding law to enforce serious consideration for a scholar who adopts that principle. What Graetz did openly has been done tacitly or unconsciously by others. Taking the case now under notice, I do not know of one instance in which the challenge of authenticity has been accompanied by an assigned reason, beyond the fact that it was heard of first in the thirteenth century: it is part of the programme to get rid anyhow of anything which goes to shew that the whole ZOHAR was not written at the period of Moses de Leon. The reason is not far to seek: the excerpts from the BAHIR, if genuine, involve the existence not merely of purely Kabbalistic but of typically Zoharic teaching prior to that date: as this proves too much for the imposture theory, they are set down as part of the imposture. One critic who espouses the antiquity of the ZOHAR has, however, rejected the BAHIR. He says: "The SEPHER HA BAHIR, attributed to Nehunya ben Ha-Kanah, contemporary of Hillel the Elder and Herod the Great, is often cited. Various fragments, manifestly unauthentic, still pass for extracts from this book."[1] Perhaps so; but why, if so? It is for some determinate and material reason that one looks and waits in vain, failing which the identity of the ZOHAR quotations with the original can be accepted as a tolerable hypothesis, because no reason has been given to the contrary. It is quite another thing to affirm that they are the work of Nehunya, or that they are older than the SEPHER YETZIRAH. Placing this cosmogony somewhere between the fourth and the ninth century, as our personal feeling prompts; regarding the ZOHAR itself as, at least, a gradual growth between the close of that period and the date of its publication, the BAHIR can

---

[1] Adolphe Franck: LA KABBALE, ou la Philosophie Religieuse des Hébreux. Paris 1843. If the unauthentic nature follows from the fact that it is falsely attributed, then the SEPHER YETZIRAH belongs to the same category.

be accepted as a production of the formative age of the work which is made to quote it until evidence to the contrary has been produced. When the extracts were inserted therein we do not know; absent from the Mantua edition, which was simultaneous with that of the Cremona codex which contains them, it is possible that they were first added when the ZOHAR was prepared for press under the supervision of R. Isaac De Lattes, that unknown but " highly learned Jew unsurpassable in all the branches of knowledge required," whom the publisher describes. In this case, they have no connection with Moses de Leon.

There is, of course, little unanimity in hostile or indeed any Kabbalistic criticism. As, on the one hand, a defender of the ZOHAR challenges the BAHIR excerpts, so the latter have been exalted as the prototype and actual inspirer of the former work. This view, though in any case of little moment, involves at least the existence of the BAHIR prior to the alleged period when the ZOHAR was produced out of the head of Moses de Leon, like Minerva out of the head of Jupiter, ready made and at one leap. Morinus, who has left on the whole a sensible review of the subject, founds his opinion that the BAHIR was a product of the thirteenth century, on the silence of writers prior to that date, and especially of Moses Nahmanides, a Kabbalistic Jew of Jerusalem, whose literary labours belong to the period before and after 1250. Morinus, however, is wrong on the point of fact, as the work is mentioned *sub voce* Midrash R. Nehunya ben Ha-Kanah in the Commentary of Nahmanides on the Pentateuch (Gen. i.). See the JEWISH ENCYCLOPÆDIA, *s.v.* BAHIR. According to Wolf the first reference to the BAHIR is made by R. Shem Tob, who was a contemporary of Moses de Leon, but belonging to a younger generation. This, however, is a mistake also, because R. Azriel, the author of a distinguished treatise on the Sephirotic system, and born, as we have seen, about 1160, in his commentary on the Song of Songs which is ascribed sometimes to Nahmanides, quotes the BAHIR, though not under its own name but under that of YERUSHALMI. The proof is that the Italian Jew Recanati, contemporary of Moses de Leon, used these quotations, and, misled by the name, inferred that they were from the JERUSALEM TALMUD, but afterwards discovered them in the BAHIR, to which a Palestinian origin is ascribed. By how much the lost treatise antedated Azriel we have no ground for conjecturing; but the position of Wolf and Morinus is destroyed by the fact here recorded, which leaves the BAHIR where we should be disposed to place it, between the date when the SEPHER YETZIRAH is first mentioned and the first report of the ZOHAR.

The name BAHIR is referred to Job xxxvii. 21 : " And now men see not the bright light which is in the clouds," according to the Authorised Version, or according to Dr. Durell's amended rendering, " And now men see not the light which is above (or within) the clouds, &c." [1] The subject-matter of the book, which—like the great bulk of the ZOHAR—is in the form of a dialogue between certain illuminated doctors, includes the mystery inherent in Divine Names, and it contains a very full exposition of the celebrated SHEMAHAMPHORAS, or Expounded Name of Deity. Some of it therefore at least must be relegated to the side of waste and scattermeal, to which extent we can sympathise with the instinctive dislike of Franck to accept the excerpts by which it is known among us. Facts, however, must have precedence of predilections, and though the later history of the doctrine of Divine Names may well make an admirer of the higher Kabbalism regret such a connection, it is far older than that of the SEPHIROTH, not to speak of the Two Countenances in the BOOK OF CONCEALMENT and its dependencies. Setting aside certain references to the parts or modes of the soul and the mythos of the Fall, it must be confessed that the other fragments are involved as theses and almost barren of suggestion; yet a few points may be noted here and there. A tradition is cited concerning a Sacred Palace in which are four Living Creatures who are the holiest of all angels and also the most ancient : they are in correspondence with the four letters of the Sacred Name and constitute therefore its image.[2] They are also a connecting link between the world above and that which is below, presumably because of their relation to the Divine Name, which unifies height and deep. Elsewhere a comparison is drawn between those Mysteries of Scripture which are concealed from all but initiates and the Mysteries of God hidden within His own being.[3] We are assured on the authority

---

[1] Compare the Vulgate version : *At nunc non vident lucem ; subito aer cogetur in nubes, et ventus transiens fugabit eas.*
[2] Z., II, 82b ; III, 344.
[3] *Ib.*, II, 83b ; III, 346.

of Rabbi Abba that three meals must be eaten on the Sabbath Day, the first while it is yet night, and this is in honour of Shekinah; the second in honour of Him Who is the Ancient of Days; the third to the glory of Him Who is begotten of Wisdom and Understanding, according to the doctrine of the IDRAS. By these meals are the people of Israel set apart from the pagan nations, and those who neglect them shall have no part in the Sacred Palace where dwell the Living Creatures.[1] It is added hereto that the Sabbath is the Name of the Holy One, which explains why the elect who observe it carry titles of admission to the presence of those angels who are in its image and likeness. We shall discern also a certain sequence of symbolism when it is said elsewhere that the Sabbath is a day favourable to the study of the Hidden Law, for that which belongs to the Name belongs also to the Law [2]: it is under such auspices that the seventy modes of interpreting Holy Writ are revealed to initiates.[3] The last word on the subject tells us that whosoever observes the Sabbath fulfils the whole Law, from which point of view it might be said that its yoke is easy and its burden light.

It remains to say, on the authority of Wolf at its value, that William Postel is reported to have rendered the BAHIR into Latin; but, if so, I can find no record that the version was ever printed, nor is there any indication of its whereabouts in manuscript form.

VII.—THE FAITHFUL SHEPHERD

The Zoharistic treatise bearing this title records conversations between Simeon ben Yohai and Moses, who appeared to the great light of Kabbalism and gave him many instructions and revelations. Elijah took part in the conference, and the witnesses included not only Abraham, Isaac, Jacob, Aaron, David and Solomon, but God Himself. This indicates that in spite of the exalted doctrine concerning AIN SOPH, the ZOHAR recurs occasionally to the same anthropomorphic conceptions that are found in the Talmud. Ginsburg says: " The chief object of this portion is to shew the twofold and allegorical import of the Mosaic commandments

---

[1] Z., II, 88a, 88b; III, 360, 361.
[2] " The Law is the Name of the Holy One."—*Ib.*, II, 90b; III, 366.
[3] *Ib.*, II, 89a; III, 362.

and prohibitions, as well as of the Rabbinical injunctions and religious practices which obtained in the course of time." THE FAITHFUL SHEPHERD is longest by far of all the supplementary texts which have been brought into the ZOHAR proper, and it has been shewn where and how the various portions have been distributed in the codex followed by the French translator. It may be added now that they are dispersed through the Cremona edition in the following order: Part I., col. 98, 104, 126, 207, 211, 214, 247, 322, 343, 346, 378, 483; Part II., col. 72, 100, 106, 165, 203, 281, 328; Part III., col. 1, 26, 32, 42, 45, 47, 56, 57, 79, 101, 122, 134, 144, 147, 171, 187, 209, 214, 218, 233, 235, 277, 289, 329, 332, 339, 343, 394, 400, 404, 408, 413, 422, 429, 430, 431, 432, 433, 434, 447, 451, 456, 457, 458, 459, 460, 461, 466, 468, 472, 519, 534. As regards their authenticity, Franck classes these excerpts along with those of the BAHIR, but, as in that instance so in this, he gives no account of his suspicions, which may be taken, however, to follow from a personal conviction that much of the ZOHAR is really attributable to the period of Simeon ben Yohai and the disciples who came after him. In either case, the DISCOURSE OF THE FAITHFUL SHEPHERD is important to our purpose in several respects. Its views on vicarious atonement and on the Messiah to come will enable us to appreciate its contribution—if any—to the profound Salvation mythos; some of its moral teachings will illustrate its ethical position; its references to the Shekinah will cast light on this *Theosophia magna* of Kabbalism; while its speculations on angels and demons might shew the Zoharistic foundation for the later system of pneumatology which was developed by Isaac de Loria. They are reserved, however, for consideration at their place in later sections.

The discourse introduces two phases of vicarious atonement, the first of which is effected through the sufferings of just men in a general sense, or in the aggregate.

"When the righteous are afflicted by disease or other sufferings in atonement for the sins of the world, it is so ordered that all the sinners of their generation may obtain redemption. How is this demonstrated? By every member of the physical body. When all these are suffering through some evil disease, one of them is afflicted [*i.e.*, by the instrument of the leech] so that the others may recover. Which member? The arm. It is chastised by the blood being drawn from it, which ensures healing in all other members of the body. It is in like manner with the children of the world; the members are in relation with each other even as those of the body. When the Holy Blessed One willeth the health of the world, He afflicts a just man therein with pain and sickness and heals the rest through him. How is this shewn? It is written: But He was wounded for our transgressions, He was bruised for our iniquities: the chastisement of our peace was upon Him, and with His stripes we are healed (Isa. liii. 5). ' By his stripes,' as by the bruises [incisions] made in bleeding the arm, are we healed, that is, recovery is insured to us as members of one body." [1]

Here, it will be said, the Kabbalah recognises the great and fruitful doctrine of the solidarity of humanity. We may register full agreement: it is one of those instances wherein Jewish Theosophy has forestalled some modern ideas. But if we take the illustration which it gives, we shall see that it is fantastic in character; the affliction of a diseased rabbi does not as a fact benefit his neighbour physically, and only on the most arbitrary hypothesis can we suppose that the patience with which he may suffer will reflect credit on any one but himself and on those in his immediate circle, who may profit by a bright example. Let us glance, however, at a more particular illustration which follows in the text immediately.

"This is also exemplified in the history of Job. For the Holy Blessed One, seeing that the entire foundation was sinful, and how Satan appeared to accuse them, said unto Him: 'Hast thou considered my servant Job, that there is none like him in the earth' (Job i. 8), 'to save his generation through him?' This may be illustrated by the parable of a shepherd who beheld a wolf approaching to rend his sheep and destroy them. What did this shepherd? Being wise, he gave unto the wolf the strongest and stoutest bell-wether, even that which the flock was accustomed to follow, and while the wolf was bearing it away, the shepherd hurried with his sheep to a place of safety, and then returning rescued the bell-wether from the wolf. So does the Holy Blessed One deal with a generation: He surrenders a righteous man into the power of the accuser for the salvation of the generation through him. But when such an one is strong like Jacob, it is said: A man

---

[1] ZOHAR, Cremona ed., part iii. fol. 101a.

wrestled with him (Gen. xxxii. 24). But he (Satan) will be unable to prevail, and in the end he will supplicate the righteous man to release him (*Ibid.* 26), for the righteous man, chosen by the Holy Blessed One, is too strong for the evil one and bears the most cruel afflictions willingly for the redemption of his generation; whence also he is held as their saviour, and the Holy Blessed One constitutes him shepherd over all the flock, to feed them in this world and to rule over them in the world to come." [1]

The clumsy and inadequate parable which thus represents the Almighty flying from Satan as the shepherd flies from a wolf, and in accordance with which the just man is at first compared to a bell-wether and afterwards to the shepherd of a flock, is something more than a literary failure. Theologians have, I believe, found some trouble in locating the accuser of Job, and it is perhaps most accurate to say with the poet that " He, too, is God's minister"; but the Zoharic commentary on Job makes Satan in most respects a match for the Almighty, Who must have recourse to a stratagem in order to save His people. The Kabbalah on the problem of evil is therefore, in this place, neither illuminating nor reassuring: it is, in fact, no better than childish. "The ancient pillars of the world [the intellectual luminaries of Israel] differ," says the same disquisition, as to the nationality of Job. One affirms that he was a righteous Gentile who was chastised for the atonement of the world. At a certain time R. Hammarumnah met the prophet Elijah and said to him: How is it to be understood that the righteous man suffers while the wicked one has joy of his life? He answered, saying: The just man of few sins receives his punishment for these in this world, and hence it is that he suffers here; but the man whose sins are many, while his good deeds are few, receives recompense for the latter in this world and hence has the joy of life." [2]

In this instance the Kabbalah offers an explanation which, however manifestly crude, is in close correspondence with findings of Latin Theology. The latter goes even further, and affirms that not only the sporadic good actions of those who

---

[1] Z., Cremona ed., part ii. fol. 100*b*.
[2] Z., Cremona ed., part ii. fol. 106*b*. Compare the Mantua edition, I, 6, 8, where it is said that the pure man is in himself a true sacrifice and that the just are the expiation of the universe.

are wicked habitually but all natural goodness can find their reward only in this world. The Kabbalah is disfigured seldom by methodised enormities of this kind. There are times also in which it loses its grotesqueness for a moment, and by some not unhappy reference to Scripture illustrates an elementary spiritual truth, as, for example, concerning the change necessary to sinners.

"Those who are oppressed with sin need a change of place, a change of name and a change in their actions, even as it was said unto Abraham: Get thee out of thy country (Gen. xii. 1.) Here is a change of place. And: Neither shall thy name any more be called Abram, but thy name shall be Abraham (Gen. xvii. 5). Here is a change of name. A change of deeds: he changed from his former evil actions to good actions."[1] The Christian Theosophist might develop the significance of this quotation in connection with the new name of the Apocalypse, the new name received in confirmation, ordination and the monastic and conventual life. But such analogies, though suggestive, are of slender value; and the change mentioned in the FAITHFUL SHEPHERD offers no point of mystical importance: it concerns only an initial aspect of spiritual life.

The Zoharistic speculations on Shekinah are a great treasury of mystical symbolism, but their study at full length belongs to a much later stage. It is said in the FAITHFUL SHEPHERD that the relation of Shekinah to other lights of creation is like that of the soul to the body, but she—for this Divine Manifestation is presented under a feminine aspect— "stands to the Holy Blessed One as the body stands to the soul." The Shekinah is the vestment of the Almighty. But the discourse of the Faithful Shepherd adds that all are one, that is, God is one with His manifestation. This may be illustrated by the profound spiritual doctrine of the Christian Eucharist: the bread is the vestment of Christ, the mode of His manifestation in His Church; but Christ, by the hypothesis of the doctrine, is one with the veil which He assumes. It is otherwise in man, says the FAITHFUL SHEPHERD. "His body is earth, but the soul is called reason. The one is death, the other is life." The death, however, is obviously emblematic or figurative. It is to be understood as imprisonment,

---

[1] Z., Cremona ed., part ii. fol. 98b.

the limitation of walls and fetters. "But the Holy Blessed One is life, and Shekinah also is life. Whence it is written: She [meaning Shekinah, but the Scriptual reference is to Wisdom] is a Tree of Life to them that lay hold upon her" (Prov. iii. 18). The Shekinah of Kabbalism is not, however, merely the visible splendour which shone in the Holy of Holies. The FAITHFUL SHEPHERD affirms that the Holy Blessed One is concealed in the Mysteries of the THORAH and is known or manifested by the commandments, for these are His Shekinah and this is His image. Herein are high intimations, and they do not need the gift of the mystic to understand and appreciate. It is one of those instances in which a depth is opened within or beneath the sacred tales of Jewry. We may not at this day feel disposed to accept literally and, so to speak, physically the alleged manifestation in the Temple; here the Zohar helps us to something truer and profounder than the letter of the legend, and we acknowledge gladly that the little people of Palestine, encompassed by the idolatrous nations, had truly something of the divine in the law which was given them. The passage continues: "As He is humble, so is Shekinah humility; as He is benevolent, so is she benevolence; as He is strong, so is she the strength of all the nations of the world; as He is the truth, so the truth is she; as He is the prophet, so is she the prophetess; as He is righteous, so is she righteousness; as He is King, so is she Queen; as He is wise, so is she wisdom; as He is intelligent, so is she His intelligence; as He is the crown, so is she His diadem, the diadem of glory. Therefore the masters have decided that all those whose inward part is not like unto the outward semblance shall have no admission to the House of Doctrine. As the image of the Holy Blessed One, whose interior He is, whose outward splendour is Shekinah; He, His interior internally, she His exterior externally, so that no difference subsists between her the outward and Him the inward,[1] as she is an outflow from Him, and hence all difference is removed between external and internal, and as, further, the inner nature of YHVH is concealed, therefore is He only named with the name of Shekinah, that is to say, Adonai;

---

[1] It follows that She is He, She as God in manifestation and He the God in hiddenness; She Who is attained and Known, He Who is unknown, except as we know in Her. Cf. Z., Part ii, fol. 118b; III, 456.

hence the Masters tell us on the part of the Holy One: Not as I am written [YHVH] am I read."[1]

The connection instituted between Shekinah and MALKUTH, in the light of the alleged unity of God and the vestment which conceals Him, suggests the identity of the divine and the universe; but it is only in the sense of immanence. The Kabbalah, in its great moments, knows that all things are One and even that the One is All; but at others it is in some respects the very opposite of pantheism.

Our quotations must close with two references to angels and demons in the FAITHFUL SHEPHERD. The first concerns the great Presence-Angel Metatron, who—in this text—is the sole occupant of the Briatic world, as the supernal Adam is of that of ATZILUTH. He is the garment of Shaddai. According to some his form is that of a boy, while others ascribe to this angel a female aspect. This shews a connection with Shekinah, and indeed Metatron, with the difference of an added letter, signifies the cohabiting glory.[2] There are secondly certain reveries concerning Samael, or Satan, and his wife Lilith. The first was once a servant of the Holy Blessed One and the second a maid of Matroneetha.[3] Their ultimate destruction is hinted; but meanwhile Lilith is the devastation of the world and the lash in the hands of the Holy Blessed One to strike the guilty. So she, too, is God's minister.

VIII.—HIDDEN THINGS OF THE LAW

The extant fragments of this tract were tabulated by Rosenroth as follows in the Cremona edition of the ZOHAR: Part I., col. 221, 258, 262, 370.[4] Part II., col. 250. Dr. Ginsburg discovered others in the Amsterdam codex, to which his references are made. The words SITHRE THORAH signify SECRET DOCTRINE, otherwise, Mysteries of the Law and its Hidden Things. The title belongs, therefore, to the Tradition at large rather than to a single text which claims to treat thereof. The tract itself has no history outside the ZOHAR, and it does not seem that a line of it is extant elsewhere. A note of the French editors affirms it to be demonstrably

---

[1] Z., Cremona ed., part ii. fol. 106a. Myer, PHILOSOPHY OF IBN GEBIROL, p. 341.
[2] ZOHAR, part iii. fol. 106b.
[3] Z., Cremona ed., part iii. fol. 134b.
[4] In the French paraphrase see II, 720-734; III, 328 et seq., 367-373.

impossible that it is earlier than the tenth century; but whether it is much anterior to the Mantua and Cremona codices is an alternative speculation which may not be devoid of likelihood. The question is not of my concern and can be left to stand at its value, nor is SITHRE THORAH calculated to detain us long, as I conceive it unnecessary to give examples of its Scriptural exegesis, which is at once monstrous and puerile. It has, however, some occasional lights, even if they shine among clouds, and there is much on the evolution of the SEPHIROTH, but it belongs to another section. There is one rather curious reverie which has been thought to distinguish certain stages of mystical vision. It is said that the glory of the King is discovered in three colours.[1] The first is above and so far away that no eye can perceive it in its clearness; but it is distinguished (dimly) by contracting the range of vision [*i.e.*, by half opening the eye]. It is of this Divine Manifestation that Scripture says: Jehovah appeared to me far off.[2] The second colour is seen when the eye is hardly opened at all. The clearness of the light could not be endured otherwise. Of this it is written: What seest thou?[3] The third colour is that bright luminous flash which cannot be suffered at all, except between the rolling of the eyes when the lids are closed altogether and the eyes move in their sockets. There can be seen then in that rolling the light as of a luminous mirror; but the colour thereof can be comprehended only by him who beholds the shining with eyes shut, and as if in recollection, whence it is written: The hand of the Lord was upon me[4]; and: The hand of the Lord was upon me in the evening.[5] It is added on the authority of another sacred text that all prophets stood in need of an explanation to make their visions intelligible, save Moses only, who could look on highest Divinity.[6] No doubt the Kabbalists had visions and means of inducing visions, as well as modes of contemplation and occasional deeper states which pass under

---

[1] Z., I, Appendix III; II, 720, 721.

[2] Jer. xxxi. 3. The Authorised Version reads: The Lord hath appeared of old unto me. Compare, however, the Vulgate: *Longe Dominus apparuit mibi*.

[3] Jer. i. 11. The prophet, however, did not see the will of God but a rod of an almond-tree.

[4] Ezek. xxxvii, 1.

[5] Ezek. xxxiii, 22.

[6] See Numbers xii. 7, 8, and especially: With him will I speak mouth to mouth, even apparently, and not in dark speeches. But the Vulgate seems stronger, clearer, and corresponds better with the mind of SITHRE THORAH: *Ore enim ad os loquor ei, et palam, et non per ænigmata et figuras Dominum videt*.

this name. So also had Böhme, St. John of the Cross and all the seers and mystics; but this delineation confuses cause and effect, while it offers no intelligible result.

The discourse proceeds, however, to another illustration of colour symbolism in the case of the three angels who appeared to Abraham.

"It is written: And lo, three men stood by him.[1] These are the three angelic emissaries, clothed in human forms, which come down to this world, and shew themselves to the children of men. They correspond to the three colours of the rainbow: white, red and green. The white is Michael, because he is the right side; the red is Gabriel, because he is the left side; and the green is Raphael. And these three colours are those of the rainbow, because it is never seen otherwise than with them.[2] . . . Thereby also was the Shekinah revealed to Abraham. . . . It is written also: And they that be wise shall shine as the brightness of the firmament.[3] They shall shine with a light which is enkindled by igniting a splendour. That brilliant light which is hidden, the spark of all sparks, of all lights, is therein invisible and hidden, concealed and made known, seen and not beheld. This shining light came out from the Supreme Fountain of enlightenment, which is shewn in the day and hidden at night. It illuminates the ordinances of the Law and all colours are concealed therein. . . . Those three colours which are beheld below are in the likeness of colours that are above and are unseen by eyes of flesh. The light is called by the Name YHVH."[4]

The account in Genesis, upon which this pretends to be a commentary, is exceedingly perplexing, and to say that the three men are three angels clothed in the light of Shekinah scarcely removes the difficulties. The explanations of Christian interpreters may not be satisfactory and may not call for recital; but in this place the colour symbolism of SITHRE THORAH leads only to a disquisition on Divine Names and Titles, and this leads nowhere.[5]

---

[1] Genesis xviii. 2.
[2] This point should interest ethnologists.
[3] Daniel xii. 3.
[4] Z., Part I, Appendix III; II, 722, 723. See also Isaac Myer, *op. cit.*, pp. 427, 428, for another form of paraphrase.
[5] The fact remains, however, and is important for the whole Zoharic subject, that when God manifests on earth He appears in the form of Shekinah. Latin theology postulates a Christ form.

For the rest, SITHRE THORAH delivers intimations there and here not only in disquisitions but also in occasional short passages and mere sentences, of which a few are worth noting. We are taken back by one of them to that colour symbolism which so far has profited little and are told that even as white is the foundation of colours, while all return therein, so is there a White Light of the Spirit, even a Light of Mercy, from which other lights emanate—meaning sacred qualities and virtues—that belong to the Divine Order. It is mysterious and concealed, is perceived by no one who depends on bodily vision and is reserved for the just alone.[1] Those who seek to know it should meditate on the precepts of the Law by day and by night.[2] We are reminded of another passage in the ZOHAR, which affirms that the world was made by Mercy, derived from the Supernal Loving Kindness abiding in the world above. It is another way of saying not alone that Mercy is greater than Judgment, but is that which moves therein and rules in all. It seems to me that we shall remember this and keep it in our hearts when we have forgotten about the three angels which appeared to Abraham, the colours to which they correspond, and that the words ADONAI ELOHENU ADONAI are composed of fourteen Hebrew letters.[3]

We are told elsewhere that the Scriptural ordinance to sanctify the Sabbath Day is not merely, as we have seen, the synthesis of all other Scriptural commandments and earns the same merit as the observance of all, but that it lifts up those who do so into a realm of everlasting memory.[4] The explanation is that forgetfulness is found only below, but in the world above that which we are is known, that which we were is with us and the future stands revealed.

It is affirmed finally that the letter ALEPH calls upon us to proclaim the unity of God, and this is clear at least, because its numerical value is one. But the text goes on to tell us that ALEPH is a letter of prohibition as well as of command, since it forbids us to acknowledge the identity of the true God with any pagan divinities. There is added, and the point may be commended to " occultists " of all classes, that the same letter

---

[1] Z., II, 78b ; III, 328, 329.
[2] Joshua i. 8.
[3] Z., Appendix III, SITHRE THORAH ; II, 723.
[4] Z., II, 91a ; III, 370.

forbids us to be seduced by Magic and the art of evoking the dead.[1] In the absence of this information it is unlikely that I should have cited the passage.

IX.—THE SECRET COMMENTARY

We know that Scott provided headings to many chapters of his romances by pretended quotations from old plays which existed only in his imagination, and it happened occasionally that these mythical excerpts contained stronger lines than some of his acknowledged versecraft. Those who believe—if indeed any are left at this day—that Moses de Leon wrote the ZOHAR out of his own head may account in a similar manner for certain fragments of unknown treatises which are found only in that work. Of some of these it may be said also that they are more curious here and there than is the ZOHAR proper. As we have seen, the student world of Kabbalism agreed in the past to exalt the BOOK OF CONCEALMENT over other discourses attributed to Simeon ben Yohai; but for the purposes of our present inquiry it must be confessed that not a little interest attaches to the SECRET COMMENTARY. The extant fragments of MIDRASH HA NEELAM are found in the Cremona edition at the following places: Part I., col. 257, 260, 261, 264, 265, 268, 269, 272, 273, 276, 296, 370. The field which they cover is chiefly that of the destiny of souls, future punishments and rewards, the resurrection of the body, the Paradise above and its relation to the Paradise below, and the doctrine concerning angels and demons. But these subjects are reserved for consideration in their proper places subsequently. It is possible, however, to offer here and now a few of the intimations concerning the soul and its destiny, as they will not detract from that which is designed to follow. At the beginning of the MIDRASH, or more properly at that point which is cited first in the ZOHAR,[2] we hear not alone of the soul in glory, because it ascends thus into heaven, but that this splendour is called a visit of the Holy One, meaning therefore that the soul is encompassed by the Divine Presence. But it is only a light which is reflected thereupon by an event to come, for it is said presently that the Holy One comes to the soul, accompanied by Abraham, Isaac and Jacob. There

---

[1] Z., II, 91a; III, 368, 369.
[2] Ib., Part I, Appendix III; II, 675 et seq.

is the authority of Rabbi Eleazar for an assurance that the souls of the just desire after that moment when they will leave the vanities of this world and enjoy the life to come; but the picture presented at this stage of the MIDRASH is more than normally anthropomorphic; and even when it is said a little later that the soul's joy in heaven is in the contemplation of the glory of God and in the nutriment of higher lights, it does not rise definitely above this level or in any wise approach the Thomist conception of the Beatific Vision, though it is unchallengeable that in the last resource, and howsoever transmuted, this also is the doctrine of separation impressed with everlasting seals. It should be added that texts outside the SECRET COMMENTARY present a different view.

Meanwhile the suggestion that Light in the celestial world becomes the nourishment of those who have been admitted therein takes us back to a subject on which we have dwelt previously, namely the Supersubstantial Bread, and it happens to be unfolded for our further consideration in the SECRET MIDRASH.[1] The epoch under discussion by various Masters in Israel is that which will follow the resurrection, a time when the Holy One will be in union with His creatures, the just will be conscious of His inward presence, and they shall know Him as if they saw Him with their eyes—an intimation which differs from all that so far has preceded. It has been handed down that at this time He Who is Holy and Blessed will prepare a Feast for the righteous, that is, a spiritual nourishment, defined as the splendour of Shekinah between the Cherubim on the Mercy-Seat. A later intimation says that it will be a food of joy, experienced by contact with the Holy One, otherwise, rejoicing in His joy.[2] There is also a wine reserved for the righteous from the creation of the world, and it is said to signify Hidden and Immemorial Mysteries which will be revealed in the age to come.

It will be seen that in this very suggestive passage the MIDRASH offers a great advance upon the monstrous Talmudic allegory of the salted leviathan, even if it be objected that the cream and marrow of the rabbinical discourse is summed up in a single sentence which affirms that " it hath not entered into the heart of man to conceive what God hath prepared

---

[1] *Loc. cit.*, § TOLDOTH; II, 713-715.
[2] There is a reference at this point to Ps. xxxiv.

for those who love Him."[1] Isaac Myer has sought to increase the significance by an indication that the word "wine" refers Kabbalistically to "the mysterious vitality and spiritual energy of created things," an opinion based on its investigation by NOTARIKON, for Wine = 70 = SOD, or secret.[2] However this may be, there is a more pregnant explanation on the part of the MIDRASH itself, according to which the leviathan of Isaiah and the TALMUD, the behemoth of Job and analogous rabbinical legends are things written for the crowd, which understands only material rewards and punishments. We know, however, what is the faith of the just and whither their aspirations tend, namely, "to rejoice with God, with a joy that shall be wholly spiritual."

For the rest, what is evident in other texts is evident also in the SECRET COMMENTARY: that the study of the Doctrine and the Study of its Secret Law was the consolation in chief which was sought by Sons of the Doctrine through the exile of the Christian centuries. The Temple was destroyed, and it was not possible to offer sacrifices; but always the Law remained, and the reward of dedication thereto was that of the world to come, understood as the Mountain of the Lord, the Mountain of Delight and Felicity.[3]

X.—MINOR TRACTS OF THE ZOHAR

We have now passed in review the more important MIDRASHIM and fragments which have been incorporated with the ZOHAR proper. It is far beyond the province of this analysis to offer an account in full of all that remains over, of texts and pieces particular to the Cremona edition, of the Ancient and Later Supplements and the additional content of ZOHAR HADASH. A few items only can be noticed briefly for the sake of comparative completeness.

A.—THE OMISSIONS

We have seen that certain השמטות = HASHMATOTH = OMISSIONS are comprised in the first Appendix to Part I. of the ZOHAR, being the Commentary on Genesis. Of these the first cannot be identified and the rest—with one exception,

---

[1] Is. lxiv. 4; I. Corinthians ii. 9.
[2] PHILOSOPHICAL WRITINGS OF IBN GEBIROL, p. 358.
[3] Z., Part I, Appendix III; II, 680.

about which something must be said later—form part of the HIDDEN LAW, the LUMINOUS BOOK and the FAITHFUL SHEPHERD. These texts, or their extant portions, having been reviewed already, the present note has reference only to a few leaves of Appendix I.[1] The subjects of consideration include: (1) The White Head in the BOOK OF CONCEALED MYSTERY, to which the Divine Name יהוה = JEHOVAH is allocated in place of יה = JAH, according to the Holy Assemblies. (2) The Glory of the Lord—that is to say, Shekinah—which was revealed in the Tabernacle is identified with what is termed the Sea of Wisdom in the Supernal World, meaning the SEPHIRA CHOKMAH = Wisdom; but we shall find that the Shekinah in Transcendence is referable to BINAH = the Sea of Understanding. (3) It is said that the Sun and Moon are placed under the presidency of two powerful angels, otherwise Planetary Spirits of old magical lore; that Esau was under solar dominion, while Jacob was under lunar influence; and that for this reason the one would rule over nations here on earth, but the other in the world to come. (4) It is affirmed yet once more that the true Sacrifice of Expiation is the study of the Law, that is, the Secret Doctrine.

B.—THE ADDITIONS

The various TOSSEFTOTH = ADDITIONS or ADJUNCTIONS, which occupy the second Appendix of Part I., are in the same position as the OMISSIONS, being extracts from the same MIDRASHIM already enumerated, one only excepted.[2] A paragraph under the title of ADDITIONS is found also in Appendix I., so that there are two left for our consideration in this place. In one of them [3] the Great Sea is again identified with Wisdom instead of Understanding; but it may be remembered in this connection and recurring to my previous note that the qualities and titles of Wisdom in the Old Testament are referred to Shekinah throughout the ZOHAR, from which it follows that Wisdom and Understanding, otherwise, CHOKMAH and BINAH, the second and third SEPHIROTH in the Tree of Life, are in a state of union, which is obvious by the nature of things; and it is shewn elsewhere in the ZOHAR

---

[1] Z., Part I, fol. 251b–253a; II, 591–597.
[2] Ib., Part I, fol. 283b, 284a; II, 657, 658.
[3] Ib., fol. 278a; II, 646, 647.

that this union or marriage produces a Son, who in fact is Divine Knowledge. By the second we learn that two spirits are provided for just men, one which animates them in this world, and one in the world to come, both now in being and presumably in joint activity. The affirmation is important, because we shall see later, on other authority than a mere gloss or annotation, that the highest part of the human soul never leaves the Supernals.

There are also ADDITIONS which constitute the first and third Appendices to the Commentary on Exodus.[1] That of Appendix I. is a conference of some length on the Celestial Tabernacle, and in certain editions of the ZOHAR it is printed as part of the eleventh and last section into which the Commentary itself is divided. The subject-matter claims to be derived from a book entitled SUPREME MYSTERIES. The Tabernacle above is built upon twelve thousand worlds, while the Tabernacle below corresponds by its material images to the Celestial Chariot; but it is in the likeness also of the Tabernacle of Adonai, even as this is in analogy with the higher Tabernacle of Jehovah. In this connection it is affirmed that the Divine Name Jehovah designates the male principle in Deity, while the Divine Name Adonai signifies the female principle; but it is added that these two are one, a pregnant doctrinal point which may be noted for future reference as regards the Mystery of Sex. It is affirmed at a later stage that the holocaust ascends to the Infinite, or to That Which is without end or beginning, a Supreme Will, more mysterious than all other Mysteries: its name is Nothing. This also should be noted, awaiting that time when we shall be called to consider the Majesty of God in Kabbalism. As regards the recurring subject of the holocaust, it is said that man was intended originally as an offering to the Supreme Spirit, but man fell and animals were substituted in consequence. The ADDITIONS of Appendix III. are drawn in part from the SEPHER HA BAHIR and in part from ZOHAR HADASH. Among subjects of consideration in those which remain over it must be held sufficient to mention (1) express prohibitions in respect of Magic, Sorcery, the Evocation of the dead and the practice of Astrology; (2) a discourse on the creation of Paradise, the Pillar which is based thereon and

---

[1] Z., Part II, fols. 235b–244b and 269b–296a; IV, 261–273 and 307–318.

goes up to the Throne of Glory, or the sapphire firmament which is above and the splendour which fills the Blessed Place when the Holy One comes down to visit the just therein; (3) a dogmatic affirmation that the tradition according to which the Law delivered to Moses on Mount Sinai was by him transmitted to Joshua and by the latter to certain Elders, alludes to the Oral Law, whereas Deuteronomy xxxi. 9, concerning transmission through the sons of Levi, refers to the Written Law.[1]

C.—REPETITIONS

There are two only which call for notice here, and one of these especially because it has reference to that Mystery of Faith which is cited continually in the ZOHAR, as we shall see in due course, though its nature never emerges in clear language. It is said in the first MATHNITIN = REPETITION [2] that those who would penetrate the Mystery must hearken concerning the well by which Moses sat and helped the daughters of Reuel to water their father's sheep.[3] On the side of external things it is the well of Jacob,[4] but on the inward side it is Adonai, even Adonai Jehovah, the Lord God,[5] and that Lord Who is Master of all the earth.[6] It is certified that this figurative well conceals a sacred spring, the Name of which is Jehovah Tsabaoth. The well in fine is the Ark of the Covenant which belongs to the Lord of all.[7] It may be thought that this is an involved way of affirming that the Mystery of Faith is revealed only in God; but we shall find in proceeding that Adonai is a name of Shekinah, that Shekinah is described emblematically as a well and is also the Ark of the Covenant. In this case Shekinah is the Mystery of Faith.[8]

The second MATHNITIN [9] claims to describe a hierarchic

---

[1] The *additamenta* or Accessions are scattered as follows through the Cremona codex: Part I, cols. 83, 87, 145, 176, 188, 189, 203, 222, 259, 265, 295, 303, 318, 367, 371, 487, 513; Part II, cols. 48, 107, 120, 163, 238, 358, 426; Part III, cols. 50, 82, 97, 98, 117, 149, 155, 163, 177, 184, 186, 191, 274, 331, 441.
[2] Rendered Traditional Receptions by Knorr von Rosenroth.
[3] Exodus ii. 15–19.
[4] Genesis xxix. 2–10.
[5] The reference cited is to Deuteronomy, iii. 24: O Lord God (Adonai Jehovah), Thou hast begun to shew Thy servant Thy greatness, and Thy mighty hand.
[6] The text quotes Daniel ix. 17: And cause Thy face to shine upon Thy sanctuary that is desolate, for the Lord's sake.
[7] Exodus ii. 16.
[8] Z., II, 12b, 13a; III, 56, 57.
[9] *Ib.*, III, 73b, 74a; V, 200, 201.

order in the empire of the Demon and would be remitted to another section if its symbolical imagery could be made intelligible. It is mentioned here because it introduces Metatron, the Great Angel of the Presence, and because above all he is said to bear a sword which changes every instant from male to female and from female to male. So far as a sword is concerned, the statement is mere nonsense; but we shall find that Metatron himself transforms in the same manner. He belongs therefore to the Zoharic Mystery of Sex, and so also does Shekinah, who is called Adonai. It is to be inferred, therefore, that the two REPETITIONS—which reveal rather than repeat—are concerned with this subject, *sub nomine* Mystery of Faith. The point may be noted at this stage in view of future references.

D.—THE SECRET OF SECRETS

The single fragment which is extant of RAZE DE RAZIN is found in Part II. of the Cremona edition, beginning at col. 134.[1] It treats, firstly, of the connection between the soul and the body; and, secondly, of physiognomy, which must be a subject of future reference in the final consideration of so-called " occult science " and the judgment of the ZOHAR thereon. It may be worth while, however, to say in the present connection that Kabbalistic physiognomy proves, as might be expected, to have little connection with any accepted principles to which this empirical subject may be supposed to have attained, and is, indeed, purely arbitrary and conventional. Lavater, the physiognomist in chief and reputed inventor of the art, was something of a Theosophist, but he borrowed nothing, as probably he knew nothing, of the ZOHAR and its connections. Four general types of the human countenance are distinguished by the text in chief, and these are referred to the faces of the Four Living Creatures in Ezekiel's vision.[2] We have thus the leonine, the bovine and the aquiline types, and another, less easy to characterise, but corresponding to the " living creature " which " had the likeness of a man." The approximation of any individual to a given type depends upon his intellectual and moral rank. Physiognomy, however, according to the SECRET OF SECRETS,

---

[1] See also ZOHAR HADASH, fol. 56a, in the Venice edition.
[2] Compare Z., Part II, 73b–75a, Section JETHRO.

"does not consist in the external lineaments, but in the features which are drawn mysteriously within us. The features of the face vary, following the form which is impressed on the inward face of the spirit. The spirit only produces all those physiognomical peculiarities which are known to the wise, and it is through the spirit only that the features exhibit meaning. When spirits and souls pass out of Eden they possess a certain form which is afterwards reflected in the face." M. Gabriel Delanne, in his day perhaps the most interesting if not most persuasive writer on the French theory of reincarnation, would say that the Zoharic fragment here refers undoubtedly to the "perisprit"—of the Kardec school of spiritism—which he holds to be the plan or type upon which the body of the man is fashioned. The SECRET OF SECRETS pretends also that every feature in a given countenance indicates to those who can read therein whether it is possible or not for the possessor to be initiated into Divine Mysteries.[1] It is, perhaps, unnecessary to say that the fragment does not disclose the rules which governed the sages in their discernment, so that the Kabbalah is not likely to be of much practical use to the few persons who may be inclined to include physiognomy within the charmed circle of any secret wisdom.

E.—THE DISCOURSE OF THE YOUTH

The little history which has passed under this name will be found in the Cremona edition of the ZOHAR, Part II., comprised in a few columns, 91 *et seq.*, which follow shortly after the BOOK OF CONCEALMENT.[2] It is the account of a rabbinical prodigy, the son of R. Hammenouna, but living at the period in question with his widowed mother in a certain village. One day two disciples of R. Simeon ben Yohai, namely, R. Isaac and R. Judah, passed through this village on a journey and paid a visit to the widow. When her son returned from school she wished to present him to the rabbis, to receive their blessing, but he declined to approach them, after the unamiable manner of prodigies. The reason assigned in the narrative is that he discerned by the odour of their garments

---

[1] In the writings of the Gaon R. Shereerah and other literature preceding the appearance of the ZOHAR we meet with notions of physiognomy and chiromancy of a parallel kind. They recur in the SUPPLEMENTS of the ZOHAR.

[2] See, however, the French translation, where it appears in Part III., sect. BALAC, fols. 186a–191b.

that they had not recited the requisite "Hear, O Israel!" in honour of the unity of God. He did not disdain, however, to converse at the table, delivering sundry discourses (1) On the symbolism of washing the hands, a function of some mystery, because it is written: So they shall wash their hands and their feet, that they die not (Ex. xxx. 21), that is, Aaron and his sons, when entering the tabernacle of the congregation; (2) On grace before meat; (3) On the Shekinah; (4) On the utterance of Jacob: "The Angel which redeemed me from all evil, bless the lads" (Gen. xlviii. 16); and on other matters. The cautious critic might not be prepared to deny that the invention of this history was beyond the genius of R. Moses de Leon. However, the discourses impressed the disciples of Simeon ben Yohai, to whom they gave account of the adventure and paid subsequently a second visit to the lad, who unfolded to them further Secrets of the Law, concerning the heave offering,[1] the Mystery of Bread and Wine, and on grace after meat. When again the facts were reported to the Lamp of Knowledge, he was of opinion that the lad would not continue on earth, for the Holy One would call him to Himself.

F.—The Mansions or Abodes

We have made acquaintance with a work anterior to the appearance of the ZOHAR in which there is a methodical description of heaven. It must not be confused with the equally methodical treatise which, under the above title, termed in the original HIKLVTh = Palaces, gives account of the structure of Paradise and the infernal region, as an Appendix to the Commentary on Exodus. There will be something to say of it in connection with the soul in Kabbalism. We shall see also that many Palaces and several series of Palaces will be found in the text and its supplements, for example, in the Cremona edition, Part I., col. 116 *et seq.*; Part II., col. 358 *et seq.*, and col. 438. According to one tabulation the mansions are seven in number and were the original habitations of the earthly Adam. After the Fall of man they were reconstituted and became the abode of the saints. Rabbi Simeon testified otherwise to nine Celestial Palaces which are of no definable form, being the Thought

---
[1] Numbers xv. 19.

of the Holy One. He should have said rather that they are forms of Divine Thought.¹

The term which signifies Mansion, Temple or Palace, is applied by later Kabbalism to MALKUTH, in which TIPHERETH is said to be concealed as in a palace. So also the name Adonai [ADNI], Lord, is the Palace of TETRAGRAMMATON, because it is the same number as HIKL = PALATIUM = 65. This name is attributed to BINAH, and in an especial manner to KETHER, on the authority of the ZOHAR proper, for HIKL, Palace, is the place in which HKL, that is, the All, is contained, seeing that KETHER includes the whole world of ATZILUTH, because the Supernals are in unity. In another sense the term is applied to the SEPHIROTH generally. In the plural, HIKLVTh = Palaces are the branches of the SEPHIROTH in the inferior worlds. The Palace of the Holy of Holies corresponds, says Rosenroth, to the Three Supernals.

The ZOHAR proper has also a good deal to tell us concerning the seven heavens, one above the other, like the layers of an onion. " Each heaven trembles with fear of its Lord, through Whom they all exist and all are taken away. Over all, the Holy Blessed One holds all in His power." There are further seven earths below, arranged after the same manner. " These earths are disposed according to their names, and between them is the Garden of Eden and Gehenna." They are inhabited by creatures of whom some have four faces, some two, while others are single visaged, like humanity. They are not the children of Adam; some of them are clothed in skins and others in shells, " like the worms which are found in the earth." It would serve no purpose to enlarge upon monstrous inventions of this kind. The concealed meaning which some dreamers once supposed them to possess is again evidently the plan upon which they are based, and to understand them is to know the method by which they can be calculated out, so to speak. For example, we have just seen that ADNI is the mansion of YHVH; by counting the numbers of these Names it appears why the Kabbalists said this, but we do not discover that it served any reasonable purpose until we find elsewhere in the medley that ADNI is God in manifestation, while YHVH stands for God in concealment. It emerges then at long last that the

---

¹ Z., Part II, fol. 269a; IV, 302.

Immanent and Transcendent are One God; and as—according to the ZOHAR—ADNI = ALHIM = SHEKINAH, we enter into a deeper sense of the doctrine that Jehovah is Elohim, or that God and His Shekinah are One. And this is THEOSOPHIA at the highest.

G.—The Commentary on Ruth

It should be understood in the first place that the Zoharic extracts are drawn from MIDRASH RUTH, which is to be distinguished from RUTH RABBAH, otherwise MIDRASH ZOUTA. They are found in SITHRA THORAH, SEPHER HA BAHIR and MIDRASH HA NEELAM; but expert knowledge has been required to distinguish them from the text of those tracts, which do not refer to their source. There are, secondly, views and notions expressed in the MATHNITIN of Appendix III to the first part of the ZOHAR which depend from MIDRASH RUTH, or, at least, are found therein. The subject-matter of the extracts may be tabulated briefly thus: (1) The libations of water made at the Feast of Tabernacles signify the grace and favour which the Holy One will pour upon the world when impurity has passed from earth.[1] (2) Wine is an emblem of Severity or Fear, and Milk of Mercy.[2] (3) Their point of meeting is Peace.[3] (4) The world was created by means of ten words, and among them are Lover and Beloved, Joy and Mirth—one of the ever-recurring testimonies to the irrepealable optimism of the ZOHAR, for which the good things of the Lord are ever in the Land of the Living.[4] (5) The word sacred belongs to all books of Scripture, but to the Song of Solomon in a peculiar manner: it is also the most beautiful book, even as the citron is fairest of all trees.[5] (6) Its versicles are subject to two hundred and sixteen interpretations, and they were communicated on one occasion by R. Eliezer to R. Abba.[6] (7) There is a Paradise on earth as well as a Paradise on high, and there is a celestial GEHENNON, even as there is a GEHENNON below. The hell which is above is the abode of Jews who have neither kept the Law nor

---

[1] Z., Appendix I, fol. 265b; II, p. 627.
[2] Ib., 270a; II, 637, 638.
[3] Ib.
[4] Ib., fol. 275a; II, 643.
[5] Ib., fol. 282; II, 653.
[6] Ib., Appendix III, 4b II, 678.

repented of their sins; the earthly hell is the place of the shadow of death, an eternal terror.[1]

My analysis of the ZOHAR, regarded as a literary document, has reached its utmost limit, and these specimens of extraneous or interpolated texts—howsoever we may choose to term them—must be held to serve for the whole. It should be added that a few only are omitted. Though he regarded the Mantua edition as *Codex correctus*, Rosenroth ingarnered all the tracts and fragments embraced by that of Cremona when he produced his own careful codex; but it must be remembered that the ZOHAR had in all probability grown under the hands of transcribers and makers of glosses during the space, approaching three centuries, which elapsed between its first promulgation and the date when it was first printed. We have no means of knowing how much of it was contained actually in the alleged script of Moses de Leon. The suspicion under which it has remained may be accounted for partly by its frequent quotation of unknown works which have been considered fictitious; but the ZOHAR was edited prior to the persecution of the Jews inaugurated by the atrocious edict of Ferdinand and Isabella, and many documents existing in Spain may have been destroyed during that fiery epoch. Again, it is impossible to say that Continental libraries contain no MSS. by which the excerpts of the ZOHAR might be justified. The unprinted literature of Jewry has been catalogued by various bibliographers, but no critical knowledge of its contents is possible by recourse to bibliographies. Let us take, for example, the passages from a commentary on the Song of Solomon, which is peculiar, as we have seen, to the Cremona *editio princeps*. These excerpts have not, I believe, been identified; but there is a manuscript in the Vatican Library which is mentioned by Buxtorf under the very same title, namely, MIDRASH HAZEETH.[2] It is the work, as he tells us, of an unknown author, but a uniform tradition assigns it to a Tanaite commentator, *circa* A.D. 100. The existence of such a work, of course, predicates nothing; but why should a commentary on the Song of Solomon be called MDRSh

---

[1] Z., fol. 2b; II, 686, 687. It should be mentioned that Rosenroth specifies passages drawn from MIDRASH RUTH in the Cremona edition of the ZOHAR, Part III, cols. 114, 124, 130, 174, 181, 184, 332, 330.

[2] Among later MS. commentaries, also in the Vatican, Bartolocci mentions that of R. Abraham ben Isaac Tze'mach Levi, the physician, and that of R. Immanuel ben Solomon written towards the end of the fifteenth century.

ChDzITh, which is understood as a reference to Proverbs xxii. 29? I speak under correction, but I know of no ground except in the idiosyncrasy of an author, and I am inclined to infer therefore that the same catchword would not have been used by two writers, but that the editor of the Zohar quoted the alleged Tanaite treatise.

XI.—THE ANCIENT AND LATER SUPPLEMENTS

The sudden appearance in public of a momentous work which either has or purports to have remained in concealment for several centuries may be expected to lead to the discovery or manufacture of continuations or connections thereof, and thus we have two series of Zoharic writings subsequent to the BOOK OF SPLENDOUR and distinguished as its Ancient and Later Supplements. When productions of this kind multiply their authenticity does not tend to assume a stronger guise, and the documents with which we shall deal in this section the reader will do well to regard as without determined claims. I should add, however, that considerable importance and authority have been ascribed always by Kabbalists to the ANCIENT SUPPLEMENTS, and according to Franck they have been known as long as the ZOHAR itself. They contain explanations of the term BRAShITh by R. Simeon ben Yohai after seventy different ways, and hence the work is divided into seventy chapters, with eleven further chapters added at the end. It was printed by Jacob ben Napthali at Mantua in 1557 under the editorship of Immanuele di Benevento, and appeared again at Cracovia.

Among notable matters in these ANCIENT SUPPLEMENTS we find the attribution of the members of the human body to the SEPHIROTH, whence the practical Magic of the West may have obtained later on its notion of Divine and Angelic Names ruling those members.[1] The apex of the head and brain is referred to KETHER, the brain as a whole to CHOKMAH, the heart to BINAH, the back and breast are attributed to TIPHERETH, the arms to CHESED and GEBURAH, the legs to NETZACH and HOD, the generative organs to JESOD, the feet to MALKUTH. Later Kabbalism recognises other corre-

---
[1] According to the ZOHAR itself the erect figure of humanity exhibits the letters of the TETRAGRAM superposed one upon the other. Part II, 42a, Mantua.

spondences, the arbitary nature of which is obscured sometimes by an appearance of methodical precision.

There are better things than this in the Supplements to the Zoharic books, and it may be well supposed that some out of all the seventy ways of interpreting the much-debated word which is rendered "beginning" in Genesis should be suggestive as well as curious. A single instance must, however, suffice. "'In the beginning God created.' This is the soul when it emerges from the bosom of its mother and is taught thereof. 'And the earth was without form, and void, and darkness was upon the face of the deep' (Gen. i. 2), because the eyes of the soul were closed. Hath it opened its eyes? 'And God said: Let there be light.' Hereafter man is gathered in from this world, and this then is written about the soul. 'And God said, Let the waters under the heaven be gathered unto one place, and let the dry land appear.' When the soul is removed from a man his body remains even as 'dry land.'"

That French school of occultism which was once beginning to recognise in the plays of Shakespeare a veiled scheme of initiation has, it must be admitted, an influential precedent in the biblical exegesis of the ZOHAR, of which the above passage seems to be a very neat instance, arbitrary beyond all words, and yet not without a certain grace of notion.

One of the most celebrated quotations from the ANCIENT SUPPLEMENTS is, however, the Prayer of Elijah, though it belongs only to the prefatory part.[1]

"Lord of the universe, One alone art Thou, but not according to number. Thou art the most sublime of all that is sublime, the most withdrawn of all things concealed, and conception cannot attain Thee. Thou hast produced ten forms which we call SEPHIROTH, and Thou guidest by means of these the unknown and invisible as well as the visible worlds. In them Thou dost veil Thyself and, permeated by Thy presence, their harmony knows not change. Whosoever shall regard them as divided one from another, it shall be accounted unto him as if he dismembered Thy unity. These ten SEPHIROTH are developed in successive gradations, so that one is long, another short and the third intermediate between them; but Thou art He who ruleth them, and

---

[1] Namely, the beginning of the second preface.

whether from above or below art guided Thyself by none. Thou hast provided the SEPHIROTH with garments which serve human souls as intermediate phases; Thou hast veiled them with bodies, so-called in comparison with their encompassing vestures, and taken together they correspond to the members of the human form. . . . Thou art the Lord of worlds, Foundation of all foundations, the Cause of all causes; Thou dost water the Tree from that source which spreads life everywhere, as the soul spreads it through the body. But Thou hast Thyself neither image nor form in all that is within or without. Thou didst create heaven and earth, that which is above and that which is below, with the celestial and terrestial hosts. All this didst Thou do that the worlds might know Thee. . . . Yet no one can conceive Thee in Thy reality; we confess only that apart from Thee, whether above or below, there can be no unity, and that Thou art Lord of all. Each SEPHIRA possesses its allotted name, after which angels are also called, but none describes Thyself, the One alone, Who dost all names inform, to all impart their force and their reality. Didst Thou withdraw therefrom, they would be left like bodies devoid of souls. Thou art wise, yet not with positive wisdom; thou art intelligent, but not with a definitive intelligence, nor hast Thou a fixed place; though all these things are attributed to Thee, so that man may conceive Thine omnipotence and may be shewn how the universe is guided by means of severity and mercy. If therefore a right or a left side or if any centre be named, it is only to exhibit Thy government of the entire universe by comparison with human actions, but not because any attribute can be really imputed to Thee corresponding either to mercy or severity."

The distinction between God and His attributes, and hence between God and the SEPHIROTH, which in a manner are His attributes emanated, is insisted on elsewhere in the Supplements by the help of a striking illustration :

" Woe unto those whose hearts are so hardened, whose eyes so blinded, that they regard God as the totality of His attributes; they are like unto a madman who should describe the King as the totality of his insignia. Behold a king wears his insignia only that he may be known through them, and verily, the King of Kings, the Concealed of all the hidden, the Cause of all causes, is disguised in a splendid garment so only that He may be known thereby, and thereby may impart to the dwellers on this earth a conception of His sacred nature." [1]

This distinction has at first sight an appearance of considerable profundity, but perhaps in the last analysis it is rather childish than otherwise, for it is obvious that even in our finite humanity there is a latent and unseen nature behind all its manifested characteristics. Man is not exhausted by any description of his attributes, and to insist that this is true also of God seems scarcely necessary.

From what has been quoted above it will be seen that the ANCIENT SUPPLEMENTS are identical in their teachings with the ZOHAR itself, as they are in resemblance throughout, from a documentary and literary standpoint; and some affirm that the original work had existed from time immemorial at Fez in Africa.[2] We have no means of checking this statement, nor is there any authority for supposing with Isaac Myer that the tracts were brought thither by disciples of Rab Hay, the Gaon of the Sages of Chirvan on the Caspian Sea.[3] There is, on the other hand, no need to say that hostile critics make use of weak points in the ANCIENT SUPPLEMENTS as if there were no distinction between these and the ZOHAR proper.

In the section on the bibliographical content of the BOOK OF SPLENDOUR we have seen what is broadly embraced by the NEW ZOHAR—ZOHAR HADASH—namely, a sequel to the HIDDEN COMMENTARY, certain additional Supplements, a Commentary on the Song of Solomon, and another on the Book of Lamentations. It was published at Cracow in 1703, or subsequently to the KABBALA DENUDATA, by Isaac ben Abraham of Neustadt. Its history seems entirely unknown. It may be noted also that later still Isaac ben Moses of Satanow, though otherwise of some literary repute, is said to have produced a forged ZOHAR which may have deceived a few persons, but it was unmasked speedily. It is difficult to conceive what is meant by the denomination "forged" in connection with a memorial which has been so described from the beginning by hostile critics, and I have failed to find particulars of the work.

---

[1] SUPPLEMENT, 21.

[2] Compare the statement which rests on the authority of the SUPPLEMENTS, that the revelation in full of the ZOHAR is reserved for the end of time. It will be the work of Moses. The prediction is utilised by Karppe (*op. cit.*, p. 323) to picture Moses de Leon, the alleged concealed author, as bringing forward himself and his work as a new prophet bearing a new revelation.

[3] PHILOSOPHY OF IBN GEBIROL, p. 47.

BOOK V

THE DOCTRINAL CONTENT OF THE KABBALAH IN RESPECT OF GOD AND THE UNIVERSE

BOOK V

THE DOCTRINAL CONTENT OF THE KABBALAH

I.—THE MAJESTY OF GOD IN KABBALISM

FROM a study of the documents at large, their age and general nature, from the names, traditional and otherwise, connected with these, but leaving over expositors of the Secret Tradition in its later developments, the research passes now to the Tradition itself, which is the subject-matter of the next four Books. The first will be dedicated to the Kabbalistic idea of God and the evolution of the universe; the second to the soul in man and the hypothesis of extra-mundane spiritual essences; the third to a consideration of the ways of God with man, from Paradise to the resurrection state; and the fourth to those deeper questions which are concerned with the Holy Shekinah and the Mystery of Sex.

A conventional division of Kabbalistic doctrines into metaphysical and physical has been proposed from time to time, and it serves for purposes of tabulation; but it must not be held to signify that there is a clear line of demarcation in virtue of which the literature branches off into divergent paths, much less that the Kabbalah offers a natural history of the universe. Its physics, so far as it can be said to have any, are transcendental physics. Admitting of no separation between God, Man and Nature,[1] the science which explains them is likewise one, and the best manner of studying it is to follow its view as to the eternal order. It begins in that Absolute which it is the purpose of all fundamental wisdom to make known or communicate to man; it attempts to exhibit the transition from the Absolute to the related, from the noumenal to the phenomenal, and to establish a chain of

---

[1] That is to say, the mystic communication is permanent, but the pantheistic doctrine of identity is quite foreign to the real position of Kabbalism.

correspondence between the infinite and the finite. It is, however, more than a philosophical attempt to bridge over the gulf which separates the timeless from the temporal; that is the side on which it connects with philosophy, as understood commonly. The intermediaries of the transition are, moreover, the ladder of ascent by which man returns to the Divine; and hence it is more than an explanation of the universe: it is, speaking correctly, a sum of religion, and as it is founded, no matter how, on those Scriptures which Jew and Christian have recognised equally as the peculiar revelation of God, the text-book of true religion, we shall see readily what depth and mystery are sought to be infused by the Kabbalah into the Bible. We shall realise also that it is described most adequately as a system of Theosophy, an application of the wisdom of Israel to the Mystery of God, beginning, as we might have expected, with a confession that it is unsearchable, that beyond our highest conceptions of all that is most divine, as beyond so many veridic illusions, there is the unknown and unknowable God.[1] Even in the mystical communication possible between the divine and man, which is an old doctrine of Jewish Mysticism, long anterior to the ZOHAR, at least in its present form, the essence escapes our apprehension. We can indeed know God, but not as He is in Himself, our knowledge being made possible—*ex hypothesi* —through the manifestation of the Deity, and this takes place after two manners—by the mediation of the Law of Nature, that is to say, in the physical universe; and by the Law of Grace, which is the manifestation of God in his relation with the souls of his elect. It will be seen that both these methods are sacramental, and the sacramental system is the outward vesture or form of all Mysticism. For the Kabbalistic Jew the Law and the Covenant were signs or mysteries capable of a plurality of interpretations, while the whole outward world was omen and metaphrasis. It is to be expected therefore that in the written word we must look for another meaning than is conveyed by the outward sense. It was also a part of Jewish mental bias to look for an inward significance which

---

[1] According to the ZOHAR, it is impossible to know that which there is in this Principle, for it never stoops to our ignorance and is above even wisdom. See THE LESSER HOLY SYNOD, when treating, for example, of the *Caput quod non est caput . . ., quod non comprehenditur Sapientia nec intellectu.* KABBALÆ DENUDATÆ TOMUS SECUNDUS, p. 528. Compare De Pauly's version in SEPHER HA ZOHAR, Vol. VI, p. 83.

was opposed to the external, and strikes unfailingly the modern observer as strained and unnatural.

In the eternity which preceded either of the manifestations that have been mentioned, the Deity was withdrawn into Himself and subsisted after a manner which transcends entirely the conception of human faculties.[1] It is said that the Glory of the Holy One is so sublime and so highly exalted that it remains eternally secret: no man can penetrate the deeps of Divine Wisdom. The place of its exaltation is unknown to men and angels [2]; and this is held to be intimated by the prophet when he said: "Blessed be the Glory of the Lord from His place." The Names which are ascribed to the Deity in this abyssal condition are not Names which present either the condition or the Divine Nature: they are conventions of the philosophical hypothesis; they are terms which serve to indicate that God, prior to manifestation, is nameless, even as He is beyond reach.[3] He is the Ancient One, and the most Ancient of all the Ancients, but this describes only the eternity of His subsistence; and He is the Hidden of all the Hidden Ones, but this concerns only His concealment. We are led in this manner to the Doctrine of the Infinite, as it finds expression in the ZOHAR on the Mystery of AIN SOPH, or the Divine Essence abiding in the simplicity and undifferentiation of perfect unity. The Latin equivalent is *fine carens*,[4] that is to say, without end; but it includes also by the separate significance of the word AIN, an abstract conception of nothingness, as a last attempt to register the ineffable nature of an infinite mode.[5] AIN SOPH is under-

---

[1] The tract entitled THE FAITHFUL SHEPHERD, which forms part of the ZOHAR, says, on the authority of R. Simeon ben Yohai, that before God created the archetypal idea which underlies the form of the world, He was alone, without form or similitude, and hence there could be no cognition of Him. See RAAIAH MEHEMNAH, in the Cremona edition of the Zohar, pt. ii. col. 73. Compare De Pauly's version, Vol. III, p. 192. There was, of course, no intelligence to comprehend Him; but the idea behind the confusion may be that the supposed period of God's immemorial rest is now beyond realisation by the human mind. We are unable to think of a state or period in which the world was not, but God alone. It is to be understood, however, that the essence of the subject escapes not only in this attempt to simplify, but also in the Zoharic position. God in the uttermost transcendence is eternally in this state which is postulated here as prior to creation.

[2] Z., Pt. I, fol. 103a; II, 18. See also Ezek. iii. 12.

[3] The interrogative pronoun *Who?* is ascribed by the ZOHAR to this state of the Supreme. Earlier Mysticism speaks of God being alone with his Name, *i.e.*, the DIVINE TETRAGRAM, which, according to Maimonides, preceded the whole creation.

[4] *Apparatus in Librum Sohar pars prima*, KABBALA DENUDATA, vol. i. p. 81.

[5] Zoharic teaching affirms this point specifically. We have just seen, according to the FAITHFUL SHEPHERD, that prior to the creation of the world, God was alone, formless and resembling nothing. It is added that in this state it is forbidden to

stood, moreover, as the limitless mystery of Divine Thought, the centre of all and the secret of all secrets.[1] The pregnant references to this state of Deity are comparatively few in the ZOHAR,[2] and we have seen that it is unknown to the BOOK OF FORMATION which preceded it. The first developments are in commentaries on that work and in the School of Isaac the Blind.[3]

According to the BOOK OF CONCEALMENT, His dwelling is the place which is not a place, or more literally, *locus qui non est*. We are here on familiar ground, with many echoes of the past about us, and it may seem even for a moment that the ZOHAR is translating pseudo-Dionysius into its own terms of symbolism.[4] The *Non-Ens* dwelling in the *Non Est* is a metaphysical subtlety which seeks, by successively stripping off every attribute pertaining to manifest existence, to attain some idea of unmanifest, unconditioned, abstract being. It is the TRACT ON MYSTICAL THEOLOGY in another form of language, but after all varied slightly, and behind this little book of the supposed Areopagite lies all the field of Neoplatonic speculation. But after the ZOHAR there came its commentators, with power to methodise and materialise all that came into their hands, and among them is R. Moses of Cordova,[5] who affirms that the Cause of Causes is called AIN SOPH because His excellence is without bound, and there is nothing which can comprehend Him. This is mere repetition; but it must

---

represent Him by any image, even by His Holy Name, or by any letter or any point.—ZOHAR, ii., 42*b*, Mantua.

[1] Z., Pt. I, fol. 21a; De Pauly, I, 129. LIBER OCCULTATIONIS, *seu Mysterii*, c. i. § 5. KABBALA DENUDATA, vol. ii. p. 348. Compare, however, De Pauly's rendering, vol. iv. p. 157.

[2] They are pregnant, however, because of TSURE, being the Supernal part of the soul.

[3] It is important to establish this point because of confusions created on the subject by several writers. In those portions of the ZOHAR which were translated into Latin by Rosenroth he has added interlinear commentary which gives a false impression as to the recurrence of the doctrine throughout the text. Franck (LA KABBALE, pp. 173–176) introduces the term AIN SOPH in the course of a Zoharic excerpt which is by no means direct translation. Lastly, Mathers (THE KABBALAH UNVEILED, 1887), who failed to render even Rosenroth's Latin correctly, produces the latter's annotations with additions of his own and increases the confusion further.

[4] The antecedents of Zoharic doctrine in past theosophies are of necessity outside my whole proposition, except where occasion offers a brief intimation from sources ready to the hand. There are obvious limits to a study of this kind. Such an undertaking, moreover, would demand qualifications to which I make no claim, and it is somewhat late on my part to serve another apprenticeship. Special proficiency is not required, of course, to recognise in how many quarters the great vistas open.

[5] PARDES RIMMONIM, *i.e.*, *Paradise of Pomegranates*, Tract iii. c. i. Moses of Cordova belonged to the more modern school of Kabbalists, and his treatise is exegetical, not authoritative in Kabbalism.

be admitted that later Kabbalism has occasional developments of consequence respecting AIN SOPH. It was located above KETHER in the Sephirotic Tree, and this first SEPHIRA—sphere or numeration—was regarded as the Throne of Ineffable Deity. It is added that AIN SOPH dwells in the hiddenness thereof.[1]

It will be seen that the Kabbalistic conception is one which is familiar to later forms of speculative philosophy under the name of the Absolute, a term, in the last analysis, which is not wanting in similar intellectual difficulties, or, rather, symbolises our intellectual recognition of that which exceeds our intelligence.[2] In this Absolute resides the essence or potentiality of all [3]; it is not accurate to say that it is the Subsistent Principle which underlies the objective state termed existence, because existence is a condition of the finite and the created, though there is a true and real sense in which God is held to encompass and indwell the whole visible world.[4] AIN SOPH is the subsistent state of Deity itself,[5] whence it follows that there is from the Kabbalistic standpoint a manifested state of the Divine Nature, and this is certainly not the visible world. How this manifestation occurs will be indicated in the next section.

It will be obvious that all ordinary notions of a personal God are transcended by this *Non-Ens* or *Non-Ego* of the Kabbalists. It is absolutely simple, unity without any multiplication, above all number, above Wisdom, which, as we shall see, is, however, one of its first emanations. It is also without sex, and it is therefore, strictly speaking, inaccurate to make use of the masculine pronouns in reference thereto. According to Moses of Cordova, the angels are

---

[1] See KABBALA DENUDATA: *Apparatus in Librum Sohar, Pars Prima*, p. 81.

[2] See, however, Dr. Noah Porter: THE HUMAN INTELLECT, London, 1868, who argues that in its proper definition the Absolute becomes knowable. Our idea of the Absolute belongs, nevertheless, to that region of our consciousness which Herbert Spencer terms indefinite and escaping formulation.

[3] Hœne Wronski, whose mathematical transcendentalism was once at least of high authority with French students of Kabbalism, affirms that the reality of the Absolute is the first principle of reason, and in the absence thereof every assertion made by reason would be valueless. On this principle, as on an indispensable condition, he establishes "absolute philosophy" in his work entitled APODICTIQUE.

[4] According to the ZOHAR, God is immanent in all that has been created or emanated, and yet is transcendent to all.

[5] It has been described absurdly by S. L. Macgregor Mathers as "negative existence." See THE KABBALAH UNVEILED, which embodies a translation of three Zoharic texts from the Latin of Rosenroth, as already noted. So far back as 1867 Herbert Spencer established clearly in his FIRST PRINCIPLES that "the Unconditioned must be represented as positive and not negative."

neither simple nor without multiplication in comparison with it. The book entitled FAITHFUL SHEPHERD [1] says: "Woe unto him who makes God to be like unto any mode or attribute whatever, even if it be one of His own; but woe still more if he make Him like unto the sons of men, whose elements are earthly, and so are consumed and perish! There can be no conception attained of Him, except in so far as He manifests Himself when exercising dominion by and through some attribute. Abstracted from this there can be no attribute, conception or ideal of Him. He is comparable only to the sea, filling some great reservoir, as, for example, its bed in the earth, wherein it fashions for itself a certain concavity, so that thereby we may begin to compute the dimensions of the sea itself."

To sum up now on the whole subject, the ZOHAR testifies (1) that God is essentially without form,[2] but in His manifestation He is seen or discerned under different aspects, according to a scale of degrees, which will be unfolded hereafter in a study of the Paths of Wisdom. (2) That the most secret of all Mysteries is that which is called Nothing,[3] being the Most Holy Ancient, from whom the Light flows forth.[4] This notwithstanding, it is affirmed (3) that in the essence of the Infinite there are neither intentions nor lights, nor brightness,[5] and the explanation is that although every light emanates therefrom, they are not in that state of clear shining which would enable man to grasp the nature of the Infinite: it is a Supreme Will. (4) That, again this fact notwithstanding, the holocaust, which has for its object an union effected with the Holy of Holies, ascends to AIN SOPH, because all perfection

---

[1] Quoted in BETH ELOHIM, or the HOUSE OF THE GODS, *Disertatio* i. c. i. See KABBALA DENUDATA, vol. ii.; *Partis Tertiæ Tractatus* i., *i.e.*, *Pneumatica Kabbalistica*, p. 187. But see De Pauly's translation, Vol. III, p. 193. It is much shorter and affirms that the forms under which God manifests are merely subjective.

[2] Z., Pt. I, 275a; II, 644. The text derives its authority in the usual amazing manner from the SONG OF SOLOMON, vii. 11, 12: "Come, my beloved, let us go forth into the field; let us lodge in the villages. Let us get up early to the vineyards; let us see if the vine flourish." This is contrasted with a Talmudic story concerning the son of Zoma, one of the four persons who penetrated into the Mysterious Garden; but he remained on the hither side of the vineyard, which is taken to mean that he did not enter the Paths of Supreme Wisdom.

[3] *Ib.*, 64b; III, 283. It is founded on Ex. xvii. 7: "They tempted the Lord, saying, Is the Lord among us, or not?"—which is supposed to contain a distinction between the Ancient and Jehovah, contrary of course to the unity of God, whether manifest or unmanifest.

[4] *Ib.*, 43b; III, 194.

[5] *Ib.*, Pt. II, 239a; IV, 267.

must tend to fusion with the Mysterious Unknown,[1] which is the Object of all desires, though in AIN SOPH there are no desires, even while they subsist only by reason thereof. (5) That AIN SOPH is symbolised by the letter ALEPH.[2] It seems to follow that later Kabbalism was well within the measures of the symbolism when it posited AIN SOPH as a Hidden Light above KETHER, at the head of the Sephirotic Tree.

II.—THE TEN SEPHIROTH

Having postulated the existence of the Absolute and the Unconditioned, the next concern of the Kabbalah is the mode of the manifestation of that withdrawn and inconceivable nature. Having attained its ultimate and fundamental conception of the Deity by the process of elimination to which reference has been made already, it was inevitable that the attribution of absolute reality to that which had been stripped of all realism should have produced as a result something which was outside intellectual comprehension, the fact notwithstanding that its methodical and elaborated antithesis of anthropomorphism was as much a convention of the human mind as that which it sought to replace. The intellectual difficulty became a ground for exaltation of the conception at the expense of the human mind by which it had been devised so laboriously.[3] Now, the Jew was confronted by at least two problems which called for the exercise of his further ingenuity as regards the *latens Deitas* of AIN SOPH. He had to account for the bond of connection between this abyss of the Godhead and the visible universe, having man for its mouthpiece; but so far this is only the common problem of all philosophy which begins and ends in the unconditioned. He had further a problem peculiar to his own inheritance and election, and this was to establish another bond of connection between the absolute transcendency of AIN SOPH, apart from all limitation, outside all human measurement, isolated from all relationship, and the anthropomorphic Lord of Israel, whose stature and measurements were not beyond the ingenuity of rabbinical calculations, and most

---

[1] Z., Pt. II, 26b; V, 74, 75.
[2] *Ib.*, 257a; V, 597.
[3] The ZOHAR says that it is called AIN, not on the ground of nonentity, but, it may be inferred, because that which is wholly outside our knowledge is for us as nothingness.

of whose members are mentioned with sufficient fullness and frequency in the sacred writings for any devout student to possess a clear notion of the " body of God," and to describe it, did he please, and we have seen already that he did, with considerable minuteness, in a book dedicated to the question. For the moment, however, we are concerned only with the first problem, namely, the difficulty of conceiving why the abyssal state in which God unmanifest had been sufficient from eternity to Himself should at any period have had another mode superadded to it. I say superadded by convention based on the notion of sufficiency; it is not an adequate term to make use of in such a relation, to which no terminology is suitable. The *non ens* dwelling in the *non est* is like the cipher of the decimal system [1]; of itself it is nothing, and its extension produces nothing; so also it is not possible to add to it, but it gives power to all numbers. The solution offered by Kabbalism does not differ materially from that which has been given by other philosophies and religions which postulate a First Cause. It is, in a word, the movement of the Divine Will. " In this," says Myer, " the Unknown Absolute, above all number, manifested itself through an emanation in which it was immanent, yet as to which it was transcendental." [2] We are dealing here with a system of speculative philosophy, and, traditional or otherwise, it must not be supposed to be free from the disabilities of other philosophies or from the crudities of its particular period. The Kabbalistic hypothesis supposes an eternity antecedent to this initial operation of the Divine Will, and in the latent subsistence of AIN SOPH it would appear an inconsequence to assume that there was either will [3] or consciousness possible.[4] Both, however, by a common and almost inevitable anachronism, are attributed to AIN SOPH, despite the warning of the ZOHAR already quoted : " Woe unto him who shall compare Him with any mode or attribute, even with one of his own." [5] The later commentators on the

---

[1] The circle is, in fact, a Kabbalistic symbol of AIN SOPH.
[2] PHILOSOPHY OF IBN GEBIROL, p. 266.
[3] The ZOHAR, however, says expressly that " in the beginning was the will of the King."
[4] " Exceeding comprehension it must be regarded as the *non-Ego* rather than the *Ego*. All that is in man depends from it, but it transcends consciousness ; it transcends what we conceive by the terms personal and individual." Myer: PHILOSOPHY OF IBN GEBIROL.
[5] Z., Pt. II, RAAIAH MEHEMNA, col. 73, Cremona edition. See also Mantua edition, Pt. II, 42b.

ZOHAR either do not recognise or are content to ignore the difficulty. Thus a treatise entitled THE ROYAL VALLEY, by Rabbi Naphthali Hirtz, says: "Blessed be His Holy Name! Before anything was, He, by His simple will, proposed to Himself to fashion the worlds. For the King is not given without the people, as it is written in Proverbs xiv. 28: 'In the multitude of the people is the King's honour.' And it is the nature of the supreme Goodness to dispense good. Now, if the world were not, on whom could He bestow it?"[1] The exegetical literature, treatises like GATES OF LIGHT, indicate that the exertion of Divine Will in the production of the emanations is a path so secret that no creature, not even Moses himself, can understand it.[2] At the same time, that will is *beneplacitum*, or good pleasure, and *beneplacitum termino carens*, without end or limit. Hence the motive by which the universe is accounted for is the same motive which communicates the mercy of God to them that fear Him, after which it will be unnecessary to say that optimism is a fundamental characteristic of Kabbalism, or that, according to the ZOHAR, this is, in some respects, the best of all possible worlds, as affirmed by Robert Southey.

Seeing then that the transition of the Divine Being from the state of the *non ens* was accomplished, like the conversion of man from the condition of a merely material creature, by an operation of the mystery of will, we have next to ascertain something of the nature of such process, and we are brought back in this manner to the word which I have had occasion to cite already, namely, emanation.[3] The Kabbalah repudiates implicitly the axiom *ex nihilo nihil fit*, for the *non ens* dwelling in

---

[1] KABBALA DENUDATA, tom. ii., *partis primæ tractatus secundus*, § 1, *De Mundo Infinito primo*, p. 152.
[2] KABBALA DENUDATA, tom. i., *Apparatus in Librum Sohar pars prima*, pp. 691, 692.
[3] In which the idea of pantheism is almost always, but not, I think, of necessity, involved. There is, of course, a certain sense in which that notion is not escaped even on the hypothesis of creation, and further there is a higher sense of pantheism from which no true Theosophist could wish to escape. But as regards Jewish Mysticism, while there is always some doubt in what way it made use of the term emanation, there seems to me no question that its system does not answer to what is commonly understood by pantheism, though it has often a pantheistic aspect. God was all for the Kabbalist, as he is for the Christian, and yet no Theosophical Jew, any more than the orthodox Christian theologian, would admit that God was one with the material world. When, therefore, Solomon Munk: DICTIONNAIRE DE LA CONVERSATION, says that the Kabbalah issued from the amalgamation of oriental pantheism with the religion of the Hebrews, we can accept this only by supposing that the pantheism in question had suffered a peculiar alteration.

the unconditioned state, wherein is neither time nor place,[1] is the fullness which contains the all. *Ex plenitudine ista omnia fiunt.* In this Divine Plenitude pre-existing eternally was the substance of all the worlds, which therefore came forth from God. Hence the Kabbalistic system is broadly one of emanation.[2] When it is said that emanation is not its only foundation, for it rests also on the identity of thought and existence,[3] or otherwise the doctrine of Divine Immanence, there is much in the literature which combines to enforce this view, after due allowance has been made for the confusion and obscurity of the originals.[4] But that which is more to our purpose and rests on Zoharic authority is that the idea of emanation belongs more especially to the Divine Nature unfolding from within Itself, that it may be revealed ultimately to and within an external universe, the relation of which to God is not that of a symbolic globe held in a king's hand, nor even a veil or a vesture, but rather a cosmic sacrament, of which He is the inward power and He the abiding grace. For the rest, at the moment it is enough to say that after the World of Emanation there is a Kabbalistic World of Creation.

The first consequence which followed the operation of Divine Will was the manifestation or unfolding of the Divine Attributes—in a word, the transition of Deity from the latent to the active mode, so far as any of these terms can be used in respect of a state where there was no universe in which manifestation could take place, no created intelligence to cognise it, and no objective for action. As in the postulated state of latency, God was above all number, so in the subsequent activity He is held to have produced numbers, and the decade— in the sense of the SEPHIROTH—is brought forth from AIN SOPH. We must not be so crude as to suppose that mere arithmetical numerals are here intended: it was powers, forces, vitalities, virtues, attributes, principles, which were thus produced or unfolded, and these are the ten SEPHIROTH,

---

[1] "The No-Thing is not, however, an absolute negative or void, but some-Thing unknown to man." Myer: PHILOSOPHY OF IBN GEBIROL, p. 378. It should be added that Nahmanides was one of the few Kabbalists who maintained creation *ex nibilo*.

[2] In Book III, § 2, we have seen that this statement is subject to a reservation regarding the most ancient document of the Kabbalah, and it should be noted in this connection that at least one capable writer has rejected the general view, and does not regard the Kabbalah as a system of emanation. See Joel: PHILOSOPHIE RELIGIEUSE DU ZOHAR.

[3] Isaac Myer: PHILOSOPHY OF IBN GEBIROL, p. 266.

[4] That is to say, the terms emanation, creation, formation and such like, signifying distinct ideas, are used somewhat indiscriminately by the Kabbalists.

THE TEN SEPHIROTH

which are tabulated as follows with their curious conventional titles:[1]

I. כתר = KETHER, the Supreme Crown.
II. חכמה = CHOKMAH, Wisdom.
III. בינה = BINAH, Intelligence or Understanding.
IV. חסד = CHESED, Mercy, otherwise גדולה = GEDULAH, Magnificence or Benignity and Greatness.
V. גבורה = GEBURAH, Severity, Judgment, Awe, Power.
VI. תפארת = TIPHERETH, Beauty.
VII. נצח = NETZACH, Victory.
VIII. הוד = HOD, Glory.
IX. יסוד = YESOD, the Foundation.
X. מלכות = MALKUTH, the Kingdom.

The conjunction of CHOKMAH and BINAH produced a quasi-emanation called DAATH, knowledge, but it is not one of the SEPHIROTH.[2]

To these ten emanations or numerations various profound meanings are attached; indeed, the study of the Kabbalistic system of the SEPHIROTH [2] constitutes a research by itself, and one which is full of complexity; but we are not engaged here in its exhaustive presentation or with more than its elementary symbolism.[3] We are concerned, in a word, not with what it may have been designed to conceal for the benefit of a presumed circle of initiates, which is the claim implied by the ZOHAR, but with what it was intended to explain, and this explanation may offer some warrant for concluding that outside it there is only a wider province of fantasy.

Beyond a certain point it is not allowable to suppose a double meaning in any literature; the theory of many-sided allegories does credit chiefly to the ingenuity of the critic,

---

[1] Azriel, in his work on the Song of Solomon, terms them "measures and organs," and in the ZOHAR itself they appear as divine emanated essences.

[2] A term derived from a word signifying "to number," though late Kabbalists offer other etymologies, as, for example, the Greek σφαῖρα. The singular is SEPHIRA. The emanations are regarded as vessels, receptacles of the Divine Power and attributes as they developed, and there is no doubt that these vessels were usually considered spherical. See especially the treatise BETH ELOHIM concerning KETHER, in which the idea of circularity is involved. The author of the GATES OF LIGHT refers the term to the Hebrew word signifying sapphire, which stone, on account of its brightness and purity, is a symbol of the SEPHIROTH. Other rabbinical authorities have supported this view. See Jellinek: BEITRÄGE ZUR GESCHICHTE DER KABBALA. Leipsic, 1851.

[3] See Appendix I.

and of its general value we have had a typical instance in Talmudic exegesis.[1]

The initial purpose of the Sephirotic system was undoubtedly to provide intermediaries between the Deity and the material world. It is that of all doctrines of emanation. But while we set aside conjectures for which no warrant is produced we must be careful not to fall into the opposite error. To bridge the gulf between the finite and the infinite, and to effect a correspondence by stages between the inconceivable purity of the Divine Nature and the uncleanness attributed to matter by all the old Theosophies, was not the sole purpose of the Sephirotic system, a point which is sometimes missed by the merely academical critic.

It is affirmed by hostile writers, for example, by Dr. Ginsburg,[2] that as the earliest Kabbalistic literature does not contain the doctrine of AIN SOPH, so also it wants that of the SEPHIROTH; but it is above challenge that the germ of the Sephirotic scheme must be sought in SEPHER YETZIRAH. The ten numerations of that treatise are, in fact, SEPHIROTH, and it seems quite impossible to maintain a contrary opinion.[3]

III.—THE DOCTRINE OF THE FOUR WORLDS

The Sephirotic system was concerned first of all, as I have indicated, with the mystery of Divine Evolution. From that unsearchable condition which is above consciousness, by a mysterious operation, the Uncreated Will moved forthward, and certain manifestations or relations of Deity became established. By a kind of flowing forth or emanation, there were produced Four Worlds in succession,[4] and as it happens that the developments of these are chiefly in later Kabbalism,

---

[1] After an exhaustive study of modern esoteric literature, I doubt much whether even French occultism of the late nineteenth century really concerned itself with the discovery of a concealed sense in the Kabbalah. It is a sufficient exercise of patience to codify and harmonise the outward sense, which is assuredly not removed. Take, for example, the conception of AIN SOPH: even the fantasiast Éliphas Lévi does not look for any notion more withdrawn than that of Divine Latency therein. The inner meaning of the Kabbalah is its proper and single sense, which has been confused by an obscurity of style and subject.

[2] More especially in his article, s.v. Kabbalah, contributed to the third edition of Kitto's CYCLOPÆDIA OF BIBLICAL LITERATURE.

[3] William Postel, the first translator of SEPHER YETZIRAH, indubitably regarded the Ten Numerations as identical with the SEPHIROTH of more evolved Kabbalism.

[4] The earliest description of these Worlds is found in a TREATISE ON EMANATION—MASSEKET ATZILUTH—which belongs to the twelfth century and has been described as the earliest literary product of the Speculative Kabbalah.

being very elaborate therein, it is desirable to see exactly what is said upon the subject in the fountain text. The references are in summary form as follows: (1) There is a Sephirotic degree entitled MALKUTH, and it seems clear that to what world soever this name is allocated, one SEPHIRA alone is signified, being that which is tenth in numeration and is actually called MALKUTH,[1] signifying the Kingdom. (2) It is testified that Scripture makes use of the three expressions " to create, to form and to make "[2] in allusion to the three worlds which are below the World of Emanation.[3] It follows that the Four Worlds are those of Emanation, Creation, Formation and Manifestation, otherwise Action, the material universe, or as it is called by Rosenroth *Mundus Factionis*.[4] The Hebrew equivalents are ATZILUTH, BRIAH, YETZIRAH and ASSIAH. (3) The union of God and His Shekinah takes place as we shall see in ATZILUTH,[5] the World of Emanation, where there is no separateness; the angels of BRIAH form the body of Shekinah,[6] when she descends therein, and this World is called the region of the Throne. It is said that the princes of Israel, the wise, the intelligent, the zealous, heroes, men of truth, prophets, just men and kings are all from the World of Emanation, but there are others from the World of Creation, whereof Shekinah is the sacrifice. This is not to be taken literally, as there can be no call to say. (4) There is also a reference to three Worlds of Divine Hiddenness.[7] The first can be neither seen nor discerned and is known only to Him Who is concealed therein; I suppose that this alludes to AIN SOPH. The second is attached to the first and the Holy One is manifested therein: it is presumably ATZILUTH. The third is the beginning of division, signifying created intelligence, and is the world of

---

[1] Z., Pt. I, 18a; I, 112. MALKUTH is supposed to be designated by the word " bow," when it is said: " I do set my bow in the cloud."—Gen. ix. 13.

[2] *Ib.*, Part I, fol. 179b; II, 298.

[3] I conceive that this must be understood in a dual sense. Divinity in the world of ATZILUTH is God in the Hiddenness and yet moving towards manifestation, because this Deific mode not only can be but is conceived, however remotely, by the human mind. Beyond is the unknowable mode of AIN SOPH, from which it emanates. But there is a state of emanation in ATZILUTH, although it is a World of Unity, for God and His Shekinah in Kether are brought forth, so to speak, into CHOKMAH and BINAH as ABBA and AIMA, the Father in Supernal Wisdom and the Mother in Supernal Understanding.

[4] KABBALA DENUDATA: *Apparatus, Pars Prima*, p. 12.

[5] Z., Pt. III, fol. 109b; V, 276.

[6] *Ib.* The Angel METATRON is called the vesture of Shekinah.

[7] *Ib.*, fol. 159a; V, 411, 412.

the superior angels: it is therefore BRIAH, according to later Kabbalism.

For the Sons of the Doctrine the Four Worlds of their conception were understood not only in their first or universal sense but in a manner particular to themselves, from which point of view the worlds in their synthesis are symbolised, in later Kabbalism, by the Hebrew word פרדס = *Pardes*, signifying a Garden and understood as that of Paradise, the consonants of which—as we have seen—are the initial letters of four words signifying (*a*) the literal sense of the word of Scripture = פשוטה; (*b*) the symbolical sense = רמז; (*c*) the allegorical sense = דרוש; and (*d*) the mystical or Kabbalistic sense = סוד.[1] It was a question of correspondence and went to show in the eloquent manner of symbolism that the Divine Word is truly Divine in all its stages and that its study is an ascent from the world of manifested things to that of Deity. So also it was out of the literal sense of Scripture that the doctors derived their exalted notion of things unseen and of Him Who reigns not alone in the world to come but in this which we see with our eyes, Who fills them both and by Whom the soul is replenished on all the planes of being.

Now it follows from the Kabbalism of every period that these Four Worlds are subdivided into those ten spheres which are called SEPHIROTH or Numerations, and have been tabulated already in brief. Their further consideration will follow, but we are concerned at the moment with the way in which these spheres are allocated to the Worlds of Kabbalism. Now the ZOHAR speaks of three Supernal Degrees or Divine Hypostases, and the first of them is called KETHER.[2] It is said also that when the world of manifest things was in the state of TOHU, God revealed Himself therein under the Hypostasis SHADDAI; when it had proceeded to the condition called BOHU He manifested as the Hypostasis TSABAOTH; but when the darkness had disappeared from the face of things He appeared as Elohim. Hereto appertain the words: " And the spirit of God moved upon the face of the waters," [3] understood as a reference to the sweet and harmonious voice

---

[1] KABBALA DENUDATA: *Apparatus Pars Prima*, p. 12. The Sons of the Doctrine made up the worlds in their minds, and—for us at least—this is the sense of their claim that the story of creation is the history of the chosen people.
[2] Z., Pt. I, fol. 22b; I, 139.
[3] Gen. i. 2.

heard by Elijah and termed: "The Voice of the Lord is upon the waters."[1] This signifies the completion of the Sacred Name Jehovah. Hence in the vision of Elijah it is said that "the Lord (Jehovah) was not in the earthquake": it was Shaddai. He was not in the fire: this was Tsabbaoth; but He was in the still small voice, being that of the Spirit of Elohim, and the Name of Jehovah was complete.[2] It is said also that this Name is composed of four letters,[3] the relation of which to the Divine Essence is like that of the limbs to the human body[4]; but this notwithstanding, the Hypostases are three only. Now, as Kether is the first it is to be inferred that Chokmah and Binah constitute the other two, and the world of Atziluth or Emanation will be completed in these. They are symbolised by the three bars of the Hebrew letter Shin,[5] which also exhibits their essential unity. We may regard the point as determined by one further statement, according to which the First Light is symbolised by the Crown and the Second Light or Hypostasis forms the second Sephira. These lights appeared to Abraham,[6] and the third, which was seen by Jacob,[7] proceeds from the two first.[8]

It has been necessary to enter at some length into this involved subject because later Kabbalism has complicated almost inextricably the Worlds of the Zohar.[9] I proceed now to establish the following Sephirotic division as that which represents the mind of the original text. To the First World of Atziluth are referred Kether, Chokmah and Binah; to the Second World of Briah are allocated Chesed, Geburah and Tiphereth; Yetzirah comprises Netzach, Hod and Yesod; while Assiah is Malkuth, as I have said earlier in this study. The ten Sephiroth are contained therefore within the Four Worlds.

According to the Zohar, the Sephiroth are comparable to chariots for the Degrees of the Divine Essence, and the word Degrees, which is used very frequently in the text, illustrates after a simple manner the idea of gradations in the nature of the Presence, as the spheres of manifestation proceed further from the Head of the Tree. The Supernal World contains the highest Degrees of which the human mind can

---

[1] Ps. xxix. 3.
[2] I Kings xix. 11, 13.
[3] Z., Pt. I, fol. 16a; I, 97.
[4] Ib.
[5] Ib., Pt. III, 194a; V, 503.
[6] Gen. xviii. 1.
[7] Gen. xxxii. 31.
[8] Z., Pt. I, fol. 21a, b; I, 130, 131.
[9] See Appendix II.

conceive by the intellection of faith, and KETHER, CHOKMAH, BINAH form an unity therein. It will be seen from previous extracts that BRIAH is the World of created intelligence, though it would seem that its content flows over into YETZIRAH. The Third and the Fourth World are not described, though they are implied obviously, in the ZOHAR, and their names indicate that as in BRIAH God created the forms of consciousness to which He could manifest Himself by Divine Modes, so in YETZIRAH He produced the pattern, idea or archetype of the visible and material cosmos, referred to ASSIAH. The names allocated to the ten SEPHIROTH are on their surface conventional and arbitrary—at least in certain cases. We can recognise that MALKUTH is appropriate in respect of the visible world, and that KETHER is the crown or summit of the entire Sephirotic system. Mercy and severity will be found to explain the reason why they are ascribed to certain SEPHIROTH when arranged as what is called the Tree of Life in Kabbalism. YESOD has a deep significance which we shall come to understand later; but the names of NETZACH and HOD = Victory and Glory are without interpretation, even in later Kabbalism, which can be said to be of moment.

The source of Zoharic information respecting the ten SEPHIROTH or Numberings is—as we have seen—in the SEPHER YETZIRAH or BOOK OF FORMATION.[1] The sequence, however, seems arbitrary to the last degree, and I have found nothing in the ZOHAR which can be held to connect therewith. It should be observed that the names allocated to the SEPHIROTH are wanting in the early text, nor do I pretend to say when or in what work they are met with for the first time. Something will depend on the date to which we assign the ZOHAR itself: if it is earlier than the earliest commentaries on the SEPHER YETZIRAH—for example, that of Ha Levi—it may have been—for all that I know to the contrary—the authority for the ten names. We have met with a story which refers their invention to Isaac the Blind, and this shall stand at its value, because it has been said also that the ZOHAR itself was either his product or that of his school at Posquières.

It should be remembered further that the SEPHIROTH are

---

[1] The little text is mentioned twice in the ZOHAR. See Pt. II, fol. 187b, where it is quoted to prove that the SEPHIROTH are not eleven but ten, and *Ib.*, fol. 289a; IV, 315, where its authorship is referred to the patriarch Abraham, in accordance with Tradition. The English reader may consult the translation of Knut Stenring, *s.v.* THE BOOK OF FORMATION or SEPHER YETZIRAH, 1923.

represented as good and evil equally, which seems reasonable in respect of that world of dimensions wherein both principles manifest. The ZOHAR has developments of its own on this subject and something must be said of them later. The diagrams which represent the SEPHIROTH in the form of the Tree of Life are unknown to THE BOOK OF FORMATION, nor can they be deduced therefrom. Here also the origin is doubtful, but a certain form is met with in the ZOHAR, or perhaps it would be more accurate to say that it is implied continually therein. Passing to this work, I will give the indications suggesting the arrangement mentioned. There is firstly the Middle Pillar and there are the Right and Left sides, corresponding to Mercy and Severity. CHOKMAH is on the right of KETHER and BINAH on the left.[1] CHESED is the right and GEBURAH the left arm. NETZACH and HOD are the right and left hips, for the Tree in this case has become a human figure. The right side is life and the left is death.[2] The Pillars of Mercy and Severity are thus completed, according to the scheme of the Tree. The Middle Pillar is one of the Hypostases in the Divine Essence, and it is called the Perfect Pillar.[3] The light of the right side, which is active, enters therein, and so does the passive light of the left. The Word issues from this union, an allusion to the Divine Son, Who, according to another text, is begotten by ABBA and AIMA, the Holy Father and the Holy Mother in the World of the Supernals. Elohim forms the Middle Pillar and therein are the union and fecundity of the waters above and below, meaning Sephirotic degrees.[4] Children, life and the means of existence come therefrom [5]: it is " mine eldest son, Israel."[6] It is to be understood therefore that Israel is in the likeness of the Highest. The four rivers of Eden seem to be CHESED, GEBURAH, NETZACH and HOD.[7] The Middle Pillar is the Tree of Life, and perhaps the two other Pillars are together the Tree of Knowledge of Good and Evil—but it is all speculation and all is high convention, as well as a jumble of notions. There is no evil when these are united with the Central Pillar, which is called the seventh day,[8] the Sabbath and the tent of peace.[9] The Central Pillar is Shekinah. It is the peace in

[1] Z., Pt, fol. 26b; I, 164, 165.
[2] Ib., Pt. I, fol. 22b; I, 139.
[3] Ib., Pt. I, fol. 16b; I, 101.
[4] Ib., fol. 17a; I, 103.
[5] Ib., fol. 24a; I, 149.
[6] Exodus iv. 22.
[7] Z., fol. 28a; I, 165.
[8] Ib., fol. 47b; I, 276.
[9] Ib., fol. 48a; I, 279.

particular between the light of the right side and that which in another place is called the darkness of the left.[1] The TALMUD and the MISHNAH come from the Middle Pillar.[2] There are many alternative allocations, as for example, when the Middle Pillar is called the Son of YOD but also the HE, which is BINAH.[3] The Middle Pillar is otherwise the Master of the House.[4] It is said of the right arm that it draws the immensity of space in love, like the arm of the male drawing the female.[5] The law of faith is on the right side.[6] The left arm draws the immensity of space in rigour.[7] The serpent constitutes the left arm and thence emanates the impure spirit. It is the side of water and the side of sadness. These engender darkness and the way of escape is by the harmony which can be instituted between the Mercy or Grace of CHESED and the Severity of GEBURAH.[8] The left side is without pity in the state of separation,[9] yet she who is Matrona according to another allocation is the left side, as well as the Middle Pillar: she is the latter apparently because she is the ground and state of union, and it is known that she is the Mother of Mercy.[10] A day will come when the left side shall disappear and good will obtain only.[11] It is said further that the Mercy and Severity of CHESED and GEBURAH are united in TIPHERETH.[12] The Holy Degrees are declared to emanate from the holy side and the impure degrees from the impure side.[13] It follows that the ZOHAR bears out the thesis of SEPHER YETZIRAH when this work describes the SEPHIROTH as the abyss of good and evil. It gives no explanation which will help us to understand this, though it speaks in one place of the union between good and evil [14] as a secret or mystery and indicates in another that there is a sense in which the left side is on the way of attainment.[15] It was possibly the difficulties arising from the allocation of evil to spheres in which God was present everywhere [16] that led some later Kabbalists to

---

[1] Z., fol. 254a; II, 599.   [2] Ib., fol. 255a; II, 601.
[3] Ib., Pt. II, fol. 115b; III, 445. We shall see that from one point of view this is supported by an independent text, one of the most ancient imbedded in the ZOHAR; but the text-general presents a different aspect.
[4] Ib., III, 272a; VI, 37.   [10] Ib., fol. 250a; II, 584.
[5] Ib., Pt. I, fol. 64a; I, 375.   [11] Ib., Pt. II, fol. 190a; IV, 175.
[6] Ib., Pt. II, fol. 82a; III, 342.   [12] Ib., Pt. III, fol. 233a; V, 563.
[7] Ib., Pt. I, fol. 64a; I, 375.   [13] Ib., I, 203b; II, 409.
[8] Ib., Pt. II, fol. 103b; II, 21.   [14] Ib., Pt. II, fol. 34a; IV, 166.
[9] Ib., fol. 198b; II, 387.   [15] Ib., 60b; IV, 268; and 114b; III, 443.
[16] The mystery deepens when it is affirmed that there is no other God comprised outside the ten SEPHIROTH, and that Shekinah, Who is a Divine Hypostasis, dwells in each SEPHIRA.—Z., Pt. III, fol. 109b; V, 276.

suppose that the ten Sephiroth were repeated in each of the four worlds; but this development does not really deal with the point at issue, and as there is no further light thereon we must be content to pass it over, remembering that, almost in the words of the text, the Middle Pillar draws the right and left sides, the good and the evil together, in which union evil dissolves as such and the good obtains entirely under the name of Benignity—which is that of the Middle Pillar. It is a question of transmutation.

The conventional Tree of Life connects the Sephiroth together by means of lines which are called paths, being twenty-two in number, and these in connection with the Sephiroth themselves constitute the thirty-two paths of the Sepher Yetzirah. As there are several forms of the Tree according to different commentators, I have reproduced those which are regarded as of authority. They do not seem to represent the mind of the Zohar, and I have therefore added one which seems to be more in consonance, especially regarding the Supernals.[1] Serving only to reconcile several statements to which no vital consequence attaches, I am of opinion that the accepted forms are generally speaking preferable. We must remember that late Kabbalism arose to account for the difficulties, omissions and discrepancies which prevail in the fountain text, and though I have had occasion to make various strictures, these are without prejudice to the fact that the work as a whole was done with sincerity and zeal, whence it is helpful in respect of occasional conciliation and from time to time as reasonable extension and inference. There is one point, however, in which I believe that my diagram is more within the logic of the symbolism than are its alternatives in the printed text-books. It is a question of the right and the left sides, which are always presented from the observer's standpoint, so that Chokmah is on the right of him when he is looking at the figure, while Geburah is on his left. On the contrary, what seems intended obviously in the Zohar is right and left in the order of procession on the Tree, or on the path of descent into manifestation. The distinction may seem unimportant at first sight, but it has enabled me to rectify the position of the consonants belonging to the Sacred Name in respect of certain Sephiroth, so that it is

---

[1] The reference is to the plate which forms the Frontispiece.

justified by a particular allocation, as well as by the reason of things.

I will now summarise the correspondences of the ten SEPHIROTH in succession. KETHER is the crown or head of the Tree.[1] It is the first Hypostasis but not apparently the First Cause or Cause of causes.[2] The meaning seems to be that the First Cause contains within itself two Hypostases, understood as male and female.[3] Jehovah manifests with Shekinah in the degree of KETHER.[4] In contradiction hereto it is said that the first and third SEPHIROTH are united as male and female.[5] It is said also that KETHER and CHOKMAH are never in separation.[6] This is true, however, of the whole Supernal Triad, or First Three SEPHIROTH.

As regards CHOKMAH, it is by the sublime and impenetrable mystery of this SEPHIRA that the world exists [7] and all other mysteries depend therefrom.[8] It is the second SEPHIRA or Hypostasis and is called Man [9]: otherwise, it is ABBA, the Father. The house is built by CHOKMAH; [10] it was concealed like the Supreme Point before the creation,[11] and it is called YOD.[12] It is Eternal Wisdom,[13] and therein is concealed the Eternal Thought, which is the Great Voice,[14] meaning the still small voice which is the House of Eternal Wisdom. In contradiction to these indications it is said to be the Sister, meaning thereby Shekinah.[15] It is also Daughter and Mother. It is the beginning of all.[16]

BINAH is intelligence or understanding,[17] and its number is said to be fifty because of the Gates of Understanding.[18] It is the concealed world,[19] and motherhood is its image.[20] It is also penitence,[21] the degree of the moon,[22] the mystery of the Supreme World,[23] and the Community of Israel.[24] The letter HE is allocated to BINAH, and it is then described as the only Daughter [25] or alternatively AIMA, the Mother. It is

---

[1] Z., Pt. I, 21b; I, 131.
[2] Ib., fol. 22b; I, 138.
[3] Ib., fol. 22b; I, 139.
[4] Ib., Pt. III, fol. 242b, 243a; V, 581.
[5] Ib., fol. 31b; I, 196.
[6] Ib., Pt. II, fol. 11b; III, 51.
[7] Ib., fol. 3b; I, 18.
[8] Ib., fol. 7; I, 38.
[9] Ib., fol. 21b; I, 131.
[10] Ib., fol. 29a; I, 183.
[11] Ib., fol. 30a; I, 188.
[12] Ib., fol. 31a; I, 194.
[13] Ib., fol. 31b; I, 195.
[14] Ib., fol. 50b; I, 293.
[15] Ib., fol. 111b, 112a; II, 50, 51.
[16] Ib., APPENDICES III, SECRETS OF THE LAW; II, 732.
[17] Ib., fol. 71a; I, 420.
[18] Ib., fol. 106a; II, 34.
[19] Ib., fol. 154a; II, 206.
[20] Ib., fol. 158a; II, 220.
[21] Ib., APPENDICES II, SECRETS OF THE LAW; II, 662.
[22] Ib., Pt. II, fol. 11b; III, 51.
[23] Ib., fol. 43b; III, 194.
[24] Ib., fol. 85a; III, 349.
[25] Ib., Pt. III, 6a, 27b; V, 76.

the Throne of Mercy and the celestial fire which descends, as MALKUTH is the Throne of Justice and the fire which goes up.[1] It is the sweetness of God [2] and constitutes the mystery of the Levirate.[3] The House is built by CHOKMAH and is established by BINAH.[4]

CHESED is the male side [5] and the patriarch Abraham is referred thereto.[6] The Divine Name Jehovah is attributed to CHESED [7] and it is even called in one place the first degree of the Divine Essence. It is merit, as demerit is GEBURAH.[8] It is the place of revelations [9] and it is the twin sister who came into the world with VAU,[10] but this allocation is contrary to the general trend of the symbolism. The VAU is the son of YOD and HE; it unites to the HE, symbolising CHOKMAH, and itself represents BINAH.[11] What, however, it represents really is the six lower SEPHIROTH.

GEBURAH or PACHAD is sometimes used in a good and sometimes in an evil sense [12]; the world is based thereon—in the sense that severity is indispensable—but it could not subsist without Mercy.[13] It is said also to be the repentance of God [14] and it seems even to connect with Samael.[15] It was by GEBURAH that Jerusalem was destroyed.[16]

TIPHERETH is beauty; [17] it is the heart of the Sephirotic Tree and is called Heaven.[18] It is also glory.[19] NETZACH and HOD come from the celestial river.[20] NETZACH is in correspondence with the Covenant,[21] according to one attribution. NETZACH and HOD represent also the two Messiahs [22] mentioned by the TALMUD. In the macrocosmic human figure YESOD is the organ of generation, and it receives

---

[1] Z., Pt. III, fol. 34a (FAITHFUL SHEPHERD); V, 89.
[2] Ib., fol. 161b; V, 416.
[3] Ib., fol. 215b (FAITHFUL SHEPHERD); V, 547.
[4] Ib., Pt. I, fol. 52b; I, 203.
[5] Ib., fol. 94a; II, 282.
[6] Ib., fol. 132b; II, 123.
[7] Ib., fol. 173b, 174a; II, 282.
[8] Ib., Pt. 8, Appendices I, fol. 265a (SECRETS OF THE LAW); II, 626.
[9] Ib., Pt. II, fol. 119b; III, 460.
[10] Ib., Pt. III, fol. 77b; V, 210, 211.
[11] Ib., fol. 247b (FAITHFUL SHEPHERD); V, 585. It must be remembered that the FAITHFUL SHEPHERD is a text imbedded in the ZOHAR and—as here—is not always in harmony therewith, while it contradicts also other imbedded texts.
[12] Ib., Pt. I, fol. 160a; II, 228.
[13] Ib., fol. 180b; II, 311.
[14] Ib., fol. 163a; II, 237.
[15] Ib., fol. 36a; I, 223.
[16] Ib., fol. 151a; II, 196.
[17] Ib., fol. 34a; I, 211.
[18] Ib., fol. 31a; I, 195.
[19] Ib., Pt. II, fol. 79b; III, 332.
[20] Ib., Pt. III, fol. 68a; V. 186.
[21] Ib., Pt. I, fol. 24b; I, 152.
[22] Ib., Pt. III, fol. 243a, 243b (FAITHFUL SHEPHERD); V, 581.

light from the supreme SEPHIROTH.[1] It is said to issue from the right and left sides—meaning that it draws from both—as MALKUTH issues from YESOD. MALKUTH is connected with Israel, regarded as Son of the King.[2] It is the rainbow, or at least the arch thereof.[3] It is also the lower firmament.[4]

The following points may be drawn together in conclusion: All Supreme Degrees and all SEPHIROTH are one, and God embraces all the SEPHIROTH. The law is CHESED. BINAH is repentance,[5] and MALKUTH is confession. God and the ten crowns are one [6]—a notable statement, which substitutes a doctrine of identity for that of mere emanation. To ascend to the Paradise above, it is necessary that souls should cleave to the Middle Pillar.[7] There is an unity of the ten SEPHIROTH, and [8] there is joy in the world when order reigns among them.[9] Finally, the Holy One manifests in the SEPHIROTH for those who comprehend them.[10]

The doctrine concerning the three Divine Hypostases is obviously that of a Trinity in Kabbalism, and the heads of this subject must be considered in the next place in view of developments towards the end of my study, not to speak of the Christian implicits suggested by the simple expression. There are three that bear testimony in ATZILUTH, and these three are one. They are described after many manners, as, for example, when it is said that they are three lights, which form a single light.[11] But the chief symbolism is drawn from the Sacred Name, being YOD, HE, VAU, HE, = Jehovah. YOD is the Father, HE is the Mother and VAU the begotten Son.[12] At the moment we will not affirm that these ineffable

---

[1] Z., Pt. I, fol. 30b; I, 191.
[2] Ib., Pt. III, fol. 223a (FAITHFUL SHEPHERD); V, 563.
[3] Ib., Pt. I, fol. 18a; I, 112.
[4] Ib., fol. 33b; I, 209.
[5] Ib., fol. 286a (SECRETS OF THE LAW); II, 662.
[6] Ib., Pt. III, fol. 70a; V, 190.
[7] Ib., Pt. II, fol. 211a; IV, 219.
[8] Ib., fol. 67a; III, 298. See also Pt. III, fol. 28a; V, 80.
[9] Ib., Pt. II, fol. 78b; III, 329.
[10] Ib., Pt. I, fol. 241a; II, 554.
[11] Ib., I, fol. 17b; I, 103.
[12] An important analogous intimation occurs early in the ZOHAR. The Scriptural reference is "Let there be light" (Gen. i. 3), which in Hebrew is ויהי אור, the first word being the verb in the imperative. It should be remembered here that Hebrew is read from left to right. This word, YOD, HE, YOD, is regarded as a symbol of the three Divine Hypostases occurring at the opening of Genesis and designed to shew that the three are one. The first YOD is the Heavenly Father, the HE is the Divine Mother, while the third Hypostasis is indicated by the second YOD and proceeds from the first two.—Z., I, 16b; I, 99, 100.

THE FOUR WORLDS

personalities are referable to KETHER, CHOKMAH and BINAH —as might seem probable—because later considerations will intervene to correct this view. Let us remember only that the Zoharic Trinity constitutes a Divine Family in the World of Heaven. Like the Christian Trinity, the letters which are their symbols are called one on account of the unity of God.

We are now in a position to advance a step further. YOD and HE are the Supreme Mystery,[1] for ever impenetrable.[2] On the YOD are all things based,[3] and it is never in separation from the HE.[4] As the prototypical male principle, it has man for another symbol.[5] HE is the female principle,[6] and it has woman therefore as its emblem; it signifies many mysteries,[7] and its true name is Shekinah. Because the letter HE is duplicated in the Sacred Name it is said to terminate both the first and second parts thereof.[8] The world was created by the HE,[9] or alternatively by the YOD and HE in the perfection of their concurrence.[10] The VAU is the " free Son,"[11] and it is this which diffuses all blessings.[12] The YOD unites with the HE, as male with female, and gives birth to the VAU as Son.[13] The three dwell together in unity.[14] VAU is the Eternal World.[15]

So far in respect of three Divine Hypostases; but there is the HE final which completes the Sacred Name, and this is called the Daughter.[16] It is said of this Daughter [17] that the HE came down to earth.[18] The first He is liberty above and

---

[1] Z., Pt. I, fol. 159a; II, 225.
[2] Ib., fol. 232b; II, 517.
[3] Ib., Pt. III, fol. 10b; V, 31.
[4] Ib., fol. 279b; VI, 54.
[5] Ib., fol. 34a; V, 89.
[6] Ib.
[7] Ib., Pt. II, fol. 180b; IV, 152.
[8] Ib., Pt. III, 89b; V, 240.
[9] Ib., fol. 298a; VI, 125.
[10] Ib., Pt. II, 22b; III, 13.
[11] Eccles. x, 17.
[12] Z., Pt. I, 124b; II, 98.
[13] Ib., Pt. II, 123b; III, 47ε.
[14] Ib., Pt. III, 92a; V, 245.
[15] Ib., fol. 252b; V, 591.
[16] Ib., Pt. I, fol. 27b; I, 174.

[17] Ib., fol. 354b; II, 600. There is another symbolism as follows: When the letter YOD is written at length in Hebrew it is composed of YOD, VAU and DALETH. YOD is the Father of all, VAU—as seen already—is the begotten Son, and DALETH is the Daughter—that is, the Daughter of Matrona. The imagery is confused on the surface, as this Daughter is said to proceed from the Father and the Son, whereas it is certain in the sense of things and is plain from the text elsewhere that the HE primal of the Sacred Name produces in union with the YOD not only the Son, being VAU, but his Sister, who is also her Daughter and in the natural succession of the Divine Name is therefore the HE final.—Ib., Pt. III, 10b; V, 31. It is not of much consequence to the purpose in view whether it is possible or not to harmonise distinct symbolisms on this subject: it is sufficient that they help to formulate the Kabbalistic notion of the Trinity in the Supernal World. As a fact, however, the Daughter proceeds from the Son in precisely the same sense as Eve proceeded from Adam, for the Daughter originally abode within the Son, in a state of ineffable union, and was brought forth afterwards from Him.

[18] Ib., Pt. I, 354b; II, 600.

the second is liberty below.¹ The High Priest depends from the HE which is above but the ordinary priest from that HE which is below.² It follows that two letters of the Name belong to the male principle—namely, YOD and VAU—two also to the female, being HE primal and final. The engendering of a whole world depends on these two principles.³ The second HE will rise from the earth, meaning that it will be united with the Divine Hypostases in the world of transcendence.⁴ The VAU will be united to the HE,⁵ and when the VAU is thus attached, as a bridegroom to the Bride, there will be union everywhere—between the YOD and the HE above, between the VAU and the HE final.⁶

The abodes of these symbolic personalities is our next question. Now, it is said that the YOD is CHOKMAH, while the HE is BINAH,⁷ this being repeated in another place, where it is added that they sustain the VAU, but without intimating the location of this letter or of the second HE which is represented as in union therewith.⁸ For information on these points we must transfer our attention from the ZOHAR proper to some of the additional materials with which I have dealt already in the previous book.

The tracts in question are THE ASSEMBLY OF THE SANCTUARY, THE SECRET BOOK—otherwise, BOOK OF CONCEALMENT—THE GREAT AND HOLY ASSEMBLY and THE LESSER HOLY ASSEMBLY.⁹ We can pass over the first of these, as Rosenroth was guided wisely in omitting it; it seems contradictory and inextricable in its symbolism and is speaking roughly a sort of summary appendix to much that has preceded in a better and fuller form. THE SECRET BOOK comprises a discourse concerning The White Head,¹⁰ the Ancient,

---

¹ Z., Pt. II, fol. 183a; IV, 109.
² Ib., Pt. III, 89b; V, 240.
³ Ib., Pt. II, fol. 228a; IV, 250.
⁴ Ib., Pt. I, 116b; II, 66.
⁵ Ib., fol. 119a; II, 76.
⁶ Ib., Pt. III, 267b; VI, 23.
⁷ Ib., Pt. II, fol. 123b; III, 478.
⁸ Ib., Pt. III, fol. 153b; V, 394.

⁹ THE ASSEMBLY OF THE SANCTUARY is inserted towards the end of Part II, § 6, and occupies folios 122b to 123b. THE SECRET BOOK, called sometimes in translation THE BOOK OF CONCEALED MYSTERY, follows Part II, § 7, and occupies folios 176b to 179a. THE GREAT AND HOLY ASSEMBLY is placed at the end of THE COMMENTARY ON NUMBERS, § I, Z., Pt. III, folios 127b to 145a. THE LITTLE HOLY ASSEMBLY follows THE COMMENTARY ON DEUTERONOMY, § 10, Z., Pt. III, folios 287b to 296b.

¹⁰ Z., Pt. III, fol. 128a; V, 334. The White Head is also without beginning and without end before its reign was established and the Crown, that is, KETHER, was assumed. The reference would seem therefore to AIN-SOPH AOUR, which pours down into KETHER, and we shall see that the White Head is called AIN. At this point the ZOHAR and the mystical theology of pseudo-Dionysius the Areopagite join hands. It should be understood, however, that the White Head is not AIN-SOPH, but the first procession therefrom.

or the Great Countenance. The same subject is continued in THE GREAT AND HOLY ASSEMBLY, and he who is symbolised therein is the Master with the white mantle and resplendent visage; he is called also Holy of Holies.

Connected by means of a white thread [1] or bond of union with the Great Countenance, there is that which is called the Lesser Countenance, Little Form or Figure, which presents, however, a complete aspect of humanity and is extended through many symbolical worlds. The distinction between the two heads is that in this case the hair and beard are black.[2] The Lesser Countenance has eyelids, because it has periods of sleep,[3] a complete visage in manifestation, because severity is one of its attributes; and a distinctive name, being Lord, whereas the Great Countenance is called AIN,[4] or Nothing, because it draws or is emanated from AIN SOPH, though it is located certainly in KETHER. These points notwithstanding, it is laid down (1) that the Lesser Countenance emanates from the Greater,[5] (2) that the Greater metamorphoses into the Lesser,[6] (3) that the latter is actually the former, as if seen through a curtain,[7] and more specifically that they are one and the same.[8] The body of this Sacred Form is described fully and is that of the male perfect in all its members.

Of this Form there is a counterpart of perfect womanhood, and these two were primordially side by side, till the Ancient of Days put the Lesser Form to sleep and detached the female principle,[9] whose name is Matrona, Bride, Daughter, Betrothed and Twin-Sister—for the Zoharic allegories institute strange marriages in the world above. The object of separation was that the Bride might come to the Bridegroom and, in the great sacrament of matrimonial union, that they might become one body and as if one flesh.[10] All is mercy in this

---

[1] Z., fol. 128b; V, 335, 336.
[2] Ib., Pt. III, fol. 132a; V, 346. The authorities are THE SONG OF SOLOMON, v. 11: "His locks are bushy, and black as a raven," and Dan. vii. 9: "The hair of his head like the pure wool," or as the ZOHAR gives it, "whitest and purest wool." It is to be noted, however, that when severity operates the hair of the White Head becomes black.
[3] Ib., fol. 136b; V, 359.
[4] Ib., fol. 129a; V, 337.
[5] Ib., fol. 131b; V, 345.
[6] Ib., fol. 135a; V, 354.
[7] Ib., fol. 128b; V, 335.
[8] Ib., Pt. III, fol. 141a; V, 365. See also THE LITTLE HOLY ASSEMBLY, ib., fol. 288a; VI, 82, and fol. 292a; VI, 99.
[9] Ib., Pt. III, fol. 142b; V, 368.
[10] Ib., fol. 143b; V, 369.

union;[1] it constitutes the Law of the Sabbath; and it is this that God blessed and sanctified.[2] The sacred organ of intercourse is called YESOD[3] on the male side, and it has access to the concealed and mysterious region on the female side which is called ZION.[4] It is a holy place and all the holiness of the male enters therein.[5]

The reference to YESOD shews that the Lesser Form is extended through the Lower SEPHIROTH. It is the Begotten Son or VAU,[6] whose place we have been seeking on the Tree; and as its name is DAATH[7] or Knowledge, being a semi-SEPHIRA which represents the junction point of the influences flowing from CHOKMAH and BINAH, the inference is that the Lesser Countenance or Head is located there, while the feet are established on MALKUTH, as later Kabbalism affirms. We have learned also where the Daughter and Bride dwells, being side by side or face to face in union with her Celestial Spouse. But she is the HE final of the Divine Name and we shall learn at a later stage that her present dwelling is in MALKUTH.

We are now in a position to establish the Doctrine concerning the Tree with as much clearness as is possible considering the subject. According to the symbolism of the IDRAS, the Great Countenance is in ATZILUTH and it encompasses therefore the three Supreme SEPHIROTH, which are KETHER, CHOKMAH and BINAH. It is located, as I have said, in KETHER, where it is at once male and female, these principles being brought forth subsequently, the male principle into CHOKMAH and the female into BINAH, who produced between them DAATH, which is the Divine Son. We have therefore in the Sephirotic Tree: (1) The first Divine Manifestation proceeding from AIN-SOPH and so interpenetrated thereby that it bears sometimes the same name. In so far as it is postulated in KETHER, it is not differentiated into male and female, but these are implied, and according to other testimony the Shekinah is certainly there. (2) But when the Sacred Ancient wished to establish all things, He constituted male and female

---

[1] Z., fol. 143a; V, 368.
[2] It is said that Matrona dwells in the Supernal Sanctuary—that is to say, in BINAH—and in the Jerusalem which is manifested on earth—that is to say, in MALKUTH; and it is because she is united to the male in the unseen world that she is joined in manifestation with man. This is defined as the quintessence of all faith, for all faith is comprised in this mystery.—Z., Pt. III, fol. 143b; V, 370.
[3] Ib., fol. 296a; VI, 118.
[4] Ib., fol. 290b; VI, 92.
[5] Ib., fol. 296b; VI, 119.
[6] Ib., fol. 291a; VI, 94.
[7] Ib.

in His supreme region,¹ namely, the Father and Mother, owing to Whom all is made male and female. These are the second Divine manifestation in CHOKMAH and BINAH.² (3) The third is in the lower SEPHIROTH, as Son and Daughter, Brother and Sister, King and Queen. According to later Kabbalism, the Great Countenance is MACROPROSOPUS, the soul of the greater world, while the Lesser Countenance or Figure is MICROPROSOPUS, the soul of the lesser world, and ADAM PROTOPLASTES, his Bride being the archetypal Eve. They form together the *habitaculum* of all created intelligences, the hierarchies of consciousness; and we can therefore sum up the whole subject by saying that THE BOOK OF MYSTERY and the IDRAS are a great allegory of man and his analogues coming forth from God. Male and female they were implied and conceived in Him; male and female He manifested Himself on account of them; male and female they came forth in Him and from Him; male and female they abide above and below; male and female they return in fine to Him, as we shall see fully and clearly in its proper place.

In conclusion, as to the Four Worlds, the consideration of which and of the Ten SEPHIROTH belongs essentially to the Majesty of God in Kabbalism, I must add that there is a Zoharic Theosophy of the Word, but how the term should be referred in respect of the Divine Hypostases is not easy to determine. The name of Elohim is allocated thereto,³ but this is a title of Shekinah. Again, it is said that the Word was manifested in the Sanctuary, because it was indispensable to the existence of the latter on earth that the Divine should be present therein ; ⁴ but that which we know to have appeared between the Kerubim on the Mercy Seat was the Presence in the form of Shekinah. In the paraphrase of Onkelos the term MEIMRA was substituted for Jehovah, Who is thus identified with the Word; but in the ZOHAR it is held that the Word in Scripture is designated under the term BERE-SHITH, because in order to fulfil the work of creation this term was engraven " under the form of a turnstile," ⁵ representing the six great celestial directions, being the four cardinal points, together with height and depth. The Word seems also to be specified under the name Sabbath ; ⁶ it had

---

¹ Z., Pt. III, fol. 290a ; VI, 90.
² *Ib*., Pt. III, fol. 290b ; VI, 92.
³ *Ib*., Pt. I, fol. 16b ; I, 99.
⁴ *Ib*., fol. 74a ; I, 439.
⁵ *Ib*., fol. 3b ; I, 18.
⁶ *Ib*., Pt. I, fol. 32a ; I, 199.

birth by the union of the active and the passive light, the latter being called darkness, and it discovers to us the Supreme Mysteries.

The Supreme Principle and the Word are distinguished as two, though at the root they harmonise as one.[1] It is said: "While the King sitteth at his table, my spikenard sendeth forth the smell thereof." It is to be understood here that the King means the Supreme Principle while the spikenard signifies the Word, Who is king below and has formed the world below on the model of the world above. Thought and the Word are held to be of the same essence; seen through the medium of one region, this essence appears as Thought, but through another as the Word. The doctrine of Israel is placed between two voices,[2] one of which constitutes the Supreme Mystery, but the other is more accessible. The first is the Great Voice, " the voice out of the midst of the darkness." It is interior, imperceptible, without cessation or interruption. Thence cometh the Secret Doctrine, which —in its manifestation—is called the Voice of Jacob, and this voice is heard. The Voice of Jacob is placed between the interior, imperceptible voice and that Word which resounds abroad and which I should identify with the Written Law. The Great Voice is the House of Eternal Wisdom and is female, as a house should always be. The Word is the House of the Voice of Jacob, that being apparently the literal and this the esoteric doctrine. When the Song of Solomon testifies that the voice of the turtle is heard in our land, the reference is to that voice which emanates from Him Who is the inward essence of all.[3] It is the Voice that utters the Word—as for example, the Word which ordained circumcision for Abraham, so that he might be made perfect. The Voice is added or joined to the Word—meaning that what is conceived in thought passes into expression, whether of speech or action—and this is held to be indicated by the appearance of the Lord to Abraham, when that tent before the door of which the patriarch was seated signified the Supreme World, on the threshold of which he rested, to receive the light thereof.[4]

---

[1] Z., fol. 74a ; *ib*., 439.
[2] *Ib*., fol. 50b ; I, 292, 293.
[3] *Ib*., fol. 97b, 98a ; II, 5.
[4] Further intimations on the Word in Kabbalism will be found in the fifth section of the present Book.

In dismissing this section, the reader is asked to observe that it offers, thus early in our subject, some vital intimations on the root-matter of the Secret Doctrine, as this has been enshrined in the Secret Tradition of Israel. As proposed more than once already, it is that which is embodied in the distinction, relation and union of male and female; but—as there should be no need to say—such root-matter is a metaphysical foundation and far removed from anything that belongs in public ways of life to the idea of sex.

IV.—THE PATHS OF WISDOM AND GATES OF UNDERSTANDING

In the Latin collection of Pistorius the marrow of philosophical Kabbalism is presented in the form of certain terse propositions or dogmas,[1] according to one of which the ways of eternity are thirty-two—*Viæ æternitatis sunt triginta duo.*[2] These are the Paths of the SEPHER YETZIRAH, namely, the ten SEPHIROTH and the letters of the Hebrew alphabet. The doctrine concerning them is a dependency of this fundamental treatise, but of much more recent date, and without even an imputed authorship. It tabulates the special graces and illuminations which may be communicated to man from above by means of these channels, and is not unimportant, because it shews that Kabbalism, even on its most speculative and formal side, had a practical application to the human mind, and was not a purely arbitrary system. It is outside the province of this work to offer translations to the student, but as in the present instance it would be difficult to summarise the tabulation more briefly, I shall give it *in extenso*, premising only that it has been translated more than once into English, and is indeed available in a number of European languages.

I. The first path is called the Admirable Intelligence,[3] the Supreme Crown. It is the light which imparts understanding

---

[1] They are extremely interesting theses of Picus de Mirandola, which will be found in Book VII.

[2] They are referred to the SEPHIRAH CHOKMAH and are termed channels, at once hidden and revealed. In the FAITHFUL SHEPHERD, CHOKMAH is called the highest of all paths, embracing and including all that are beneath it, and the influx of all is derived therefrom. The same treatise connects with CHOKMAH the words in Job xxviii. 7: "The bird hath not known the path, neither hath the eye of the vulture beheld it."—KABBALA DENUDATA, *Apparatus*, i. 601, 602.

[3] Stenring gives Mystical Intelligence, following the French version of Comtesse Calomira de Cimara.

of the beginning which is without beginning, and this also is the First Splendour. No created being can attain to its essence.

II. The second path is called the Illuminating Intelligence. It is the Crown of Creation and the splendour of the Supreme Unity, to which it is most in proximity. It is exalted above every head and is distinguished by Kabbalists as the Second Splendour.

III. The third path is called the Sanctifying Intelligence and is the foundation of Primordial Wisdom, termed the Creation of Faith. Its roots are אמן. It is the mother of Faith, which indeed emanates therefrom.

IV. The fourth path is called the Arresting or Receiving [1] Intelligence because it arises like a boundary to receive the emanations of the higher intelligences which are sent down to it. Herefrom all spiritual virtues emanate by the way of subtlety, which itself emanates from the Supreme Crown.[2]

V. The fifth path is called the Radical Intelligence, because it is more akin than any other to the Supreme Unity and emanates from the depths of the Primordial Wisdom.[3]

VI. The sixth Path is called the Intelligence of Mediating Influence, because the flux of the emanations is multiplied therein. It communicates this affluence to those blessed men who are united with it.[4]

VII. The seventh path is called the Hidden Intelligence, because it pours out a brilliant splendour on all intellectual virtues which are beheld with the eyes of the spirit and by the ecstasy of faith.

VIII. The eighth path is called the Perfect and Absolute Intelligence. The preparation of principles emanates therefrom.[5] The roots to which it adheres are in the depths of the Sphere Magnificence, from the very substance of which it emanates.

IX. The ninth path is called the Purified Intelligence. It

---

[1] Receptacular is an awkward variant which has been used by more than one translator.

[2] Westcott, following the text of Rittangelius, makes this rendering: "The fourth path is named Measuring, Cohesive, or Receptacular; and is so-called because it contains all the holy powers, and from it emanate all the spiritual virtues with the most exalted essences; they emanate one from the other by the power of the primordial emanation," i.e., KETHER.

[3] Or, "the primordial depths of CHOKMAH."—Westcott, SEPHER YETZIRAH, p. 28.

[4] According to Comtesse de Cimara, the sixth path is the Intelligence of Separated Emanation.

[5] According to Westcott "it is the means of the primordial."—Ibid., p. 29.

purifies the numerations, prevents and stays the fracture of their images,[1] for it establishes their unity, to preserve them from destruction and division by their union with itself.[2]

X. The tenth path is called the Resplendent Intelligence, because it is exalted above every head and has its seat in BINAH: it enlightens the fire of all lights and emanates the power of the principle of forms.[3]

XI. The eleventh path is called the Fiery Intelligence. It is the veil placed before the dispositions and order of the superior and inferior causes. Whosoever possesses this path is in the enjoyment of great dignity; to possess it is to be face to face with the Cause of Causes.[4]

XII. The twelfth path is called the Intelligence of Light,[5] because it is the image of magnificence. It is said to be the source of vision in those who behold apparitions.

XIII. The thirteenth path is called the Inductive Intelligence of Unity. It is the substance of glory, and it manifests truth to every spirit.[6]

XIV. The fourteenth path is called the Illuminating Intelligence.[7] It is the institutor of arcana, the foundation of holiness.

XV. The fifteenth path is called the Constituting Intelligence, because it constitutes creation in the darkness of the world.[8] According to the philosophers, it is itself that darkness mentioned by Scripture (Job xxxviii. 9), cloud and the envelope thereof.

XVI. The sixteenth path is called the Triumphant and Eternal Intelligence, the delight of glory, the paradise of pleasure prepared for the just.

XVII. The seventeenth path is called the Disposing Intelligence. It disposes the devout to perseverance and thus prepares them to receive the Holy Spirit.[9]

---

[1] Or, " proves and corrects the designing of their representations."—*Ibid.*
[2] Or, " disposes their unity with which they are combined without diminution or division."—*Ibid.*
[3] " Causes a supply of influence to emanate from the Prince of Countenances."—*Ibid.*
[4] Westcott gives an entirely different version: " It is the essence of that curtain which is placed close to the order of the disposition, and this is a special dignity given to it that it may be able to stand before the face of the Cause of Causes."—*Ibid.*
[5] Or of Transparency, in the French version.
[6] " It is the consummation of the truth of individual spiritual things."—Westcott.
[7] Otherwise, Luminous Intelligence.—De Cimara.
[8] " It constitutes the substance of creations in pure darkness."—Westcott, p. 30.
[9] Stenring terms it " the path of Life and Death."

XVIII. The eighteenth path is called the Intelligence or House of Influence,[1] and thence are drawn the arcana and the concealed meanings which repose in the shadow thereof.

XIX. The nineteenth path is called the Intelligence of the Secret or of all spiritual activities. The fullness which it receives derives from the highest benediction and the supreme glory.

XX. The twentieth path is called the Intelligence of Will. It prepares all created beings, each individually, for the demonstration of the existence of the primordial glory.

XXI. The twenty-first path is called the Rewarding Intelligence of those who seek.[2] It receives the divine influence, and it influences by its benediction all existing things.

XXII. The twenty-second path is called the Faithful Intelligence, because spiritual virtues are deposited and augment therein, until they pass to those who dwell under the shadow thereof.[3]

XXIII. The twenty-third path is called the Stable Intelligence. It is the source of consistency in all the numerations.

XXIV. The twenty-fourth path is called the Imaginative Intelligence. It is the ground of similarity in the likeness of beings who are created to its agreement, after its aspects.

XXV. The twenty-fifth path is called the Intelligence of Temptation or Trial, because it is the first temptation by which God tests the devout.

XXVI. The twenty-sixth path is called the Renewing Intelligence, for thereby God—blessed be He!—reneweth all which is capable of renovation in the creation of the world.[4]

XXVII. The twenty-seventh path is called the Natural Intelligence, whereby the nature of everything found in the orb of the sun is completed and perfected.[5]

XXVIII. The twenty-eighth path is called the Active Intelligence, for thence is created the spirit of every creature

---

[1] Westcott adds: "By the greatness of whose abundance the influx of good things upon created beings is increased."—*Ibid.*

[2] Westcott gives "the Conciliating Intelligence," and De Cimara "the Intelligence of Desire."

[3] Westcott's rendering reads: "by it spiritual virtues are increased, and all dwellers on earth are merely under its shadow."—*Ibid.* The version lacks discernment.

[4] "All the changing things which are renewed by the creation of the world."—*Ibid.*, p. 31. But this seems nonsensical.

[5] "The twenty-seventh path is the Exciting Intelligence, and it is so called because through it is consummated and perfected the nature of every existent being under the orb of the sun, in perfection."—*Ibid.* A redundant rendering.

of the supreme orb, and the activity, that is to say, the motion, to which they are subject.[1]

XXIX. The twenty-ninth path is called the Corporeal Intelligence; it informs every body which is incorporated under all orbs, and it is the growth thereof.

XXX. The thirtieth path is called the Collective Intelligence, for thence astrologers, by the judgment of the stars and the heavenly signs, derive their speculations and the perfection of their science according to the motions of the stars.

XXXI. The thirty-first path is called the Perpetual Intelligence. Why is it so called? Because it rules the movement of the sun and the moon according to their constitution and causes each to gravitate in its respective orb.[2]

XXXII. The thirty-second path is called the Assisting Intelligence, because it directs all the operation of the seven planets, with their divisions, and concurs therein.

The comparatively modern accent of this tabulation will occur to the reader, but its quotation was necessary to exhibit the intellectual profit believed to follow from the study of Kabbalism, and still more that it was in the last resource the understanding of man methodised,[3] embracing, as such, the entire circle attributed to human knowledge.[4] After what manner the Paths correspond to their various affirmed offices, how they communicate the powers and graces which abide therein, and for what reason they bear their distinctive titles, must remain open questions. The thesis concerning them constitutes a body of dogma, and is to be taken or left as such. The Paths are those of the Tree and its SEPHIROTH.

---

[1] This path is omitted both in the text of Rittangelius and in Westcott's version.

[2] According to Éliphas Lévi, this verse contains the secret of the Great Work of Alchemy. The reason assigned is that path thirty-one corresponds to the Hebrew letter SHIN (Sh), which represents the magic lamp, or the light between the horns of Baphomet. "It is the Kabbalistic sign of God or the Astral Light, with its two poles and equilibrated centre." The sun mentioned in the paragraph represents gold, the moon silver, and the planets correspond to the other metals.—LA CLEF DES GRAND MYSTÈRES, p. 234. It is needless to say that the SEPHER YETZIRAH and its developments have nothing to do with Alchemy. As regards the Great Work and Lévi's pretended discovery of its secret, see my annotated translation of his TRANSCENDENTAL MAGIC, pp. 345-347.

[3] "Man is the Kabbalistic balance," according to W. B. Greene.—THE BLAZING STAR, p. 51.

[4] However, it fell, as may be expected, into superstitious uses and became a kind of theosophic divination, based on the first chapter of Genesis, wherein the name Elohim is mentioned thirty-two times. The consultation of this chapter was accompanied by prayers extracted from the divine name in question, and, according to Kircher, by suitable ceremonies.

A word must be added concerning a still more arbitrary Kabbalistic classification, entitled the FIFTY GATES OF UNDERSTANDING. It is referable to BINAH, the third SEPHIRA, and is an attempt—as developed—to sketch the outlines of universal science, to embrace, as Éliphas Lévi observes, all possible departments of knowledge and to represent the whole encyclopædia. At the present day such fantastic experiments have something more than a ghostly aspect. There is, however, no intention to methodise human science after the manner of Raymund Lully and his *Ars Magna Sciendi*. I infer also that, in spite of the exalted themes which are included in the scheme, it concerns only intellectual knowledge, acquired by the external way, and thus constitutes a kind of scholastic introduction to the Paths of CHOKMAH or of Wisdom,[1] by which the holy men of God may, as Kircher observes, after long toil, long experience of divine things and long meditation thereon, penetrate to the concealed centres.[2] The principle of the enumeration must be sought in the symbolism of the Hebrew word כל = KOLL, which signifies All, and the consonants of which are equivalent to the number fifty.

The Gates of Understanding, considered as an introduction to the Paths of Wisdom, which diverge, as we have seen, from CHOKMAH, are essential *ex hypothesi* to the higher knowledge approached by these.[3] It would serve no purpose to enumerate them all categorically; they begin with the first matter, the Hyle or Chaos, proceed through the various elements of ancient science to the theory of composite substances, thence to organic life and the physical, intellectual and psychic nature of man, afterwards to the heaven of the planets, that of the fixed stars and the *primum mobile*, then to the nine orders of the angelic world, and, finally, to the supermundane and archetypal world, that of AIN SOPH, unseen by mortal eye, transcending human intelligence. It is said that Moses did not attain to this, the fiftieth, gate, and some stress seems to be laid on the point, one would think a little superfluously, as it is obvious that what is beyond all finite capacity

---

[1] According to Papus, the thirty-two paths are deductive like the SEPHER YETZIRAH itself, which starts from the notion of God and proceeds thence to natural phenomena, while the fifty gates are established on the inductive principle, ascending from Nature to Deity.—LA KABBALE, p. 132.

[2] Athanasius Kircher: ŒDIPUS ÆGYPTIACUS, Rome, 1623, *Pars Prima*, p. 321.

[3] They are called gates, because no one can attain to the paths unless he enters by these.—*Ibid.*

must have been beyond the law-giver of Israel. We shall meet however with a more particular and indeed curious explanation at a later stage.

The scheme in full of the Gates of Understanding is late in Kabbalism; it is found in the treatise entitled THE GATES OF LIGHT,[1] which is full of references to the mystery of the word כל = KOLL (All). All created things, it explains, have come out of these gates, so that in a sense their knowledge connects with the mystery of universal generation, in reference to which it may be observed that the addition of the feminine letter H = 5 to the word KL = 50 gives KLH = the Bride of MICROPROSOPUS, the Lesser Countenance, whence follows the whole mystery of spiritual generation in man, for KLH = BRIDE, connects with כנסת = KNST = Church, *i.e.*, the Church, ECCLESIA ISRAEL, and brings us back to that place called mystically Zion and Jerusalem, in which the Divine is communicated to man, as seen in an earlier section. It is by living gleams of suggestion after this kind that the dull art of GEMATRIA is lighted up from time to time, or is refreshed and fructified by the waters of Secret Doctrine. We seem to be contemplating from a distance some greater subject than an arid tabulation of sciences, more especially when it lies far apart from any method of attainment; and it happens that we shall come later on to the Gates of Understanding in the light of another Mystery and shall enumerate the intimations of the ZOHAR apart from the formulæ of later Kabbalism.

V.—THE DOCTRINE OF COSMOLOGY

If the Four Worlds of Kabbalism are held in a very true sense to correspond with a path in consciousness by which the mind of the dedicated seeker after Divine things may pass from the " sacred and beautiful Kingdom " of the literal sense or the surface of the Word of God, and through world on world of experience may attain at last that place or state of realisation where all meanings are unified in the light of the Eternal Word, we shall find no difficulty in understanding those who devised this analogy when they go on to tell us not only that *Deus non pars est sed totum*—as Raymund Lully expressed it—but that all whatsoever of the realms in which

---

[1] By R. Joseph Gikatilla ben Abraham.

He is immanent or is held to have revealed Himself are part of that law of election in virtue of which those who are drawn by God are journeying in Him for ever. So is the spiritual history of Israel the sole concern of Scripture, from the moment when Elohim said "Let there be light," that the minds of the chosen might be enlightened. The same motive manifests, as a fact, through all the story of creation, nor was there other reason needed for the Kabbalist to account for God passing from the withdrawn state of AïN-SOPH to the manifestation which begins in KETHER and reaches its limit in MALKUTH.

The thesis of creation is as follows, but I should explain that I am drawing from many quarters of Zoharic texts and simplifying at every point, so that no remediable difficulties may be left in respect of expression. We are not concerned at the moment with the respective share in the work taken by any or all of the three Divine Hypostases. It will be more intelligible at this point to speak of the cosmos in a general sense, as created by the Holy One, which is indeed a recurring affirmation of the ZOHAR. When therefore the Holy One, Who is the Mystery of all mysteries, willed to manifest Himself, He constituted in the first place a point of light, which became the Divine Thought [1]—that is to say, in its application to the purpose then in view. Within this point he designed and engraved all things, but especially that which is termed the Sacred and Mysterious Lamp, being an image representing the Most Holy Mystery.[2] About the nature of this mystery, situated—if one may so speak—at the heart of all the manifested world, we may derive some light of speculation at a later stage. Here indeed is one of those allusions through which a vista opens into the unwritten Secret Doctrine. It follows in the meantime that the universe was created by and from thought.[3] The authority for this revelation is the prophet Elijah, and the development is an excursus on the

---

[1] Z., Pt. I, fol. 2a ; I, 8. See *ib.*, II, 98a ; III, 395, where it is said that the words "Lord my God" (Ps. civ, 1) are the foundation of the mystery concerning the unity and indivisibility of the world at the moment when it was conceived in the Supreme Thought.

[2] We shall see that this is identical with what is called so frequently the Mystery of Faith, and it is to be distinguished therefore from what is called otherwise the Lamp of God, being simply the general notion of merit.—*Ib.*, III, 28b ; V, 80.

[3] It may be noted here—though the statement belongs to another part of the text—that thought and the word by which it is formulated are of the same essence : seen under one aspect, this essence appears as thought and under another as the word,

words: "Behold Who hath created these things."[1] In the beginning, however, that is to say, in the point of Divine Thought, the creation was only in the subject of the Divine Mind, or—as the text says—it existed, yet existed not. In other words, it was hidden in the Divine Name, and it would seem to follow that this also was hidden. The symbolism of the thesis is very curious and deep withal herein. The Sacred Name of God presupposes those who can pronounce, or at least conceive it.[2] In this sense the Name exists for man and as antecedent of necessity thereto are the letters which are images of the Word. Now the world is said to have been created by the help of the Hebrew letters,[3] whence it follows that these were produced in the first place—or rather their archetypes. They are said to have emanated from one another,[4] presumably on account of the fact that it is possible to reduce them to a few primitive simple forms. After their emanation, the Sacred Letters, the Great Letters—the letters that are above, of which those on earth are a reflection—remained in concealment for a period which is specified as 2,000 years before the Holy One proceeded further in His work.[5] When He willed so to do the letters came successively before Him, to shew cause why each one of them should be utilised as an instrument in the task. This is mere comedy in the literal understanding and is one of the curiosities of literature in its form of expression, as it is all easy to say; but let us mark what issues therefrom. The letter BETH was chosen, but not because it is the initial of the word BARA, meaning to create, nor yet because it is that of BERESHITH, or "In the beginning," with which the BOOK OF GENESIS opens, but because it is the initial letter of the word BARACH, which signifies to bless.[6] It serves therefore to illustrate the ineradicable optimism of Jewish philosophical thought, which maintains that in the root-sense all is "right with the world," because for ever and ever God is "in His heaven."

---

which may really mean that, for the processes of the human mind, they are inseparable.—Z., Pt. I, fol. 74a; I, 439. It is obviously, as we have seen, the transition from conception to expression.

[1] Isaiah xl. 26.
[2] In other words, it is recognised that manifestation can be only to consciousness.
[3] Z., Pt. I, fol. 204a; II, 411.
[4] Ib., fol. 2a; I, 9.
[5] Ib., fol. 2b; I, 12 et seq.
[6] See the Talmudic treatise entitled HAGHIGHA, cap. II, which affirms that the world was created by the letter BETH. But a counter-affirmation on the authority of another rabbi substitutes the letter HE.

It is indeed something more than optimism, which is often a characteristic rather than a ground in reason; it is something more than instinct; it is an apprehension in consciousness, the beginning of a work in knowledge. It is so permeating and so paramount that there are moments when the catholic sense of goodness seems to cast down the last barrier, and one or another rabbi thinks in his zeal that even the punishment of the Gentile in the world to come shall be for this or that period or season, but not world without end. It is in virtue of *beneplacitum termino carens* that the letter BETH was used in creation, and I care not by what devious or grotesque path of thought such a truth is reached, so long as it emerges at last on the Pisgah height with such a sun shining in the eyes.

The ZOHAR is like the Hebrew Scriptures, canonical and sub-canonical: it is sealed with sanctity. The writers had passed that sacred initiatory degree in which the soul looks for " good things of the Lord in the land of the living ": [1] they had come to see with their own eyes. Amidst the sorrows and rogations of the Greater Exile, their hearts never faltered nor failed over that faith which opens into sight, or in that hope which begins already to realise itself in participation. The ZOHAR is therefore like Osiris: it is " true of voice," and is inspired on every page, not only with the sense of immortality but with that of a conscious communion subsisting ever and continually between the Holy Assembly that is above and the Assembly which has attained holiness below. There is hence a consolation throughout it which seems—for the most part—to be implied only under veils by the Law and the Prophets.

The Divine intention to make use of the letter BETH, for the reason stated, does not concern further the mind of the ZOHAR,[2] because it has done its work in delineating the motive of the worlds, shewing that the instrument of creation was the power to bless all things. The intention was further to manifest the Divine Name therein as an Indwelling Presence of the universe and as a glory standing above the four quarters thereof. The procedure is symbolised by reciting that the Holy One engraved in the ineffable world those letters which

---

[1] Ps. xxvii. 13.
[2] I ought to say that there is one instance of recurrence to the general notion when the story of the letters and their pleading is mentioned, with variations respecting the letters RESH and TETH; but they do not now concern us.—Z., Pt. I, fol. 204a; II, 411.

represent the Mystery of Faith, being YOD, HE, VAU, HE, the synthesis of all worlds above and below.¹ God represents the central point and the cause of all things, concealed and unknown for ever, being the Supreme Mystery of the Infinite.² It is that point of Divine Thought which has been mentioned previously, and from it there issues a slender thread of light which is itself concealed but contains all lights, receiving vibrations from Him Who does not vibrate and reflecting light from Him Who does not diffuse light—that is, the mysterious point, or God centralised in thought on the world about to be produced. The slender light—*lumen exile*—gives birth to a world of light, which enlightens the other worlds. It is affirmed that when the central point—the thread of light and the light-world—are united, then is union perfect. This is the office of the Great Name shadowed forth in part, but the primordial elements which were produced at the beginning of creation were without feature—as it is said that " the earth was without form and void," ³ like " the sign drawn by a pen overcharged with ink," and it was by the grace of the Sacred Name of forty-two letters that the world assumed shape.⁴ All forms emanate from these letters, which—in a manner—are the crown of TETRAGRAMMATON—that is to say, the Sacred Name of four letters already enumerated. By their combinations, their superposition, and by the figures thus obtained above and below, the four cardinal points had birth, with all other images. The letters of the Sacred Name were the moulds of the work of formation, and as such they were arranged in a reverse order to that which obtains here.

Many things, however, were united or drawn together in the mind of the Holy One for the perfect purpose of His providence in respect of all that which was to come into being. He contemplated in His foresight the Mystery of the Law, and because it was impossible for the world to subsist without

---

¹ The Mystery of Faith is once more the hidden doctrine that there is male and female above, as there is male and female below.
² Z., Pt. II, fols. 126b, 127a ; IV, 5, 6.
³ Gen. i. 2.
⁴ Z., Pt. I, fols. 30a, 30b ; I, 189. The name of forty-two letters is an expansion of TETRAGRAMMATON, for if the consonants of that Name are written at length thus— YOD, HE, VAU, HE = ה, וו, ה, יוד, their sum in numbers is forty-two. After what manner the letters themselves are extracted to make up the expanded Name it is scarcely worth while to consider, being not only outside our subject but of no consequence in itself. I will refer, however, to Athanasius Kircher : ŒDIPUS ÆGYPTIACUS, Tomus III, pp. 261 *et seq.*

it,[1] He created that Law to rule in all things above and below, and to sustain them. But because of the Law, in which the possibility of transgression is implied, He created also repentance [2] as a path of refuge in Himself, of return at need to Him. But the Law is said to be contained in the Sacred Name and to be summarised by the Decalogue, the ten sections of which correspond to ten other Names. These appear to be described alternatively as ten creative words,[3] which are reducible to three, for it is said: " With the Spirit of God, in wisdom and in understanding."[4] The end in view was that God might manifest Himself and be called by His Divine Name.[5]

It is easy to say that all this is arbitrary in the extreme, and certainly many developments, which I forbear to cite, represent the casuistry of words pushed into a region of distraction; yet one is inclined to think that almost any peg will serve to support a discourse on Divine Things—though some devices are to be preferred before others—and if it be found to serve the purpose it is then a good peg. Whether it so does depends upon the quality of thought which is extracted in such strange manners as these, and of course it has to be realised that the peg is only a pretext—whether Jewish Theosophy understood it as such or not. From the manner in which the Secret Doctrine is externalised in the ZOHAR one cannot help feeling that some of its authors knew this in their day, and in no very different manner from that in which I realise it now. The changes are rung after many manners by the great bells of tradition when they peal out the work of creation. The truth which emerges from the far-spreading tissue of reveries is the operating efficacy of the Divine Will in all the manifest universe, together with that which may be

---

[1] Z., fol. 207a ; II, 429.
[2] Ib., fol. 290a ; II, 670.
[3] Ib., Pt. II, fol. 14b ; III, 66, 67. It is said, however, elsewhere that the words by the help of which the world was made were not established until it pleased God to create man. The intention was that he should be dedicated to the study of the Law, by which the world subsists. In this study man is said to sustain creation.—Ib., Pt. II, fol. 161a, b ; IV, 101. In this manner the ZOHAR seems to stultify itself intentionally, establishing a contradiction in terms, as if to indicate that its concern was not with cosmology *per se* but with a mode of regarding creation imposed on the elect. Alternatively it might be intimating that the mind creates its world.
[4] Exodus xxxi. 3.
[5] Z., Pt. I, fol. 2a ; I, 8. It is to be noted in this connection that this Name was not revealed to the angels, which is one instance only of a recurring pretension that man was in a position of superiority to all other hierarchies of being.—Ib., Pt. III, 78b ; V, 214. See also ib., Pt. I, fol. 25a ; I, 157.

held to be within the measures of the Doctrine of Correspondences, which obtains everywhere in the Secret Doctrine—whatever the schools thereof—and has been reflected thence into systems which cannot be included in the same category. It would seem further to have been discovered at first hand by a few seers—as, for example, Jacob Böhme [1] and perhaps Swedenborg. It is the erection of an inevitable anthropomorphism into a philosophical doctrine, though when I say this I may be sanctifying the seeming limitation. It is at least true that man is, for all concern of man, the measure of the whole creation, and if the testimony of creation is true—as Leibnitz would have held—then that which we discern intellectually is in the likeness of the truth of things. But this is the Doctrine of Correspondences.

Nature, according to the ZOHAR, is the garment of God [2]; it is that in which He appears and wherein He is veiled, so that we can look upon Him and know Him in His vestured aspect; but it is not the body of God—which is more properly Shekinah, at least in one of her aspects—and it is still less God manifest. It is that which He took upon Himself for the purpose of appearing. Prior to the period when the Divine Name was formulated for the ends of creation He was apart from the kind of definition implied therein and this non-defined state is termed "Who" by the ZOHAR, as in the words: "Behold Who hath created," [3] while the product of creation is called "That": "Behold Who hath created That"—or these things. The Hebrew words are respectively MI and ELAH. The product specified was not, however, for the ZOHAR, that which we understand by creation but the Elohim below,[4] who thus came into being when the letters emanated from each other. The explanation is that by the pairing of ELAH and MI the Sons of the Doctrine contrived

---

[1] A comparison between Böhme's MYSTERIUM MAGNUM, which is a commentary on Genesis, and the ZOHAR on the same text would bring out some extraordinary parallels and would increase the zeal of speculation concerning the glass of vision into which the German mystic looked. It was assuredly a glass which was common in several respects to other seers besides himself. His intimations on the first estate of man, on the making of woman, on Paradise and the Mystery of the Fall offer recurring analogies with Jewish Theosophy.

[2] Z., Pt. I, fol. 2a; I, 8.

[3] Isaiah xl. 26.

[4] It is not difficult to follow the reverie, though it seems involved at first sight. In the transcendence God and Elohim are inseparable, being male and female, and the first movement towards the production of a manifested universe was to send forth their living images below. That which was of the nature of God became of the nature of the Cosmos.

to obtain the word Elohim, and out of this verbal juggle arise the following conclusions: (1) Even as in creation MI, or Who, the Unnamed, remains always attached to ELAH = That, so (2) in God these two descriptions are inseparable, and (3) it is, thanks to this mystery, that the world exists. We have here at the very inception of the ZOHAR that identification of Jehovah and Elohim which we shall find of such capital importance at a later stage of our research. At the moment we have only to observe that what I have called the juggle educes a doctrine of Divine Immanence in the cosmos of manifested things. Apart from this there could be neither the things themselves nor the harmony which produces the music, the accord, the grace, the beauty of creation. It was to make known this doctrine that Elijah once shewed himself to Rabbi Simeon on the sea-shore, after which he took flight, as the text says, and the Master of Kabbalism saw him no more, leastwise at that time.[1]

The passage of Isaiah which I have quoted twice already is affirmed elsewhere to express the whole work of creation. By "Who" above and "That" below has all been made.[2] When we read in yet another place that Scripture was the Architect under God,[3] the reference is also to Elohim, either in the vesture of the Written Law or in that of the Secret Tradition. But I have spoken of the word BERESHITH and how it is rendered sometimes " in Wisdom," which is recognised by the ZOHAR on the authority of the Chaldaic Paraphrase of Onkelos. But Wisdom is regarded more correctly as the analogical interpretation of the Word,[4] and it is added that the world exists owing to the " sublime and impenetrable mystery of CHOKMAH." It follows that creation is a work of wisdom, operating by means of benediction. He Who is ineffable, according to the Secret Doctrine, He Who is mysterious and unknown,[4] delineates Himself in vesture, as a priest assuming pontifical clothing. He unfolds Himself in the Voice of Blessing and passes continually from the unknown into the range of apprehension by means of this Voice, uttering the speech of wisdom.

But God said: " Let there be light," and it is affirmed that

---

[1] Z., Pt. I, fol. 2a; I, 9.
[2] Ib., fol. 29b, 30a; I, 186.
[3] Ib., Pt. II, fol. 161a, 161b; IV, 100, 101.
[4] Ib., Pt. I, fol. 3b; I, 18.

all celestial legions and powers emanate therefrom. When first manifested, its brilliance filled the world from end to end; but when God foresaw the number of the guilty He concealed and rendered it inaccessible.[1] The sweet smell of the spikenard in the SONG OF SOLOMON signifies the celestial light,[2] while it is said elsewhere that it is designated by the word goodness.[3] This is an illustration of the way in which from many ingenuities of interpretation some appealing lesson is educed. Again, it does not signify that the methods are artificial in their nature; Zoharic Theosophy is in a very marked and particular sense an illustration beforehand of Matthew Arnold's idea that God has put " a heap of letters " into the hands of man and has bade him make with them " what word he would." The distinction between Arnold's hypothetical case and the one now under notice is that in place of a painful consciousness on the part of humanity through the ages that the true Word has never been formed with the letters, the rabbinical masters believed that their sacred ciphers produced true words invariably and could be used in any manner which would extract a refulgent and Divine idea. BERESHITH has served on more than a single occasion in this manner, but its capacities are not exhausted, and so also in respect of the first created light. If that word signifies goodness, it means also Perfect Love,[4] the Grand and Divine Love, that Love of man for God, the correspondence of which is God's Perfect Love for man. This Love of the Divine in man is not grounded on the self-questing hope of personal benefit, but is something constant in affliction and in joy, rooted in the perfection of God. Hereof is the ground of union between the Divine Creator and the creature divinely fashioned by the hands of Him.[5] And because of this union the word Light is said also to be the symbol of Unity.[6] It is in the sense of all these considerations that our world is held truly to form the centre of that which is celestial and to be surrounded by doors which open thereon.[7] Like all the streets of thought, all paths and

---

[1] Z., Pt. I, fol. 30b; I, 190, 191.
[2] Ib., fol. 30a; I, 188, 189.
[3] Ib., fol. 7a; I, 3b.
[4] Ib., fol. 11b; I, 66.
[5] The authority is THE SONG OF SOLOMON, i. 2: "Let him kiss me with the kisses of his mouth"; and these words are held to express the perfect and eternal joy which all worlds shall experience in their union with the Supreme Spirit. The condition of this union is said to be the prayer of man.—Z., Pt. I, fol. 44b; I, 262.
[6] Ib., fol. 12b; I, 70.
[7] Ib., fol. 172a; II, 275.

vistas of the cosmos, the portals in their tens of thousands open on God.

I must append hereto the symbolism of a certain myth which connects with the primæval formulation of the Divine Name and has its origin in the TALMUD.[1] As developed in the ZOHAR, it presents another aspect of that point of Divine Thought about which we heard at the beginning of this section. It concerns a mysterious stone called SCHETHÍYÂ which was originally in the Throne of God [2]—that is to say, it was a precious stone or jewel —and was cast by Him into the abyss, so to form the basis of the world and give birth thereto. One might say otherwise that it was like a cubical stone or altar, for its extremity was concealed in the depth, while its surface or summit rose above the chaos. It was the central point in the immensity of the world, the corner-stone,[3] the tried stone, the sure foundation, but also that stone which the builders rejected.[4] The last allocation, however, passes understanding, as by the hypothesis of the legend it was used in the building from the beginning. Finally—but this is not less inscrutable—it was that stone which served Jacob as a pillow and thereafter for an altar.[5] It was the good stone, the precious stone and the foundation of Zion.[6] The Tables of the Law were made from it,[7] and it is destined for the salvation of the world.[8] Jacob called it the House of the Elohim,[9] meaning that the Hypostasis to which this name is attributed transfers her residence from the world above to that which is below.[10] It is like the *lapis exilis* of the German Graal legend, and of Alchemy according to the Second Raymund Lully, for it appears to be a slight stone; it is supposed to have been carried by Aaron [11] when he entered the Holy Place, and it was held in the hands of David when he desired to contemplate close at hand the glory of his Master.[12]

---

[1] See the tracts called YOMA and SANHEDRIN.
[2] Z., Pt. II, fol. 222a, 222b; IV, 243.
[3] *Ib.*, Pt. I, fol. 231a; II, 511. See also Job xxxviii. 6.
[4] Ps. cxviii. 22. See also Z., III, 152b; V, 392.
[5] Z., Pt. I, fol. 72b; I, 429.
[6] *Ib.*, fol. 231a; II, 512.
[7] *Ib.*, fol. 231b; II, 514.
[8] *Ib.*, fol. 231a; II, 512.
[9] Genesis xxviii. 22.
[10] Z., Pt. I, fol. 231a; II, 512.
[11] Leviticus xvi. 3. The reference is merely to Aaron's entry, and does not tolerate the suggestion indicated.
[12] Z., Pt. I, fol. 72a; I, 427.

In a sense it fell from heaven, like the Stone from the crown of Lucifer, and again it was overturned by the iniquity of man, until Jacob restored it to an upright position. Solomon was also one of those who restored it, and thereon he built the Sanctuary.[1] We may not know how to harmonise these references which seem to exhaust all that is said of the Stone in the Old Testament, but its connection with other and less fabulous elements belonging to the Zoharic myth of creation resides in the fact that this Stone was inscribed with the Divine Name before it was cast into the abyss.[2] For the rest, it seems part of the inherent notion that the world was created for Israel and that the Story of its making is a part of the Story of election. So is it said in one place that the world did not obtain stability until Israel received the Law on Mount Sinai[3]; that God created the worlds after He had delivered the Law; that He ended his work in the Levitical Law, which is the basis of the world, and is therefore that legendary Stone with which we have been dealing, for the Secret Doctrine is a Sabbath; and that Abraham is also the foundation, the one just being on whom it rests, by whom it is made permanent, and who nourishes all creatures.[4] It would be not less idle work to try and harmonise these references than to shew that they are not to be taken blindly. They are things that Stand by themselves, unrelated one to another, and they serve their purpose as such, being loose lines of thought turning the Student's attention in one direction. If we look in this direction and read with the heart therein, I think that we may come to understand how the mystic Stone is the central point of the world and how at this point there is the Holy of Holies.[5]

---

[1] Z., fol. 91b; I, 429.
[2] Ib., Pt. II, fol. 91b; III, 370.
[3] Ib., Pt. I, fol. 89a; I, 511. Within the measures of the romantic hypothesis, it is obvious that the world was created for the elect of Israel, for it is the scene in which their election finds its field of action. The fantasy would obtain more widely in its application to that greater Israel which is the elect of all ages and peoples.
[4] Ib., Pt. II, fol. 86b; I, 498.
[5] Ib., Pt. I, fol. 231a; II, 511.—There is also the Stone "cut out without hands" of Dan. ii. 34, and it is said in the ZOHAR to represent Him Who is "the shepherd, the Stone of Israel" (Gen. xlix. 24). It is the Community of Israel—that which shall be called the House of God (ib., xxviii. 22). The Stone of Jacob is that Stone which forms the bond of union between the Divine Essences—blessed on the right, blessed on the left, blessed above and below. According to THE FAITHFUL SHEPHERD, Z., Pt. III, fol. 279b, the Stone of Daniel was engraved with the letters of TETRAGRAMMATON, and it is not to be identified with the Stone of Moses, being that rock which he smote twice.—Num. xx, 8-11.

I have spoken of the Word in its relation to the Divine Transcendence. It is said that the six days were created thereby, being lights emanating from the Word and illuminating the world. It is also the Divine Seed from which manifest things came forth. The specific affirmation is, however, that the world was created by the Word united to the Spirit,[1] that which operated being the sound of the Word as a voice which spoke and it was done. For the dispensation of the light this Word was joined with the Father, the light itself proceeding from the Father and being as such incompatible with matter.[2] In the union of the Father and the Word it became accessible thereto, seeing that henceforward it proceeded from both. Before the manifestation of the Word the light proceeding from the Father formed seven letters, which—in some inscrutable sense—were without body and for this reason were inaccessible to matter. When the sacred, nebulous, clouded fire which is called " darkness upon the face of the deep "[3] appeared for the transmutation of matter, seven other letters were formed, also from pure light and hence inaccessible to matter, like the first seven. When the Word manifested, the remaining eight letters were formed, and then the whole alphabet was rendered accessible by the casting down of that barrier which separated matter from the celestial rays. It is for this reason that, according to Scripture, Elohim said : " Let there be light."[4] The firmament was made likewise and the waters were separated from the waters, or the light above from the light below.[5] It was subject to this separation that matter became susceptible of light, and I infer that a spiritual mystery is here indicated which might be comparable to the distinction between material light of reason and that of the higher mind. Now, the Word is said to be designated by the name Elohim.[6]

---

[1] It is taught that the one is not without the other, and the authority is Ps. xxxiii, 6: " By the word of the Lord were the heavens made and all the hosts of them by the breath of his mouth."—Z., Pt. I, fol. 156a ; II, 213, 214.
[2] Z., Pt. I, fol. 16b ; I, 98 *et seq.*
[3] Gen. i. 2.
[4] *Ib.*, v. 3.
[5] Z., Pt. I, 16b ; I, 100.
[6] The greater light which God made to rule the day is a symbol of Jehovah, while the lesser which rules the night is the Word, regarded as the end of thought.—*Ib.*, fol. 20a ; I, 123. It is said elsewhere that if the world had been the work of the Divine Essence called Jehovah, everything would have been everlasting therein, but being the work of the Divine Essence called Elohim, it is all subject to destruction. This curious statement arises from Ps. xlvi. 9, but it has been pointed out that in this Psalm the

The firmament constituted the line of division: thereunto matter could ascend and thereunto could the light come down; but while it is thus a limit in both directions, the firmament is also a bond of union between the one and the other, so that both are united thereby in Elohim. It is said also that the Word assumed the form of the alphabetical signs, presumably because it is in this form that thought passes into written expression.[1] The six days of creation are lights emanating from the Word for the illumination of the world.[2] It is thanks, in fine, to the Word that the waters of the celestial river flow for ever to irrigate the worlds that are below.[3]

So far therefore concerning the work of God in creation and the instruments appertaining thereto. But there are certain final intimations which belong more especially to our subject and lead therein. When the Holy One created the world He engraved the Mystery of Faith in letters of sparkling light; He engraved it above and below, because it is the same Mystery and because the world below is the mirror of that which is above. By means of the Mystery of Faith He created the worlds. Now, in another place it is asked: What worlds? The answer is matrimonial unions.[4] These are the worlds which God does not cease from creating. It follows that creation, as the story is told, is a veil of the sex mystery; it follows also that something is understood of which physical union is the shadow as this is known here: the intimations concern union as the result of a law, which law is literal on the plane of expression and mystical on a higher plane. Another Key is given in these words: The union of the male and female principle engendered the world [5]—as indeed it was impossible that it should do otherwise within the measures of Zoharic symbolism. So also in the emanation of the letters, ALEPH and BETH are postulated, from which two come forth the rest of the alphabet, and hence

---

Divine Name used is not Elohim but Jehovah. In the text itself a debate follows and there is a divided view.—*Ib.*, fol. 59b; I, 337.
[1] Z., Pt. I, fol. 21a; I, 129.
[2] *Ib.*, fol. 31b; I, 196. The ZOHAR is sometimes like scholastic philosophy in its lighter moments, and seeing that the six days of creation are mentioned by Genesis but not the six nights which are implied therein, it inquires what has become of the latter and concludes that God holds them in concealment for some good purpose of His own.
[3] *Ib.*, fol. 33b; I, 208.
[4] *Ib.*, fol. 89a; I, 511.
[5] *Ib.*, Pt. II, fol. 228a; IV, 250.

it is said that these two are male and female.[1] Here is a further reason why BETH was the instrument of creation, as already explained. Another story intimates that God took the "heap of letters" in His hands and began to make worlds therewith over and over, but they had no consistence, the reason being that the Covenant had not yet been made.[2] The world under the law of circumcision must be understood as a specific dispensation within the manifest order, and the destroyed worlds are previous dispensations which arose and decayed unceasingly. This is illustrated when it is said that their destruction was because those who dwelt therein did not accept the commandments of the Doctrine. It is not that God undoes His works, but the works undo themselves by refusing salvation. Why, it is asked, should God put an end to those children whom, according to tradition, He created by the Second Hypostasis, called HE?[3]

It is only under the Law and the Doctrine, or in virtue of that Inward Covenant of which circumcision was once the shadow, that man is hereby made male and female by the Elohim, which is another manner of saying that the cosmic harmony is established in him. We shall see in a later division that he was created prototypically in the likeness of the world below and in that of the world above. He was also so made that he represents the Celestial Lover and Beloved, Who are symbolised by the letters YOD and HE, and are united by VAU.[4] In another form of symbolism he was designed to be the Spouse or Beloved of God who was never to be separated from the Lover. So proceeds the mystery with which we are concerned from stage to stage of unfoldment; but we are at present concerned only in seeing how it belongs to all.

---

[1] Z., Pt. I, fol. 30a; I, 187. It is said elsewhere that the letters expressing the male principle are not susceptible of transformation, while those expressing the female principle can be counterchanged by means of certain combinations.—*Ib.*, Pt. II, fol. 134a; IV, 29. Which letters are male and which are female, we are not told. A note to the French version suggests that the uneven are masculine and the even feminine, which is theoretically plausible but is not borne out in fact because it is certain that HE, the fifth letter, is female in the ZOHAR, while the sixth or VAU is masculine.

[2] *Ib.*, fol. 25a; I, 154.

[3] *Ib.*

[4] Z., Pt. I, fol. 26a; I, 161, 162.

BOOK VI

HIERARCHIES OF SPIRITUAL BEING

BOOK VI

HIERARCHIES OF SPIRITUAL BEING

I.—THE SOUL IN KABBALISM

WE have ascertained the heads of Kabbalistic instruction as to the essential nature of God, the transition from the Divine Unmanifest into the manifestation of Divinity, the extension of the powers and attributes thus developed through the archetypal, creative, formative and material worlds, the Kabbalistic hypothesis of creation and the doctrine of transcendental and natural science. It remains for us to present in brief outline the doctrine of spiritual essences according to Jewish Theosophy. This is one of the favoured and certainly most recurring subjects found in the ZOHAR, as it is that also which was destined to receive fuller development than any other in the later literature of Kabbalism. The history of its growth is also worth noting. Pre-existence and the sub-division of the spiritual nature in man are found in the TALMUD, but the SEPHER YETZIRAH has nothing to tell us on the subject, and there is very little in the first commentators on that treatise. It may be said, with considerable truth, that the book and its connections were concerned rather with the physical forces which produced the universe; but the commentaries at least are sufficiently discursive to have included it in their scheme if they had anything to say upon the subject. It remains therefore that the curious and involved speculations with which we are dealing here are in the main a later growth. The distinction between a holy intelligence and an animal soul in man is found in the BOOK OF CONCEALMENT,[1] which, so far

---

[1] "When the inferior man descends (namely, into this world) there are found (in him) two spirits, according to the supernal form. Man (therefore) is constituted from the two sides, the right and the left. As from the right side he has a holy mind, as from the left an animal soul." The extension of the left side was the consequence of the Fall.—BOOK OF CONCEALMENT, c. iv. par. 7-9. This is according to the Latin version of Rosenroth, his expansions in brackets included. Compare, however, De Pauly's translation, Vol. IV, p. 143, as follows: "When 'Adam' came here below the

as can be judged from its form, is among the most ancient portions of the ZOHAR. The latter cycle may be regarded, broadly speaking, as the chief source of metapsychical hypotheses in Kabbalism proper. The indications contained therein became a vast and ponderous system in the schools of Isaac de Loria and Moses of Cordova. This system has exercised at all times a particular influence on writers who have approached Kabbalism from an occult standpoint, and—chiefly, perhaps, because it has been made available in Latin by Rosenroth—has superseded that of the ZOHAR itself. Franck states that it is not Kabbalism proper, and affirms very truly that it is full of distorted rabbinical reveries, but it cannot be denied that the roots are in older texts. The later speculations are in other words developed from the ZOHAR, and the following slight sketch contains the general elements of the subject.

Belief in the soul's immortality, which is not found in the Pentateuch or the prophets, was held by the Israel of later times in connection with that of the resurrection of the body, and appears freely in the TALMUDS.[1] Makers of occult speculations, who remember that Moses was learned in all the wisdom of the Egyptians, conceive it to be impossible that he should have known nothing of doctrines which were known to all Egypt, and they hold accordingly that he communicated them secretly to a circle of initiation, by which they were perpetuated in the oral way. Others incline to the notion that they were acquired by the Jews in Babylon. In the Græco-Egyptian period it was, of course, impossible that the learned rabbins of Alexandria should not have been acquainted with the great speculation of a future life. In one way or another it was inevitable that the Jews should have acquired it, which they did accordingly, and the particular date or circumstances are a minor question, about which there can be no certainty. The doctrine, as taught by the TALMUD,

---

Celestial Figure had two spirits, one on the right destined to man and the other on the left destined to animals. But after the sin of Adam the left side was so extended that it penetrated even to man."

[1] " The immortality of the soul and the resurrection of the body figure in the TALMUD as tenets of the Synagogue. They form the thirteenth and last article in the profession of faith of Maimonides."—Leroy-Beaulieu, ISRAEL AMONG THE NATIONS, p. 17. This is not quite accurate, as that article concerns the resurrection only. " I firmly believe that there will be a resurrection of the dead, at the time when it shall please the Creator, blessed be His name ! "—M. Friedländer, TEXT BOOK OF THE JEWISH RELIGION. 4th ed. London. 1896.

though recognising five divisions of the soul having names familiar to Kabbalism, is comparatively of a simple kind : it does not possess, for example, that philosophical aspect which we find in Philo, and even those who dwell upon Greek influence in early Kabbalism must admit that its pneumatology, after allowing for pre-existence, shews very little trace of Platonism.[1]

It should be understood that the story of the soul in Kabbalism is part of that central doctrine which the ZOHAR calls the Mystery of Faith, or at least the one is in close connection with the other and they arise together.[2] I shall proceed at once to my subject and consider it under four heads, being (1) Pre-existence, (2) The parts of the soul, (3) The soul in the world to come, but here only in respect of the blessed state, and (4) Reincarnation. The doctrine concerning Sheol will call for separate treatment.

As regards pre-existence, I will establish first what may be termed the general thesis, with that which belongs thereto, and will then illustrate it by such distinctions and variations as may seem to deserve mention. When the Holy One willed to create the universe, He formed [3]—and apparently in the first instance—those souls which were intended subsequently to dwell in human bodies.[4] The place of their tarrying is said in more than one place to be the Paradise below, which is the Earthly Paradise or the Lower Eden.[5] This is also an abode of disincarnate souls who have entered that path which leads to the blessed life ; but it is not their final home.[6] Like the Christ of Nazareth, the ZOHAR seems to know that there are

---

[1] For a good summary of Kabbalistic pneumatology the German student may consult, *inter alia*, Leiningen's LEELENLEHRE DER QABALAH. Leipsic. 1887.

[2] It speaks at once for the genesis and term of the mystery : there is that which must be done in heaven, brought down amongst the similitudes of earthly things and finally restored to heaven.

[3] This is the method of expression in the place from which I derive, but the idea, in its more adequate Zoharic expression, is not one of formation ; it is rather of begetting. The point is that souls are affirmed to have a father and mother, and they are produced in virtue of the union between male and female. The basis of the idea is Gen. i. 24 : " Let the earth bring forth the living creature," this " creature " being held to mean the soul of the first celestial man.—Z., Pt. II, fol. 12a ; III, 53. The fundamental point to be noticed is that the ZOHAR teaches the pre-existence, as it does also the foreknowledge of the soul.

[4] *Ib.*, fol. 96b ; III, 387. " Each has its form like that of the body which it is destined to animate."

[5] Z., Pt. II, fol. 11a ; III, 48. It is also said poetically that souls are formed in Paradise of the four winds which breathe therein, but the reference is really to that psychic vesture which gives form to the soul.—*Ib.*, fol. 13b ; III, 59, 60.

[6] Z., Pt. II, fol. 11a ; III, 48.

many mansions in the House of the Father. Before they left the presence of the Maker, all souls—meaning those destined to incarnate under the obedience and election of Israel—were conjured to keep the precepts of the Law.[1] While they await incarnation in Paradise they are clothed with bodies and have countenances like those which they are destined to possess hereafter, but these vestures are of course of a psychic or spiritual kind.[2] When the time arrives for embodiment each soul in its turn is called before the Holy One and is told which physical envelope to inhabit.[3] Paradise is a place of blessing, and it may be that " from the gold bar " thereof it has leaned out and seen no reason to descend of its own accord, or to quit present happiness, as it is said, " for bondage and temptation." It is assured, however, that from the day of its creation it had no other mission than to come into this world.[4] It submits therefore and is stripped of the paradisaical body, that it may be clothed with veils of earth. It takes the road of earth sorrowing [5] and proceeds into the exile of human life.

Souls descend in a pre-established order of succession, though there are certain exceptions.[6] As in all the great events of human life and the universe the precedence must be taken by Palestine, it is held that descent to earth reaches its term therein, and this invariably, after which the souls are thence

---

[1] Z., Pt. I, fol. 223d ; II, 520. See also Pt. III, fol. 13a ; V, 38, and Pt. II, fol. 161b ; IV, 101, where the soul is pledged to the study of the Law and the attainment of the Mystery of Faith.

[2] *Ib.*, Pt. II, fol. 150a ; IV, 70. There is no real joy for the soul, save in the body of Paradise ; in that of earth it is shut out from communication with the Supreme Mysteries. See also *Ib.*, Pt. I, fol. 90b, 91a ; II, 515, 516.

[3] *Ib.*, Pt. II, fol. 96b ; III, 388.

[4] *Ib.* Seeing that the Earthly Paradise is the house of pre-existing souls and the place to which they return after death, it might seem that the Fall which took place therein was in the prototypical humanity, or ADAM PROTOPLASTES of later Kabbalism, in whom all souls fell, as Recanati maintained. He speculated also that they are detached from the parent body in succession for incarnation on earth. This is not Zoharic symbolism but individual reverie. There is a sense in which the man of the Eden myth was ADAM PROTOPLASTES, as the first of human beings, but the prototypical ADAM PROTOPLASTES is the Divine Son, conceived in DAATH and so extended through the Lower SEPHIROTH that He stands on MALKUTH.

[5] It is even declared that all which is learned by man as a consequence of his habitation here below was known previously by him in the world above, but this is apparently the case—more especially or only—with those who love the truth and are righteous in earthly life. My authority is the COMMENTARY ON LEVITICUS, and it puts an end to the question of freewill by adding that those who are wicked below have been already set aside by God, their incarnation being delayed through frequent enforced visits to the abyss. So also those who are headstrong here were headstrong prior to their incarnation.—Z., Pt. III, fol. 61b ; V, 169. This was said in the presence of Rabbi Simeon and was suffered to pass unchallenged.

[6] *Ib.*, Pt. II, fol. 101a ; III, 407.

distributed to the whole world.[1] What is much more important is that all souls awaiting incarnation are arranged in pairs; the one which is destined to animate a male is by the side of one who is to animate a female, so that those who are united below have been united previously above,[2] because, according to Scripture, there is nothing new under the sun. They descend also together, but they pass into the charge of an angel who presides over the pregnancy of women and they are then separated.[3] Sometimes the male soul animates a man first, sometimes the reverse.[4] When the time of marriage comes, the Holy One unites them as before and proclaims their union. After the espousals, and apparently when intercourse has taken place, they become—mystically speaking—one body and one soul. If, this, however, is the law, we shall see later on that it is illustrated chiefly by exceptions.[5] At the moment I will mention only a variant of the last notion, which says that, prior to their descent on earth, all souls form an unity, and are part of the same mystery; separation into male and female takes place by reason of incarnation, but they are again made one in marriage.[6] This recalls the Adamic legend and would seem its application to the history of individuals above and below.

I have now given the general thesis, supplemented by counter-theses, but it should be realised that it is drawn from several places. Among questions which must be left open when the text is collated at large there is that which locates the soul prior to incarnation in the Paradise below, as I have said. Other accounts substitute the superior Eden,[7] and

---

[1] Z., Pt. I, fol. 205b; II, 424. The exceptions correspond to the ideas of those who are born out of due time. It is said that male souls come from the Tree of Wisdom and female souls from an Inferior Tree, but it is a sporadic suggestion which is at issue with recurring notions.—*Ib.*, Pt. II, fol. 101a; III, 408. It is explained in another place that just souls attached to the Sacred King by true love are longer than others in coming to this earth.—*Ib.*, Pt. III, fol. 68a, b; V, 186.

[2] This is the blessed union.—*Ib.*, fol. 91b; I, 520. But it is to be understood almost unquestionably that the allusion, here and elsewhere, is always to the souls of Israel.

[3] *Ib.*

[4] It is not said that a mistake ever occurs, though this is recognised by one form of occultism and is held to account for certain sex-aberrations. I have not found any Kabbalistic warrant for the opinion. See Éliphas Lévi, in my translation of his TRANSCENDENTAL MAGIC, *Its Doctrine and Ritual*, 1923, pp. 109, 110.

[5] As the Zoharic considerations on the subject of sister-souls who have been, so to speak, mismarried bear ample witness.

[6] Z., Pt. III, fol. 43b; V, 121. See also *ib.*, Pt. I, fol. 85b; I, 493, 494, where it is stated that whether or not a man shall meet in this life with the soul predestined to himself in union, even from the beginning, depends on his own desert.

[7] *Ib.*, Pt. III, fol. 43a; V, 120. Here it is said that when the soul is in the act of

according to one of these the descent for a period into the Earthly Garden takes place just prior to incarnation. The time is thirty days.[1] One of the alternatives has no explicit concern with either Paradise but affirms that from an epoch which preceded the creation of the world all souls have been in the presence of the Holy One and there remain till they are called to go down on earth.[2] According to tradition all emanate from the same region and during their sojourn in heaven they share in the government of things above and below.[3] There are also certain souls which are kept in the hiddenness and are guarded in a particular manner. When these enter into earthly bodies they have power to reascend into heaven without dying.[4] Of such were Enoch and Elias. Speaking for the majority of cases, there is some trouble in effecting a harmonious junction between the soul and its earthly envelope[5]; it is not definitely established therein until after thirty-three days, and for the first seven it goes in and out continuously. One reason seems to be that circumcision does not take place till the thirtieth day and that for three days thereafter the body is in a state of suffering.[6] These reveries are drawn out of two texts: "She shall then continue in the blood of her purifying three and thirty days,"[7] which is of course a reference to the purification of women after childbirth; and: "It shall be seven days under the dam,"[8] which is a reference to the birth of animals—bullocks, sheep, or goats. The "blood of her purification" is in some obscure way the blood of circumcision.[9]

---

descending towards this world it visits the Earthly Paradise, where it sees the souls of the just who have left this life. It goes also to SHEOL and sees the souls of the wicked. These are object-lessons, and the inference is that they may act as a guide in life. It is said in another place that the Soul is from the Sanctuary on high.—*Ib.*, Pt. I, fol. 205b; II, 424. It is that Temple which is mentioned in Ex. xv. 17, as "the Sanctuary, O Lord, which Thy hands have established."—Z., Pt. I, fol. 7; I, 38.

[1] According to another account, they pay only a flying visit—also for purposes of inspection.—*Ib.*, Pt. III, fol. 13a, b; V, 39.

[2] *Ib.*, Pt. II, fol. 282a; IV, 310. It was especially the union of male and female souls which existed before creation. The time of intercourse corresponds to midnight on earth. It is an union in the contemplation of God and the joy thereof brings forth other souls, which are those of Gentiles who become converts to Jewry.

[3] *Ib.*, Pt. III, fol. 68a; V, 186.

[4] *Ib.*, fol. 68b; V, 186, 187. See also *ib.*, fol. 182b, 183a; V, 475, 476.

[5] It is said to be attached to the body by one end only. The soul and its envelope develop simultaneously, meaning that their union becomes more perfect, but care of the soul is needed for this purpose, just as the body needs care. The soul, however, is in the care of heaven.—*Ib.*, Pt. I, fol. 197a; II, 381.

[6] Z., Pt. III, fol. 43b; V, 121, 122.

[7] Leviticus xii. 4.

[8] Ex. xxii. 30.

[9] Z., Pt. III, fol. 43b, 44a; V, 122.

Hereof is the ZOHAR in one of its exceptional moods; but these things are weariness, and I will conclude therefore on pre-existence with one further reference. It is said that the souls of the patriarchs pre-existed in the thought of God before the creation and were connected in the other world, whence they came forth in their due day.[1] The text apposite hereto is: "The flowers appear on the earth,"[2] meaning that the souls of the patriarchs appear in this world. One would say that these souls were the thoughts of God dwelling in divine men, but if we debated the subject, we should see, I think, that the ZOHARIC hypothesis really comes to this; that the soul-world is a world of thought in God; that the thought precedes the Word, as it is shewn to have done in respect of creation generally; and that souls are uttered forth continually, passing ultimately into expression in flesh.

Though it is closely connected with pre-existence, the mode followed in the generation or creation of souls is hypothetically at least independent and there are important reasons why it should be postponed for consideration till I treat of the mystery of sex in Zoharic Theology. I proceed therefore to the parts or divisions of the soul. It is taught in a summary way that man is composed of three things[3]: Life, or NEPHESH; Spirit, which is RUAH or HAÏÂ; and Soul, that is, NESHAMAH. By these he becomes "a living spirit"— a term, however, which is applied more especially to NESHAMAH. They are called also three degrees, or vital spirit, intellectual spirit and soul proper.[4] NEPHESH is the fallible part, for sin is suggested neither by RUAH nor NESHAMAH.[5] It is said elsewhere and more plainly that the vital spirit sins, but not the soul. The three degrees are superposed one upon another in the order already given,[6] and NESHAMAH is attached

---

[1] Z., Pt. I, fol. 1a; I, 5.
[2] Song of Solomon ii. 12.
[3] Z., Pt. I, fol. 27a; I, 169. The "living spirit" is said to proceed from the mouth of Shekinah, who is called "living soul." Here is another aspect of souls being uttered forth by the Divine, and seeing that this is the Shekinah in transcendence, who is (a) the Third Hypostasis and (b) the Mother = AIMA, in the Supernal SEPHIRA BINAH, we shall understand the kind of union which subsists between her and the Father, who is ABBA in CHOKMAH. There is the Divine Thought in KETHER: it is formulated as if mentally in CHOKMAH: and it is uttered in BINAH, producing the living intelligences, who are therefore begotten into the higher Paradise.
[4] Ib., Pt. I, fol. 205b, 206a; II, 424.
[5] Ib., Pt. III, fol. 16a; V, 46. It is said, however, elsewhere that the defilement of Nephesh defiles Ruah and Neshamah.—Ib., Pt. II, fol. 182a; IV, 155.
[6] Ib., Pt. II, fol. 206a; II, 425.

to God¹; but all these are not the imprescriptible possession of every person in life: the higher parts are earned by serving the Master.²

Unfortunately, this thesis—which may seem intelligible enough in itself—leads to very grave complications in respect of that which pre-existed and that which constitutes man a living being in manifestation. It is said that some persons are judged worthy to possess a NESHAMAH, others a RUAH only, while yet others have a NEPHESH and nothing more.³ These last, by reason of their deficiency, are attached to the impure spirit.⁴ The NEPHESH alone is imprescriptible, or necessary to the man's existence.⁵ If he comports himself worthily with this gift another spirit is poured into him, which is like a crown of NEPHESH, and this is RUAH. The man is then illuminated by light from a superior region and is in a position to discern the laws of the Secret King. If he still continues worthy he receives the crown of RUAH, the name of which is NESHAMAH; but it is called also Soul of God. Now, it seems obvious that it is this only of which pre-existence, paradisaical life and the Divine Vision can be predicated, and the point is therefore that—contrary to the very clear doctrine concerning the descent of souls—NESHAMAH does not come down and incarnate at birth in any human being.⁶ It seems in this case to be mere fantasy with which we have been dealing previously.

There is, however, an attempt elsewhere to harmonise these disparities, for it is said that when the soul, meaning NESHAMAH, leaves the celestial region and comes down

---

¹ Z., Pt. III, fol. 25a; V, 64.
² Ib., Pt. I, fol. 206a; II, 424.
³ Ib., fol. 25a; V, 65.
⁴ We have to check this by other statements as follows: (a) Man is endowed with a NEPHESH in the first place and it is given him as a preparation for leading a holy life.—Ib., Pt. I, fol. 206a; I, 424. (b) The three degrees constitute one soul and are attached one to another.—Ib., Pt. III, fol. 70b; V, 191. But in further contradistinction hereto, another ruling suggests that the possession of NEPHESH and RUAH leaves man useless for the purposes of Shekinah in captivity and of Moses who abides with her.—Ib., Pt. I, fol. 28a; I, 175, 176. But the reason seems to be that they are unskilled in the Secret Doctrine.
⁵ Z., Pt. III, fol. 70b; V, 191, 192.
⁶ Alternatively, the successive addition of higher parts of the soul must be understood as gifts of grace, and there is authority for this view in the text, though I do not propose to consider it, as the multiplication of aspects beyond what is actually needed must tend only to the reader's confusion. I have registered the fact for the use of those who would carry their research further. When it is said elsewhere that NESHAMAH cannot sin, the reference—from such point of view—is to a state of attained sanctity in which lapse is—by this statement—impossible, meaning unlikely. It has become not less difficult to sin than before it was to abstain from sin.

towards earth it is joined to the intellectual spirit; afterwards both are joined to the spirit of light—that is, NEPHESH.[1] The spirit of light and the intellectual spirit dwell together and depend one upon the other; but the soul is independent of both. Another thesis is that when man proposes to live in purity, heaven comes to his aid, granting him the holy soul, by which he is purified and sanctified; but if he be unworthy and will not live in purity, he is animated only by NEPHESH and RUAH. It is obvious that this fails to concur with the earlier statement, which represents RUAH as a gift to be earned; but we can read between the lines of contradiction and conclude that the real intention is to represent the permanent part of man as descending and overshading the personality, when this is born into the world; it draws nearer with his growth and improvement; and it may be, so to speak, incorporated with him, or it may not. Understood thus, the speculation will stand at its value: it is a primitive crudity of materialism, but the ZOHAR sometimes exceeds such notions and ascends into a clearer region.

Before giving two or three casual examples, I will cite another classification because of the extraordinary consequences which follow.[2] NEPHESH is the soul which forms the body and presides over the propagation of beings; RUAH is the soul which causes NEPHESH to act and determines its kind of action[3]; NESHAMAH is the supreme force issuing from the Tree of Life.[4] These three degrees separate after death, each returning to the place from which it was brought. NEPHESH is presumably of the earth earthy, for it is said to remain in the tomb[5]—but any statement seems to serve which is made on the spur of the moment; RUAH passes to

---

[1] Z., Pt. I, fol. 62a; I, 365. According to Adolphe Franck, NEPHESH throughout the Old Testament signifies the body of man, so long as it is alive.—LA KABBALE, p. 61. It is identified with the PSYCHE by ADUMBRATIO KABBALÆ CHRISTIANÆ, which is one of the rare supplements to Rosenroth's KABBALA DENUDATA. It is here regarded as the vitality inherent in the natural and instrumental body, and it is vegetative and sensitive in its nature. There seems to be no Zoharic authority for the other definitions.

[2] Z., Pt. I, fol. 287b, Appendix II, containing TOSSEFTA or ADDITIONS: I, 664.

[3] Late Kabbalism sometimes termed RUAH the Spirit, meaning the human soul itself. It was held to extend through the body, to be rational and self-subsisting, but its mode of comprehension was by intermediaries and not direct. It was also the seat of good and evil, and hence of the moral attributes.

[4] NESHAMAH is understanding in late Kabbalism, the individual intellect communicated by the Catholic and Divine Intellect.

[5] Z., Pt. I, fol. 287b; I, 664, 665. This statement is subject to considerable modification in other places.

the Earthly Paradise, where the High Priest Michael offers it as a holocaust to the Holy One and it remains in the joy of Paradise[1]; NESHAMAH ascends on high.[2] What purpose has been attained by its experience below does not appear in the text: it cannot sin, and it is not in search of merit. There is no need to add that—here again—this version of the tripartite personality, postulating independent survival in three separate directions—for NEPHESH is alive in the tomb—cannot be reconciled with the alternatives that have gone before. I conclude that the Secret Doctrine in Israel was unsettled on the subject of the soul and its divisions, that there is no guide for the perplexed therein, and that we shall come in the end to recognise only one truly and pregnant Secret Doctrine in Jewry, which is the secret concerning sex.

Among several intimations which are better than formal attempts to classify there is one which says that man acquires the soul of soul by fear of the Lord and by wisdom. He acquires the soul by penitence. Abraham represents the soul of soul; Sarah is the soul; Isaac is the intellectual spirit; and Rebecca is the vital spirit.[3] Another speculation designates NEPHESH as the soul in a state of sleep, and this definition seems excellent. RUAH is the soul in a waking state, by which I understand the earlier stages of becoming alive to things above. It is said that these two do not differ in essence. Above them is NESHAMAH, which is the soul proper.[4] These grades of the spirit of man are the image of the Mystery of Wisdom, and to fathom them is to discover that Wisdom. When NESHAMAH is pre-eminent in man he is called holy.

The parts of the spiritual personality are by no means exhausted in any triadic enumeration,[5] for ascent in the

---

[1] This also is qualified; it remains in the Paradise for a period and then returns whence it came, because the spirit—*i.e.*, RUAH—goes back to God Who gave it.
[2] It returns to the Tree of Life, because it came therefrom.
[3] Z., Pt. I, fol. 264a; II, 622.
[4] *Ib.*, fol. 83a, b; I, 480, 481.
[5] A more simple extension than here follows is given in Pt. II, fol. 158b; IV, 95, where it is said that the soul has five names, being NEPHESH, RUAH, NESHAMAH, HAÏA and YEHIDAH. This is an extract from THE FAITHFUL SHEPHERD. But—as we have seen—HAÏA is sometimes a synonym for RUAH. Isaac Myer gives the following definition: "YE'HU-DAH, the only one, is the *personality* of man; HAÏA is the life in man; NESHAMAH the soul or intellect; RUAH the spirit; NEPHESH the animal soul or vital *dynamics*, the *anima*.—PHILOSOPHY OF IBN GEBIROL, p. 397. Such a classification makes for confusion only as the distinctions do not correspond to separable aspects of human nature. Late Kabbalism said that YEHIDAH is individuality—the unity or correspondence by which man becomes like unto his First Cause. HAÏA is a condition of unity between the particular and catholic intellect, the union apparently

grades of sanctity can provide additionally to these and in succession: (1) a soul from the world of emanation on the side of the Daughter of the King[1]; (2) a soul from the world of emanation on the side of the Son of the King[2]; (3) a soul from the side of the Father and the Mother[3]; and (4) a soul which reflects the four letters of the Sacred Name Jehovah.[4] This is one specimen extension, but there are others, some of which I will omit and some are transferred to their proper place elsewhere. I may add here, however, that there is a casual supplementary soul[5] added to the Students of the Doctrine on the Sabbath Day, after which it returns whence it came. It appears to be a sacred soul issuing from the Tree of Life, and it is adapted to the works of the recipient. An alternative account attaches it to all good Israelites who fulfil the Law, whether they are students of the Doctrine in the deeper mystical sense or not.

The state of the soul in the world to come is described in several ways, as we should expect assuredly; but those which concern the blessed life of the departed can be harmonised, or at least there is nothing of essential discrepancy. When the good soul is preparing to leave this world, and while it is suspended from the body only at the larynx, it beholds three angels, to whom the dying man confesses his sins.[6] These spirits engarner the souls of the just and they accompany the glorious Shekinah, for no man leaves this world without seeing the Shekinah at the last moment of life.[7] The soul prostrates itself before her and praises God.[8] It seems then to enter a cavern wherein is a door leading to the Earthly Paradise[9]; there it encounters Adam, the patriarchs and all the just, who rejoice with her and she is admitted within the Garden. Either then or previously, she has been furnished

---

of our life with that life which is Divine. Franck says that it is the vital spirit, that its seat is in the heart, and that it is distinct from the principle of animal life.—LA KABBALE, p. 235.

[1] Z., Pt. II, fol. 94b; III, 379.

[2] *Ib.*, the authority being: "Ye are the children of the Lord your God."—Deut. xiv. 1.

[3] Z., fol. 94b; III, 379, 380. The versicle appertaining hereto is "breathed into his nostrils the breath of life; and man became a living soul."—Gen. ii. 7.

[4] A man in possession of this soul is the image of the Heavenly Master. Of him it is said: "And have dominion over the fish of the sea."—Gen. i. 28.

[5] See Z., Pt. II, fol. 88b; III, 361—among many other places.

[6] Z., Pt. I, Appendix III, SECRET MIDRASH, fol. 3b; II, 677.

[7] *Ib.*

[8] *Ib.*, fol. 2b; II, 676.

[9] *Ib.*, Pt. I, fol. 127a; II, 103. See also fol. 287b; II, 664.

with an envelope other than the fleshly body but still having the form thereof.[1] It is said as to this that the days of life are a vesture, and the days of man's life on earth are his vesture in the world to come, in so far as he has lived them worthily.[2] The odours given forth daily in the Garden of Eden perfume the precious vestments woven out of the days of man.[3] This again is a clear issue at its value, but it is superseded in other accounts and it complicates its own position by adding that there is one vesture [4] for NESHAMAH, another for RUAH, and one finally of an external and scarcely perceptible kind for NEPHESH [5]—all formed from the days of life. At the same time the commandments of the Law are the vesture of NESHAMAH.[6]

In this way we are taken to another point of spiritual progression which may be perhaps without prejudice to what has gone before. When the soul of a man who has been consecrated to the study of the Law during life quits this world, it goes up by the roads and pathways of the Law,[7] so that his knowledge is a guide in attainment, while the souls of those who have neglected such study go astray in the paths which lead to the region of GEBURAH, where they suffer punishment.[8] In another manner of symbolism the Law goes before the soul when it rises into the celestial regions, and it opens to him all the doors.[9] The Law remains with the soul till the day of resurrection, when it will take up the defence of the soul. This is again in reference to the Students of the Law,

---

[1] Z., Pt. I, fol. 91a; I, 516.

[2] See *post*, p. 285; and Z., Pt. I, fol. 224a, b; II, 482–484. It is said elsewhere that the soul cannot have two vestures at one and the same time, even as the spirit of good and the spirit of evil cannot dwell together. The heavenly envelope is assumed, or the soul is clothed therewith, when that of earth is decomposed as well as laid aside. It is a curious theory of vehicles, but it rests—*ex hypothesi*—on the authority of Rabbi Simeon. The object of Samael is to hinder man from receiving the garment of heaven, and this he can do until the fleshly body has dissolved.—*Ib.*, Pt. I, fol. 169b, 170a; II, 441. But the reference is apparently to NEPHESH. The RUAH is itself not at rest; it is only after the complete return of the earthly part to earth that it is drawn back to the Holy Spirit Which gave it.

[3] *Ib.*

[4] It is admitted that the wise in doctrine have not reached a full agreement on the subject, yet the number of vestures is three.—*Ib.*, fol. 225a; I, 485.

[5] Because, notwithstanding previous testimony, NEPHESH is bound up with the body in its tomb for twelve months only, after which it goes wandering and enters into communication with those who are still incarnate, to inquire respecting their sufferings and to pray at need for them.—*Ib.*, Pt. II, fol. 141b; IV, 48.

[6] Presumably NESHAMAH is so clothed with righteousness because it cannot sin.

[7] *Ib.*, fol. 175b; II, 290. See also fol. 27a; I, 170.

[8] *Ib.*, Pt. I, fol. 175b; II, 290.

[9] *Ib.*, fol. 185a; II, 329.

and it is said that after their resurrection they will preserve intact all knowledge which they had during their antecedent life.[1] Indeed such knowledge will be extended, so that they will be able to penetrate mysteries which were concealed from them previously.[2] It would seem also that those who are dedicated to the study of the Law on earth will be so occupied also in the world to come, and this apparently apart from the resurrection life.[3]

I will make an end of these economies by condensing one more parable of the soul.[4] There are Seven Palaces on high containing the Mystery of Faith, and I understand these as seven stages of union, like a tower going up to God. In case I am correct herein, it is said that six of them are accessible to the understanding of man, but the seventh is secret and forms part of the Supreme Mysteries.[5] The reason is the old reason, namely, that " eye hath not seen "; and considering that in this state the union is altogether ineffable, it may be worth while saying that we have no title to term it absorption, identity, or by any other word which is within the measures of things expressible. There are also Seven Palaces below, and among these one is superior to the rest, as it holds both from heaven and earth. For the rest, they are postulated in relation to certain grades of advancement in the world to come. When the souls of the just leave material life they enter the first Palace and are occupied with preparations for the next stage of their experience, but there are no particulars.[6] The second Palace [7] is the sojourn of those who have suffered

---

[1] Z., fol. 185a; II, 330.
[2] Ib.
[3] Ib. When stripped of its conventions, the real meaning which issues from these extracts is that the pursuit of the Law is the following of the will of God and that the union hereafter therewith is a penetration of the Divine Mystery, in which the soul progresses for ever.
[4] Ib., fol. 38a; I, 235.
[5] Ib.
[6] Z., Pt. I, fol. 38b; I, 236.
[7] There are several systems of Palaces described by the ZOHAR; there are those in which speech prevails but in others thought or intention. The latter are more exalted in order, presumably because silence is better than speech, seeing that it stands for the contemplation of God in the heart. I do not find for what reason *per se* or in what manner, but the object of all the Palaces above is to preserve Shekinah in the world below. The variant accounts are somewhat confusing, as it is not invariably too easy to see whether the subject of discourse is the Palaces which are above or those which are below. (See, for example, Z., Pt. I, fol. 38a; I, 236.) It is said (Ps. xxvii. 4): " That I may dwell in the House of the Lord all the days of my life, to behold the beauty of the Lord, and to inquire in His Temple." The beauty of the Lord is held to designate the Palaces above, but the word " beauty " is rendered " delights " by the ZOHAR. The Temple means the Palaces below. The seven superior Palaces are

morally and physically in the present world, but have given daily thanks to their master, this notwithstanding, and have not neglected prayer.¹ The Messiah descends into this abode and thence he draws souls into the third Palace. It is the place of those who have suffered extremely in earthly life as the result of serious disease. It contains also the souls of young children and of such as have shed tears over the destruction of the Temple. They are consoled by Messiah, who brings them into the fourth Palace, where are the souls of all those who have shared the sorrow of Zion and those also who have been slain by heathens. The fifth Palace is the sojourn of true penitents, who have restored their souls to a state of purity, and of those who have sanctified the Name of their Master by going to meet death for His glory.² There also are the souls of those who have repented on their deathbeds, since the Doctors of Kabbalism insist no less on the possibility of saving the situation of life thus at the last moment than do the Doctors of the Latin Church: for the one and the other the great fatality resides in final impenitence. The sixth Palace is the sojourn of the souls of ZELATORES who have proclaimed the Master's unity, and have loved Him with a true love.³ The seventh Palace is that which I have called superior in respect of the rest; it is also more secret and mysterious. It is not unlike that glimpse of the Beatific Vision which according to Catholic Theology is seen for a moment by souls on the threshold of purgatory, or it is like the vision of Shekinah which is granted *in articulo mortis*, according to Kabbalism—as we have seen. The soul on its

---

(1) the basis and beginning of the Mystery of Faith; (2) the abode of Faith; (3) the place in which worthy souls are offered in sacrifice; (4) the place of judgment, whether propitious or otherwise; (5) the Palace of Love; (6) the Palace of Mercy; and (7) the Holy of Holies and final end of souls.—See TRACT PALACES, being Appendix II., Z., Pt. II, fol. 244b, 261a; IV, 277-294. There are also Seven Palaces of Prayer, provided with doors by which the prayers of man ascend to the Great Master. The first corresponds to the " paved work of a sapphire stone."—Ex. xxiv. 10. It leads to the heaven of heavens. The second is like " the body of heaven in its clearness " (*ib.*). The third is a Palace of pure untinctured light, having a point of golden splendour. The fourth is a Palace of 70 lights, while the splendour of the fifth is like that of the lightning and thunderbolt, combining purple with many colours. The sixth is the Palace of Will, and it diffuses 12 lights; its mystery is expressed by the words: " Thy lips are like a thread of scarlet " (SONG OF SOLOMON iv. 3). It is also the Palace of Love. But the seventh Palace is devoid of all form; it constitutes the Mystery of Mysteries; and it is separated from the other habitations by a veil. Herein sojourns the Infinite Will.—Z., Pt. I, fol. 41b-45b; I, 248-265.

¹ Z., Pt. I, fol. 38b; I, 237.
² *Ib.*, fol. 39a; I, 239.
³ *Ib.*, I, 240.

departure from earth enters this Palace for a moment—though there seems no assignable reason and though it is not said to see anything: it is then immediately relegated to that place of sojourn which corresponds to its state at death. It will be noted that the parable has no logical consistence—as it has no concurrence with previous accounts: if those who have suffered martyrdom for the glory of God have a particular abode assigned them, it is obvious that others who have died naturally, for example, have no title therein; and so of the rest. Were it worth while to exercise one's mind on the subject, it might be suggested that souls which have reached a certain grade in life do not pass through the Palaces below that grade, while those who are below work upward and attain that grade after a given period in the world to come. But the ZOHAR is really concerned only with enforcing the idea of ascent in the scale hereafter, and the logic of its fiction is of no consequence in comparison with the main object. It is therefore idle to rectify on our part; let us realise rather that the ZOHAR is establishing another point of correspondence between the lesser and greater world. We have seen how early in the Christian centuries it forestalled the modern doctrine of macrocosmic evolution, and this now is a story of evolution in the microcosm, working on the basis of six periods corresponding to those of creation; and as the latter was followed by a period of rest, so is the seventh Palace a place of secrecy and mystery, suggesting a Sabbatic state. But above it there is the other and ineffable order of Supernal Palaces, and beyond the present epoch in created things there is the Messianic age to come, in which the story of the world and man reaches its end for Zoharic Theosophy, as it does in the Apocalypse for Theosophy according to Christ.

The idea of reincarnation in Kabbalism has been the subject of much confusion in the modern occult schools, which have depended, firstly, on the vague and incorrect vestige of elucidation offered by Adolphe Franck [1] and, secondly, on the obvious misstatements of Éliphas Lévi.[2] It is dismissed by

---

[1] LA KABBALE, pp. 244-247. There is postulated in the first place the fact of metempsychosis in Kabbalism on the authority of Z., Pt. II, fol. 99b, and afterwards the author gives a very imperfect account of the Zoharic doctrine concerning overshadowing, impingement, or embryonic states of souls, with which I am proceeding to deal.

[2] See A. E. Waite: THE MYSTERIES OF MAGIC: *A Digest of the Writings of Éliphas Lévi*, second Edition, 1897, where it said that a multiplicity of incarnations has never been recognised by Kabbalists of the first order.—pp. 131, 132.

the one in a few paragraphs and the other states that the doctors of traditional science in Israel did not admit the subject. On the contrary, there is a clear system of reincarnation scattered throughout the ZOHAR, but it calls to be distinguished from those later developments with which I must deal otherwise.

To some extent the doctrine hinges on questions of paternity, for it is stated plainly that when a man has failed to have children in this world, the Holy One will send him back, and many times at need, to fulfil what has been neglected, so that he is compared to a plant which is removed continually from the ground and located elsewhere—in the hope that it will do better.[1] Reincarnation is not, however, an universal law, or at least it is contingent in other cases than the particular case which has been just specified. Those who have accomplished their mission during a single sojourn on earth rest near to the Holy One; those who return are those who have not finished their work, whether it be that of parentage or otherwise.[2] It is rather obvious that the perfect fulfilment of the Law was a matter of great difficulty, and we know that St. Paul regarded it as an intolerable burden; we know also that failure in certain points voided the entire fulfilment; and the inference would seem to be that reincarnation for the doing of that which had been previously left undone and for the undoing of that which was amiss formerly must, by the hypothesis, have been the rule rather than the exception. Hence it is said in one place that the words " seeing that he also is flesh "[3] signify that the spirit of man, meaning his soul, will be many times reclothed with flesh, until the time comes when the soul shall be susceptible of receiving the spirit of God. In order that the significance of the expression should not remain doubtful, it is added that the Holy One will some day ransom the world and will grant the spirit in question to men generally, so that they may live eternally.[4] This is said to be shewn by the words: " For as the days of a tree are the days of my people,"[5] and also: " He will swallow up death in victory: and the Lord God will wipe away all tears from

---

[1] Z., Pt. II, fol. 186b; II, 337.
[2] Ib., fol. 187b; II, 341.
[3] Gen. vi. 3.
[4] An allusion apparently to the permanence of the resurrection state.
[5] Is. lxv. 22.

off all faces; and the rebuke of His people shall He take away from off all the earth: for the Lord hath spoken it."[1] Reincarnation or transmigration would seem also to be the invariable fate of the Gentiles. The souls of Pagans who deliver up their bodies in the Holy Land are not received in heaven: they wander about in the universe, transmigrate many times and finally return to the unclean place whence they came.[2] The souls of Israel which leave the body outside Palestine have also transmigrations and wanderings before reaching the region assigned them.[3] If this is to be taken as definite—and I do not think that the view is revised subsequently—one side of the law of reincarnation depends upon a merely external accident.[4] It will be useful to remark here that the ZOHAR knows nothing concerning spaces of time intervening between death and rebirth; the question does not seem to have arisen within their consciousness; the period elapsing may have been variable, as it is regarded in Eastern doctrine; but the new event is sometimes at least immediate. Seth, for example, was animated by the soul of Abel, which thus returned to earth.[5] At the birth of Benjamin, however, his soul left the body of his mother, which it had animated previously.[6] At the death of Rachel, her soul animated the son of Benjamin.[7] It seems to follow that in each case there were two souls at one time in the same body. It is said further that Phineas received the soul of Nadab and Abihu, who were alive at the time.[8] Rabbi Simeon testifies that this is a mystery, meaning that their soul did not find refuge under the wings of Shekinah, because they left no children and had thus diminished the figure of the King.

I have spoken already of the place—whatever it is, for it is indeed described variously—in which souls are reserved, awaiting the period of their primary embodiment in flesh; and I have mentioned the notion that at the Messianic period

---

[1] Is. xxv. 8.
[2] Z., Pt. II, fol. 141a; iv. 46.
[3] Ib.
[4] See post, p. 320, regarding final reincarnation, which must take place in Palestine.
[5] Ib., Pt. I, fol. 55a; I, 315. Adam is said to have called his son Seth to mark the end of a situation, the consonants of his name being the two last letters of the alphabet.
[6] Z., Pt. I, fol. 155b; II, 211.
[7] Ib.
[8] Ib., Pt. III, fol. 216b; V, 550. The suggestion is difficult to follow and would scarcely deserve the pains. It is added that when Phineas slew Zimri and Cozbi the tribe of Simeon were keen on avenging the death of their chief; the soul of Phineas fled and the two wandering souls took possession of its vacant place.

the fount of souls will be exhausted, leading to the creation of entirely new cohorts.[1] But it is said also that there will come a time when old souls, meaning souls in migration, will be renewed for the renewal of the world.[2] Each of these souls who have been incarnated previously will be united to a new created soul, as it is written: "And it shall come to pass that he that is left in Zion, and he that remaineth in Jerusalem, shall be called holy, even every one that is written among the living in Jerusalem."[3] We see by these extracts that reincarnation according to Kabbalism is complicated by several considerations and that the word impingement or overshadowing would be a better description of that which occurred in certain cases. The subject is not developed in the text itself, and it came into the hands of later Kabbalists who manufactured mighty systems thereon. The testimony of Isaac de Loria in his BOOK OF THE REVOLUTIONS OF SOULS is an instance of the lengths to which it could be carried and I shall have to deal with it at a later stage.[4]

The question of resurrection in connection with reincarnation created difficulties of its own. It was alleged that in the case of souls who take flesh several times the body which shall rise will be that in which the soul has succeeded in taking root, meaning presumably that it has fulfilled the Law in perfection.[5] Those bodies in which the soul fails to reach its ends are like dried up trees which fall to dust, and they will rise no more. There is some subtlety in this as a way out of the difficulty created by the idea of resurrection in connection with the idea of rebirth. But it will be observed that nothing is said as to those who have been rooted only in wickedness. I may add that the Zoharic doctrine of the world to come and the recompenses and punishments therein is quite independent of any reincarnation hypothesis and cannot be adjusted thereto. The two notions were developed almost certainly in complete independence of each other. As regards resurrection, there is a variant of the above view, according to which the soul will return into the last body that was animated, but the previous bodies will rise also and will be animated with new souls. "If these bodies have fulfilled meritorious works"—I give the literal words in this instance—"they will continue,

---

[1] Z., Pt. I, fol. 28b; I, 179.
[2] *Ib.*, Pt. I, fol. 119a; II, 76, 77.
[3] Is. iv, 3.
[4] See Book IX, § 1.
[5] Z., Pt. I, fol. 131a; II, 114.

but if not they will return again to dust," and as no purpose will have been served, this reverie does not seem less than imbecile.[1]

Some incidental points may be summarised as follows. On the basis of the words: " One generation passes away, and another generation cometh,"[2] it is said that the generation which comes is that also which has passed.[3] Reincarnation is sometimes despite the soul and sometimes apparently otherwise.[4] In one place it is formulated in the terms of uttermost simplicity by affirming that souls are sent for a second time on earth, that they may repair faults committed on the first occasion.[5] They come back also through the workings of Grace, as for example when husband and wife have been sterile through no fault of theirs in a previous lifetime[6]; on the next occasion they will be enabled to fulfil the Law, though it is not suggested that they will do so one with another. This implies that the axiom once an Israelite always an Israelite obtains automatically, and though I have not had occasion to mention it previously, it may be said now that what may be called the primordial generation of the chosen people insures this—supposing that rebirth occurs. There is another point: reincarnation is good because good reasons are, by the hypothesis, behind it; but as it is not good in itself, it is well to be spared therefrom. In conclusion, rebirth befalls those who do not study the Law, the inference being that those who do and who at the same time fulfil the other precepts do not suffer transmigration.[7]

II.—ANGELS AND DEMONS

We have seen that the world of BRIAH is that of Creation so-called, that is, of the emanation of creative forces. These forces are Elohim, and in this sense BRIAH is therefore the Elohistic world. It is called also the world of archangels, but

---

[1] Z., Pt. I, 131a; II, 114.
[2] Eccles. i. 4.
[3] Z., Pt. I, fol. 268b. LUMINOUS BOOK or BOOK OF BRIGHTNESS; II, 635.
[4] Z., Pt. II, fol. 96b; III, 387, 388.
[5] Ib., Pt. II, fol. 54a; III, 244.
[6] Ib., fol. 109a; III, 429, 430.
[7] Ib., Pt. III, fol. 178b, THE FAITHFUL SHEPHERD; V, 464. According to the testimony in this text, incarnation may take place thrice, because of the words: " Lo, all these things worketh God oftentimes with man."—Job xxxiii. 29. The ZOHAR renders the passage: " Behold what God doeth in respect of each man, even to the third time." Compare the Vulgate: *Ecce haec omnia operatur Deus tribus vicibus per singulos.*

this is in later Kabbalism. It would not be exact to say that the archangels are ELOHIM, much less that Michael, Raphael, Gabriel, Metatron and so forth are deities according to the Kabbalah.¹ In a general way it may be affirmed perhaps that the intelligent forces of the Briatic World, when assumed, so to speak, by the Divine World, can be regarded as ELOHIM, in the speculations of later rabbinical minds. Thus, according to Kabbalism, the three men who appeared to Abraham in the vale of Mamre to announce the destruction impending over the cities of the plain were three archangels, but they were also ADONAI, the Lord, for they were forms assumed by Divinity. Even at the risk of forestalling some part of that which is to come, it seems important to register at this stage that Shekinah is ELOHIM as well as ADONAI, according to recurring testimony of the ZOHAR, and that she under God made the world by CHESED, which is the highest of Briatic SEPHIROTH, and it is in this sense that BRIAH is the Elohistic world.

Of the hierarchy of spiritual beings outside humanity we meet with various classifications by different rabbinical writers, and they are not to be regarded as mere inventions, for they have their roots or vestiges in Talmudic times. As regards the descending or demonological scale, later authorities do not hesitate to contradict Zoharic statements. It should be understood that what follows depends from Zoharic expositors and not from the ZOHAR itself. They are tabulated on the Tree of Life and the Four Kabbalistic Worlds, which are complicated, moreover, by assuming an evolution of the Ten SEPHIROTH in each. The archangels of BRIAH, corresponding to the extension in question through that world, are usually enumerated as follows :

I. METATRON, Angel of the Presence, World-Prince, corresponding to KETHER.²
II. RAZIEL, the Herald of Deity, corresponding to CHOKMAH.

---

[1] Isidore Loeb, however, describes METATRON as a species of *Demiourgos*, following presumably the heterodox opinions of the Talmudic R. Acher. Franck also regards him as a Divine Hypostasis.

[2] When written with a JOD (MITTRVN), the name METATRON signifies SHEKINAH ; without that letter it signifies the angel who is " legate of SHEKINAH," also called NGHR = Boy, and hence METATRON has been said to be a boy-angel.—KABBALA DENUDATA, *Apparatus*, i. 528. We shall see later that he has other and more pregnant titles.

III. TSAPHKIEL, Contemplation of God, corresponding to BINAH.
IV. TSADKIEL, Justice of God, corresponding to CHESED.
V. SAMAEL, Severity of God, corresponding to GEBURAH.
VI. MICHAEL, Like unto God, corresponding to TIPHERETH.
VII. HANIEL, Grace of God, corresponding to NETZACH.
VIII. RAPHAEL, Divine Physician, corresponding to HOD.
IX. GABRIEL, Man-God, corresponding to YESOD.
X. SANDALPHON, Messias, the second phase of Metatron, corresponding to MALKUTH.

The world of YETZIRAH or Formation is said to be that of the angels, who are divided into nine choirs, which are very nearly identical with the hierarchy of pseudo-Dionysius, whose scheme has become part of Christianity.[1] Those who attribute a high antiquity to Kabbalistic Tradition say that Dionysius drew from the oral doctrine of Israel; others pretend that Dionysius and the Kabbalah both derive from Neoplatonism; but Greek and Hebrew thought had come to know one another before the date of the Areopagite. Dionysius, perhaps, may be taken to represent the point of contact between Hellenism and Jewry after modification by Christianity. The Kabbalah may represent, but at a much longer distance, in the form of its extant literature, the point of contact between Hellenism and Israel unmodified by Christianity.

According to the most usual attribution the choirs of YETZIRAH are as follows:—

I. HAYYOTH HA KADOSH, the holy living creatures, or animals of Ezekiel and the Apocalypse, corresponding to KETHER and to the Christian Seraphim.
II. OPHANIM, or Wheels, also mentioned in Ezekiel, corresponding to CHOKMAH and the Cherubim.
III. ARALIM, or Mighty Ones, corresponding to BINAH and the Thrones.
IV. HASHMALIM, or Brilliant Ones, corresponding to CHESED and the Dominations.
V. SERAPHIM, or Flaming Serpents, corresponding to GEBURAH and the Powers.

---

[1] It should be remembered, however, that unlike Christian angelology, that of the ZOHAR represents the divine messengers as altogether inferior to man and most certainly to the souls of the just, which ascend higher and attain a superior rank. See the Mantua edition, iii. 68*b*.

VI. MELACHIM, or Kings, corresponding to TIPHERETH and the Virtues.

VII. ELOHIM, or Gods, corresponding to NETZACH and the Principalities.

VIII. BENI-ELOHIM, or Sons of God, corresponding to HOD and the Archangels.

IX. CHERUBIM, the Seat of the Sons, corresponding to JESOD, the Foundation, and the Angels.

The tenth order required to complete the Sephirotic attribution is found in the ISHIM, or beatified souls of just men, corresponding to MALKUTH and the great multitude of the redeemed seen by St. John in the Apocalypse.

These orders are also summarised in the notion of a third Adam, YETZIRAH, represented by the MALKUTH of the Yetziratic world, man in the likeness of the angels—in a word, the ADAM Microprosopus of the IDRAS.

The world of ASSIAH, or of matter, is that into which Adam descended at the Fall, and beneath it is the abode of evil spirits, the Shells, Envelopes and CORTICES of the later Kabbalah.[1] It contains the orders of retrograde spirits corresponding by inversion to the angels of YETZIRAH and the arch-fiends corresponding after the same manner to the archangels of the Briatic world.[2] They are usually enumerated as follows:

I.—THAUMIEL, the doubles of God, said to be two-headed and so named, because they pretend to be equal to the Supreme Crown. This is properly the title of the averse SEPHIRA corresponding to KETHER. The cortex is CATHARIEL, according to the Supplements of the ZOHAR. Satan and Moloch are said to be the arch-demons, but the attributions are hopelessly confused throughout, partly owing to the obscure classifications of the ZOHAR and the contradictions of later Kabbalists.

II.—CHAIGIDIEL, a term connecting with the significance of *placenta*, or, according to other authorities, with that of obstruction, in the sense of an impediment to the heavenly influx. This averse SEPHIRA corresponds to CHOKMAH. Its cortices are the OGHIEL or GHOGIEL, which cleave to illusory

---

[1] For some information on Kabbalistic demonology, see DIE KABBALA: *ihre Hauptlehren und ihr verhältnüs zu Christenthum*. Innsbruch, 1885.

[2] But there are also many material correspondences which are not of shells and demons.

or material appearances in opposition to those of reality and wisdom. This explanation is, of course, very late. The arch-demon is said to be ADAM BELIAL, and so again is Beelzebuth. The Dukes of Esau are connected with this number.

III. SATHARIEL, the concealment of God, meaning that this averse SEPHIRAH, unlike BINAH or Intelligence, hides the face of mercy. In the Supplements of the ZOHAR it is termed SHEIREIL, from the hirsute body of Esau. The Dukes of Esau are referred alternatively to this number, instead of to the averse correspondence of CHOKMAH, by the same work. LUCIFUGE is said to be the arch-demon, but this is obviously not a Kabbalistic term: it is known, however, to the grimoires and to some late demonologists of the Latin church.

IV. GAMCHICOTH, or GOG SHEKLAH, disturber of all things, the averse correspondence of CHESED. According to the Zoharic Supplements the cortex seems to be AZARIEL. The arch-demon is ASTAROTH in late Kabbalism.

V. GOLAB, or burning, in the sense of incendiarism. This is the averse correspondence of GEBURAH and the antithesis of the Seraphim or Fiery Serpents. The cortex is USIEL. The arch-demon of late Kabbalism is ASMODEUS.

VI. TOGARINI, wranglers, because, according to Isaac de Loria, this averse correspondence of TIPHERETH strives with the Supernal GEBURAH. The cortices are called ZOMIEL and the arch-demon is BELPHEGOR.

VII. HARAB SERAP, dispersing raven, referring to the idea that this bird drives out its young, the averse correspondence of NETZACH. The cortices are the THEUMIEL and the arch-demon is BAAL CHANAN.

VIII. SAMAEL, or embroilment, corresponding to HOD, the supernal Victory. The cortices are THEUNIEL according to the Supplements of the ZOHAR, and ADRAMELEK is the name assigned to the arch-demon by late writers.

IX. GAMALIEL, the obscene, in averse correspondence with JESOD, which signifies generation of the higher order. OGIEL, which other classifications attribute to the averse correspondence of CHESED, seems to be the cortex mentioned in the Zoharic Supplements, and the arch-fiend is LILITH, according to late Kabbalism.

X. LILITH [1] is, however, according to another tabulation,

---

[1] According to the ZOHAR she is a stryge who slays infants.

the averse correspondence of MALKUTH, with whom later Kabbalism connects NAHEMA,[1] the demon of impurity.

In Zoharistic doctrine, however, the chief personalities of ASSIAH are SAMAEL, who is to some extent the averse Adam Kadmon, and his bride LILITH. The Sephirotic attributions are obscure and incomplete, but in a general way it is said that as in the Holy Kingdom so is it in that of iniquity,[2] as in the circumcision so also in the uncircumcision. SAMAEL is said to be the uncircumcised and his bride is the prepuce, which, it adds significantly, is the serpent.[3]

I have given space to this portion of the psychical hypotheses of Kabbalism, most of which is post-Zoharic, not because it is of inherent importance, or can be regarded otherwise than as a disfigurement of the metapsychical doctrine, but because we shall have later on to give account of the connection between the Kabbalah and Ceremonial Magic, and the doctrine of angels and demons is necessary to the understanding of this connection.[4] It should be added that not only is a methodised doctrine of the Celestial and Infernal Hierarchies not found in the ZOHAR, but there is no adequate material for the construction of such a doctrine.

---

[1] A succubus who brings forth spirits and demons after intercourse with men, says the ZOHAR, which in various places develops this idea further.

[2] Hence the true name of Satan is said to be that of YHVH reversed.—Pike, MORALS AND DOGMA, p. 102. He is reproducing Éliphas Lévi.

[3] R. Simeon ben Yohai in TIKKUNIM, or Supplements, No. 18. See BETH ELOHIM, by R. Abraham Cohen Irira, c. ii., KABBALA DENUDATA, ii., Part 3, Tract 1, i.e., PNEUMATICA KABBALISTICA, pp. 188 et seq.

[4] The TALMUDS abound with legendary history and teaching on this subject, for they are like a storehouse of folk-lore as well as of jurisprudence. It has been even proposed that the mediæval notion of vampirism is to be traced to Talmudic fables concerning stryges. See A. Brierre de Boismont, DES HALLUCINATIONS, &c. Second ed., p. 395. Paris. 1852.

BOOK VII

WAYS OF GOD WITH MAN

BOOK VII

WAYS OF GOD WITH MAN

I.—THE MYTH OF THE EARTHLY PARADISE

IN some previous chapters I have been content to lead up as I could to certain intimations which have formed part of each concerning that Mystery of Sex which is called Mystery of Faith and Supreme Mystery in the ZOHAR; but in the present consideration it will be with us even from the beginning. It is a matter of some difficulty to disassociate the subject from that Divine Personality—the Indwelling Glory—which is the central figure of the Aramaic text and the full discussion of which I have decided for good reasons to postpone till much later in our study. It must be remembered in the first place that there are two Gardens of Eden which are in communication one with another, while the one leads to the other.[1] The one is the Mystery of Sex as it was established or rather formulated originally on this lower earth, by the hypothesis of the Secret Doctrine, but this Garden was ravished; the other is a Mystery in Transcendence, as it subsists in the Eternal World, the World of the Supernals. In the symbolism of the whole subject, the ward of both is womanhood; she is the Garden in transcendence and she is also the Garden[2] below, or alternatively their

---

[1] According to later Kabbalism, the Superior Paradise is referrable to BRIAH in respect of souls and to YETZIRAH in respect of angels, but this is manifestly opposed to Zoharic teaching, by which it is allocated to BINAH and is therefore in the Supernal World of ATZILUTH. The Inferior Paradise is in ASSIAH according to both forms of Kabbalism. We have seen also that the Higher Eden is the abode of souls awaiting incarnation and that the Lower Eden is, so to speak, the threshold of entrance into the life of earth. So also on the return journey through the gate of death the Lower Paradise is a tarrying-place for the souls of the just before they ascend higher, that is to say, into the Supernal Eden, where perfect liberation is enjoyed.—Z., Pt. III, fol. 196b; V, 506.

[2] According to Franck, Paradise is always termed by the Kabbalists either גן עדן = the Garden of Eden or עולם הבא = the World to Come and never פרדס = PARDES = Garden, this being the word of the modern Kabbalists.—LA KABBALE, p. 57. GAN

mystery is she; and their image amidst the exile and penitence of this present order is also woman—woman in her betrothals, woman in her espousals, woman as wife, mother, daughter and sister. We shall see at a later stage that all these designations are titles of Shekinah—as the Divine Personality which I have mentioned—and she can be regarded from two points of view, being (1) as woman in the archetype and (2) as the Mystery of Sex. Speaking essentially, these two are reducible to one. But the male is not without the female, nor is the woman apart from man in respect of this mystery, which includes all. It is that of God in His concealment—being, however, the concealment of KETHER and not that of AIN SOPH—of God also as He is manifested in the Secret Doctrine, and of prototypical humanity. It is the mystery of the Traditional Fall of man and of all the banishments which the elect are postulated as having suffered; but as it is owing to this mystery that each one of us is incarnate here so is it also through this that we return homeward into the refuge whose name is Shekinah: it is with us at this day in the bondage of our mortality, but it is also the law of our liberation. The Zoharic Legend of the Earthly Paradise may be held to formulate the mystery, but without expounding it. The Paradise above is called "the Sanctuary, O Lord, which Thy hands have established."[1] The Paradise below has the Holy of Holies for its image and both are at the centre of the earth, called Zion and Jerusalem—the place and house of peace.[2] As regards the making of man we know that there are two accounts in Genesis, one dovetailed into the other, a fact which the Zoharic doctors did not realise, and with the difficulties which thus arose they dealt as they could. According to the Elohistic text man was made in the likeness of the Elohim—that is to say, male and female, for which reason we shall see that Shekinah—whose title is Elohim—is presented as male on a few very rare occasions, but so invariably other-

---

EDEN is applied in the Zohar both to BINAH and MALKUTH as the Sephirotic locations respectively of the Superior and Inferior Eden.
[1] Z., Pt. I, fol. 7a; I, 38.
[2] See *note*, p. 210. The Palace or Paradise below is modelled on the pattern of that which is above, for the Divine Presence in MALKUTH, as the Kingdom of this world, does not differ from the Divine Hypostasis in BINAH, which is the World to Come. The Lower Garden was formed and planted by the Holy One, that He might have joy with the souls of the just who dwell therein; but the Garden which is placed in the transcendence, under the Wings of Shekinah, is the place of contemplation for souls in the sweetness of the Lord, and herein is the Blessed Vision.—Z., Pt. II, fol. 127a; IV, 8.

wise as female that the alternative has the aspect of a mere blunder or a wilful confusion of issues. In so far as she represents the Mystery of Sex, it might be said that she is of both sexes, is male on the right side of the Tree of Life—which is the masculine side—and female on the left side. But the myth of the Earthly Paradise is a Jehovistic text, and by its hypothesis Adam, being the male in distinction from the female, or having the female latent within him, was made in the first place. Now, it is said that when the Holy One created Adam He exhorted him to walk in the way of goodness and revealed to him the Mystery of Wisdom, by aid of which he could attain even to the Supreme Degree.[1] He gave him also the Law and taught him His ways.[2] This is not, however, Adam in distinction from Eve but refers to humanity in its two primordial forms: so also in respect of what follows. Man was crowned with celestial crowns and was so formed that he could rule over the six directions of space; he was perfect in all things and bore the seal of the heights on his countenance. The angels encompassed him and honoured him, revealing mysteries relating to the knowledge of their Master. But he on his part beheld all Supreme Mysteries and all wisdom—exceeding, as we have seen already, the science of the angels—and he knew the glory of God. The intention was that he should remain united in heart and mind to Him Who was his model, thus being preserved unchanged, like God Who is the synthesis of all things and in Whom all is unified.[3] If it be said that this is mere fantasy in distraction, because man, by the hypothesis of the legend, did not know good or evil and much less one from another, I can point out only that authorised Christian doctrine on the same subject is in the same case precisely, since it is obvious (*a*) that in such state no person can be accountable for disobedience, or (*b*) if he be so accountable he is at least aware that obedience is on the side of goodness and its opposite on that of evil: but this spoils the postulate. The unreason is of course to treat a pure myth as if it were literal history. By so much, however, as we elect to exalt the state of man in Paradise, by

---

[1] Z., Pt. I, fol. 140b; II, 147.
[2] *Ib.*, fol. 199a; II, 338.
[3] Z., Pt. I, fol. 321c, 221b; II, 470. It is said also that God encompassed Adam with glory from on high (*ib.*), meaning the resplendent vesture or vehicle in which he was manifested before he was clothed with skins as one consequence of his Fall.

so much our construction crucifies further the story with which it professes to deal.[1]

In respect of the Garden itself, we learn that the whole world is watered by that mysterious river which went forth out of Eden—meaning the Paradise that is above.[2] It came from a secret place on high, and brought life to things below.[3] This place is symbolised by the letter BETH, when it appears for the first time in Genesis. The meaning is that this letter contains all letters in its womb, even as the river vivifies all things else. The secret place resembles a narrow path along which it is difficult to travel, but there the treasures of the world are hidden. The river brings sanctity from on high; and when the Kingdom of Heaven shall have come under the form of first-fruits of the earth, the latter will be raised and made equal with Heaven. One might call this a keynote for the whole doctrine of cosmology, except that a keynote of one or another kind seems to emerge everywhere. Holiness is life, and the world subsists by holiness. If this, its correspondences and analogues, were not the beginning, middle and end of Zoharic Theosophy, I should have no cause to write about it, because it would not belong to the Secret Doctrine of God, which is my concern in the old literatures.

As regards the formation of Eve from the side of Adam, we meet in the ZOHAR with another presentation of a tradition which is found in many places of legend.[4] Adam and Eve were joined side by side originally. The explanation—which is given in one place only, or perhaps I should say rather that there is no alternative—is after the most inscrutable manner of the text—*i.e.*, that they were not face to face because as yet

---

[1] We are told in Gen. ii. 15, that "the Lord God took this man, and put him into the Garden of Eden to dress it and to keep it." With this it is interesting to contrast the Zoharic ideas of those duties which fell to Adam in his original state of radiance. He was set to offer sacrifices in the Garden, and for such purpose an altar is postulated therein, which he profaned by his Fall, and so became a tiller of the ground.—Z., Pt. I, fol. 57b; I, 331. It is said in another place that he was set to grow roses. These things occurred by the hypothesis before the institution of blood offerings; we can infer therefore that the sacrifices of Adam were offerings of aspiration, and I think that what is indicated is part of the Mystery of Union. We shall see otherwise the kind of altar that was profaned by the Fall; it is simply another aspect of the mystery of womanhood—that Garden which man was given to cultivate.—*Ib.*, Pt. II, fol. 109a; III, 430. The roses were children of Shekinah, because she is the Rose of the World, and under another aspect is herself the Garden.

[2] *Ib.*, fol. 30b; I, 192.

[3] In other terms, it brought the celestial waters, and thus gave birth to the plants and fruits which flourished in the Garden.—*Ib.*, fol. 59b; I, 348.

[4] Z., Pt. I, fol. 35a; I, 216.

"the Lord God had not caused it to rain upon the earth."[1] This is on the authority of Rabbi Simeon, who forgot, as one might think, for a moment that the same verse adds: "And there was not a man to till the ground." Too much attention must not be given to inconsistencies of this kind—whether or not some means of escape happens to be found subsequently—as the purpose of the ZOHAR is always to make known a point of its Secret Doctrine which can be hooked on to a text, and the context—for this purpose—is seldom held to signify.[2] The point in this case is (*a*) that man being superior to all the works of creation,[3] the union of man and woman must be modelled on that of Nature—meaning, however, the Arch-Nature that is above; but (*b*) their union face to face could not be accomplished till after that of heaven and earth, which was manifested by rain. It is obvious that a spiritual mystery is indicated, and one that is part of the intercourse which constitutes the transcendental unions. The physical basis is of course that the sex-union of humanity takes place in an opposite position to that of all the animals, which was certain to suggest deep symbolism to ZOHARIC doctors, though they do not formulate the contrast. Another intimation is that in their original state not only was Adam made male and female but so also was the woman attached to his side.[4] I suppose that this notion is the antechamber or threshold of that "Supreme Mystery" which is believed to be expressed in the words: "Male and female created He them."[5] It is said to constitute the glory of God and to be the object of faith. In the root-nature it is regarded as inaccessible to human reason, perhaps in the sense that it has not entered into the heart of man to understand what God has prepared for those who love Him, or, from another standpoint, it is a matter of experience and not of dissertation. By this mystery was man created, as well as the heaven and the earth. It is inferred that every figure which does not represent male and female

---

[1] Gen. ii. 5.
[2] As a matter of fact, the discrepancy is recognised speedily, and the same master of doctrine explains that there was no man because Eve had not yet been created, and man was as if non-existent, seeing that he was incomplete in her absence. The last point is not a subtlety of the moment, but a doctrine which obtains everywhere regarding our human nature.—Z., Pt. I, fol. 35a; I, 217.
[3] *Ib.*, fol. 34b; I, 216.
[4] Z., Pt. III, fol. 117a; V, 301.
[5] Gen. i. 27.

has no likeness to the heavenly figure.¹ We shall see in due course that the Holy One does not make His dwelling except where male and female are united, and there only His benedictions are disposed. This is why Scripture says: And God "blessed them and called their name Adam, on the day when they were created." ²

It is recognised by the ZOHAR in no uncertain manner that the condition of side to side was one of imperfection, because it was not a true union in the likeness of heaven; the latter is eye to eye and beyond it there is another state, in which heaven and earth pass away, like all the former things, since the distinctions of THIS and THAT are at an end. Eve was joined to Adam until he was put to sleep,³ and here the text dwells especially on the fact that the place of his entrancement was that place where the Temple was built subsequently.⁴ As regards the formation of Eve, it is said that "He took one of his ribs," and here the ZOHAR develops a great subtlety, inferring that the second pronoun alludes, like the first, to Jehovah Elohim. It says, further, that the plural "ribs" signify the virgins of MATRONA, meaning her maids of honour, one of whom was taken to be the "helpmeet" for Adam.⁵ However this story is forgotten soon afterwards and yet others are substituted; but I do not think that we need attach importance to any.

When the time came for man and woman to be joined face to face the text which here follows is applied to the intercourse: "They stand fast for ever and ever, and are done in truth and uprightness." ⁶ The reference is to the state of true nuptials, ineffable in the holy transcendence, when between the male and the female, as between the wings of the two cherubim, the glory of Shekinah manifests, when within and without are over and there is neither marrying nor giving in marriage because those which were once in separation have entered into the heaven of union. The words

---

¹ Meaning the Great Adam, the Cosmic Son, himself a reflection of what subsists but is not explicated in the World of ATZILUTH.
² Gen. v. 2.
³ Z., Pt. I, fol. 34b; I, 215.
⁴ Ib., fol. 31b; I, 215.
⁵ Ib., fol. 28a, b; I, 176-178. The reference is to Gen. ii. 21. It is even said that "bone of my bones and flesh of my flesh" (Gen. ii. 23) are words that signify Shekinah, so close is the connection recognised between the Indwelling Glory who is the guide of man on earth and the womanhood which is part of him.
⁶ Ps. cxi. 8.

"stand fast" are said to designate male and female, whose union here below will subsist through all eternity in the world that is above.[1] It consists in a sacred union face to face, for Zoharic similitudes seldom transcend this, though it is only the court of the Temple, where the Lover and Beloved are still clothed in their vestments. The words: "There went up a mist from the earth, and watered the whole face of the ground"[2] signify the desire of the female for the male, and here it is added cryptically that man was taken from his place and transplanted, or changed about, that man and woman might attain perfection. Now, it is claimed in one place that the sleep of Adam signifies the captivity, so that it is another episode in the long history of creation; but it is to be questioned whether these scattered intimations can be drawn into a true memorial.

A word must be added concerning the Trees of the Garden, though I do not know that the Secret Doctrine offers lights of the first magnitude on this subject. The Tree of Life is identified with the Doctrine,[3] presumably in its inward form, or that which is inculcated by the surface sense and by the sense within: it is the Holy Law, which offers aspects of truth in all its interpretations. The fruits of this Tree subsist for ever and give life to all[4]; it gave life in particular to the twelve tribes who issued therefrom.[5] It covers those vessels which are pure souls with its wings. It is Knowledge in the true sense, which is supernal, the Knowledge that is above reason: those who are attached thereto possess life in the world to come as well as life in this world.[6]

The Tree of the Knowledge of Good and Evil is reputed to have been a vine and the forbidden fruit was the grape,[7] as to which it is added elsewhere that Scripture interdicts wine and fermented drink: but this is obviously untrue. It is said also to be the female principle,[8] which, I suppose, may mean when it is unsanctified and in the state of separa-

---

[1] Z., Pt. I, fol. 35a; I, 217.
[2] Gen. ii. 6.
[3] Z., Pt. I, fol. 106b, 107a; II, 36.
[4] Ib., Pt. II, fol. 2a; III, 3. They are sweeter than honey.—Ib., Pt. I, Appendix 3; II, 730.
[5] At the end of time the purified Israel will depend from this Tree only.—Ib., Pt. III, fol. 124b; V, 322.
[6] It is the centre of all life.—Z., Pt. II, fol. 11a; III, 48.
[7] Ib., Pt. III, 158b; V, 410, fol. 127a; V, 327.
[8] Ib., Pt. I, fol. 36a; I, 223.

tion.¹ Among the fables concerning it there is that which relates how it invited many spirits to revolt before they were furnished with bodies, meaning possibly in the state of pre-existence about which we have heard previously. When so furnished, these spirits conceived a plan to descend on earth and assume possession thereof. God classed therefore the spirits in two categories, the good being placed on the side of the Tree of Life and the evil on that of mixed knowledge. He provided the first with bodies, but when the time had come to do likewise in respect of the second, the Sabbath interrupted the work of creation ²—otherwise there would have been wreck and ruin from end to end of the world. By this intervention the Holy One provided the remedy before the evil, advancing—that is to say—the hour of the Sabbath, so that evil spirits had the mortification of seeing good spirits invested with desirable bodies, whilst they in their deprivation were impotent. It would seem to follow that the desire of the evil side is towards sex, but in the iniquity to which it may be debased. The infernal hosts are therefore in a state of inhibition, arrestation and unsatisfied longing.

Generally as regards both Trees, the Secret Doctrine looks forward not only towards that time—and because of it is glad in all its aspects—when the elect will depend no longer on the Tree of Good and Evil, when they will not be subject longer to a Law which legislates on things permitted and forbidden, on clean and unclean things.³ Our entire nature will be drawn in that day from the Tree of Life and there will be no further debates about the evil and impure, for concerning this state to come it is written: "I will cause . . . the impure spirit to pass out of the land."⁴ Herein is the rest which remains for the people of God and the fruition is herein of those good things of the Lord which are gathered into the Land of the Living.⁵ Now, there is a strange thing said in another place which seems to connect with the subject and to issue therefrom in a mystery that seems yet like a path of light.

---

¹ As a matter of fact, the passage referred to, which is curious in all respects, seems to suggest that the Tree of Knowledge is that evil woman who is the wife of Samael and intercourse with whom is incest, idolatry and murder. It is the averse side of the Sex Mystery.
² Z., Pt. I, fol. 14a; I, 82.
³ Z., Pt. III, 124b; V, 322.
⁴ Zechariah xiii. 2.
⁵ The Tree of Knowledge being the Tree of Death, in contrast to the Tree of Life.—Z., Pt. III, fol. 157a; 405.

Between the spirit of good and the spirit of evil " she must stand who is called woman," and they shall then abide in harmony or in the turning of the evil to account on the part of goodness. It is by the help of woman that the spirit of good preponderates over that of evil. After this manner does the Mystery of Faith proceed from more to more in the law of its self-unfoldment.

In conclusion, I infer that the Tree of Life is over the female principle in the state of *sacramentum ineffabile*, preserving all who are attached to it from death for ever.[1] My reason is that when it is said of the other Tree that those who are attached to it cleave also to death, the text quoted is: " Her feet go down to death; her steps take hold on hell."[2] As this is woman on the side of the devil, so is the other womanhood also, but on the side of God.

II.—THE SERPENT, SON OF THE MORNING, AND FALL OF THE ANGELS

An adequate study of Kabbalistic speculations on the subject of angelology, the fall of the angels and the hierarchy of demons which came about as a consequence would begin in Talmudic literature and would be itself an undertaking of no inconsiderable magnitude, for behind that literature lies all oriental belief. I do not pretend to know what remains to be said on the subject when I recall the vast histories which have been written already, counting only from the days of Van Dale at the end of the seventeenth century.[3] It is fortunate that such an inquiry does not belong to our subject for there is very little in the Zohar or its expositors which is important hereon from the standpoint of Secret Doctrine, though there is a mass of curious speculation and ingarnering of bizarre superstition. It would be arid and wearisome to collect it without commentary of any kind, and as certain tabulations have been made in a previous Book I shall confine

---

[1] Here it is fair to mention that in one place the letter VAU is said to be the Tree of Life.—*Ib.*, fol. 121a ; V, 309. But the point is that VAU in the perfect state—which I have called *sacramentum ineffabile*—is in union with the second HE of the Sacred Name, as we have seen already.

[2] Prov. v. 5.

[3] Antonio van Dale : DISSERTATIONES DE ORIGINE ET PROGRESSU IDOLATRIÆ . . . *et de Divinationibus Idolatricis Judæorum*. Quarto, pp. 762. Amsterdam, 1696. It offers a mass of information on angels and demons according to Jewish ideas, on false Messiahs and on the magical side of Kabbalism.

my remarks under a few general heads, to elucidate things which led up to the Fall of Man and some which followed therefrom. I suppose that in the first place a word must be said upon the subject of evil and how it is regarded in the text.

It seems to follow expressly or by implication from several statements—some of which have been cited previously—that there is at least a sense in which God is the Author of evil.[1] A system being given in which not only do all things come from God but He is present immanently in all, it is not unnatural to accept the direct consequences without debate or refinements, and in this particular respect no difficulty is created thus in the Kabbalistic mind. The Pauline consciousness that all Nature groaneth and travaileth, the sense of suffering in all animate beings had never entered therein, though there was a very keen sense of the burdens on election in Israel. It is admitted quite freely, and indeed the notion is implied in several places, that the Holy One has created both the just and the unjust,[2] or still more plainly that He formed man of a spirit of good and a spirit of evil. The exoneration resides in the fact that evil is of service to good, because good turns evil to account.[3] Moreover, God created a certain Tree, the eating of which meant that the full understanding of the evil side of things entered into the life of humanity; but the saving clause is that it imparted also the knowledge of good. There can be no question—and we have seen already—that from this point of view the Tree of the Trespass is a synonym or image of the Written Law, for this is prohibition above all things, which defines evil and separates that which is so imputed from what is recognised as good. It is understood, however, that the definition is on the formal side and stands therein at its value, without reference to essentials.[4]

---

[1] We have seen also that there is no difficulty in the SEPHER YETZIRAH on the subject, and it is this primitive text which is responsible for Sephirotic Theology throughout the ZOHAR proper. The evil which is created by God is to be distinguished, however, from that which man works on his own part. It is woe to those who make themselves wicked. This is on the authority of Is. iii. 11. It is ruled, however, that "He hath made everything beautiful in His time" (Eccles. iii. 11), because He is glorified by the works of the just and the occasional good acts of the wicked.—Z., Pt. II, fol. 11a; III, 47.

[2] Ib.

[3] Ib., Pt. I, fol. 49a; I, 283.

[4] The exoneration in chief is, however, in a discourse of R. Simeon, who maintains that merit and demerit would have been equally impossible for man if God had not (1) created the Spirit of Good and the Spirit of Evil, and if He had not (2) composed our nature of both.—Z., Pt. I, fol. 23a; I, 142. The Spirit of Good and the Spirit of Evil are on the right and left of man. If the last lives in purity, the first acquires an

THE SERPENT AND FALL OF THE ANGELS

There is no tabulated account of the Hierarchy of the Blessed Angels in the ZOHAR, but we hear generically of great hosts and cohorts, battalions of guardians, usually for purposes of honour—as when angels accompany Shekinah on some of her missions [1]—and there are also clouds of messengers. It is specified that METATRON is the leader of the Invisible Host and that his place is immediately beneath the throne of God [2]; but we are told nothing of legions like those of the Nine Choirs of Dionysius,[3] though there are divisions and subdivisions with correspondences of this kind in late Kabbalism. As regards the Infernal Hierarchy there are various categories consisting of angels who kept not their first estate and of demons generated in several ways.[4]

They are specified as comprising ten degrees or ten crowns below [5] and corresponding as such to numerous hierarchic grades,[6] separated in appearance yet communicating one with another, being ramifications of a single tree. There are ten crowns to the right and ten also to the left,[7] for there is a right and there is a left side in the empire of the demons, this being modelled throughout on that of God.[8] There is even an infernal triad in correspondence as such with the Sacred Triad that is above, and the observance of the Paschal Lamb was instituted to break its bonds.[9] There are averse Seraphim in the form of serpents, emanating from the evil serpent.[10] There are finally seven averse Palaces corresponding, on the

---

ascendency over the second, so that both combine to protect him in all his ways.—*Ib.*, fol. 165b; II, 250. The Spirit of Evil is in a state of incompleteness unless man nourishes him by sin.—*Ib.*, fol. 201a; II, 398. Apparently, those who thus nourish their master are maintained in turn by him, whence the happiness and prosperity of the Gentiles is a fruit of the union between Samael and his prostituted wife.—*Ib.*, Pt. II, 11a; III, 47. It is admitted, on the other hand, that evil is stronger than good.—*Ib.*, Pt. III, fol. 263b; VI, 24. But even the demon contains a particle of sanctity, without which he could not exist.—*Ib.*, Pt. II, fol. 203b; IV, 205.

[1] It is mentioned, for example, that 42 sacred angels, commissioned for her service, came down with SHEKINAH when she accompanied Israel into Egypt. Each bore a letter of the Divine Name of 42 letters.—*Ib.*, fol. 4b; III, 15.

[2] *Ib.*, fol. 294b; IV, 318. It is here that METATRON is said to be the name assumed by Enoch when he was raised to heaven.

[3] It is just, however, to say that Picus de Mirandula, in his CONCLUSIONES KABBALISTICÆ, manages to extract nine hierarchies in the following order: KERUBIM, SERAPHIM, CHASMALIN, ARALIM, TARSISIM, OPHANIM, ISHIM, MELACHIM and ELOHIM, but it is a purely arbitrary classification. See Book X, *s.v.* PICUS.

[4] Speaking generally, the Empire of the Demons is supposed to be under the presidency of three chiefs or princes, who are described as three impure branches, from which depend seventy minor branches, and these are the leaders or angels of the seventy Gentile nations.—Z., Pt. III, fol. 194a; V, 503.

[5] Z., Pt. I, fol. 167a; II, 256.
[6] Z., Pt. I, 277a; II, 296.
[7] *Ib.*, Pt. III, fol. 207a V, 527.
[8] *Ib.*, Pt. II, fol. 37b; III, 179.
[9] *Ib.*, Pt. II, fol. 40b; III, 189.
[10] *Ib.*, fol. 247b; IV, 281.

one hand, to the Palaces that are above [1] and on the other to the seven names which are attributed to the tempting spirit: Satan, Impure, Enemy, Stumbling-block, the Uncircumcised, Wicked, Crafty.[2]

What I may call the metaphysical account is as follows:

When the passive light, designated as darkness in Scripture, was joined to the active light on the right side,[3] following the ordinary arrangement of the Sephirotic Tree, many celestial legions—concluding that there was antagonism between the modes—in place of harmony or equilibrium by virtue of the Middle Pillar—declared themselves for the light of the left side and made ready to revolt against the other. When the Middle Pillar manifested the Perfect Unity of God, the good legions renounced the struggle and submitted, but those which were evil [4] persisted and gave birth as a consequence to hell. In this manner discord was introduced into the world on both sides, and the sense of the text seems to suggest that its vibrations remained on that of the good powers, though apart from any spirit of rebellion. The Scriptural allusion is: "And God made the firmament, and divided the waters which were under the firmament from the waters which were above the firmament," [5] a text which does duty on many sides of interpretation, and signifies, in this sense, that He separated the discord which had its source in the angels who kept not their first estate from that which was introduced into the world by those who were cast into the abyss. Both disruptions had, however, their result below; but that which belonged to the first class redounded to the glory of heaven, had this as its end in view and disappeared apparently when the end in question was reached. This is so far concerning one category of souls rejected from heaven and enchained below. There was another class, the downfall of which was consequent on the Holy One assembling several legions of superior angels and advising them that He intended

---

[1] Z., fol. 245a; IV, 278.
[2] Ib., fol. 363a; IV, 295, 296.
[3] Ib., Pt. I, fol. 17b; I, 105.
[4] The inference seems to be that, belonging to the passive side, their potentiality for evil was greater than that of the active side, though it subsisted also in this, or the imputed conspiracy could not have been shared by the intelligences of both sides, as the case was apparently. It is said also elsewhere that the "Sons of God" (Gen. vi. 2) were angels of the evil side who were in a state of perversity from the beginning.—Ib., fol. 270a; II, 638.
[5] Gen. i. 7.

to create man.¹ They appear to have replied by quoting the Psalmist when he said: "Nevertheless man being in honour abideth not: he is like the beasts that perish."² Thereupon the Holy One stretched forth a finger and burned these blessed legions, after which He called others into His presence and made the same statement, to which they answered on their part: "What is man that Thou art mindful of him and the son of man that Thou visitest him."³ The Lord explained that man should be made in His image and would be superior to those whom He addressed. It does not appear what happened to these legions.⁴ There were, moreover, those Sons of God who "saw the daughters of men that they were fair,"⁵ and they included Aza and Azael, who entered into a dispute with Shekinah on the advisability of creating Adam, seeing that he would end by sinning with his wife, to which Shekinah replied that before they could make accusations of this kind it must be postulated that they would prove more chaste in their own persons.⁶ This was the conclusion for the moment; but the children of God had recourse to the daughters of men and "took them wives of all that they chose."⁷ The result was that Shekinah stripped them of their sanctity and of all part in eternal beatitude,⁸ which had been the case also with the rebellious angels belonging to the first category: these are burnt eternally in Sheol.⁹ According to one version Aza and Azael became enamoured of the evil daughters of Cain,¹⁰ but the text says also that the Sons of Elohim or of God were actually Sons of Cain. We can take our choice among alternatives over matters of no consequence. Elsewhere it is affirmed that before the corruption of the

---

¹ Z., Pt. III, fol. 207b, 208a; V, 529.
² Ps. xlix. 12.
³ Ps. viii. 4.
⁴ It must be confessed that these ridiculous fables have neither an inward sense nor an outward light. We know that Latin Christianity has a legend of the Fall of the Angels which connects that event in some clouded manner with the scheme of human redemption; but it speaks with the tongue of seraphs in comparison with these inventions, in which the superior sense of the hierarchies is punished by burning and expulsion.
⁵ Z., Pt. I, fol. 23a; I, 141.
⁶ Certain codices of the ZOHAR cause the Shekinah to intimate at this point that Adam will indeed end by sinning with a single woman, but it will prove also with her that he will be able to repair the fault, while the lost angels will sin with many women and will be deprived of all reparation.
⁷ Gen. vi. 2.
⁸ Z., Pt. I, fol. 25b; I, 157.
⁹ *Ib.*, fol. 17b; I, 108.
¹⁰ *Ib.*, fol. 37a; I, 230.

world all men were called Sons of Elohim.[1] When Aza and Azael were cast down, they assumed bodies on earth and were imprisoned therein.[2] It was subsequently—according to this version—that they were seduced by women and are alive at this day, still instructing men in the Art of Magic, which they had begun to teach soon after their descent. They were chained on certain black mountains, which Laban and Balaam frequented for instruction in the forbidden art.[3] There were in all five orders of intelligence which seem to have been cast out of heaven, and some of them were incarnated as men.[4] These were the Giants of Genesis, the NEPHILIM, the descendants of AMALEK, the Intruders of the TALMUD, and so forth. It is on record that they caused the destruction of the Temple.

There is a distinction made in the ZOHAR between the serpent mentioned in Genesis and him who rode thereon. It is said that the serpent was female and was she who is called the Prostituted Woman.[5] She was the wife of him who rode upon her back,[6] and this was Samael the death-angel. It comes about in this manner that there is male and female on the evil, even as on the sacred side [7]—though in a rough and general sense the right side is sometimes said to be masculine and the left feminine. Samael is the tempter-spirit whose purpose is to put man to the test, and his other name

---

[1] Z., Pt. I, fol. 37a; I, 230.

[2] Ib., fol. 58a; I, 334. They belonged to that class who appeared under the form of men, and it was possible therefore for them to exist on earth. They assumed bodies to come down and because of their revolt they could not unclothe to reascend. By their union with women they engendered giants, the "mighty men of old," and "men of renown," mentioned in Gen. vi. 4. Compare, however, the previous section, p. 268.

[3] Z., Pt. III, fol. 208a; V, 530. According to another version Naamah, the sister of Tubal Cain, was from the side of Cain the murderer; she was a seducer of men and spirits, including Aza and Azael, who again were of the children of God mentioned in Genesis. She became the mother of demons and is still abroad in the world, exciting the desires of men, more especially in dreams of the night. She is associated with Lilith, of whom we shall hear shortly in connection with the Fall of Adam. It is testified by this tradition that demons are subject to death in the same way as human beings, but this must apply to the progeny and not to the first parents, as Samael, Lilith and Naamah are still in activity.—Z., Pt. III, fol. 55a; I, 317.

[4] Ib., fol. 25a; I, 156. See also TARGUM of Jonathan to Gen. vi. 4.

[5] Ib., APPENDICES, Pt. III, SECRETS OF THE LAW; II, 727. See also ADDITAMENTA (TOSSEFTA); II, 734. It is she whose "feet go down to death."—Prov. v. 5.

[6] It is said also that the adulterous woman by whom the world is seduced is the sword of the destroying angel.—Z., Pt. III, fol. 231b; V, 571.

[7] Ib., Pt. I, 153a; II, 201. They are impurity taking shape as such; and from their union issue powerful spiritual leaders who are spread abroad in the world and defile it. Samael mounted on the serpent's back is a symbol of the evil side of sexual intercourse—that is to say, after the manner of the beasts.

THE SERPENT AND FALL OF THE ANGELS

is the End of Darkness, which is equivalent to " the end of all flesh." [1] But when the ZOHAR speaks of the spirit of evil generically, it affirms that this is an old and insensate thing [2]—much as European folk-lore was accustomed to represent Satan as a poor and witless creature who is cheated easily in the end. When the serpent was condemned to go upon her belly this means that God took away those feet which are the support of the body, and here the text affords one of its profound intimations when it goes on to say: But Israel, who would not be supported by the Law—which was built up to encompass it, as the hills stand round Jerusalem—has lent feet to the serpent for the support of her.

As there is a serpent below which is still at work in the world, so there is a sacred serpent above which watches over mankind in all the roads and pathways and restrains the power of the impure serpent.[3] It is one of the adornments of the heavenly throne. From the kind of union which is predicated concerning Samael and the evil serpent, they seem to pass easily one into another, and it is presumably in this way that we hear of a great serpent—the dragon of later Kabbalism—which was cast into the abyss with his legions when the Sacred Name of forty-two letters was first graven upon the seal of God. But the abyss subsequently gave up the demons and the surface of the earth was covered with darkness till celestial light illuminated the world.[4] This spirit of evil has chiefs and messengers under his orders, intervening in all acts of man; yet the serpent can only defile the soul by special authorisation therefrom.[5] Hence Israel still suffers on account of the impurities which came from the side of the first serpent; from the impurities of ill-doing spirits; and from those of demons; but especially from the impurities of that particular reptile which is called " the other god " and is identified with AMALEK.[6] He is said to be the cause of all uncleanliness in the world, in all the degrees thereof. He is apparently on the male side and as such is an assassin, while his wife is a mortal poison, because she incites to idolatry. It is curious in this connection that the name Samael—סמאל—is held to signify

---

[1] Z., Pt. I, fol. 152b; I, 201.
[2] Ib., fol. 179a; II, 307. The reference is to the " old and foolish King " of Eccles. iv. 13. See also Z., Pt. II, fol. 33b; III, 163, and Pt. III, fol. 219a, THE FAITHFUL SHEPHERD; V, 553, from which it seems to follow that the demon is a fool.
[3] Z., Pt. I, fol. 243b; II, 563.   [5] Ib., fol. 152b, 153a; II, 200, 201.
[4] Ib., fol. 30b; I, 190.   [6] Ib., fol. 28b, 29a; I, 181, 182.

the "venom of God." He is also the Angel of Death, who destroys men with a single drop of poison. AMALEK is apparently his synonym. There are said, however, to be two demons, *sub voce* AMALEK and the Divine malediction of the first serpent applies to both.

For the rest, demons are the excrement of the earth and are designated by the word TOHOU, while BOHOU signifies that part of the world which is free from demons.[1] It follows that the first state is that of the infernal cohorts, so confused with matter that they formed one body therewith. A separation was accomplished by the fire which is referred to under the name of darkness, when it is said that " darkness was upon the face of the deep."[2] But to make the clarification complete, the Holy Spirit brooded upon the face of the waters.[3] It is added that so long as the purification was unfinished, the spirit of the demon still interposed between heaven and matter, to deprive man of the pure vision of God [4]—another suggestion that the history of creation is one of states of the soul. Unfortunately the ZOHAR—amidst all its casual information of this kind—does not furnish one per cent. of the materials necessary to elucidate it at length, and the same remark applies to the general history of election of which it is a part, so that this phase of the Secret Doctrine cannot be developed.

We shall meet with the Serpent and Samael again in the next chapter and shall ascertain after what manner they enter into the Mystery of Sex. As a conclusion to this part, it seems desirable to say that the Zoharic prince of demons is never compared to the morning star or to any other luminary in heaven. I do not remember that the word הילל=Day-Star= Lucifer occurs anywhere in the text as a synonym of Satan. Finally, the world will not be set free from the serpent until the coming of Messiah the King, who will cast down death for ever.[5] As to what may happen thereafter, the mind of the doctors is divided, which it seems to have been invariably

---

[1] There is apparently a light of the world below which is in separation from the world above, and this is said to generate demons without number.—Z., Pt. I, fol. 156b; II, 214. As regards TOHOU and BOHOU, it may be useful to compare Book VI, § 2.
[2] Gen. i. 2.
[3] *Ib.*
[4] Z., Pt. I, fol. 16a; I, 94–96.
[5] Z., Pt. I, fol. 113b, 114a; II, 58, 59. The authority is Is. xxv. 8; Zech. xiii. 2. The point is that Samael is the death-angel, and it is one of those places in the ZOHAR where he and the serpent on which he rides are identified on account of their union.

on all matters that concern eschatology. We shall have to take back into our hearts every primitive form of thought before we shall consent to believe that the Holy One, blessed be He, created the tempter-spirit so that He might put man to the test[1]; but this is one of the theses, as we have seen, and it follows in course " that he is also God's minister." Perhaps it is for this reason that there is a counsel not to affront the demon, since in virtue of such an imposed office he would be saved, like the executioner. Moreover, as the infernal male and female principles symbolise the Sex Mystery in the deeps of corruption, we have to remember that even in these deeps it is a reflection of the Mystery that is on high, and to say that it may not be without an inward element of redemption seems to connect with the truth of things, working towards a justification of the Divine Ways in all the quarters of the universe.[2] *Si descendero ad infernum, ades.* One of the fragmentary texts incorporated with the ZOHAR affirms therefore that even the evil spirit will be restored at the end of days.[3] The inference is extracted with an all too common perversity out of the words : " He brought back all the goods, and also brought again his brother Lot."[4] The imputed authority matters nothing and the idea which has begotten the interpretation signifies everything. I have indicated that the ZOHAR as exegesis was conceived and born in a house of distraction.

III.—THE FALL OF MAN

Matthew Arnold was of opinion that it was impossible to dispense with Christianity or to be satisfied with it in the current and accepted forms. A similar impression has been created through all the Christian centuries by the Myth of Paradise, and especially that part of it which concerns the Fall of Man[5]; but it will be understood that I am not

---

[1] Z., Pt. I, Appendix III, THE SECRET MIDRASH, fol. 2a ; II, 686.
[2] Between good and evil the mediating and reconciling principle is held to be womanhood, and hence it is said—in rather cryptic language—that the Spirit of Good and the Spirit of Evil can only abide in harmony so far as the female is between them, she having part in both. It is then only that the Spirit of Good, which constitutes pure joy, attracts the female and thus preponderates over the Spirit of Evil.—*Ib.*, fol. 49a ; I, 284. Cf. *ante*, p. 269.
[3] *Ib.*, SITHRE THORAH, Pt. I, fol. 287b ; II, 664.
[4] Gen. xiv. 16.
[5] There is a feeling at the present day in certain schools of interpretation that the idea of a genuine difference between man in the first estate of Paradise and in the exile of the world beyond has no authority in Scripture and that it was adopted by the

alluding to persons for whom it is folk-lore or fable. As to these there is no difficulty: it is only among those who regard it as in some sense a veil of man's spiritual history that the problems offered by this myth are of real consequence, and it is these naturally who have expended their skill in seeking to construct it rationally. Very few have done otherwise than distort the materials placed in their hands, so that if it is hard to be satisfied with the plain story, it is impossible to accept the attempts by which the literal body has been buried, so that it might be raised a spiritual body. The resurrections are worse than the form which used to move among us in some manner of the life of faith. I believe that at this day the Latin Church imposes on its members an acceptance of the simple story, exactly as it is given in Genesis, so that it is a clear issue and deserving of our respect as such.[1] It is to be taken or left; those in the faith take it amidst silence in the heaven of faith, though there may be many wry faces turned to the wall for concealment; the rest leave it no doubt. I have spent many years among the mystics who have made excursions into this subject and have produced their various versions, "to perplex the sages" and others. The versions stand at their value, and I do not know that there is much to choose between them, from those of St. Augustine to Saint-Martin. Readers who are acquainted with the theses of Jacob Böhme on the Paradisaical state will remember that Adam, in his system, began to degenerate before the specific occasion of his Fall is supposed to have arisen and, as part of his declension, that a state of inactivity supervened.[2] One consequence was that Eve had to be removed from within him and manifested in a mode of separation. I do not know how this is harmonised with the Lord God's statement that

---

Church early in the Christian centuries as a working hypothesis of doctrine. However this may be, the ZOHAR has very plain instruction on the subject, and the present section of our research, taken in connection with that on the Myth of Paradise, will show that a life of glory and divinity was followed by a life of shame. The word Fall is of course technical and as such particular to Christian Theology, with all its cloud of developments, but about that which is meant thereby no question will be found in the ZOHAR.

[1] It makes a clean sweep of the whole fantastic mass of private interpretation and throws us back on the first principles of the story, forbidding us to exercise our personal and putative wisdom above that which is written. While it is not possible to accept the asylum offered, there is no desire to make salvage in respect of the baggage which has been " heaved over among the rubbish."

[2] It is said that the "tincture" of Adam was quite wearied: THE THREE PRINCIPLES, c. 13. The reason is given at length in MYSTERIUM MAGNUM, c. 18, being his hunger to eat of good and evil, not indeed in the mouth but with the imagination.

"it is not good that the man should be alone," [1] nor does it perhaps signify. In any case the provision of a helpmeet did not save him, for in the obscure providence of the dealings woman was the occasion of his literal fall. The ZOHAR also recognises a gradual degeneration of Adam,[2] because apparently the workings of the beast "more subtle than any" were in process prior to the manifest temptation of Eve. I do not know why a time-limit should be drawn about the story so closely, but it is stated more than once that Adam fell on the very day of his creation,[3] the notion being drawn in the usual inscrutable manner from this text of Isaiah: "In the day shalt thou make thy plant to grow, and in the morning shalt thou make thy seed to flourish,"[4] though the reading differs in the ZOHAR.

It appears that the original union of man, male and female, was apart from fleshly sensation, and it was therefore an union in modesty.[5] When Adam said: "This is now bone of my bones and flesh of my flesh"[6] he was seeking to dispose Eve in favour of such intercourse, because they were one only. It was out of this that the temptation is represented as having arisen, for immediately after these words of tenderness the spirit of evil awoke, to substitute carnal pleasures for its own profit in place of pure affection.[7] The object was also to sully the sanctity above by defiling man below in the first place.[8] As regards what Theology would call the matter of the sin, there is no need to say that the apple is not understood literally.[9] It is called sometimes—as we have seen—the fruit of the vine, that is to say, grapes; but this is a veil also and is to be understood as the explanation of a certain Mystery of Knowledge, which Knowledge belongs to the dominion of

---

[1] Gen. ii. 18.
[2] Z., Pt. II, fol. 262b; IV, 295.
[3] *Ib.*, Pt. I, fol. 35b; I, 219. According to Jacob Böhme, the period was forty days. We shall see elsewhere that the First Sabbath followed the decree of expulsion.
[4] Is. xvii. 11. The Zoharic rendering is: "The day that you have planted, your seed shall produce only wild fruits."
[5] There is an obscure suggestion that children were born to Adam in the Garden of Eden, that is to say, souls, and if they had come with him out of the Garden, man would have had eternal life. He was expelled, however, to engender children outside. —Z., Pt. I, 60b, 61a; I, 356.
[6] Gen. ii. 23.
[7] Z., Pt. I, fol. 49b; I, 287.
[8] *Ib.*, fol. 52a; I, 301.
[9] After the Fall of Man, it is said that the Tree of the Trespass was banished from Paradise, which sounds fantastic; but the whole Tree is allegorical and moves with man through the places of his exile. See the Cremona ed., Pt. I, fol. 126b.

sex. These are the fruits that are said elsewhere to be agreeable, on the authority of Genesis, but they trouble the spirits of those who make bad use of them, as Noah did in the case of his own vine.[1] He who rode upon the serpent, the Tempter-Spirit or Samael,[2] who is said also to have descended from heaven so mounted, as if he were an accredited messenger, approached Eve and testified that the Holy One created the world by help of the Tree of Knowledge;[3] that by eating thereof and so only was He able to create the world; and that if the woman ate of it, on her own part, she would attain the same power.[4] In a work so multifarious as the ZOHAR and so free of all responsibility created by the precedents of its own sections, it will be understood how there are alternative accounts as to the kind of temptation. In another case it is said that Eve was seduced by the peculiar atmosphere of the demon which encompassed the mythical fruit, as if it lay in a hot bed;[5] but this is additional detail rather than alternative. In a third there is exactly the kind of intimation which we should expect in relation to the mystery which the text reads into the myth: it was a seduction arising from the bewrayment of love, which had not appeared in the world till Adam and Eve were set toward one another, face to face;[6] it was also an outcome of the blind turning towards conception and generation; so that in this sense Eve was made victim as a result of her own womanhood. By reason of one or another cause, she decided to taste the fruit, which had the faculty of opening the eyes, in those who approached it, meaning in things concerning the Tree itself.[7] The result was a division between life and death,[8] as if the peace-insuring Middle Pillar had been removed from the Sephirotic Tree and Shekinah had ascended to KETHER, leaving the SEPHIRA MALKUTH

---

[1] Z., Pt. I, fol. 192a; II, 356. See also Deut. xxxii. 32: "Their grapes are grapes of gall, their clusters are bitter." And see Z., Pt. I, fol. 36a; I, 225.

[2] Ib., fol. 35b; I, 221. It is said that all creatures took fright when he appeared.

[3] The allusion is to the Mystery of Faith and Sex; the universe was a work of generation, and in this sense therefore the testimony of Samael was true, but that to which it was a preface proved—by the hypothesis of the legend—a lying travesty of the true practice.

[4] Z., Pt. I, fol. 36a; I, 222.

[5] Ib., Pt. II, fol. 203b; IV, 205.

[6] Ib., fol. 231a; IV, 253. It is suggested again in this place that Adam and Eve began to engender children from the moment that they were put face to face.

[7] Ib., Pt. I, fol. 36a; I, 224.

[8] Ib., fol. 36a; I, 225. The threatened death seems always to have been understood spiritually. It is said elsewhere that "the Serpent takes away the higher souls—NESHAMOTH—of all flesh."—Z., Cremona ed., Pt. I, fol. 28a.

without God in the world. There was division also between the Voice and the Word, so that the Voice spoke yet the Word was not uttered.[1] God was asleep therefore in the heart of man. To speak of events like these in whatever immemorial past is of course to remind the Sons of the Secret Doctrine how it fares with them in the actual present; and so it is added that since Israel has been in captivity the Voice has been divided from it, whence the Word is audible no longer.[2] The inference is that the Word remains in the heart, but the lips which should speak are paralysed.

Recurring to the substitution of a mystical vine for the apple-tree, another tradition certifies that Eve pressed grapes and gave the juice to her husband. The opening of their eyes was to behold all the ills of the world.[3] I suppose that I need not specify in what sense these grapes are to be understood as a sex-symbol, and it follows that she shewed Adam how they might be enjoyed. Obviously, according to this version—*Traditum est genitales partes adæ existere*, in some sense, at that period, though neither he nor his wife had as yet been clothed with skins, which are understood sometimes as material bodies. They discerned also their nakedness, and of this fact there are several explanations, the most important of which must be cited. In the act which constituted the trespass they lost that celestial lustre and decoration of sacred letters which had covered them previously and they clothed themselves with leaves of the same Tree of which they had eaten—that is to say, with leaves of the vine or fig![4] They knew now all secrets of the lower world—*vel infra cingulum*—and seeing that the leaves of the Tree were the most pleasurable of that region, they sought to acquire force therein by the means thereof.

---

[1] Z., Pt. I, fol. 36a; I, 225. It was the consequence of separating life from death, the analogy of which is separation between man and woman by the chastisement of the *menses*, so that she is in hiding like the moon, which is taken away from the heaven of stars for a week from month to month. But I question whether the symbolism is true in this case, for as the phenomenon concerned is a line of demarcation in sex between woman and the world of animals, it is in the proper sense a dignity rather than a punishment.

[2] The suggestion comes from Ps. xxxix. 2: "I was dumb with silence. I held my peace, even from good."

[3] Z., Pt. I, fol. 36b; I, 226.

[4] These leaves are said in more than one place to signify demons, meaning probably the evil side of fleshly desires. It is difficult not to think that the Doctors of the Secret Law who invented a cloud of parables to explain the parables of Scripture in its literal sense had a meaning behind this grotesque woof of symbolism, and sometimes it shines through the texture.

Another account renounces symbolism utterly, so that he who runs may read. "And when the woman saw that the tree was good for food and pleasant to the eyes ... she took of the fruit thereof, and did eat."[1] These words are held to designate the first union of Adam and Eve.[2] "She consented originally to union as a result of her reflections on the values of conjugal relations and by reason of that pure affection and tenderness which united her to Adam."[3] But the intervention of the serpent had as its result that Eve "gave also to her husband with her," which means that their conjugal relations changed and that she filled him with carnal desires.[4] Henceforth desire was first on the part of the woman, she alluring the man. This evil notwithstanding, the acts performed between them subsequently were in correspondence with those which obtain above, for the Spirit of Evil imitates the Spirit of Good, and that which it occasions below in malice the spirit of good fulfils in holiness above. This correspondence implies, however, "a sublime mystery," which is said to exceed the capacity of most men.[5] When Adam and Eve had sinned the Holy One stripped off the cuirass formed by the light of the sacred letters with which they had been invested: it was then they saw that they were naked.[6] Previously the cuirass had shielded them from all attacks, whilst they were free therein. "And they sewed fig-leaves together and made themselves aprons."[7] This means that they betook themselves to the delights of the lower and material world, leaves of the Tree of Good and Evil, fleshly pleasures and the consequences thereof.[8] But it is to be observed that the evil is not without the good in the Tree of Knowledge: it was the profanation of a Great Mystery, but the seeds of redemption remained. It is for this reason that

---

[1] Gen. iii. 6.
[2] Z., Pt. I, fol. 49b; I, 287.
[3] I have put this sentence literally, to shew that the early Victorian accent existed prior to the congeries of motives and manners belonging to that period. This statement is by allusion to that which remains after due allowance has been made for the habit of paraphrase which beset the French translator De Pauly.
[4] Z., Pt. I, fol. 49b; I, 287, 288.
[5] Z., Pt. I, fol. 49b; I, 288. It is obvious *ex hypothesi* that the correspondence existed previously in the putative spiritual intercourse already mentioned, and the fact that the likeness remained in the alleged grosser union constituted its title to redemption. That the Sons of the Doctrine practised that which they regarded as the path of its transmutation we shall see later.
[6] *Ib.*, fol. 53a; I, 307.
[7] Gen. iii. 7.
[8] Z., Pt. I, fol. 53b; I, 307.

THE FALL OF MAN

the ZOHAR discerns a promise of salvation hidden in the words: " And the Lord God commanded the man, saying, Of every tree of the garden thou mayest freely eat: but of the Tree of the Knowledge of Good and Evil, thou shalt not eat of it: for in the day that thou eatest thereof thou shalt surely die."[1] The interpretation itself is extracted against all simple sense and reason; but the fact remains that the Sons of the Doctrine recognised a way of escape.[2]

A third version affirms that the forbidden fruit signifies woman herself,[3] and the versicle appertaining hereto is: " Her feet go down to death; her steps take hold on hell."[4] But we know that the extract applies only to a " strange woman," and the application must have reference to intercourse in unredeemed bonds of the body of death, as if the *ficus religiosus* of the Tree of Life had become the barren fig-tree which Christ cursed, or as if the letter of the Law remained without one vestige of its spirit. Woman is also signified by the Garden,[5] when it is said: " And a river went out of Eden to water the Garden."[6] Prior to the trespass this river penetrated into the woman and irrigated her waters. It is added—obscurely enough—that when men are in such a degree of sanctity there is perfect unity, and of this unity it is said: " In that day there shall be one Lord, and His Name one."[7] Subsequently to their sin the Holy One clothed Adam and Eve with vestments belonging to flesh alone.[8] The suggestion is that previously the flesh was glorified by

---

[1] Gen. ii. 16, 17. This was prior to the creation of Eve, according to the literal account in Genesis and therefore, as a technical point, it is to be noticed that he alone was commanded and he alone forbidden.

[2] Z., Pt. I, fol. 35b; I, 219.

[3] *Ib.*, fol. 35b; I, 220. The Tree is said, moreover, to signify man. *Ib.*, fol. 35b; I, 222. It must follow in the sense of things that, in this case, the forbidden fruit is an act common to man and woman. It is not less certain that in the logic of such symbolism the Tree of Life is another postulated act performed by male and female according to a law and life of perfection. I must add, after weighing all the counter-symbolism, that we must be on our guard how we accept in all its literal bearings the somewhat casual and certainly isolated suggestion that the forbidden fruit was woman. It is true in a certain sense, but that sense postulates the kind of relations between the woman and the serpent, between the man and Lilith, of which we hear otherwise, and which is the recurring symbolism. I think, in conclusion as to this matter, that woman was the forbidden fruit in the same way that she is said to be the Garden of Eden. Here again there is a sense in which the statement is true assuredly: she is the Garden in the Kingdom of MALKUTH and she is meant to become the Garden in BINAH when man has been redeemed in her and she in man; but this is high mysticism and would be nonsense according to the letter, if it were so taken.

[4] Prov. v. 5.
[5] Z., Pt. I, fol. 35b; I, 221.
[6] Gen. ii. 10.
[7] Zech. xiv. 9.
[8] Z., Pt. I, fol. 36b; I, 226, 227.

light of the spirit; but what is stated otherwise is that they had garments of light, thanks to which they were raised above the higher angels—who had recourse to them in order to enjoy light.[1] A non-Zoharic tradition declares that the beauty of Adam was reflected from the glorious Throne, while the beauty of Eve was such that no creature could look on her. Even Adam could not do so till after the trespass, when both lost their supernatural loveliness.[2]

According to yet another account, the sin of Eve was one of separation, and this would no doubt have been endorsed by the Böhme school of Christian Mysticism. Separation, on the other hand, according to the ZOHAR, designates death.[3] This is on the one side, and on the correlative it is said elsewhere that when Adam ate of the Tree of Good and Evil he provoked the separation of woman from man.[4] On the day of transgression both heaven and earth sought to flee away, because they were established only on the covenant of God with man, as it is written: " If my covenant be not with day and night, and if I have not appointed the ordinances of heaven and earth,"[5] &c. When Adam forsook the way of faith and the Tree which is the synthesis of all trees, he lapsed from a region of stability into one susceptible of variation, exchanging life for death.[6] The Tree of Life preserves all who are attached to it from death for ever. Humanity was made originally in the likeness of the Elohim, which likeness was obscured by the Fall, so that the faces of men were transformed, with the result that they began to fear the beasts who had been afraid previously of them.[7]

I will put separately another intimation which is distinct

---

[1] Z., Pt. I, fol. 36b; I, 226, 227. Towards the close of the ZOHAR, Rabbi Eleazar, in the course of a discussion with another doctor of the Secret Law, allows that Adam and Eve were clothed with garments of skin before the Fall, but they were then glorious vestments which became gross subsequently. He adds that their eyes were opened by the trespass to the material form of this world, whereas previously they had beheld in all things only the celestial side.—*Ib.*, Pt. III, fol. 261b; VI, 11.

[2] *Ib.*, Pt. III, fol. 83b; V, 227. The physical beauty was theirs afterwards and is the subject of several allusions.

[3] *Ib.*, Pt. I, fol. 12b; I, 70, 71.

[4] *Ib.*, fol. 53a; I, 306. The intention may be to signify that the union of physical intercourse is of times and seasons only, but above it there is a spiritual union, once enjoyed by man, and this is unceasing, like that of Jehovah and Elohim. We have seen that this union is postulated in a pre-natal state, and it may well be that the myth of the Earthly Paradise is an allegory thereof, embodying a delineation of things which led up to the life of earth.

[5] *Ib.*, fol. 56a; I, 321, 322. Jer. xxxiii. 25.

[6] *Ib.*, Pt. III, fol. 107a, b; V, 269, 270.

[7] *Ib.*, Pt. I, fol. 71a; I, 419.

from these and belongs to a variant order of symbolism, though it seems to me a moral consideration rather than a secret doctrine. It depends from the reverie that innumerable pleasant odours are diffused for ever throughout the Garden of Eden, to prepare the precious vestments of the soul which are formed from the good days spent by man on earth.[1] " And they knew that they were naked." [2] This means, according to tradition, that they were aware of being without the precious vestures which are formed of stainless days.[3] As a result of the trespass, no such day was left to Adam, and it is in this sense that he was naked.[4] When he repented, the Holy One clothed him with other garments, but they were not garments of days.[5] If, however, the garments of skin are on the whole to be understood as vehicles of manifestation, material in place of spiritual bodies, the question of nakedness remains in the absence of a covering belonging to the origin of artifice. Alternatively, if the bodies were not already of flesh, in what sense did the trespass open the eyes of Adam and Eve to the fact that they were naked? There are two places in which the garments of skin are said to be robes of glory with which they were clothed by God, in which they left Paradise, in virtue of which they resembled those who are on high, and wherein they were ultimately buried.[6]

There is one more point of view before I come to the suggestion in chief of the story. It is said that when Adam sinned the evil serpent cleaved to him and defiled him, as well as all future generations.[7] The serpent was able to penetrate

---

[1] The Earthly Paradise is a place of sojourn for the departed on the return whence they came.
[2] Gen. iii. 7.
[3] Z., Pt. I, fol. 224a, b; II, 482, 483.
[4] It is rather an unhappy similitude, for so long as he had not eaten of the Tree of Knowledge, he was incapable of good days, and furthermore—according to another myth—that which was stripped from him was a robe of glory, wherein he had no need for the vesture of stainless days.
[5] Z., Pt. I, fol. 224a; II, 483.
[6] *Ib.*, Pt. II, fol. 39a, 39b; III, 184, 185. They were permeated with the odours of Paradise. See also *ib.*, Pt. III, fol. 261b; VI, 11, already quoted.
[7] *Ib.*, Pt. I, fol. 53b; I, 309. As regards the serpent, it is said—Cremona ed., Pt. I, fol. 28a—that Samael descended with all his hosts, and he sought upon the earth a companion like unto himself, but it had an appearance even as a camel. This curious comparison is based on the fact that the Hebrew G M L means camel when certain vowel points are added to these consonants, and reward or recompense with others. The significance of this is developed in the PEKUDE section of the ZOHAR, commenting on Gen. xxiv. 64: " And Rebeccah lifted up her eyes, and when she saw Isaac, she lighted off her camel." The camel is here said to signify the mystery of death, referred to in Prov. xix. 17: " That which he hath given will He pay him again." The connecting idea is, firstly, that reward, in the sense of retribution, came into the world by

secretly into man's interior, and Adam submitted to this so that he might know the mysteries of things below. The serpent shewed him all the pleasures of the world [1]—presumably as Satan took Christ into a high mountain whence He beheld all the Kingdoms. These intimations depend from a thesis which recurs many times in the ZOHAR. It is testified by the colleagues that the Fall of man was one of sin with a woman,[2] in the normal sense which attaches to this expression. It is added almost immediately that sexual desires have caused all evils, but a correction or modification follows in the course of debate—namely, that in themselves they are good or evil according to the spirit which inspires them. Now, seeing that it is to Eve that sin of a sexual order was first imputed, the question is who instructed or initiated her? The answer is that the serpent—meaning Samael—had "criminal relations" with her and injected his defilement into her,[3] Adam not being affected until she communicated in turn to him.[4] She cohabited with Samael, who corrupted her and by him she became with child, bringing forth Cain.[5] It is obvious that this is in clear contradiction to the text of Scripture, which says: "And Adam knew his wife Eve; and she conceived, and bare Cain."[6] But the anomaly is so glaring that it must be assuredly of set purpose, or, in other words, that to develop the sexual nature of the Fall the history on which it is founded is ignored at need. The ZOHAR is content equally to contradict itself, for it

---

the serpent, and, secondly, that the peculiar nature of the Fall is indicated by the alleged hidden sense of the term camel, which represents the *pudenda*. Compare Cazotte's DIABLE AMOUREUX, where the impure demon is revealed at last with the head of that animal.

[1] Z., Pt. I, fol. 52a; I, 301.
[2] *Ib.*, Pt. I, fol. 23a; I, 142. This transpires in the course of a conversation, already mentioned, between Shekinah and the two fallen angels Aza and Azael. Some of the codices add, as we have seen, that with woman man will repair his fault, which is a very important statement from the standpoint of the Mystery of Faith, and involves the reintegration of nuptial union in the order of Divine things.
[3] *Ib.*, fol. 54a; I, 311.
[4] *Ib.*, fol. 126a; II, 101.
[5] *Ib.*, fol. 37a; I, 230. The story of this cohabitation is of Talmudic origin and will be found in the TRACT SABBATH, among other places. It is also of general rabbinical authority otherwise, and is stated by R. Abraham de Seba in his commentary on the Pentateuch. The MIDRASH RUTH affirms that both Adam and Eve were defiled by the serpent. Finally, it is mentioned categorically in the PARAPHRASE of Jonathan ben Uzziel (Gen. iv. 1) that when Adam knew Eve his wife she had conceived already of the angel Samael. Apparently as a result of the dual intercourse, she brought forth Cain, who is said to have resembled the beings who are above, not those who are below. Eve is also recorded to have said: "I have gotten a man, an angel of Jehovah," and not: "I have gotten a man from the Lord" (Gen. iv. 1).
[6] Gen. iv. 1.

THE FALL OF MAN

affirms in another place that Adam was defiled by the impure spirit before his union with Eve, and the son whom he begot in this state of impurity was from the left side: so was Cain born. But when Adam repented he engendered a son from the right side: so was Abel born.[1] It is of course arbitrary to postulate such repentance between the two nativities, rather than before or after. All that we know from the text of Genesis is that at the birth of Cain, Eve was of opinion that she had " gotten a man from God." [2] Another account, on the authority of Rabbi Eleazar, recurs to the earlier thesis, specifying that Cain was begotten from the serpent but that after intercourse with Adam, Eve conceived again, and so brought two sons into the world—one of the works of the serpent and one of the works of Adam. The image of Abel was from on high and that of Cain from below.[3]

We have not finished, however, with the complications of this subject, for another story recites that the relations of Samael continued for a long time with Eve, who bore him many children—presumably after the expulsion from Paradise.[4] They were not in human likeness. So also, after the death of Abel,[5] Adam separated from his wife and began to receive visits from two female demons, with whom he had relations, and engendered those evil spirits and demons which infest the world.[6] It is pointed out that there is no need for surprise at this, because every man in his dreams sees such women occasionally, observes them smiling at him, and if

---

[1] Z., Pt. I, fol. 54a; I, 311.
[2] Gen. iv. 1.
[3] Z., *ib*. It will be seen that this is at issue with the PARAPHRASE of Jonathan. According to ZOHAR HADASH, § YITHRO, the seduction of Adam by Lilith and of Eve by her companion Samael caused our mortal condition. This is the sense in which death was brought into the world, " and all our woe." *Ex hypothesi*, the springs of generation were tainted.
[4] Z., Pt. I, fol. 53a; I, 315, 316.
[5] It is taught, much after the manner of Christian Theology, that if Adam had never sinned man would never have tasted death as the condition of his entrance into the world beyond. But Christian Theology does not encourage us to suppose that in such case the union of Adam and Eve would have produced children—so far at least as I am aware. On the other hand, the separation of the sexes was primarily for this purpose, according to Kabbalism.—See Z., Pt. III, 159b; V, 412. I should add that in another place one of the doctors maintains that Adam and Eve would have remained alone in the world in the unfallen state, but another answers him that they would have engendered children emanating from the Holy Spirit.—*Ib.*, Pt. I, fol. 61a; I, 356, 357. See also Pt. III, fol. 189a; V, 495, 496.
[6] Z., Pt. I, fol. 54b; I, 314. The Talmudic story is different in this sense, that the sin of Adam in eating of the forbidden fruit was punished by an excommunication which lasted 130 years, and it was thereafter that he began to engender children in his own image.

they excite his concupiscence they conceive and bear demons. I suppose that one of these demons was the black Lilith and the other Naamah, who are both mentioned in the ZOHAR, though not actually in this connection. We shall see shortly that presumably another Lilith was the wife of Adam in Paradise. Adam remained separated from his true wife for one hundred and thirty years, continuing to engender, and so long as he was defiled by the infection of the impure spirit, he had no desire for union with Eve. It returned, however, when he purified himself, and he begot "a son in his own likeness, after his image"—that is to say, Seth.[1] Dwelling still upon the mystery behind sex, the ZOHAR generalises on this matter, saying that so long as man follows the path which leads to the left side, his desire is towards the impure only, but the just who walk in the right way have children worthy of themselves. The important point to fix in our minds is that the Fall of man was not the result of human intercourse taking place between Adam and Eve but of some aberration in sex variously described, most accounts being exclusive one of another. There is an alternative not mentioned previously which balances the copulation of Eve and Samaël by the relations subsisting for a long period of time between Adam and Lilith amidst all the splendours and perfections of Paradise, prior to the creation of the helpmeet. It was to substitute human for impure pleasures that she was taken ultimately from the side of Adam, and from this point of view we discern another sense in which it was "not good that the man should be alone."[2]

---

[1] Z., Pt. I, fol. 5a; I, 316.
[2] *Ib.*, fol. 34b; I, 216. There are many scattered references to this female demon, who—in one of her forms—appears to have been of the Melusine and mermaid type, for when it is said that "God created great whales" (Gen. i. 21), the reference is to Leviathan and his wife Lilith.—*Ib.*, fol. 34b; I, 213. She is a *negotium perambulans in tenebris*, for she goes abroad in the night.—*Ib.*, fol. 34b; I, 214. She is the instigator of punishments, clamouring daily for their infliction.—*Ib.*, fol. 106a; II, 33. She is said to preside over all fish who are charged with missions to this world—presumably other amphibious demons, though the ZOHAR says that they are called "the first-born in the land of Egypt" (Ex. xii. 29). The sacred angels of the waters that are above were separated by God from the emissaries of Lilith in the waters below. It may be noted here that she is distinct from the "adulterous woman" who was the wife of Samael, as the latter is to be distinguished from Leviathan.—*Ib.*, Pt. II, fol. 35a, b; III, 169, 170. She is termed "servant" in one place, which is in opposition to that servant who is Shekinah. The latter is like the conjugal Venus and presides over the birth of children, but Lilith devours them.—*Ib.*, fol. 96a, b; III, 387. Also *ib.*, fol. 111a, b; III, 435. She is the mother of demons.—*Ib.*, fol. 267b; IV, 301. She is the most terrible of all evil spirits, but she took refuge in the deep when God created and adorned Eve.—*Ib.*, Pt. III, fol. 19a; V, 51, 52. See also *ib.*, Pt. I, fol. 169b;

THE FALL OF MAN

To illustrate further that, from the first page of Genesis to the last of the prophets, the importance of Holy Writ is in its adaptation to the history and election of Israel, it is said that when the Tables of the Law were broken, it was then man perceived that he was naked [1]—as he was literally, according to the account in Exodus. It is said further that the words: "They heard the voice of the Lord God," is an allusion to the voice of God on Mount Sinai. And finally: since the Day when Adam fell the world was in a condition of poverty [2] until the arrival of Noah, who—having offered a sacrifice—restored it to the normal state. Now, it is obvious that there had been sacrifices previously—*e.g.*, the acceptable offering of Abel. There must have been therefore something particular about that of Noah—I mean, in the mind of the ZOHAR—and we shall see in the next chapter that there was something particular also about his drunkenness, which was an exploration of Divine Mysteries. We know the indignity which befell him, and I shall shew presently the kind of sin which led, *ex hypothesi*, to the Deluge. I believe that all these allusions touch upon the same mystery.

The ZOHAR contains no suggestion of importance in respect of the expulsion from Eden or the Flaming Sword.[3] Adam is said to have chanted the 92nd Psalm in his flight and the Sabbath intervened to protect him, so that he was not entirely driven out until the end of that day. I do not know what purpose this version is supposed to serve; but the Secret Lamp of Israel did not diffuse always the same light. The way of the return to the Garden was barred, lest worse evils might be brought upon the world.[4] The "Flaming Sword which turned every way"[5] signifies angels set over

---

II, 266.—Pt. II, fol. 114b; III, 442.—Pt. III, fol. 222b; V, 562. A Talmudic legend relates that Lilith was created from the same earth as Adam and refused in the end to serve him through pride respecting her origin. I should mention that the word which the Authorised Version renders "screech-owl" in Is. xxxiv. 14, and the Vulgate *lamia* is Lilith in the original Hebrew, the root of which is a word signifying night. Rabbi Elias recognised four mothers of demons, namely, Lilith, Naamah, Ogeret and Mahalath.

[1] Z., Pt. I, fol. 28b; I, 181.
[2] *Ib.*, fol. 63b; I, 371.
[3] A certain supposed confusion of pronouns in the Hebrew text of Gen. iii. 24. enables the ZOHAR to suggest that it was not the Lord God who drove out Adam but rather that the latter expelled the Divine Being, presumably from his own heart and also, as a manifest Presence, from that world which man had ravaged by his trespass.—Z., Pt. I, fol. 53b; I, 307.
[4] Z., Pt. I, fol. 53b; I, 308.
[5] Gen. iii. 25.

the chastisement of man in this world.¹ Now, there is no true grace herein and there is no mystery; but if the temptation and the Fall signify an aberration of sex, a declension or a materialisation therein, there is no question that the Tree of Life is the perfect way of nuptials; and the ascent of the Sephirotic Tree, which—according to the Secret Schools—is a return into union, we shall find at the proper time to be a journey in the graces and glories of the Sacred Shekinah, who presides over the intercourse which, if begun on earth, is completed in the World of the Supernals. For there is a grade of perfection attainable in these Mysteries which was known to the Sons of the Doctrine, and in view of it they said that a day shall come when the world will be avenged of the serpent:² this will be the day of the coming of the Tree of Life, which will obtain the remission of sins and will enchain the serpent. The male and female will be united in the Garden of Eden as they were before the Fall. But now the nakedness of the natural Adam is a nakedness of good works and of obedience to the commandments of the Law—understood as that Secret Doctrine which is concerned with the Mystery of Faith.³

IV.—THE LEGEND OF THE DELUGE

The way of human generation⁴ had replaced the higher intercourse which is outlined faintly, at a far distance and amidst all confusion by the Secret Tradition, and so outlined only in deference to the covenants expressed and implied, because it is admittedly a mystery that cannot be revealed to

---

[1] It is said also to have symbolised the trials with which God overwhelms man, that he may be restored to the way of goodness.—Z., Pt. II, fol. 167a; IV, 114.

[2] Z., Pt. I, fol. 145b; II, 173, 174. It is an exceedingly suggestive intimation, and its seeming Christian implicits are plain, almost on the surface. The world will remain in the toils of the serpent until that day shall come when a woman who is comparable to Eve and a man corresponding to Adam shall vanquish not only the serpent but the angel of death and destruction who rides thereon.

[3] It is quite extrinsic to my subject at this point, but as there will be occasion for a subsequent reference, I may add here that Adam and Eve were interred together in a cave having a door which opened on the Garden of Eden; and there also some of the patriarchs were buried.—Z., Pt. III, fol. 164a; V, 423. There are several other references.

[4] It should not be inferred that the way of human generation is ever reduced in its importance or tampered with in its high symbolism. This is why I have termed it important to observe that the Fall of man was not a sin of natural intercourse with a woman. Under certain prescribed conditions, that is rather the way of his return into the true likeness of God—though not so much for what it is in itself as for that which it intimates.

the world. The way of humanity had become a sacred way, a sacrament in virtue of its correspondence with things above, in virtue also of its reflections from that which was the design of Nature when it came forth resplendent at its first birth.¹ Had this been maintained there would have been no path of regeneration, for men would have walked in union, as Enoch walked with God. It is implied more especially that in the birth of Seth ² human generation was uplifted into the sacramental world, and the path of nuptials was followed by the saints of old in accordance with a practice of wisdom which will be indicated hereafter—towards the end of the present study. But it was not the way of the world, and we have next to consider those stages of the downward path which led up to the Deluge, as this is understood in Zoharic Theosophy. It will be found that the mystery of sex belongs thereto, but it is here on the averse side.

In the explanation of this cataclysm the text dwells naturally on the wickedness of man and has the authority of Scripture that it was very great over the whole world. The particular mystery of iniquity indicated by the ZOHAR is peculiar thereto. The patience of God was extended until the evil began to take that form which is described as the spilling of blood vainly on the earth.³ The sex aberration here designated will be understood by the expression used. It is the crime attributed to Onan, and the Zoharic doctrine affirms that no man who is sullied in this manner shall enter the Heavenly Palace or behold the face of Shekinah.⁴ The Shekinah is driven away thereby, and because of its prevalence the world fell into corruption, in part through the sin itself and for the rest by the absence of Shekinah. It was as if the principle of life had been withdrawn or that the loss of the head caused the body to decay. The world had become like

---

¹ The point is that the ZOHAR postulates a mystery of spiritual intercourse belonging to the state of Paradise and in the body of our present life a natural intercourse which can be raised into a sacrament of things Divine: between these was a sexual iniquity described in the language of earthly lust and constituting the Fall of Man.

² Because he only—according to the ZOHAR—was in the image and likeness of his father, who was in the likeness and image of God.

³ Z., Pt. I, 56b; I, 326.

⁴ *Ib.*, fol. 57a; I, 327. I believe that some *Theologia Moralis* of the Latin Church is not in agreement with the ZOHAR respecting the nature of the offence recorded in Gen. xxxviii. 9, and offers a particular alternative which there is no need to specify. I mention the matter because the alternative probably represents an old understanding of the subject. For the rest, it may be suggested that the specific enormity is possibly the veil of a larger complex and would include aberrations connected with the cities of the plain and Lesbos.

an unclean woman who has to hide in the presence of her husband.[1] Yet this was not the last state, for a time came when corruption reached such a point that there was neither shame nor concealment longer. The sin of Onan is held to have corrupted the earth as well as man,[2] *quia semen fundebat in terram*. Now, the waters above represent the male principle, while the female principle answers to the waters below, which is a very simple allegory of posture in the act of intercourse. The sin postulated was concerned with the waters of the male principle and it was necessary therefore that the whole contaminated earth should be purified by those of the Deluge.[3] But the waters above, which are spiritual, and the spiritual waters below both concurred therein, for the floodgates of heaven were opened and the fountains of the great deep were broken up.

One explanation of the vicious state of the world is that at the Deluge period it had as yet not been purified fully from the infection of the serpent.[4] The generation was also without faith —more especially concerning the secret subject matter of that which is called the Mystery of Faith. Men were attached to the leaves of the Tree of Good and Evil, meaning the spirit of the demon.

There is something very strange implied in the symbolism of the Ark, and one is inclined to ask : What was this Ark, or who ? It is a symbol of the Ark of the Covenant, and Noah had to be shut up in such a vessel here below because this comes to pass also in respect of the Mystery which is on high.[5] He could not be so inclosed until God had entered into a covenant with him.[6] He was then able to save the world, and this corresponds with the Supreme Mystery. It is said that Noah walked with Elohim, Who is the Covenant of Peace in the world : he was predestined from the day of creation to be shut up in the Ark. But it is unbecoming for a wife to

---

[1] Z., Pt. I, fol. 61a ; I, 359, 360.
[2] *Ib.*, fol. 61a, 61b ; I, 359, 360. This, however, is qualified later on, when it is said that the earth is called corrupt when man is in a state of decadence.—*Ib.*, fol. 62a ; I, 363.
[3] *Ib.*, fol. 62a ; I, 363, 364.
[4] *Ib.*, fol. 63b ; I, 371. The complete purification took place for a moment at the foot of Mount Sinai.
[5] It is obvious that the meaning of this passage is not on the surface. It will be seen from what follows that the Noetic Ark was feminine, because it was a house for those who were saved from the waters of the Deluge, and we know already that a house is always feminine.
[6] Z., Pt. I, fol. 59b ; I, 349.

receive any one as a guest at her house without the consent of her husband, so when Noah proposed to enter the Ark, it was necessary that Jehovah, the Spouse or Master of the House, should authorise his union therewith.[1] It was therefore at the invitation of God that he so entered. The reason is found in the words: "For thee have I seen righteous before me in this generation."[2] But Elohim is the celestial Bride, who is Shekinah, and it was by her permission, as Bride, Wife and Mistress of the house, that he had a permit to leave the Ark when the Deluge was over. It would seem that in some mystical sense he had dwelt within her precincts. After leaving those hospitable quarters, Noah made a present to the lady of the house, but it reached her by the mediation of her Spouse, because Scripture tells us that it was to Jehovah and not to Elohim that Noah erected an altar and offered sacrifice thereon. It was direct, however, from the lady of the house that Noah received his reward, because it is said that Elohim blessed Noah and his children, saying: "Increase and multiply and fill the earth."[3] It follows, as we shall see otherwise, that Shekinah presides over the fruit of nuptials, as well as over the nuptials themselves. In respect of the altar itself, it may be remembered that the ZOHAR has occasional references to an offering made by Adam and to that on which he sacrificed. The Deluge either destroyed or overturned everything, and when the time came for Noah to sacrifice on his part he is supposed to have raised up for this purpose the overthrown altar of Adam.[4] We see that his sacrifice is connected, though obscurely enough, with that Mystery of Sex which is the subject of allusion throughout. This would seem to be the case with every kind of burnt-offering, and it is even said that Leviticus i. 17, should be translated to signify that the holocaust is a woman and as such an agreeable odour to God.[5] The Authorised Version, reads: "A burnt sacrifice, an offering made by fire, of a

---

[1] Z., Pt. I, fol. 67a; I, 394; and *ib.*, fol. 70b, 71a; I, 418.
[2] Gen. vii. 1.
[3] Gen. ix. 1. The name which the Authorised Version and the Vulgate translate "God" is "Elohim" in the Hebrew. But the name in Gen. viii. 20, 21, which is translated "Lord" in the Authorised Version and Vulgate is Jehovah in the original.
[4] Z., Pt. I, fol. 69b, 70a; I, 412.
[5] The translators point out that the ZOHAR in this passage alters the sense of Scripture by substituting other vowel-points. But the question for us is whether it succeeds in conveying its own designed intimation. We shall see in due course that Shekinah, the Divine Woman, is termed more than once the Sacrifice of the Holy One.

sweet savour unto the Lord." It is admitted at the same time that the victim of the holocaust is male, according to the text, a male without blemish. It is admitted also that the word translated " burnt " is correct according to the literal sense; but if this were its true meaning it is argued that the orthography would have been different. The real purpose of the holocaust was the union of the male and female principles, as these should never be in separation. Noah offered a sacrifice because he represented the male principle which the Holy One united to the Ark, the latter representing the female principle.[1]

There are two other points which may be mentioned for the sake of completeness, and the first of these is that the Holy Land was not covered by the waters of the Deluge.[2] An authority is found in the words: " Thou art the land that is not cleansed, nor rained upon in the day of indignation." [3] The second is that the Deluge came to be called the waters of Noah, because he prayed for himself only and not for the world. I believe that this idea attaches to a Talmudic story, for there is no indication in Genesis of especial prayer on the part of Noah. The thesis is, however, that had he chosen he could have prevailed with God to spare the whole creation.[4]

We know from Genesis that Noah planted a vineyard, and according to one Zoharic opinion he transplanted the vine which had grown in the Garden of Eden; but whether this signifies the Tree of Knowledge does not transpire—except by inference from the legends. According to another view, he moved an ordinary vine of earth to a more favourable place. The fact that Noah pressed the grapes—as Eve is said also to have done—partook of the juice and so became drunken, is affirmed to contain a mystery of wisdom.[5] We have seen that *ex hypothesi* the lady of all our race was making an experiment of knowledge, and we shall understand further that what followed was an intoxication after its own kind. So also Noah was concerned with an experiment, having set himself to fathom that sin which had caused the fall of the first man. His intention was to find a cure for the world,

---

[1] Z., Pt. I, fol. 70a ; I, 413.
[2] *Ib.*, P. II, 197a; IV, 192.
[3] Ezek. xxii. 24.
[4] Z., Pt. III, fol. 14b, 15a ; V, 43. The manner in which he saved the world, as we have seen that he was supposed to do, proved wanting therefore in the seals and characters of perfection.
[5] Z., Pt. I, fol. 73a ; I, 433.

"in place of Eve and her poison"[1]; but he became drunken by laying bare the Divine Essence without having the intellectual strength to fathom it. This is why Scripture says that he was drunken and was uncovered within his tent. The meaning is that he raised a corner of the veil concerning that breach of the world which ought always to remain secret. The physical symbolism is obvious in this place. Moreover, the tent of Noah was really the tent of the vine.[2]

I do not pretend that the last sentences are intelligible from any point of view, nor that the materials as a whole of this section convey anything of especial importance beyond the postulated experiment made by Noah for the purpose of restoring the Mystery of Sex to its proper place in the spiritual life of man. The rest only continues the tale of lapse and degradation from the perfect union signified by the state of Paradise. I will add here a few vestiges of symbolism on the subject of the confusion of tongues, which was the next event of importance after the Deluge. The builders of Babel are said to have found a book containing certain Mysteries of Wisdom, which book had belonged to the generation destroyed by the Deluge.[3] The text is very loosely worded and it might seem at first sight that it was the primeval memorial of secret knowledge which, as we have seen, was transmitted to Adam and thence to the chiefs of the people, leaders of sanctity in the early generations. I do not think that this is the case, but that it was rather a record of magical art as this was attained by Enos, according to another Zoharic account.[4] It is said that his knowledge and ability in occult science exceeded that of his predecessors from Adam downward, and this is the sense in which we are to understand the scriptural statement that he, Enos, began to "call upon the name of the Lord"[5]—that is to say, he used the Divine Name to compel

---

[1] But not of course Eve apart from the serpent's poison. I cannot help feeling that it would have been a great relief to the Sons of the Doctrine and a material simplification of their system, if they had not been compelled to follow the legend of Genesis which ascribes the Fall to the woman.

[2] Z., Pt. I, fol. 73b; I, 434. The Ark was the means of transmitting the true knowledge concerning the Mystery of Sex from one epoch of the world to the other. Certain "literati" of the early nineteenth century, like Jacob Bryant, the Rev. G. S. Faber, Godfrey Higgins and Edward Davies seem to have recognised that it conveyed somehow certain profound Mysteries of Knowledge, but of what nature they had no conception.

[3] Ib., fol. 76a, b; I, 449, 450.

[4] Ib., fol. 56a; I, 323.

[5] Gen. iv, 26. The Authorised Version reads: "Then began men to call upon the Name of the Lord"—apparently at the time of the birth of Enos, or soon after. The

spirits in accordance with the recognised procedure of magical operations. The progress of this science ended by assuming such proportions that the wicked generation of the Deluge expected to escape Divine chastisement by recourse thereto. With the help of its mysteries they prepared even to make war on the Holy One, which was also the intention of those who planned the tower of Babel.[1] Like their predecessors, they had great trust in Magic: it was enough for them to pronounce words and things were accomplished. But the project had its source in a limited knowledge concerning the Mystery of Ancient Wisdom,[2] and I conclude therefore that there were two primeval books recognised in the legend—one that of Adam and the other one of knowledge which was either evil in itself or could be converted readily to evil.[3] At the dispersion which arrested the building those concerned therein lost even their partial knowledge. The confusion of tongues was of course a punishment adjudged[4]; but the apocryphal prophecy of Sophonia assures us that at the end of days the Lord will change the tongues of all the people into a pure tongue, so that all may invoke His Name and all pass under His yoke in one spirit.[5] This is quoted by the ZOHAR and is, I think, the only instance in which it cites a scriptural text outside the greater canon.

V.—THE COVENANT WITH ABRAHAM

The considerations arising in the ZOHAR out of the history of Abraham fall into two sections, the first of which is con-

---

Revised Version agrees, but the Vulgate translates the verse in the sense of the Zohar: *Iste—i.e.,* Enos—*cœpit invocare nomen Domini.* I should mention that the ZOHAR always recognises the claim of Magic as the art of a secret power, but, as we shall see more fully, it is condemned in all its branches and all its modes.

[1] Z., Pt. I, fol. 75b *et seq.*; I, 445, n.
[2] *Ib.*, fol. 76a; I, 447.
[3] It must be admitted that this does not agree with a statement in fol. 76a; I, 446, where it is said that the celestial book containing the Mystery of Wisdom was transmitted by Adam to other men who penetrated this Mystery, and seem to have imitated God thereby; but this is not in agreement with the succession of the keepers of the treasure, already enumerated.
[4] The union between thought and the word already mentioned seems to have been symbolised by the original existence of one language only. When men became separated from God, unity was no longer possible among themselves. The plan of Babel was elaborated with ingenious perversity, as the builders desired to quit the celestial domain for that of Satan and so substitute a strange glory for the glory of God.
[5] But the Vulgate rendering of the PROPHETIA SOPHONIÆ reads, *Quia tunc reddam populis labium electum, ut invocent omnes in nomine Domini, et serviant ei humero uno.* This is rendered by the revised Douay version: "Because then I will restore to the people a chosen lip, that all may call on the name of the Lord, and may serve Him with one shoulder."

THE COVENANT WITH ABRAHAM

secutive, coherent in a certain sense and of great length, but it is not of our especial concern, while the second, on account of its content, is scattered throughout the text and is of prime importance to the subject of this study. The first may be said to open with an interpretation of the call that came to the patriarch, in answer to which he left " the land of his nativity, in Ur of the Chaldees " [1] and entered into the land of Canaan. The journey was literal no doubt for the doctors in Kabbalism and stood as such at its value, but it was also a mystical travelling, and in this respect it belongs to a higher currency. Abraham had been endowed with a spirit of wisdom [2] and by the use of its talents had attained a knowledge of the celestial chiefs [3] who govern the various divisions of the habitable world.[4] He had gone further also than this, having discovered that Palestine was the centre of the earth, as well as the point of departure in its creation. He had not as yet ascertained by what chief it was ruled but concluded that such a president must be head over all the cohort. The study of the Holy Land was therefore the intent of his journey and he drew for the purpose on all his stores of astrological knowledge, but still was unable to penetrate the essence and importance of that Supreme Power which ruled the worlds innumerable and was postulated in his mind as the Spiritual Chief of Palestine. When at the end of his resources, however, the Holy One manifested on His own part, counselling that he should enter into himself, learn how to know himself and forsake all the false occult sciences to which he had recourse previously. This is another sense in which he was to come out of his own country. The words : " Go into a land that I will shew thee " [5] mean that Abraham was to be occupied henceforth only by those things which God would make known to him, though the essential nature of the Supreme Power which rules the world could not be included in the revelation, being above human understanding. It was there-

---

[1] Gen. xi. 31 ; xv. 7.
[2] Z., Pt. I, 77b, 78a ; I, 457.
[3] It is not quite certain whether this carries the implicit that he was addicted to the kind of Magic which is an art of dealing with spirits and is usually called ceremonial because it follows a ritual and prescribed verbal formulæ. If so, the sequel shews that he was held exonerated in virtue of his intention.
[4] Z., Pt. I, fol. 78b ; I, 458.
[5] Gen. xii. 1. The direction to leave his country signified that he should abandon his studies of the moral influences connected with different regions ; to leave his kindred was to abandon the science of astrology ; to leave the house of his father was to cease from the manner of life observed therein.—Z., Pt. I, fol. 78b ; I, 458.

fore a journey in the Divine obedience rather than one of the soul in God; but this path of conformity is itself a ladder of sanctity, by which man can be united to the Holy One, and is indeed the one way of our ascent. Abraham went up this ladder stage by stage [1] until he attained that point which was designed in his case, as it is written: " And Abram journeyed, going on still toward the South " [2]—being the Holy Land, wherein he was to reach the highest degree of holiness. But it is said that there was famine therein, which means that the country was not as yet consecrated, and he proceeded therefore to Egypt which is assimilated to the spiritual Garden of the Lord,[3] for it is written: " As the garden of the Lord, as the land of Egypt." [4] Abraham knew the mystery of this Garden,[5] the degrees of which are in correspondence with those that are below—that is to say, with Egypt, which is therefore said to be assimilated. But the nearer that he drew to Egypt the more did he cleave unto God. This notwithstanding, as the journey had not been authorised divinely, he was destined to suffer therein in respect of Sarah.[6] It is stated in this connection that Abraham had lived so modestly with his wife, and in such holiness, that he had never looked upon her face previously. Only as they drew near to Egypt did she raise a corner of her veil, and then he saw that she was fair.[7] In Egypt he found a great centre of the occult arts and again betook himself to their study, but this time he penetrated the secret of evil without being led away thereby. He returned thence to his own grade or degree, which is indicated by the words [8]: " And Abram went up out of Egypt . . . into the South " [9]—meaning the inward height of his

---

[1] Z., Pt. I, fol. 80a; I, 468.
[2] Gen. xii. 9.
[3] Z., Pt. I, fol. 81b; I, 469.
[4] Gen. xiii. 10.
[5] The knowledge of Abraham was the consequence of his absolute faith in God.
[6] Gen. xii. 14–20. It is said that the Holy one was seeking to prove Abraham and for this reason allowed him to act on his own initiative in visiting Egypt.—Z., Pt. I, fol. 82a; I, 474.
[7] Sarah was under the protection of Shekinah and during the night that she passed in the palace of Abimelech she was accompanied by angels belonging to the superior degrees, who gave thanks to God.—Z., Pt. I, fol. 82b; I, 476. See also ib., fol. 81b; I, 470, by which it appears that the beauty of Sarah was a reflection of the Divine Presence. I may mention here that the verbal economy or subterfuge to which Abraham had recourse in respect of his wife and sister occasions no comment in the ZOHAR, although it enlarges on the account and adds miraculous elements. It is affirmed that the description of Sarah as Abraham's sister was a description of Shekinah, who was with her.
[8] Ib., fol. 83a; I, 478.   [9] Gen. xiii. 1.

sanctity. From this time forward he knew the Mystery of Supreme Wisdom and became the right hand of the world. This is indicated by the words: "From the South even to Beth-el," [1] which is the integral stone—that stone of the world and Jacob, about which we have heard already. Abraham—in other words—had attained what the ZOHAR understands by perfect faith. But he was yet to proceed further, " going on still toward the South," [2] rising from grade to grade, as one experiencing the infinite and winning his aureole.[3] So did the Holy One become his patrimony, and after Abraham was parted from Lot he " dwelled in the land of Canaan," [4] which is the place of faith.

When the time comes for the ZOHAR to speak of Melchizedek King of Salem it says that his offering of bread and wine symbolised the world above and the world below.[5] The sense in which he was " priest of the Most High God " is that in the sanctification of himself he raised the world below to the height of that which is above. For once, as it seems to me, the ZOHAR has exceeded its own measures at this point and has announced a spiritual truth, the full purport of which it did not realise. Concerning the mission of the priesthood it gives, however, a proper definition when it says that this conjoins the world below to that which is above by an indissoluble bond.[6]

I believe that I have indicated sufficiently the qualities of interpretation which appertain to the first section in the history of Abraham; but the second covers that period which opens with the making of the Covenant between God and the patriarch, or the whole of his later history. The subject at this point passes from personal narration to the " token " or signing the Covenant and the mystery foreshewn thereby.[7]

The characteristic physical sign of all Israel on the male

---

[1] Gen. xiii. 3.
[2] Gen. xii. 9.
[3] Z., Pt. I, fol. 83b; I, 482.
[4] Gen. xiii. 12.
[5] Z., Pt. I, fol. 87a; I, 502. It seems to follow that according to another manner of Zoharic symbolism bread and wine signify male and female. The bread and wine of Melchizedek were also symbols of nutriment and blessings for the world.—*Ib.*, fol. 87b; I, 505.
[6] *Ib.*, fol. 87a; I, 502.
[7] I have called Abraham throughout by his name in its later form, but it is said that the addition of the letter HE, by which Abram was transformed, was not added until he had suffered circumcision, and it was thereafter that the Shekinah became attached to him.—Z., Pt. I, fol. 93a; I, 529. The letter HE was added also to the name of Sarah, as a symbol of the female principle.—*Ib.*, fol. 96a; I, 546, 547.

side has issued in the ZOHAR from the region of arbitrary ordinance into that of most sacred symbolism. If at first it was a hygienic observance or one that might act as an aid to continence, it has become in the Secret Tradition a seal of purity, and though it is not expressed it is implied indubitably by the text that it had reference also to the purity of womanhood, because her protection was therein. The proof is that, according to the ZOHAR, the male side of humanity in its separation from the female had no true title to the name and prerogative of man. There is little need to add that the woman was not without the man, but this is not discussed in the ZOHAR, for, with all its illuminations and its strong tendencies towards the liberal side, it represents the last development of a purely oriental religion.[1] It remains that while the masculine shares in humanity, it is true man only in union with womanhood.

When Abraham was circumcised [2] he separated himself from the impure world and entered into the Sacred Covenant, into that Covenant on which the world is based; and seeing that he so entered, it follows that the world is founded on him. Expanding this fantasy it is affirmed sometimes that Genesis opens with the words: "By Abraham God created," &c., and therefore the Covenant of circumcision is the origin of heaven and earth.[3] The HE added to the name of Abram after he had fulfilled the ordinance is said to symbolise the five books of the Law, which are the records at length of the Covenant. But that which begins on earth is raised gloriously into heaven and prolonged through all the worlds. The Sign of the Covenant constitutes the foundation of the Sacred Name and of the Mystery of Faith—the root of the notion being probably the shape of the letter YOD with which the Name commences, or this at least is the material root. It is said further that the Sacred Sign of the Covenant is fixed at the base of the Throne, between the two thighs and the trunk [4] —a reference to the SEPHIRA YESOD, when this is placed on

---

[1] It is said, however, that the Covenant implies the union of the two principles.—Z., Pt. II, fol. 26a; III, 127.
[2] Ib., fol. 91b; I, 519.
[3] Z., Pt. I, fol. 93a; I, 529.
[4] When it is said in Gen. xxi. 1: "And the Lord visited Sarah," the Divine Name used in the Hebrew is Jehovah, but according to the ZOHAR it was that Degree of the Divine Essence which was symbolised by the VAU. It is added that all is contained in the mystery of VAU, and thereby all is revealed.—Z., Pt. I, fol. 117b; II, 69.

the Tree.¹ As the sun enlightens the world, so the Sacred Sign enlightens the body; as a buckler protects man, so does this: no evil spirit can approach him who preserves it in purity.² By the fact of circumcision man enters under the wings of Shekinah.³ He who preserves the Sign as I have just said, and fulfils the commandments of the Law, is righteous from head to foot, and his life in continence is his title to a part in the world to come.⁴ It is said also that so long as a man is uncircumcised, he cannot unite himself to the Name of the Holy One; but after circumcision, he enters that name and is joined therewith.⁵ Those who do not preserve the sign in purity make separation, in a manner, between Israel and the Heavenly Father.⁶ All the forces of Nature centre in the organ of the Covenant, and in the metaphysical principle of the Covenant it is said ⁷ that there was subsequently hidden and enclosed that light created when God said: " Let there be light " ⁸—the alleged reason being that it symbolises the fructifying principle, *qui semen injicit fæminæ*. It is this which is called in Scripture " the fruit of a tree yielding seed." ⁹

It is counselled: " Suffer not thy mouth to cause thy flesh to sin," ¹⁰ and the exhortation is understood as a restraint placed upon speech lest this should generate evil thoughts, calculated to soil the consecrated flesh which is marked with the Seal of the Holy Covenant. When the Psalmist says: " The firmament sheweth His handiwork," ¹¹ it is to the Mark of the Covenant that reference is made—that is " the work of His hands." So also those other words: " Wherefore should God be angry at thy voice and destroy the work of thine hands ? " ¹²—are an allusion to those who keep the Seal in purity. In yet other terms, the firmament publishes the names of those holy men who have lived in chastity, and our part is to plead for their intercession with God, Who hears them always. Their names are written in the Book of God, which

---

¹ Z., Pt. I, fol. 149b; II, 190. It is very difficult to allocate sporadic symbolism of this kind to its proper source elsewhere in the text, but the allusion is almost certainly to the extension of the Divine Son through the lower SEPHIROTH, having the head in DAATH, as explained in a previous section.
² *Ib.*, fol. 8a; I, 45, 46.
³ *Ib.*, fol. 95a; I, 543.
⁴ *Ib.*, fol. 162a; II, 235. The text is: " Blessings are upon the head of the just."—Prov. x. 6. But the head of the just signifies the Sign of the Covenant.—Z., *in loco cit.*
⁵ *Ib.*, fol. 89a; I, 510.
⁶ *Ib.*, fol. 189b; II, 348.
⁷ *Ib.*, fol. 1a; I, 4.
⁸ Gen. i. 3.
⁹ Z., Pt. I, fol. 1a; I, 4.
¹⁰ Eccles. v. 6.
¹¹ Ps. xix. 1.
¹² Eccles. v. 6.

is the great firmament of stars: they are the company which follow the Heavenly Spouse.[1]

It is said otherwise concerning the Sign of the Covenant that holy flesh is marked with the letter YOD,[2] referring to the obvious analogy between the " organ of sanctity " and this letter, when circumcision has been performed upon the first. The letter YOD symbolises also the configuration of the celestial river which is the source of souls. The words: " Sanctify unto me all the firstborn, whatsoever openeth the womb among the children of Israel," [3] is a commentary on the letter YOD, which is the first-born of all the heavenly sanctities.[4]

Finally, there is a curious train of thought which requires to be followed carefully.[5] " Through wisdom is an house builded." [6] This is termed an allusion to the mystery expressed in those other words: " And a river went forth from Eden to water the garden." [7] It is said further: " Thy tabernacle is holy," [8] but our English rendering is not literally the same. This tabernacle is termed the union of all. The verse in question enumerates three enclosures, one within the other— the Courts, House and Tabernacle—and the ZOHAR says, unexpectedly enough on the surface, that whosoever subjects his son to the holocaust of circumcision may be assured that the Holy One will draw the child to Himself and make his abode in the innermost of these enclosures, while the father will earn no less merit than if he had offered all other sacrifices in the world and had raised up the most perfect altar. The explanation of these things can rest only, as I have said, in a most profound understanding of the Mystery of Sex, and the final place of that Mystery is indicated by the correspondence alleged in another part between the Sign of the Covenant and the Sacred Crown.[9]

---

[1] Z., Pt. I, fol. 8b; I, 48.
[2] Ib., fol. 13a; I, 74.
[3] Ez. xiii. 2.
[4] Z., Pt. I, fol. 13b; I, 79.
[5] Ib., fol. 94b; I, 539.
[6] Prov. xxiv. 3.
[7] Gen. ii. 10.
[8] See Ps. lxv. 4: " Even of Thy Holy Temple." Compare, however, the corresponding passage in the Vulgate, Ps. lxiv. 5: *Sanctum est templum tuum.*
[9] Z., Pt. I, fol. 95a; I, 542. The following points may be gathered from other parts of the text: (1) The mark of the Covenant is imprinted above as well as on man below; but this is probably a reference to the mark on the Throne, already given. (2) The Kingdom was removed for a period from David because he had not preserved the sign in perfect purity. (3) He who so keeps it has nothing to fear from severity— *i.e.*, judgment—being united thereby to the Name of the Holy One. (4) He who defiles it cannot aspire to the mark of God, which is royalty and Jerusalem. (5) The

It was said at the beginning of this section that the history of Abraham is for the ZOHAR the actual story concerning the father of nations, and this obtains throughout; but for the great theosophical commentary its living value lies in the way of its understanding as an inward text of election, applicable to every soul in Israel.

VI.—OF MOSES, THE MASTER OF THE LAW

The Biblical story of Moses issues in a mystery, for he " whom the Lord knew face to face," [1] having died in the Lord on Mount Nebo, was also by Him buried, and " no man knoweth of his sepulchre unto this day." [2] But, according to the ZOHAR, the story of Moses begins in a mystery also, for he, about whom it is said that " there arose not a prophet since in Israel like unto Moses," [3] was not in his conception after the manner of men who had preceded or of those who came after him. The distinction belongs more properly to another part of my subject and will be found therein. I will therefore say only that his parents—the " man of the house of Levi " [4] and she who was " a daughter of Levi " [5]—had their hearts uplifted unto Her who is called Shekinah, second of the Divine Hypostases—at the time of that union when it is said that " the woman conceived and bare a son." [6] The consequence of this was that Shekinah reposed on the nuptial bed of his parents.[7] He was therefore born, " not of blood, nor of the will of the flesh, nor of the will of man " merely, " but of God " [8]; and even from the day of his birth the Shekinah never quitted him.[9] He ascended into that region

---

sign is the gate of the body, to hold which in sanctity is to find the gate of heaven always open.—Z., Pt. I, fol. 94a; I, 535, 536; and fol. 150b; II, 193. But that to which all this applies is surely the idea which lies behind circumcision.

[1] Deut. xxxiv. 10.   [2] *Ib.*, v. 6.   [3] *Ib.*, v. 10.
[4] Ex. ii. 1.   [5] *Ib.*   [6] *Ib.*, v. 2.
[7] See Z., Pt. II, fol. 11a–12a; III, 48–52. It is said in the most cryptic manner of the text that the " man of the house of Levi " was the angel Gabriel, who is called " man," as it is written : " Even the man Gabriel, whom I had seen in the vision at the beginning " (Dan. ix. 21). The house of Levi signifies the Community of Israel—referring probably to the School of Sanctity above in the SEPHIRA BINAH. The daughter of Levi is the soul. The meaning is that the parents of Moses stood for these symbolically.
[8] St. John i. 13.
[9] The father of Moses is said to have been espoused to Shekinah—apparently in the sense that she was attached to or overshadowed him. Otherwise he would have been unworthy to beget the Lawgiver. But it is added that the daughter of Levi whom he espoused was the Shekinah—perhaps in the sense of being her symbol below.—Z., Pt. II, fol. 19a; III, 92.—*Ib.*, Pt. I, fol. 120b; II, 83.

where she is said to extend her wings,[1] as it is written: "He did fly upon the wings of the wind."[2] The Lawgiver is affirmed, moreover, to have been the first man who attained perfection, even as Messiah will be the last[3]; but there are good reasons—*e.g.*, the story of Abraham—from the standpoint of Zoharic Kabbalism, why it was requisite to qualify this statement, and so it is said elsewhere that he was not perfect in all things, the reason being that he was separated from his wife.[4] There is no authority in the Pentateuch on this subject, but there is that of Talmudic Tradition which says that they ceased to cohabit. It is probably an arbitrary inference from the fact that neither she nor his two sons, Gershom and Eliezer, are mentioned in Exodus or elsewhere after they were brought back to Moses, " when he encamped at the Mount of God " in the wilderness of Sinai.[5] So it is said otherwise that the Lawgiver attained the degree of BINAH but not that of CHOKMAH[6]; in other words, he did not open the 50th Gate of Understanding which gives upon the path of DALETH, leading from BINAH to CHOKMAH in the Sephirotic Tree.

It is difficult, however, to judge clearly as to the earthly espousals of Moses, according to the ZOHAR, for we learn elsewhere that he separated himself from Zipporah by the ordinance of God, that he might be joined to the heavenly light of Shekinah.[7] Hence it is intimated elsewhere, on the authority of Rabbi Simeon, that to attribute children to him was in some sense beneath his dignity, as he had entered into spiritual espousals.[8] It is a question of the Mystery of Faith and a case of extraordinary exception from the prevailing mind of the ZOHAR, which makes children according to the flesh an indispensable title to union with the glory of that

---

[1] Z., Pt. II, fol. 78b; III, 329.
[2] Ps. xviii. 9.
[3] Z., Pt. III, fol. 260b; VI, 7.
[4] *Ib.*, Pt. I, fol. 234b; II, 523. The explanation is that in order to perfection there must be union not alone with that which is above but also with that which is below. A Talmudic Tradition on the subject will be found in the Tract SABBATH, but this is at issue with the ZOHAR as it reckons the fact of his separation among his titles of honour.
[5] Ex. xviii. 5.
[6] Z., Pt. III, fol. 223a; V, 564.
[7] Z., Pt. III, fol. 180a; V, 472.
[8] *Ib.*, Pt. II, fol. 69b; III, 308. The argument is purely casuistic, pretending that Scripture attributes the children of Moses to the mother only, and afterwards—on the authority of Rabbi Simeon, wresting Ex. xviii. 5—maintaining that Jethro brought his own sons to Moses.

Second Hypostasis which stands for the nuptials that are above. It should be understood at this point that the Mystery of Faith consists, according to the French translation of the ZOHAR, " in the union of God with a Female whom He fructifies, after the manner of the union of male and female." This is true assuredly, yet it is only a part of the Mystery, or rather it is the doctrinal aspect, and arising therefrom is a practical side about which we receive intimations at many points of the text, though it enters into complete expression nowhere. Its real nature is the sole end of our research. To conclude as to the marriages of Moses, there was a moment when God said to the Lawgiver: " Let it suffice thee "[1]; but that which was sufficient, says the ZOHAR,[2] was the prophet's union with Shekinah, to Whom he was nearer in truth than hands and feet, for—as we have seen—they were not in separation prior to his birth in this life. So also he was under the guidance of no angel and no messenger from heaven but under that of God Himself,[3] because God and His Shekinah are one. He represented the male principle,[4] though in virtue of his union with Shekinah he was the light of the moon, the moon being his symbol, for albeit that she and God are one—as I have said—she shines in the light of the Eternal Sun of Justice, more especially in her manifestation below, or in the work of her providence concerning the children of men. It is by Moses that the men of this world are held to have found salvation, for he communicated the vital spirit of the Tree of Life. If Israel had not sinned this spirit would have been preserved for ever in Israel.[5]

There was no servant so faithful as he who is called in the Secret Tradition the Faithful Shepherd. He knew all the celestial degrees and was never tempted to join himself otherwise than to the Highest.[6] His fidelity was greater than that of Ezekiel, for the latter is said to have divulged all the treasures of the King.[7] This statement is not explained by the ZOHAR,[8] but I suppose that it refers to what is called

---

[1] Deut. iii. 26.
[2] Z., Pt. III, fol. 260b; VI, 7.
[3] Ib., fol. 286b; VI, 72. This is held to follow from the words: " And he said unto Him, If Thy Presence go not with me, carry us not up hence."—Ex. xxxiii. 15.
[4] Z., Pt. II, fol. 37b; III, 178.
[5] By virtue of the gracious Law contained in the First Tables.
[6] Z., Pt. I, fol. 76a; I, 447.
[7] Ib., Pt. II, fol. 5a; III, 19.
[8] Except indeed to say that if Ezekiel so acted he had authority from the Holy One.

Kabbalistically the Work of the Chariot, being that of Ezekiel's vision, and it seems to me that in this respect the later prophet may be held to deserve exoneration. The title of Moses was that he kept the Secret Law secretly, transmitting it only to the elect,[1] and that he made public the Exoteric Law, which does not contain the Mystery of Faith. In this sense he is called the elder son of Adam,[2] and the reason—which is not readily translatable—is *quia verenda patris sui operaverat*. It is the keeping of the Mystery.

I pass now to the promulgation of the Law, and it would seem that Moses ascended Mount Sinai clothed in the vesture of Shekinah, being that cloud which he entered and in virtue of which it was possible for him to go up.[3] The intention of the Law was to place man under the domination of the Tree of Life,[4] which means that there would have been no mysteries, the Law in this aspect being the Spouse of God, and therefore it is Shekinah herself, or the Mystery of Faith expounded. It is that Mystery which is beheld in contemplating the face of Shekinah, in the state which is eye to eye.[5] If this intention had been fulfilled, there would have been no distinction of an Oral and Written Law, and the question is therefore as to what intervened so that another order followed, contrary to the design of Providence. Now, it is affirmed by the ZOHAR that a change took place in Israel at the foot of Mount Sinai,[6] and this is insisted upon so frequently in terms which never vary as to the alleged fact that one cannot help feeling some principle is involved, some unstated matter of Secret Doctrine. It is testified that Israel was joined anew to the Tree of Life, so that it beheld the heavenly splendours and realised their lights; it experienced the ineffable joy which fills the hearts of those who desire to know and understand the Supreme Mysteries. The nation was reclothed by the Holy One with that cuirass formed from the letters of His Sacred Name which was the protection of Adam and Eve before their fall. The serpent could cleave no longer to Israel, and it is affirmed to

---

[1] Z., Pt. I, fol. 28b; I, 179.
[2] Ib.
[3] Ib., Pt. II, fol. 99a; III, 398.
[4] Z., Pt. III, fol. 261b; VI, 10.
[5] Ib., Pt. II, fol. 40b—THE FAITHFUL SHEPHERD; III, 189.
[6] Ib., Pt. I, fol. 52a, b; I, 302, 303. See also *ib.*, fol. 36b; I, 226. It may be that an arbitrary mode of reasoning is all that lies behind this subject. In the view of the Zoharic doctors, there was something so great and beyond all experience of fallen human nature which it was designed to promulgate in the first Tables of the Law that for them it was the Law of Paradise, and its proposed reception by Israel involved for them a restitution of the paradisiacal state.

have disappeared from the world. We must understand all this as a reflection rather of the Divine Intention in its union with the covenant made by the people on their part: "All that the Lord hath spoken we will do."[1] They were washed also and sanctified. To go beyond this point is unreason, and I know not how the ZOHAR, regarded as commentary, can postulate such exaltations of Israel either on the basis of the text or of that which followed.[2] For we must remember that in the absence of Moses, and in the uncertainty as to what had become of him, but—*ex hypothesi*—in the absence otherwise of all temptation, Israel adored the golden calf; the old evil order was thus reinstated, and I conclude that the serpent returned. It is to be understood further that the riot of the feast which followed the idol-worship signifies a sexual orgy, so that she who presides over the Mystery of Sex in sanctity was driven from the people, and her secret was taken from them. When therefore Moses came down from the mountain carrying the Tables of the Law he broke them in the presence of the people, which, according to Scripture, was because "his anger waxed hot"[3]; but it is understood otherwise in the ZOHAR. The thesis is that the original Tables constituted the liberation of all,[4] meaning the separation from that serpent who is called "the end of all flesh."[5] They were formed originally from a single block of sapphire, but God breathed upon them and the precious stone was divided into two parts.[6] They were created prior to the world by the coagulation of the sacred dew which is said to fall on the Garden of Apples.[7] They were written before and behind, and were symbolised by the loaves of proposition.[8] It is

---

[1] Ex. xix. 8.

[2] The canon of criticism seems to be reached by the contrast of two passages of Scripture: "And Israel saw that great work which the Lord did" (Ex. xiv. 31)—which the French translation of the ZOHAR renders: "And Israel saw the mighty hand of the Lord," following apparently the Vulgate (*et manum magnam quam exercuerat Dominus contra eos*)—this being reputed to mean that Israel was able to contemplate the celestial splendour and enjoy the vision of the supernal lights. The other passage is this: "And when Aaron and all the children of Israel saw Moses, behold, the skin of his face shone, and they were afraid to come nigh him" (Ex. xxxiv. 30). As to the value of the contrast, it is enough to point out that the first text belongs to the period when the Red Sea had just been crossed and has nothing to do with the sojourn at the foot of Mount Sinai, which was reached three months after (Ex. xix. 1).

[3] Ex. xxxii. 19.

[4] Z., Pt. I, fol. 63b; I, 371.

[5] *Ib.*, Pt. I, fol. 63b; I, 371. It is understood that one consequence of this separation would have been that there should be no more death.

[6] *Ib.*, Pt. II, fol. 84a, b; III, 347.

[7] *Ib.*, fol. 84b; III, 348.

[8] *Ib.*, Pt. III, fol. 271b; VI, 27, and fol. 273; VI, 39.

noted in another place that the writing thereon was like black fire on white fire,[1] while according to yet another it would appear that the stones were transparent[2]: the writing in front, or on the obverse side, was read from behind, and that on the reverse, or behind, was read from in front.[3] It is an allusion to the inter-connection of the written and oral Law. The Tables were given to Moses on the Sabbath Day. It is recorded by Scripture[4] that they were cast from the hands of Moses and were broken, and here it is explained by the ZOHAR that this was because the letters took flight[5]—a device designed to point out that no writing remained upon them which could possibly be seen by Israel in contemplating the fragments. The Tables were broken because Israel was not worthy to profit by them,[6] and that which was shattered is said to have been not only the written but the inward and oral Law.[7] The meaning is that the higher order of liberation and mercy which included these, the revelation of the secret union, was taken henceforth into concealment. The malediction brought upon the world by the trespass, and removed for a moment as the people passed under the shadow of Mount Sinai,[8] descended again upon them. The Tables came out of that region from which all liberties issue and on which they all depend.[9] Over the mystical mountain they diffused a sweet odour, because the sanctities of the world of sanctity inhered therein; but this passed away when the golden calf was set up for the worship of the nation.[10]

It is recognised by the ZOHAR that the second Tables embodied another record, which was the Law of opportunism, the Law of mine and thine—of prohibition and denial, being that of bondage. It was sacred after its own manner, because it was a shadow of the first intention, but it reflects at a very far distance. I do not know whether it is affirmed

---

[1] Z., Pt. II, fol. 226b; IV, 248.
[2] Ib., fol. 84b; III, 348. See also fol. 84a; III, 347.
[3] Ib., fol. 84a; III, 347.
[4] Ex. xxxii. 19. According to the ZOHAR, they fell of themselves from his hands.—Z., Pt. II, fol. 195a, b; IV, 188.
[5] Ib.
[6] Ib., Pt. I, fol. 26b; I, 167.
[7] Ib., fol. 28b; I, 181. "And the Lord said unto Moses, ... I will give thee tables of stone, and a law, and commandments which I have written.—Ex. xxiv. 12. According to the ZOHAR, the word "law" signifies that which is written, while the word "commandments" refers to the Oral Law.—Ib., Pt. III, fol. 40b; V, 109.
[8] Ib., fol. 26b; I, 22b.
[9] Ib., Pt. III, fol. 6b; V, 17.
[10] Ib., fol. 61b; V, 170.

literally that it is a work of the Tree of Knowledge, but this must be held to follow from numerous impressive intimations. And the Secret Doctrine, with all the Oral Law by which that Doctrine is encompassed, is the Tree of Life; but the art of its mastery is long, and of all the Sons thereof, of all the heirs at law, I suppose that only Rabbi Simeon could have been said to possess it in the fullness.[1] We know that after him the reign of certitudes was over and the great quest in the hiddenness was pursued in the attitude of groping, not erect as heretofore with the light of sure enlightenment shining from a meridian sun on the heads of the initiates. There is much more that could be said upon this subject, but I feel that my purpose is served. I would add only that amidst the clouded splendours and substitutions of the surface sense we can understand readily the great and pressing need for that study of the inward meaning which is imposed everywhere in the ZOHAR on those who would enter into the real heritage of the elect. To sum up therefore: Moses gave other Tables to Israel, and these were from the side of the Tree of the Knowledge of Good and Evil, from which the Law emanates. *The other Tables emanated from the Tree of Life.*

I should add that the Written Law seems to be represented by the word DAATH, or Knowing [2]: it is completed by that which is traditional. The Doctrine is sometimes called CHOKMAH, or Wisdom, and sometimes BINAH, or Understanding.[3] The Traditional Law has come out of the Written Law, as woman was brought forth from man, according to the Mystery of the Garden—but this we have seen already. It can exist only in unison with the Written Law; but I think that the Zoharic treatment of the latter shews that it was regarded rather as a beast of burden—that ass of a certain comparison—already cited—on which the King and Queen of the Secret Mysteries must never be set to ride.[4] There is,

---

[1] I mean, of course, since the days of patriarchs and prophets. As regards the work of this Tree of Knowledge, the Law—from this point of view—was to preserve the species of the chosen people according to the mode of human generation in the world beyond the mystical Garden of Eden; but the work of the Tree of Life, for those who would dwell beneath it, was one of mystical generation and fruition. It is not suggest·d that the Sons of the Doctrine attained the secret in its fullness: they raised a corner of the veil.

[2] Z., Pt. I, fol. 48b; I, 282.

[3] The reason given is that it has been formed by the "Complete Name"—*i.e.*, Jehovah Elohim, being the Divine Male and Female.

[4] It was like the mule in THE HIGH HISTORY OF THE HOLY GRAAL—" a beast on God's side."

however, one more memorable point concerning the Oral Law, and this is that although it is a balm of life for the just, for the unjust it is a mortal poison.[1] I believe that as much has been said concerning the Elixir of Alchemy. The aphorism is not therefore *vel sanctum invenit, vel sanctum facit*, yet I think that there is a heart of the Doctrine in which the good must fill us entirely, as the student enters more deeply into its understanding. But the sorrow of it is that after eating of the Tree of Knowledge through the years and the ages we are still untutored children, knowing little in the essential manner either of good or evil.

I have reminded my readers already that Moses was interred outside the Holy Land and that "no man knoweth of his sepulchre unto this day."[2] But this sepulchre, according to the ZOHAR, signifies the MISHNA.[3] The Secret Doctrine was interned in the written word—that end of all revelations.[4] But the tradition says that the inner meaning—like the spirit of Moses—remained with the elders and was handed on secretly. The Scripture mentions that "the children of Israel wept for Moses in the plains of Moab thirty days."[5] They might have mourned him, had they known, through the triumphs and the exiles continued thenceforward, for they lost the Secret Doctrine of which he was the personification. It was withdrawn when he left, as if into a secret sanctuary, and no voice issued therefrom until the days of Rabbi Simeon. He was even as a Rose of Sharon which blossomed on the ruins of Jerusalem in the days of Vespasian. I wonder not that there was sorrow on occasions amidst the Sons of the Doctrine, as with Marius over the ruins of Carthage. Moses was the life of the Doctrine, and hence it is affirmed that when he ascended to the height of Pisgah "his eye was not dim, nor his natural force abated."[6] It is recorded also of his figure in its prime that this resembled the sun in its splendour [7] —so perfectly did his moon reflect that glory.

One legend says, however, that he did not die,[8] though the

---

[1] Z., Pt. I, fol. 268a; II, 633, 634.
[2] Deut. xxxiv. 6.
[3] Z., Pt. I, fol. 27b; I, 175.
[4] The MISHNAH is the maid-servant who takes the place of the mistress.—*Ib.*, fol. 28b; I, 175.
[5] Deut. xxxiv. 8.
[6] Deut. xxxiv. 7.
[7] Z., Pt. I, fol. 28a; I, 177.
[8] *Ib.*, fol. 28a; I, 176, and *ib.*, Pt. II, fol. 174a; IV, 129.

text repeats it on an authority which is not its own, and it adds —rather in the manner of a casuist—that no man does who is graced by faith. As a fact, the authority is the MIDRASH RABBA on Deut. xxxiv., and the ZOHAR quotes it again in another place but in a less questioning mood. Perhaps there is a deeper heart of meaning than transpires on the surface, for if we accept the Secret Doctrine on the subject of Moses and the Law there is an aspect of failure about the great mission of the Lawgiver. His stiff-necked generation prevailed against him to the extent that he could fulfil only the shadow of that which he proposed. His intention was to deliver the truth which makes men free, but they were fit only for a substitute. Now, this is set forth very curiously in a single passage of the text, where it is affirmed that Moses sought to bring the Shekinah out of exile, but he failed.[1] The Shekinah signifies here the Secret Doctrine and this implies that the First Tables were written *ad clerum*, but the context was destined to remain in exile so long as Israel was incorporated as a people in its own place and land, while there is no suggestion that the debates of the Doctors brought Shekinah into liberation.[2] It is said therefore, in yet another place, that Moses will return on earth at the end of time to complete his mission by revealing the True Name of Shekinah[3] which is also in the hiddenness, and there is no pretence that it was known to the Doctors. Those whom he brought out of Egypt he will then lead into knowledge. This is why it is exclaimed by Job: " The Lord hath given and the Lord hath taken away: Blessed is the name of the Lord."[4] That will take place which was to have been fulfilled at first: the elect will be set free from the death-angel by the true Tables of the Law. Meanwhile Moses obtained the degree of BINAH—as we have seen—but not that of CHOKMAH. His death was from what is called in the ZOHAR the other side, which means the right side, the left being the side of the serpent.[5] It was not caused by the sin of Adam but by the operation of a

---

[1] Z., Pt. I, fol. 28a; I, 176.
[2] On the contrary, so long as the Shekinah is in captivity, she is never left by Moses.—*Ib.* That which he did on earth was, however, to attract her to Israel.—*Ib.*, fol. 68a; I, 400.
[3] *Ib.*, fol. 28b; I, 180. See also, for the return of Moses, *ib.*, Pt. II, fol. 255a; I, 602.
[4] Job i. 21.
[5] Z., Pt. I, fol. 53a; I, 306.

Supreme Mystery. It is also recorded of Joshua that he did not die through his own sinning, but through the serpent's counsel to Eve, and this is said to be expressed in the words : " His servant Joshua, the son of Nun, a young man, departed not out of the Tabernacle." [1]

VII.—THE TEMPLES IN JERUSALEM

Looking back upon the chequered history of their nation and on the purport of its life generally, the mystical doctors of Israel did not fail to discern the uplifting of strange portents in their spiritual sky, the full significance of which was not rightly to be recognised beforehand, supposing that they were real prognostics. It is only after the event that most of us become wise in this manner. In retrospect the portents were everywhere ; in retrospect the world's creation, the great myth of the Garden, the judgment of the Flood, and the rest of the Divine Providences were like tocsins and trumpet voices concerning all that was to follow. Not alone were the seeds therein, but it was Israel delineated throughout. Abraham might turn to the South and again he might turn therefrom, but the reason in either case was of that or of this to come in respect of the twelve tribes. Yet it was not only to come ; already it was in a sense there, so that the stories of old look weirdly in a light which suggests that they were recorded before the events with which they are supposed to deal. The occurrences of the past were also fateful in respect of later things that were to come. For example, when the Tables of the Law were broken by Moses, this is said to have occasioned the ultimate destruction of the First and Second Temples.[2]

There are two aspects under which the Temples come before us in Zoharic texts, and as happens so often, they do not harmonise together, while it is impossible rather than difficult to believe that an adjustment can be effected between them. I will collate them under what may be called the motives attaching to each. There is firstly that wherein there is no shadow of vicissitude as to the glory and the plenary grace which inhered in the design and execution of Solomon's Holy House. The Inner Sanctuary constituted the

---

[1] Ex. xxxiii. 11.   [2] Z., Pt. I, fol. 26b ; I, 167.

heart of the world;[1] the Shekinah dwelt therein after the manner of a virtuous and faithful wife who never leaves the abode of her husband.[2] It was therefore well with Israel during this period. The building plan was sketched by a supernatural hand and was delivered—as we are aware—to David, by whom it was shewn to Solomon.[3] The Temple was erected on seven pillars,[4] the craftsmen following the design, point by point, until the work was finished.[5] There was a sense in which they followed blindly, but there was also another sense in which the work was self-executed. This is suggested by the silent nature of the building, about which we hear in Scripture.[6] The analogy is that of creation, for the world evolved of itself, with God as the beginner of the work.[7] Hence David said: "Except the Lord build the house, they labour in vain that build it."[8] The meaning is that the Lord designed the Temple and the work went on of itself. It is said also: "Except the Lord watch the city, the watchman waketh but in vain."[9] This is Jerusalem in its building. The moon is symbolised as shining at the full during the whole period.[10] The Temple was built for the union of the King and Matrona,[11] God and His Church in Israel. Of the structure in its completeness we are told that the earth inhabited by the Gentiles encompasses the Holy City, which is the centre of the habitable world; the town encircles the Holy Mountain; the Mountain surrounds the session-house of the Sanhedrin; this in its turn stands about the Temple; and the Temple encompasses the Holy of Holies, where dwells the Shekinah and where are the Propitiatory, the Kerubim and the Ark of the Covenant.[12] The Holy of Holies itself was built on that foundation stone which, as we know already, is held to form the central point of the world. It is identified with the celestial throne of Ezekiel, and in

---

[1] Z., Pt. I, fol. 84b; I, 487.
[2] *Ib.*
[3] *Ib.*, Pt. II, fol. 164a; IV, 107.
[4] *Ib.* It was guarded by the archangel METATRON.
[5] *Ib.*, Pt. I, fol. 74a; I, 438.
[6] "And the house, when it was in building, was built of stone made ready before it was brought thither: so that there was neither hammer nor axe nor any tool of iron heard in the house, while it was in building."—1 Kings vi. 7.
[7] Z., Pt. II, fol. 226a; IV, 247.
[8] Ps. cxxvii. 1.
[9] *Ib.*
[10] Z., Pt. I, fol. 150a; II, 190.
[11] *Ib.*, Pt. III, fol. 74b; V, 203.
[12] *Ib.*, fol. 161b; V, 416.

appearance it was like a sapphire.¹ Solomon is said to have united Matrona to the Supreme King by the building of the Temple and there was joy everywhere, both above and below.² The Temple itself is understood as the spiritual union of male and female apart from any fleshly union.³ It symbolises therefore the Mystery of Sex at its highest, and this is a point to be memorised in respect of all these reveries.

Here is the first picture, but the alternative as follows is drawn from the FAITHFUL SHEPHERD and not the ZOHAR itself. The First and Second Temples were transitory things in their nature; they should have been the work of God Himself, but because of Israel's sin in the wilderness, the First Temple was built by Solomon, and hence it did not subsist.⁴ Contrary to the former intimation, the Lord was not its builder. So also at the epoch of Ezra, again on account of sin, the Second Temple was erected by men and there was no ground of subsistence. It follows that so far no holy house has been built in reality at all,⁵ nor has even the city of Jerusalem been as yet constructed. The world is still awaiting that promise of the Lord: "I, saith the Lord, will be unto her a wall of fire round about, and will be the glory in the midst of her." ⁶ There are suggestions however which go much further than mere questions of substitution. It is said that from the day when the Holy One raised the Supreme Sanctuary the celestial favours were never manifested in the terrestrial Temple, built of stones and mortar.⁷ I suppose that here is the house not made with hands which is termed elsewhere a place of spiritual nourishment which the kingdom of heaven accords to those in need of it and that sanctuary which brings all the poor under the shadow of Shekinah.⁸

The Temple of Solomon was a symbol of penitence as well as a house of prayer, and its destruction signifies an impenitent state.⁹ The cause of its destruction is said otherwise to have been the separation of the HE and VAU in the Divine Name

---

¹ Z., Pt. I, fol. 71b, 72a; I, 425. See Ezek. i. 26: "And above the firmament that was over their heads was the likeness of a throne, as the appearance of a sapphire stone." This stone, according to the ZOHAR (*ib.*), signified the celestial throne, and the throne of the vision signified the Traditional Law, while "the appearance of a man" who sat thereon was the Written Law.
² *Ib.*, Pt. III, fol. 74b; V, 203.
³ *Ib.*, Pt. II, fol. 258b; IV, 292.
⁴ *Ib.*, Pt. III, fol. 221a; V, 559.
⁵ Z., Pt. III, fol. 221a; 559.
⁶ Zech. ii. 5.
⁷ Z., Pt. II, fol. 108b; III, 427.
⁸ *Ib.*, Pt. I, fol. 208a; II, 434.
⁹ *Ib.*, Pt. III, fol. 75a; V, 204.

as the result of sin.¹ The people were sent into exile and the Shekinah was driven out.² The VAU went in search of the HE, but she was in a distant place; it looked towards the sanctuary, but it was burnt; it looked for the chosen people, but they were in exile; it turned towards the source of benedictions, but this was dried up.³ It is said otherwise that the destruction of the First Temple dried up the sources of the Shekinah above and that of the Second Temple those of the Shekinah below.⁴ All light was clouded, so that the saints of this world were no longer enlightened.⁵ During the exile in Babylon the wings of the Mother in Transcendence did not cover her children;⁶ there was therefore a separation between the YOD and first HE of the Divine Name. The reference is of course to the spiritual state of Israel, and behind it lies a strange spiritual understanding of the Fall of man. During the present and greater exile the Divine Name is divided now as it was divided then,⁷ albeit that which it signifies is one eternally above. In another form of symbolism the First Temple was destroyed because it wanted light,⁸ which was absent also from the Second Temple, but in a still greater degree, the Second Temple signifying the fleshly union of male and female.⁹ The priests of the First Temple ascended on the walls of the Sanctuary, holding their keys in their hands and said to God: Hereunto we have been Thine administrators; henceforth take back Thy possessions.¹⁰ The sun turned away from the moon and enlightened it no longer; there was no day without maledictions and sufferings.¹¹

These are the lamentations of the ZOHAR over its Holy Places and Houses; but another day will come when the moon shall resume its primal light.¹² It will be that period

---

¹ Z., Pt. I, fol. 122a; V, 316.
² Ib., fol. 75a; V, 204.
³ The reason was that the male was united no longer to the female.—Ib.
⁴ Ib., Pt. I, fol. 255a; II, 601.
⁵ Ib., Pt. II, fol. 9b; III, 40.
⁶ Ib., fol. 9b; III, 39, 40.
⁷ Ib., fol. 9b; III, 41.
⁸ Ib., fol. 179b; IV, 150. The obvious commentary hereon is that Shekinah, by the hypothesis at least, was reigning on the Mercy Seat.
⁹ Z., Pt. II, fol. 258b; IV, 292.
¹⁰ Ib., Pt. I, fol. 202b, 203a; II, 406. This is " the burden of the valley of visions."—Is. xxii. 1.
¹¹ Ib., fol. 181a, b; II, 315.
¹² Ib., fol. 181b; II, 316.

mentioned in Scripture: " Behold, My servant shall deal prudently, he shall be exalted and extolled and be very high." [1] The reference is to the Messianic epoch, when the world will be restored, impurity will disappear therefrom, and death shall be cast out for ever. The Holy One will remember His people Israel and the Temple shall be rebuilt.[2] Formerly it was based on severity and wrath, but it will be restored in charity and will be founded thereon.[3] Meanwhile, since the destruction of the Sanctuary here below, the Holy One swore never to enter the Jerusalem above until Israel returned into the Jerusalem below.[4] No blessings have gone forth, either in the world above or in that which is below, for these worlds depend on one another.[5] The consolation of the elect is however that, in the absence of a place of sacrifice, devotion to the study of the Law will bring the forgiveness of sin more readily than the burnt-offerings of old." [6]

VIII.—THE COMING OF MESSIAH

There is no question that the Kabbalistic teaching concerning a Deliverer to come should begin by a consideration of Talmudic intimations on the subject; for these are many and important within their own measures. There is unfortunately no space for such an extension of the materials already in my hands, but there are several sources of information which are open to any reader, and indeed the whole subject is available if he can have recourse to the French rendering of the JERUSALEM TALMUD [7] and even to the unscholarly English version of the BABYLONIAN TALMUD [8] which appeared some years since in America. Outside this question of the past, the first thing for us to realise on our own part is that there is not one line, and much less one page,

---

[1] Z., Pt. I, fol. 181b; II, 316; Is. ii. 13. See also Gen. xxiv. 2.
[2] Ib., Pt. I, fol. 134a; II, 128.
[3] Ib., Pt. II, fol. 59a, b; III, 263, 264.
[4] Ib., Pt. I, fol. 231a; II, 511.
[5] Ib., fol. 70b; I, 415.
[6] Ib., APPENDICES III, SECRET MIDRASH, fol. 6a; II, 680.
[7] M. Schwab: LE TALMUD DE JÉRUSALEM, 11 vols., Paris, 1871-1889, 8vo. See also LE TALMUDE DE BABYLONE, traduit par l'Abbé Chiarini, 2 vols., Leipsic, 1831. It embodies a condensed account of both recensions and may serve some general purpose.
[8] New edition of the BABYLONIAN TALMUD: English Translation. Original Text edited, formulated and punctuated by Michael L. Rodkinson, vol. I, TRACT SABBATH, 1896. In all 18 volumes, various years.

in the ZOHAR which can be constructed according to its proper sense on the assumption that a Messiah has appeared already in Israel, while there is consequently nothing that can be applied to a Second Advent of the Christ of Nazareth. These things are dreams, and recent pleadings on the subject are if possible of less consequence than those of the old scholars who filled Europe with their debates in the sixteenth and seventeenth centuries.[1] The points of analogy between Kabbalistic and Christian doctrine are many and eloquent in their way, but they belong to another order. There is an attractive hypothesis with which I shall attempt to deal later on, and its whole design is to construct Zoharic Theosophy in a direction opposite hereto, or not only in a Christian sense but in one which would place the texts under the particular obedience of Latin Theology; and I who, of all things else, would desire, were it possible, to look through such enchanted glasses, have concluded that there is no evidence, so I would therefore warn others. It should be added in justice to the interests at large that the Roman Church is much too wise to lend countenance—officially or extra-officially—to the interesting view, which is therefore the outcome of private zeal only.

The first question which concerns us is that of Messianic expectations in mystical Israel. The elect—and if these are more especially the Sons of the Doctrine it is in the sense that the greater imitate the lesser, meaning the race of chosen people—the elect must hope always for the coming of the man of holiness,[2] for it is said: " I will wait upon the Lord, that hideth His face from the house of Israel, and I will look to Him." [3] He is the man in transcendence, the man who is allocated in one place to the SEPHIRA CHOKMAH,[4] but the point is of great complexity and its elucidation belongs to a subsequent part of our research. It is said further that He is the " man more precious than fine gold " who is mentioned

---

[1] See Benedictus Poscantinus: DIALOGUM DE MESSIA, Venice, 1548, and Antonius Hulsius: IN THEOLOGIAM JUDAICAM DE MESSIA, Bremen, 1580. There is a still earlier work, but I can only claim to know of a report concerning it: EPISTOLA R. Samuelis Judæi missam ad Isaac, Mantua, 1475. It claims to have been translated from the Arabic by a Dominican, Alphonsus Bono-Homo, and is an argument from the prophets that Jesus Christ was the Messiah expected by Jewry.
[2] Z., Pt. I, fol. 204a; II, 413.
[3] Is. viii. 17.
[4] I should mention that this reference depends on certain SUPPLEMENTS, which are a later addition to the ZOHAR.

by Isaiah;[1] and it is on record also that He shall be raised above all the inhabitants of the world, who will adore Him, prostrated in His presence.[2] As a further witness respecting His eternal generation, the Spirit of Elohim which brooded over the face of the waters is sometimes regarded as the Spirit of Messiah, who has washed His robes in heavenly wine from the creation of the world.[3] He is also the sacred moon on high, having no other light than that which it receives from the sun above;[4] but it is to be noted that the Shekinah is also symbolised by the moon and this has led to a precarious and indeed impossible identification of the Messiah as the Shekinah incarnate. It might be said on the same evidence that Solomon was an incarnation of Messiah and Moses also, for both had the moon as a symbol.

According to MIDRASH TALPIGOTH, the Messiah will bring eternal peace, which of course was understood by the Israelites as peace for Israel, *plus* that which may follow extermination for all who did not enter by conversion into the House of Jacob. It is said in the ZOHAR that, according to tradition, wherever Solomon is mentioned in the Song of Solomon this King of Peace is designated.[5] Conversion at the Messianic period will be apparently on a great scale, because all the nations of the world will gather about the King Messiah when He shall be manifested,[6] seeing that these words of the Scripture must be fulfilled:[7] "And in that day there shall be a root of Jesse, which shall stand for an ensign of the people; to it shall the Gentiles seek; and his rest shall be glorious." It will be a time for the revelation of mysteries which the will of God has concealed through the ages, but as the day of the King approaches even little children shall know the Mysteries of Wisdom.[8] It will be also a time of union, for in the Sabbatic millenary the Holy One will accomplish union between souls.[9] All the blessings of Israel will be realised in Israel,[10] which will form one people only on earth, " and I will make them one nation in the Lord." [11] The meaning seems to be that all nations shall become one nation of the Holy One; but the great war of the world will precede this.

---

[1] Is. xiii. 12.
[2] Z., Pt. I, fol. 107b; II, 39.
[3] Ib., fol. 240a; II, 548.
[4] Ib., Pt. I, fol. 238a; II, 540.
[5] Ib., fol. 29a; I, 182, 183.
[6] Ib., Pt. II, fol. 172b; IV, 127.
[7] Is. xi, 10.
[8] Z., Pt. I, fol. 118a; II, 71.
[9] Ib., fol. 119a; II, 77.
[10] Ib., fol. 145b; II, 172.
[11] Ezek. xxxvii. 22.

It is unfortunate that the annotations to the French ZOHAR are largely polemical in character and elucidations which would have been valuable on difficult points of fact are too often wanting. It would seem at first sight that there are several Messiahs to come. There is he who is to be the Son of Ischaï, said to be master of all, by whom the earth is nourished.[1] There is secondly the Son of Ephraïm, of whom it is testified that he will be driven back from Rome.[2] Three personalities are mentioned, each of them once or twice only, and it is suggested in the notes—but without offering a reason—that the second is identified with the third Messiah, who is the Son of Joseph. The fourth is the Son of David,[3] and both are mentioned in the TALMUD;[4] but one of the "Omissions" given in the first appendix to the first part of the ZOHAR affirms that the last two are one.[5] Certain MIDRASHIM are said to agree, but the distinction for what it is worth remains perfectly clear in the Talmudic references, according to which the Son of Joseph will suffer a violent death[6] and will be succeeded by the Son of David. Elsewhere in the ZOHAR it is denied that the Son of Joseph will be killed because he is compared to an ox and evil has no hold over him.[7] It is of this Messiah that it is said in Scripture: "He was wounded for our transgressions... and with his stripes we are healed."[8] On the contrary, the fact that he will die is reaffirmed a few folios subsequently. It is said also that one of these alternative deliverers is poor and mounted on an ass, while the other is the first-born of a bull.[9] They are the two Kerubim stationed before the Garden of Eden; the Flaming Sword is METATRON,[10] but at this point the symbolism passes into a wilderness of confusion where it

---

[1] Z., Pt. I, fol. 29b; I, 185, 186. Eternal life is possible through him only. The authority cited is 1 Kings xx. 31, and a supposed statement therein that "the son of Ischaï lives upon the earth," but it is not to be found.

[2] Z., Pt. II, fol. 120a; III, 461. See also Part III, fol. 153b; V, 394.

[3] The Son of David is said to be the SEPHIRA NETZACH, while the Son of Ephraim is HOD.—*Ib.*, Pt. III, fol. 243a, b; V, 581.

[4] Tracts ABODA-ZARA, SUCCA, YEBAMOT and SANHEDRIN.

[5] *Ib.*, Pt. I, fol. 267b; II, 633.

[6] The ZOHAR agrees in one place, but adds that he will rise again.—*Ib.*, Pt. III, fol. 203b; V, 520. See also *Ib.*, Pt. I, fol. 267b; II, 633, from which it follows that there is one Messiah and that he will suffer death. But this is contradicted in Pt. III, fol. 279a; VI, 52, where a distinction is made between the Son of David and the Son of Joseph, who will be slain.

[7] *Ib.*, fol. 276b; V, 48.

[8] Is. liii. 5.

[9] Z., Pt. III, fol. 279a; VI, 52, 53.

[10] *Ib.*, Pt. I, fol. 267b, 268a; II, 633.

is impossible and would serve no purpose to follow it. I do not know that we need come to any decision as to the number of Messiahs; it does not look in the ZOHAR as if they can mean states of one personality, which is the opinion of the editors, for in another place the text explains by an accident what is meant by a previous identification: it is said that the Messiah who is the Son of Joseph will be united—that is, in his mission—to the Son of David but will be slain.[1] The one is the conqueror of the great Rome and the other of the little Rome [2]—whatever the distinction between these cities may signify. The number 60 is fixed for the manifestation of the first and the number 6 for that of the second.[3] I do not pretend to explain the mysticism of these numbers, but I note that the number 6 is represented by VAU and the Son of David is connected with this number.[4] It is obvious that it is convenient for purposes of Christian interpretation to identify the Son of David and Joseph, as Jesus of Nazareth was both.[5] I should add in this connection that the words: "Lowly and riding on an ass, and upon a colt the foal of an ass," [6] which are referred to Messiah are not understood literally, for the ass represents that demon which shall be curbed by the King to come.[7]

The time of the coming of Messiah will be when all souls who are kept in the treasury of souls against the day of their incarnation shall have actually come hither in flesh.[8] Thereafter it would seem that new souls will be incarnated in Israel. Then shall the chosen people deserve to find—and shall not fail herein—the beloved and sister-soul predestined to each from the beginning of creation. It is in allusion to this that the Scripture says: " A new heart also will I give you, and a

---

[1] Z., Pt. III, fol. 203b; V, 520.
[2] Ib., fol. 252a; V, 589.
[3] Ib., fol. 252a; V, 590.
[4] Z., fol. 203b; V, 520. The letter VAU—as we have seen—is said to symbolise the Eternal World.—Ib., fol. 252b; V, 591.
[5] The Chevalier P. L. B. Drach concludes that the TALMUD speaks of the suffering Messiah as Son of Joseph and of the victorious Messiah as Son of David; but the evidence which he quotes from the TRACT SUCCA seems, on the whole, against him.—DE L'HARMONIE ENTRE L'ÉGLISE ET LA SYNAGOGUE, T. 1ᵉʳᵉ, pp. 184, 185.
[6] Zech. ix. 9.
[7] Z., Pt. III, fol. 238a; V, 577. The explanation given is that the demon, who is called the ass, can be made subject with the Sacred Name SHADDAÏ. This reference and extract belong to THE FAITHFUL SHEPHERD. It follows that Messiah, who connects with the Ox symbolically, will overcome the ass or demon, and hence it is forbidden in Deut. xxii. 10, to yoke an ox and an ass together.—Z., Pt. III, fol. 207a; V, 528.
[8] Ib., Pt. I, fol. 28b; I, 179.

new spirit will I put within you."[1] And again: "It shall come to pass that I will pour out my spirit upon all flesh; and your sons and your daughters shall prophesy, your old men shall dream dreams, your young men shall see visions."[2] The Intruders[3] shall be exterminated at the time when this shall be accomplished, which is said to be of old tradition.[4] To this period there is referable also that text of Genesis which says that Adam and Eve were "naked and not ashamed,"[5] the reason being that the Intruders are the cause of luxury and when they disappear all leaning towards incontinence will vanish in like wise.[6] Now all this is utterly stultifying disquisition and mania of interpretation in the literal sense, so far as it can be said to have any; and yet through all one feels that the Secret Doctrine is sealing and veiling the simplicity which is of all grace in Nature and Mystical Art. It is a change come over the dream of Israel, so that it shall enter into its own on all the planes and in all the worlds by the help of the "right spirit" renewed within them. This is the Spirit of Messiah,[7] as it is written: "Renew a right spirit within me."[8] And as we know that the Christ Who is to come in each one of us, Who is of Nazareth and of all the local habitations of the mastery, Who is son of David, son of Joseph, Heir of the true legitimacy, stands ever at the door and knocks, that rectified period is the one when all portals shall open, so that He shall be welcomed in all the ways. Out of the heart and the mind shall the Intruders be cast once and for all, and the soul shall find the Spouse. We might come to a pause at this point on the subject of the Messiah in Israel, according to the lights and shadows of the Secret Doctrine. It is a forecast of that time when the Mystery of Union which is now a Mystery of Faith shall have entered into realisation in experience on this earth of ours:

---

[1] Ezek. xxxvi. 26.
[2] Joel ii. 28.
[3] The reference is primarily to the mixed crowd which followed Israel during the Exodus from Egypt and were not afterwards separated from the chosen people. There are recurring allusions, and in one place it is said that these aliens were souls in transmigration from antecedent, destroyed worlds.—Z., Pt. I, fol. 25a; I, 155.
[4] See next section.
[5] Gen. ii. 25.
[6] It will be seen therefore that the alien people are understood spiritually as the prompters towards evil which are within us.
[7] It is also the Spirit of God which "moved upon the face of the waters" (Gen. i. 2). It is to this Spirit that David aspired.—Z., Pt. I, fol. 192b; II, 357, 358.
[8] Ps. li. 10.

as in the world above there is no distinction between Shekinah and the Holy One, so in that which is below there will be such a spiritual communion between the Lover and the Beloved that the voice of the turtle, which is the Song of Solomon, shall be heard everywhere, and of that time it may be said: "The male with the female, neither male nor female."

There are, however, some further points which, being of an external kind, are of the shadows rather than the lights, though there is one which is a light of symbolism, so it shall stand first in the sequence.

In the time of the letter HE [1]—that is, when the HE shall rise from the earth—God will fulfil that which is mentioned in Isaiah. The reference is to c. lx, at the end of verse 22, and it reads in the Authorised Version: "I the Lord will hasten it in his time"; [2] but the Zohar gives: "I am the Lord; and it is I who will hasten these marvels when the time thereof shall have come." When Israel was driven from its abode the letters of the Sacred Name were separated one from another, if it be permissible so to speak; the HE was separated from the VAU, and hence the Psalmist said: "I am dumb with silence." [3] When the VAU is separated from the HE the Word is stilled. The day of the letter HE is the fifth millenary—the period of Israel in exile. When the sixth millenary comes, the VAU shall raise up the HE, and Israel shall be lifted also from the dust. [4] After six hundred years of the sixth millenary the Gates of Supreme Wisdom shall open, and the springs of Wisdom shall begin to pour upon this world, which will make ready to enter worthily into the seventh millenary, and this latter will constitute the Sabbath of creation.

Assuming that we have a proper point of departure for calculation, we have in another place [5] the exact year of the

---

[1] Z., Pt. I, fol. 116b, 117a; II, 66–69.
[2] The Vulgate agrees: *Ego Dominus in tempore ejus subito faciam istud.*
[3] Ps. xxxix. 2.
[4] To understand this passage, it is necessary to remember that, according to more than one Zoharic testimony, the second HE of the Divine Name יהוה = Jehovah, fell, as I have mentioned in Book VI, § 3, with a promise to recur in the future, when we pass to the consideration of Shekinah. We have seen also that the second HE is the Daughter and that whereby she will be raised is the VAU, or Son. It is well to observe here how remote these intimations are from the Christian scheme which is based on the resurrection of the Son.
[5] Z., Pt. I, fol. 119a; II, 75, 76.

Messiah's advent. When sixty years shall have elapsed after the sixth century of the sixth millenary, it is said that heaven shall visit the daughter of Jacob. In the seventieth year the King Messiah shall be revealed in the province of Galilee. The portents will be as follows: (1) The rainbow—which is now tarnished, because it serves only as a memorial that the world will be destroyed no more by a deluge—will shine with very brilliant dyes, like a betrothed lady adorning herself to enter into the presence of her spouse.[1] (2) A star will rise in the East and swallow up seven stars in the North.[2] (3) Presumably after a period, a fixed star will appear in the middle of the firmament and will be visible for seventy days. It will have seventy rays and will be surrounded by seventy other stars.[3] (4) The city of Rome will fall to pieces [4]—an intimation which should be of moment to the hot gospel of certain protestant second-advent preachers, whose vestiges remain among us. (5) A great King will rise up and will conquer the world.[5] There will be war against Israel, but the chosen people shall be delivered. According to one account, the seventy celestial chiefs who rule the seventy nations of the earth will marshal all the legions of the world to make war on the sacred city of Jerusalem, but they will be exterminated by the power of the Holy One.[6] It is written: " And the house of Jacob shall be a fire, and the house of Joseph a flame, and the house of Esau for stubble." [7] As such stubble, by such fire and flame shall the nations perish. Thereafter the King Messiah will cause Jerusalem to be rebuilt; [8] the Holy One will remember that Covenant which He has made with Israel; and in such day will David be also raised up.[9] The Messiah will draw to him the whole world; it shall be so to the end of the century; and then the VAU shall be united with the HE.[10] It will be the period of true bridals; the Messiah will bring about union between the Palaces above and below, as also between EL and SHADDAI.[11]

The soul of Messiah is pre-existent in common with all souls, and its present place, according to the prevailing opinion, is in the Garden of Eden, but the testimony is not in

---

[1] Z., Pt. I, fol. 72b; I, 429, 430.
[2] Ib., fol. 119a; II, 76.
[3] Ib., Pt. III, fol. 212b; V, 536.
[4] Ib.
[5] Ib., fol. 212b; V, 537.
[6] Z., Pt. II, fol. 58b; III, 260, 261.
[7] Obadiah, v. 18.
[8] Z., Pt. III, fol. 212b; V, 536.
[9] Ib., Pt. II, fol. 72b; I, 430.
[10] Ib., fol. 119a; II, 76, 77.
[11] Z., Pt. II, fol. 253a; IV, 286, 287.

full accord and it must be left open as to whether this is the Eden above or that which is below. Wheresoever it be, there is a most secret place in the hiddenness which is called the Bird's Nest, and therein he abides.[1] In the Paradise there is also a certain place which is called the Palace of the Sick;[2] the Messiah enters therein and calls upon all the diseases, sorrows and troubles of Israel in exile to assail himself, and this comes to pass accordingly. Were it otherwise there is no one who could suffer the penalty due to his misdeeds. Hence it is said: "Surely he hath borne our griefs, and carried our sorrows."[3] So long as Israel dwelt in the Holy Land, and sacrifices were offered therein, Israel was preserved thereby from all maladies and penalties : now it is the Messiah who bears them—as it is affirmed, for the whole world; but I fear that this can be understood only as the world of Israel.[4]

I have left one statement till the last, that it may stand for the present by itself, because we shall recur thereto at a point which is still far away. It is said, almost at the beginning of the ZOHAR, and in that part which is called PRELIMINARIES,[5] that God created man with the object of preparing for the advent of the Lesser Countenance—that Divine Son corresponding to the letter VAU, about Whom we have heard in several of the previous sections. It is obvious that this is Messiah, and if the fact is not in undiversified agreement with a few other intimations, about which we have heard also, there will be an opportunity to contrast them in the proper place, and perhaps also to reach a conclusion on the subject.

IX.—THE DOCTRINE CONCERNING SHEOL

If there be any subject on which it might seem reasonable to expect something like unanimity of opinion on the traditions of Kabbalism, I should have thought that it would have been the question of rewards and punishments in the world to come—the latter perhaps more especially. The very contrary happens to be the case, and it is the more difficult to account for as by no extension of language can the question

---

[1] But he visits various Palaces and the School of Doctrine.
[2] Z., Vol. fol. 212a; IV, 222.
[3] Is. liii. 4.
[4] Z., Pt. II, fol. 212b; IV, 222.
[5] Z., Pt. I, fol. 19b; I, 119.

of the temporal or eternal punishment reserved for disincarnate souls be regarded as a real part of the Secret Doctrine. It seems to me that the Doctors testified very often with unmeasured words of enthusiasm and that the emotion of the moment gave the inward meaning to the written word much more frequently than any abstruse law of interpretation. I will speak first of that which is held to occur at the time of death and then of punishment in SHEOL, with special reference to its duration.

Many things which are hidden from the mind and heart of man so long as the body is in health are beheld by the soul when it is hovering between life and death.[1] Three messengers descend who begin to count up the days that he has lived, the sins that he has committed, and all the works which he has accomplished here below. The dying man confesses with his lips to the facts so related and signs the *procès-verbal* with his own hand, psychic or not, as you please.[2] Thereon is he judged, for Zoharic Theology, like that of the Latin Church, recognises a particular as well as a general judgment at the end of time. On quitting this lower world the man gives account to his Master on the basis of the record which has been mentioned. Having crossed the threshold, he recognises many persons whom he knew on earth. As we have seen otherwise, he beholds also Adam seated before the Garden of Eden, so that he may rejoice with those who have observed the commands of their Master. Adam is ever encompassed with a multitude of the just who have learned how to avoid the path going down to hell and who have been gathered into the abode of Paradise.[3]

---

[1] Z., Pt. I, fol. 79a; I, 462. This is held to be the " spiritual interpretation " of Job xxxvii. 7, which reads thus in the Authorised Version : " He sealeth up the hand of every man ; that all men may know His work." In the Revised Version there is the following variant of the last words : " That all men whom He hath made may know it." *Cf.* the Vulgate : *Qui in manu omnium hominum signat, ut nesciunt singuli opera sua.* But the ZOHAR reads : " He causes every man to sign with his own hand, that each may know His acts."

[2] The thesis is that sins are committed while spirit is united to body, and the account must be taken therefore before their separation is completed.—Z., Pt. I, fol. 79a ; I, 463. Zoharic pneumatology is sometimes almost inextricable, but we may remember that, according to one testimony, NESHAMAH cannot sin, whence it cannot be under the judgment ; NEPHESH remains with the body for twelve months, and it would seem therefore that it is RUAH only which enters into reward or punishment as a result of the particular judgment ; that in contrast hereto, we must remember further that all parts of the inward personality are one, by another account, so that the ZOHAR, like Latin doctrine, recognises fundamentally only (1) body and (2) soul. The so-called parts are therefore states of soul.

[3] *Ib.*, fol. 65b ; I, 386.

Another account says that when the soul leaves this world, it is stopped by a number of angels who preside over the offices of severity, and is prevented from passing through that door by which it would attain a place on high if the person has left no pledge on earth, meaning no son.[1] Those who would enjoy the inheritance of God and be united with Him for ever in the land of life must have produced male issue, so that the Divine Law may continue to have its servants through all generations.[2]

It is said also elsewhere that the day of death is the day of the Lord.[3] When the Holy One desires that the soul should return to Him, it does so return if worthy.[4] In the case of the just man his approach by the gate of death is proclaimed in the Garden of Eden throughout the thirty days which go immediately before the event.[5] During these days the soul is separated nightly from the body and ascends to heaven for the purpose of inspecting the place reserved for it in the world to come.[6] It follows also from a tradition mentioned by the ZOHAR that at the actual hour of death man is allowed to see his departed relations and friends, that he recognises these and that they appear to him with the same countenances which they wore here below.[7] If the man is worthy, his relations and friends salute him full of joy; in the contrary case, he beholds only the guilty whom he has known and who are expiating their offences in hell. They are all plunged in sadness. Relations and friends accompany the soul into the other world and shew him the place of his reward or punishment.

This is one side of the story,[8] but another is that when the

---

[1] Z., Pt. I, fol. 115b; II, 63.
[2] This is the higher side of the desire which prevailed in Israel towards the increase and predominance of the people; it was not alone that they might inherit the earth but that the Law might prevail therein. The production of children was therefore for the glory of God. It was a continuous building of houses not made with hands which might become meet for His habitation. Here is one sense in which the Zoharic Mystery of Sex was a Great Mystery of Sanctity and a Divine Work in the world.
[3] Z., Pt. I, fol. 217b; II, 457.
[4] There is firstly a purgation by fire according to fol. 217b; II, 457, for those who are imperfect and yet not deserving of entire condemnation. The purgatorial state of catholicism is therefore recognised.
[5] Z., Pt. I, fol. 217b; II, 457.
[6] Ib.
[7] Ib., fol. 218b; II, 463. The point is of interest in connection with death-bed visions in Jewry at the period to which the text is referable.
[8] It is said also that the highest place in the world to come is kept in reservation for those who have (a) penetrated the mysteries of their Master and (b) learned how to cleave to Him during life. It follows that the illumination of mind by Divine Things has a greater reward than works, but the works are necessary.—*Ib.*, fol. 130b; II, 111.

souls of those who have studied the Doctrine relinquish the body which is composed of the four elements they ascend into heaven—or into that part and region which is allocated to the Four Living Creatures.[1] The more general thesis is that the spirit which man attracts during life will draw his soul after death. Should it have been the Holy Spirit he will be raised thereby into the higher realms, and there—incorporated in the legion of sacred angels—he will become a servant of the Holy One.[2] He enjoys in the world above that light which he has desired here on earth. It is called "the splendour of light in reverberation,"[3] reflected by that which is in the region above all regions. Souls are clothed in what is characterised as the Mantle of the Master, in the absence of which they would be incapable of approaching the light and contemplating it.[4] I suppose that this mantle is that which is called vestments in another place. These are said to be stored in a certain Palace, each being adapted to that soul for which it is reserved.[5] All the good works which have been performed by him or her are, so to speak, embroidered thereon. The soul is not clothed, however, until the thirtieth day after death, because the sins committed on earth have to be expiated during this period, indifferently by bad and good. It is an expiation by fire and a passage through a river of fire.[6] There is, moreover, a punishment of the body in the grave [7] for a period of twelve months,[8] during which the so-called animal spirit—or NEPHESH—is attracted

---

[1] Z., Pt. I, fol. 27a, b ; I, 170.

[2] Ib., fol. 100a ; II, 8. The authority is : "I will give thee places to walk among these that stand by."—Zech. iii. 7. Cf. Vulgate : *Et dabo tibi ambulantes de his qui nunc hic assistunt*. The Zoharic version is : "I will give thee access among those who stand before me."

[3] Z., Pt. I, fol. 65b, 66a ; I, 387.

[4] Ib., fol. 66a ; I, 388.

[5] Z., Pt. II, fol. 210a ; IV, 217. The vestments seem to be different from that which Latin theology terms "the form of the soul" and from that which occultism—or its derivatives—calls the astral and psychic body. They are rather the soul's clothing in its literal sense, corresponding in things above to that worn by the High Priest in the ceremonies of the Sanctuary. I note further that in the Earthly Paradise souls are clothed with good works but in the Paradise above they are clothed more gloriously, namely, with purity of intention, rightness of heart and prayers.—Ib., fol. 210b ; IV, 218.

[6] Ib., fol. 211b ; IV, 221.—Pt. I, fol. 201a ; II, 397.

[7] Ib., Pt. III, fol. 53a ; V, 144.

[8] Ib., Pt. I, fol. 225a ; II, 487. The NEPHESH knows also the sufferings of survivors but cannot go to their aid. After the twelve months it is clothed with that envelope to which I have referred previously and passes on wings through the world, learning from the RUAH the misfortunes which befall man and seeking to communicate with these so that they may pray for the evil to be averted.

thereto and suffers therewith; but the just are not subject to this. As there does not seem to be any purgation in view the intervention of this ordeal is idle.

And now with regard to those who go down into hell I will endeavour to tabulate the distinctions and counter-distinctions under two heads, collating firstly those statements which predicate the everlasting nature of their torments. It is laid down that the Holy One forgives every man who repents of his sins; but it is woe to those who will not and who persist in their evil conduct. They will be precipitated after death into hell and will not issue therefrom through all eternity.[1] The same idea is expressed analogically in another place as follows. The souls of those who defile their bodies, and of the evil generally, go down into hell and never come forth therefrom.[2] Of these it is said: "As the cloud is consumed and vanisheth away: so he that goeth down to the grave shall come up no more."[3] But the ZOHAR here understands the grave—SHEOL—in the sense of hell, against the obvious meaning of the verse. Again, to fall into the hands of him who is called the Angel of Vindication is defined to be death in eternity.[4] These instances will suffice as to one aspect of the subject, and it will be observed that they are sufficiently unqualified.[5]

As much can be said of those in the opposite category, though if possible they seem more salient. There are only two extracts which need especially concern us; the first is an unqualified statement that the guilty are chastised in the fires of hell, but that they are not damned for all eternity.[6] Indeed the period has been fixed by tradition at twelve months, being that of the sufferings of Job.[7] This is the first statement, and

---

[1] Z., Pt. I, fol. 66a; I, 389, 390.
[2] *Ib.*, fol. 77b; I, 455.
[3] Job vii. 9.
[4] Z., Pt. I, fol. 94a; I, 535. The Angel of Vindication is DOUMÂ, and the Gentiles seem to be his victims *en masse* (*ib.*), while that which is the protection of Israel against him and his consequences is the Sign of the Covenant, on the understanding that it is preserved in purity.
[5] Respecting punishment in the other world, man was not considered to have attained his majority—and therefore to be capable of punishment—till he had reached the age of thirty years.—*Ib.*, fol. 118b; II, 74.
[6] Z., Pt. II, fol. 21b; III, 105. There is some undemonstrable way in which this assurance and its consolation are drawn from Is. xxxiii. 12: "And the people shall be as the burnings of lime: as thorns cut up shall they be burned in the fire." But the ZOHAR gives "thorn-bush" and institutes a comparison with the burning but unconsumed bush on Mount Sinai.
[7] And also of NEPHESH with the body.—Z., Pt. I, fol. 130b; II, 111.

the second is that at the end of time all the guilty will be saved, with the single exception of Canaan.¹ It is said that this mystery is not unknown to those who are familiar with the highroads and bypaths of the Secret Doctrine.² We are acquainted with the pre-Zoharic tradition respecting Caanan, which is part of a sex-mystery. It belongs to the same realm of reverie as the mystery which presided over the marriage of Bathshebah and Uriah before she was espoused to David.³ It is added that those who know this mystery will be in a position to see why the Holy Land was given as a patrimony to Canaan before the coming of the Israelites.

The question is whether there is any middle term by which we can reconcile the two series of conflicting testimonies, and if it be granted beforehand that the Doctors of the Secret Law, as they are reported in the ZOHAR, were frequently very loose in their statements, we may find what we seek almost at the end of the great text.⁴ There, on the authority of yet another tradition, it is affirmed that there are various compartments in hell, one beneath another, and corresponding to the different degrees of culpability found among men. The lowest of all bears the name of ABADDON, and the man who is cast therein is lost through all eternity, because it has no door through which he can go out therefrom. It is about this place that it is said : " As the cloud is consumed and vanisheth away : so he that goeth down to the grave—SHEOL—shall come up no more." ⁵ This notwithstanding, says the ZOHAR, we learn otherwise from Scripture that " He sends down into hell and again He brings forth therefrom." ⁶ The first of these verses refers to the lowermost pit and the second to one of those places from which escape is possible.⁷ Canaan is not located and the darksome picture of the deep below the deep is relieved by the unconscious grotesquerie which testifies that the denizens of this region are those who,

---

¹ Z., Pt. I, fol. 73b ; I, 435. See also fol. 114b ; II, 60, 61, where it is argued that all men will be acquitted at the celestial judgment.
² *Ib.*
³ *Ib.*, fol. 73b ; I, 436.
⁴ *Ib.*, Pt. III, fol. 285b, 286a ; VI, 67.
⁵ Job vii. 9.
⁶ I Sam. ii. 6. The French translators follow the Vulgate, which says, *Liber Primus Samuelis, quam nos Primum Regum dicimus*.
⁷ But as a travesty of the whole situation—as we shall see immediately—the abysmal hell is reserved to punish acts of irreverence. I make a point of this because one is inclined to speculate whether Rabbi Simeon—who is the supposed speaker—was not secretly insinuating the opposite of that which he expressed.

prompted by disdain, have omitted the word AMEN which completes the forms of prayer.

Two other points deserve to be mentioned in this connection as they tend to shew that the ZOHAR might have furnished some useful material to the pious author of HELL OPENED TO CHRISTIANS. It is said [1] that the impure soul which is cast into SHEOL is sometimes drawn out therefrom and carried through celestial realms, with this cry going before it: "Such is the lot of those who transgress the commandment of their Master." It is then returned to its place. There may be some justice in adding that this moral diversion is meted out in that part of the text which limits the period of damnation to twelve months, after which the soul is remitted to a suitable region. Here is the first point, and the second is a brief picture [2] of souls located in Paradise proceeding to view ceremonially the chastisement of the guilty. So does eschatology reproduce itself independently in the minds of its makers. I do not suggest that the ZOHAR in this place is really a post-Thomist text or that St. Thomas Aquinas was acquainted with the Zoharic COMMENTARY ON EXODUS, but I say that the same notion is found in both.

In conclusion as to the whole matter: (1) There are three chiefs in hell, acting as overseers of those who are doomed for murder, incest, and idolatry.[3] If this is to be taken literally, Barabbas would have left the premises without a stain upon his character; but the inference is doubtless that greater crimes stand at the head of a long list in their respective sequences. (2) The chastisement is by fire and ice,[4] but an elucidation in another place [5] explains that the waters which fall from above are cold as ice, while the fire which comes up from below is water which burns. (3) The souls of the heathen will never come out of hell.[6]

I suppose that things more ridiculous have never been said on the subject of retribution, but there are gleams here and there of a better sense. It is recorded for example that those who have been guilty on earth but have been also punished

---

[1] Z., Pt. I, fol. 130b; II, 111.
[2] *Ib.*, Pt. II, fol. 212a; IV, 221, 222. As regards both these points they constitute solitary statements in the text, but the second is on the authority of Rabbi Simeon, by which I mean that it is imputed to him and occurs in one of his discourses.
[3] *Ib.*, Pt. III, fol. 237a, THE FAITHFUL SHEPHERD; DE PAULY, V, 576.
[4] *Ib.*, Pt. I, fol. 238b; II, 542.
[5] *Ib.*, fol. 68b; I, 405.
[6] *Ib.*, fol. 4b of Appendix III, to Pt. I, *i.e.*, SECRET MIDRASH; II, 687.

on earth will not suffer in eternity if they have shewn resignation here.[1] And I observe rather frequently a disposition in the doctors to lean towards human mercy and to forget very often even their sentence on the heathen in general. There is a feeling that all men will be acquitted at the general judgment,[2] and there is one place from which it seems to follow that Satan himself will become again an angel of light.[3] So is the " broken circle " made whole by fits and starts.

There are the following supplements and alternatives which have suggestive points, and they serve, moreover, the unintended purpose of proving that eschatology in the ZOHAR is in a state of complete flux: all views were possible and the alternatives of all views. The souls of those who die impenitent go forth naked and find no envelope,[4] but it is set forth pretty plainly elsewhere that some kind of vesture is essential to personal existence. They suffer punishment in hell, but many of them are saved at the end of time, being those who intended to repent but did not get to the work. They take up their task in SHEOL and its gates are opened subsequently in their respect. There is nothing more agreeable than this to the Sacred King, a view that is illustrated amply in another place. It is laid down furthermore that even those who are just and nearly approach perfection go down into hell (1) because all have been guilty of some offences at least; but (2) because it is theirs to bring forth those very sinners who had proposed to repent in this life and have succeeded only on the other side of the grave.[5] So and continually does the ZOHAR lean towards mercy, as I have said, though it holds out little hope for persons who have planned no atonement:[6] they remain in the place of perdition for ever.[7] This is the case especially with those who have led a life of debauch; they do not have respite on the Sab-

---

[1] Z., Pt. I, fol. 108a; II, 42.
[2] Ib., fol. 114b, 115a; II, 60, 61.
[3] It is even said that while we are to be on our guard against the attacks of the demon we are not authorised to treat him with contempt.—Ib., Pt. II, fol. 237b; IV, 265. See also Pt. III, fol. 265b; VI, 19.
[4] Ib., Pt. II, fol. 150a; IV, 70.
[5] Ib., Pt. III, fol. 220b; V, 558. We have seen already that intention is greater than works and the uttermost sacredness is ascribed thereto. It may be said therefore that the ZOHAR is inclined to pave the way to God with good intentions rather than the road to hell, as the old proverb puts it. But it is implied of course that such intentions pass continually into work; it is a question therefore rather of a permanently right direction of heart and mind.
[6] Ib.
[7] See Pt. II, fol. 150a, b; IV, 70, 71.

bath—like the rest of the damned.[1] However, another thesis shows that the flames of hell are stilled of necessity on that day.[2] By these and all other considerations we are justified in applying the most liberal sense to the vague suggestions that all men—Jew and Gentile—will enter ultimately into some kind of salvation and that hell will give up all its prey at the end of days, whether demons and the prince of demons or men, including Canaan.

One last word: the doctors of the ZOHAR countenanced prayers for the dead, one of them asking another to visit his tomb for seven days following his burial, there to plead for his soul.[3]

X.—CONCERNING RESURRECTION

Seeing that the doctrine of physical resurrection remains to our confusion as something of a blot on the 'scutcheon of Catholic Theology—though it was almost inevitable for the period in which it grew up—it may be reasonable to ascertain that which is advanced on the subject by Zoharic Theosophy. We shall find that it is pleased to be particular—I was about to say—in no common degree; but my readers may judge for themselves. It will be thought, and this naturally, that a Secret Doctrine which offers no enlightenment on the subject —in the sense that we should attach to this term—is scarcely one that can appeal to the modern mind and much less that of the mystic; but I trust that I have done nothing throughout the present study to reduce the difficulties, or—if it should be preferred—the impossible nature of much that has been transmitted from this source. To say otherwise would be to pose as unserious. We are concerned, however, in reality only with the root-matter of the Tradition and we have yet to reach a decision thereon. If the central testimony should prove of moment, it is of little importance—however regrettable otherwise—that there should be a considerable accretion of waste and drift from all sources encrusted over

---

[1] Z., Pt. II, fol. 150b; IV, 72.
[2] Ib., Pt. I, fol. 14b; I, 84.
[3] Ib., fol. 217b; II, 458. It is testified also that the faithful departed pray for those who are alive, without which the latter would be unable to subsist for a single day, or even part of a day.—Ib., Pt. II, fol. 16b; III, 75. This is another side of a very clear Christian reflection—the intercession of the just above for those who need help below.

it.¹ I believe that so far in our quest we have come across much that is at least of a certain value, while the curiosities—taken as such—are not in themselves idle. In respect of physical resurrection we shall find, in the first place that it is physical above all things, and as the Sons of the Doctrine happen to be acquainted with the *modus operandi* of the whole process, we may have great expectations on the wonder-side, and though we can scarcely look to be edified, the lessons in other respects may not be without significance.

I should record in the first place that it must be left as an open question whether the Gentiles are included in the scheme of resurrection.² This is negatived categorically in one place,³ while in another it is added by way of re-expression that only the circumcised will subsist at that dreadful day.⁴ But even here there are reservations, for certain persons belonging to the past of Israel—persons conspicuous for their ill-doing—are regarded as blotted out completely, so that for them there is neither judgment nor rising.⁵ The restrictions would be still greater if several casual statements were to be construed literally—as when it is said, for example, that resurrection is by the merit of chastity.⁶ The vesture of holy days—about which we have heard—is a particular aid of the just ;⁷ but as it is certain that many of the wicked will also come to judgment it is possible that evil days may serve in their case, while making for their condemnation of course.⁸

---

¹ The point is that the root-matter is not one of metaphysical speculation or dogmatic teaching merely : it is a practice connected with a theory, the latter on account of the practice belonging to a category apart.

² For example, when it is said without qualifying the statement that the guilty will rise with the just, will do penance and will enjoy thereafter the light of God, there can be no question that the reference is to Israel alone.—Z., Pt. I, Appendix III, MATHNITIN ; II, 711.

³ The words are that God will command His Servant who is charged with the work of resurrection not to restore their souls to the Gentile peoples.—*Ib.*, fol. 181b ; II, 317. The servant is METATRON.

⁴ *Ib.*, Pt. II, fol. 57b ; III, 256.

⁵ *Ib.*, Pt. I, fol. 69a ; I, 406. The allusion is especially to the sin of Onan, the enormity of which is ever present to the mind of the Doctrine. See also fol. 66a ; I, 390.

⁶ *Ib.*, fol. 220a ; IV, 234. The remark should perhaps be taken in the sense of the previous extract.

⁷ Another account tells us that when a man has maintained his soul in its pristine purity, on leaving this world many lights are poured upon him and he is preserved against the day of resurrection in a hidden Palace of Love where the King of Heaven kisses the holy souls.—*Ib.*, Pt. II, fol. 97a ; III, 389. The Scriptural authority is Ex. xxi. 9, very curiously adapted : " He shall deal with her after the manner of daughters." It follows that all souls in respect of God are held to be female by the ZOHAR, and the kind of Divine Union here adumbrated is remarkably like that which we meet with in many recognised aspects of Christian Mysticism.

⁸ Z., Pt. I, fol. 224a, b ; II, 483, 484.

The general thesis of the subject is put very clearly as follows: When circumstances required it, a simple morsel of wood—the reference is to Aaron's rod—was transformed by the Holy One into a thing having body and life. With how much the more reason will He change into new creatures those forms which possessed previously a vital spirit and a holy soul, fulfilling the commandments of the Law, consecrated to its study.[1] It is the same bodies that have existed heretofore which will be resuscitated, as it is written: "Thy dead men shall live;"[2] and they will be animated by the same souls.[3] There is a sense, however, in which they will be formed anew, but they will have the aspects of old and will be therefore recognisable.[4] The new formation is more especially a Divine act of healing, so that the lame and the blind will be disqualified thus no longer.[5] This will be effected by the rays of that primitive sun[6] which shone at the beginning, embracing the whole world from one extremity to the other.[7] After God had beheld the generations of Enoch, with those of the deluge and confusion of tongues, He concealed this light, which had curative properties. Its future restoration as stated signifies the restoration and enlightenment of Israel. It is said that "in that day shall there be one Lord, and His Name one."[8]

We should read between these lines to our destruction, did we seek to spiritualise any of the statements made: there is nothing so full as their literalness, and the details to which I have alluded rise up here and there for our complete confusion. The resurrection of the dead will take place in the order of their interment:[9] if a wife was the first to be buried, it is she who will rise first, and this rule seems to prevail through the

---

[1] Z., Pt. II, fol. 28b; III, 135, 136.
[2] Is. xxvi. 19.
[3] Z., Pt. I, fol. 130b; II, 112.
[4] Ib., Pt. III, fol. 91a; V, 243.
[5] Ib., see also Pt. I, fol. 203b; II, 410. The robes of glory, or psychic vestures and vehicles with which the disembodied soul is clothed in the state of beatitude, being psychic garments, would, by the hypothesis, serve in the transfiguration of the risen physical body, though there would not be two envelopes one within the other, this idea being set aside by the ZOHAR, as we have seen.
[6] The Gentile nations will be consumed by its fire.—Ib., fol. 203b; II, 410.
[7] Ib., fol. 203b; II, 410. The light of this concealed sun encompassed Moses as an infant among the bulrushes; it surrounded him on Mount Sinai, whence the children of Israel could not look upon his countenance; and in some sense it remained with him for the rest of his life.—Ib., fol. 31b; I, 198.
[8] Zech. xiv. 9.
[9] Z., Pt. III, fol. 164a; V, 423.

ages, with an exception in favour of those who died in the desert: the trumpet will sound for these sooner than for the earliest of humanity.¹ When the great day approaches it will be the task of METATRON to embellish or glorify the bodies in the sepulchres and presumably to prepare them for rising;² but when the hour sounds the Holy One will cause a dew to fall, and it is thanks to this that the event itself will be accomplished. It will be a dew of light and it will emanate from the Tree of Life.³ There is, however, a special dispensation in respect of students of the Doctrine. Whether or not without prejudice to those who died in the desert, it is those who will be raised first,⁴ and they will bear witness in favour of the rest. The instrument in their case will be a wind which shall be the synthesis of all winds.

These things stand at their value, but there is a sort of central fact—*ex hypothesi*—which may be held to explain everything: each man who is born into the world is provided with an imperishable bone in his present physical body, and it is from or on this that his organisation will be built up anew at the time of the resurrection ⁵—it is like the rib taken from the side of Adam. The bone in question will be to the risen body that which the leaven is to the dough. So is it sown a natural body and raised miraculously enough, though scarcely—on the evidence—spiritually. Now, it is said in one place that by virtue of the dew of light, already mentioned, the resurrection of bodies will be as the upspringing of flowers; ⁶ but this is the poetry of the subject, and there is another side of the question. It was essential for the peace of the doctors that such an event as resurrection should take place only in Palestine, and it became necessary to devise a particular scheme for the great majority of Israel dying outside the precincts of that sacred land. This was done by

---

¹ Z., Pt. III, fol. 168b; V, 437.
² *Ib.*, Pt. I, Appendix III, MATHNITIN, fol. 6a; II, 705. But it is MATRONA who preserves souls until the resurrection.—*Ib.*, Pt. III, fol. 222b; V, 561.
³ Z., Pt. I, fol. 130b, 131a; II, 113. It is said elsewhere that at the time of resurrection (1) the waters of that heavenly fountain which is represented by the letter YOD will flow forth afresh; (2) the 32 paths of communication between things above and below will be open freely; and (3) all letters of the Sacred Name will be complete, which has not been the case in the world heretofore.—*Ib.*, fol. 10a; I, 42.
⁴ *Ib.*, fol. 175b, 176a; II, 290, 291. The risen bodies of these will subsist always, because the Law will be their protection.
⁵ Z., Pt. I, fol. 69a; I, 406. See also Appendix III to Pt. I, SECRET MIDRASH; II, 716.
⁶ *Ib.*, fol. 130b, 131a; II, 113.

postulating that, after their reconstitution, the bodies of such persons will be transported underground to the Holy Land, and there only will they receive their souls.[1] The complete resurrection will begin in Galilee.[2] Souls will come down through the gates of heaven and rejoin their bodies.[3] At first it will be a day of severity, for the Holy One will demand an account of all actions prior to the separation of soul and body; the books of record will be opened and the chiefs of severity will stand ready to act.[4] But Israel is a nation of the elect; the guilty who rise with the just will do penance and thereafter will enjoy the Divine splendour.[5] It is even testified—as we have seen—that the tempter-spirit will be transformed,[6] though whatever is understood by extermination is meted out to him in other passages.[7] The Holy One will bless the bodies of the just and will render them like the body of Adam in the state of Paradise. Such souls will bring with them the higher lights which nourish them during their sojourn in heaven, between the death and the rising, and those lights will make their bodies radiant.[8] Soul and body in fine shall know their Master.[9] A great festival will follow; but in place of the salted leviathan promised to the elect by the TALMUD the refection will be spiritual, because those who are truly just have no need to eat or drink but are nourished by the splendour of Shekinah.[10]

I am no doubt exceeding the restricted province which I have chosen, but it seems to me difficult to deny that Zoharic eschatology is tinctured by that of the Christian scheme, as presented by the Latin Church. Subject to the distinctions—not always maintained—on the question of the duration of punishment, all souls at death go to the place prepared for them and the judgment connected with the resurrection

---

[1] Z., Pt. I, fol. 131a; II, 115.
[2] Ib., Pt. II, fol. 10a; III, 42.
[3] Ib., Pt. I, Appendix III, SECRET MIDRASH; II, 712.
[4] Ib., Pt. I, fol. 201b; II, 401. It is said also that the "Serpent will rise up to bite and man shall tremble in all his members."—Ib.
[5] Ib., Pt. I, Appendix III, MATHNITIN; II, 711.
[6] Ib., Appendix III, SECRET MIDRASH; II, 716. The passage is a good example of the ZOHAR in its most cryptic mood. "The tempter spirit and his two daughters will be transformed. Formerly he was called Lot, meaning malediction, but hereafter he will be called Laban, meaning white."
[7] In one place it is said merely that he will disappear.—Ib., Pt. I, fol. 131a; II, 114.
[8] Ib., Pt. I, Appendix III, SECRET MIDRASH; II, 696.
[9] Ib., II, 713.
[10] Ib., p. 714.

determines once and for all the state of humanity for ever. There is neither change nor vicissitude thereafter. The just in their risen bodies will behold the Divine, so that the earth shall be filled with the knowledge of God.[1] In this world—as it now is—they are in a state of imperfection, but after the resurrection they will be perfect and will rejoice with Shekinah.[2] Their bodies will be like the splendour of the firmament, or like silver that has no alloy.[3] So will the earth be renewed.[4]

---

[1] Z., Pt. I, Appendix III, SECRET MIDRASH; II, 713. *Ib.*, p. 696. It is affirmed also that those bodies shall be unto them as a lasting habitation.—*Ib.*, Pt. I, fol. 80, Cremona ed. Again—*ib.*, fol. 66—the body shall be made wholly, even as it was formerly—meaning the body of Adam unfallen—that it may be like unto the holy angels.

[2] *Ib.*, p. 698.

[3] *Ib.*, Pt. I, Appendix III, SECRET MIDRASH; II, 699.

[4] *Ib.*, p. 697. I will mention in this connection for the students of numerical mysticism that the number 40 seems to be a resurrection or renewing number.—*Ib.*, Appendix III, SECRET MIDRASH; II, 715, 716, where the recurrences of the number in the Old Testament are tabulated. It will be remembered that the Ascension of Christ occurred 40 days after the Resurrection.

BOOK VIII
THE HIGHER SECRET DOCTRINE

BOOK VIII

THE HIGHER SECRET DOCTRINE

I.—THE MYSTERY OF SHEKINAH

THERE is a very true sense in which the Secret Doctrine of the ZOHAR must be said to centre in that Mystery, whatsoever it may be, which lies behind the wonder and glory of Shekinah —a recurring, and speaking literally, incessant subject of reference in adoring honour throughout the great text. There is a very true sense furthermore in which it may be said that out of this Mystery all Kabbalism seems to issue and, moreover, goes back therein. It would have been very reasonable, if indeed it had been possible, to have opened my study of the Doctrine with this subject; but it would have involved entering at once into its most recondite and difficult part, one also which might have made the whole undertaking insuperable for the general and not too critical reader.[1] As it is, I must proceed carefully, not only on account of the difficulties but because the Keys of the Mystery open into a region about which there are grave motives for speaking with considerable reserve, when it is possible to speak at all. It is here, if anywhere in our subject, that we shall find whether as mystics we are coming into something which may be our own in the matter of Jewish Theosophy or whether we must relegate it to the curiosities of past speculation that are not of our vital concern.

---

[1] The old maxim of the mystical alchemist, Khunrath, seems to obtain in every direction without variation or reduction: *Sigillum Naturæ et Artis simplicitas*, and I quote it here, as I have quoted it on several occasions elsewhere, to indicate that it is one which applies in a paramount manner to the root of the Secret Doctrine in Israel; for the vast body of cryptic writing and the practice concealed behind it arose out of that one verse in Scripture which says: " So God "—that is to say, Elohim—" created man in His own image, in the image of God created He him; male and female "— defining the nature of the image—" created He them."—Gen. i. 27. The difficulty therefore to which I have alluded above is not in respect of the fact wherein the Doctrine centres but in the complications of its development and in the details of the practical part.

"The sole object with which the Holy One, blessed be He, sends man into this world is to know that Jehovah is Elohim."[1] Herein is also all true joy of heart.[2] Now, it is in this manner that I open the high conference respecting the Mystery of Shekinah, which is a Mystery of man and God, of man in the likeness of the Elohim, of the relation between things above and things below, of intercourse for union upon earth performed in the spirit of celestial union, and the transmutation of one by the other for the work of God in the world. In this union abides the Mystery of Faith, which is the synthesis of the whole Law—Written and Oral Law—and of all that exists whatsoever. But union is not identity,[3] whence it is said further that Jehovah and Elohim are distinct, not synonymous, though together they form an unity.[4] It must be remembered in the first place that Elohim is a title of Shekinah and so also is Adonai,[5] in which sense—but presumably for us in manifestation—she is called the Mirror of Jehovah.[6] Like the First Matter of the Great Work in Alchemy, Shekinah is almost myrionymous in respect of her designations, but, almost without exception, the ascriptions are feminine. She is now the Daughter of the King; she is now the Betrothed, the Bride and the Mother, and again she is sister in relation to the world of man at large.[7] There is a sense also in which this Daughter of God is—or becomes—the Mother of man. In respect of the manifest universe, she is the architect of worlds, acting in virtue of the Word uttered by God in creation. In respect of the myth of Paradise, the Shekinah is the Eden which is above, whence the river of life flows forth

---

[1] Z., Pt. II, fol. 161b, 162a; IV, 101, 102. There is also a marriage of the two names in Kabbalism, producing the Sacred Name of nine letters, the consonants succeeding one another alternately, thus—אױחהוחים: YOD, ALEPH, HE, LAMED, VAU, HE, HE, YOD, MEM.—*Ib.*, iv, 151. It is said also: "And the Lord God formed man" (Gen. ii. 7)—*i.e.*, Jehovah Elohim, the male principle united to the female, according to the ZOHAR. Man is said to be grafted on Elohim, as the latter is grafted on Jehovah.—*Ib.*, Pt. II, fol. 260a; IV, 293.

[2] *Ib.*, Pt. III, fol. 8b; V, 23.

[3] *Ib.*, Pt. II, 162a; IV, 102.

[4] *Cf.* Deut. iv. 35: "Unto thee it was shewed, that thou mightest know that the Lord He is God"—or, as the ZOHAR quotes it, that Jehovah is Elohim. It will be observed that the Scriptural text does not tolerate the Zoharic dogma, though *ex hypothesi* one of its sources.

[5] Z., Pt. I, fol. 101a; II, 10.

[6] *Ib.*, Pt. II, fol. 124b; III, 482.

[7] *Ib.*, Pt. I, fol. 81b; I, 470. See also Pt. III, fol. 297b; VI, 124, for Shekinah and Matrona; Pt. I, 276a, SEPHER HA BAHIR, OTHERWISE, LUMINOUS BOOK or BOOK OF BRIGHTNESS; II, 644, for Daughter of the King; and Pt. II, fol. 100b; III, 406, for all the synonyms.

that waters the Garden below, and this is also Shekinah as she is conceived in external things—or Bride, Daughter and Sister in the world below. Considered in her Divine Womanhood, in the world of transcendence, she is the Beloved who ascends towards the Heavenly Spouse, and she is Matrona who unites with the King, for the perfection of the Divine Male is in the Divine Female. Hence it is said that the perfection of Jehovah is in Elohim.[1] She is a trinity in respect of her title as Elohim, for there is an Elohim in transcendence—concealed and mysterious—an Elohim that judges above and one who judges below; but these three are one.[2] As such, the Oral Law is her image, while the image of Jehovah is the Written Law[3]—a distinction at once eloquent and pregnant, for the Inward Law is life, while the Outer is the body of life. So also she is the waters that are above the firmament in respect of her title of Elohim, but she is the waters below the firmament when she manifests as Adonai.[4] As Elohim she is the Middle Pillar,[5] and all the various aspects of the one thing that is needful from the standpoint of the Secret Tradition are collocated, their seeming exclusiveness notwithstanding, to shew that she abides in all, is at once above and below, without even as within. She is that Divine Presence which walked in the Garden of Eden in the cool of the evening, which went before Israel in the desert and protects the just man who has fulfilled the precepts, dwelling in his house and going forth with him in his journeys.[6] As Elohim, in fine, she is the middle degree of the Divine Essence [7] corresponding to the Pillar of Benignity in the Tree of Life.

Now, in all the references cited up to this point the intention of the ZOHAR has been to shew in the most positive and unqualified way that the Shekinah—as affirmed already in the present section—is female in essential aspect, whether as the Bride of God in that transcendent state wherein there is no distinction between her and the Holy One,[8] or whether as the

---

[1] Z., Pt. III, fol. 5a; V, 11.
[2] Ib., Pt. II, fol. 257a; IV, 290.
[3] Ib., fol. 161b; IV, 102. Elsewhere the ZOHAR seems to say that the Kabbalah is actually Shekinah and that the MISHNA is its humble servant.—Pt. III, fol. 279b.
[4] Ib., Pt. I, fol. 17b, 18a; I, 108.
[5] Ib., fol. 278a, THE FAITHFUL SHEPHERD; II, 647. See also fol. 241a; II, 552.
[6] Ib., Pt. I, fol. 76a; I, 448.
[7] Ib., fol. 150b; II, 194.
[8] " She and God are one."—Ib., Pt. II, fol. 118b; III, 456.

tutelary guide of humanity.[1] But in preparation for another part of our subject it is necessary to glance at certain alternative allocations which appear in the ZOHAR. The Shekinah is the Liberating Angel who delivers the world in all ages,[2] who is ever near to man and never separated from the just.[3] Of her it is said: " Behold, I send an angel before thee, to keep thee in the way, and to bring thee into the place which I have prepared."[4] But it is stated that this Liberating Angel manifests as male and female, being male when it dispenses the celestial benedictions on the world below, because it then resembles a male nourishing the female; but when charged with offices of judgment it is called female, as a woman who carries her child in the womb of her.[5] It is said elsewhere that those who understand these male and female attributions know the great wisdom.[6] But the exposition as to this wisdom is given much later on, when it is stated that MATRONA is feminine in so far as she is not in union, but in that state she is identified with the male principle, and this is how the interchange of sex in divine things must be understood throughout.[7] So also METATRON, who is an aspect of Shekinah, is indifferently male and female, changing incessantly according to the vibrations of the union.[8] Now, it is said that Shekinah is to METATRON what the Sabbath is to the weekdays.[9] In other words, she is rest and the rapture of rest, yet it is that rest in which there is the intercourse of spiritual union. The same vibrations which are mentioned in the case of METATRON constitute the beatitude of the soul in heaven.

There are two points which should be memorised on this subject. At the apex of the union between male and female—which is to be understood only in a spiritual sense—the sex distinction has ceased: it can be only from this point of view

---

[1] See Z., Pt. II, fol. 207a; IV, 210.
[2] Ib., Pt. I, fol. 228b; II, 502.
[3] Ib., fol. 230a; II, 508.
[4] Ex. xxiii. 20.
[5] Z., Pt. I, 232a; II, 516. The " Flaming Sword which turned every way, to keep the way of the Tree of Life " (Gen. iii. 24) is a symbol of this Angel and of Shekinah in the dual sex of both. Mercy is always counted as masculine and severity or judgment as feminine.
[6] Z., Pt. II, fol. 100b; III, 406.
[7] Ib., Pt. III, fol. 31a; V, 84. It is said distinctly that, in this respect, whether the feminine or masculine form is used by Scripture, the same degree is always and only designated.
[8] Ib., fol. 73b; V, 201.
[9] Ib., fol. 243b; V, 581.

that the Shekinah is mentioned sometimes as if she were on the male side. Here is the first point, and the second is that in characteristics and in mission, she is always typically female; it is she who comprises all women in her mystery,[1] and this is why—as we shall see—she does not abide except with him who is united to a woman.[2] In conclusion, so far as there is a dual aspect on the sex side in the notion of Shekinah, it may be noted that the Divine Name Adonai would answer to the male aspect, Shekinah to the female and Elohim to the combination of both. There is, however, no Zoharic authority.

We have next to consider her relation to the letters of Tetragrammaton. The HE which is above, meaning the first HE of the Sacred Name, is the symbol of the Shekinah in transcendence, while the HE final represents the Shekinah below, or in manifestation, connected with the idea of MALKUTH[3]—understood as the world of ASSIAH. According to one account, she has been in manifestation so long as the world was created.[4] She is, however, above and below at one and the same time—there encompassed by twelve sacred legions and the supreme HAYOTH, or Living Ones, here by the twelve sacred tribes of Israel.[5] The YOD and the HE constitute the Father and the Mother: these are Jehovah and Elohim.[6] She is the Mother, MATRONA, above and MATRONA or Mother below.[7] From the constant and ardent love of HE for YOD there issues VAU, conceived and born of HE, who also nourishes VAU. But VAU came into the world with a twin sister bearing the name of Grace; the two took root on earth and constituted the HE final—a reference to the metaphysical conception of their affirmed union. Then and thus was the VAU united to the HE, meaning the second HE of the Divine Name.[8] It follows that there is a descent of VAU into

---

[1] Z., Pt. I, fol. 228b; II, 501.
[2] *Ib.* The task of lighting the Sabbath candles devolved on the matrons, because they are in the service of MATRONA. The act was regarded as an earnest (a) of long life for the husbands and (b) of a holy posterity for both, as well as (c) great personal rewards for themselves.—*Ib.*, fol. 48b; I, 281.
[3] *Ib.*, Pt. I, fol. 27b; I, 174, where it is said also that the HE final is the child of the first HE.
[4] *Ib.*, fol. 85a; I, 489.
[5] *Ib.*, fol. 159b; II, 227.
[6] *Ib.*, fol. 28a; I, 177. That is to say, in CHOKMAH and BINAH, as we have seen by the evidence collected in Book V, § 5, especially p. 226.
[7] *Ib.*, Pt. III, fol. 10b; V, 31.
[8] *Ib.*, fol. 77b; V, 210, 211.

manifestation, but there should be no need to add that this notwithstanding the VAU has its place in the Supernal World and so also has the final HE, because it is obvious that the Divine Name must be perfect above before it can manifest below, and from this point of view, though there is no Zoharic authority, and other allocations are paramount, the place of the HE final is with the VAU in DAATH.[1] As the HE in manifestation, the Shekinah is the repose of beings below and in transcendence of beings above,[2] referring more especially to souls who have attained beatitude, which is defined as the vision of her.[3] The VAU is the male child or the Son.[4] The YOD of the Sacred Name is ever united to the primal HE, and when the VAU is also joined thereto it is union everywhere, including that which should obtain between the VAU and the HE final.[5] Owing to the present state of the world, we shall see that this union has been broken. In a withdrawn sense the YOD of the Sacred Name designates the Supreme Thought, while the HE designates Shekinah, as the Heart of Love in that Thought.[6] To conclude as to the Divine Name, its consonants bear the vowel points of the Name Elohim,[7] from which two things seem to follow: (1) That the intimate union between Jehovah and Elohim is here indicated by the silent eloquence of verbal symbolism, and (2) that the degree or hypostasis, or that part of the Divine Nature with which man is in communion on earth, is that which the Secret Tradition understands as Shekinah. It is she who enables the Name to be expressed on earth, or God to be realised in the heart. I conclude that in the perfect state, the manifestation of the HE final on earth would be in espousals with VAU, but there is separation in the present order until that which now hinders shall be taken out of the way.[8]

The next point which is posed for our consideration is the

---

[1] I have put this on record in respect of the Sacred Name in the Supernals, but it need not concern us further. In the scheme of Divine Names allocated to the ten SEPHIROTH by late Kabbalism, JEHOVAH is referred to CHOKMAH.
[2] Z., Pt. III, fol. 108a, b; V, 274.
[3] Ib., Pt. II, fol. 40b, THE FAITHFUL SHEPHERD; III, 189, 190.
[4] Ib., Pt. III, fol. 118b; V, 305.
[5] Ib., fol. 267b; VI, 23.
[6] Ib., fol. 230a; V, 570.
[7] Ib., Pt. I, fol. 90a; I, 511, 512. Otherwise this Divine Name has the pointing of Adonai.
[8] My reference is to the period, foretold in the ZOHAR, when the VAU shall raise up the HE.

place of Shekinah in the Sephirotic Tree, and it will be well to state at the inception that the attributions throughout Kabbalism seem almost as many as the references, though there is only one which is predominant. She is the Middle Pillar—as we have seen—the Pillar of Benignity, extending from KETHER to MALKUTH,[1] and she takes up the SEPHIROTH to God, or into the place which is no place, beyond the infinite height and depth, the infinite of all directions embraced by the Tree. This is the place of AIN SOPH.[2] The Middle Pillar is described otherwise as the trunk of the Tree,[3] it being understood that the root is in KETHER, so far as the genesis and legend of the soul are concerned; but it is in MALKUTH in respect of the return journey to God, which is a journey through the Shekinah, or under her glorious leading. Shekinah is, in another form of symbolism, the body of the Tree;[4] and the elect—summarised as Israel—are the cloud of witnesses forming the branches. But it is said also that she is the crown of the Middle Pillar,[5] the synthesis of all the SEPHIROTH and of every Sacred Name expressed or implied in the wisdom of the Secret Doctrine. She is to God that which the vowel point is to the letter—a thing not distinct therefrom but the means of its utterance. She is further the crown of the seven lower SEPHIROTH, and this would account for the allocation of the semi-SEPHIRA DAATH or Supernal Knowledge to the centre of the influence coming from CHOKMAH and BINAH, as tabulated by later Kabbalism.[6]

---

[1] This is likely to cause some mental confusion, for which the text is too often responsible. We have seen that, according to the IDRAS, the Son or VAU is extended through the three worlds which are below the world of ATZILUTH, and He is called also the Middle Pillar; but He is in union with the HE final, or Bride, therein. I have spoken in the present tense, but this was during the perfection of the manifest world. They are in separation now, for the HE is fallen to earth—that is, to MALKUTH—and has to be raised by the VAU. It is never said that the VAU also has fallen, but as the method and terminology chosen to illustrate the notion are an adaptation of the Myth of Paradise symbolism, the VAU is certainly involved, as Adam in the calamity of Eve. The undoing of the evil rests also with her—as the ZOHAR itself intimates in one place. The whole account is an allegory of man and woman involved by a fatal construction respecting the Mystery of Sex but intended to redeem the trespass, with the life belonging thereto.

[2] This is a matter of inference from one isolated statement, which says that Shekinah in her ascent draws up the ten SEPHIROTH, and it is a matter of logic that thither where she draws them is beyond KETHER. Now, beyond KETHER is AIN SOPH by the hypothesis of the Tree.—See Z., Pt. I, fol. 24a; I, 149, where it is said that when she rises towards God she causes all the ten SEPHIROTH to go up with her.

[3] Ib., Pt. I, fol. 241a; II, 552.

[4] Ib., fol. 241b; II, 555.

[5] Ib., Pt. II, fol. 158a; IV, 94.

[6] This again leads to confusion, for we have seen that the head of the Son is in DAATH. I am not, however, attempting to harmonise the innumerable statements

Now, we know that there is an appendix to the SEPHER YETZIRAH concerning 50 Gates of Understanding—referred to BINAH, also by late Kabbalism; but this ascription is countenanced by the ZOHAR when it is said that these Gates are in the region of the Supreme Mother, who gives power to the Mother below[1]—a reference to the Shekinah in transcendence and in manifestation. This determines absolutely that the Shekinah is in BINAH and that the first HE of the Divine Name is also therein. It is said further that the side of severity emanates from her, though she is not herself severity,[2] and we know that the Pillar of Severity is on the left side of the Tree, at the head of which is BINAH.[3] " Shekinah emanates from the left side."[4] The 50 Gates are another symbolism concerning the return of man to the heights by the operation of Shekinah, as by a journey through the great distance, for the first gate is in matter and the last is in God Himself; but this gate was not, according to tradition, opened by Moses—presumably because another tradition affirms—as we have seen—that he ceased to cohabit with his wife on earth. It is to be observed that it is a Gate in BINAH, so that God is attained by man in and because of Shekinah, for which reason her number is said to be 50,[5] though from another point of view she is not contained in number.[6] There are, however, various allocations. Two Supernals, namely CHOKMAH and BINAH, are disposed on the right and the left, and these are said to be united in Shekinah.[7] But the complete integration in her of all branches of the Sephirotic Tree will not take place till He comes Who shall be called Man, that is, Adam or SHILOH.[8] It follows that

---

and counter-statements. Our object is to study the bent of the symbolism, and the glaring discrepancies—seeing that they speak for themselves—must take care of their own differences.

[1] Z., Pt. III, fol. 262a; VI, 12. As regards the number 50 which is allocated otherwise to Shekinah, it should be noted that the jubilee year, occurring once after every 49 years, is allocated to the Divine Mother in BINAH, as the Sabbatic year—occurring every 7 years—is referred to the Mother below—that is, the Shekinah in manifestation, so that her number on earth is 7.—See *ib.*, fol. 108b, THE FAITHFUL SHEPHERD; V, 274.

[2] *Ib.*, fol. 262b; VI, 13.

[3] That is to say, in the ordinary diagrams of the Sephirotic Tree—left and right referring to the observer.

[4] Z., Pt. III, fol. 275b; VI, 44. But this is looking towards the observer—as, for example, when he is faced by the two Countenances of the IDRAS. See Bk. V, § 5.

[5] Z., Pt. III, fol. 108b, THE FAITHFUL SHEPHERD; V, 274.

[6] *Ib.*, Pt. II, fol. 164b; IV, 108.

[7] *Ib.*, fol. 165a; IV, 109.

[8] *Ib.*, Pt. I, fol. 25b; I, 160.

THE MYSTERY OF SHEKINAH

there is a sense in which Shekinah is in CHOKMAH,[1] and it is supposed to be of her that it is said: "She openeth her mouth in wisdom."[2] For the purpose of this attribution wisdom is the letter HE and all depends therefrom.[3] The Shekinah in this relation is called concealed and visible, conciliating the mysteries above and the mysteries below.[4] Her hiddenness is in respect of the Supreme Degree of the Divine Essence, which exceeds understanding. She herself is revealed in wisdom by the mode of the Law of Mercy, so that she is Mercy on one side although Severity proceeds from her on the other. As the mouth which is opened with wisdom, she is the HE final of the Sacred Name, and this is the word which emanates from wisdom.[5] Again it is said that Elohim is seated on the right side, suggesting that the Shekinah is in CHOKMAH—according to the familiar diagrams. Moreover, wisdom is the glory of and is revealed in the Tabernacle [6]—that is to say, by Shekinah. We must deal with this as we can, seeing that in another place Elohim, who is Shekinah, is said definitely to designate BINAH.[7] Fortunately the harmony between these statements is given elsewhere in the ZOHAR itself, when it is said that the mother below is sometimes called the Betrothed and sometimes Sister. If she comes from the side of the Father she is called CHOKMAH, but if from that of the mother she is BINAH.[8] The truth is that Shekinah is on both sides of the Tree, and the explanation is that she is the spirit of all the Holy Assem-

---

[1] Because she is indubitably present in things that are united in her; because, in so far as she represents sex conceived transcendently, she is male and female; and because—as we have seen—in the Supernals there is no distinction between her and the Holy One.

[2] Prov. xxxi. 26. The reference is to a virtuous woman—accentuating in this manner the feminine aspect of Shekinah. We ought, I think, to remember in this connection that, in the physical order, it is woman who conceives, contains and brings forth both male and female—a point which must have been present assuredly to the minds of Zoharic doctors.

[3] But the attribution is casual or transient and as such fantastic. There is no question that in the natural allocations of the Tree it is the YOD that is in CHOKMAH, and for this—as we have seen—there is full evidence. Compare THE ASSEMBLY OF THE SANCTUARY, Z., Pt. II, fol. 123b; III, 478.

[4] Ib., Pt. I, fol. 145a; II, 171.

[5] Ib., Pt. I, fol. 145a; II, 171.

[6] Elsewhere the Tabernacle is said itself to be Shekinah.—Ib., Pt. III, fol. 114; V, 285.

[7] Ib., Pt. I, fol. 263a, SECRETS OF THE LAW; II, 620. It is all a very simple question of transposing the diagram and bearing in mind what follows above.

[8] Ib., Pt. III, fol. 77b; V, 212. She is known by many names, as we are told in another place—sometimes as an angel simply, sometimes as the angel of Jehovah and sometimes even as Jehovah.—Ib., Pt. I, fol. 113b; II, 58.

blies above and below.[1] It is in this sense and this only that CHOKMAH is sometimes said to be female and is that Mother who is allocated alternatively to BINAH, while she is Daughter, Sister and Bride in the worlds below. There is also a question of the unity which obtains throughout the Supernals. For the same reason she is now located in her manifestation at the foot of the Middle Pillar—that is to say, in the fallen world; but we have seen that she is also at the head and is therefore in KETHER—that is to say, as AIMA ELOHIM, covering the Supernals with her wings. Hence it is mentioned that the Holy One is covered by His Shekinah, both within and without.[2] I conclude that there are the Father, the Mother and the Begotten Son, being CHOKMAH, BINAH and DAATH, overshadowing the lower SEPHIROTH, though other allocations are made and stand at their value. These three are symbolised by YOD, HE and VAU in the Sacred Name, while the HE final, the Bride in manifestation, is in MALKUTH since the legendary Fall, but so that the kingdom of this world may become in the fullness of the Messianic day the Kingdom of Heaven. Outside these there is KETHER, and it should be noted in this connection that Jehovah abides, in the deep hiddenness, with Shekinah in that Supernal SEPHIRA.[3] The seeming attribution of feminine descriptions to the Shekinah in her threefold aspect, so far from leading to confusion, really provides the key. She is the catholic nature of womanhood in all degrees and grades. In so far as everything proceeds from KETHER, it is in virtue of the union between God and His Shekinah therein. That which was produced is male and female also, being the Father and Mother in CHOKMAH and BINAH, but because of this twofold procession there is a sense in which these two may be called Son or Word and Daughter. They beget on their own part the King and the Queen below, Lover and Beloved, the Son and Shekinah in manifestation. But the Supernals are in unity, and this is why the ZOHAR is

---

[1] Z., Pt. III., fol. 103b; V, 262.

[2] *Ib*., Pt. II, fol. 159a, THE FAITHFUL SHEPHERD; IV, 96. The Shekinah is represented also by the initial letter of the word Sabbath, but this would be, I think, the Shekinah below, because of the Sabbatic year already mentioned.

[3] This is a most important point and is on the authority of THE FAITHFUL SHEPHERD.—Z., Pt. III, fol. 243a; V, 581. It determines affirmatively a suggestion which I made in considering the symbolism of the White Head, as this is found in THE BOOK OF MYSTERY and the IDRAS. There is no aspect of the manifest Godhead in which the Male is without the Female, but the distinction is lost in AIN SOPH, about which nothing can be posited, except that it is shewn forth in KETHER.

THE MYSTERY OF SHEKINAH

so careless seemingly in its allocation of Shekinah, so that it is in CHOKMAH or BINAH as the one or the other mood happens to prevail. There are moments even when it looks as if Father, Word and Spirit abide in the SUPERNAL SEPHIROTH.[1] We must beware, however, of being misled by apparent correspondences with Christian Trinitarian doctrine and must remember in this connection that the Zoharic hypotheses are never spoken of as proceeding eternally one from another. The Word, for example, is strictly a time concept, postulated in respect of creation and preceded by the indwelling thought of God.

Shekinah herself in the state of distinction which—as we have seen—is affirmed concerning her, is either the first of created things or may be such when she assumes the vesture of METATRON.[2] In the state of ineffable union and in that conception which lies behind her name, she can be only eternal like the Holy One, save in so far as the Holy One, postulated in KETHER, is also a time conception in respect of AIN SOPH, the Inaccessible God, compared with Whom even the world of ATZILUTH is a conditioned state, and its conditioning is in respect of manifestation.

I have mentioned in another connection the work of Shekinah in creation. In her office as architect of the world, the Word was uttered to her, was by her conceived and brought or begotten into execution. We have seen that Shekinah below concurred with the architect above and was also a builder—in what sense does not signify, nor is it explained by the ZOHAR.[3] In so far, however, as creation is the history of the elect symbolised, it is obvious that the work remains unfinished till the great day of restitution, and coincident therewith is the history of Shekinah herself. On the manifest side it begins in the Garden of Eden—in that Garden which is she, according to another symbolism [4]—and it continues for the Theosophical Jew through the whole period of the

---

[1] Z., Pt. III, fol. 10b ; V, 31.
[2] *Ib.* We have seen that METATRON is the vesture of SHADDAI, but this Divine Name, with those of Adonai, Elohim and Shekinah herself, are evidently interchangeable. See Z., Pt. III, fol. 231a ; V, 571, in respect of METATRON, by which it appears that they are so related because the numerical value of the one name is the same as that of the other.
[3] *Ib.*, Pt. I, fol. 22a, b ; I, 136–138. It is said, however, that she is the object of the mysteries relative to the works of creation.—*Ib.*, Pt. III, fol. 231a ; V, 571.
[4] The counterpoise to this is that Shekinah was the companion of human exile when Adam and Eve were expelled from the Garden—as we shall see immediately.

Greater Exile. I have mentioned that it was Shekinah who walked with Adam in Paradise under the title of Lord God,[1] that is to say, of Jehovah Elohim, the union above communicating to the union below and prescribing the first law of life. This is the Shekinah in manifestation. But we know that the trespass followed and that our prototypical parent was driven out of the Garden. This might appear to mean that he was cast out from under the wings of Shekinah; but he was not deserted in his need, for she followed him into the captivity of the senses. This is one side of the Zoharic doctrine that Shekinah suffered with mankind,[2] but it is put much more explicitly when it is said: "Therefore the man was driven out and the Mother was driven out with him."[3] This was the primal captivity, and many captivities followed, wherein Shekinah shared; for it is said that she is the sacrifice which God has placed on His right and on His left hand, and about Him.[4]

There was separation between the King and Matrona in respect of the outer world and so came about a separation in the Divine Name, for the final HE was detached and came down on earth, the source of graces coming with her.[5] Though it is forbidden to separate the Heavenly Bride and Bridegroom, even in thought, it is this which has come to pass by reason of the sufferings of Israel,[6] with whom Shekinah was destined—as we have seen—to endure even from the beginning.[7] "When Israel is in exile the Shekinah is also in exile. It is for this reason that the Holy One will remember Israel," meaning that He remembers His covenant, "which is Shekinah."[8] The symbolical position is summed up in the

---

[1] Z., Pt. I, fol. 76a; I, 448.
[2] Ib., fol. 120b; II, 84, 85.
[3] Ib., fol. 22b; I, 137. The authority is: "Behold, for your iniquities have ye sold yourselves, and for your transgressions is your mother put away."—Is. l, 1.
[4] Ib., fol. 256a; II, 603.—Ib., Pt. III, fol. 109a; V, 275.—Ib., Pt. I, fol. 24a; I, 149. Sometimes it is a question of drawing into the deeps and heights of Divine Union. Sometimes it is the same conception symbolised by the female offering all her members and all the parts of her personality to the corresponding members and parts on the male side.
[5] Z., Pt. I, fol. 254b; II, 600. The point is expressed in a very curious way—namely, that the world could not exist until the HE final detached itself from the other three letters of the Divine Name and descended on earth. The authority seems to be: "I have said, Mercy shall be built up for ever" (Ps. lxxxix. 2), which the ZOHAR renders: "The world shall be built by mercy." Cf. Vulgate: *In aeternum misericordia aedificabitur in caelis.*—Ps. lxxxviii. 3.
[6] Z., Pt. II, fol. 9a, b; III, 39.
[7] Ib., Pt. I, fol. 120b; II, 84.
[8] Ib., Pt. I, fol. 120b; II, 84. Compare Deut. xxx. 3: "The Lord thy God will turn thy captivity, and have compassion upon thee."

THE MYSTERY OF SHEKINAH

statement that the second HE was obscured and fell,[1] becoming a symbol of penitence.[2] The meaning is that she is with the elect, for better, for worse, for richer, for poorer;[3] and as in their attainments so is she with them in their sins, though not after the same manner, for she is then on the wrath side. Her shame is the defiled body of man.[4] Again, she is in separation from the King owing to the wickedness of man, and though she does not leave him the sin of Israel causes her to turn away.[5] To sum up on this subject, she was driven out of the Garden of Eden with Adam, like a wife sent away by her husband; but it was for the salvation of the world.[6]

In glancing at the concurrent history of Israel and that of Shekinah, considerable care is needed to distinguish between the allusions to her who is enthroned in BINAH, never leaving the Supernals, and the exiled servant of God,[7] for there is a Shekinah called servant and a Shekinah called Daughter of the King.[8] The one is above the angels, like her who in Christian doctrine is called *Regina Angelorum*,[9] and in respect of all other lights of creation is that which soul is to body, though in relation to the Holy One she is as the body to the soul, notwithstanding that she and God are one.[10] She is the Mistress of the Celestial School, called the Abode of the Shepherds, and this is a school of METATRON, understood as a vesture or form assumed by Shekinah.[11] In another aspect of symbolism she is that great and wide sea mentioned in Ps. civ. 25, and she embraces the whole world, which is concentrated in her.[12] She is the jubilee above—presumably on account of joy.[13] All this is in the world of procession or

---

[1] Z., Pt. II, fol. 9b; III, 40.
[2] *Ib.*, fol. 114b; III, 442.
[3] *Ib.*, Pt. III, fol. 74a; V, 202. She is weighed down by the sin of Israel.—*Ib.*, fol. 28a; V, 79.
[4] *Ib.*, fol. 75a; V, 204.
[5] *Ib.*, fol. 155a, b; V, 397.
[6] *Ib.*, Pt. I, fol. 237a; II, 535, 536. It is written: "O Lord our God (Jehovah Elohim), other lords beside Thee have had dominion over us; but by Thee only will we make mention of Thy Name," or—as the ZOHAR has it—"but, thanks to Thee, we have remembered Thy Name only."—Is. xxvi. 13. This verse is held to contain the Supreme Mystery of Faith. JEHOVAH ELOHENOU is the source of highest mysteries, and when Israel attains perfection it will make no distinction between Jehovah and ELOHENOU. It is forbidden to separate these Names even in thought. Yet is there separation now on account of the sufferings of Israel, and because it is apart from God.—*Ib.*, Pt. II, fol. 9a, b; III, 38–40.
[7] Z., Pt. III, fol. 223a; V, 563.
[8] *Ib.*, Pt. II, fol. 94b; III, 378.
[9] *Ib.*, fol. 116b; III, 450.
[10] *Ib.*, fol. 118b; III, 456.
[11] *Ib.*, Pt. III, fol. 197a; V, 508.
[12] *Ib.*, Pt. I, fol. 236a; II, 530, 531.
[13] *Ib.*, fol. 252a; II, 593.

emanation—the hypostatic world, which is ATZILUTH.[1] But Shekinah is said otherwise to receive a body in YETZIRAH [2] and so is empowered to manifest in ASSIAH, wherein—among other titles—she is the Lady of Battles,[3] who also obtains remission of the sins of Israel, after the manner of the *Agnus Dei qui tollit peccata mundi*.[4]

The Shekinah is held to connect in a particular sense with the patriarchal age. It was after his circumcision that the letter HE was added to the name of Abram and it was also thereafter that he was united—as we have found—with Shekinah.[5] Most of the divine visions beheld by Abraham were visions and manifestations of Shekinah,[6] who dwelt constantly in the tent of Sarah, and this is why Abraham—as we have seen—on appearing in the presence of Pharaoh, described Sarah as his sister, not as his wife, his reference being really to Shekinah, who bears this title in respect of man and who accompanied Sarah.[7] When he went to the rescue of Lot,[8] on leaving his house, Abraham beheld Shekinah lighting the way before him and encompassed by many celestial legions.[9] She was present when Isaac blessed Jacob;[10] it was she who conferred upon Jacob the name of Israel,[11] and she was with him when he set up the mystic stone as a pillar.[12] When seeking a wife it was with Shekinah that Jacob united his intention, and hence it is said—in characteristic Zoharic symbolism—that when he married Rachel he united heaven and earth.[13] Shekinah, however, did not ignore or forget Leah but—as the Holy Spirit—inspired her, so that she knew respecting her part in the bearing of the twelve tribes.[14] Rachel died when the progenitors of these tribes were completed and her place was taken by Shekinah, but after the death of Leah she removed to the house of Bala, so that she might be near Jacob, though she could not dwell in his house because—as we know—she resides only where

---

[1] Z., Pt. III, fol. 109a; V, 276.
[2] Ib.
[3] Ib., fol. 75b; V, 205. It is of course obvious that Shekinah as Daughter of the King did not fall into sin and hence her exile is willing, or she is empowered, as this text says. But that of which she is prototype—incarnate womanhood—did—*ex hypothesi*—fall, and that son who is incarnate manhood fell with her.
[4] Z., Pt. I, fol. 191b; I, 353.
[5] Ib., fol. 93a; I, 529.
[6] Ib., Pt. II, fol. 105a; II, 27.
[7] Ib., fol. 111b; II, 50.
[8] Gen. xiv. 14.
[9] Z., Pt. I, fol. 112b; II, 55.
[10] Ib., fol. 144b; II, 168.
[11] Ib., fol. 173b; II, 283.
[12] Ib., fol. 148b; II, 186.
[13] Ib., fol. 153a; II, 203.
[14] Ib., fol. 157a; II, 216.

the man is united to the woman.[1] When Jacob lost Joseph he lost the Shekinah also, either because joy had left him, and she dwells only with the glad heart, or because it is said that he ceased to cohabit with his wife, as a mark of grief and desolation.[2] The part of joy returned to him after reunion with his son and presumably also Shekinah, for she accompanied Jacob and his family into Egypt, and forty-two sacred angels destined for her service came down with her, each bearing a letter belonging to the Divine Name of forty-two letters.[3] So long as Joseph was with the Israelites the Shekinah was with them also, and they were not enslaved by the Egyptians; but when the day came for him to die, it is said that she departed,[4] and we know how it was with the people until the advent of Moses. It was he who attracted again the Shekinah to Israel[5]; it is said that she never quitted him from the day of his birth[6]; but more even than this, one of the doctors affirms that the father of Moses was espoused to Shekinah, or alternatively that both father and mother aspired towards her in their hearts during the intercourse which was followed by his conception.[7] This is what is meant by the statement, already cited, that the Shekinah reposed upon the nuptial bed of the parents of Moses.[8]

The nature of the union which subsisted between Moses and Shekinah is set out very curiously, for it is said that in a manner she had three husbands, namely, Jacob, Joseph and Moses. But the first abode with his wives on earth and was only united with her after his death. The espousals were not dissolved between her and Joseph until the bones of the latter were interred in Palestine. It was for this reason that Moses carried them out of Egypt, and they accompanied the children of Israel during the wanderings in the desert. It was somehow in virtue of their presence that Moses was united to Shekinah, so that she cohabited with him, and in connection with this it is observed that he detached himself from his wife—a very strange intimation if the Indwelling Glory abides only with man in so far as he is wedded in the ordinary and lawful sense.[9] Indeed in another place the fact

---

[1] Z., Pt. I, fol. 175b; II, 289.
[2] Ib., fol. 197a, b; II, 381, 382.
[3] Ib., Pt. II, fol. 4b; III, 15.
[4] Ib., I, fol. 184a; II, 327.
[5] Ib., fol. 67b, 68a; I, 400.
[6] Ib., fol. 120b; II, 83.
[7] Ib., Pt. II, fol. 19a; III, 92.
[8] Ib., fol. 11b; III, 49.
[9] Ib., Pt. I, fol. 21b, 88a; I, 133–135. I am only giving a very slight sketch of the whole subject, which would seem to the general reader a record of utter unreason.

stated is not counted to Moses exactly as righteousness.[1] The whole point rests on that Talmudic tradition which we have met with concerning the separation of Moses from Zipporah.[2] Another account, which is in opposition to much that has preceded, says that the Holy One espoused Matrona to Moses, and this was the first time that she made contact with the world below.[3] We may compare herewith the remark on the Daughter of God in another place, where it is said that until she became a Bride, no one spoke with God face to face[4]: it is another reference to the espousals of Moses, contradicting her alleged union with Abraham and Jacob and her presence in the world before its creation. The meaning is that Shekinah was united with Moses after a new and more intimate manner than had been the case previously, just as God revealed Himself to the lawgiver in another way and in a sense under a New Name. The exodus brought about by Moses occasioned, moreover, the manifestation of Shekinah before the people of Israel, she being the pillar of fire by night, as Jehovah was that of cloud by day.[5] According to another account, she was also a cloud, and it was through this cloud that Moses passed on his ascent of Mount Sinai.[6] Finally, and most important of all, Moses caused Shekinah to manifest in the Ark of the Covenant over the Mercy-Seat, between the figures of the Kerubim. The Tabernacle was erected to serve as her residence; and at the moment when it was set up by Moses, there was another erected in the world above. What seems to have happened, however, was that the Mosaic Tabernacle became the residence of METATRON, who connects so curiously with Shekinah.[7] The latter was also that cloud which abode on the tent of the

---

The fact that the bones of Jacob were interred in Palestine means that they belonged to the "celestial beings": it was otherwise with those of Joseph, and he was still counted as belonging to the earth. The bones are symbols of the celestial legions, and these only needed to be interred in Palestine. The Sons of the Doctrine did not know how a man in the position of Joseph would have been embalmed after his death. A still more inscrutable suggestion is worded literally as follows: "Moses cohabited with Shekinah, who is symbolised by the moon, even while the spirit dwelt in his body, and he subjected her to his desires."—*Ib.*, fol. 22a; I, 134. After his death he ascended to the degree of the Jubilee, which—as we have seen—is BINAH and the Shekinah in transcendence therein. She who was the spouse of Moses was the Shekinah in manifestation, and it is said that after his death she returned to Jacob. With all this compare *ante*, Book VIII, § 6, where it is said that Moses failed to open the 50th Gate of Understanding because he had ceased to live with his wife.

[1] Z., Pt. I, fol. 234b; II, 523.
[2] See *Tract Sabbath*.
[3] *Ib.*, Pt. II, fol. 145a; IV, 59.
[4] *Ib.*, fol. 22b; III, 115.
[5] *Ib.*, Pt. III, fol. 191b; V, 499.
[6] *Ib.*, Pt. I, fol. 176b; II, 293.
[7] *Ib.*, Pt. II, fol. 143a; IV, 54.

congregation while the glory of the Lord filled the Tabernacle.[1] Alternatively it was a cloud that rose up to veil her presence, and dissolved when she went forth. It is called smoke by the ZOHAR, which also gives the reason, according to its own fantastic symbolism—namely, that Shekinah had been drawn into this world by the fire which burns in the hearts of the patriarchs.[2] The male principle or Jehovah is said further to have spoken from the Tabernacle by the intermediation of Shekinah, who is the female principle.[3] The Tabernacle itself—as we have seen—is Shekinah under another aspect,[4] much as the tent of Sarah is so called on occasion, because she and the Divine Bride dwelt therein.[5] The Shekinah considered as the Tabernacle is in pledge for the sins of man.[6]

We know by the scriptural account that in the temple of Solomon the Shekinah continued to repose between the wings of the Kerubim.[7] She is described as resident throughout the Holy of Holies,[8] yet is connected in an especial manner with the western wall of the temple.[9] The Holy of Holies was guarded moreover by METATRON[10] and was built for the union of the King and MATRONA. It is written: "Those of the country shall utter cries, and the angels of peace shall weep bitterly."[11] This is the Zoharic version of Isaiah xxxiii. 7. It refers to the weeping of the angels when the Sanctuary was destroyed and the Shekinah was exiled into a foreign land.[12] She underwent transformation and assumed another form than that which she had worn previously. So also the Spouse of Shekinah—referring to the VAU of the Sacred Name, she in manifestation being the second HE—reduced that light which enlightens the world,[13] as it is written: "The sun at his rising shall be covered with darkness, and the moon shall give no light."[14]

These are naturally the heads, and such only, of the history of election in Israel and the glory of all in connection there-

---

[1] Ex. xl, 34, 35.
[2] Z., Pt. I, fol. 1, 76b; II, 294.
[3] Ib., fol. 239a; II, 545.
[4] Ib., Pt. III, fol. 114a; V, 285.
[5] Ib., Pt. I, fol. 101b; II, 11.
[6] Ib., Pt. III, fol. 114a; V, 285.
[7] Ib., Pt. II, fol. 16b; III, 76.
[8] Ib., Pt. III, fol. 161b; V, 416.
[9] Ib., Pt. II, fol. 116a; III, 447.
[10] Ib., fol. 164a; IV, 107.—Ib., Pt. III, fol. 74b; V, 203.
[11] Cf. Vulgate: *Ecce videntes clamabunt foris, angeli pacis amare flebunt*. The Authorised Version is: "Behold, their valiant ones shall cry without: the ambassadors of peace shall weep bitterly." The Revised Version agrees.
[12] Z., Pt. I, fol. 203a; II, 407.—Ib., fol. 182a; II, 319.
[13] Ib.
[14] Is. xiii. 10.

with. In the Second Temple the Shekinah had no part,[1] though by the hypothesis of the subject she had followed her people into the exile of Babylon and helped them to remember Zion by its sad waters. Albeit the Sons of the Doctrine had their dark moments during that day of a thousand years or over which followed the destruction of Jerusalem, at some period of which the ZOHAR entered into record, and though some of their sayings in these moments haunt the heart with their catholic sense of unavailingness, the mood and its clouds lifted ever and unerringly. Deeper still in their own hearts they knew that they had not been deserted, that on account of the Betrothed of God Israel was not forsaken by Him.[2] Were they not conscious also—I think in my soul, most surely—as by all the waters and in all the Babylons of the greater exile, they made up their dream of Shekinah, that she was more vitally and efficaciously with them than she had been with patriarchs of old; that she was married to them not less closely than to Moses, prince of lawgivers; and that she was realised better as a presence than when she sat between the Kerubim? Ever in BINAH her celestial fire abode on the Throne of Mercy[3] for those who dwelt in her covenant, and by her mediation an union was still possible, as indeed actual, between the Holy One and the Community of Israel.[4] This is one of the senses in which the souls of Israel are said to be attached to Shekinah.[5] That is not true therefore *quod unus doctor dixit in excessu suo*: " Israel is dead for the Shekinah which is above by the destruction of the First Temple; it is dead a second time for the Shekinah which is below by the destruction of the Second Temple."[6] And again: " The destruction of the two Temples dried up the sources of the Shekinah above and below."[7] She and Israel are in exile together, in sorrow and loss together,[8] and the path of penitence trodden by the one is the path of emancipation for both. Meanwhile, " the earth is the Lord's, and the fullness thereof; the world, and they that dwell therein ";[9] but the fullness thereof is a reference to Shekinah, as an ample moon enlightened over its surface by the sun. She is full also of

---

[1] The First Temple was destroyed, because light failed therein, but the Second Temple seems never to have had the light.—Z., Pt. II, fol. 95b; IV, 150.
[2] *Ib.*, Pt. III, fol. 115b; V, 297.
[3] *Ib.*, fol. 34a; V, 89.
[4] *Ib.*, fol. 37b; V, 102.
[5] *Ib.*, Pt. I, fol. 25a; I, 154.
[6] *Ib.*, Pt. I, fol. 26a; I, 164.
[7] *Ib.*, fol. 255a; II, 601.
[8] *Ib.*, Pt. II, fol. 189b; IV, 175.
[9] Ps. xxiv. 1.

THE MYSTERY OF SHEKINAH

celestial benefits, like a treasury; and in her manifestation to Israel she is a treasury which belongs to the Lord.[1] Moreover, the exile of Shekinah with Israel, and her residence among other peoples, has its train of extrinsic consequences in the peace and benefits which are enjoyed by the latter.[2] This is the sense in which it is said that other nations have attracted the Shekinah towards them.[3] Indeed her perfection is throughout the whole earth and her benedictions are over all the world,[4] for Elohim is a Mystery of Life.[5] and the Source of all life. She never separated from man so long as he observed the commandments of the Law;[6] but in connection with this we must take and qualify freely a number of counter-statements: (1) Every sin committed in public drives away Shekinah from the earth;[7] (2) the generation of Noah sinned in the sight of the whole world, and the Shekinah was far from the world;[8] (3) when owing to the wickedness of the world the latter has been left by Shekinah it is deprived of all defence, and the severity of justice reigns therein;[9] (4) after the guilty have been exterminated the Shekinah returns.[10] It is obvious that these statements do not obtain generically on the literal side; the consequences, like the acts, are individual, or, in the case where they are collective, it is only in a restricted way.

To sum up: the wounds of the world and the wounds of the Church in the world may be wide and deep; but the Church and the world go on, for ten persons in the House of Prayer constitute the body of Shekinah;[11] and there is a very much truer sense than was ever conceived by the ZOHAR in which those ten are never wanting: the elect are everywhere the true Israel, and it is thanks to Israel that Shekinah resides on earth, Israel being its bodyguard.[12] In thousands and tens of thousands of cases, all the wide world over, it is true and glorious that man acknowledges the kingdom of heaven and submits thereto; that the Shekinah rests upon his head, assisting him in the quality of witness; that she testifies before the Sacred King how this man proclaims the Divine Unity—or, in other words, that Jehovah is Elohim—above

---

[1] Z., Pt. I, fol. 67a; I, 395, 396.
[2] Ib., fol. 84b; I, 488.
[3] Ib.
[4] Ib., Pt. I, fol. 166a; II, 251.
[5] Ib., fol. 227b; II, 497.
[6] Ib., Pt. I, fol. 231a; II, 516.
[7] Ib., fol. 57b; I, 333.
[8] Ib.
[9] Ib., fol. 68b; I, 406.
[10] Ib.
[11] Ib., Pt. III, fol. 126a; V, 324.
[12] Ib., Pt. I, fol. 61a; I, 358.

and below, twice every day;[1] that so far as these are concerned the earth is perfect and all joy is found therein.[2] Thus is Jerusalem rebuilt for ever in the heart; the Shekinah goes up into the high mountain and announces its reconstruction to the patriarchs.[3] In these also she herself is delivered,[4] and they dwell together henceforward in the Holy Land.[5] It is a foretaste of that time when all peoples shall enter under the wings of Shekinah,[6] as also of the day to come when evil shall be exterminated entirely and there shall be the same solemnity of festival as when the Holy One, blessed be He, created heaven and earth.[7] Let us therefore join our voice to those of the doctors who say that the Covenant with Shekinah will endure for ever.[8]

Before attempting to place a reasonable interpretation on the materials that are now in our hands, it is necessary to complete the collection by certain additional particulars which to some extent stand by themselves.

The created Law is called the garment of Shekinah[9]—a vesture, as METATRON is also, being perhaps the same vesture. It follows that she herself is something that dwells within it—as, for example, the Traditional, Oral and Secret Law which is not disclosed to the rank and file of believers because of the wickedness of the world. When the Created or External Law is broken below it is as if the sinner rent or removed the vestments of Shekinah, while alternatively those who observe the commandments have the same merit as if they clothed the Shekinah with garments.[10] Such is the work of sanctity in the higher conventions, according to the reverie of Israel. The MISHNA is the servant of Shekinah[11] and is also that helpmeet for man which is promised in Scripture.[12] Whether this interpretation could be elucidated by explaining in what sense the MISHNA—as part of the story of Israel—may be said to have tempted men, understood as those who are elect or are at least capable of election, and may have led them into the exile of the Fall, is another question; but the *tour de force* is not attempted in the ZOHAR. It might be affirmed truly that

---

[1] Z., Pt. II, fol. 160b; IV, 99.
[2] Ib., Pt. I, fol. 61a; I, 357.
[3] Ib., Pt. III, fol. 173b; V, 451.
[4] Ib., Pt. II, fol. 216b; IV, 229.
[5] Ib., fol. 222a; IV, 242.
[6] Ib., fol. 69b; III, 308, 309.—Is. ii. 2, 3.
[7] Ib., Pt. I, Appendix III, SECRET MIDRASH; II, 714.
[8] Ib., Pt. III, fol. 257a; V, 597.
[9] Ib., Pt. I, fol. 23a, b; I, 143.
[10] Ib., Pt. I, fol. 23a, b; DE PAULY, I, 143.
[11] Ib., fol. 27b; I, 174.
[12] Gen. ii. 18.

it took him further and further into the bondage of the letter. The text itself says only that the MISHNA was the spouse of Israel during his adolescence,[1] spouse also during his exile, though sometimes for and sometimes against him. The marriage was imperfect at best. During the adolescent period the MISHNA was pre-eminent over MATRONA, so that the King and MATRONA were separated from the Celestial Spouse.[2] It was the servant who took the place of the mistress. Perhaps the meaning is that the literal explanation in its excessive development clouded the spiritual sense of holy doctrine;[3] but if it be this, it is also more. Who then is the mistress? The answer, according to the ZOHAR, is that the Oral Law is the image of Elohim, and this we know to be Shekinah.[4]

There is one practical application of all this cloud of doctrine, and it may be summarised in a few words. It is prayer that attaches man to Shekinah, and as the Holy One is united constantly to her, it follows that by prayer man is attached to the Holy One.[5] All the angels open their wings to receive the Shekinah by prayer, and those on earth who wish their prayers to reach heaven should unite themselves with the Shekinah.[6] Whereas the gates of the palaces to which prayers ascend commonly have numerous guardians, those of the palace of Shekinah have none, and prayers enter unhindered.[7] It will seem at first sight that she occupies in Kabbalism the same position of intercessor which is ascribed to the Blessed Virgin by the devotion of the Latin Church, yet having regard to Shekinah's incorporation with the Divine Hypostases, I incline to think that the analogy is misleading. In view of all that has been done to Christianise Kabbalism by every good means, and by so many that are bad intellectually, one has to be very careful about reading Christian implicits into the text of the literature.[8]

---

[1] Z., Pt. I, fol. 27b; I, 174.   [2] *Ib.*, fol. 27b, 28a; I, 175.
[3] We have had one example previously to shew that the sense of darkness and uncertainty alternated with the sense of light. The successors of Rabbi Simeon were not like that doctor himself, who had apparently William Postel's key of things kept secret from the foundation of the world. They were rather like the second circle of Brothers of the Rosy Cross, of whom it was said to be doubtful whether they were admitted to all things. It is clear, by their own confession, that they did not understand all things.
[4] Z., Pt. II, fol. 161b; IV, 102.   [5] *Ib.*, Pt. I, fol. 24a; I, 148, 149.
[6] *Ib.*, fol. 279b, 280a; II, 648.   [7] *Ib.*, fol. 24a; I, 148.
[8] Undesigned Christian reflections are another matter, and I have mentioned a few out of many possible examples.

There is a question whether my next and last point of analysis had better be taken here or in a later chapter; but as I have mentioned Christian implicits, and as what I have to say seems to connect with this subject, I will incorporate it under that motive, though it has also other issues. We have come across already in our quest many allusions to the Divine Father, the Divine Son, being two of the Christian Hypostases, and as we know that the Shekinah in transcendence is also the Divine Mother, the question arises naturally whether this is the Holy Spirit, the Third Person of the Christian Trinity.[1] Those who are acquainted with Theology will know that the Third Person is not recognised as feminine, though there has been a tendency in several modern departments of semi-Christian Transcendentalism to regard the Holy Spirit in this light and thus complete the triad of the Divine Family. They forget, however, that neither in the East nor the West—under the ægis of the Greek or Roman Orthodoxy—is the Son held to proceed from the Father and the Spirit, but on the contrary that the last is postulated as proceeding from the Father and the Son. Albeit the *Filioque* clause of the Nicene Creed was a ground of division between the two branches of the Church Catholic, as not of apostolical authority, I have heard that it is not denied otherwise in the Greek Rite. One alternative would be the co-equal and co-eternal procession of the Son and the Spirit from the Divine Father, and the symbol in this case would be a triangle with the apex upward, not in the reverse position which characterises Latin Theology. Now it cannot be said that either doctrinal position represents the mind of Kabbalism. We have seen that Jehovah Elohim, Spouse and Bride, Father and Mother, God and His Shekinah are in KETHER in a state of oneness, without separation and without distinction. There are very few references to this state in the ZOHAR. I have intimated indeed that there is only one which can be quoted with complete certainty in the wording, but I am justified thereby in saying that it is a state corresponding to that of parentage. They reproduce themselves immediately below as ABBA and AIMA, referred to CHOKMAH and BINAH.

---

[1] I have said that it arises naturally, but I do not mean that we should do much in this manner to complete the Christian Triad in Kabbalism. Readers who have followed my study up to this point will find little ground for comparison between Those who dwell in the Sephirotic Supernals and Father, Son and Holy Ghost in the Heaven of St. Thomas Aquinas, or other of the Latin Doctors.

But as in the Supernals the Divine Persons are not in a state of separation, so the male and female in these SEPHIROTH are one with those which are in KETHER. It follows that Shekinah is on both sides of the Tree, as I have said elsewhere in this section, and it is difficult to postulate in such a triad either a time conception or passage from subject to object. But the Trinity was working towards manifestation, and the result was that ABBA and AIMA begat the Son, who is VAU in DAATH, from which His personality was extended through six of the lower SEPHIROTH. They begat also the Daughter and Bride, at first implied in the Son, but afterwards separated and extended with him through the three worlds below ATZILUTH. Later Kabbalism locates the conception of YOD in CHOKMAH, excogitated as King and Father; HE in BINAH, as Queen and Mother; VAU posited in the Six Briatic and Yetziratic SEPHIROTH from CHESED to YESOD inclusive, but enthroned especially as the Son in TIPHERETH; while the HE final is in MALKUTH. So far as I have been able to see, the particular variations of arrangement are not destitute of Zoharic authority. It must be recognised perhaps that there are two separate arrangements of the Tree of Life in the text. There is that which I have followed, drawing largely from THE BOOK OF MYSTERY and the three IDRAS, and there is its alternative which can be extracted—not without some confusion—from other parts of the collection. According to this the Father and Mother are in KETHER, the Son Who is the Word is in CHOKMAH, the Daughter and Bride is in BINAH. Now the Divine Name attributed to KETHER is JAH, formed of JOD and HE primal belonging to the TETRAGAM. It is said to be the Unknown God for whom the Name in question is that which the Propitiatory was for the Tabernacle—a summary of the male world above and the female world below. It is the Name of the Ancient of Ancients; it is the synthesis of all things below and above. It follows in the arrangement that the VAU is referable to CHOKMAH and the HE final to BINAH, who descended to MAKLUTH, as the Bride or Shekinah in manifestation. Once more, Shekinah is really in every part as well as on both sides of the Tree, being the Mistress of the height and the deep, President over the four quarters of the universe of created things and all that led up thereto.

Now the French editor and translator of the ZOHAR have an arrangement peculiar to themselves, by virtue of which

YOD or the male principle, understood as the Father, is allocated to KETHER; HE, understood as Shekinah, is in CHOKMAH; while VAU in BINAH is the Holy Spirit. The Christian Trinity is thus complete, though the question of procession is left to account for itself as it may. The attribution is part of a scheme for decoding the mystery of Shekinah along a particular line in connection with Zoharic doctrine respecting Messiah, and it will be considered in full later on. The question which arises here is whether Shekinah, by us allocated to BINAH, is or is not the Holy Spirit. The editor and translator maintain that she is not, and the fact that two opinions are possible on the subject implies that the ZOHAR is either not at one with itself or utters an uncertain voice. There are many references, and perhaps there is a mean between them. It is manifest in the first place that the Holy Spirit is personified in the ZOHAR, and a preliminary point is whether we can find authority for this in the Old Testament. "Take not thy Holy Spirit from me," [1] says David, and according to Isaiah the people of Israel vexed God's Holy Spirit.[2] He asks also: "Where is He that put His Holy Spirit within him?"[3]—meaning Moses, adding that "The Spirit of the Lord" caused Moses to rest. I do not know whether these can be called personifications, but they exhaust the allusions in the Old Testament which are connected with the distinctive qualification of "holy." We know that "the Lord put his spirit upon them";[4] that "the spirit rested upon them and they prophesied";[5] that Joshua was "a man in whom is the spirit";[6] that God hardened his spirit";[7] that "the spirit came upon Amasai";[8] that David gave to Solomon all the designs for the temple "that he had by the spirit";[9] that by His spirit God "garnished the heavens";[10] that God sends forth His spirit;[11] that there is a spirit poured from on high,[12] and Isaiah also says that "the Lord God and His spirit hath sent me," *i.e.*, on the prophet;[13] that "the spirit of the Lord God is on me," *i.e.*, Isaiah;[14] that the spirit took up Ezekiel;[15] and that according to Zechariah God sent in His spirit by former prophets.[16] There is a sheaf of other

---

[1] Ps. li. 11.
[2] Is. lxiii. 10.
[3] Is. lxiii. 14.
[4] Numbers xi. 29.
[5] *Ib.*, xi. 26.
[6] *Ib.*, xxvi. 18.
[7] Deut. ii. 30.
[8] 1 Chron. xii. 18.
[9] *Ib.*, xxviii. 12.
[10] Job xxvi. 13.
[11] Ps. civ. 30.
[12] Is. xxxii. 15.
[13] Is. xlviii. 16.
[14] Is. lxi. 1.
[15] Ezek. iii. 12.
[16] Zech. vii. 12.

allusions, but enough has been quoted for the purpose in hand. They may be kept in mind by the reader in connection with the Zoharic allusions which will follow hereon. He shall decide for himself—as I have no wish to adjudicate—whether there is more explicit personification in the Kabbalistic text, and if so whether it is to be accounted for by (1) natural development of ideas; (2) Jewish tendencies prior to the TALMUDS, represented roughly by Philo and, as such, a possible common source for Kabbalistic Jew and Christian; (3) Talmudic evidence; or (4) the atmosphere of Christian doctrine in which the Kabbalistic Jew lived and moved for the most part and which he can have scarcely failed to absorb in some degree.

I will take first of all those references which are either dubious or appear to suggest that the Holy Spirit is not synonymous with Shekinah.

The ZOHAR asks: what is signified by the words: "And the Spirit returns to Elohim who gave it?"[1] The answer is that one of the words designates Shekinah, that word being אלהים = Elohim, while another word designates the Holy Spirit, *i.e.*, the word רוח = "spirit." It might seem therefore that the Holy Spirit is not Shekinah but is in close connection therewith, like a breath that goes forth and returns.[2] It does not signify for our purpose that the ZOHAR is making a false interpretation—seeing that the spirit mentioned in Scripture is that of man. Again, it is said that when man is circumcised he is joined to the sacred crown of Shekinah and the Holy Spirit rests upon him.[3] In another place three spirits are distinguished: (1) The Spirit below, which is called the Holy Spirit; (2) the Spirit of the Middle Way, which is that of Wisdom and Understanding; (3) the Spirit which sounds the trumpet and unites the fire to the water, this being the Superior, Concealed and Mysterious Spirit, whereunto are suspended all sacred spirits and all luminous countenances.[4] Now, it is stated, after the prevailing manner of the ZOHAR, which cannot postulate a triad apart from an inward unity, that these three are one and that

---

[1] "And the spirit shall return unto God who gave it."—Eccles. xii. 7. Authorised Version, for which the Revised Version substitutes: "And the spirit returns." *Cf.* Vulgate: *Et spiritus redeat ad Deum, qui dedit illum.*
[2] Z., Pt. II, fol. 97b; III, 390.   [3] *Ib.*, Pt. III, fol. 14b; V, 42.
[4] *Ib.*, Pt. III, fol. 26a; V, 73, 74.

they form a holocaust which is the Holy of Holies.¹ This, however, is explained elsewhere to be Shekinah, for—as we have seen—she is the sacrifice which God has placed on His right and His left hand, and about Him.² Again, " she is the sacrifice of the Holy One," and prayer is the holocaust which in turn is offered to her.³ Once more, it is said that when the Shekinah resided in the Holy Land the impure spirit took flight and found refuge in the abyss, while the Holy Spirit was diffused throughout the world, so that the one would seem to be associated closely with the other, if we can presume that there is indeed distinction.⁴ In this connection the Holy Spirit is spoken of as the cloud that covered the Tabernacle; but the same cloud has been identified otherwise with Shekinah and with Metatron. It will be seen so far that it would be difficult to quote anything more indecisive. There is, however, one memorable passage which I have reserved to the last, and must cite almost *in extenso*. " A tradition tells us that at the hour when Moses, the true prophet, was about to be born into the world, the Holy One caused the Holy Spirit to come forth from the Tabernacle "—elsewhere that which seems to be the abode of Shekinah in transcendence. God entrusted all power thereto and innumerable keys of power, together with five diadems, the splendour of which enlightened a thousand worlds. " The Sacred King exalted the Holy Spirit in His palace and set Him above all celestial legions "—even as Shekinah is placed above all angels. " These were in great amazement, for they saw that the Holy One was resolved to change the face of the world by the intermediation of the Holy Spirit." They began to inquire concerning " Him," and were told to prostrate themselves, because " He " would descend one day among men, and the Law—till then hidden—should be revealed. They did homage accordingly, and thereafter the Holy Spirit ascended towards the King. The three letters, MEM, SHIN and HE, belonging to the name of Moses, offered their worship also; and then the Holy Spirit, in fulfilment of what had been fore-

---

¹ Z., Pt. III, fol. 26a; V, 73, 74.
² *Ib.*, Pt. I, fol. 24a; I, 149.
³ *Ib.*, fol. 256a; II, 604.
⁴ *Ib.*, Pt. II, fol. 269a; IV, 503. I may add that when Joseph saw Benjamin with the rest of his brethren, as related in Gen. xliii. 16, he is said by the ZOHAR to have discerned by the Holy Spirit (a) that Benjamin would have part in the Holy Land, and (b) that the Shekinah would reside therein. Whether this tends to identification or to the opposite might be difficult to affirm.—See *ib.*, Pt. I, fol. 202b; II, 405.

told, came down to earth, bearing the arms necessary to smite Pharaoh and his entire country. On reaching this world He found the Shekinah already here, radiant of aspect and spreading light through all the house.[1] It will be observed that the last sentence looks like an unqualified and conclusive distinction, though in its absence and from what has preceded in the extract one would have said that the Holy Spirit was actually a synonym of Shekinah. We hear nothing more, however, of any office in distinction, for that which henceforward abode with the Lawgiver was not the Holy Spirit but the glory of his Spiritual Spouse, who had been with him from his beginning on earth.

Let us now take the evidence in the contrary sense, proceeding in the same manner and remembering that there is only one testimony at most on the negative side of the subject.

In the first place, it is said—as we have seen indeed already—that the Holy Spirit inspired Leah concerning her work in connection with the foundation of the twelve tribes;[2] but we know otherwise that it is Shekinah who presides over birth, seeming to be in analogy with the chaste and conjugal Venus. In connection with the daughter of Jethro—who was the father-in-law of Moses—the Holy Spirit is affirmed to have been always with Moses,[3] which we may read in the light of another statement—that the Shekinah was associated with the orders which Moses gave to the experts charged with building the Tabernacle, because such work could not be accomplished properly without the inspiration of the Holy Spirit.[4] The association of Shekinah meant the enlightenment of the Holy Spirit. Here again is at least the close connection in virtue of which the one is not without the other, and the kind of nearness is illustrated more clearly by another passage which speaks of that day when God shall pour upon us the Holy Spirit of His Shekinah.[5] It would seem again to be the breath of Shekinah. Once more it is said that the Holy Spirit is called ZOTH,[6] being the name which designates the sign of the Sacred Covenant imprinted on man;[7] but we

---

[1] Z., Pt. II, fol. 53b, 54a; III, 241, 242.
[2] Ib., Pt. I, fol. 157a; II, 216.
[3] Ib., Pt. II, fol. 13b; III, 61.
[4] Ib., Pt. II, fol. 179b; IV, 149, 150.
[5] Ib., Pt. III, fol. 219a; V, 555.
[6] זאת = This, in its opposition to זלה or זה = That, understood as on the evil side. The ZOHAR cites a number of Biblical passages.
[7] Z., Pt. I, fol. 228a; II, 498.

shall see that this sign is connected especially with Shekinah. So also when Balaam lifted up his eyes,[1] he is supposed to have beheld Shekinah resting with poised wings above the twelve tribes of Israel, and to have questioned how he could prevail against them, seeing that the Holy Spirit was thus their stay and their protection. There seems no doubt that this is an equivalent of identification.[2] It is only at the end of the ZOHAR that we obtain a still more decisive voice on the affirmative side. The question is one of alleged or suggested criminal relations between Esther and Ahasuerus, which are characterised as slander, the ZOHAR adding that " she was clothed with the Holy Spirit,"[3] as it is written : " Esther put on her royal apparel "—or, as the passage renders it, " clothed herself with royalty." The interpretation follows immediately thus : " The Holy Spirit—this is the Shekinah with which Esther clothed herself."[4] It is an opportunity for a favourite form of testimony, and the great text adds : " Woe to those who feed upon the husk of the Law, while the grain of wheat is the mystical sense." It will be observed that, if words signify anything, this is not less than an unqualified and conclusive identification. If anyone will read over with care similar to my own the references which I have provided now on both sides of the question, I believe that they will conclude with me, as against the one definite statement on the negative side, that there is a cumulative affirmative evidence crowned by a most clear affirmation : " The Holy Spirit—this is the Shekinah."

When therefore the editor and translator of the ZOHAR allocate this Spirit to BINAH, it means that they are referring the Shekinah thereto, as I have done also, even if their design is in the opposite sense. But this Spirit is not the Third Person in the Blessed Trinity of Christendom, though it is impossible that it should not have aspects of likeness, in so far as the root of both doctrines is in the Holy Scriptures of Israel. I conclude on the authority of the text itself—which for once I must repeat at this point—that " from the constant and ardent love of HE " in BINAH " for YOD " in CHOKMAH " there issues VAU " in DAATH, conceived and born of HE,

---

[1] Num. xxiv. 2.
[2] As a fact, it is actually more than a simple equivalent.
[3] Z., Pt. III, fol. 275b ; VI, 47.
[4] *Ib.* See Esther v. 1.

THE MYSTERY OF SHEKINAH

by which also it is nourished.[1] "But VAU came into the world with a twin-sister bearing the name of Grace," which is CHESED, because Grace is Mercy. "The two took root on earth and constituted the HE final"—that is to say, in MALKUTH—because the male is not without the female—as we shall see—either above or below. "Thus was the VAU united to the HE" final. But in the completion, the perfection and harmony of the Divine Name, letter by letter and letter within letter, all these are one at the root: there would be separation proclaimed in the Divine Nature if YOD, HE, VAU, HE did not bear witness to His unity.[2]

The most important consideration which arises out of the whole subject is after what manner we are to regard essentially this Cohabiting or Indwelling Glory which is termed Shekinah in Scripture and in the sacred texts of the ZOHAR. We know that it dwelt between the Kerubim in the Tabernacle or Ark of Moses, and the Kerubim are said to have been male and female, types in the Sanctuary of Israel of things manifested on earth as types in their turn of the union that is above. When a mean is taken between all the cloud of references, it calls for no gift of interpretation to discern what lies with uttermost plainness on the surface; but we have explained nothing which is vital if we say that Shekinah is the principle of Divine Motherhood—that is, the feminine side of Divinity, implied in the logic of our symbolism when we speak of the Fatherhood in God. It is a case of being true to our symbols, and though this is of consequence intellectually, it remains thereat. If we turn to the analogy which subsists in virtue of the symbolism between womanhood above and that which is found below, we shall not proceed much further if there is brought home to us merely the notion that the office of the mother on earth is made sacred in a sense that is above the hallowed sense of Nature by the conception of its archetype in heaven. It has been present to us through all the Christian centuries in the popular and most catholic devotion to the Queen of Heaven, which, like so many other popular interests,

---

[1] Z., Pt. III, fol. 77b; V, 210, 211.
[2] The passage is important to my purpose, but it must be admitted that it is exceedingly confused. The meaning may be that in the extension of VAU through the worlds below ATZILUTH, the head of the Son is in DAATH—as we have seen otherwise—while that of his Bride and Sister is in CHESED, which, however, is on the male side of the Tree. I do not pretend to explain fully how the descent of the Son and Daughter constituted the HE final, for the VAU is distinct from the HE. But this has been touched upon in a previous note.

but those more especially that are consecrated by the greatest of all the Churches, adumbrates a vital truth in the spiritual life and a first principle in the world of reality. It has been a very sincere and whole-hearted devotion in those who have been drawn thereto; but the particular doctrine of miraculous and virgin birth, though eloquent and suggestive within its own measures, creates a clear line of demarcation between subject and object, so that there is a world-wide distinction between the honour paid to her who is ever outside ourselves and the adoration of Him Who is never understood essentially until He is realised within. Now, there are no prayers to Shekinah in the official liturgies of Jewish religion; but in the Secret Church of Israel, frequented in spirit and in truth by the Sons of the Doctrine, she is either the House of Prayer or else abides therein, and we have seen that her doors are open to prayers for ever. She was the great object of prayer, though it is to be questioned whether it was by the way of prescribed forms: it was rather by that prayer in the stillness of unexpressed thought about which we hear in the ZOHAR. The reason is ready to our hands, and the first light which may be said to fall on our subject is that the Shekinah is an Indwelling Glory. The Latin Kabbalists made use of the term *cohabitans* by an imperfect understanding on their own part of the mystery involved—that is to say, by a consideration of the external side which obtains in espousal-relations on earth. The proper word is *inhabitans*, for it is said that the Shekinah dwells in man,[1] being in the hearts of those who seek after good works zealously.[2] And more definitely: Man is the House of Shekinah.[3] The beginning of this inhabitation is when man makes a firm effort towards self-amendment, for by such turning the Shekinah is drawn towards him,[4] and to this condition are applied the words: " I am my beloved's and his desire is towards me."[5] Those with whom she dwells are those who are humbled and even broken by suffering.[6] Yet does she reign only where there is joy rather than sadness, an allusion to the support of trials with resignation. The suffering is, however, more especially that of which the root or cause is in love, being the state of those who are consumed by the love of the Divine: these

---

[1] Z., Pt. I, fol. 166a; II, 250.
[2] *Ib.*, Pt. II, fol. 128b; IV, 11.
[3] *Ib.*
[4] *Ib.*, Pt. I, fol. 88b; I, 509.
[5] Song of Solomon vii. 10.
[6] Z., Pt. I, fol. 181a; II, 315.

are the Brothers of Shekinah.¹ Again, it is said that the work of Shekinah below is comparable to that which the soul accomplishes in the body: more accurately still it is the same work,² and this enables us to understand in what sense she is termed the soul of the Tabernacle below,³ which Tabernacle is the sacred body of man.

I have called these intimations a first light, but I have not intended to exaggerate their value as such. I speak as a mystic; we have heard for two thousand years that God is within and His kingdom, yet the world remains comparable rather to the wilderness without the Holy City than to the blessed Zion; and if Shekinah is offered to us in the secret literature of Jewry as that aspect of the Divine Nature or Principle which is realisable by the heart of man, I do not see that we have added anything to our subject. It is idle to decode books of Secret Doctrine unless they have something more definite to tell us concerning the way, the truth and the life. So also it is beautiful to hear that whosoever wrongs a poor person is guilty of wrong to Shekinah, because she is the protectress of the poor;⁴ but we know too well already about things which grieve the Spirit. I might multiply these quotations, and it would serve no greater purpose; the question would remain then which remains now: the Secret Doctrine of Israel either covers a mystery of knowledge wherein there lies possible a mystery of certitude in experience or it is a temple in a waste of thought, far from any city of refuge and filled only with confused rumours or raving of empty words. Now, I have performed many arid journeys in my time and have returned with an empty wallet; but if this had been one of them I should not have written its itinerary in the present study of the ZOHAR. There have been recurring intimations there and here in these pages concerning a Mystery of Sex; it is imposed upon me now to affirm that this is the Mystery of Shekinah; and the nature of such Mystery corresponds—according to its veiled claim—with the definition which I have just given concerning a knowledge and an experience. The point and centre of the whole subject is the Indwelling Glory; it is declared everywhere,

---

[1] Z., Pt. I, fol. 181a; II, 315.
[2] *Ib.*, Pt. II, fol. 140b; IV, 45.
[3] *Ib.*
[4] Z., Pt. II, fol. 86b; III, 355. See also Is. lvii. 15.

but everywhere also it is concealed : one aspect of its presentation—amidst great hiddenness of wording—suggests that the entrance of the High Priest into the Holy of Holies belongs to the Mystery of Sex [1]; but I do not propose to pursue this intimation, as it seems to me like that fiftieth gate which was not opened by Moses, and, moreover, the fitting time is not yet. I will resume rather the conference by saying that, according to the ZOHAR, the union of male and female is Modesty,[2] and that the title to behold the face of Shekinah is one of purity.[3] It seems true therefore to say that she is the Law of the Mystery, and the ZOHAR quotes concerning her, " When thou goest, it shall lead thee ; when thou sleepest, it shall keep thee ; and when thou awakest, it shall talk with thee." [4] The study of this Law is life eternal.[5] Considered as a law, it implies a covenant, and of this covenant Joseph is said to be the image, because of his continence in respect of Potiphar's wife.[6] Having tabulated these premises and thus secured a point of departure, we have to approach again the great text and see after what manner it will shed light on the research.

It is specified that Shekinah dwelt with Israel prior to the captivity, meaning probably the captivity in Babylon, and the sin which brought about this exile was equivalent to the uncovering of the hidden physical centre of Shekinah. I am speaking here under great difficulty and am somewhat exchanging terms, for this Minerva and Diana of Israel is a woman, like Isis, and her veil is not to be lifted. The French translators finish the quotation under notice with the help of the Latin tongue, and it reads : *Traditum est . . . genitales partes Shekinæ existere*.[7] This also is a sacrament, but we can understand the meaning by assuming that Shekinah in such a connection signifies the Secret Doctrine in so far as it was a mystery of sex, and the ZOHAR goes on to particularise the alleged sin as a crime of incest, by which we must understand some illegal and reprobate application of the sex doctrine. It matters nothing to our subject if on the surface of Scripture the accusation seems without warrant : to justify the hermeneutics of the ZOHAR would be a task as much beyond my

---

[1] Z., Pt. III, fol. 66b ; V, 182. The hour of entrance is when the Sacred King is united to MATRONA.
[2] *Ib.*, fol. 145b ; V, 375.
[3] *Ib.*, Pt. II, fol. 60b ; III, 268, 269.
[4] Prov. vi. 22.
[5] Z., Pt. I, fol. 175b ; II, 290.
[6] *Ib.*, fol. 184a ; II, 327.
[7] *Ib.*, fol. 27b ; I, 173.

province as beyond my powers of pleading.[1] But we begin to see in this manner the kind of problem that has been taken in hand.

It is said further that the Mystery of Shekinah comprises all women, and this—as we have seen—is why she does not abide except with him who is united to a woman.[2] She is fixed definitely in the house of man when he marries, *et quum fœderis suum signum in locum ponit*.[3] This is why the HE and the VAU follow each other in the alphabet—VAU being the symbol of the male and HE of the female principle. Husband and wife are one, and a ray of celestial grace covers them; it descends from CHOKMAH, penetrates the male principle, and the latter communicates it to the female.[4] We can understand therefore in what sense her shame is the defiled body of man,[5] and how she is weighted by the sin of Israel.[6] The reason is that she is a virgin betrothed to the Middle Pillar,[7] and of her it was said by Adam in the great day of his perfection: "This is now bone of my bones and flesh of my flesh,"[8] which is to affirm that in one of her aspects she is the type of stainless womanhood; but she passes ever into espousals below—as she is ever in espousals above—for the fulfilment of herself in humanity, and of all humanity in her. The evidence is that when there is a just man on earth the Shekinah cleaves to him and does not leave him henceforth.[9]

It will be observed that in order to gain the particular point at a given moment the ZOHAR is valiantly careless of that which goes before, as of that which may be designed to come after. The history of the Fall of man through the intermediation of woman, acting under the virus of the serpent, is by no means the history of Shekinah, unless under a special aspect and as a remote reflection; but when it is sought to shew that she is nearer to the elect than hands and

---

[1] As a matter of fact, the idea is drawn from the TALMUD, which enumerates various cases of the crime in question, but the reference in the ZOHAR is to be understood spiritually, as of an assault on Shekinah, who—as we have seen—is the sister of all men. From all modern points of view and feeling, this kind of symbolism is unfortunate and disconcerting enough; but I think that the Sons of the Doctrine, if they had been challenged on the subject, would have replied with Gerald Massey that Nature is not ashamed of her emblems.

[2] Z., Pt. I, fol. 228b; II, 501.
[3] *Ib.*, fol. 94a; I, 536.
[4] *Ib.*, fol. 94a; I, 537.
[5] *Ib.*, Pt. III, fol. 75a, b; V, 205.
[6] *Ib.*, fol. 28a; V, 79.
[7] *Ib.*, Pt. I, fol. 28a; I, 178.
[8] Gen. ii. 23. The interpretation of this text in this strange manner is like an opening into a great vista of the Secret Doctrine.
[9] *Ib.*, fol. 66b; I, 391.

feet are near, it is difficult to find anything more complete in its correspondence than such words as "bone of my bones and flesh of my flesh,"[1] and the use of the text—so long as it is apart from the context—happens to be a true one, though it is about as literal in its application as is the tale of the Garden of Eden. So also when the ZOHAR wishes to apply that idea of a "field which the Lord hath blessed"[2] to the Mystery of Sex, it is not above saying that the King who "tills the field"[3] or is "served by the field" is the Shekinah, sex-contradiction notwithstanding. The object is to indicate that the dwelling of Shekinah in the house of those who are married is to bring about the descent of souls to animate children under her presidency.[4] But perhaps there was never an instance so much to our purpose as the statement that on the day when the Song of Solomon was revealed below, the Shekinah descended[5]—as if for the first time, though we know that she had been with man from the beginning and had shared in the whole creation. The object, however, is to shew that this glorious canticle is the world's history of her in man, the beginning and end of all that belongs to the union, the Mystery of the Lover and the Beloved throughout the ages of election. It is the summary of Holy Scripture; it is the work of creation, the mystery of the patriarchs, the exile in Egypt, the exodus of Israel, the Decalogue and manifestation on Sinai, the emblem of all events during the sojourn in the desert, thence to the entrance into the Holy Land and so forward to the building of the Holy Temple. It is also a summary of the Mystery contained in the Sacred and Supreme Name, of the dispersal of Israel through the nations, of its deliverance to come, the resurrection of the dead and the events leading up to that day which is called the Sabbath of the Lord. In a word, it contains all that hath been, is and ever shall be, for it is the story of that Isis who is Shekinah, from the first verses

---

[1] Gen. ii. 23.
[2] *Ib.*, xxvii. 27.
[3] Eccles. v. 9. The Authorised Version says: "The King is served by the field." Cf. Vulgate: *Et insuper universæ terræ rex imperat servienti*, and the Douay rendering: "Moreover there is the King that reigneth over all the land subject to him."—Eccles. v. 8.
[4] Z., Pt. I, fol. 122a; II, 91, 92.
[5] *Ib.*, Pt. II, fol. 143b; IV, 55. The putative authority is I. Kings viii. 11: "So that the priests could not stand to minister because of the cloud; for the glory of the Lord had filled the house of the Lord."

concerning the kisses of his mouth to the last rapture on the mountain of spices.[1]

Now, it is said that there is desire on the part of man to be united with the Mother in transcendence as well as with the Mother below, to attain her by perfection and to be blessed on account of her.[2] We know that this is a desire for Divine Union because Jehovah is Elohim, and in case such testimony should not be found full or sufficient, the ZOHAR adds elsewhere that the memorable words : " I am that I am " signify in their inward sense : " I, the Holy One, blessed be He, am the Shekinah."[3] It is certain that the state of union is not only deeper than the state of vision but differs generically therefrom, and I cannot say that I have found plenary Zoharic authority for the attainment of Divine Union in that proper sense of the term which is to be desired by the heart of the mystic. But the implicits are in many places, for we have seen that Shekinah is within. It is more often vision which is promised to the blessed in the world beyond, to gaze upon the face of Shekinah,[4] as in a substituted state of union, and the title must be earned in this life by the following of the path of purity.[5] It is affirmed in reference to this that those only who quit the lower world in the grace of Shekinah are judged worthy of eternal life.[6] So also there are some who do not die as men die commonly, but are ravished by the attraction which Shekinah exercises on their souls.[7] The Mother in transcendence is, however, like the Mother below, and spiritual communion with her is in so far as man has become a house or abode by attaching himself to the female : it is then that the Divine Mother pours down her blessings on both.[8]

There is—in the true sense of this term—a spiritual union below for the Sons of the Doctrine, so that they are encompassed by two females [9]—the wife who is on earth and the Unseen Helpmate. After what manner her presence is

---

[1] Z., Pt. II, fol. 144b ; DE PAULY, IV, 55, 56. It should be understood that while I have not given an actual translation of the passage I have kept faithfully to its sense. My readers may recognise with myself at this stage that, with due regard to the logical inviolability of distinct schools of symbolism, all Sufic imagery concerning the Lover and Beloved belongs to Shekinah and might have come forth with all its adornments from the Secret Tradition in Israel and its intimations on MATRONA and TABOONAH.

[2] It is a question of integration in the Zoharic law of correspondences.
[3] Ib., Pt. I, fol. 23a ; I, 140.
[4] Ib., Pt. II, fol. 40b ; III, 189.
[5] Ib., fol. 60b ; III, 268, 269.
[6] Ib., Pt. I, fol. 82a ; I, 473.
[7] Ib., fol. 16b ; II, 99.
[8] Ib., fol. 50a ; I, 292.
[9] Ib.

realised never transpires definitely in the text, but—as there is no need to say—it is by spiritual apprehension only. Curiously enough, this does not appear at its best in connection with views on the nuptial state itself but in discourses of the Sons of the Doctrine on the Traditional Law : they are conscious then of the presence of Shekinah and testify respecting it continually with no uncertain voice. It must be said that the women of Israel are never present at the debates,[1] but their place in the house insured that of the Divinity. When, however, the master of the Law was going by himself upon a journey, and when, technically speaking, the male was to be apart from the female, he was not for that reason in a state of separation from Shekinah, supposing that he had prayed to the Holy One before starting,[2] in order to maintain the union between male and female abroad as well as at home. Another condition was that he must watch over all his actions in every phase of life :[3] otherwise he might be separated from his Spiritual Companion, putting a stop to the union and rendering himself an incomplete being.

It is scarcely desirable at this stage to speak of anything so obvious and familiar as the known characteristics of oriental imagery, to recall for example the personifications of Wisdom in the books ascribed to King Solomon ; but the literary vestures of these experienced two curious developments. The titles and offices of the Hebrew CHOKMAH were raised bodily from their setting and transferred to the Blessed Virgin by the compilers of the Roman Breviary, while through another channel they passed over to the Gnostic SOPHIA and by a last transition into the Virgin Wisdom of Jacob Böhme and the later mystics of his school. The correspondences between Shekinah and the Christian Mother of God are rather plausible on the surface and may be deceptive to that extent, because shallow analogies still deceive many ; but even the unusual predispositions which led up to the French translation of the ZOHAR have not permitted its editors to postulate that Shekinah is a veil of Mary. The correspondences between the Indwelling Glory and the Virgin Sophia of Böhme are so much closer that they cannot fail to create an impression that

---

[1] I remember, however, that there is a solitary exception in favour of an innkeeper's daughter, who was present when her husband exhibited his knowledge of the Hidden Law before a company of adepts.—Z., Pt. II., fol. 166a ; IV, 111.
[2] Z., Pt. I, fol. 49b ; I, 289.   [3] Ib., fol. 50a ; I, 289.

the German Theosophist owed something to this source. There is nothing in his life to suggest that he was taught in any secret schools or was in communication with persons who were acquainted with the Secret Doctrine in Israel, though there were many Kabbalistic scholars at his period. There is one possible alternative—that the root-matter of Jewish tradition in the Scriptures of the Old Testament developed in his own consciousness, to some extent after the same manner as it did in that of the Sons of the Doctrine, so that in his case, as in others without number, it proved that true men and seers spoke the same language because they belonged to the same region of thought. They saw also in the same glass of vision. But the question, however interesting, is not of our real concern.

We have now considered the Shekinah in the light of all her attributes. I do not believe that I have omitted a single reference of the least importance found in the text of the ZOHAR, while all have been regarded critically. The conclusion reached is that Shekinah, as the president of a Mystery of Sex, is the direction in which we must look if—as labourers in this strange field—we are to obtain our wages. The other intimations are excellent and agreeable in their way, but that which we seek, in what is for us an untrodden region of thought, is some new message, which is not to be found in the other offices, qualities and virtues that characterise the Holy Guide of Jewry. I suppose that, here in conclusion, I have no real need to say that the Secret Doctrine in Israel is not one of sex only, though intimations concerning the latter are found everywhere. Eschatology, for example, is not of this order, nor are the parts of the soul in man, but with these things and with several others that are like them I have dealt at their value.

II.—THE MYSTERY OF SEX

I am entering in this division upon that part of my task which is at once most important and difficult. It may be an open question whether I should begin at the highest point of the research and thence work downward or take the opposite course and so—as the proverb counsels—proceed from small beginnings to the greater end. That is best which seems the simplest, and I have therefore chosen to work upwards from below. I will cite in the first place certain great axioms of the whole subject—as these have been proclaimed on the authority of the masters. It is testified that the union of the male and female must be a perfect union in the Mystery of Faith.[1] There is also another testimony, and this is that the title to behold the face of Shekinah is one of purity,[2] the scholium on which—though it lies far away in the text—is that modesty is the union of the male and female;[3] and it may be remembered in this connection that the most cryptic of all texts in the ZOHAR—containing the mysteries of Divine Personalities—is called THE BOOK OF CONCEALMENT OR OF MODESTY. These things being so, we may consider in the next place what is said on the subject of espousals, as these are known on earth. There is one definition which is in keeping with the Tradition at large, and this is that marriage is the union of the Sacred Name here below[4]—that is, its completion in each person. The thesis appertaining hereto is that circumcision is the symbol of all purity in sexual intercourse;[5] that Israel is placed on this account in purity as a starting-point and enters under the wings of Shekinah.[6] This sacred sign of the Covenant constitutes the root-matter of the Sacred Name and of the Mystery of Faith.[7] As the sun enlightens the world, so the sacred sign enlightens the body; as a buckler protects man, so does this: no evil spirit can approach him who preserves it in purity.[8] But as the advantage is greater with which the children of Israel begin their earthly life, so is the responsibility greater if they make the Covenant of no effect in their own persons.

Now, the Sacred Name is never attached to an incomplete man, being one who is unmarried, or one who dies without issue.[9] Such a person does not penetrate after death into the vestibule of Paradise,[10] on account of his incompleteness. He is like a tree that is rooted up, and he must be planted anew—that is to say, he must suffer rebirth, as we have seen, in order

---

[1] Z., Pt. I, fol. 101b; II, 11.
[2] Ib., Pt. III, fol. 213a; V, 542; ib., Pt. II, fol. 60b; III, 268, 269.
[3] Ib., Pt. III, fol. 145b; V, 375. Man is perfect only when he comprises male and female; it is then that he fears sin and then that the title of modest is conferred upon him. But here is the sum of the whole subject passing into expression at the highest.
[4] Ib., Pt. III, fol. 7a; V, 18.
[5] Ib., Pt. I, Appendix III, SECRETS OF THE LAW; II, 721, 722.
[6] Ib., fol. 95a; I, 543. [9] Ib., Pt. I, fol. 48a; I, 278.
[7] Ib., Pt. II, fol. 3b; III, 10. [10] Ib., fol. 66a; I, 388; ib., fol. 48a; I, 278.
[8] Ib.

that the Sacred Name may be completed in all directions.[1] The command to increase and multiply, which means the procreation and engendering of children, is to spread the radiance of the Sacred Name in every direction, by collecting spirits and souls which constitute the glory of the Holy one—above and below. Whosoever fails to apply himself to the fulfilment of this command diminishes the figure of his Master and prevents it descending here below.[2] The last statement refers of course to the making of man, male and female, in the likeness of the Elohim. It is said also that the paucity in the descent of souls is the reason why Shekinah does not come down into this world,[3] with which is to be compared the affirmed presence as the Indwelling Glory throughout the whole creation. God blessed Adam because they were made together male and female, and blessings are found only where male and female are united for the fulfilment of the purpose of creation,[4] which—according to the counsel of the Elohim—was to increase, multiply and replenish the earth. It was not good for man to be alone because this end was in a state of frustration. It may be even that the Zoharic legend concerning male and female being originally side by side is only a veiled way of indicating that they were not in the marital estate.[5] Afterwards they were face to face, signifying the fulfilment of the precept.

I have now dealt briefly with what may be called the principles at issue, and we have next to see after what manner those who exalted so highly the nuptial state gave instruction, so to speak, on its practice here below. The doctrine was that no marriage is made on earth before it is proclaimed in heaven, and that the Holy One accomplishes unions in the world above before the descent of souls on earth.[6] About

---

[1] Ib., Z., Pt. I., fol. 66a; I, 388; ib. fol. 48a; I, 278. [2] Ib., fol. 272b; II, 641.

[3] Z., Pt. I, fol. 272b; II, 641. The reference is really to her manifestation and not to her immanence. She stands at the door and knocks, but those who should welcome her in keep fast their precincts and tyle their portals. This, however, is symbolism; it is more true to say that we fail to realise her presence in our consciences.

[4] Ib., Pt. I, fol. 165a; II, 245.

[5] I have put this tentatively, as I wish to leave some conclusions in the hands of my readers; but there is no question that Zoharic teaching is clear on the point, not only in what it implies but in what is expressed frequently. Whether there was ever such an epoch in the history of the human soul is another question. We must remember that the object of the soul's legends is not the delineation of putative histories, but the symbolical administration of possibilities inherent in the soul. That which is indicated here is a transcendental union between the Lover and Beloved, of which the nuptial union on earth is a type and to which it may be a path of approach.

[6] Ib., fol. 229a; II, 503.

the last point we shall see at a later stage. In practice the Sons of the Doctrine were separated as far from the uninitiated world of Israel as the chosen people at large were separated *ex hypothesi* by the fact of their circumcision. There is a particular sense in which it is held that the union here below between husband and wife is the work of the Holy One, and herefrom, as from other considerations, arises the sanctity and necessity of that act which is implied by the word union.[1] After what manner the Divine is said to intervene therein, or perhaps I should say to overshadow it, is indicated by the theory that man is formed below on the model of that which is above.[2] It follows that he who, in Zoharic terminology, suffers his fount to fail and produces no fruits here—whether because he will not take a wife, whether his wife is barren, or whether he abides with her in a way that is against Nature—commits an irreparable crime.[3] " It is vain . . . to sit up late "[4] are words that designate those who do not marry till an advanced age, for it is woman who constitutes the repose of man.[5] Hereof, according to the text, is the peace of espousals, and in further variation of the testimony which recurs continually, it is added that man shall participate in the world to come because he has entered during this life into the joy of living honourably with his wife.[6] The reason is that soul as well as body shares in the *gaudium inexprimabile* by which children are engendered. This is the eroticism which characterises the ZOHAR, according to commentators : but as the Doctors of the Law beheld the Supreme Mystery in sex, it is obvious that whatever belongs thereto is explained thereby.[7]

And now as regards the practice, the thesis is that whoever

---

[1] Z., Pt. I, fol. 186b ; II, 337.
[2] *Ib.*, fol. 186b ; II, 338.
[3] *Ib.*
[4] Ps. cxxvii. 2.
[5] Z., Pt. I, fol. 187a ; II, 340. See also Pt. III, fol. 108a ; V, 274, where it is said, on the authority of Rabbi Eleazar, son of Rabbi Simeon, that the HE is the repose of beings above and below—above being the rest of the Shekinah in transcendence and below of the Shekinah in manifestation.
[6] *Ib.*, Pt. I, fol. 90b ; I, 515 ; *ib.*, Appendix III, SECRET MIDRASH, fol. 14b, 15a ; II, 694 ; *ib.*, fol. 187a ; II, 340.
[7] It is about the worst word that could be selected by a scholar and a critic who is alive to the issues of his subject. Coventry Patmore's young lady thought that the sacrament of marriage was rather a wicked sacrament, but the Zohar raises it into realms of which Christian Churches have never dreamed, though I have met with some rare aspects of Latin Theology which seem to indicate that a Redeemer may live hidden therein.

sanctifies himself at the moment of intercourse shall have children who will not fear the tempter-spirit. This is the consequence respecting the fruit of marriages, but there is also a consequence within the measures of the union itself, so that it is raised from the physical into a spiritual degree, from the mode of Nature into the mode of Grace.[1] The fulfilment of a particular precept is the condition attaching hereto and this is the raising of the heart and mind on the part of the Lover and Beloved, to the Most Holy Shekinah, the glory which cohabits and indwells, during the external act.[2] The *absconditus sponsus* enters into the body of the woman and is joined with the *abscondita sponsa*.[3] This is true also on the reverse side of the process, so that two spirits are melted together and are interchanged constantly between body and body. The sexes are then interchanged also in a sense, as the sex of METATRON is said to be transformed momently before the veil of palms and pomegranates on the threshold of the Inmost Shrine in the Supernals.[4] In the indistinguishable state which arises it may be said almost that the male is with the female neither male nor female: at least they are both or either. So is man affirmed to be composed of the world above, which is male, and of the female world below.[5] The same is true of woman.

Now according to the ZOHAR those words in the Song of Solomon: "Thy breasts are better than wine"[6] refer to that wine which provokes joy and desire; and seeing that—in an alternative manner of language—all things are formed above according to a pattern which is reproduced faithfully below, it is held to follow that when desire awakens beneath it awakens also on high.[7] Herein lies the sanctity of espousals

---

[1] It is added significantly that herein the Holy One exercises such providence over man that he may not be lost in the world to come.

[2] There are many references, but perhaps the most signal is Z., Pt. I, fol. 50a; I, 290.

[3] *Ib.*, Pt. II, fol. 101b; III, 410.

[4] This intimates what, by the hypothesis, can be accomplished in nuptials, through the purification of body and mind, towards the union of souls. The statement in the ZOHAR on which my words are based seems to contain the elements of the whole mystery on the manifest side and after what manner that which is now only mutual in a complete distinction may be unified by experience in consciousness. I am somewhat veiling my meaning because it is not possible to speak *ad clerum*.

[5] Z., Pt. II, fol. 173b; IV, 128.

[6] In the majority of Scriptural quotations the translator of the Zohar has done his best to conform his rendering to the Vulgate: it was of course unlikely that he would follow any other version, and I am stating the fact only to shew that he has seldom translated *de novo*. Our Authorised Version of I, 2, reads: "Thy love is better than wine," and the Vulgate: *Quia meliora sunt ubera tua vino*.

[7] Z., Pt. I, fol. 70a, b; I, 415.

on earth and herefrom depends the need for exalting that sanctity and all that belongs to espousals into the highest grade. There are however two classes whose respective duties differ with the degrees of their election; there are those who are termed ordinary mortals, meaning the rank and file of the chosen people, but there are also the Sons of the Doctrine, chosen among the chosen out of thousands. The counsel imposed on the first class is to sanctify their conjugal relations in respect of the time thereof, which is fixed at midnight, or forward from that hour, the reason being that God descends then into Paradise and the offices of sanctity are operating in the plenary sense. But this is the time when the counsel to the Sons of the Doctrine is that they should arise for the study of the Law, for union thereby with the Community of Israel above and for the praise of the Sacred Name of God.[1]

The Sons of the Doctrine are described as reserving conjugal relations for the night of the Sabbath, being the moment when the Holy One is united to the Community of Israel.[2] The thesis is that God is One and as such it is agreeable to Him that He should be concerned with a single people. Out of this arises the question as to when man may be called one, and the answer is that this comes about when the male is united to the female in a holy purpose: it is then that man is complete, is one and is without blemish.[3] It is of this that the man and the woman must think at the moment of their union; it is in uniting bodies and souls that the two become one; man in particular is termed one and perfect; he draws down the Holy Spirit upon him and is called the Son of the Holy One, blessed be He.[4] According to Rabbi Simeon, the

---

[1] Z., Pt. III, fol. 81a; V, 224.
[2] *Ib.*, Pt. I, fol. 14a, b; I, 82. *Ib.*, Pt. III, fol. 81a; V, 224.
[3] *Ib.*
[4] *Ib.*, fol. 81b; V, 224. The intention here seems obvious, and it is to shew that beyond that process indicated by Gen. ii. 24, when it is said that " they shall be one flesh," there is another and higher process, in the fulfilment of which it is possible that they shall be one soul. The one is not, however, without the other, and this is a point to be marked because the contrary idea may be presented to some minds. The following curious speculation should be noticed in this connection. It is affirmed that the words: " In the beginning God created " (Gen. i. 1) conceal the same mystery as those other words: " And the rib which the Lord God had taken from man made He a woman " (*Ib.*, ii. 22). In " God created the heaven " the two last words conceal the same mystery as the words: " And brought her unto the man " (*Ib.*, ii. 22). In " God created the heaven and the earth " the three last words conceal the same mystery as " bone of my bones " (*ib.*, ii. 23). All designate " the earth of life."—Z., Pt. I, fol. 50b; I, 293, 294. But it is said also that the words " the heaven " signify Shekinah

relations of the patriarchs with their wives were actuated by a Supreme Mystery.[1] So long as Jacob was unmarried, God did not manifest to him clearly, and this mystery is familiar to those who are acquainted with the ways of the Law. After marriage he arrived at the perfection which is above, as distinguished from the perfection which is below, and God manifested to him clearly.[2] The explanation seems to be that the Supreme Wisdom is a Mystery of Sex,[3] as intimated on my own part previously.

Out of these considerations there arose a very curious question, of which I must speak at some length because—in its way—it is a characteristic development on the practical side and, within certain measures, it carries our subject further. The principle is that the male must be always attached to the female for the Shekinah ever to be with him.[4] All holiness might be practised, the Secret Doctrine might be studied by night and by day, and the illuminations thereof might overflow the intellectual part; but failing fulfilment of this radical counsel a man was not on the way which leads into true life.[5] He was in that condition in which " it is not good for man to be "[6]—alone, like Adam in the Garden.[7] But those who had the precept at heart and were therefore complete men, by their union with women on earth, remind us in one particular of many Sons of Israel and Students of Doctrine in the Middle Ages: they were travellers in search of wisdom; and they were also men of affairs, workers in the vineyard of this world as well as in the Garden of God. The ZOHAR is full of their little journeys and these, so far as possible, were taken one with another, that the Secret Doctrine might be studied on the way and that the presence of Shekinah might be secured thus for their consolation, protection and instruction as they fared forward. Great adventures befell them in the sense of the Mysteries of Doctrine, for strange

---

above, while the words " and the earth " denote Shekinah below, whose union shall be as perfect on a glorious day to come as the union of the male and the female.—Z., Pt. I, fol. 50b; I, 295.

[1] Ib., Pt. I, fol. 133b; II, 126.   [3] Z., Pt. I, fol. 150b; II, 193.
[2] Ib., fol. 150a; II, 192.   [4] Ib., fol. 49b; I, 289.
[5] There was otherwise a certain dispensation for the Sons of the Doctrine in respect of the fruit of intercourse. On the assumption that there was no issue they appear to have been spared the penalty of return into incarnation.
[6] Gen. ii. 18.
[7] He was held to be in a state of sickness, and as such was to be isolated from the offices of the altar. Only a man completed, and in this sense made perfect, by union with a woman, could offer sacrifice.—Z., Pt. III, fol. 5b; V, 12.

people went about in those days carrying, unknown to one another, the treasures of hidden knowledge. It was after all an unincorporated fraternity, and though it looks differently there and here, initiation was by a segregating principle, not by communication from a common centre of knowledge. The son of an instructed doctor might have advanced a great distance unknown to others, while occasionally an isolated student entered by his own reflections, and by grace descending into the heart, into the golden chain of tradition, so that he was not less in an illuminated state than if he had sat at the feet of Rabbi Simeon through the days and the years.

Now, journeys in search of wisdom or in the prosecution of business—which, it may be mentioned, was often of a humble kind—meant separation from the wife of the doctor's household, and this would seem at first sight to involve separation from Shekinah.[1] To remove this difficulty it was held sufficient (a) that the doctor should pray to the Holy One before starting, and (b) should watch over all his actions during the period of absence from home.[2] He would not be separated then from his spiritual companion, nor would he put that stop to the union between male and female which would render him an incomplete being. It was understood further that the counsel which prevailed abroad must prevail at home also, so that what was inculcated was really a precept of life. I feel that this might have been almost taken for a point of departure in respect of the Cohabiting Glory, if considerations of a different kind had not intervened. It occurs early in the ZOHAR—as a fact, in the first section—and concerning the Great Presence it postulates the dwelling of Shekinah with man.[3] The word cohabiting seems to be the correct word here, though it was obviously in an inward

---

[1] The position is a little fantastic, because in such case the same danger might arise from the isolation of a single hour: moreover, the notion discounts the whole value of unions realised in spirit and in truth, appearing to make physical contiguity more important than that nearness of heart which spatial considerations do not help or hinder. But the question seems raised in reality because it is an opportunity to enforce a practice of inward dedication after the best manner of the ZOHAR. As usual, the peg answers because it supports this lesson.

[2] Z., Pt. I, fol. 49b, 50a; I, 289.

[3] It is said elsewhere that Shekinah never separates from man so long as he observes the commandments of the Law.—Z., fol. 232a; II, 516. The authority is: "Behold I send an angel before thee, to keep thee in the way" (Ex. xxiii. 20); and: "I will send an angel before thee" (ib., xxxiii. 2). This is held to be the Liberating Angel to whom Jacob made allusion (Gen. xlviii. 16), who watches over man, who receives blessings from above and distributes them below.—Z., Pt. I, fol. 230a; II, 508; and fol. 228b; II, 502.

sense only that the Shekinah accompanied the Sons of the Doctrine in their recurring voyages and ventures. If not indwelling, she was their overshadowing grace and power; but they seem to have been conscious of a certain marriage state—spiritually realised—in their relation with her, though it was of course collective and not personal. Alternatively, there is a sense in which it was peculiar and catholic at one time, and this is an important point of analogy between the Holy Guide of the Sons of the Doctrine and that Christ Who is the Spouse of the soul. That this, however, is *per se* an insufficient ground for the identification of the two Divine Principles we are likely to see at the end. I need not add that the Shekinah appears throughout this section of the symbolism as distinctively feminine.

Recurring to the text, after having made these lawful inferences therefrom, the ZOHAR—with Rabbi Simeon as the mouthpiece of its teaching—is comprehensive and precise in its justice after the manner which obtains throughout. It is not in virtue of the man being side by side with the woman, as the legend depicts him previously, that Shekinah abides with man.[1] We have seen that this ancient mode was before all things imperfect. The man and the woman must be face to face, at once in the continuity and restrictions of the sacred mystical act. So also when, after days and weeks of travel, the Son of Doctrine returns to his home he must procure nuptial gratification to the wife of his heart, seeing that he has had the advantage of mystical union in his absence with the Companion or Helpmate who is on high.[2] In the deepest understanding of the subject, the one belongs to the other, that which is without being Zoharically as that which is within, and all the correspondences being aspects of one thing seen and done upon different planes of being. The external and expressed reason is, however, twofold : (1) be-

---

[1] See, among other places, Z., Pt. I, fol. 49a ; I, 284. I suppose that the reason is obvious from the Zoharic standpoint : contiguity is not union. It is obvious also, or should be, that we are not considering a Siamese-Twins symbolical legend. What lies at the heart of the story, regarded as hypothetically something of the far past, would be very difficult to decide if it were to be regarded as one of fact. It belongs to " the hunger and thirst of the heart " after a way to the blessed life through earthly espousals. Surely the Sons of the Doctrine must have found in their own marriages pearls of great price which their heirs have lost now, and of which we have not even dreamed. And yet we continue to hear rough things about the position of womanhood in Israel, sometimes even from converted Jews like that Chevalier Drach who chaffered and trafficked in his conversion—as it seems to me, more than enough.

[2] Z., Pt. I, fol. 50a ; I, 290.

cause there is Talmudic authority that conjugal relations on returning from a journey constitute a good work [1] and (2) every pleasure resulting from a good work is shared by Shekinah.[2] Furthermore, it is in such pleasure that the peace of the house is maintained, for the ZOHAR is much too modest and inclined spiritually to have any shyness over the physical and emotional facts of daily life. The Scriptural authority, obtained after the usual manner, is contained in the words: "Thou shalt know that thy tabernacle shall be in peace; and thou shalt visit thy habitation, and shalt not sin."[3] To abstain from conjugal relations in such a case would be indeed sinful, depreciating the work of the Companion on high, who cleaves to the man, but thanks only to his own union with his wife.[4] If subsequently there be fruit of this intercourse, the Heavenly Companion will provide a holy soul for the new-born child, the Shekinah being that Covenant which is termed: Covenant of the Holy One. The rule on return from a journey must be fulfilled therefore with the same zeal as the ordinance laid down by the wise regarding the restriction of conjugal relations to the day of the Sabbath, and it is apparently the only recognised exception thereto in the matter of times and seasons, unless of course an exception is made by Nature.

Finally, and this, which is assuredly a most strange, and within my experience of the sacred literature, an unique counsel, has been cited already: when man has in view the Shekinah [5] at the moment of his conjugal relations the pleasure which he experiences is a meritorious work. The reason—which has been explained also—is that the union below is an image of the union that is above. The mystery of the whole subject is the now familiar dogma that the Mother in transcendence abides with the male only in so far as he has constituted himself a house by his attachment to the female: there must be a local habitation, an union below to offer a point of contact with the union that is on high, and

---

[1] See Talmud, Tract YEBAMOTH.
[2] Z., Pt. I, fol. 50a; I, 290. She who suffers with Israel enters into joy with him.
[3] Job v. 24.
[4] Z., Pt. I, fol. 50a; I, 290.
[5] It is part of the contemplation of the absent and higher beauty in union with that beauty which, albeit lower, is present, manifest and is or may become sacramental. It is a memorial also that the union which is of time has, or may attain, a part in the union which is eternal, described in one place as the contemplation of the beauty of Shekinah, already mentioned.—*Ib.*, Pt. II, fol. 116a; III, 448, 449.

then the Divine Mother pours down her blessings therefrom—that is to say, on male and female in equal measures.¹ So is the male below said to be encompassed by two females, and all the ways of blessing in the two worlds are open before him.² He reads the Secret Doctrine in the womanhood on earth, and it is read to him by her who sits between the Pillars of the Eternal Temple with the Book of the Secret Law lying open on her sacred knees.³

Among its lesser objects the counsel concerning the Sabbath Day and the relations therein offers proof to the spirits of the evil side respecting the superiority of those on the side of goodness, meaning mankind, who being provided with bodies can fulfil the duties of procreation.⁴ Whosoever has intercourse with his spouse, on what day soever, must obtain her consent beforehand with words of affection and tenderness; failing consent, he should proceed no further, for the act of union must be willing and not constrained.⁵ Nuptial intercourse is interdicted during the day because of the words: "And he lighted upon a certain place, and tarried there all night, because the sun was set."⁶ Subject to these and the rest of the provisions, some of which I have omitted, because of their difficulties of expression,⁷ it is affirmed that blessed are those who sanctify the Sabbath Day by intercourse with their wives; for the Sons of the Doctrine it is a work consecrated to the Holy One, because the union of Matrona with the heavenly King has for its object to send

---

¹ Z., Pt. I, fol. 50a; I, 291. It is said also that Shekinah does the will of the master of the house.—*Ib.*, fol. 236b; II, 532. The reference on the surface is to Moses.

² *Ib.*, fol. 50a; I, 292.

³ It is important to note here what is involved by the illustration as a whole—namely, that man in his union with woman becomes a house in which the Divine Presence can dwell. Let us take another illustration, which is excellent and indeed admirable in its symbolism. The eye of man is said to be an image of the world; the white of the eye is an image of the great ocean by which earth is encompassed, and the latter is represented by the " internal circle " of the eye. Within this there is another circle, and it is called the image of Jerusalem, centre of the whole world. Finally there is the pupil, which corresponds to Zion, and this is the abode of Shekinah.—*Ib.*, fol. 226a; II, 490, 491. So also there are the parts of human personality—physical and mental parts—and there is the conscious centre wherein is the Divine Presence, awaiting realisation within us. The thesis is that marriage is a condition of realisation.

⁴ Z., Pt. I, fol. 14a, b; I, 82, 83.

⁵ *Ib.*, fol. 49a, b; I, 286.

⁶ Gen. xxviii. 11. Z., Pt. I, fol. 49b; I, 286.

⁷ In view of the sanctity which the Zohar attributes to the sex-act under the obedience of purity—which is marriage—there was a prohibition respecting its performance *in nuditate personarum*. Those who ignore it are subject to the visitation of demons and will produce epileptic children obsessed by Lilith. This is the case more especially if the light of a lamp is used. I do not know whether this has Talmudic authority.—Z., Pt. I, fol. 14b; I, 83.

down holy souls into this world, and the colleagues on earth seek to attract these sacred souls into their own children.[1] The theory of conception is that the Holy One and His Shekinah furnish the soul, while the father and mother provide the body between them [2]—heaven, earth and all the stars of heaven being associated in the formation, together with the angels.[3] By the desire which the man experiences for the woman and the woman for the man at the moment of their intercourse, their seeds are interblended and produce a child which is said to have two figures, one within the other. The child in this way draws life from father and mother, and this is why there should be some kind of sanctification for all classes at the moment of conjugal union, so that the child about to be born may be perfect and complete in figure.[4] The Secret of Divine Generation is however a Secret of the Doctrine and is reserved for the initiated therein; it is apparently they alone who draw down the holy souls which are the fruit of the union between God and His Shekinah. But there are various kinds and generations of souls, some being superior to others, and when the desire—apparently of the ordinary man—provokes in an equal degree the desire of the male soul for the female soul, the child born of this union will have a soul superior to that of other men, since its birth has come about by desire of the Tree of Life.[5]

These things are clear issues at their value, and in looking at them from the standpoint of Israel we must make allowance for national exclusiveness in what is said about holy souls which can only become incarnate in Jewry. We must make allowance also for that which by inference from the teaching might be supposed to befall the barren woman. In conclusion as to this part, it is affirmed that the Sons of the Doctrine, knowing the Mysteries of the Doctrine, turned all their thoughts to God, and their children were called Sons of the King.[6] But those whose marital relations were not

---

[1] Z., Pt. I, fol. 50a; I, 290. *Ib.*, Pt. II, fol. 89b; III, 363.
[2] *Ib.*, Pt. III, fol. 219b, THE FAITHFUL SHEPHERD; V, 556.
[3] *Ib.*
[4] *Ib.*, Pt. I, fol. 90b; I, 514, 515.
[5] *Ib.*, fol. 209a; II, 437. This also is important because of that which it implies. The frigid, uninspired unions of *pro forma* marriages are, by this hypothesis, useless for the higher purposes: there must be mutual and equilibrated desire, upspringing from love, and such desire must be transmuted by the tincture of Divine Aspirations.
[6] Here then is the counsel of espousals: *Mens sana in corpore sano et spiritu Deo adhærens;* but such cleaving is in virtue of love uplifted through all the worlds.—See Z., Pt. III, fol. 78a; V, 213.

encompassed with sanctity caused a breach in the world above.[1]

The religion of earthly espousals, if I may so term it, is the part in manifestation of that which is called so frequently the Mystery of Faith, and I will proceed next to the consideration of what is intimated there and here on this subject. In the words "male and female created He them"[2] there is expressed the Supreme Mystery which constitutes the glory of God, is inaccessible to human intelligence and is the object of faith. By this mystery was man created, as also the heaven and the earth.[3] It is inferred that every figure which does not represent male and female has no likeness to the heavenly figure. This is why Scripture says that God "blessed them and called their name Adam in the day when they were created."[4] The Scriptural authority for the affirmation that there is a Mystery of Faith is drawn from several sources, but without exception on the *lucus a non lucendo* principle, as it is impossible to conceive where it lies in the texts or what it can be on the evidence of their surface meaning. I will group a few of them together and let them speak for themselves. (1) "O Lord, Thou art my God; I will exalt Thee. I will praise Thy Name; for Thou hast done wonderful things; Thy counsels of old are faithfulness and truth."[5] (2) "And his hand took hold on Esau's heel."[6] (3) "Thus the heavens and the earth were finished, and all the host of them,"[7] *et seq.* This is said to be the Great Mystery. (4) "I will sing unto the Lord, for He hath triumphed gloriously: the horse and his rider hath He thrown into the sea,"[8] *et seq.* Among the intimations which rest upon the ZOHAR there are many which seem designed almost obviously to confuse the issues and misdirect research thereon. The Mystery is said to consist in the examination of good and evil and then in cleaving to the good.[9] It is

---

[1] It is said also that woman is the image of the altar, from which it seems to follow in the symbolism that man is the priest, and then of the oblations there should be no need to speak. It is said further, in this connection, that divorce makes a breach in the altar—in the altar below, because there is separation between male and female, and in the altar above, by the Kabbalistic hypothesis of correspondence between things above and below.—Z., Pt. II, fol. 102b, 103a; III, 415. See also *ib.*, Pt. III, fol. 78a; V, 213.
[2] Gen. i. 27.
[3] Z., Pt. I, fol. 55b; I, 320.
[4] Gen. v. 2.
[5] Is. xxv. 1.
[6] Gen. xxv. 26. Z., Pt. I, fol. 199a; II, 387.
[7] Gen. ii. 1.
[8] Ex. xv. 1.
[9] Z., Pt. II, fol. 34a; III, 166.

said again to be contained in the fact that Zion constitutes the foundation and beauty of the world and that the world draws its nourishment therefrom.[1] There is Zion, which is severity, and there is Jerusalem, which is mercy; but the two are one.[2] We may say in respect of both that goodness and mercy are on the male side of the Sephirotic Tree, while evil and severity are on the female side; that these two must be united by the Middle Pillar: that this is entering under the wings of Shekinah; and that when they are thus joined, goodness, joy and beauty are found everywhere. We shall speak in this manner the characteristic language of the ZOHAR and might deserve the blessing of Rabbi Simeon; but we shall not have advanced our subject by one line or syllable belonging to a line. We must therefore go further and test the values of a few less obdurate extracts.

There are forty-nine gates of compassion which connect with the mystery of the perfect man, composed of male and female, and with the Mystery of Faith.[3] These are the Gates of Understanding referable to BINAH,[4] wherein dwells the Spouse in Transcendence, who is Shekinah; but there is a fiftieth Gate which Moses did not open, according to the legend. This Gate is the Mystery of Espousals in the Divine

---

[1] Z., Pt. I, fol. 206b; II, 427. *Ib.*, fol. 186a; II, 335.
[2] *Ib.*
[3] *Ib.*, Pt. II, fol. 139b; IV, 41, 42.
[4] It seems desirable at this point to collect the references to these Gates which occur throughout the text, so that there may be no misunderstanding on the subject. The indications are these in summary: (1) It is through 50 openings of the mysterious heavenly palaces that the Word of YOD—which, as we have seen, is in CHOKMAH—penetrates to the HE (in BINAH).—Z., Pt. I, fol. 13b; I, 79. (2) There is one Gate which is the synthesis of all Gates and one Degree which is the synthesis of all Degrees; by this Gate and Degree do we enter into the glory of the Holy One.—*Ib.*, fol. 103b; II, 19. (3) This Gate is unknown because Israel is in exile, and the result is that all the Gates are shut.—*Ib.*, fol. 103b; II, 20. (4) The 50 Gates of Understanding are or may become salvation for the whole world.—*Ib.*, Appendix I, OMISSIONS; fol. 260a; II, 611. (5) The Gates emanate from or are referable to the side of severity.—*Ib.*, Appendix III, SECRETS OF THE LAW; II, 723, 724. (6) It is owing to the evil Samael that Moses could enter only 49 of the 50 Gates of BINAH.—*Ib.*, Pt. II, fol. 115a; III, 443. (7) The union of the Father and the Mother produced 5 lights, which gave birth in their turn to the 50 Gates of Supreme Lights.—*Ib.*, ASSEMBLY OF THE SANCTUARY, fol. 122b, 123a; III, 473. (8) The light of the Mother above reaches us by 50 Gates.—*Ib.*, fol. 137b; IV, 37. (9) He who devotes himself to the study of the Law opens the 50 Gates of BINAH, which correspond to the YOD multiplied by the HE.—*Ib.*, Pt. III, fol. 216a; V, 548. (10) By such multiplication Moses attained these Gates.—*Ib.*, fol. 223b; V, 565. (11) In the absence of these Gates Israel would have remained always in the bondage of Egypt. They are in the region called the Supreme Mother, who gives power to the Mother below.—*Ib.*, fol. 262a; VI, 12. It will be seen that the subject is left at a loose end and does not emerge in fact; but it becomes clear at least that the Zoharic Gates of Compassion belong to another mode of Understanding than was evolved by late Kabbalism, as summarised in Book V.

World. Another reference tells us that there are Seven Degrees above which are superior to all others, and they constitute the Mystery of Perfect Faith.[1] The attachment of Israel to the good side is attachment to the Supreme Mystery, the Mystery of Faith, so that Israel is one therewith.[2] By the hypothesis that the Mystery of Faith is a Sex Mystery, the practice of perfection therein, on the terms already indicated, should give a title to the knowledge of these Degrees and thereby the Mystery of Faith would pass into a perfect Mystery of Experience. Probably these Seven Degrees are identical with the seven firmaments the purpose of which—as we are told elsewhere—is to reveal the Mystery of Faith.[3] They are called also Seven Palaces.[4] There is a kingdom to come after that which is termed symbolically the end of the world; it is a sacred region, and this also is said to constitute the Mystery of Faith;[5] but we have heard otherwise that the advent of Messiah means perfect conformity in the nuptial state, above as well as below.

It has been necessary to make these citations; but it will be seen that the most which they tell us is (1) the fact that there is a Mystery of Faith, and (2) that it is concerned with the union of male and female. We may take the question one step further by the collation of some final references. The priestly garment with fringes [6] and the phylacteries on head and arms [7] designate the Supreme Mystery, because God is found in that man who wears them.[8] It is the Supreme Mystery of Faith. A spring which flows unfailingly is another image of the Mystery,[9] and we shall remember in this connection the sex-interpretation placed on the river which came forth from Eden to water the Garden—in which man was created male and female—and which was afterwards parted and became into four heads. A well fed by a spring also symbolises the Mystery of Faith, because it symbolises the union of male and female,[10] and here again we shall remember (1) the "fountain of gardens," [11] (2) the "garden inclosed" which is "my sister, my spouse," [12] (3) the

---

[1] Z., Pt. I, fol. 204b; II, 414.
[2] Ib., Pt. I, fol. 205a; II, 217.
[3] Ib., fol. 85b; I, 494.
[4] Cf. Book IV, § 10, p. 176.
[5] Z., Pt. II, fol. 134a, b; IV, 30. The Feast of the Paschal Lamb is said to contain the Mystery of Faith.—Ib., fol. 135a; IV, 32.
[6] Numbers xv. 38.
[7] Deut. xi. 18.
[8] Z., Pt. I, fol. 141a; II, 150.
[9] Ib., fol. 141b; II, 151.
[10] Ib., fol. 141b; II, 152.
[11] Song of Solomon iv. 15.
[12] Ib., iv. 12.

"fountain sealed,"[1] and (4) the "well of living waters and streams from Lebanon."[2] Whoever contemplates such a well is said to contemplate the Mystery of Faith.[3] The moon is said finally to be another image, and we know that this luminary is a symbol of Shekinah.[4]

I conclude on all the evidence that the doctors of the ZOHAR had no intention of communicating under the formula which they used so often more than a broad and general definition of what their convention symbolised.

Again therefore we must go further, and the key to the matter before us will be found, under another form of symbolism, by the collation of two passages which are separated widely from each other. It is affirmed [5]—as we have seen—that when the YOD is united to the HE they give birth to that river concerning which it is said: "And a river went forth from Eden to water the Garden."[6] The other extract tells us that from the union of the male and female—meaning, of course, in the transcendence—come all souls which animate men.[7] The inference is that the Eden-river is that of life, or

---

[1] Song of Solomon iv. 12.
[2] *Ib.*, iv. 15.
[3] Z., Pt. I, fol. 141b; II, 152.
[4] *Ib.*, fol. 142a, b; II, 157. As I have by no means exhausted the references and as so much seems to be implied in the formula, I will make a further selection as follows: (a) That the Supreme Mystery, which is synonymous with the Mystery of Faith, is the law of the whole world is taught in the words: "These are the three sons of Noah: and of them was the whole earth overspread" (Gen. ix. 19), as if the Zohar were indicating that the event in question marked a new epoch in the mode of generation.—Z., Pt. I, fol. 73a; I, 432. (b) The Mystery of Faith is represented by Jacob.—*Ib.*, fol. 138b; II, 143. (c) Every word in Scripture conceals the Supreme Mystery of Faith, because all the works of the Holy One are based on equity and truth.—*Ib.*, fol. 142a; II, 154. (d) The Supreme Wisdom is by implication the Mystery of Sex.—*Ib.*, fol. 150b; II, 193. (e) The Mystery of Faith and all celestial sanctities emanate from the union of male and female principles.—*Ib.*, fol. 160a; II, 229. (f) One Mystery of Supreme Wisdom is that the world's salvation must issue from the union of Juda and Thamar, as if there were a secret sanctuary somewhere in the world which overwatched that true legitimacy belonging to the line of David.—*Ib.*, fol. 188b; II, 344. (g) The union of the worlds above and below is of the Mystery of Faith.—*Ib.*, fol. 206b; II, 426. (h) The Supreme Mystery concealed in the Law is the Secret of the Lord, and this is a secret of the Holy Covenant.—*Ib.*, fol. 236b; II, 533. (i) The Cup of Blessings comprises the Mystery of Faith, which Mystery embraces the four quarters and the Sacred Throne.—*Ib.*, fol. 250b; II, 585. (k) The Sacred Reign to come constitutes the Mystery of Faith—meaning union sanctified everywhere.—*Ib.*, Pt. II, fol. 134a; IV, 30. (l) The Mystery of Faith is to know that Jehovah is Elohim.—*Ib.*, fol. 161a; IV, 100. As I have now omitted only references that are trivial or obscure and calling for considerable explanation, the two collections are in all respects adequate and it will be seen that they are quite clear as to the nature of the Mystery, whether it is qualified as Supreme or characterised as that of Faith.
[5] Z., Pt. I, fol. 95b; I, 545.
[6] Gen. ii. 10.
[7] Z., Pt. II, fol. 70a; III, 310. It is said here that the creation of man in the likeness of the Elohim is an allusion to the Mystery of the Male and Female Principles.

synonymously it is the river of souls,[1] and in this case we shall understand that the Higher Eden is the place of Divine Nuptials, while the Garden which was watered by the river was the place of nuptials below. We have found this illustrated already by various speaking images—as, for example, in the higher degree by the analogy instituted between Shekinah and the Seed of Solomon,[2] the tent of grace,[3] and so forth; but in the lower degree by the identification of the Garden with womanhood.[4] We are not left, however, to mere inferences on the subject, for it is said elsewhere that at the moment of the union of the Spouse and Bride all souls came forth from the celestial river.[5] The one is "the Sanctuary, O Lord, which Thy hands have established" and the other is the repose of man.

It is said elsewhere—and we have seen indeed already—that souls are produced by the union of male and female,[6] whence it follows that they have a father and mother—*ex hypothesi* in God—even as their bodies have when they enter into incarnate life. We learn also that all souls emanate from the celestial region called JAH, which is explained to be the Unknown God.[7] As seen already, this name is for God that which the Propitiatory is for the Tabernacle—a summary of the male world above and the female world below.[8] We can understand now in what sense the Shekinah is termed so often the Supreme Mother; we can understand also why it is joy of heart[9] to know that Jehovah is Elohim and why the attainment of such knowledge is the object with which the Holy One sends man into this world.[10] It is said—as we have seen also—that this is the Mystery of Faith which is the synthesis of the whole Law. It is said further that Eden is

---

[1] It is the river of life and of souls in the sense that it issues from the letter YOD, regarded as the organ of the Covenant in the Supernal World—*semen superinexprimabile*. Sometimes this idea is expressed almost literally.

[2] Z., Pt. II, fol. 66b; III, 292.

[3] *Ib.*, Pt. I, fol. 101b; II, 11, where the tent of Sarah is understood as the tent of Shekinah, or as Shekinah herself. There are other instances: The Jerusalem above is said to be designated a tent in Is. xl. 22, and to signify Shekinah.—*Ib.*, Pt. II, fol. 65b; III, 288.

[4] It was also the Synod of Israel.—*Ib.*, Pt. I, fol. 63a; I, 369.

[5] *Ib.*, Pt. I, fol. 207b, 208a; II, 432. They came forth male and female, descending confusedly. This intimation is of some importance in the legend of the soul.

[6] See Z., Pt. I, fol. 207b, 208a; II, 432, among other places.

[7] *Ib.*, Pt. II, fol. 165b; IV, 111. The reference is to KETHER, where Jehovah is in union with Elohim, or God and His Shekinah are one. We have seen that the letters YOD and HE primal of the Divine Name are allocated to this SEPHIRA.

[8] *Ib.*

[9] *Ib.*, Pt. III, fol. 8b; V, 23.

[10] Z., Pt. II, fol. 161b; IV, 101, 102.

the Mother above and the Garden which was watered by the river coming forth out of Eden is the Shekinah or Mother below, while the river itself is the Middle Pillar of the Sephirotic Tree.[1] It follows that descent into manifestation is by the central path which communicates between KETHER and MALKUTH. It is the path of Shekinah, and when it is testified that she was destined from the beginning to suffer with Israel [2] this means that the nuptial intercourse which was infinite and holy in the world above, which was pure, spiritual and holy for a period—*ex hypothesi*—in the world below, descended through what is termed the Fall of man into the region of the shells, or the order of animal things. The physical sign of the Covenant is held to symbolise Shekinah [3] because it symbolises the path of purification by which man may return into the perfection of spiritual union.[4]

We have heard that the Supreme Mystery of Faith is the union of Jehovah and Elohim, which union is the source of all other Mysteries. We have heard also that when Israel shall become perfect, it will make no distinction between Jehovah and Elohim—the male with the female being neither male nor female. It follows that the Supreme Mystery and the Mystery of Faith are one and are also the Mystery of Union of Male and Female in the Divine Nature, behind which I infer that there is a Mystery of Experience in man.

Let us now take another legend of the soul which is not quite in consonance with some things that have preceded, as it postulates a continual generation as fruit of the eternal union between the Father and Mother in transcendence [5] in place of a creation of souls once and for all, prior to the

---

[1] Z., Pt. I, fol. 26a, b; I, 164.

[2] *Ib.*, fol. 120b; II, 84. It is said here that Shekinah is the first of all that is, which is affirmed also of METATRON.

[3] *Ib.*, fol. 278a, b, THE FAITHFUL SHEPHERD; II, 647. So also it is said, as we have seen, that the Covenant with Shekinah will endure for ever.—*Ib.*, Pt. III, fol. 257a; V, 597.

[4] I ought to mention here that in one place only of the text it is said that in forming the prototypical Eve and placing her face to face with man, it was intended that the union between male and female should be accomplished after the same manner as that of Jehovah with Elohim, or in the absence of any fleshly and impure sensation.—Z., Pt. II, fol. 258b; IV, 291, 292. This seems to me an allusion to a pre-natal state, for things must be referred to their natures: the spiritual unions are one thing and have their own end; the physical union is another and Nature insures thereby the perpetuation of species.

[5] Hence it is said that man—understood as male and female—is the synthesis of Jehovah and Elohim.—Z., Pt. III, fol. 48a; V, 134.

evolution of the created universe. That which follows is more in consonance with the Mystery of Faith, and is in fact one of its aspects. It is said that at every birth new souls are created and detached from the Celestial Tree.¹ Thanks to these new souls, the legions of heaven are increased,² for which reason the Scripture says: " Let the waters bring forth abundantly the moving creature that hath life," ³ meaning the waters of the celestial river which has its source in the Holy and Eternal Alliance.⁴ It should be understood that this Alliance, which is the union of Jehovah and Elohim, has its correspondence below in the Covenant between God and man on the basis of circumcision—as symbolising the great postulate concerning purity. The Scripture adds: " And fowl that may fly above the earth," ⁵ because at the moment when the newly-created soul traverses the heavenly region called " living "—meaning the Land of Life—it is accompanied by many angels, who have followed it from the time that it was detached from the Tree of Heaven.⁶ Those who abstain from practising the precept " Increase and multiply " diminish—if it be permitted so to speak—the Celestial Figure, centralisation of all figures: they arrest the course of the celestial river and defile the Holy Alliance.⁷ We have seen that this is a sin against God Himself; the soul of such a man will never penetrate into the vestibule of Paradise and shall be repulsed from the world above.⁸ After this manner does the ZOHAR indicate yet again that from the beginning of the sacred text it is concerned with the history of man rather than the external cosmos and, by inference, with the history of Israel rather than of man at large. We on our part are in a position to understand it in a higher sense as

---

¹ It is repeated also that all souls issue from the celestial region called JAH, which is the source of wisdom. This is called the Holy Spirit, and all souls are comprised therein.—*Ib.*, Pt. II, 174a; IV, 129. According to another version, those souls which animate men issue or emanate from Him Who is called the Just.—*Ib.*, fol. 70a; III, 310.
² *Ib.*, Pt. III, fol. 168a; V, 434, and elsewhere.
³ Gen. i. 20.
⁴ They are the waters of CHOKMAH and BINAH, the YOD and the HE in their union, or alternatively—according to another form of the symbolism—they are those waters proceeding from KETHER under the presidency of the Divine Name JAH.
⁵ Gen. i. 20.
⁶ This notion is expressed in one place only and seems only semi-poetical adornment.
⁷ Z., Pt. I, fol. 273a, a, Appendix I, BOOK OF BRIGHTNESS; II, 641.
⁸ *Ib.*, fol. 48a; I, 278. The guilt of such abstinence is exaggerated in the prevailing manner of the ZOHAR, and if we come to discriminate thereon we shall remember that the man returns—*ex hypothesi*—to this life in another body and has the chance to do better.

the catholic history of souls; it is this on the inner side, though it is cosmic history of course on the surface of the outward sense. This also is the construction of the ZOHAR, which naturally does not deny that on the literal side the first chapters of Genesis are the story of creation; but the vital or palmary interest rests in the internal sense—as if the one were a question of accidents and the other of essence.

The souls of all Gentiles emanate from the demons under circumstances which are not explained in the ZOHAR.[1] The suggestion is sometimes that they are from the left side of the Tree; but the question is exceedingly obscure,[2] because God and His Shekinah are everywhere in the Tree of the SEPHIROTH, and though there is a sense in which God is allowed to have created evil, the position is by no means maintained with any consistency throughout. It was left for late Kabbalism to contrive its own way of escape from the difficulty, for which purpose it conceived the idea of postulating ten SEPHIROTH in each of the four worlds, as also in each SEPHIRA. There is practically no warrant for this in the original text, though there is a trace of some septenary repetition of SEPHIROTH in the individual SEPHIROTH. The case of those who were converted from Paganism to Jewry and fulfilled the whole law thereafter raises another question: it was necessary that they should be reconciled on all the planes or it would serve no purpose to receive them into the fold; and it was therefore postulated that after undergoing circumcision they entered under the wings of Shekinah and were separated from the side of the Demons.[3] They did not participate, in the world to come, in the full beatitude of the elect who were such by their right of birth; they remained under the wings of Shekinah, but the latter was like a chariot for Israel, in which Israel passed higher, namely, into the Land of the Living. The Gentiles had no part in the Heavenly Tree and could not therefore return to it.[4] The view is naturally at

---

[1] It is affirmed elsewhere, on the contrary, that they come from the Divine World; but the question is negligible, as anything that is found in the ZOHAR on the subject of unbelievers is antecedently known to be worthless. The literal statement is that, all differences notwithstanding, human souls come from heaven.—Z., Pt. I, fol. 13a; I, 77.

[2] There is one place at least in which the right and the left side seem to be two paths of coming out into manifestation apart from any Sephirotic notion.—Z., Pt. I, fol. 160a; II, 229.

[3] Ib., fol. 13a; I, 76.

[4] The records are obscure and contradictory, but I have suggested previously that the Sephirotic Tree is really the Tree of Life, and there may be a sense intended in which

THE MYSTERY OF SEX

issue with much that has preceded; but the question does not concern us in any important way.

Returning to the generation of souls, it is said that there are three souls in the superior degrees;[1] the first is the Supreme Soul, which is unintelligible even to beings on high: it is the Soul of all souls, it is concealed eternally and all depends therefrom. The second soul is the female principle, and by the union of these two Divine Works are manifested to the whole world, even as all acts of the human soul are manifested by the human body. The third soul is that of all holy souls emanating from the Male and Female in the transcendence.[2] The multiplication of symbolical modes for the expression of the same speculative doctrines is disconcerting enough and sometimes tends to confusion, but the meaning is in no sense remote, as it happens in the present instance. We see in the first place the root-postulate belonging to the Mystery of Faith—that the union of male and female in the Ineffable Persons causes conception and birth everlastingly; that what are born are souls; that these descend, and that they are male and female. One account

---

the Tree of the Knowledge of Good and Evil is also Sephirotic in its attributions, the good being the right and the left the evil side. Zoharic Kabbalism recognised, moreover, an averse Tree under the title of Inferior Crowns, in analogy with the Crowns that are above, namely, the true SEPHIROTH. The salient allusions are as follows: (a) There were ten averse Crowns and they were in analogy with ten varieties of Magic, all understood as infernal, for the ZOHAR very properly recognises no distinction between Black and White in the occult arts.—Z., Pt. I, fol. 167a; II, 257. (b) The Inferior Crowns are ramifications of one and the same Tree.—*Ib*., fol. 177a; II, 296. (c) The Law of Correspondence obtains in these things, for—as we have seen—the empire of the demon is modelled on that of God.—*Ib*., Pt. II, fol. 37b; III, 179. (d) There is further a demoniacal triad in imitation of that Triad which is Supernal.—*Ib*., fol. 40b; II, 189. (e) There are also inferior palaces corresponding to the Palaces that are above and—like these—they are seven in number.—*Ib*., fol. 245a; IV, 278. (f) There are hierarchies of demons answering to the Hierarchies of Blessed Angels—Seraphim to Seraphim, and so forth.—*Ib*., fol. 247b; IV, 281. (g) The titles of the averse SEPHIROTH are the same as those above—Wisdom and so forth, all the qualities being illustrated by their opposites.—*Ib*., Pt. III, fol. 70a; V, 190. (i) It is said finally, and this is a further light on another subject which has been under consideration just previously, that there are ten averse SEPHIROTH on the right and ten upon the left, even as in the Holy World. Here is another way of understanding the right and left side in the ZOHAR. I do not affirm that there is a single ruling idea throughout the references, yet if there be, the modes of expression are not less obscure than they are otherwise misleading.—*Ib*., Pt. III, fol. 207a; V, 527.

[1] *Ib*., Pt. I, fol. 245a, b; II, 570, 571.

[2] Though there has been no occasion to dwell upon it, seeing that I am not concerned with the maintenance of orthodox theological views or their opposites, I think that the reader has abundant proof in his hands by this time that the Zoharic system as a whole is no more emanationist than pantheistic. That which proceeds from AÏN-SOPH into the complete concealment and yet comparative manifestation of the Three Supernal SEPHIROTH may be called an emanation from AÏN-SOPH, but as it is a question of Divine Essences, that is an orthodox view at its value. In the present instance the symbol is one of begetting, which is not synonymous with emanation.

says that at the moment of earthly marriage the souls must sort themselves out, each male soul discovering the female who was its companion before incarnation; but this is so rough and crude that it is set aside tacitly, without, however, establishing any general law in its place. The implicit is of course that the male body contains a male soul and that the soul of a woman is female, though there is an obscure sense in which any soul is male to any material body but is female to the degree which is above it.[1] Another implicit can be recognised which is more to our purpose—that he who abides in the true way will meet in marriage with the woman-soul which was his pre-natal companion.[2] If he has deviated it may happen that the woman predestined to him is espoused to another; but in the event of his repentance a time will come when the alien male will disappear, thus yielding the woman to her true mate.[3] In a scheme like this it is obvious that there must be fatalities and mischances innumerable when it comes to be worked out: among others there is that in virtue of which a male soul will come into this world without a sister-soul, and presumably *vice versâ*. It is held that such a person will not marry and cannot therefore have children; but in the event of his keeping the Law and proving worthy, he will find the means of rehabilitation in another earthly life. In the alternative case, he will be judged unworthy of a new transmigration.[4] It is part of the Divine Plan for the salvation and felicity of man that a sister-soul is not permitted to remain the wife of another.[5]

The considerations with which I have been dealing lead up to other dreams that are significant of the concern of Israel on another and higher side of the sex mystery. It is not to be supposed, the union of humanity below according to the manner of flesh being, at least in its consecration, a reflection of the Divine Union, that there should not be an union of souls in the world to come, so that in the beatitude of the true

---

[1] Z., Pt. I, Appendix III, MATHNITIN; II, 703.
[2] See on the general subject *ib.*, Pt. III, fol. 283b, 284a; VI, 64, 65. Also, *ib.*, fol. 43b; V, 120, 121, and Pt. I, Appendix III, MATHNITIN; II, 703.
[3] See on the general question *ib.*, Pt. III, fol. 283b; V, 64. And on this special point, *ib.*, Pt. II, fol. 229a; II, 503.
[4] We have seen that reincarnation is not in itself desirable but that it is justified—*ex hypothesi*—by adequate reasons. It follows from the above statement that there is a less favourable alternative. That which is suggested or proposed is, however, only a sporadic or casual notion, and it is quite out of harmony with much that goes before and comes after.
[5] This is discounted somewhat fully in other places of the text.

region of life they should not continue to reflect the Supernal Work and its Mystery. This is why, as we shall see, the union between God and the soul is so often in the sense of vision, though there are indications of deeper stages. That which is substituted is the union in heaven of souls who have been espoused on earth—being those who were espoused previously before the world began.[1] When it is said that the Blessed Vision is the sight of Shekinah and the contemplation of her Divine Face,[2] we are to understand apparently that the union of sister-souls is under her eyes and in her presence. It is said that in the heights of heaven there is yet another union of two born of love and for ever inseparable.[3] It is contemplated by those who have part in the life to come. The way which leads to the Tree of Life, the Tree which is kept by the Kerubim and the Flaming Sword, are the Grand Matrona herself. She is the way of the Sacred City, the way of the Heavenly Jerusalem, the intermediary of communication between things above and below in both directions: she is the perfect Mediatrix, to whom all the Divine Powers are confided.[4] The intimation is vague, but as the contemplation

---

[1] It is a recurring subject of reference and we see that the triad obtains here as otherwhere. There are (a) Pre-natal union; (b) Union on earth and (c) Union in the risen life of the spirit. Two things are to be observed, firstly, that we hear nothing concerning marriage-life after the resurrection, or in that state wherein the perpetuation of a physical envelope seems to pronounce separation for ever between God and man, so far as all that is understood by Mysticism respecting the union is concerned; but, secondly, following all the analogies, there can be no doubt that the risen bodies will enter into the life of intercourse, because they are complete bodies.

[2] Z., Pt. II, fol. 40b, THE FAITHFUL SHEPHERD; III, 189, 190. But there are other references.

[3] *Ib.*, Pt. II, fol. 50b; III, 229.

[4] *Ib.*, fol. 51a; III, 230. The same Divine Powers were said to be entrusted to Enoch when he became METATRON, concerning whom I will now collect the following references: (a) He is charged with the government of the earth.—Z., Pt. I, fol. 143a; II, 161. (b) He sets all his legions in motion by the power of a single letter in his name—presumably any letter, as none is specified.—*Ib.*, Appendix III, MATHNITIN; II, 705. (c) He is the Serpent above.—*Ib.*, Pt. II, fol. 28a; III, 134. (d) This is explained by *ib.*, Pt. I, fol. 27a; I, 171, which says that he is favourable to man when he is transformed into a wand—*e.g.* that of Aaron or Moses—but as a serpent he is against man. (d) The river which went out of Eden to water the Garden (Gen. ii. 10) is Enoch, who is called otherwise METATRON; but it is the Lower Eden and not that in the Supernal World. It is the place called PARDES, which name—according to Franck—was never so used in the ZOHAR.—*Ib.*, fol. 27a; I, 168, 169. (e) He is to the cohorts above apparently that which is Samael to the cohorts below.—*Ib.*, Pt. II, fol. 42a; III, 191. (f) He is called Server and he embraces the six directions of space.—*Ib.*, fol. 94a; III, 377. (g) It is said that souls proceed from the side of METATRON and from the side of Shekinah, but it does not seem to be by the way of generation, as between male and female.—*Ib.*, fol. 94b; III, 379. (h) He is also called "Young Man," and it was he who dwelt in the Tabernacle of Moses.—*Ib.*, Pt. II., fol. 143a; IV, 54. (i) He helped to build the Tabernacle.—*Ib.*, fol. 159a; IV, 96. (j) He guarded the Temple of Solomon.—*Ib.*, fol. 164a; IV, 107. (k) The School of

of Matrona sanctified nuptials below, so is the path by which the elect enter into the higher nuptials as if they ascended that Middle Pillar of the SEPHIROTH which is so often said to be she. We can proceed therefore to glance at another question of those palaces for which the ZOHAR has a natural attraction, while their number is most usually seven. When souls leave the lower world they enter into a certain palace which is above, if they carry the proper warrants, and therein those which are male are again united to the female, in which union they radiate light as in sparkles.[1] This palace is said to be the throne of Faith and, I infer, is the place of its mystery. Yet another story of palaces tells us that there are four which are exclusive to women, or at least to holy mothers, but it is forbidden to reveal their nature.[2] During the day the females are separated from the males; but the spouses are in union at night, and in their mutual embrace the lights of both dissolve into a single light. The conclusion reached on this subject is that blessed is the lot of the just, male as well as female, for they shall enjoy all delights in the world to come.[3]

We are led on in this manner to the great mystery of the subject, as to which there are several testimonies. It rests on the witness of a testament bequeathed by Rabbi Eleazar the Great [4] that when the Holy One comes down into Paradise

---

METATRON is the School of the Holy One.—*Ib.*, Appendix III, fol. 287a; IV, 314. (l) The curtain of the Tabernacle was his symbol.—*Ib.*, fol. 293a; IV, 317. (m) He is like Michael, for he offers the souls of the just to God.—*Ib.*, Pt. III, THE FAITHFUL SHEPHERD, fol. 29a, b; V, 81. (n) There is an obscure suggestion that he may be the Angel of the Sun, and it is said also that he draws milk for his purification from his mother, as if she were the MATRONA in BINAH and he were the Begotten Son or VAU.— *Ib.*, fol. 64b; V, 177. (o) He has the Keys of Heaven.—*Ib.*, fol. 171b; V, 445. (p) During the exile, he has the government of the House; he is the rainbow, and he is called SHADDAI.—*Ib.*, fol. 215b; V, 547. (q) He is old and he is again young.—*Ib.*, fol. 217a, b; V, 530. (r) He is the Man of the Lesser Countenance; that is to say, he is the tenth SEPHIRA, MALKUTH; and here we must remember that there is a sense in which the VAU came down to earth in union with the HE final.—*Ib.*, fol. 223b; V, 565. (s) As otherwise noted, he is the vesture of SHADDAI.—*Ib.*, fol. 231a; V, 571. (t) As noted also, he is to Shekinah that which are the week days to the Sabbath—as if he were activity and she rest.—*Ib.*, fol. 243b; V, 381. (u) He is poor in exile— that is to say, in the exile of Israel, and his nourishment is prayer.—*Ib.*, fol. 278a; V, 51. I have omitted only a few minor allusions and one fantastic comparison which would tend to confuse the issues. Apart from the stultifying intervention of the Enoch motive, I think that these extracts tend very clearly towards the identification of METATRON with the Son who is extended through the worlds below ATZILUTH, and who is not exactly in union with Shekinah and yet not apart from her during the fall and exile of the elect. At times—perhaps generally—they are distinct from one another; at times they are found together; and their end is complete union.

[1] Z., Pt. II, fol. 246a; IV, 279.
[2] *Ib.*, Pt. III, fol. 167b; V, 434.
[3] *Ib.*
[4] It is not clear whether this means the son of Rabbi Simeon.

at midnight the male souls are united to the female; fecundation follows from the joy which they experience in the contemplation of God, and they bring forth other souls [1] which are destined to occupy the bodies of Gentiles who will become converts to the Law of Israel.[2] In another place this is explained after a different manner: the souls born of celestial unions are reserved in a palace, and when a man is converted one of them takes flight and comes under the wings of Shekinah, who embraces her—because she is the fruit of the just in their intercourse—and sends her into the body of the convert where she—or he—remains, and from that moment the convert acquires the title of just.[3] This is the mystery of those words in Scripture: " The fruit of the just is the Tree of Life."[4] There is, however, by yet another testimony, a general sense in which the Holy One affects the union of twin-souls so that they may engender other souls, themselves animated by those sacred forces which are above them.[5]

The fact that these passages are all less or more irreconcilable is of no consequence; the object is to indicate the nature of beatitude in the world above, and they are all independent fables belonging to the motive, inspiration or casual spur of the moment:[6] no one would have been more astonished possibly than a Son of the Doctrine, had he heard that they were to be collated and harmonised, were that possible.

There are a few minor points which may be mentioned at this stage. It is said that all depends on thought and intention; holiness is attracted by good thought; but he who defiles himself by thought, and he who at the moment of fulfilling the act of intercourse with his wife thinks of another woman changes the Degree above—the Degree of Holiness—into one that is impure.[7] We may compare the elective

---

[1] I must not omit to mention that this is contradicted in THE FAITHFUL SHEPHERD, which says that in the world to come there is neither eating nor drinking, that there are no conjugal relations, and that the beatitude of the just—as we have seen—is to contemplate the beauty of Shekinah.—Z., Pt. II, fol. 116a; III, 448, 449.
[2] *Ib.*, Pt. III, fol. 168a; V, 434.   [4] Proverbs xi. 30.
[3] *Ib.*   [5] Z., Pt. I, fol. 186b; II, 337.
[6] I must except, however, conditionally at least, one other quality of testimony which seems to suggest that the way of the generation of souls has been always by conception and birth, following intercourse.
[7] Z., Pt. I, Appendices III, SECRETS OF THE LAW; II, 730. Yet it would seem permissible on occasion to think of another, because in cohabiting with Leah, Jacob thought of Rachel, though unintentionally, as it is said.—*Ib.*, p. 731.

affinities of Goethe, for the child born of such union is called a substituted son: soul and body are held alike to be substituted. The second point is that there are rare occasions when conjugal relations seem forbidden, even on the Sabbath, and periods of famine are a case in point:[1] the child born at such a season will be from the side of the demon. Lastly, there is the question of virginity—by which I mean among women.[2] That such a condition on earth should be considered as tolerable, much less as a title of sanctity, never entered into heart or mind of any Son of the Doctrine. The only Zoharic reference to virgins in an exalted state specifies that the third among several legions is composed of celestial virgins who are in the service of MATRONA and adorn her when she is presented to the King: these are her maids of honour. It is a very simple transfer of an earthly image; but the legion does not consist of human souls.[3]

We are now at the end of our inquiry into the Mystery of Sex, so far as the statements in the text are concerned, and that which remains is to determine whether the path which was followed by the early Kabbalists may have led them into any experience of a spiritual kind that is implied rather than expressed in the records before us. I will suppose that they followed the counsel on which those records insist, and as it involved a distinct mode of procedure in connection with an important fact of life, the insistence, as it seems to me, must indicate that in the experience of things the method had proved of practical service. In other words, they had found that there is a mystery of nuptials of which it has not entered into the heart of man to conceive in the ordinary ways and under the common motives of desire.[4] There is one beautiful point to observe in this connection—that their mystery lay within the pure offices of Nature, under all the accepted warrants. Those who conceived it had fulfilled already the Law in respect of marriage; they sought no new way of the physical kind; they were not lovers at white heat on the

---

[1] Z., fol. 204a; II, 412, 413. The consequence threatened seems arbitrary, as usual, but—according to Rabbi Simeon—a Supreme Mystery is involved. Ordinary sense would assume that the regulation was a question of doing penance.
[2] Ib., Pt. II, fol. 131b; IV, 23.
[3] Ib., Pt. II, fol. 131b; IV, 23.
[4] We must remember that there is no lawful act of life and no law of Nature which cannot be raised above its own degree by the consecration of motive, or otherwise that the will of man in all its authorised ways and places can be united to the Divine Will.

quest of the ideal beloved;[1] they were not in search of an excuse for setting aside old pledges and old bonds; they were content with that which they had; they made use of the elements which had been given already into their hands, like true craftsmen and masters. The genesis of their practice is of course outside our knowledge: it may be that those who sought to make all things holy in their life had sanctified by intention of their own the fulfilment of that Law which told them to "increase and multiply," and that which they experienced in its sanctification may have developed subsequently the sequence of theosophical speculations with which I have been dealing; alternatively, it may be that they had come across teaching in unfrequented paths, something handed down from the past. I know nothing of written records on the subject outside the ZOHAR; but I do know that there is some vestige of teaching in the East [2] which is communicated on rare occasions, though I believe that it is concerned with the act itself rather than with the fruit thereof, and it is not the kind of secret which the East keeps to itself exclusively. Two things followed in respect of Kabbalistic doctrine and practice. Marriage for the mystical Jew had become a sacrament, and I care nothing if scholarship—supposing that it were to take up the question—should decide in its wisdom that the Zoharic notion of marriage owes something to the sacramental system of the Catholic Church. I reject the proposition in advance—for what my view is worth—and I do not think that it will be put forward; but it would signify nothing if it were true. There has been no failure so great on the register of Latin orthodoxy as its consecration of marriage; there has been nothing that is so skin deep, nothing so reluctant and half-hearted. It never did a wiser thing, a greater or a truer, than when it instituted the seventh sacrament; how it ever came to do it is another question, having regard to all the conflict of interests, the so-called counsels of perfection, the intolerable and melancholy burden brought over from Theban deserts and everything that has been collected into that strange edifice which is termed the Paradise of Palladius.[3] The result has been that

---

[1] More correctly, they had an inward, spiritual and godly ideal, on which they dwelt, and by which they seem to have accomplished transmutations below.

[2] It is precisely the same teaching as that of the ZOHAR, though not of course in the same terms.

[3] Dr. E. A. Wallis Budge: THE PARADISE OR GARDEN OF THE HOLY FATHERS . . .

after nearly two thousand years of so-called Sacramental Rites there is nothing less consecrated either in the East or West than are the offices of earthly marriage. On the other hand, the ideal presented in the ZOHAR stands for true and life-long consecration on the highest plane: it is not the ceremonial of a moment which puts a kind of ecclesiastical veneer over something that was less or more abhorred. Here is the first point, and the second in all simplicity is added on the hypothesis, at its value, that the ideal did more than exist on paper and may represent the practice of a secret school. We are told by the records that the fruit of the mystical intercourse was the begetting of children from what is called the Holy Side, as against the side of the demons, and I believe that this was a Kabbalistic way of accounting for the literal fact that children born of such unions belonged to another category than we are accustomed to meet with in the streets and byways of daily life all the world over, or—for that matter—to be familiar with in our own homes. They were Children of Grace, rather than what we call Nature, though Grace is only Nature better understood.

There is one word more: of the personal consequences which befell the Sons of the Doctrine in their delineated life of espousals we hear nothing directly, but the claim is that they came to realise the Divine Presence in their hearts as the general recompense of their consecrated lives. They were not ascetics and they were not solitaries: truly they were a company of scholars in the city and along the countryside, in village and in wilderness. For them the world of Nature was Grace externalised; the Presence was about them therein, and they attained it after their own manner—which was one of very life and testimony—each of them in his proper heart and mind. I conclude that they had found the true meaning of the words: " It is not good for man to be alone." [1] and that there is a very secret path in which " the joy of living honourably with his wife " [2] may bring the completed man—male and female—into the

---

Compiled by Athanasius Archbishop of Alexandria, Palladius Bishop of Helenopolis, Saint Jerome and others. Translated out of the Syriac. 2 vols., 1907. I do not wish to be understood as making a sweeping condemnation; I speak chiefly of processes and atmosphere. There are other respects in which the text is worthy to rank with THE GOLDEN LEGEND.
[1] Gen. ii. 18.
[2] See page 380.

spiritual city of joy, great city of praise,[1] wherein is the joy of the Lord.[2]

So the souls go up male and female into the world beyond: if they are prepared souls, they find one another; and the union that is everlasting begins in the light of God.

---

[1] Jer. xlix. 25. [2] Is. xxix. 19.

BOOK IX

THE WRITTEN WORD OF KABBALISM: THIRD PERIOD

BOOK IX

THE WRITTEN WORD OF KABBALISM: THIRD PERIOD

I.—EXPOSITORS OF THE ZOHAR

THE works—already cited—which are recommended by Rosenroth as assisting to a better comprehension of the ZOHAR fall under two heads—namely, those which are designed to elucidate technical matters and those which may claim to be original expository treatises. In the first are included WORDS OF UNDERSTANDING, which is actually a Zoharic lexicon or vocabulary; the GATE OF THE EYES, which is concerned with the Scriptural passages in the ZOHAR and ANCIENT SUPPLEMENTS; and the *ZER ZAHAB*—by the hypothesis, a Golden Crown, a wreath of gold, but it is not otherwise described than the title itself indicates, the reason being that the APPARATUS of Rosenroth borrows various extracts from its pages. The second section contains the famous GARDEN OF POMEGRANATES, the WAY OF TRUTH, with its sequel the FOUNT OF WISDOM, and a digest of the ZOHAR proper, entitled the VISION OF THE PRIEST. Outside these there are a few texts which may be regarded as extensions or developments of Zoharic doctrine, but more especially of that part which is concerned with spiritual essences. The scope of this inquiry excludes the discussion of such technical matters as the claims of word-books and anthologies of Biblical quotations: they will be found by those who are concerned in the *Apparatus* of Rosenroth. To mention them in this place will be therefore sufficient, and we may proceed to the consideration of those commentaries and developments which arose out of the ZOHAR and to the names, illustrious in later Kabbalism, which are connected with these.

A.—Moses of Cordova

Assuming that the ZOHAR first became known in Spain towards the end of the thirteenth century, there was a lapse of two hundred and fifty years, according to the dates fixed by modern scholarship, before any literature followed thereon. Hence this literature may be regarded largely as a consequence of the Cremona and Mantua editions. Franck says [1] that two Zoharic schools were founded about the same time in Palestine, namely, the middle of the sixteenth century, the first by Moses of Cordova and the second by Isaac de Loria. On the other hand, Bartolocci [2] and Basnage [3] agree in assigning Moses of Cordova to the fourteenth century. The earlier date would be of importance to the history of Kabbalism, because certain side issues of documentary criticism, untouched in this study, depend upon it; but, as it happens, there is no question that Moses ben Jacob, called Remak, was born in 1522 and died on June 25, 1570. He is the first commentator on the ZOHAR, for Joseph ben Abraham Gikatilla, called the divine Kabbalist and Thaumaturge, who was of the time of Ferdinand and Isabella, was a writer on the SEPHIROTH, and connects with the SEPHER YETZIRAH rather than Zoharic Theosophy, though he refers to the Kabbalistic Work of the Chariot.[4]

As his name indicates, Moses of Cordova was a Spaniard, but he travelled to Palestine, and it is conjectured that he was instrumental in founding the Academy of Sapeth in Upper Galilee, nine miles from Bethsaida. In either case he was one of its teachers and helped to make it illustrious, for he was regarded by his fellow theosophists as the greatest light of Kabbalism since Simeon ben Yohai. Franck says that he adhered to the real significance of the original monuments of Kabbalism; but, although this appears worthy of praise, the French critic seems to complain that R. Moses was wanting in originality. However this may be, the work by which he is known is of high authority in Kabbalism. It is entitled the

---

[1] LA KABBALE, p. 4.
[2] BIBLIOTHECA MAGNA RABBINICA, t. iv. p. 230.
[3] HISTOIRE DES JUIFS, livre vii. c. 24, t. v. p. 1942.
[4] He was born in Old Castile *anno* 1248 and died at Peñafiel *circa* 1305—perhaps somewhat later. His views on the relation between the Divine Names JHVH and Elohim shew that he was unacquainted with the doctrine of Shekinah, as this is found in the ZOHAR.

GARDEN OF POMEGRANATES (*Pardes Rimmonim*), referring to the versicle in the Song of Solomon, iv. 13 : " Thy plants are an orchard of pomegranates." Basnage says that, after the manner of Kabbalists, he discovers whatsoever he pleases in that single sentence.¹ The pomegranate, with its innumerable seeds, is a favourite object for symbolism, and the garden, orchard, or paradise has produced a wealth of imagery for all Mysticism. Here, in a general sense, it is the treasury of Scriptural meanings, and the Hebrew word by which it is described having four consonants, these meanings are classified as four : פרדם = PRDS ; the P signifies the literal sense, R the mystic sense, D the enigmatic sense, and S the secret and concealed sense.

Dwelling upon these involved meanings, as may be imagined, the GARDEN OF POMEGRANATES ² is an obscure and difficult treatise, and the attempt made by Rosenroth to dismember it for the purpose of his APPARATUS, while it gives no idea of its contents, creates a lively image of its complexity. The attribution of the letters of TETRAGRAMMATON to the SEPHIROTH, the mystical meaning of words deprived of their context, the names applied to SEPHIROTH, the superincession of these and their union with AIN SOPH, the Mystery of the Throne and of Shekinah, primæval TOHU and BOHU, the unknown darkness—these are specimens here and there of the subject-matter. But as the heart of the Kabbalist, in opposition to the ascribed character of his nation, was fixed with peculiar intentness on the eternal destinies of Israel and not on temporal concerns, so his chief interest was the soul, ever recurrent in his writings, as if it were impossible to atone sufficiently for the silence of his sacred books. There is hence no need to say that a special tract in the GARDEN OF POMEGRANATES ³ is dedicated to the subject of the soul, discussing the region from which it emanates, its purpose in the world, the profit of its creation, its union with matter, its superiority over the angels, its chief divisions, their relation one with another, the SEPHIROTH to which they are referred, the places to which they resort after death, the absence of one or both

---

¹ HISTOIRE DES JUIFS, l. vii. c. 24, vol. v. p. 1943.
² It appeared at Cracow in 1591, and Samuel Gallico published an abridged version under the title of ASIS RIMMONIM, which is cited often by Rosenroth, but I have failed to trace its date.
³ Namely, Tract xxxi., translated in the KABBALA DENUDATA, *Apparatus in Librum Sohar pars secunda*, i. 100 *et seq*.

of the higher divisions in many individuals—following Zoharic doctrine—and the good and evil angels accompanying each human being. The tract devotes also a very curious chapter to the *simulacrum* which presides at generation, a phantasmal image of humanity which descends on the male head *cum copula maritalis exercetur inferius*. It is affirmed to be sent from the Lord, and no procreation can take place without its presence. It is not, of course, visible, yet might be seen if licence were given to the eye. This phantom or *imago* is prepared for each man before he enters the world, and he grows in the likeness thereof. With the Israelites the *simulacrum* is holy, and it comes to them from the Holy Place. To those of another religion it descends from the side of impurity, and hence the chosen people must not mingle their seed with that of the Gentile.[1]

Another curious speculation is founded on that thesis of the ZOHAR, according to which the good works performed by a person in this world become for him vestments of price—as we have seen—in the world to come. Here was a poetic sentiment which had to be methodised and made literal inevitably by a late Kabbalist. When a man who has performed many good works falls away finally from righteousness and is lost, what becomes of his earlier works? Though the sinner may perish, they, says R. Moses, remain, and if there be a just man walking in the ways of the Supernal King, yet wanting something in his vestments, God will supply the deficiency from the good works of the impious one. The preference is given to those who, taken in their youth, have been unable to fulfil all the precepts of the Law.

B.—ISAAC DE LORIA

Of this Kabbalist Bartolocci and Basnage have very little to tell us, and it is not necessary to say that he is ignored by writers like Graetz. He is referred by Basnage to the seventeenth century [2] and by Franck to that which preceded it. As a fact, he was born at Jerusalem of German parentage in 1534, and he died at Sapheth or Safed in 1572, having pub-

---

[1] This fantasy rests on the authority of the ZOHAR, which states that the *simulacrum* is an emanation of the celestial form of each man, *i.e.*, JECHIDAH.—Mantua edition, iii. 107.

[2] HISTOIRE DES JUIFS, l. vii. c. 31, p. 2089, vol. v. He was a pupil of David ibn Abi Zimri, and has been regarded as the greatest rabbinical doctor at his period in Germany.

lished nothing himself except some Aramaic poems. The substantial authenticity of the great body of his doctrines collected by his disciple, R. Hayyim Vital, has not been challenged, however, and Franck bases thereon his hostile judgment of Loria,[1] on the ground, firstly, that he was, like Moses of Cordova, not original; and, secondly, that he departed from Zoharic Kabbalism to indulge in his own reveries, a criticism which stultifies itself. It is certain, however, that Loria—otherwise Luria—did innovate or extend, and that this is also his title to interest. He is not a mere echo or reflection, and he makes good reading because he is a wild fantasiast. Rosenroth terms him the eagle of the Kabbalists. It is, of course, impossible to say how far his scribe and disciple, R. Chaïm, may have developed his developments and elaborated his fantasies. Subject to one reservation, as will appear shortly, the vast thesaurus which represents both made its first printed appearance in KABBALA DENUDATA, where the excerpts, embodying whole treatises, fill some three hundred quarto pages.[2] They include:

I. The first tract, so called, of the LIBER DRUSHIM,[3] *i.e.*, BOOK OF DISSERTATIONS, forming the second volume of the collection. It occasioned a curious correspondence between Rosenroth and Henry More, who was surprised, as he expresses it, by the unexpectedness of its doctrine, but found much with which he could sympathise, as we shall learn later on in the book devoted to Christian students of the Kabbalah.

II. A commentary on the BOOK OF CONCEALMENT,[4] forming the second tract in the sixth volume of the collection. It is not given in its absolute integrity—*cujus maximam partem infra exhibemus*, says Rosenroth.[5]

III. The BOOK OF THE REVOLUTIONS OF SOULS,[6] forming the first tract in the fifth volume of the collection, which seems to have been even larger than the ZOHAR itself—in fact, almost the camel's load of the legend. A portion of this tract is said to have been printed in DE PERCUSSIONE SEPULCHRI, at Venice in 1620, together with DE PRECIBUS, recalling a further

---

[1] The modern orthography is Luria and the full name Isaac ben Solomon Ashkenazi Luria. I have followed that of Rosenroth for the convenience of those who may have occasion to consult his great collection.
[2] A printed edition in full appeared at Volkiev in 1772.
[3] KABBALA DENUDATA, *Apparatus . . . pars secunda*, i. 28 *et seq.*
[4] *Ibid.* ii. *pars secunda, tractatus quartus*, pp. 3 *et seq.*
[5] In the *Præfatio ad Lectorem*, p. 16, vol. ii.
[6] KAB. DEN. ii., *partis tertiæ tractatus secundus pneumaticus*, pp. 234 *et seq.*

subject treated in the collection. I have been unable to trace the volume or to find any particulars concerning it.[1]

The LIBER DRUSHIM is a metaphysical introduction to the Kabbalah, which discusses a variety of subtle and abstruse questions much after the manner of scholastic philosophy, and there is no doubt that Isaac de Loria might have diffused a great light of reasoning at Salamanca, had he been a Christian Doctor instead of a Jewish Rabbi. His first point, as he tells us, is one over which Kabbalists, late and early, had outwearied themselves already, namely, for what reason were the worlds created and was their creation of necessity? Assuredly from the period of the Angel of the Schools, the halls of Salamanca, of Padua, of Louvain and the other seats of scholastic learning, had echoed with similar debate. Perhaps the Kabbalists owed something to the Scholastics, perhaps they drew both from one another. The Wisdom of the Exile was encompassed on all sides by the great debate of Christian speculation. It would be interesting to discriminate the extent of interchange between them and to determine whether the plummet of Kabbalism sounded lower depths than the schoolmen; but I doubt whether the dimensions of a volume would suffice for this one excursion. Let me indicate therefore the answer of Isaac de Loria, and perhaps some student at large among scholastic quartos will find illuminating parallels in the Scholastics.[2] The answer is that God cannot fail of perfection in all the works and names of His magnificence, His excellence and His glory; but unless those works had been brought from potentiality into act they could not have been termed perfect, as regards either works or names. The Name TETRAGRAMMATON signifies perpetual existence, past, present and future, in the condition of creation before the creation, and thereafter in the immutability of things. But if the worlds had not been created, with all that is in them, it could not have signified thus the continuity of existences in every instant of time, and TETRAGRAMMATON would have been an empty formula. How very curious is the treachery of this reasoning, which ascribes to a Name of the Deity an existence independent of the intelligent creatures whose convention it is! But we should probably find many

---

[1] This is the subject of my reservation on the previous page.
[2] He must go further, however, than B. Hareau in his treatise DE LA PHILOSOPHIE SCHOLASTIQUE. Paris. 1880.

parallel treacheries among scholastic reasoners, were there any one at hand to disinter them. So also the name of ADONAI, or the Lord, involves the idea of ministers or servants, and if there were no ministers God could not be called by this title. But after the creation of the worlds and the production of the divine works from potentiality into accomplishment, God has fulfilled His perfection in every operation of His powers, and in all His Names without any exception.

The next point discussed by LIBER DRUSHIM is why the world was created at the time and moment that it was, and not at an earlier, or, for that matter, at a later epoch. The answer is that the Supreme and Most Excellent Light is infinite, exceeding comprehension and speculation, and that its concealed foundation is far from all understanding. Before anything was produced by emanation therefrom, there was no time or beginning therein. This is the solution of the difficulty which is offered by most official theology, and it could have no aspect of novelty at the late period of Isaac de Loria. It may be affirmed in a general way that when Kabbalists touch any common ground of speculation they surpass their epoch but seldom in profundity or subtlety, I might add also in the adequacy of their views, though metaphysical sufficiency was not, of course, to be expected on any side.

But it is not often and it is not for long that works like LIBER DRUSHIM confine themselves to the common ground of speculation, and the Kabbalist in this instance passes speedily into the transcendental region of the SEPHIROTH, including the manner of their emanation, another question, as he tells us, which has involved all Kabbalists in controversy. In so far as such speculations are of consequence to our purpose, they belong to an earlier stage and have been noted at least therein. Do they proceed from one another in the simplicity of a successive series, or is their emanation in columns? We have found that there is authority for both views and also for a third, which represents them as a series of concentric circles. These questions, says R. Isaac, are hard and difficult to determine, but he offers a solution on the ZOHAR, namely, that before the order of things was instituted, they were disposed one over the other, but after that time in three pillars, those of Mercy and Severity, with the central column of which KETHER is the summit and MALKUTH the base. The hypothesis of circles adopted by a German expositor in Cœlum Sephiroticum is thus implicitly set aside.

In subsequent chapters the Sephiroth are considered under a dual aspect, namely, as regards the portion of Divine Light contained in each and as regards the containing vessel, while these again are distinguished into an ambient and an inward Light, and an external and internal vessel. The existence of many worlds prior to the Sephirotic emanations is affirmed, herein following, as we have seen, both Talmudic and Zoharic tradition. Finally, several classifications of the Sephiroth are considered in the last chapter.

The study of Liber Drushim may be recommended to those —if any remain among us—who have been taught to regard the Kabbalah, on so-called " occult " authority, as a doctrine of certitude, whereas it is largely empirical, its leading theorems giving rise to as much disputation regarding their proper meaning as the principles of any other speculative philosophy.

The commentary on the Book of Concealment, as might be expected, is written undesignedly on the *lucus a non lucendo* principle. It does not yield readily to an analysis of contents, as it takes various paragraphs of the text and exposes their meaning consecutively, with the help of the Idra Rabba and Idra Zouta. The peculiar designation of the treatise is said to arise out of Proverbs xxv. 2 : " It is the glory of God to conceal a thing," [1] and *Ibid.* xi. 2 : " With the lowly is wisdom." The second reference explains why it is termed both the Book of Concealment and that of Modesty. On the authority of the Zohar, section Pekude, the balance symbol, which has made this treatise so famous in Kabbalism, is affirmed to represent the Male and Female principles, which indeed follows from the developments of the Lesser Holy Synod. The male denotes Mercy, the right-hand Pillar of the Sephiroth, and the female Severity, the Pillar on the left hand. These principles are termed the Father and the Mother, and in the Hebrew Alphabet are referable to Jod and He. The Father is perfect love and the Mother perfect severity. The latter had seven sons, namely, the Edomite Kings, who had no foundation in the Holy Ancient One.[2] These are empty

---

[1] Or according to the Vulgate : *Gloria Dei est celare verbum.*
[2] See Book IV, § 3, p. 141.

lights dispelled by the source of lights concealed within the Mother. Male and female are conformations of the Holy Ancient One, corresponding to KETHER, and represented mystically by three heads signifying: (*a*) the Unmanifested Wisdom, which is so withdrawn that it is as though it were not, in contradiction to that which is manifested in the thirty-two paths; (*b*) the Supreme Crown, which is the Holy Ancient One; and (*c*) the Head which neither knows nor is known, namely, AIN SOPH. Thus on the one side of KETHER is CHOKMAH, or Wisdom: this is the Father; while on the other is BINAH, the Mother or increment of Understanding; and above is the *latens Deitas*.

These instances of Loria's skill in developing and distorting the Zoharic symbolism of the three supernal SEPHIROTH must suffice as a specimen of the whole commentary, which, it may be added, does not proceed—in this its Latin version, beyond the first chapter of the BOOK OF CONCEALMENT. Loria affirms, as the sum of the whole mystery, that man in his prayers should fix his mind upon the foundation of all foundations, that he may derive to himself a certain influence and benediction from the depths of that source. In this manner the obscurities of Kabbalism are redeemed at times by the simplicity and depth of the lesson which is extracted from them.

THE BOOK OF THE REVOLUTIONS OF SOULS is obviously of more living consequence than an obscure exposition of so obscure a work as SIPHRA DI ZENIOUTHA; but it is difficult to give account of it in a small space because the system which it develops is involved, even for a Kabbalistic work. The greatest importance has been attached to it by speculators like Éliphas Lévi, who made no distinction between Zoharic and later doctrine.

The basis of its scheme is the doctrine of the BOOK OF CONCEALMENT and its expository synods concerning the Seven Edomite Kings who emanated and passed away prior to the production of the present universe. In these Kings there was good as well as evil, and a separation therefore was made, that which was good being used for the material of the Four Kabbalistic Worlds as they are now constituted. Each of these Worlds, according to Isaac de Loria, has its MACRO-PROSOPUS, Supernal Father, Supernal Mother, MICROPROSOPUS and Bride, all derived from the Seven Kings. A like origin is attributed to souls, and they are disposed similarly in the Four Worlds, some corresponding to the Bride, some to MICROPROSOPUS, some to the Father Supernal, some to the Supernal Mother and some again to MACROPROSOPUS in the World of ASSIAH. The totality of these souls constitutes Psyche in ASSIAH, which in reference to the Supernal Personalities of that World has therefore five parts: the Psyche in the Psyche, or NEPHESH of ASSIAH, the *mundus factivus;* the medial spirit, or RUAH of the *Psyche factiva;* the *mens,* or NESHAMAH; the *vitalitas,* or HAÏA; and the *singularitas,* individuality, or YEHIDAH, all belonging to the *Psyche factiva,* or NEPHESH of ASSIAH. There is a similar distribution through the Three Superior Worlds, RUAH and its five-fold division being referred to YETZIRAH, NESHAMAH to BRIAH, CHIAH to ATZILUTH, and JECHIDA, possibly to the World of Unmanifest Deity which is beyond ATZILUTH; but Loria's system is not extended above the measures of the Tree of Life. Each of the five divisions is again attributed as follows in the Sephirotic scheme:

I. NEPHESH to MALKUTH, the Kingdom, *i.e.*, the Bride.
II. RUAH to the SEPHIROTH of MICROPROSOPUS.
III. NESHAMAH to the Mother, *i.e.*, BINAH.
IV. CHIAH to the Father, *i.e.*, CHOKMAH.
V. YEHIDAH to KETHER, *i.e.*, the Crown.[1]

We are now in a position to appreciate the standpoint of Franck when he observed that Loria added his own reveries to Zoharic teaching. The developments have at the same time been considerably simplified in this digest.

All these souls were contained in the Archetypal or Protoplastic Adam at the time that he was formed, some corresponding to the head, others to the eyes, and so with all the members. But these souls are those of the Israelites, who are *gens unica in terram.* We must look elsewhere for the origin of the nations of the world. The recrements, the evil and rejected parts of the Edomite Kings are the *cortices* or shells which compose the averse Adam Belial, evolved by our late expositor from rare Zoharic allusions to the SEPHIROTH

---

[1] It follows that each of the Four Worlds has the Four Worlds within it, and the Ten SEPHIROTH tabulated in the authentic Tree of Life. Other Loria speculations shew each SEPHIRA as containing all SEPHIROTH. Compare Book VI, § 2, p. 254. There is perhaps a certain vestige of this notion in the ZOHAR.

of the shadow. When the Adam and Eve of Genesis partook of the forbidden fruit, their fall confounded the good with the evil of the *cortices*, that of Adam with the male shells of Samael or Adam Belial, and that of Eve with the evil of his bride Lilith, the *spurcities* of the serpent; for the serpent had commerce with Eve according to Issac de Loria, which is a recurring but not invariable doctrine of the ZOHAR. It was after this fall that the nations of the world were produced from the shells. This is the doctrine which certain dreamers of the late nineteenth century accepted by implication when they spoke of the connection between later Kabbalism and the Secret Traditions on which their devotion was fixed. To put the position tersely, the souls of the Israelites were distributed in the members of the protoplastic Adam, regarded in his mystical extension through the four worlds, and the souls of the Gentiles in the members of Adam Belial, belonging to the Averse Tree. It is not seemingly affirmed that if man had remained in perfection he would have procreated according to the way of Nature and brought an Israel of super-election into the world; but the Fall at least was responsible for the souls of the nations taking flesh on earth. Liberation from the foulness and venom of the serpent—as things are—is by generation and death only, whereby the good is separated from the evil, until all nations of the world shall have been brought forth from the evil and the Israelites from the good kind.

From the time when the good and evil were thus confounded two things have been necessary: (1) that the good man should be separated from the evil; (2) that the portion of the good should be restored. The first is accomplished by observation of the prohibitive precepts of the Law, and the second by that of the affirmative. Both classes must be accomplished in all their number, and in thought, word and deed, by every soul, whose revolutions therefore must continue until the whole Law has been fulfilled. This Law must be studied also in each of its four senses, failing which the revolutions of the deficient soul will further be prolonged. This scheme seems to apply exclusively to the Israelites, as the nations of the world can be destined only to return whence they came, and Adam Belial is obviously not under the Law. The scheme, however, is subject to a certain mitigation, as revolution proper is sometimes replaced by *status embryonatus*.

Revolution is the entrance of a soul into the body of an infant at birth, to experience the pain and trial prepared for that body. The alternative condition is the entrance of a soul into the body of a grown man, who must be at least thirty years old,[1] *i.e.*, when he is obliged to fulfil the precepts. The *status embryonatus* is entered either (*a*) because the soul in question has something to fulfil which was neglected in the preceding revolution; or (*b*) for the benefit of the man who is impregnated, *i.e.*, to justify and direct him. Revolution occurs (1) for the cleansing of sin; (2) for the fulfilment of a neglected precept; (3) for the leading of others into the right way, in which case the returning soul is perfect in justice; (4) to receive the true spouse, who was not deserved by the soul in the prior revolution. Four souls may revolve in one body, but not more, while the *status embryonatus* may associate three alien souls with a single man, but again no more. The object of all revolutions and all Kabbalistic embryology is the return of the Israelites into the stature of the first Adam, all having been involved in his fall since he included all.

The Kabbalistic doctrine of revolution according to Isaac de Loria is not Zoharic doctrine—though it has a certain ground therein—nor is it a scheme of reincarnation peculiar to any other school of theosophy in the past or at the present day. In so far as it differs from the ZOHAR, it would be unreasonable to regard it as a fuller light of any old Tradition; it is greatly curious, yet fitly described as a reverie, written by R. Hayyim Vital out of the head of Isaac de Loria, and perhaps owing something to the scribe.

C.—NAPTHALI HIRTZ

This German Kabbalist, who is known otherwise as Napthali Herz ben Jacob Elhanan, was born at Frankfort-on-the-Main in the second half of the sixteenth century, but he is said to have lived in Palestine and presumably died there at an uncertain date, few biographical particulars being extant concerning him. His work, entitled THE VALLEY OF THE KING, was made great use of by Rosenroth, who gave, firstly, a compendium of its content [2] in the form of one hundred and

---

[1] The Jewish age of reason.
[2] So far at least as the first part is concerned, being that which was printed at Amsterdam, 1648, under the title of EMEK HA-MELEK. The second part, or GAN HA-MELEK, has remained in manuscript.

thirty KABBALISTIC THESES,[1] arranged with considerable perspicuity; in the second place, the first six sections of the treatise, designed as an introduction to the ZOHAR for the better comprehension thereof;[2] and, thirdly, all that part of it which is concerned with the BOOK OF CONCEALMENT and the two Synods as a commentary on these works.[3] A large part of the ROYAL VALLEY is included therefore in KABBALA DENUDATA, the excerpts extending over several hundred pages. Its author belonged to the school of Isaac de Loria, and he appears to have traversed a portion of the ground covered by the Lorian MSS. of R. Hayyim Vital. After the same manner that these develop and exaggerate Zoharic metapsychical teaching, so the ROYAL VALLEY extends Kabbalistic cosmology, and classifies it in correspondence with the parts or divisions of the human soul, as these are found in the ZOHAR. The *mundus prior* of Kabbalism, *i.e.*, the emanation of the Seven Edomite Kings, is termed the world of NEPHESH, and it was destroyed with the souls belonging to it because evil prevailed therein. The actual world is that of RUAH, in which good and evil are confused, but good comes out of the evil and at last all shall be good. Then a new world shall succeed, being that of NESHAMAH, and this will be the Sabbath of Grace. It follows therefore that the present order must pass away, and this is symbolised by the death of the second Hadad, the eighth Edomite King, as recorded in 1 Chron. i. 50, 51. In the day of this destruction the spirits of impurity, namely, the shells, shall be burnt up entirely, God will establish a new creation and will bring forth from His glorious light the mystery of the NESHAMAH of His Great Name. The dominion of this NESHAMAH is the King who shall reign over Israel, and in that day the Lord shall be one, and His Name one.

The hypothesis of the creation of the world begins with the contraction of the Divine Presence, producing that space which is termed primæval air. " Before the emanations issued forth and the things which are were created, the Supreme Light was extended infinitely. When it came into the Supreme Mind to will the fabrication of worlds, the issue of emanations and the emission as light of the perfection of

---

[1] KABBALA DENUDATA, *Apparatus in Librum Sohar pars secunda*, i. 150 *et seq.*
[2] *Ibid.* ii. 152 *et seq.*
[3] *Ibid.* ii. *partis secundæ tractatus quartus*, pp. 47 *et seq.*

His active powers, aspects and attributes, then that Light was in some measure compressed, receding in every direction from a particular central point, and thus a certain vacuum was left in mid-infinite, wherein emanations might be manifested."

It is to this treatise that Kabbalism owes the curious conception of the evolution of SEPHIROTH by a process of explosion, through the excess of light which distended them. From the fragments of the broken vessels originated the Four Worlds, the shells both good and evil, and myriads of souls. This notion is fundamentally similar to that of Isaac de Loria, and becomes identical in its developments. As it is impossible to compress the scheme of the treatise within the limits that are here possible, I will add only that the ROYAL VALLEY regards KETHER as containing *in potentia* all the remaining SEPHIROTH, so that originally they were not distinguishable therefrom. "Precisely as in man there exist the four elements in potence but undistinguishable specifically, so in this Crown there were all the remaining numerations." It is added that in the Second World, called that of restoration, KETHER became the Cause of Causes and the Ancient of the Ancients. We see therefore that, according to this late school of Kabbalism, the first attempt at manifestation by the *latens Deitas* went utterly astray, and that the evil of the whole world is the result of the failure of God—a peculiar reverie which is found also in the Talmud.

D.—ABRAHAM COHEN IRIRA [1]

This Spanish Jew was another and late follower of the school of de Loria, but tinctured by Platonic philosophy, which he sought to harmonise with Kabbalism in his GATE OF THE HEAVENS.[2] His other treatise is BETH ELOHIM, the HOUSE OF GOD, containing three dissertations in exposition of the doctrines of Loria, but founded upon and citing at considerable length the metapsychical portions of the FAITHFUL SHEPHERD, the PEKUDE section in the ZOHAR, and the

---

[1] The name is given in the form adopted by Rosenroth and as such familiar. It is otherwise Abraham Cohen de Herrera and accurately Alonzo de Herrera, who was of Spanish birth, but died at Amsterdam in 1631.

[2] KABBALA DENUDATA, *Apparatus . . . pars tertia*, t. i.

ANCIENT SUPPLEMENTS of that work.[1] So much space has been given already to Kabbalistic psychology that it will be permissible to dismiss this writer in a few words. The first dissertation in the HOUSE OF GOD rests chiefly on Zoharic utterances attributed to R. Simeon ben Yohai, who is termed the mouthpiece of holiness and the angel of the Lord; it recites the emanation of the SEPHIROTH according to the received doctrine, develops the system of the hierarchy of evil spirits, who are termed *cortices*, or shells, and of the ten sinister or impure Numerations—otherwise, the AVERSE SEPHIROTH. It examines also in a special chapter the opinion of R. Isaac de Loria concerning eleven classes of shells, and of R. Moses of Cordova concerning the connection of the angels with the celestial bodies, and concerning their physical vestments. The second dissertation treats of the different angelical orders and the seven heavens, while the third deals with elementary spirits and the nature of the soul.

We have seen that the HOUSE OF GOD has been included unaccountably by some occult writers [2]—who did not know their subject—among the books which constitute the ZOHAR, but it is a commentary or development, of considerable importance in its own sphere, yet neither possessing nor claiming any pretension to antiquity. Both works were written in Spanish and remained in manuscript till they had been translated into Hebrew, in which form they appeared at Amsterdam in 1665.

E.—ISSACHAR BEN NAPTHALI

This expositor of Kabbalism seems to have been a contemporary of Loria, and, like him, was a German. His chief work, the VISION OF THE PRIEST, was printed at Cracovia in 1559.[3] It is a synopsis of the entire ZOHAR, or, more properly, a methodised analysis of its contents, distributed under a number of titles, each of which is sub-divided according to the Mosaic books. It has been found almost impossible to make use of it for the purposes of this study, and it is indeed designed only for the assistance of the scholar who may

---

[1] KABBALA DENUDATA, ii. *partis tertiæ tractatus I.*, pp. 188 *et seq.*
[2] As, for example, S. L. MacGregor Mathers in the introduction to his KABBALAH UNVEILED.
[3] Translated in the KABBALA DENUDATA, ii. *pars prima ejusque tractatus primus*, p. 1. *et seq.*

desire to consult the ZOHAR on a given subject. The other works of R. Issachar are of similar character, and are, in fact, those technical treatises mentioned at the beginning of the present section as outside the scope of the present inquiry. I find no particulars concerning him, even in the JEWISH ENCYCLOPÆDIA, which fails to follow up a cross-reference s.v. Napthali Herz ben Issachar.

II.—THE BOOK OF PURIFYING FIRE

When a given order of mystical symbolism, possessing distinct objects and a sphere of application more or less defined, is applied to the purposes of another order, we may expect to derive some curious results from the analogy thus instituted if we can get to understand the method, though, as I have indicated, this superincession of typology tends to be somewhat dazing in its results. The treatise entitled ÆSH MEZAREPH, which signifies Purifying Fire, is an instance of the application of Kabbalistic apparatus to the purposes of Alchemy, and is, so far as I am aware, the sole instance of its kind. In this connection, however, we shall do well to remember that Hermetic and Kabbalistic philosophy are ascribed by some authorities on occultism to a common source,[1] while the rabbinical influence on Alchemy is illustrated by such inventions as that about Rabbi Abraham and Flamel, not to speak of a work under the title of THE PHILOSOPHICAL STONE, which is attributed idly to Saadiah by Moses Botrel, and is known only by a single quotation. A few metallic allusions are to be found in the ZOHAR, which recognises the existence of an archetypal gold, and regards the metals generally as composite substances. But these references are almost less than incidental, and it is needless to say that there is no cryptic chemistry whatever in the great theosophical storehouse.

The treatise on Purifying Fire is said to have been written in Aramaic Chaldee. It was made use of so largely by Rosenroth in his LEXICON that practically the whole work is affirmed to have been rendered into Latin in the pages of

---

[1] Thus Thomas Vaughan (Eugenius Philalethes), see Book X, § 11, affirms in his MAGIA ADAMICA that the learning of the Jews, i.e., their Kabbalah, was chemical, and that Flamel's BOOK OF ABRAHAM THE JEW is the best proof thereof. See A. E. Waite: THE WORKS OF THOMAS VAUGHAN, London, 1919, pp. 171, 172.

KABBALA DENUDATA.[1] It was reconstructed from this source in the early part of the eighteenth century by an Unknown Hermetic Student, styling himself a Lover of Philalethes, and was by him put into an English vesture.[2] In the year 1894 this translation was included in a series of Hermetic reprints under the editorship of Dr. Wynn Westcott.[3] The preface and notes which accompany this edition appear under the denomination of *Sapere Aude*, being one of his pseudonyms, and have certain points of interest. No information is given, however—and of course none was to be expected—as to the Chaldee original, either by the English translator or his modern editor.

There is further no evidence available by which we can fix with any degree of precision the period at which this treatise was composed.[4] It is subsequent, of course, to the promulgation of the ZOHAR, which it quotes frequently. It is subsequent to the GARDEN OF POMEGRANATES by R. Moses of Cordova, a treatise belonging to the middle of the sixteenth century, which it quotes also. It borrows processes from R. Mordechai, a Kabbalistic alchemist, whose date I have failed to discover,[5] and it refers to the Latin treatises of Geber. We may conclude that it does not antedate Rosenroth by any considerable period, and that it may be placed conjecturally at the beginning of the seventeenth century, or a little earlier. Finally, it contains expressions which are common to most of the Latin alchemists, and were by them derived from the Greeks, such as, " He that is wise may correct natures." It does not possess the interest or importance which would attach to a chemico-Kabbalistic treatise of the ZOHAR period,

---

[1] The authority—such as it is—is that of Dr. Westcott, but no one has seen the original since Rosenroth, and the statement represents therefore not merely a personal speculation, but one of a hazardous kind.

[2] ÆSH MEZAREPH, or Purifying Fire. A Chymico-Kabbalistic treatise collected from the KABBALA DENUDATA of Knorr von Rosenroth, London, 1714. Perhaps it should be added that the translator's pseudonym is an allusion to Eirenæus Philalethes, a famous English adept of the seventeenth century, whose identity, like that of his admirer, has never been discovered.

[3] COLLECTANEA HERMETICA, vol. iv. London, 1894.

[4] It is mentioned by Claverus in his OBSERVATIONS ON THE MOST USEFUL THINGS IN THE WORLD, 1706, pp. 72 *et seq*. He gives an account of it designed to shew that the Jews accommodated the Kabbalistic SEPHIROTH to CHRYSOPŒIA, *i.e.*, the Art of Alchemy. He states also that the Jews hold the ÆSH MEZAREPH in such high esteem that they consider no Christian worthy of reading it.

[5] A number of writers, mostly Kabbalistic, are classed under this name in the bibliography of Bartolocci, but there is no alchemist among them, the statement obtaining also for the JEWISH ENCYCLOPÆDIA, its cross-references included.

and I have not been able to find any evidence on the authority ascribed to it.[1]

In the supplement to his KEY OF THE GREAT MYSTERIES, Éliphas Lévi gives, firstly, what he calls the fragments of the ÆSH MEZAREPH, terming it one of the most important books of Hermetic science; secondly, the complements of its eight chapters, being further fragments which he claims to have discovered; thirdly, a hypothetical restitution of the original.[2] The methods of the brilliant French occultist are well illustrated in each case. It should be observed that the fragments are designed to exhibit the difficulties and the weariness which his researches have spared to his readers, and to illustrate the conscientious and serious nature of his studies. The first section proves when examined not to be fragments of the ÆSH MEZAREPH, but a loose paraphrase which has a very slender correspondence with the original. The second section, which is similarly paraphrase, is substantially to be found in Rosenroth and the English version. The hypothetical reconstruction serves only to shew that Lévi, like every one else, never saw the original which some have said is still extant, or he would not have so misplaced his ingenuity. Lastly, he attributes the work to Rabbi Abraham of the Flamel mythos, thus investing it with an antiquity which is contradicted by its own references.[3]

Before indicating, however briefly, the heads of its contents, it is necessary to observe that ÆSH MEZAREPH must be for the ordinary student only a curious memorial of the connections instituted between two orders of cryptic symbolism. It is described by its latest editor as "suggestive rather than explanatory," and he adds that its alchemical processes are not set forth "in such a way that they could be carried out by a

---

[1] Dr. Gerhard Scholem published an interesting and important study of ALCHEMY AND THE KABBALAH in the MONATSCHRIFT FÜR GESCHICHTE UND WISSENSCHAFT DES JUDENTUMS in 1925 and reprinted it subsequently as a pamphlet. He affirms that after examining every Kabbalistic text which came within his reach, it is certain that Alchemy and Kabbalism cannot be reconciled, if only because gold is the perfect metal for the one and silver for the other. As to ÆSH MEZAREPH, it is concerned with producing silver rather than gold, but it is not a treatise on actual processes of transmutation. Its Kabbalistic parts may be circa sixteenth century. It should be noted that, according to the ZOHAR, II, 147b; IV., 65, gold is superior to silver.

[2] LA CLEF DES GRANDS MYSTÈRES. See RENSEIGNEMENTS sur les grands mystères de la philosophie hermétique, pp. 405 et seq.

[3] Firstly, in the title, which reads, Fragments de L'ASH MÉZAREPH du Juif Abraham; secondly, in the hypothetical recomposition of the treatise which connects it with the mystical book possessed by Flamel. The ÆSH MEZAREPH is entirely anonymous, and is included as such in the bibliography of Wolf, ii. 1265.

neophyte; any attempt to do so would discover that something vital was missing at one stage or other." The fact is so true of all alchemical literature that it does not need stating, and the ÆSH MEZAREPH has the common difficulties of purely Hermetic books complicated further by the system of Gematria and the Sephirotic correspondences of metals.

On the correspondences here indicated the treatise is based mainly, and it is in this sense that the mysteries of alchemical transmutation are said to "differ not from the superior mysteries of the Kabbalah." The SEPHIROTH of the material world are identical with those of the archetypal, and they are the same in the mineral kingdom. The alchemical root of the metals corresponds to KETHER; all metals originate therefrom, as the other SEPHIROTH are all emanations from the Crown. The metallic root is concealed, and so also is the Crown. Lead is referred to CHOKMAH, which proceeds immediately from KETHER, as Saturn from the metallic root. Tin has the place of BINAH, Silver that of CHESED, and these three are the white metallic natures. Among the red, Gold is is in correspondence with GEBURAH, Iron with TIPHERETH, and the hermaphroditic Brass with NETZACH and HOD. Quicksilver is referred to JESOD, and "the true Medicine of Metals" to MALKUTH. The attribution will appear in some cases a little conventional, and it depends upon a curious use of Scriptural authority. However, the writer adds: "If any one hath placed these things in another order, I shall not contend with him, inasmuch as all systems tend to the one truth." In illustration of this, he cites another attribution, as follows:

"The three Supernals," namely, KETHER, CHOKMAH and BINAH, "are the three fountains of metallic things." "The thick water," that is, Mercury, "is KETHER, Salt is CHOKMAH and Sulphur is BINAH." These are the Three Principles of the alchemists. This attribution, says the treatise, is "for known reasons." CHESED, GEBURAH and TIPHERETH correspond as before to Silver, Gold and Iron; NETZACH is Tin, HOD is Copper, JESOD is Lead, while MALKUTH is the "Metallic Woman," the "Luna of the Wise" and the "Field into which the seeds of secret minerals ought to be cast, that is, the Water of Gold." The attribution in either case has a concealed sense which "no tongue may be permitted to utter." It seems to follow that superficial explanations offered at one and another point should not be taken literally, as, for example, that Silver is referred to CHESED " on account of its whiteness, which denotes Mercy and Pity." The KAMEA or Magical Squares of the planets are given in connection with each of the seven metals, but not always correctly in the printed copies.

The peculiar genius of the work is illustrated in the third chapter, where Daniel's vision of the beast with ten horns is interpreted alchemically by the help of *gematria*.[1]

III.—THE MYSTERIES OF LOVE

With the sole exception of Abraham Cohen Irira, the succession of Kabbalistic writers whom we have thus passed in review never descended to the use of a vulgar tongue. To that exception we must now add the case of R. Juda, son of Isaac Abravanel, better known under the designation of Leo the Hebrew. His inclusion in an account of developments which find their place in Kabbalism is to be justified only as an example of the distance which was travelled at times. Leo is, comparatively speaking, early, though I have placed him later, for it is only at a far distance that he offers any link with the ZOHAR, which obviously he had never seen. He was born in the kingdom of Castile shortly after the middle of the fifteenth century, and it is even stated that he broke away from all Jewish tradition by becoming a Christian. At the same time there are two additional points by which he is forced upon our notice: in the first place, he has been a favourite subject of allusion with some modern esoteric writers, and should not be overlooked therefore in a work which is compelled to recognise the recurring fact of occult interest in Kabbalism; in the second place, his dialogues on love have been more popular than any Kabbalistic treatise—actual or imputed. According to the best opinion, they were written originally in Italian: in any case, they appeared in this language at Rome in the year 1535. They were reprinted at Venice in 1541. Then they were translated into Latin by Sarrazin, being published, according to Wolf, in 1564 at Vienna. This version, which has been praised for its elegance, was included by Pistorius in his famous ARTIS

---

[1] For another excursus of my own on ÆSH MEZAREPH the reader may consult THE SECRET TRADITION IN ALCHEMY, Appendix II, pp. 377-394.

CABALISTICÆ SCRIPTORES, Basle, 1587. They were rendered twice into Spanish, the first version, and the only one of my acquaintance, being that of Juan Costa, in 1584. Lastly, there have been at least three French translations, namely, by Pontus de Thiard, 1580; the Seigneur du Parc Champerrois; and Alexander Weill, 1875.

Though he wrote, as it is said, in Italian, Abravanel was Portuguese by birth, but was removed by his father to Spain and thence to Italy, through the edict of Ferdinand and Isabella. This was in 1492. His first refuge was Naples, where he entered the king's service; but the king died and his realm fell into the hands of Charles VIII., after which the " Spanish Jew " became once more a wanderer. Some say that he retired to Sicily, afterwards to Corfu and Ponilles, and, finally, to Venice, where he died in 1535. Others relate that he fixed his abode at Genoa, and there practised medicine with honour for a long period. As to the change, real or pretended, in his religious opinions there is also serious confusion. Basnage says that he was a man of a mild nature who mixed familiarly with Christians, but inveighed against them in his writings, especially against the priests and the Pope.[1] Pistorius, on the other hand, represents him as a converted Jew.[2] He is the subject of high praise, based on intimate knowledge, in the bibliography of Bartolocci.[3]

The interest in Leo the Hebrew can be only of a mystical kind, and it is on this basis presumably that he was included by Pistorius in his ambitious and unfinished attempt to engarner the signal treatises of Kabbalism. Even so, it is difficult to see that such a text has any title to a place among records of the Secret Tradition in Israel. We look in vain for the essential doctrines of Jewish Theosophy, as these are enshrined in the ZOHAR; we have in their place the elegant sentimentalism which characterised Italian literature at the period; we are reminded now of Boccalini, and now of the declamatory Latin exercises of Palingenius. The machinery of the dialogues, if they can be said to possess machinery, belongs to classical mythology; the allusions, the illustrations,

---

[1] HIST. DES JUIFS, l. vii. t. v. pp. 1898, 1899.
[2] So also does Drach in his notice of the Kabbalah in L'HARMONIE ENTRE L'ÉGLISE ET LA SYNAGOGUE.
[3] BIBLIOTHECA RABBINICA, iii. 86. There is no mention of his conversion in the notice, but the original edition of the Dialogues describes their author as *di natione Hebreo et di poi fatto Chriſtiano*. There seems to be good evidence against the testimony.

the images are echoes of Greek and Latin poets; when the philosophical authority is not Aristotle, it is Plato; there is only one direct reference to the Kabbalah in the whole three hundred folio pages which the dialogues occupy in Pistorius, and it is then a slender allusion to successive renewals of the world, which suggests that the author had misconceived the "restoration" of the BOOK OF CONCEALMENT. As against this there is not one trace of characteristic Hebrew thought or influence; there is nothing which would lead us to suspect a Jewish authorship, except such negative evidence as the absence of any Christian reference. If the work can be said to recall anything outside the *belles lettres* of the sixteenth century in Italy, it is certain Sufic poets adapted to the understanding of Venetian ladies in the days of the Doges. And here, indeed, is the true secret of its popularity. It is not only so pleasing, so educated according to the lights of its period, so correct in its sentiment and breathing too often so little but mere sentiment, so refined in its amorous passion and so much above reproach, that it does not contain a single indelicacy or a single recondite thought, until it passes towards the heights of its subject, as the undertaking draws to a close. One of its French translators has thought it worth while to append a glossary of its difficult words, but it has no difficulties and its words are simplicity itself. It has many passages which even at the present day may be called delightful reading, and it is redeemed from the commonplaces of sentiment by tender suggestions of shallow allegory. The Philo and Sophia of the dialogue are enough by their mere names to suggest transcendentalism to an occult student, and more than one criticism has supposed it to be concerned *ab initio* and only with the love of God. As a fact it discerns in all things the activity, the influence and the power of the master passion, and another of the secrets of its popularity in the warm-blooded world of the South is that however much love is transcendentalised in the dialogues, it is always sexual, as it is throughout the ZOHAR. So also the philosophy of this love is the doctrine of delectation and felicity. Delectation is union with the beloved, and the good and the beautiful are identified in words that recall the light metaphysics of Cousin and the blessed life of Fichte.

The general definition of love is that it is a vivifying spirit which permeates all the world, and a bond uniting the entire universe. But the proper definition of the perfect love of man and woman is the concurrence of the loving with the beloved to this end, that the beloved shall be transformed into the lover. When such love is equal between the partakers it is described as the conversion of the one into the other being. Below such human love in apotheosis, there is not only that which subsists among mere animals, but in things insensible, in the hypothetical first matter, in the elements and in the heavenly bodies, which are drawn one to the other and move in regular order by the harmonious impulse and interaction of a reciprocal affection.

Hereof is the form and the spirit, and—for the rest—though I have spoken plainly, this Book of Love and its Mysteries moves forward to deeper things, when the knowledge of God is presented, as regards language and images, under a transcendentalised sexual aspect. God is loved in proportion as He is known, and as He cannot be known entirely by men, nor His wisdom by the human race, so He cannot be loved as He deserves, for such an exalted sentiment transcends the power of our will. The mind therefore must be content to know God according to the measure of its possibility and not that of His excellence. The knowledge and love of God are both necessary to beatitude, for He is the True Intellectual Agent with Whom consists felicity, which is not to be found in the knowledge of all things, but in the One alone Who is Himself all others. This felicity does not consist in the cognoscitive act of God, which leads to love, nor in the love which succeeds such knowledge, but in the copulation of the most interior and united Divine Knowledge, for this is the sovereign perfection of the created intellect, the last act and happy end in which it finds itself rather divine than human. Such copulative felicity with God cannot be continuous, however, during our present life, because our intellect is here joined to the matter of our fragile body.

It may be added that Leo the Hebrew, like Raymund Lully, accounts for the self-sufficiency of the Divine Nature on the ground that the love, the lover and the beloved are all one in God; that God alone is the end of all love in the universe; and that His love towards His creatures is the stimulation of a desire of good for their sake and not for His own. It may be inferred also that a mystical meaning is not improbably contained in such speculations as that of the sleep of love, of amorous contemplation, of the graving of the image of the beloved in the thought of the lover, and of the ravishment of this state. In other terms and in another setting, it could be said that all this belongs to the root-matter of highest Mysticism. It is here and there like a door which opens on the Infinite; but it is to be feared that if Abravanel had conceived something in the mind on these great subjects, he had not conceived in the soul.

IV.—MINOR LITERATURE OF KABBALISM

We have now completed our study of the chief Kabbalistic writings to which any currency has been given; but we have by no means exhausted the literature either before or after the appearance of the ZOHAR. It has been classified in chronological order, but otherwise uncritically enough, in a special list by Bartolocci at the beginning of his vast work, and those who desire to pursue the subject further will there see how impossible it is to deal with in this place. It is, moreover, outside the purpose of our inquiry. A few names, however, may be mentioned which are to some extent typical of the minor literature of Kabbalism.

When the ZOHAR was on the verge of the historical horizon, in the reign of Alphonso X., we find at Toledo Rabbi Mevi, the son of Theodore, Prince of the Levites of Burgos. Though a Kabbalist and a light of Kabbalism, he opposed Nahmanides, thus shewing that at a comparatively early period there was little unanimity among the doctors of Theosophy and the voices of Tradition, on the subject of Tradition or Theosophy. His book is entitled BEFORE AND BEHIND, which is supposed to indicate that he had approached the Kabbalah from every point of view.[1]

Side by side with philosophical Kabbalism the spurious practical part, the ARS KABBALISTICA, never wanted its professors. As neither worse nor better than the rest we may mention R. Chamai of Arragon, in the early part of the fifteenth century. One of his practical secrets was the determination of the sex of an unborn child by placing the nuptial couch from North to South, thus indicating respect

[1] Bartolocci, BIBLIOTHECA MAGNA RABBINICA, iv, 18; Basnage, HISTOIRE DES JUIFS, v, 1773.

for the majesty of God, which resides between East and West, and might suffer dishonour by marital intercourse taking place in the same direction. Such consideration, it was deemed, would not go without its reward in the birth of male children.[1]

In the reign of Ferdinand and Isabella, and a victim of their edict of expulsion, flourished Joseph Gikatilla, called the divine Kabbalist and the Thaumaturge, who wrote on the attributes of God, the Divine Names and the SEPHIROTH.[2] He has been mentioned already.

At the period of Picus de Mirandula Kabbalists abounded in Italy, many of whom were refugees from persecution in Spain and Portugal. Picus in his APOLOGIA affirms that his demonstrations of Christian dogma in Jewish Theosophy effected the conversion of a Kabbalist named Dattilius. As it is one of few instances on record, the sincerity of the change may be allowed to pass unchallenged.[3] Long afterwards, that is to say, in 1613, Samuel Nahunias, a Jew of Thessalonica, but residing at Venice, also abjured Judaism and wrote the PATH OF FAITH. So also, about 1672, Mordekai Kerkos composed a treatise directed against the Kabbalah; but it has not been printed. Basnage hints that such an action at that period seemed scarcely less subversive in Israel than to embrace Christianity. On the other hand, Judas Azael, about the same period, contributed to the literature of the Tradition by his THRONES OF THE HOUSE OF DAVID, a treatise dealing with the Fifty Gates of Understanding, while in Germany Nathan of Spire, better known, however, for a treatise in praise of the Holy Land, produced a Kabbalistic commentary on Deuteronomy iii. 13, under the title of MEGILLAH HAMNEOTH. In Holland, a few years previously, the famous Manasses composed his work on the resurrection of the body, which connects with Jewish esoteric theology

---

[1] Bartolocci, BIBLIOTHECA MAGNA RABBINICA, ii, 840; Basnage, HISTOIRE DES JUIFS, v, 1895.
[2] Ibid. v, 1899.
[3] In the sixteenth century Paul Elhananan became a convert to Christianity, and in his MYSTERIUM NOVUM sought to prove from the Kabbalah that Jesus of Nazareth was the true Messiah. Petrus Galatinus also abjured Judaism; so did Johannes Fortius, who wrote on the mystical meanings of the Hebrew Letters. Paul de Heredia was a convert of the fifteenth century. Bartolocci (iv, 420) mentions Louis Carret, a Frenchman of the sixteenth century, who in his VISIONS OF GOD defended the truth of the Catholic faith by means of the Kabbalah. Later names are Aaron Margalita, whose many works attempted to Christianise the Kabbalah. There are also Rittangelius, the editor of the SEPHER YETZIRAH, who turned Protestant; and Prosper Ruggieri, the astrologer.

by its defence of metempsychosis; and Isaac About, a Brazilian settled in the Low Countries, translated the PORTA CŒLORUM of Abraham Cohen Irira from the original Spanish into Hebrew.

These meagre memoranda, which do not pretend to represent a serious study, may close with the name of Spinoza, who connects also with Kabbalism, though it must be confessed that the tincture which he exhibits is little more than the memory of early reading.

BOOK X

SOME CHRISTIAN STUDENTS OF THE KABBALAH

BOOK X

SOME CHRISTIAN STUDENTS OF THE KABBALAH

I.—INTRODUCTORY

So far as our inquiry has proceeded no theosophical system would seem less connected with what is known conventionally as Magic than is the Kabbalah to all outward appearance. That there was, however, an imputed connection, there can be and is no doubt, for side by side with the Secret Tradition in Israel, as understood and set forth here, there was a so-called Practical and Thaumaturgical Kabbalah which not only belongs to Magic but has helped to create its forbidden arts in the West, as stated summarily in an early part of the present work. We owe our mediæval witchcraft chiefly to this source; we owe also our mediæval demonology; and the Jew, hounded out of Spain by the iniquitous edict of Ferdinand and Isabella, left to the Inquisition and its devildom another pretext for extermination, more fuel for the burning—in a word, the tremendous legacy of sorcery. The Jew was avenged in the magician.

When enumerating the alleged branches of Esoteric Tradition in Israel I endeavoured to distinguish that of Magic from Theosophy. While the traces of Theosophical Tradition are met with nowhere in remote antiquity, those of Magic abound: be it observed that the reference is to rumour and vestige, not to records at large, since these are mostly late. It was to be expected that the newer order of ideas should become interfused with the older. But the SEPHER YETZIRAH and the ZOHAR are not Magic, and that which drew the Christian students of the literature and made them seek to fathom the Kabbalistic Mystery was assuredly its Theosophical, transcendental indeed, but not its thaumaturgic part.

We are on the track here of another misconception which prevails among that class of thinkers who have discovered most reason to concern themselves with the claims of the Kabbalah. It is useless for the expositors of occult views and their too easy disciples to continue, as they have done in the past, appealing to Christian authorities as to great names supporting their notion of the subject. Those who accepted and those who vindicated the authenticity of the Secret Tradition had never dreamed of a religion behind all religions, nor did they look to Sanctuaries of Egypt for any light but that which perchance was carried into it by the descendants of Abraham. Persons of the class referred to have fallen into two major among many minor errors. In the first place, they cite as Christian Kabbalists various alleged authorities, within and without the mystical circle, who have no claim to the title; in the second place, they misconstrue entirely the position of those whose title itself may be beyond any challenge. Over and above these points, many names, great and otherwise, which it looks well to engross on the deeds of a brief for the defence, bear witness only to prevailing ignorance.

The purpose of the brief studies which follow is to demonstrate these facts, which are not without importance and are therefore an integral part of my scheme. They are not biographical sketches, and they are not bibliographical notes. They are designed to exhibit that among the names commonly cited in connection with Kabbalism, some should be removed from the list; some belong to a Quixotic attempt at discovering an *eirenicon* for Christendom and Jewry; some are not worth citing, because, despite their imputed authority, they have nothing of moment to tell us; and some, a bare residuum, with a handful of recent writers, may be left on the otherwise vacated benches.

II.—RAYMUND LULLY

The name of Raymund Lully has been cited as that of a considerable authority on the Kabbalah, as upon several other departments of secret knowledge. It is time to affirm that few ascriptions seem to possess less foundation in fact. It must be said, first of all, that there is indubitable evidence for distinguishing between two persons at least who bore this name: otherwise it was assumed for a second time at a later date. The original Raymund Lully was that seneschal of Majorca whose legend is narrated in a monograph on the *doctor illuminators* which I wrote in recent years.[1] He was born during the first half of the thirteenth century.[2] The second Raymund Lully was an alchemist.[3] His legend, enshrined in the deceitful memorial of a so-called Abbot of Westminster,[4] was unknown, so far as I can trace, till the beginning of the seventeenth century,[5] but the works by which he is distinguished from his prototype are certainly much earlier, possibly by two centuries.[6] There is a third and modern legend, which bears all the marks of invention on the part of its narrator, Éliphas Lévi, and this identifies the two personages by prolonging the life of the first through the instrumentality of the Great Elixir.[7] It is described as a popular legend, but Raymund Lully and his namesake were never of enough importance to impress the imagination of the people. The first was known chiefly as a scholastic reformer and a Christian evangelist, martyred for an ill-judged attempt at the propagation of the faith among the Mussulmen of Africa. The second has been described as a "Jewish neophyte," the denomination on its surface suggesting a proselyte of the gate. This is therefore the personality which would connect naturally with Kabbalism. The second Raymund Lully connects, however, exclusively with Alchemy, and his works are evidence that he did not renounce the Christian faith.[8] It is to him must be attributed those Keys,

---

[1] RAYMUND LULLY, ILLUMINATED DOCTOR, ALCHEMIST AND CHRISTIAN MYSTIC, 1922.

[2] The dates attributed to some of his works, if accurate, would shew that he was separated from his successor by more than a century, but they are in a sad state of confusion, and all popular sources of information are misleading. See, for example, Blackie's *Popular Encyclopædia*, *s.v.* Alchymy.

[3] See my SECRET TRADITION IN ALCHEMY, 1926, pp. 131, 132.

[4] TESTAMENTUM CREMERI, *Abbatis Westmonasteriensis, Angli, Ordinis Benedictini*.

[5] It was published at Frankfort in 1618, by Michael Maier, being the third tract of TRIPUS AUREUS, *hoc est tres tractatus chymici selectissimi*. In 1678 it reappeared in MUSEUM HERMETICUM *Reformatum et Amplificatum*, and is known in English by a translation of that collection, edited by myself, 2 vols. London. 1893.

[6] They contain a few personal memoranda, but of a mythical order.

[7] With material derived from Éliphas Lévi, and a pyrotechnic terminology from M. Huysman, a bizarre work entitled LE SATANISME ET LA MAGIE, by Jules Bois, compresses all the legends into one small pellet of fable which, published in 1895, was, I suppose, the last memorial on the subject of Raymund Lully till the Catalan poet of that name began to attract attention from the students of early Spanish literature.

[8] Witness the address to the Deity at the head of the TESTAMENTUM *Magistri Raymundi Lullii* (Mangetus: BIBLIOTHECA CHEMICA CURIOSA, i. 707, 708); the last words of its theoretical division—*Laus honor et gloria Jesu* (*ibid.* 762); the TESTAMENTUM NOVISSIMUM, addressed to King Charles: *Ideo mi Carole dilecte, te in filium sapientiæ dilectissimum ut*

Compendiums, Testaments and Codicils of Alchemy which are found in all the great collections of Hermetic treatises. He was so far imbued with the apostolic spirit of his predecessor that his great ambition was to engage some Catholic monarch in another barren crusade for the recovery of the Holy Sepulchre. According to his legend he transmuted into gold sufficient base metal for the minting of six million nobles, and gave it to an Edward, King of England, on condition that the latter assumed the Red Cross. The king did not keep his promise, and the adept escaped as he could from the extortion of further projections.[1]

The confusion of the two Raymunds is perhaps more excusable among occultists than for ordinary biographers. That Alchemy connects with Kabbalism, or that Kabbalism became identified with Alchemy, the treatise on Purifying Fire stands forth to bear its witness; but the alchemist *per se* is not, as we have seen, a Kabbalist, and there is no single word of Kabbalism in the Hermetic treatises of Raymund Lully the second. The doctor of Majorca does connect artificially with the esoteric tradition of the Jews, by the arbitrary use of certain words and methods, though he was not a proselyte of the gate; but his intellectual system is a mechanical introduction to the sciences, and has no title to the name, having nothing to do with a tradition, exoteric or esoteric, Jewish or Gentile. It has, moreover, no mystical foundation, and is concerned wholly with an educational method. It is untrue therefore to say that Raymund Lully was one of the grand and sublime masters of transcendent science, as Éliphas Lévi describes him. In the ARS MAGNA SCIENDI and the ARS NOTORIA there is as much occult significance as in the scholastic jest concerning *chimæra bombinans in vacuo*. The NOTARY ART of Solomon, which Robert Turner first printed in English, connects remotely with Kabbalism, and the ARS NOTORIA of Raymund Lully has a verbal connection, and no more, with this enchiridion of Jewry. It is the same with the treatise entitled DE AUDITU KABALISTICO, an *opusculum Raymundinum*, or particular application of the method of Lully, which has been ignorantly included among his works. The name alone

---

fidei catholicæ ampliatorem eligam; and again: *Accipe igitur in nomine sanctæ Trinitatis et æternæ Unitatis,* &c. (*ibid.* p. 790).

[1] See my *op. cit.*, caps. iv, v and vi. It contains a full discussion of the two Raymunds.

is occult, and its selection is beyond conjecture.[1] The work proves on examination to be a late offshoot of the great vacant pretentious system which enabled those who mastered it to dispute on all subjects with success, though perhaps without knowledge of any. Some great minds were captivated by it, but such captivities are among the weaknesses of great minds. The best that can be said for the ARS MAGNA is that it was discoursed upon by Cornelius Agrippa, that it was tolerated by Picus de Mirandula, and that the encyclopædic mind of Athanasius Kircher had embraced it sufficiently to produce a *summa magna* on the subject in one of his vast folios. And of these facts, at the present day, not one possesses a consequence. The chief philosophical mission of the first Raymund Lully was to protest against the school of Averroes;[2] his chief practical work was the exhortation of prelates and princes to found schools for the study of languages so as to facilitate the conversion of the heathen; but there were few who heard or heeded him. It was only after his death that his system obtained for a time a certain vogue. The collapse of the process of his beatification is one of the escapes of the Latin Church, because it would have helped to accredit a system which began and ended in words. It was not, as it has been described erroneously, an universal

---

[1] It is fair to say that Franck takes the opposite view, but with what qualification for judgment may be gathered from the fact that he accepts the attribution to Lully of the work mentioned above. He says that Lully was the first to reveal the name and existence of the Kabbalah to Christian Europe, for which there is no ground in fact; he thinks that it would be difficult to determine how far Lully was " an initiate of this mystical science " or the precise influence which it exercised on his doctrine. " I refrain from saying with a historian of philosophy (Tennemann) that he borrowed thence his belief in the identity of God and Nature " (I think that Tennemann has here misconstrued his author), " but it is certain that he had a very high idea of it, considering it a divine science, a veritable revelation addressed to the rational soul, and it may perhaps be permissible to suppose that the artificial processes used by Kabbalists to connect their opinions with the words of Scripture, such as the substitution of numbers or letters for ideas or words, may have contributed in no small degree to the invention of the Great Art. It is worthy of remark that more than two centuries and a half before the existence of the rival schools of Loria and Cordova, at the very time when some modern critics have sought to place the origin of the Kabbalah, Raymund Lully makes already a distinction between ancient and modern Kabbalists." The passage on which Franck seems to depend for his general view is as follows: *Dicitur hæc doctrina Kabbala quod, idem est secundum . . . Hebræos ut receptio veritatis cujuslibet rei divinitus revelata animæ rationali . . . . Est igitur Kabbala habitus animæ rationalis ex rectâ ratione divinarum rerum cognitivus. Propter quod apparet quod est de maximo etiam divino consequutivè divina scientia vocari debet.* This extract is derived from the *Opus Raymundinum* already mentioned.

[2] I am speaking throughout here of him who was Lully of the schools, whether or not he was also that Catalan poet, whose title to greatness has emerged of recent years, under the auspices of scholars who are content so far to know nothing of ARS MAGNA.

science, or a synthesis of knowledge; it was chaffer and noise; its egregious tabulations are a mockery for the modern understanding. Even the martyrdom of this eccentric Spanish enthusiast had a strain of the folly of suicide, if the martyrologists have told it truly. It had, however, its defenders, and it had in time its miraculous legend. So also, and for the space of some centuries, there was a quiet and intelligible cultus of Raymund Lully in the Balearic Islands, which, like other local sanctities, seems even at the present day to be something more than a memory.

I should add, in conclusion, that there are works by or attributed to the original Raymund Lully[1] which have no connection with his ARS MAGNA SCIENDI, as they have none with imputed occult science: they belong to a higher category. When we turn over the vast, uncompleted collection of his OPERA OMNIA, and dwell, as the devout student will do, on certain passages concerning the eternal subsistence of the lover and the beloved in God, concerning contemplation in God—*quomodo omnis nostra perfectio sit in perfectione nostri Domini Dei*—and the deep things of Divine Union, we begin to discern the existence, so to speak, of a third Lully, who has qualities which recommend him to our admiration that are wanting in the *Doctor illuminatus*, though he invented *Ars Magna*, and in the *Doctor alchemisticus*, even if he transmuted metals.[2]

III.—PICUS DE MIRANDULA

Magical legend has availed itself of the name of Mirandula, and on the warrant of his Kabbalistic enthusiasm has accredited him with the possession of a familiar demon.[3] His was the demon of Socrates which a late Cardinal Archbishop brought within the limits of natural and clerical orthodoxy.[4] His marvellous precocity furnished a thesis to the ingenuity of the late Gabriel Delanne, for, as with the music of Mozart and as with the mathematics of Pascal, it remains a ground of speculation how this Italian Crichton acquired his enormous

---

[1] The reference is here to the Catalan poet and the author of BLANQUERNA.
[2] See my *op. cit.*, c. vi. Some texts cited therein have been translated since into English from their Catalan originals by Professor Peers, but apart from all reference to Lully of the ARS MAGNA and the Hermetic Lully.
[3] Migne's DICTIONNAIRE DES SCIENCES OCCULTES, t. ii. col. 308.
[4] See Manning's brochure, *s.v.* THE DAIMON OF SOCRATES. London, 1874.

eruditon. Delanne would assure us [1] that he brought it with him at his birth, that it was an inheritance from a previous life and that Picus de Mirandula Kabbalised in a college of Babylon. On the other hand, Catholic writers, for whom his studies are unsavoury, affirm that he was swindled by an impostor who sold him sixty bogus MSS. on the assurance that they had been composed by the order of Esdras. "They contained only ridiculous Kabbalistic reveries." These MSS. have been enumerated and described by Gaffarel, and his monograph on the subject will be found, among other places, in the bibliography of Wolf.[2] As Mirandula, who was born on February 24th, 1463, and died mentally exhausted in 1494, is the first true Christian student of the Kabbalah, it is important to know what he derived from his studies in this respect. Now, unfortunately, we are met at the outset with a difficulty only too common in such inquiries. Of the Kabbalistic Conclusions arrived at by Picus de Mirandula, and actually bearing this name, there are two versions extant; there is that which we find in the collected editions of his works, both late and early, reproduced in the garner of Pistorius with a voluminous commentary by Archangelus de Burgo Nuovo, and there is that which we find with another commentary, though curiously by the same writer, in a little volume, published at Bologna in 1564—prior to the collection of Pistorius which belongs to 1587—and again at Basle in 1600.[3] The evidence is in favour of the first version, but nothing attaches to the question: it is that in any case which came to be known and used, the Bologna codex being so utterly obscure that I have not seen it mentioned. We may accept either without prejudice to the point which it is here designed to establish, and that is the nature of the enthusiasm which prompted Picus de Mirandula. In the first place, though he speaks of Magic in terms which may be held to indicate that he possessed a tolerant and open mind as to some of its claims and, like a learned man as he was, did not regard

---

[1] See in particular ÉTUDE SUR LES VIES SUCCESSIVES, *Mémoire présenté au Congrès Spirite International de Londres* (1898), *par Gabriel Delanne*, p. 61, where Mirandula is a case in point.

[2] Joh. Christophori Wolfii: BIBLIOTHECA HEBRÆA ... *Accedit in calce Jacobi Gaffarelli* INDEX CODICUM CABBALISTIC. MSS. *quibus* Jo. Picus, Mirandulanus Comes, *usus est*. 1715. The Index in question is reprinted from the Paris edition of 1651.

[3] *Archangelus de Burgo Nuovo agri Placentini*: APOLOGIA PRO DEFENSIONE DOCTRINÆ CABALÆ, &c. Ostensibly a reply to an impeachment of Mirandula by Peter Garzia.

it from the standpoint of Grimoire Sorcery, he is not to be considered as a disciple of any alleged Higher Magic. The only department of the putative Secret Arts which he has treated at any length is Astrology, and to this he devoted a long and undermining criticism, which in some of its salient parts is as good reading as Agrippa's VANITY OF THE SCIENCES, and on its special subject takes much the same point of view. We should not expect therefore that he betook himself to the esoteric speculations of Jewry because he was attracted by supposed supernormal powers ascribed to Divine Names, because he intended to compose talismans, or because he desired to evoke. I must not speak so confidently as to possible fascinations in the direction of GEMATRIA and THEMURAH, for his was a subtle and curious intelligence which found green spots or rather enchanted cities of mirage in many deserts of the mind, and he might have discovered mysteries in beheaded words and achroamatica in acrostics. There is, however, no proof that he did. The bibliographical legend which represents him purchasing MSS. on the assurance that the prophet Esdras had a hand in their production will disclose his probable views as to the antiquity of Kabbalistic literature. He took it, we may suppose, at its word, and the legend indicates also that he was persuaded easily: it was a common weakness in men of learning and enthusiasm at the period. On the other hand, it is more than certain that he did not regard this antiquity as a presumption that the Kabbalah was superior to Latin Christianity; the wisdom which he found therein was that of Christian doctrine: [1] when he hung up his famous theses in Rome and offered to defray the expenses of every scholar who would dispute with him, those theses included his KABBALISTIC CONCLUSIONS, but that which he sought to establish was a *via media* between Jewry and Christendom. When he turned the head of Pope Julius with Secret Mysteries of the THORAH, the enthusiasm which was communicated for a moment to the Chair of Peter was, like Lully's, that of the evangelist. The *servus servorum Dei* found other zeal for his ministry, and the comet of the schools blazed itself out. The KABBALISTIC CONCLUSIONS alone remain to tell that Rome had a strange dream in the evening

---

[1] The existence of Christian elements, or at least of materials which might be held to bear a Christian construction, is admitted by several Jewish writers of the post-Zoharic period.

of the fifteenth century.[1] They lie in a small compass and, as I believe that it will be of interest to shew what Picus de Mirandula extracted from his sixty MSS., I will translate them here for the reader. It ought perhaps to be premised that Éliphas Lévi rendered some of them in his own loose fashion and published them with a suggestive commentary, in LA SCIENCE DES ESPRITS,[2] ascribing them to the collection of Pistorius but without mentioning the name of Mirandula. He gave also what purports to be the Latin originals, but these he has polished and pointed. To do justice to his skill, they are occasionally much better than the quintessential Kabbalism of Picus, but as they are neither Picus nor the Kabbalah, I shall not have recourse to them for the purposes of the following version, except by some references in footnotes.

Kabbalistic Conclusions

I.

As man and the priest of inferior things sacrifices to God the souls of unreasoning animals, so Michael, the higher priest, sacrifices the souls of rational animals.

II.

There are nine hierarchies, and their names are CHERUBIM, SERAPHIM, CHASMALIM, ARALIM, TARSISIM, OPHANIM, ISHIM, MALACHIM, and ELOHIM.

III.

Although the Ineffable Name is the quality of clemency, it is not to be denied that it combines also the quality of judgment.[3]

IV.

The sin of Adam was the separation of the kingdom from the other branches.

V.

God created the world with the Tree of the Knowledge of Good and Evil, whereby the first man sinned.[4]

---

[1] They appeared originally at Rome in 1486, the volume being entitled: CONCLUSIONES PHILOSOPHICÆ, CABALISTICÆ ET THEOLOGICÆ. Picus wrote also CABALISTARUM SELECTIONES, which seems to have been printed for the first time at Venice in 1569.
[2] Part II, c. iv. pp. 147 *et seq.*
[3] As Lévi puts it tersely: *Schema misericordiam dicit sed et judicium.* He utilises it to denounce the doctrine of everlasting punishment.
[4] Hence Lévi infers that the sin of Adam was educational.

VI.

The great North Wind is the fountain of all souls simply, as other days are of some and not all.[1]

VII.

When Solomon said in his prayer, as recorded in the Book of Kings: "Hear, O Heaven," we must understand by heaven the green line which encircles all things.[2]

VIII.

Souls descend from the third light to the fourth day, and thence issuing, they enter the night of the body.[3]

IX.

By the six days of Genesis we must understand the six extremities of the building proceeding from Brashith as the cedars come forth out of Lebanon.

X.

Paradise is more correctly said to be the whole building than the tenth part. And in the centre thereof is placed the Great Adam, who is TIPHERETH.

XI.

A river is said to flow out from Eden and to be parted into four heads signifying that the third numeration proceeds from the second, and is divided into the fourth, fifth, sixth, and tenth.[4]

XII.

It is true that all things depend on fate, if we understand thereby the Supreme Arbiter.[5]

---

[1] I have given this literally without pretending that it has much meaning. Lévi reduces it to *Magnus aquilo fons est animarum*, explaining that souls enter this world to escape idleness. Archangelus de Burgonuovo, in his *Cabalistarum Selectiora, Obscurioraque* DOGMATA affirms that *Aquilo* signifies GEBURAH, the fifth SEPHIRA. See Pistorius: ARTIS CABALISTICÆ SCRIPTORES, 1587, p. 753.

[2] Lévi renders this *Calum est Kether*, which does not, at first sight, seem to represent it. See, however, CONCLUSION 48, and note thereto.

[3] This is mangled by Lévi, who seems to have misunderstood its meaning. For the night of the body he substitutes the night of death.

[4] CONCLUSIONS 9, 10, 11 signify, according to Lévi, that the history of the earthly paradise is an allegory of truth on earth.

[5] Lévi gives, *Fatum fatum quia fatum verbum est*, an admirable specimen of polishing.

XIII.

He who shall know the Mystery of the Gates of Understanding in the Kabbalah shall know also the Mystery of the Great Jubilee.[1]

XIV.

He who shall know the meridional property in dextral co-ordination shall know why every journey of Abraham was always to the south.[2]

XV.

Unless the letter HE had been added to the name of Abram, Abraham would not have begotten.[3]

XVI.

Before Moses all prophesied by the stag with one horn (*i.e.*, the unicorn).[4]

XVII.

Wheresoever the love of male and female is mentioned in Scripture, there is exhibited mystically the conjunction of TIPHERETH and CHIENSET (or CHENECETH) ISRAEL, or BETH and TIPHERETH.[5]

XVIII.

Whosoever shall have intercourse with TIPHERETH in the middle night shall flourish in every generation.[6]

XIX.

The letters of the name of the evil demon who is the prince of this world are the same as those of the name of God— TETRAGRAMMATON—and he who knows how to effect their transposition can extract one from the other.[7]

---

[1] The significance evaporates in Lévi's shortened recension, *Portæ jubilæum sunt*. He explains the Jubilee as the joy of true knowledge.

[2] Lévi's explanation is feeble, namely, that the South is the rainy quarter, and that "the doctrines of Abraham, *i.e.*, of the Kabbalah, are always fruitful."

[3] *Per additionem* HE *Abraham genuit*, this being " the feminine letter of the Tetragram."

[4] *I.e.*, says Lévi, they saw only one side of truth : Moses is represented bearing two horns. Lévi adds that the unicorn is the ideal.

[5] Lévi substitutes *Mas et fæmina sunt* TIPHERETH ET MALKUTH, and gives a sentimental explanation which has no connection with Kabbalism. It is to be observed, for the rest, that the fruitful union on the Tree of Life in Kabbalism is between CHOKMAH and BINAH.

[6] Lévi interprets by distinguishing the marriage of mere animals, human or otherwise, from the true human and divine marriage of souls, spirits and bodies.

[7] Lévi substitutes *Dæmon est Deus inversus* and argues with characteristic logic that could the former be said to exist, then God as his opposite could certainly have no existence.

XX.

When the light of the mirror which shines not shall be like the light of the shining mirror, the day shall become as the night, as David says.[1]

XXI.

Whosoever shall know the quality which is the secret of darkness shall know why the evil demons are more hurtful in the night than in the day.

XXII.

Granting that the co-ordination of the chariots is manifold, nevertheless, in so far as concerns the mystery of the PHYLACTERIES, two chariots are prepared, so that one chariot is formed from the second, third, fourth, and fifth, and these are the four Phylacteries which VAU assumes; and from the sixth, seventh, eighth and ninth, a second chariot is made, and these are the Phylacteries which HE final assumes.[2]

XXIII.

More than the quality of penitence is not to be understood (or applied) in the word (which signifies) " He said." [3]

XXIV.

When Job said: "Who maketh peace in his highest places," he signifies the austral water and boreal fire, and their leader, concerning which things there must be nothing said further.[4]

---

[1] This apparently puzzled the commentator, so he invented a substitute which partly reproduces an apocryphal saying of Christ.

[2] That is to say, CHOKMAH, BINAH, CHESED and GEBURAH form the chariot, seat, or throne of the third letter of the Tetragram; while TIPHERETH, NETZACH, HOD and JESOD constitute the chariot of the fourth letter. This is the explanation of Archangelus; but it is not Sephirotic doctrine according to the ZOHAR, nor is it reflected from Picus into later Kabbalism. Moreover, VAU is TIPHERETH, and TIPHERETH cannot be used to build a chariot for HE final, which is MALKUTH. The idea is that the Phylacteries were like chariot wheels on which the soul ascends in prayer; but it is rather nonsense symbolism.

[3] This is the best rendering which I can offer of the obscure original—*Supra proprietatem panitentia non est utendum verbo dixit.* It is quite certain that its intention is not represented by Lévi's substituted aphorism *Panitentia non est verbum,* which he translates, "To repent is not to act." According to Archangelus de Burgonuovo, the meaning is that he who seeks the forgiveness of sins must not have recourse to the Son, nor to the Holy Spirit. The proof offered is that the word rendered *dixit* belongs to the Son, and that which stands for *dicens* to the Holy Ghost. This refers to certain sayings of Christ. Forgiveness is to be sought from the Father. The Kabbalah is not, however, a commentary on the New Testament.

[4] Lévi substitutes: *excelsi sunt aqua australis et ignis septentrionalis et præfecti eorum. Silo.*

XXV.

BERESHITH—*i.e.*, in the beginning He created, is the same as if it were said: " In Wisdom He created." [1]

XXVI.

When Onkelos the Chaldean said: BECADMIN—*i.e.*, with or by the Eternals, he understood the Thirty-two Paths of Wisdom. [2]

XXVII.

As the first man is the congregation of the waters, so the sea, to which all rivers run, is the Divinity. [3]

XXVIII.

By the flying thing which was created on the fifth day we must understand angels of this world, which appear to men, and not those which do not appear, save in the spirit. [4]

XXIX.

The name of God, composed of four letters, MEM, TSADE, PE, and final TSADE, must be referred to the Kingdom of David. [5]

XXX.

No angel with six wings is ever transformed. [6]

XXXI.

Circumcision was ordained for deliverance from the impure powers wandering round about.

XXXII.

Hence circumcision was performed on the eighth day, because it is above the universal bride.

---

[1] Pointed by Lévi, this appears as *In principio, id est in* CHOKMAH.
[2] This is given boldly by Lévi as *Via aeternitatis sunt triginta duo*.
[3] Lévi sums the idea by writing *Justi aqua, Deus mare*, and shews in his annotation how God becomes man and man God after his familiar Voltairean fashion.
[4] Lévi gives, *Angeli apparentium sunt volatiles cæli et animantia*, which exceeds the Kabbalistic idea. I do not think it was intended to say that birds are angels of the outer form, but that the flying things created on the fifth day are symbols of the angels who have appeared to men, wearing the likeness of humanity, as to Abraham and to Lot, not those seen in the interior state and in vision.
[5] Lévi reads Daniel.
[6] Meaning, says Lévi, that there is no change for the mind which is equilibrated perfectly; but this is mere ingenuity.

XXXIII.

There are no letters in the entire Law which do not shew forth the secrets of the ten numerations in their forms, conjunctions and separations, in their curves and direction, their deficiency and superfluity, in their comparative smallness and largeness, in their crowning, and their enclosed or open form.[1]

XXXIV.

He who comprehends why Moses hid his face and why Ezekias turned his countenance to the wall, the same understands the fitting attitude and posture of prayer.[2]

XXXV.

No spiritual things descending below can operate without a garment.[3]

XXXVI.

The sin of Sodom was the separation of the final branch.

XXXVII.

By the secret of the prayer before the daylight we must understand the quality of piety.

XXXVIII.

As fear is outwardly inferior to love, so love is inwardly inferior to fear.

XXXIX.

From the preceding conclusion it may be understood why Abraham was praised in Genesis for his fear, albeit we know by the quality of piety that all things were made from love.

XL.

Whensoever we are ignorant of the quality whence the influx comes down upon the petition which we put up, we must have recourse to the House of Judgment.[4]

---

[1] *Literæ sunt hieroglyphicæ in omnibus*, according to the shorter recension of Lévi.

[2] *Absconde faciem tuam et ora*, writes Lévi, connecting the praying shawl in his comment with the veil of Isis!

[3] *L'esprit se révêtent pour descendre et se dépouille pour monter*, says Lévi elsewhere in his writings. Here in his annotation he reasons that, as we cannot live under water, so spirits without bodies are unable to exist in our atmosphere.

[4] Literally, *Domum Naris*; and hence Lévi's abridgment is *Nasus discernit proprietates*, which he defends from the BOOK OF CONCEALMENT.

XLI.

Every good soul is a new soul coming from the East.[1]

XLII.

Therefore Joseph was buried in the bones only and not in the body, because his bones were virtues and the hosts of the Supernal Tree, called ZADITH, descending on the Supernal Earth.

XLIII.

Therefore also Moses knew no sepulchre, being taken up into the Supernal Jubilee and setting his roots above the Jubilee.

XLIV.

When the soul shall comprehend all that is within its comprehension, and shall be joined with the Supernal Soul, it shall put off from itself its earthly garment and shall be rooted out from its place and united with Divinity.[2]

XLV.

When prophecy by the spirit ceased, the wise men of Israel prophesied by the Daughter of the Voice.

XLVI.

A king of the earth is not manifested on the earth until the heavenly host is humbled in heaven.[3]

XLVII.

By the word את = ATH, which occurs twice in the text: "In the beginning God created the heaven and the earth," I believe that Moses signified the creation of the intellectual and animal natures, which in the natural order preceded that of the heaven and the earth.

---

[1] The distinction between new souls and old is developed at some length by Isaac de Loria. Éliphas Lévi overlooks this point and has recourse to a sentimental explanation. He takes occasion also to deny that reincarnation was taught by the best Kabbalists; but he is not quite correct as to his facts.

[2] Lévi gives *Anima plena superiori conjungitur*, and understands this to mean that a complete soul is united with a superior soul, whereas the reference is undoubtedly to the Divine Soul.

[3] The version of Lévi is an entirely different aphorism, namely, *Post deos rex verus regnabit super terram*.

XLVIII.

That which is said by Kabbalists, namely, that a green line encircles the universe, may be cited appropriately as the final conclusion which we draw from Porphyry.[1]

XLIX.

Amen is the influence of numbers.[2]

We have seen that a rival series of Kabbalistic Conclusions has been referred to Picus, and so also the number of the above series is occasionally extended to seventy. The collection of Pistorius contains only those which have been cited, and they are possibly intended to connect with the Fifty Gates of Understanding, less the one gate which was not entered by Moses. To develop any system from these aphorisms would appear almost impossible, and this difficulty has occurred to earlier critics, despite the labours of their commentator, Archangelus de Burgo-Nuovo, who was himself a Christian Kabbalist, but disputatious, verbose, and with predetermined theological motives.

IV.—CORNELIUS AGRIPPA

The untimely death of Picus de Mirandula took place in the early childhood of another Christian Kabbalist, Cornelius Agrippa of Nettersheim, born at Cologne in 1486. It is to him that we owe the first methodical description of the whole Kabbalistic system, considered under the three heads of Natural Philosophy, Mathematical Philosophy and Theology. Agrippa is therefore of importance to our inquiry, and his three books, entitled DE OCCULTA PHILOSOPHIA, are practically the starting-point of Kabbalistic knowledge among Latin-reading scholars of Europe. It is needless to say that his treatise enjoyed immense repute and authority. We must remember, however, that it is professedly a magical work,

---

[1] According to Lévi, the Kabbalists represent KETHER as a green line encompassing all the other SEPHIROTH. I do not know his authority, but Azriel, in his commentary on the SEPHER YETZIRAH, says, as we have seen, that KETHER is the colour of light seen through a mist. I assume that this is not green, though Zoharic observations on the rainbow seem to indicate that some Kabbalists at least were colour-blind. It should be noted that Norrelius in his PHOSPHORUS ORTHODOXÆ FIDEI, 4, Amsterdam, 1720, translating from an elegy on R. Simeon ben Yohai, given in the SEPHER IMRE BINAH, explains that the *linea viridis* is the new moon.

[2] An affirmation of the mind, an adhesion of the heart, a kind of mental signature, says Lévi.

by which I do not mean that it is a Ritual for the Evocation of Spirits, but that it unfolds the philosophical principles upon which all forms of Magic were supposed to proceed, and this is so true that the forged FOURTH BOOK, which was added to it soon after the death of Agrippa, and does provide a species of Magical Ritual, is so much in consonance with the genuine work that it might have been almost by the same hand. We must expect therefore that the magical side of Kabbalism, that which deals with the properties and virtues of Divine Names and so forth, is developed much more fully than the cosmology of SEPHER YETZIRAH or the Divine Mysteries of the ZOHAR. We have to remember also that, albeit Agrippa was the first writer who elucidated the Kabbalistic system, he was better acquainted with the philosophy of Greece and Rome than with that of the later Hebrews. He was in a position, however, to understand and expound the Mysteries of Divine Names and the NOTARICON connected therewith. Of the literature itself he gives no information from which we could infer his textual knowledge; he does not mention the SEPHER YETZIRAH or the ZOHAR, both of which were then only accessible in manuscript, and I am inclined to think that his acquaintance with Kabbalistic subjects was formed chiefly through the CONCLUSIONES CABALISTICÆ of Mirandula, which, as we have seen, appeared at Rome in the year of Agrippa's birth. It should be added also that there are serious errors in his division of the Hebrew alphabet which would not have been made by one who was acquainted with any authoritative source of knowledge, as, for example, the BOOK OF FORMATION, not to speak of mistakes without number in the lettering of Divine Names, when the time came for his work to be printed.

It is noticeable in this connection that the doctrines of occult virtues residing in words and names is expounded on the authority of the Platonists.[1] It is only in the scales of the twelve numbers, dealt with somewhat minutely in the second book, that a Kabbalistic system is developed, but this has remained a chief source of information among writers on occult subjects up to this day.[2] The most important gleanings

---

[1] It should be noted, however, that he preceded the chief Hellenising schools of later Kabbalism.
[2] On the general question of Agrippa's connection with Kabbalism, see Frederich Barth: DIE CABBALA des Heinrich Cornelius Agrippa von Nettersheim, Stuttgart, 1855.

are, however, in the third book, devoted to Theology and the doctrines, mainly Kabbalistic, concerning angels, demons and the souls of men, but creating correspondences with classical mythology wherever possible. Thus, AIN SOPH is identified with the Night of Orpheus and the Kabbalistic Samael with Typhon. The ten SEPHIROTH are described as vestments, instruments or exemplars of the Archetype, having an influence on all created things from high to low, following a defined order.

It would serve no purpose here to attempt a summary account of the instruction, while tables of commutations shewing the extraction of angelical names would require elaborate diagrams. My object is to note rather than illustrate exhaustively the character of Agrippa's exposition, which is concerned largely with the so-called Practical Kabbalah, and very slightly with the theosophical literature. It brought him no satisfaction, and before his troubled life drew to its disastrous close he recorded his opinion that the Kabbalistic art, which he had "diligently and laboriously sought after," was merely a "rhapsody of superstition," that its mysteries were "wrested from the Holy Scriptures," a play with allegory proving nothing. As to the alleged miracles wrought by its practical operations, he supposes that there is no one so foolish as to believe in any such powers. In a word, "the Kabbalah of the Jews is nothing but a pernicious superstition by which at their pleasure they gather, divide and transpose words, names and letters in Scripture; and by making one thing out of another dissolve the connections of the truth." What was done by the Jews for the literature of the Ancient Covenant was performed, he goes on to say, for the Greek documents of Christianity by the Ophites, Gnostics and Valentinians, who produced a Greek Kabbalah, as Rabanus, the monk, later on attempted with the Latin characters.

I do not know that a modern writer could have put the position more clearly, but its chief value to ourselves lies in its clear exhibition of the author's limits in respect of Kabbalistic knowledge. He was acquainted with its artificial side and with that only. Agrippa adds another argument which also, from its own standpoint, could not be expressed better: "If Kabbalistic Art proceed from God, as the Jews boast, and if it produce to the perfection of life, the health of men and the worship of God, as also to the truth of understanding, surely that Spirit of Truth which has left their synagogue, and has come to teach us all truth, would not have concealed it from His Church even until these last times, and this the more, seeing that the Church knows all things which are of God, while His Mysteries of Salvation are revealed in every tongue, for every tongue has the same power, if there be the same equal piety; neither is there any name, in heaven or on earth, by which we can be saved, whereby we can work miracles, but the one Name Jesus, wherein all things are recapitulated and contained."

Of course, in the last analysis this argument proves too much. There is either a peculiar virtue in Divine Names or there is not. If there be, the Christian cannot well deny it to Jehovah; and if there be not, any thaumaturgic doctrine of the Great Name in Christianity is a subtlety no less idle than the TETRAGRAMMATON or the SCHEMAHAMPHORASH. We know, however, that, in so far as names represent ideas, they are moving powers of the intellectual world; when they are used without inspiration and without knowledge they are dead and inert, like other empty vehicles. The Kabbalistic Jews believed that they could dissect the name without losing the vital essence which informs it, and they erred therein. The name of Jesus spells grace and salvation to millions, but it spells nothing when lettered separately and nothing when it is transposed. To say otherwise is to rave.

V.—PARACELSUS

Among the great names of occultism which are cited in support of the influence exerted by the Kabbalah and the authority which it possessed, that of Paracelsus is mentioned. We are given to understand, for example, by Isaac Myer, that it is to be traced distinctly in the system of the great German adept.[1] Statements like these are themselves a kind of Kabbalah, which are received by one writer from another without any inquiry or any attempt at verification. In this way we obtain lists of authorities, references and testimonials which seem at first sight to carry great weight, but they will bear no examination and defeat their own purpose when they

---

[1] PHILOSOPHY OF IBN GEBIROL, p. 171.

come into the hands of a student who has sufficient patience to investigate them. In the present instance we have to remember that Paracelsus occupies an exceptional position among occult philosophers; he was not a man who respected or quoted authorities; he owed very little to tradition, very little to what is understood commonly by learning.[1] If we take his alchemical treatises and compare them with Hermetic literature, we shall find that they are quite unlike it, and that he was, in fact, his own alchemist. When he concerns himself with Magic, he has few correspondences which will enable him to be illustrated by other writers on this subject: again, he was his own magician. And as regards the question of the Kabbalah, if we discover, on examination, that he has something to say concerning it, we should expect that it would be quite unlike anything that went before him, and quite foreign to the known lines of Kabbalism. Once more, we should find that he would prove to be his own Kabbalist. In every department of thought he illustrated his characteristic maxim: *Alterius non sit qui suus esse potest.* It must be added also that any contributions which he offers are seldom helpful. They do nothing to elucidate what is obscure in previous authorities, and they constitute new departures which are themselves in need of explanation.

Nearly two centuries elapsed between the death of Moses de Leon, the first alleged publisher of the ZOHAR, and the birth of Theophrastus of Hohenheim, and though no attempt to print it took place till some forty years after his turbulent life closed sadly at Strasburg, or wherever it occurred actually, there can be no doubt that it was accessible in manuscript, or that Paracelsus, had he known Aramaic, could have made himself acquainted with its contents. It seems certain, however, that he never acquired the language from which it had not been translated, and that his knowledge of the Kabbalah would be limited to what he could gather from authors who wrote in Latin or some current tongue; but his own works shew that he was at very little pains of this kind. As to this, it is only necessary to collect the few references on the subject which they contain.

The study of Magic and the Kabbalah is enjoined several times on the physician, and old medical authorities are scouted

---

[1] He is said, indeed, to have boasted that his library would not amount to six folio volumes.—Gould's HISTORY OF FREEMASONRY, vol. ii. p. 77.

on the ground that they were unacquainted with either.[1] The "Cabala" is in one place identified with Magical Astronomy,[2] which, I presume, refers to the Paracelsic theory concerning stars in man and the stars of disease, and connects with the contextual statement that all operations of the stars in all animals centre at the heart. It is identified also with Magic itself, of which it forms a part.[3] But from indications given in another place, Kabbalistic Magic seems to have signified some obscure operations with the faculties of the astral body.[4] Subsequently this point is exposed more plainly, when the Kabbalistic Art is said to have been built up on the basis of doctrines concerning the sacramental body, which appears after the death of the corruptible, and accounts for the phenomena of spectres, visions, apparitions of a supernatural character, &c.[5] The art of judging what is concealed by certain outward signs—in a word, the theory of signatures—is said to be the Kabbalistic Art, "once called 'caballa,' afterwards 'caballia.'" It has also been termed falsely Galamala, from its alleged author—of whom one has heard nothing otherwise—and is of Ethnic origin, having been transmitted to the Chaldæans and the Jews, by whom it was corrupted, "for the Jews were exceedingly ignorant in all ages."[6] Finally, the use of certain prayers and *signacula* —*i.e.*, talismans in the cure of diseases is connected with the Kabbalah.[7]

These meagre instances exhaust the three folio volumes which constitute the Geneva collection of the works of Paracelsus, and shew little relation even to the debased and thaumaturgic side of the Secret Tradition in Israel. I should add, however, that there is a short section entitled CABALLA, which forms part of a treatise on the plague, but it is concerned with the official elements of early science and with the alchemical principles, Salt, Sulphur and Mercury. There is a reference also in one place to some "books of the Caballa," apparently the work of Paracelsus and in this case presumably no longer extant. By the student of Paracelsus that loss may

---

[1] DE CAUSIS ET ORIGINE LUIS GALLICÆ, Lib. iv. c. 9, OPERA OMNIA, Geneva, 1658, vol. iii. p. 193, *b*. Also *De Peste*, Lib. ii., *præfatio, ibid.*, vol. i. p. 408.
[2] DE PESTILITATE, Tract. i., *ib., ib.*, p. 371, *b*.
[3] DE PESTE, Lib. i., *ib., ib.*, p. 405, *b*.
[4] DE VITA LONGA, Lib. i. c. 6, *ib.*, vol. ii. p. 56, *b*.
[5] DE NATURA RERUM, Lib. viii., *ib. ib.*, p. 101, *b*.
[6] PHILOSOPHIA SAGAX, Lib. i., *ib.*, vol. ii. p. 565, *b*.
[7] DE VULNERIBUS, Lib. v. in CHIRURGIA MAGNA, Pars. iii., *ib.*, vol. iii., p. 91 *b*.

be regretted, but it is not of moment so far as the Kabbalah proper is concerned, for it is evident that this term, like many others, was made use of in a sense which either differs widely from its wonted meaning, or is the lowest form of that meaning. The Kabbalah for Paracelsus, when it is not something quite fantastic and unimaginable, is a species of Practical Magic, and here we shall do well to remember that the adept of Hohenheim flourished at a period when the spurious literature of Clavicles and Grimoires was abroad already in the world.

It is very difficult to judge Paracelsus, and many false statements have been made concerning him by friends and enemies. But it is well to know that he was not a student of the Kabbalah in any sense that we should care to associate therewith.

VI.—JOHN REUCHLIN

As these sketches are not constructed biographically, there will be no difficulty in regarding the subject of the present notice as the representative of a group, which group illustrates most effectively the standpoint and purpose of our inquiry as regards the Christian students of the Kabbalah. They have been mentioned already in my preface. The missionary enthusiasm which may be said to have begun with Mirandula, which, if Lully had been a Kabbalist, would have been already at fever heat in the *doctor illuminatus* of Majorca, which ceased only in the early part of the eighteenth century, assumed almost the aspect of a movement between the period of Reuchlin and that of Rosenroth. It was not a concerted movement; it was not the activity of a theosophical society or a learned body; it was not actuated by any occult interests, and perhaps still less by those of an academic kind. The shape which it assumed in its literature was that of a deliberate and successive attempt to read Christian dogma into the written word of Kabbalism. It does not appear so strenuously in the work of Rosenroth as it does in the collection of Pistorius,[1] because in the days of the KABBALA DENUDATA there was, perhaps, more reason to hinder such intellectual excesses. Nor is it so strong in the writings of Reuchlin as in those of Archangelus de Burgonuovo. It is impossible

---

[1] ARTIS CABALISTICÆ, *hoc est, recondita theologiæ et philosophiæ Scriptorum*, Tomus I., Basiliæ, 1587.

to survey the vast treatises, extending in some cases to hundreds of folio pages, by which the enthusiasm is represented, and it is fortunately not necessary. We have only to establish their proper connection with Kabbalism and to shew that it has been so far misconceived by occultists of the past.

We are justified in regarding Éliphas Lévi as to some extent a mouthpiece in his day of modern occult thought: it is to him more than to any one that such thought owes its impulse towards the Jewish Tradition as to a so-called absolute of philosophy and religion, "the alliance of the universal reason and the Divine Word."[1] It was he who first pretended that "all truly dogmatic religions have issued from the Kabbalah and return therein," that it has "the keys of the past, the present and the future, etc."[2] In order to "receive initiation" into this great tradition he has counselled us, among other books, to have recourse to the "Hebrew writers in the recollection of Pistorius."[3] Following this direction, occultists have been taught to regard the famous Basle folio as a storehouse of genuine Jewish Tradition. No impression could well be more erroneous. The works engarnered by Pistorius are neither the Jewish tradition nor valid commentary thereon. It is well also to add that they are not the work of occultists or of persons who believed that "Catholic doctrine," or Lutheran, is "wholly derived" from the Kabbalah. The writers are of three types: I. The Jew who had abjured Israel and directed his polemics against it. He is represented by Riccius, and his presence is fatal to Lévi's standpoint. Lévi recommended the Christian to become a Kabbalist; Riccius thought it logical for the Kabbalist to turn Christian.[4] II. The born Christian, who believed that the Jew was in the wrong for continuing in

---

[1] DOGME DE LA HAUTE MAGIE, p. 95, 2me édition, Paris, 1861; TRANSCENDENTAL MAGIC, p. 20; MYSTERIES OF MAGIC, second edition, p. 502.
[2] See my translation of the DOGME ET RITUEL, s.v. TRANSCENDENTAL MAGIC: its Doctrine and Ritual, second edition, 1923, pp. 24, 25.
[3] Ibid. Students who know the collection of Pistorius will be aware that a large part of it is Christian in authorship, and that, with the exception of PORTA LUCIS and a version of SEPHER YETZIRAH, none of its treatises was written originally in Hebrew.
[4] After his conversion this German repaired to Padua, where he taught philosophy with great credit. He was invited back to Germany by the Emperor Maximilian. He belongs to the sixteenth century. His chief work treats of CELESTIAL AGRICULTURE. It occupies nearly two hundred pages in the folio of Pistorius and offers very curious reading to those who can tolerate it at this day; but it is to be noted that the ZOHAR is not cited through all its length.

Judaism when the Kabbalah taught—as it was argued—the doctrine of the Trinity, the Divine Word and so forth. He also is in opposition to Lévi, who thought that the Jew was in the right because the germ of all dogmas could be found in the traditions of Israel. This type is represented by Reuchlin,[1] who is learned, laborious and moderate, but also by Archangelus de Burgonuovo, who does frequent outrage to good sense, and seems to regard the Kabbalah as a note-book to the New Testament. Reuchlin toyed with Lutheranism; Archangelus was a Catholic prelate. III. The purely natural mystic, who might be either Jew or Gentile, who has no Kabbalistic connections worth reciting, and to whom Christianity does not seem even a name. He is represented by a writer who, as a fact, was born a Jew and seems to have been included by Pistorius because of his supposed conversion. I refer to Abravanel, whose PHILOSOPHY OF LOVE is the subject of special mention by Éliphas Lévi as if it were a text-book of Kabbalism. The DIALOGUES have been dealt with already, and here it is enough to say that their citation annihilates Lévi, because a student of the Kabbalah might as well be referred to an " Art " of Ovid Spiritualised.

As regards Pistorius himself, the only point at which he makes contact with occult follies is in the fact that his enterprise was undertaken, among other reasons, as a counterblast to the superstitions which the Kabbalah had promoted in Christendom; a reference, we may presume, to the juvenile budget of Agrippa and to the increasing grimoire literature. The Kabbalistic studies of the editor began in his boyhood; but, so far from leading him to the boasted certitude of Lévi, he passed under their escort into Protestantism, and there was conferred upon him the august distinction of figuring as one of the deputies charged to present the Lutheran Confession of Faith to the Diet of Augsbourg. Having registered the fact itself as an illustration of the quality of his progress towards the Absolute, it is of course permissible to regard his sympathies with the attempted purgation of the Church in a spirit of clemency, perhaps even of interest, or to confess, at least, that they were excusable on the ground of natural

---

[1] A successful politician, diplomatist and man of the world. He also belongs to the sixteenth century. Some account of his life will be found in Basnage, t. v. pp. 2059 *et seq.*

infirmity, seeing that he was for long subjected to persecution, fostered by a monkish inquisitor, because he had saved the books of Jewry from confiscation and burning throughout all Germany. In place of them, as opportunity afforded, they burnt DE VERBO MIRIFICO and DE ARTE CABBALISTICA, contributions of Reuchlin to the right understanding of the Secret Tradition in Israel.[1] The treatises remain all the same as witnesses of the standpoint of Christian students in the sixteenth century, and they help to warrant us in affirming that the largest Latin collection of Kabbalistic writers, outside KABBALA DENUDATA, contains no evidence in support of any occult hypothesis.

I must by no means leave this brief and confessedly inadequate notice of Reuchlin and his connections without a word of reference to his learned pupil, J. A. Widmanstadt, whose collection of Hebrew manuscripts, for the most part Kabbalistic, is one of the great treasures of the Library of Munich. In the course of his life-long studies he gave special attention to the ZOHAR and to the theurgic side of Jewish Tradition.

VII.—WILLIAM POSTEL

A philosophical, or rather an occult legend has gathered in an unaccountable manner round the name of William Postel, and it is supplemented by a popular legend which has depicted this peaceable, though perhaps somewhat puerile monk in a vestment of thaumaturgic splendour. The philosophical legend we owe almost exclusively to Éliphas Lévi, and to a few later writers in France who have accepted his leading and, with him, appear to be impressed honestly by Postel's well-intended but too often inane writings, among which is included a KEY OF THINGS KEPT SECRET FROM THE FOUNDATION OF THE WORLD. Postel was the son of a poor Normandy peasant: by his perseverance and self-denial he contrived to obtain an education, and became, on the authority of his chief admirer, the most learned man of his time. " Ever full of resignation and sweetness, he worked like a labouring man to insure himself a crust of bread, and then returned to his studies. Poverty accompanied him always, and want at times compelled him to part with his books; but he acquired

---

[1] They will be found in the collection of Pistorius.

all the known languages and all the sciences of his day; he discovered rare and valuable manuscripts, among others the Apocryphal Gospels and the SEPHER YETZIRAH; he initiated himself into the mysteries of the transcendent Kabbalah, and his frank admiration for this absolute truth, for this supreme reason of all philosophies and all dogmas, tempted him to make it known to the world." [1]

So far Éliphas Lévi, whose undeniable influence upon all modern occultism has done more than anything to exaggerate the true philosophical position of Jewish secret literature and to place some of its supposed expositors in a false light. The redeeming point of Postel is his exalted piety; the points to be regretted are his extravagance, his transcendental devotion to a religious and homely nun of mature years, and his belief that he underwent a process of physical regeneration by the infusion of her spiritual substance two years after her death.[2] To the Council of Trent, convened for the condemnation of heresies connected with the Reformation, he addressed a benevolent but unpractical epistle, inviting it to bless the whole world, which seems outside the purpose of a deliberative assembly considering doctrinal questions. The result of these errors of enthusiasm was that Postel was shut up in some convent, a course dictated possibly as much by a feeling of consideration, and even of mercy, towards a learned man unfitted for contact with the world, as by the sentiment of intolerance. The seclusion, in any case, offered him the kind of advantages that he most needed, and he died in peace, having retracted, it is said, everything that was disapproved by his superiors.

As seen already, Postel connects with Kabbalism by the great fact that he discovered and made known in the West that celebrated BOOK OF FORMATION which contains some of its fundamental doctrine.[3] He expounded also its principles in a species of commentary to which I shall recur shortly.[4]

---

[1] HISTOIRE DE LA MAGIE. Paris, 1860, liv. v. c. 4, p. 347. See also my annotated translation, s.v. HISTORY OF MAGIC, second edition, 1922, p. 336.

[2] *Ibid.*, p. 250.

[3] "Postel was the first, to my knowledge, who translated into Latin the most ancient and, it must be confessed, the most obscure, monument of the Kabbalah; I refer to the BOOK OF FORMATION."—A. V. Franck, LA KABBALE, p. 16. He adds: "So far as I am in a position to judge of this translation, which at least equals the text in obscurity, it appears faithful in a general way."

[4] We have seen that tradition refers also to him a Latin translation of the ZOHAR, for which Franck sought vainly in the public libraries of Paris.

His own doctrine has also some remote traces of analogy with Zoharistic tradition, but its summary by Éliphas Lévi is loose and inexact, like all literary and historical studies undertaken by this modern adept.

"The Trinity," his interpretation begins, "made man in Its image and after Its likeness. The human body is dual, and its triadic unity is constituted by the union of its two halves; it is *animus* and *anima*; it is mind and tenderness; so also it has two sexes—the masculine situated in the head, and the feminine in the heart. The fulfilment of redemption must be dual therefore in humanity; mind by its purity must rectify the errors of the heart, and the heart by its generosity must correct the egoistic barrenness of the head. Christianity has been comprehended heretofore only by reasoning heads; it has not penetrated hearts. The Word has indeed become man, but not till the Word has become woman will the world be saved. The maternal genius of religion must instruct men in the sublime grandeurs of the spirit of charity; then will reason be conciliated with faith, because it will understand, explain and govern the sacred excesses of devotion." [1]

The particular fatuity of Postel was that he recognised the incarnation of this maternal spirit in the person of the pious nun before mentioned. Éliphas Lévi, who took no illuminations and no enthusiasms seriously, terms this spiritual ardour a lyrical puerility and a celestial hallucination, but there is no lyrical element in the Latin of Postellus, and, whatever the source of the hallucination, the lady died making no sign. Into the question of their subsequent reunion after a manner which recalls the *status embryonnatus* of Kabbalistic abnormal psychology, it would be ridiculous here to enter. From the period of its occurrence the mystic always termed himself *Postellus Restitutus*; it is reported that his white hair became again black, the furrows disappeared from his brow, and his cheeks reassumed the hues of youth. Derisive biographers explain these marvels as derisive biographers might be expected, as if, Lévi well observes, "it being insufficient to represent him as a fool, it was necessary also to exhibit this man, of a nature so noble and so generous, in the light of a juggler and charlatan. There is one thing more astounding than the eloquent unreason of enthusiastic hearts, and that

---

[1] HIST. DE LA MAGIE, liv. v. c. 4, p. 348.

is the stupidity or bad faith of the frigid and sceptical minds which presume to judge them."[1]

A less unsympathetic historian than those confounded by Lévi reduces the doctrines of Postel under two heads, (1) "That the evangelical reign of Jesus Christ, established by the apostles, could not be sustained among Christians or propagated among infidels except by the lights of reason," which appears wholly plausible. (2) That a future King of France was destined to universal monarchy, and "that his way must be prepared by the conquest of hearts and the convincing of minds, so that henceforth the world shall hold but one belief and Jesus Christ shall reign there by one King, one law and one faith." Given universal monarchy as a possibility of the future, no Frenchman who is true to his traditions would assign it otherwise than to a King of France. However, one or both of these propositions led the biographer in question to infer that Postel was mad, and I cite this conclusion less on account of its essential merit than because it afforded Lévi the opportunity for a rejoinder of characteristic suggestiveness. "Mad, for having dreamed that religion should govern minds by the supreme reason of its doctrine, and that the monarchy, to be strong and lasting, must bind hearts by the conquests of the public prosperity of peace! Mad, for having believed in the advent of His Kingdom, to Whom we cry daily: Thy Kingdom come! Mad, because he believed in reason and justice on earth! Alas, it is too true, poor Postel was mad!" He wrote little books at intervals which, I must admit frankly, are almost impossible to read, and in the case of the SEPHER YETZIRAH the printer has done his best to make the difficulties of Postel's translation absolute; but as I have promised to speak of the commentary which accompanies the version, I must say at least that it should be described rather as a collection of separate notes. Franck recommends no one to be guided by the views which it expresses, but they scarcely suggest leading, as they contain nothing of real importance, and some of them are almost childish. Among the points which may be noted are:—(a) Defence of the lawfulness and necessity of the concealment of sacred things; (b) A pertinent and useful distinction between the terms creation, formation and making,

---

[1] HIST. DE LA MAGIE, liv. v. c. 4, p. 348.

as used in the SEPHER YETZIRAH; (c) The antiquity of the belief in ten spheres of the heavens; (d) The recourse to numerical mysticism, to shew why the SEPHIROTH are, in the words of SEPHER YETZIRAH, "ten and not nine," the necessity of the number ten being shown by the progression from the unit to the quaternary, as follows :—$1 + 2 + 3 + 4 = 10$. And this, according to a mystical mode of calculation, brings us back to the unit, even as the external universe brings back the soul to God; (e) The attribution of angelic choirs to the SEPHIROTH, thus shewing that Postel's study of the Kabbalah was not confined to the one document which he is known to have translated.

Of Postel's original writings, that entitled DE RATIONIBUS SPIRITUS SANCTI *Libri Duo*, 1543, seems on the whole the most soberly reasoned; if, unfortunately, it has no connections with the Kabbalah, it has at least some with good sense. It is useful also for those—if any remain among us, except in France—who are disposed to be influenced by Lévi, and hence to regard Postel as an adept of their mysteries. While it is quite true that he was more than fanciful in his notions, which are extravagant in the philological as well as the conventional sense of that term, it is not at all true that he had set aside or exceeded the accepted doctrinal views of his period, nor does he appear to have possessed a specific light on given points of teaching which can be regarded as considerable for his period. He upheld, for example, the doctrine of eternal damnation, and justifies it in such a manner that no room is left for the conjecture that he was not saying what he meant. For the rest, Postel was a good and single-minded Christian, who, in spite of his CLAVIS ABSCONDITORUM A CONSTITUTIONE MUNDI, and in spite of the panegyrics of Éliphas Lévi, had no knowledge whatsoever of any so-called BOOK OF THOTH, and had never dreamed of looking for a doctrine of absolute religion beyond the Seat of Peter.

VIII.—THE ROSICRUCIANS

Among many adventurous statements advanced concerning this mystical Fraternity, we are not infrequently told that it gave a great impetus to the study of the Kabbalah. The assertion is so far from being founded on any accessible fact, that one is tempted to rejoin that it gave no impetus to anything except a short-lived curiosity and a certain pleasant fantasia in romantic fiction.[1] The truth is that no statement should be hazarded on either side. In the first place, the historical evidence for the existence of the Order, though it points to certain conclusions, is in a very unsatisfactory state,[2] and were any knowledge of another kind conceivably still in existence it would be in the custody of those unlikely to commit themselves. I have never met in literature with an express statement designed to indicate knowledge and to represent authority which could bear investigation. On the contrary, I have found invariably that those which most assumed the complexion of certitude were only the private impressions of persons who had no title to conviction, nor even a sufficient warrant for an estimable opinion by their acquaintance with the exoteric facts. I have therefore to say that there is no known student of the Kabbalah,[3] with one tentative and barely possible exception, who can be cited on evidence as the member of a Rosicrucian Fraternity, laying any claim to antiquity. It is of course well known that there have been, as there still are, various corporate societies, some semi-Masonic, as in England, some occult, as in France, which have formulated their particular interests and purposes by adopting the name. There is no great mischief in such adoption, provided the limits of the pretension are clear, and, with the exception of recent impostures which have appeared there and here in America, this, I think, has been the case.

The few great names of the past which connect with Rosicrucianism and at the same time with Kabbalism are not to be identified with the Fraternity, except on a common ground of sympathy.[4] Such was Thomas Vaughan. More-

---

[1] See, however, my BROTHERHOOD OF THE ROSY CROSS, 1924, in which the history and claims of the Order, more especially on their external side, are examined in an exhaustive manner.

[2] It is open therefore to numerous fantastic constructions, one of the most curious being that placed on it by Mrs. Henry Pott, in FRANCIS BACON AND HIS SECRET SOCIETY, London, 1891. See c. xii. especially, and compare Clifford Harrison, NOTES ON THE MARGINS, London, 1897, p. 49: "There is every good reason to suppose that the founder of Inductive Philosophy was a Rosicrucian."

[3] The term is sometimes used loosely in connection with the Rosicrucians, as if meaning a tradition of any kind. Thus, Mr. W. F. C. Wigston speaks of "German philosophers and writers . . . who each and all held up Freemasonry as a branch of their own Rosicrucian Kabbalah."—THE COLUMBUS OF LITERATURE, p. 203, Chicago, 1892. The Rosicrucian Kabbalah, understood in this sense, was Divine Magia.

[4] In a paper read before the Quatuor Coronati Lodge, and published in its transactions, Dr. Wynn Westcott, Supreme Magus of the English Rosicrucian Society,

over, the memorials which we possess of it, especially those belonging to the eighteenth century, indicate that it was engrossed mainly by alchemical processes. The barely possible exception mentioned, namely, the one case in which a well-known student of the Kabbalah, or rather a well-known expositor of Kabbalistic subjects, may have received initiation into a Rosicrucian Order going back through the last century, is Éliphas Lévi. It is not perhaps improbable that he received initiation of some kind, though I must be disassociated with all clearness from the pretence of a certain French occultist, who claimed access to secret sources of information, namely, that the scattered groups of Rosicrucian Societies were reorganised by Éliphas Lévi, presumably about the year 1850. But this solitary instance, supposing that it could be called valid, does not save the situation, more especially as I shall establish more fully later on that Éliphas Lévi, though he obtained a reputation among occultists as a Kabbalist, was not entitled to it by any tolerable acquaintance with the literature which contains the Kabbalah. The point of fact has been noted, as the need arose, already in preceding pages.

IX.—ROBERT FLUDD

The name of Robert Fludd stands high among esoteric philosophers and "philosophers by fire" in England; he was a man of wide learning, of intellectual ambition, of exalted spiritual faith. He was also a theosophical writer in the catholic sense of the term. If we add to this that he is an accessible figure, not too remote in time, and that a short pilgrimage in Kent will lead us to the site at least of that house in which he lived and died, it will not be difficult to understand the fascination which he has exercised on many who, for the rest, have never dared to stir the dust from his folios. I have had occasion already in more than one work to account for this Kentish "philosopher by fire," and as there is only a single mystery in his life, on which no one is likely to give light, I shall not need here to retrace ground that has been travelled.[1] The one mystery is whether he did ultimately enter the Fraternity of the Rose-Cross. It is

---

describes Rosicrucianism as a new presentation of Gnostic, Kabbalistic, Hermetic and Neo-Platonic doctrines. At the beginning, middle and end, it happens to have been nothing of the kind.

[1] See HAUNTS OF THE ENGLISH MYSTICS, No. 1, in THE UNKNOWN WORLD, vol. i. pp. 130 et seq. Also THE BROTHERHOOD OF THE ROSY CROSS, 1924, cap. x.

clear from the first tracts which he wrote in defence of this Order that he had not been then initiated into its mysteries.[1] Perhaps so much energy and devotion earned its reward in the end, as there is ground for supposing was the case with his friend Michael Maier, who espoused the same cause in Germany. But we do not know, and modern occult writers who pretend that he was a Rosicrucian are either misled or are romancing.

His connection with Kabbalism is, however, the only point with which we are concerned here, and as to this there is no doubt of his proficiency along certain lines, for he occupied himself a great deal with vast cosmological hypotheses, which were drawn to some extent from this source. He was forty years of age when the Rosicrucian controversy first gave opportunity to his pen, and the COMPENDIOUS APOLOGY, which he published in reply to Libavius, a German hostile critic, exhibits his Kabbalistic studies. I must add also that it gives evidence of his besetting intellectual weakness, an inordinate passion for the marvellous, which leads him to dwell unduly on the thaumaturgic side of Jewish Secret Knowledge. Having given the usual Legend of the Tradition, its reception by Moses from God and its oral perpetuation till the time of Esdras, he divides the Kabbalah into two parts. There is firstly that of Cosmology, dealing with forces operating in created things, both sublunary and celestial, and here he expounded also on philosophical grounds the arcana of the written law. This division, he observes, does not differ materially from the Natural Magic in which Solomon is recorded to have excelled, and he adds that the magical powers of natural things, concealed in their centre, can be brought forth by this species of Kabbalah. The second division is entitled MERCAVAH, which contemplates things Divine, angelical powers, Sacred Names and *signacula*. It is sub-divided into NOTARICON and THEOMANTICA. NOTARICON treats of angelical virtues and names, of demoniacal natures and of human souls; THEOMANTICA investigates the Mysteries of Divine Majesty, of Sacred Names and pentacles. Those who are proficient therein are invested with strange powers, can foretell future things,

---

[1] Perhaps the *Valete Nostrique Memores estote* of the *Epilogus Autoris ad Fratres de Rosea Cruce* may create a different impression in the minds of some readers. See APOLOGIA COMPENDIARIA, Leyden, 1616.

command entire Nature, compel angels and demons, and perform miracles. By this art Moses worked his various signs and wonders, Joshua caused the sun to stand still, Elijah brought fire from heaven and raised the dead to life. But it is a gift of God, through His Holy Spirit, which is granted only to the elect.

It will be seen that this classification presents not the exalted if bizarre traditions of the ZOHAR, but the debased and superstitious apparatus of SEPHER RAZIEL and of later Kabbalism, ignored if not unknown by writers like Rosenroth. In folios which followed the COMPENDIOUS APOLOGY the Kabbalistic connections of Fludd's philosophy are implicit and suggestive rather than patent and elaborated, and I think are positive proof that he had no acquaintance with the ZOHAR. In his Cosmology of the Macrocosmos,[1] which deals with its metaphysical and physical origin, he has recourse chiefly to Platonic and Hermetic writings, and although many other authorities are cited, nothing is borrowed from Kabbalists, except indeed the TETRAGRAMMATON, which figures within a triangle in one of the illustrations. The complementary treatise on the Microcosm recalls Kabbalism in its doctrine of angels and demons. Slight correspondences may be traced in his other writings; but they indicate no real knowledge. In discussing the properties of numbers [2] (*i.e.*, the SEPHIROTH) and the Divine Names attributed to these, the diagram which accompanies the remarks shews that he misconstrued totally the Kabbalistic scheme of emanation. So also some later observations concerning METATRON and the positive and negative sides of the Sephirotic Tree[3] suggest no special knowledge. When replying to Father Mersenne, Fludd defends what he terms his Kabbalah, but the term is used loosely and has certainly very little to do with the Kabbalah of Jewry.[4] It may be observed, in conclusion, that the Kentish mystic was pre-eminently a Christian philosopher, and, like other subjects, that of the Esoteric Tradition in Israel was approached by him from the Christian standpoint.

---

[1] *Utriusque Cosmi Majoris scilicet et Minoris* METAPHYSICA, PHYSICA *atque* TECHNICA HISTORIA, 2 vols., Frankfort, 1617 and 1629.
[2] PHILOSOPHIA SACRA *et vere Christiana, seu Meteorologica Cosmica*, 1626.
[3] MEDICINA CATHOLICA, *seu Mysticum Artis Medicandi Sacrarium*, 2 vols., Frankfort, 1629, 1631.
[4] DE SOPHIÆ CUM MORIA CERTAMINE, 1629.

X.—HENRY MORE

The Cambridge Platonic philosopher is regarded by Basnage as a great Kabbalist and his contributions to KABBALA DENUDATA as in some sense discovering the sentiment and spirit of Jewish Theosophy.[1] Franck, on the contrary, regrets their inclusion by Rosenroth on the ground that they are personal speculations which are not at all in harmony with Kabbalistic teaching.[2] While there can be no question that the just view belongs to the later critic, More is thinly interesting because of his enthusiasm and earnestness. His point of view is also of importance to our inquiry, because his name belongs undeniably to the literature of English Mysticism—or at least its outskirts. Let us begin therefore by stating that he approached the subject as a Christian who desired the conversion of the Jews, who regarded the Kabbalah as a fitting instrument to effect it, and not in the case of the Jews only, but even of Pagans. He came therefore to its study and elucidation not as an investigator of things esoteric, not as a seeker for an absolute doctrine of religion, nor even for a higher sense of Christianity, but like Picus and Postel and Reuchlin, or like his correspondent and editor Rosenroth, as one imbued with an evangelical spirit.[3]

The introduction of More to the Kabbalah was brought about, as it has been supposed, by means of Isaac de Loria's LIBER DRUSHIM. There is no reason to believe that he could or did undertake an independent study of the ZOHAR, and hence as his contributions to the subject are all prior to the appearance of KABBALA DENUDATA, it follows that his acquaintance was not exhaustive, nor was it altogether good of its kind. At the same time, his study of LIBER DRUSHIM called forth a well-reasoned letter from his pen, addressed to Rosenroth,[4] in which the description of the SEPHIROTH under the form of spheres is condemned as a fiction of the later rabbis and their relation to the denary is affirmed. The critical position of the writer is established, however, by the attribution of the Pythagorean denary to a Kabbalistic origin.

---

[1] HISTOIRE DES JUIFS, Livre iii. c. 10, tom. ii., p. 786.
[2] Ad. Franck : LA KABBALE, p. 22.
[3] And desiring the *Ecclesiæ emolumentum*, as the same correspondence shews.
[4] EPISTOLA AD COMPILATOREM, *Apparatus in Librum Sohar, Pars secunda*, pp. 52 et seq. KAB. DEN. t. i.

This letter was accompanied by a number of questions and considerations in development of the debated point and other difficulties, all which are duly printed by Rosenroth, to whom space seemed no object, together with his AMICA RESPONSIO, which cites the authority of the ZOHAR in support of the circular form of the SEPHIROTH.[1] More replied with an ULTERIOR DISQUISITIO and an accompanying letter, in which he announces his belief that he has hit upon the true Kabbalah of the Jewish BERESHITH. This epistle is in English and quaintly worded. The conclusion entreats Rosenroth to intimate to his readers " how beneficiall this may prove for the preparing of the Jews to receive Christianity, the difficultyes and obstacles being cleared and removed by the right understanding of their own Cabbala."

There is no need to follow this friendly discussion, which, it must be confessed, becomes exceedingly tedious in the ULTERIOR DISQUISITIO. More, however, contributed another thesis in exposition of the Vision of Ezekiel, *i.e.*, a Kabbalistic Catechism and a refutation of the doctrine that the material world is not the product of creation *ex nihilo*, in which last the Platonist seems scarcely to have understood the Kabbalah.

Of all these the most interesting is the MERCAVÆ EXPOSITIO, which contains nineteen postulates, fifty-two questions arising out of the text of Ezekiel and the replies thereto. It affirms, (*a*) That all souls, angelical and human, that of Messiah included, were created at the beginning of the world;[2] (*b*) That the material world in its first estate was diaphanous, or lucid; (*c*) That it had two chief elements, the Spirit of Nature and the vehicle of the Holy Spirit; (*d*) That it was divided into four parts, which are the Four Worlds of the Kabbalists; (*e*) That all souls were at first enclosed in ATZILUTH, but were subject to revolution in the other Worlds; (*f*) That souls which the Divine decree has sent into ASSIAH, but are free from willing sin, are sustained by Divine Virtue, and will assuredly return to ATZILUTH; (*g*) That in ATZILUTH the souls and the angels are absorbed wholly in the Beatific Vision, but that in BRIAH they have a tendency to external things; (*h*) That the soul of Messiah in ATZILUTH made such progress in the Divine Love that it

---

[1] In *Caput* ii., *Consideratio tertia, ibid.*, p. 91.
[2] For this there is Talmudic as well as Zoharic authority.

became united with the Eternal Word in a Hyper-Atzilutic or Hypostatic manner, and was thus constituted Chief of all souls and King of the Four Worlds, an event which took place at the beginning of the Briatic World, the special heritage of Messiah. At this point the Christian Kabbalist introduces the compact of the cross and dissolves all connection with the scheme of Jewish Theosophy.

The MERCAVÆ EXPOSITIO contains numerous references to another work of More, entitled CONJECTURA CABBALISTICA,[1] which preceded his correspondence with Rosenroth. It is a presentation of the literal, philosophical and mystical, or divinely moral sense of the three initial chapters of Genesis. It was received, so the author assures us, neither from men nor angels, and as a fact the "conjecture" illustrates the criticism of Franck, for it has very little in common with any ancient or modern Kabbalah ever received in Jewry. The literal section is a bald paraphrase of the scriptural account of the creation and fall of man. The PHILOSOPHIC CABBALA is established on the denary after the following fantastic manner:—

The Archetypal World = Monad, 1.
The First Matter = Duad, 2.
The Habitable Order = Triad, 3.
The Making of the Starry Heavens = Tetrad, 4.
The Making of Fish and Fowls, or Union of the Passive and Active Principle = Pentad, 5.
The Making of Beasts and Cattle, but chiefly of Man = Hexad, 6.

What becomes of the rest of the denary does not appear. In his first estate Adam was wholly ethereal, and his soul was the ground which was blessed by God, whereby it brought forth every pleasant tree and every goodly growth of the heavenly Father's own planting. The Tree of Life in the garden of man's soul was the essential will of God, while the Tree of Knowledge was the will of man himself. We have here the keynote of the allegory, which is merely pleasing and altogether unsubstantial. It may be noted, however, that the sleep which fell upon Adam was a lassitude of Divine

---

[1] A CONJECTURAL ESSAY *of interpreting the Mind of Moses according to a threefold Cabbala, viz., Literal, Philosophical, Mystical, or Divinely Moral*, London, 1662. The attempt was dedicated to Cudworth.

Contemplation. The MORAL CABBALA recognises two principles in man, namely, spirit and flesh. It gives apparently a synopsis of the work of regeneration, depicting, firstly, the spiritual chaos, when man is under the dominion of the flesh; next, the dawning of the heavenly principle, corresponding to the *Fiat Lux;* but the analogy in most instances seems at once weak and laboured. For example, the fruit-bearing trees are good works, the manifestation of the sun is the love of God and our neighbour, and so forth. On the whole, it may be concluded that More's connection with the Kabbalah is an interesting episode in the life of an amiable scholar, but it was without real increment to either.

XI.—THOMAS VAUGHAN

With the questionings, difficulties and tentative expositions of Henry More it will be useful to contrast what is said on the subject of Kabbalism by his contemporary Eugenius Philalethes, otherwise Thomas Vaughan. It will not be forgotten by students of the byways of literature in the seventeenth century that the two writers came into collision in pamphlets. When Vaughan began his theosophical labours by the publication of two tracts on the nature of man and on the universal Spirit of Nature, More, who was after all more Platonist than mystic and had scant tolerance for mystical terminology, published some acrimonious observations concerning them, to which the Welsh mystic replied in satires with the polemical virulence of his period. The dispute itself deserves nothing less than oblivion, but Thomas Vaughan has been regarded, and not, I think, with exaggeration, as the chief mystic, theosopher and alchemist, with one exception in the last respect,[1] produced at his period in England; and as he died nearly twenty-five years before the appearance of KABBALA DENUDATA, the source and extent of his Kabbalistic knowledge will help us to fix the state of scholarship in England on the subject before the formation of the group of Cambridge Platonists. Vaughan, in his early works, confesses himself a disciple of Agrippa,

---

[1] The exception is Eirenæus Philalethes, that truly "Unknown Philosopher," with whom Eugenius has been so often identified, and from whom of late years he has been so often and carefully distinguished by myself, that it is unnecessary in this connection to say anything concerning him, except that his numerous works have few points of contact with Kabbalism.

and the THREE BOOKS OF OCCULT PHILOSOPHY [1] represent the general measure of his knowledge concerning the Esoteric Tradition of the Jews, while the opinion which he had formed thereon must be referred to the Retractation of his master, that admirable work on the VANITY OF THE SCIENCES AND THE EXCELLENCE OF THE WORD OF GOD. I must not say that he shews no independent reading; he quotes on one occasion a passage in PORTA LUCIS [2] which is not to be found in Agrippa, and there are one or two other instances,[3] but for the most part he is content to represent his model and his first inspirer. If my readers accept this judgment, they must interpret his own statement that he spent some years in the search and contemplation of the Kabbalah reflectively and not bibliographically, which further will assist them to see how the peculiar Mysticism of Thomas Vaughan can offer distinct points of contact with the ZOHAR without that text-book of Kabbalism, then untranslated, having been read by the mystic, except in some Latin extracts.

In his discourse on the Antiquity of Magic we find him alive, like the students who had preceded him, to the distinction between a true and a false Kabbalah. The latter, described after the picturesque manner of his period, as the invention of dispersed and wandering rabbis "whose brains had more of distraction than their fortunes," consists altogether " in alphabetical knacks, ends always in the letter where it begins and the vanities of it are grown voluminous." But in respect of the " more ancient and physical traditions of the Kabbalah," Thomas Vaughan tells us that he embraces them for so many sacred truths.[4] He recognises also a metaphysical tradition in which the greatest mystery is the symbolism of Jacob's Ladder. " Here we find two extremes— Jacob is one, at the foot of the ladder, and God is the other, Who stands above it, *emittens formas et influxus in Jacob, sive subjectum hominem*. The rounds or steps in the ladder signify the middle nature, by which Jacob is united to God." [5] With this symbolism he contrasts the " false grammatical Kabbala " which " consists only in rotations of the alphabet and a

---

[1] Translated into English one year after the appearance of Vaughan's first treatises.
[2] Concerning the restraint of superior influences occasioned by the sin of Adam.
[3] Of which some are sufficiently erroneous, as, for example, in MAGIA ADAMICA, when he states that MALKUTH is the invisible, archetypal moon.
[4] THE WORKS OF THOMAS VAUGHAN, edited by A. E. Waite, London, 1919, p. 167.
[5] *Ibid.*, pp. 169, 170.

metathesis of letters in the text, by which means the scripture hath suffered many racks and excoriations." The true Kabbalah only uses letters for artifice, thas is, with a view to concealment.¹ Of the physical side of the genuine Tradition he gives an unfinished presentation in alchemical language, which is transfigured, however, for Thomas Vaughan regarded Alchemy as at once a spiritual and physical science, having its operations in the infinite as well as in the mineral kingdom. For him the SEPHIROTH are ten secret principles, of which the first is a spirit *in retrecesso suo fontano*, while the second is the Voice of that Spirit, the third is another Spirit which issues from the Spirit and the Voice, and the fourth is "a certain water" proceeding from the third Spirit, and emanating Fire and Air.² It will be seen that the reflections of the Welsh mystic on the apparatus of Kabbalism are not elucidating, and while recording the Sephirotic attributions of the SEPHER YETZIRAH are not fully in consonance therewith.

We shall be inclined, on the whole, to confess that Vaughan's connection with Kabbalistic texts is like his communications with the brethren of the Rosicrucian Order. He knew nothing of the latter "as to their persons," so he tells us in his preface to a translation of the FAMA and CONFESSIO of the Fraternity, and it was mainly by report and consideration on things heard at second hand that he was aware of Mysticism in Jewry. As time went on and he outgrew the simple leading-strings of Cornelius Agrippa, so he strayed further from Kabbalistic interests, and though he never lost the fascination betrayed in his earlier works, he passed far away over fields of Spiritual Alchemy, where no ÆSH MEZAREPH could help him. When he published EUPHRATES, *or the Waters of the East*, in 1655, he shews no longer any trace of the Tradition in Israel. In LUMEN DE LUMINE, which appeared some four years earlier, there are, however, a few references to the subject, and one indeed constitutes an adumbration of the Christian Kabbalah as impressed on the curious mind of the mystical royalist. The pretext by which it is introduced is a speculation concerning the "Fire-Soul," or informing spirit of the earth, which is described as an influence from the Almighty derived through

---

¹ WORKS OF THOMAS VAUGHAN, p. 171. ² *Ibid.*, p. 168.

the mediation of *terra viventium*. The mediating being thus described darkly, is said to be the Second Person, and that which "the Kabbalists style the Supernatural East." To explain this symbolism Vaughan adds: "As the Natural Light of the sun is first manifested to us in the East, so the Supernatural Light was first manifested in the Second Person, for He is *Principium alterationis*, the Beginning of the ways of God, or the First Manifestation of His Father's Light in the Supernatural Generation. From this *Terra Viventium* or Land of the Living comes all Life or Spirit."[1] The Kabbalistic warrant of this notion is the axiom: *Omnis anima bona anima nova filia Orientis*.[2] The East in question is CHOKMAH, which is contrary to Kabbalistic statements, and CHOKMAH is the Son of God. This also is opposed to the Sephirotic ascriptions with which we are familiar, but there is some trace in early Kabbalistic writers of an attribution of the Three Supernals to Father, Son, Bride, with which later rabbins are said—a little egregiously—to have tampered so as to elude its Christian inferences. In either case Vaughan is interesting as a strange light of Christian Mysticism rather than as an expositor of the Kabbalah.

XII.—KNORR VON ROSENROTH

It is, perhaps, more interesting to ascertain the motives which led the editor of KABBALA DENUDATA to the consideration of Jewish Theosophy than those of any other student of the subject. To Christian Knorr von Rosenroth the occultist of Victorian days owed nearly all his knowledge of the ZOHAR, for the bibliographical writers who preceded him give only meagre notices of that Kabbalistic *magnum opus*, and it is not even mentioned by, *e.g.*, Cornelius Agrippa. Now Rosenroth occupies a position which "occult" persons like Mathers and Westcott, as well as their inspirer Lévi, have failed to remark, because they seem to have known nothing about their chief illuminator in the theosophy of Israel. I propose to shew that he was actuated by the same missionary enthusiasm which characterised all Christian expositors who

---

[1] LUMEN DE LUMINE, London, 1651, pp. 80–82.
[2] CONCLUSIONES KABALISTICÆ, No. xli. Vaughan also cites the obscure eighth conclusion of Mirandula, and says that the third light is BINAH, the Holy Ghost.—*Ibid.*, p. 83.

preceded him,[1] but I shall begin by enumerating one or two points which indicate that he may have had one occult connection. Born in the year 1636, a German noble bearing the title of baron, he appears on the scene of history shortly after public curiosity had almost died out on the subject of the Rosicrucian mystery. Joachim Junge, Johann Valentin Andreas and Ægidius Gutmann, three persons to whom rival theories have attributed the invention of that Mystery,[2] were still alive; Robert Fludd, the English apologist of the Faternity, was on the threshold of death, but had not yet passed away; Thomas Vaughan was a schoolboy; Eirenæus Philalethes had just written his INTROITUS APERTUS to shew the adepts of Alchemy that he was their brother and their peer;[3] Sendivogius had exhausted his projecting powder and was living in seclusion, an aged man, on the frontiers of Silesia;[4] John Baptist van Helmont, who long before had testified that he had seen and touched the Philosopher's Stone—of a colour like saffron in powder, but heavy and shining like pounded glass [5]—had christened his son Mercurius; and Mercurius van Helmont, the contemporary and friend of Rosenroth, divided his laborious existence between a tireless search after the secret of transmuting metals and the study of the Kabbalah. Rosenroth, Kabbalist like Helmont, was, like Helmont, probably a chemist—in the sense of the seventeenth century—and on the crowded title-page of his great work, we find it described as *Scriptum omnibus philologis, philosophis, Theologis omnium religionum, atque philochymicis quam utilissimum*. The justification is that the *Loci Communes Cabbalistici* include a *Compendium Libri Cabbalistico-Chymici*, ÆSCH MEZAREPH *dicti, de Lapide Philosophico*. I have had occasion in the sixth book to give some account of this treatise.

We have reason therefore to suppose that Rosenroth was infected—slightly or otherwise—with the alchemical zeal of

---

[1] It was indeed, both before and after, the conventional *raison d'être* of almost every work on the subject. See, for example, Beyers' CABBALISMUS JUDAICO-CHRISTIANUS *Detectus Breviterque Delineatus*. Wittemberg, 1707.

[2] REAL HISTORY OF THE ROSICRUCIANS, by A. E. Waite, c. viii., especially pp. 220–222. Compare my later work on THE BROTHERHOOD OF THE ROSY CROSS, consulting the references to these names in the Index.

[3] See *Præfatio Authoris*, which appears in all editions of the INTROITUS APERTUS *ad Occlusum Regis Palatium*.

[4] A. E. Waite: THE SECRET TRADITION IN ALCHEMY, p. 295.

[5] In his treatise DE VITA ETERNA.

his friend, the second generation of an alchemical family. We may suspect, however, that he was more theosophist than Hermetist; we are told also that he loved meditating on the Holy Scriptures and that he knew them by heart. Like his countryman Khunrath, he was a Lutheran, and Éliphas Lévi would have said of him, as of the author of AMPHITHEATRUM: "herein he was a German of his period rather than a mystical citizen of the eternal kingdom."[1] In matters of religion his peculiar bent is determined by the fact that he wrote an EXPLANATION OF THE APOCALYPSE, about which I will forbear from wearying my readers. More to our purpose is a dialogue on evangelical history, in which a Kabbalistic catechumen proposes questions on the four Gospels and a Christian replies. With this also we may connect a treatise entitled MESSIAS PURUS, in which the life of Jesus Christ, from his conception to his baptism, is explained according to the doctrines of the Kabbalah. In a word, the motto of his correspondent Henry More was that also of Rosenroth: "May the glory of our God and His Christ be the end of all our writings!" In conformity with this he begins his enumeration of the reasons which justify the appearance of a Latin version of the ZOHAR [2] by affirming that at a period when the divisions of Christendom are traceable to diversity of philosophical opinions and metaphysical definitions it must be important to investigate a philosophical system which flourished during the age of Christ and his apostles, and from which fountain the sacred oracles have themselves drawn largely. In the preface to his translation of three texts of the ZOHAR he founds his opinion that Kabbalistic dogmas may be of Divine revelation on the ground of their sanctity and sublimity, as well as their great use in explaining the books of the Old and New Testaments. He affirms also that, unlike later Jewish writings, the ZOHAR does not contain a single utterance against Christ. Finally, after enumerating twenty-four reasons why the Jews should enjoy toleration at Christian hands, he mentions the chief things which will assist their conversion. They include, of course, the ordinary commonplaces of piety and the ordinary devices of proselytism, but there is stress laid upon the promotion of the study of Hebrew

---

[1] HISTOIRE DE LA MAGIE, Introduction, p. 33. Paris, 1860. See also my translation, s.v. THE HISTORY OF MAGIC, second edition, 1922, p. 29.
[2] APPARATUS IN LIBRUM SOHAR, *Pars Secunda*, pp. 3 *et seq.*, KAB. DEN., Tom. i.

and Chaldaic, and on the translation of the New Testament into those languages.[1] The disquisition is conventional enough, but it is important because it indicates, firstly, the project which was ever near to the heart of Rosenroth, and, secondly, how little he dreamed either of an esoteric Christianity or of a withdrawn Wisdom-Religion, how little he looked to find in Kabbalistic doctrine a deeper sense of Christian doctrines, or indeed anything but their consecration in the eyes of Jewry, by demonstrating that they were to be found in the ZOHAR. He did not wish the Christian to become a Kabbalist, but he longed very much for the Kabbalistic Jew to become a Lutheran. He is said to have endured great sacrifices, outside the vast labour involved, over the publication of KABBALA DENUDATA, but there is no need to add that it missed its aim entirely; it has enabled a few students to get a confused notion of the ZOHAR, and it has in this way done immense service to occultists by furnishing material for their reveries: it is outside probability that it ever brought a single Jew into the Church of Christ, and as Rosenroth failed in his public aim, so at the close of his life he had the misfortune to see his daughter depart from the reformed religion and embrace, under the influence of her husband, the faith of the Catholic Church. Taken altogether the story of Christian Rosenroth has a touch of heroism and tragedy, and seeing that with all its faults his gift to scholarship is one of permanent value, so it is, I think, a useful task to indicate the circumstances under which he gave it and the motives by which he was prompted.[2]

---

[1] With this description the reader may compare a little treatise which belongs to KABBALA DENUDATA, though unfortunately it is met with very rarely in extant copies, *i.e.*, ADUMBRATIO KABBALÆ CHRISTIANÆ, *id est Syncatabasis Hebraizans, sive Explicatio ad dogmata Novi Foederis pertinens, pro formanda hypothesi, ad conversionem Judæorum proficientis*. It is an addendum to the second volume, separately paged, and is in the form of a dialogue between a Kabbalist and a Christian philosopher. It has been translated of recent years into French. Even at this day the little work seems to me of singular interest, and it is written with limpid clearness. The disquisition on the parts or grades of the soul in man may be noted in this connection as a case in point.

[2] At a later date the same motives inspired two small treatises—the work of other writers—which are interesting in their way, and are worth mentioning for the benefit of students who may wish to pursue the subject. (1) PHOSPHORUS ORTHODOXÆ FIDEI *Veterum Cabbalistarum, seu Testimonia de Sacro-Sancta Trinitate et Messia Deo et Homine, ex pervetusto Libro Sohar deprompta, qua nunc primum Latiné reddita, suisque et R. Johannis Kemperi Judæo-Christiani animadversionibus concinné explicata, Judais æque ac Christianis speciminis loco edidit Andreas Norrelius Suecus, qui item commentarios Kemperianos suis illustravit notis*. *Amstelodami*, 1720. This has been cited previously, but by name only. The prolegomena are concerned with the praise of R. Simeon ben Yohai, shewing the authority of the ZOHAR and its superiority to the Talmud on the ground that its author

I should add that over the antiquity of Kabbalistic doctrine and literature he was by no means credulous for his period, seeming indeed to admit that there may have been an admixture of late material with the ancient fragments of the ZOHAR. He regarded the BOOK OF CONCEALMENT as the oldest and most important of its treatises, and this is the only one in which he was inclined to recognise the direct authorship of R. Simeon ben Yohai. Of the rest, some may have been the work of R. Abba and some of the school which succeeded these masters.

XIII.—RALPH CUDWORTH

The honoured name of Ralph Cudworth, perhaps the greatest theosophist of his age on the side of scholarship, is still a memory in English theological literature of the higher type, though, except among rare students, the TRUE INTELLECTUAL SYSTEM OF THE UNIVERSE is remembered rather than read. It is a mine of Platonism, learning and sapience, and more than this, it is a deeply reasoned treatise of its period in opposition to the atheism of that period; its points are established victoriously, and turning over the leaves of the colossal folio one almost regrets that the difficulties of the seventeenth century disturb us no longer and that their solutions no longer help us. It must be confessed that Cudworth connects but superficially with Kabbalism, and the connection, such as it is, need not detain us long. The chief thesis of the INTELLECTUAL SYSTEM is that behind all

---

flourished before Judah the Prince. The Talmud is quoted (p. 10), to prove that R. Simeon studied the Kabbalah in the cave, and that he and his son wrote the ZOHAR therein, or that part of it which is in the Jerusalem dialect. The Hebrew portions are referred to other authorships (p. 16). The translated matter is chiefly from the FAITHFUL SHEPHERD, and follows the Mantua edition of the ZOHAR. (2) LUX IN TENEBRIS, *quam Zohar Antiquum Judaorum Monumentum, genti suæ occoccata præbet, in densissimis rerum divinarum tenebris, ad mysterium SS. Trinitatis eo facilius appræhendendum, et Majestatem Christi Divinam non pertinaciter oppugnandam, et Honorem Spiritus Sancti Recentiorum more non fœdandum* ... *Studio M. Nicolai Lutkens* (without place or date, but about the same period as the treatise of Norrelius). In the first two chapters there is an attempt to prove that the Mystery of the Trinity is concealed in Leviticus xvi. 18, and Deut. vi. 5. The third chapter investigates Gen. xix. 24—*De Domino qui a Domino pluit,* in the same interest. The fourth chapter treats of the Lord God of Hosts, Is. vi. 3; and the fifth of the Lord God, *ib.* xlviii. 16. The sixth chapter seeks to prove that the three supernal SEPHIROTH were names and characters under which pre-Christian Jews distinguished the Three Persons of the One Divine essence. (3) Compare with these DIATRIBE PHILOLOGICA *de R. Simeone Filio Jochai auctore Libri Sohar, in qua viri celeberrimi Christiani Schoettgenii Dissertatio docens R. Simeonum Filium Jochai Religionum fuisse Christianum modeste examinatur et contrarium potius evincitur, auctore Justo Martino Glasenero,* Hildesia, 1736. A pamphlet of twenty-two pages.

the tapestries and embroideries of pagan mythology there is the doctrine of monotheism, and that civilised man in reality has never worshipped but one God, whose threefold nature was a " Divine Cabbala " or revelation, successively depraved and adulterated till it almost disappears for Cudworth among the " particular unities " of Proclus and the later Platonists.[1] Among the cloud of witnesses who are convened in support of this view are included the later Rabbinical writers, the HALACOTH of Maimonides, the OLAT TAMID = PERPETUAL OFFERING of Moses Albelda (sixteenth century), the IKKARIM or PRINCIPLES of Joseph Albo (fifteenth century), the commentaries of R. David Kimchi (1160-1235), and the book NITZACHON, references and extracts which at least serve to shew that this Christian divine had attempted some curious exploration in the world of Hebrew literature. His conclusion was " that the Hebrew Doctors and Rabbins have been generally of this persuasion, that the Pagan Nations anciently, at least the intelligent amongst them, acknowledged One Supreme God of the whole world, and that all their other Gods were but Creatures and Inferior Ministers, which were worshipped by them upon these two accounts, either as thinking that the honour done to them redounded to the Supreme, or else that they might be their Mediators and Intercessors, Orators and Negotiators with Him, which inferior Gods of the Pagans were supposed by these Hebrews to be chiefly of two kinds, Angels and Stars or Spheres, the latter of which the Jews as well as Pagans concluded to be animated and intellectual." The question at the present day is chiefly archaic or fantastic, but it has its interest, for it serves to illustrate the strange contrast which exists between the Hebrew mind at the period of Maimonides and at that far distant epoch when the song of the Psalmist described the idols of the Gentiles as " silver and gold, the work of the hands of men."

In addition to the TRUE INTELLECTUAL SYSTEM OF THE UNIVERSE Cudworth published some sermons and a discourse on the TRUE NOTION OF THE LORD'S SUPPER,[2] afterwards translated into Latin by Mosheim, with a confutation representing the consubstantial doctrine of Lutheran theology,[3]

---

[1] For the purposes of this notice I have used the original edition of the TRUE INTELLECTUAL SYSTEM OF THE UNIVERSE, London, 1668.
[2] London, 1676.
[3] This translation appeared in 1733.

and yet again enlarged upon by Edward Pelling in his DISCOURSE ON THE SACRAMENT. The drift of the thesis is represented sufficiently by the summary of the first chapter: "That it was a custom of the Jews and Heathens to feast upon things sacrificed, and that the custom of the Christians in partaking of the Body and Blood of Christ once sacrificed upon the Cross, in the Lord's Supper, is analogous thereto." It is outside my province to pronounce upon this view, but as a Christian Mystic who holds that sacramentalism is the law of Nature and the law of Grace, it may be remarked in passing that no theory which reduces the Eucharist to a memorial or a religious banquet can be mystically acceptable. Cudworth was by no means a mystic, and the most that his subject afforded was an opportunity to give further evidence of his unusual erudition, and it may be added of no inconsiderable skill in its management. The thesis is mentioned here because it has recourse so frequently to the Rabbinical writers, to the glosses of Nahmanides, the writings of Isaac Abravanel, the MISHNA, the commentary on that work by Rabbi Obadiah, the scholiasts on Judges, rare MSS. of Karaite Jews and so forth. The Zoharic writings are not quoted, but it was because they contained nothing bearing on the matter in hand: had occasion arisen, no doubt Ralph Cudworth would have given evidence of passable familiarity with that great cycle of Kabbalistic literature.

XIV.—THOMAS BURNET

With the Cambridge school of Platonists the name of Thomas Burnet, some time master of the Charterhouse, connects by association rather than the similarity of intellectual pursuits. He entered Christ's College in 1654, when Ralph Cudworth was master, while Henry More was just in his fortieth year. It was probably to the last-named divine that he owed his slight knowledge of the subject which entitles him to mention in this place. The amicable discussion between More and the editor of KABBALA DENUDATA appeared, as we have seen, in that work in the year 1677, but the INTERPRETATION OF THE MIND OF MOSES had preceded it by a number of years. When Burnet published his TELLURIS THEORIA SACRA, he gave no evidence of interest in Platonic or Kabbalistic subjects: it has been described by Brewster as a beautiful geological romance. It is, of course, concerned with the Mosaic scheme of creation, and the more important work which followed it, dealing as it does with the ancient doctrine concerning the origin of things, is really its extension or sequel.[1] In this interesting volume, written elegantly in Latin of the period, *tout un grand chapitre*, as the bibliography of Papus describes it, is devoted to the Kabbalah. As hinted already, it bears no evidence of original research, or indeed of any first-hand knowledge, but it is justifiable by our purpose to ascertain how a literature which fascinated, though it did not convince, the Cambridge Platonists, impressed the liberal mind of a bold and not unlearned thinker belonging to the next generation. We find, as might be anticipated, that Burnet raises no question as to the wisdom of Moses, by which he understood what all other Kabbalistic students have understood also, a knowledge of natural mysteries derived from the Egyptian education of the Jewish lawgiver. He differs, however, from Kabbalists by questioning seriously how much of this wisdom came down to the Israelites. Assuming some tradition of the kind, there could be no doubt that it was depraved in the lapse of time.[2] In particular, the Kabbalah, as we now possess it, abounds in figments of imagination and in nugatory methods. From this statement of a general position, which may be regarded as common ground of criticism, he proceeds to a more detailed examination, and reaches conclusions which are not likely to be challenged at the present day. The debased character of Jewish Tradition in some of its developments must be recognised by those, critical and otherwise, who maintain most earnestly its mystical and theosophical importance.

If we attempt, says Burnet, to separate anything which may remain uncorrupted in the Kabbalah, to divide the genuine from the spurious, we must first of all purge away that numerical, literal, grammatical part which seeks to extract arcane meanings from the alphabet, the Divine Names and the word-book of the Scriptures. The magical and superstitious element must be also purged away. We should bear further in mind, and this, I think, is the most

---

[1] ARCHÆOLOGIÆ PHILOSOPHICÆ, *sive Doctrina Antiqua de Rerum Originibus*, LIBRI DUO, *editio secunda* (the best), London, 1728.
[2] *Fædissime licet à Neotericis corrupta et adulterata.*

sensible of several secondary points raised in the criticism, that the enunciation of common notions in uncommon language cannot be accepted as any true Kabbalah. The warning which it implies was not less needed a mere generation ago than in the days of Thomas Burnet. The delight in unintelligible language because it is unintelligible was as characteristic of Victorian occult writers, even as of gloom-wrapped Hades according to the Ritual of the Dead, and it is a tendency which has an inscrutable foundation in the entire subject. It would seem indeed that the sphinx who propounds the arcana in terms as monstrous as herself needs only a commonplace to overwhelm her, as in the case of Œdipus.

In accordance with his intention Burnet proceeds to divide the Kabbalah into the Nominal and Real. The first is that which he has specified as worthless—GEMATRIA, TEMURAH, NOTARICON, VOCABULA. Its devices, he says, are the diversions of our children, and in truth it would seem hard to decide whether intellectual superiority and philosophical seriousness should be ascribed to rabbinical anagrams or to the apparatus of " Tit: Tat: To." In any case, " they do not belong to sane literature, much less to wisdom."

So far we can accept readily the judgment of Burnet, but there was no novelty in the line taken, even so far back as the second half of the seventeenth century. When he comes, however, to consider what he has agreed to regard as the real Kabbalah, his insufficiency is evident, and his slender knowledge, drawn only from KABBALA DENUDATA, when it does not arrest his judgment, leads him into manifest error. Thus, he tells us that the real Kabbalah contains two things which are important for our consideration, the doctrine of the SEPHIROTH and that of the Four Worlds, but he complains that the conception which underlies the former does not appear clearly. With the help of the Lexicon of Rosenroth he decides finally that they are emanations from God.[1] He sets forth what he can glean from that source concerning KETHER and CHOKMAH, and then surrenders the inquiry in the hope of finding more intelligible statements concerning the Four Worlds.[2] He concludes, however, that the con-

---

[1] Elsewhere, he attempts to consider their significance in connection with the axiom—*ex nihilo nihil fit*.

[2] He mentions in addition to the SEPHIROTH and the Four Worlds, the thirty-two Paths of Wisdom, from the SEPHER YETZIRAH and its commentary, and the Fifty Gates

demnation of all the pseudo-mystics of Kabbalism, Theosophy and Hermeticism is that of the unbelievers who continued to love the darkness rather than the light when the light was come already into the world.[1] He assumes, as might be expected, that the BOOK OF OCCULTATION is the most important part of the ZOHAR and, glancing at the commentaries of Isaac de Loria and of Hirtz on the tract in question and its developments, confesses his inability to understand either from text or interpreters what is meant by the symbolism of the Vast and the Lesser Countenance. "We are all of us liable some time or other to be distracted by reasoning, but it is a common complaint of the mind among Orientals to be distracted by allegories."

To sum his general position: We know from Maimonides that the Hebrews once possessed many mysteries concerning things divine, but that they have perished.[2] It is at the same time scarcely possible that all foundation should be wanting to the Kabbalah, yet if its doctrines were openly and clearly set forth, it is hard to say whether they would move us to laughter or astonishment.

Thomas Burnet has higher claims on our tolerance than his ability as a critic of Kabbalism, and his mind was not of that order which could be expected to understand or sympathise with the aspirations embraced by Theosophy. He was one of the rare precursors of liberal Theology, and he is said to have closed the path of his promotion by venturing to express an opinion that the story of the Garden of Eden should not be understood literally. In a later treatise on the FAITH AND DUTIES OF CHRISTIANS,[3] he is thought to have excluded so much which seemed to him doubtful or unimportant in accepted doctrine that it is questionable whether even Christianity remained. A posthumous work on eschatology and the resurrection [4] maintained that the punishment of the wicked would terminate ultimately in their salvation. I should add that some pretended English versions of the Archæological Philosophy do not represent the original, and in particular omit altogether the Kabbalistic section.

---

of Providence " through which Moses attained his marvellous science, and concealed the same in the Pentateuch," *i.e.*, according to the Kabbalists.

[1] John iii. 19–21.
[2] THE GUIDE OF THE PERPLEXED. Part i, c. 71.
[3] DE FIDE ET OFFICIIS CHRISTIANORUM.
[4] DE STATU MORTUORUM ET RESURGENTIUM.

XV.—SAINT-MARTIN

The life and doctrine of Louis Claude de Saint-Martin, the Unknown Philosopher, who at the end of the eighteenth century and amidst the torch-lights of the Revolution diffused in France the higher spirit of Mysticism, having been the subject of my studies elsewhere,[1] I shall refer to him here only as the recipient of an Esoteric Tradition through Martines de Pasqually, the genesis of which remains undetermined, though it was termed Rosicrucian by his initiator, and has been designated Swedenborgian subsequently by one of his interpreters in France. It is a Tradition which differs from other presentations of Theosophical Doctrine, and it has little in common with what we know or may infer concerning Rosicrucian teaching. In the RÉINTEGRATION DES ÊTRES of Pasqually,[2] and in the Catechisms of the Masonic Rite propagated by him, which are also most probably his work, the Tradition is presented in a crude manner. It was developed by Saint-Martin, who indeed brought to it a gift of genius which was wanting in his instructor. Now, Saint-Martin was a man who cared very little, and does not scruple to say so, for purely traditional doctrines, at least as traditional, nor did he shew much deference towards doctors of authority therein. He considered books at best a makeshift method of instruction, though he wrote many; he preferred learning at first hand from God, Man and the Universe. Till he came under the influence of Jacob Böhme he neither quoted nor possessed "authorities," with the exception of the Scriptures. He drew, of course, from the source of his initiation, but he never mentions it in any clear manner, except in his correspondence and his life-notes, both published posthumously. There is nothing to indicate that he had read Kabbalistic literature: there is every presumption that he did not. Some of his lesser doctrines possess notwithstanding a certain Kabbalistic complexion. There is that in particular concerning the Great Name which I have developed at some length in a study to which I have referred, but it has lost all

---

[1] See A. E. Waite: THE LIFE OF LOUIS CLAUDE DE SAINT-MARTIN, *the Unknown Philosopher, and the Substance of his Transcendental Doctrine*, London, Philip Wellby, 1901. See also my SAINT-MARTIN, *the French Mystic*, 1922.

[2] It is right to say that Kenneth Mackenzie, in his CYCLOPÆDIA OF FREEMASONRY, attributes to him three published works which, so far as I am aware, are unknown.

touch with Kabbalism in the hands of Saint-Martin. So also he has a complex system of mystic numbers which might suggest the Rabbinical NOTARIKON, but it is entirely out of line with all anterior speculations on this subject, and makes the question of its origin one of the problems in his history.[1] I conclude that Pasqually, whom I take to have been a sincere and perhaps even a saintly man, as his Masonic school was almost a seminary of sanctity, derived from a source which retained some filtrations of Kabbalism, and that they were brought over by Saint-Martin without any historical associations whatever.[2] He has therefore little title to be included among defenders and expounders of Kabbalistic doctrine, which would have come as a surprise to himself. This was done, however, by French occult writers[3] belonging to so-called Martinist and other groups of the late nineteenth and early twentieth centuries, and by Dr. Papus especially, who seemed anxious to annex anyone, from Shakespeare to the author of SUPERNATURAL RELIGION.

XVI.—ÉLIPHAS LÉVI

Between the period of Saint-Martin and that of Alphonse Louis Constant, who is the subject of this notice, the French literature of Kabbalism may be said to have been initiated rather than to have received a new impetus by the publication of Adolphe Franck, to whose views on the subject of post-Christian religious philosophy among the Jews, I have made frequent reference already.[4] I have indicated also that its superficial value remains unimpaired after the lapse of eighty years, and indeed modern criticism has in certain definite respects reverted unawares to his standpoint, as regards not only the antiquity of Zoharic Tradition but of much of the body of the ZOHAR. Franck's work has, of course, its limitations, and it is known that his excerpts from Kabbalistic books were subjected to severe strictures in Germany; but for an accomplished and luminous review of the whole

---

[1] It is not impossible that it derives from his first school and therefore from Pasqually, who was sole instructor therein.
[2] That man is superior to the angels, and may even instruct them, is, I think, the most convincing instance in Saint-Martin of such a filtration. This notion is found in the ZOHAR, and developed by some of its commentators.
[3] More especially in the case of the so-called facetious allegory LE CROCODILE, in which it may be said safely that there is not a single trace of Kabbalism.
[4] LA KABBALE ou la Philosophie Religieuse des Hébreux. Par Ad. Franck, Paris, 1843.

subject nothing of later date can be said to have superseded it. Its analyses of the SEPHER YETZIRAH and of the ZOHAR, together with its delineations of correspondences between the philosophical school of Kabbalism and the schools of Plato, of Alexandria, of Philo, created French knowledge on the subject, and together with the researches of Munk, published some few years subsequently, have been the main source of that knowledge down to recent times, the part of dream and reverie being provided by the writings of Éliphas Lévi. As regards both methods and motives, Franck and Lévi are located at opposite poles. The first was an academic writer having no occult interests; the second claimed not only initiation but adeptship, not only the ordinary resources of scholarship focussed on a literary and historical problem but all advantages which could be derived from an exclusive possession of its master key.

Among the lesser difficulties of recent Kabbalistic criticism the proper allocation of Alphonse Louis Constant in the throng of students and expositors was not without its gravity till I sought on my own part to reflect some light thereon. Whether in France or in England few had approached the subject with sympathies in the direction of occult arts and speculations who did not owe their introduction to Éliphas Lévi. I speak, of course, of the period subsequent to 1850,[1] and I may add that few persons thus initiated did anything but read the interpretations of their first leader into the obscure body of dogma which comprises the Esoteric Tradition of the Jews. If it be necessary, therefore, to make void rather

---

[1] Although the treatise of Franck had, as we have seen, preceded Lévi's interpretations by several years. So far as I can recollect the professed adept never referred to the sympathetic criticism and defence of the more academic writer. Prior to 1843 the most extraordinary ignorance must have prevailed upon the subject in France, since it was possible for a distinguished philosopher to write as follows:—" When Christian philosophy made its appearance in the world it crushed Paganism and Theurgy, and in the second century humanity was made subject to a severe régime, which set aside Mysticism. It did not reappear till the fourteenth and fifteenth centuries in certain schools of Italy and Germany. This new Mysticism, called Kabbalah, from a name known already in the schools of Alexandria, but since entirely disappeared, and signifying oral tradition, issued from the bosom of the scholastic, and acted with the instruments of the scholastic, as formerly the neoplatonist Porphyry evoked with Platonic words. The Kabbalah of the fifteenth century put in operation bizarre formulæ, magic squares and circles, mysterious numbers, by the power of which the demons of hell and the divinities of heaven were compelled, as it was pretended, to appear in obedience to the wand. Hence the mystical ecstasies of Raymund Lully, who attracted such zealous partisans and furious enemies, causing blood to flow; hence the delirium which brought Bruno to the stake." Victor Cousin: COURS DE PHILOSOPHIE, Paris, 1836. It would seem impossible to record a greater number of inaccuracies, or to display more signal ignorance, within the dimensions of a paragraph.

than reduce largely the authority attributed to Éliphas Lévi, I must expect even now to alienate the sympathy of his remaining French admirers; but this is only a question of the moment, and so far as it is possible to take a plain course in the matter there can be no need for hesitation.

I do not think that Lévi ever made an independent statement upon any historical fact in which the least confidence could be reposed. He never presented the sense of an author whom he was reviewing in a way which could be said to reproduce that author faithfully. As in the one case he embroidered history by the help of a decorative imagination, so it occurred frequently that he attributed to an old author the kind of sense which it would be interesting to find in old authors, but it is not met with except by the mediation of a magician with the transmuting power of Abbé Constant. He takes, for example, a perfectly worthless little book by Abbot Trithemius, which does not reflect the opinions of that learned Benedictine, but is simply a trifle addressed to a German prince explaining how some persons in antiquity distributed the government of the world among certain planetary intelligences, ruling successively and reassuming rule in rotation. He invests it with the importance of a grand and sublime achievement of prophetic science, whereas it does not shew half the acumen of our empirical friend Nostradamus, and is equalled in any year of grace by the almanacks of Raphael and Zadkiel. Here is an instance of what Lévi reads into an author. Nor do we need to depart from this unhappy little treatise to test Lévi's reliability over an express matter of fact. He tells us that the forecast of Trithemius closes with a proclamation of universal monarchy in the year 1879. Trithemius says nothing of the kind, but modestly remarks that the gift of prophecy, so generously attributed to him by his reviewer, would be required to discern anything beyond that period. I mention this matter, to which I have drawn attention long since,[1] because it is necessary to exhibit the quality of mind which was brought by Éliphas Lévi to the illumination of Kabbalistic and occult literature. The deliberations of the Holy Synods will be found to have suffered many transfigurations through the medium of their interpreter, and any matter of

---

[1] MYSTERIES OF MAGIC, a Digest of the Writings of Éliphas Lévi. Second and revised edition, 1897.

sharp fact in the hands of this unaccountable juggler is brought over into the realm of myth.

I need not dwell upon the miserable plight of every Hebrew quotation in those works which he may be supposed to have passed for press. No ordinary carelessness would account for such blunders, nor need they be explained by supposing that he was utterly ignorant of their language. His acquaintance must have been slender enough, but it is not necessary to be proficient in Hebrew or indeed in Chinese to ensure the accuracy of a few excerpts. The excerpts in Éliphas Lévi " no one can speak and no one can spell." But even in simpler matters his blunders are incredible. He gives the three mother-letters of the Hebrew alphabet inaccurately,[1] which for an accredited student of SEPHER YETZIRAH is almost as inexcusable as if an English author erred in enumerating the vowels of our own language.

The instance, however, which seems impressive and even final, occurs in a posthumous work entitled the BOOK OF SPLENDOUR.[2] Of this the first part is intended as a compressed translation of the GREATER HOLY SYNOD. Now, Lévi says that the deliberations of this Conclave are contained in a Hebrew treatise entitled IDRA SUTA, and these words appear accordingly at the head of his version. But the IDRA SUTA, or more correctly ZOUTA, is the name of the LESSER SYNOD, while IDRAH RABBA is that appertaining to the record of the Greater Assembly. What should we think of the qualifications of a commentator on the books of the Old Testament who informed us that the word BERESHITH was applied to Deuteronomy?

That in spite of his slipshod criticism, his careless reading and his malpractices in historical matters the writings of Éliphas Lévi are not without a certain interest is true up to a certain point. What seems to distinguish him from all other occult writers is not his knowledge as occultist, but the peculiar genius of interpretation which he applied to that knowledge, the surprising results which he could obtain from an old doctrine, even as from an old author. They were not reliable results; they were not in harmony with any secret knowledge; they represented the standpoint of the

---

[1] LA CLEF DES GRANDS MYSTÈRES, Paris, 1861, pp. 199, 200.
[2] LE LIVRE DES SPLENDEURS, *contenant le Soleil Judaïque* . . . *Études sur les Origines de la Kabbale*, &c., Paris, 1894.

agnostic rather than the transcendentalist; and they afflicted the transcendental standpoint in consequence, but they wore the guise and they spoke the language of occultism, and it is they which have fascinated his students, they which once multiplied his admirers, they also which imparted at their period a new impulse to the study of occult speculations. This is equivalent to saying that the influence of Éliphas Lévi does not make for a proper understanding of occult reveries, and as concerns the Kabbalah that it reads a meaning into the Esoteric Tradition of Israel which is not in harmony therewith.

Let us take, for example, his inverted text of the first chapter of Genesis, for which he claims a Kabbalistic foundation.[1] It is needless to say that it neither has nor could have any rabbinical authority and that it first occurred to the imaginative mind of a Frenchman in the second half of the nineteenth century. As it exceeds quotation in this place I must refer the reader to the work in which I have rendered it at length.[2] It may be described shortly as replacing the history of creation by God with that of God's creation by man. It is, if you prefer it, the evolution of the God-idea in humanity. As an exercise of ingenuity it is notable and high diversion, but the point at which the sober critic must diverge from the interpreter is that " this occult Genesis was thought out by Moses before writing his own."

Let us take another case which, though it brings us to the same question, is more perhaps to our purpose, because it is a construction placed upon Zoharic symbolism. For Éliphas Lévi the MACROPROSOPUS or Great Countenance of the ZOHAR is the evolution of the idea of God[3] from the shadow divinities represented by the Kings of Edom. MICROPROSOPUS is the grand night of faith. The one is the God of the wise, the other the idol of the vulgar. The one is the great creative hypothesis, the other the dark figure, the restricted hypothesis. As it is to the Lesser Countenance that the name of TETRAGRAMMATON is attributed,[4] it follows that the secret of the ZOHAR is the alleged utterance of the adept to the recipiendary of the Egyptian Mysteries : " Osiris is a black god." MICRO-

---

[1] LA CLEF DES GRANDS MYSTÈRES, pp. 334 *et seq.* MYSTERIES OF MAGIC, second edition, London, 1897, pp. 108 *et seq.*
[2] *i.e.*: THE MYSTERIES OF MAGIC, first and second editions, London, 1886, 1897.
[3] It follows that he was either unacquainted with the hypothesis of AIN SOPH or elected to ignore it.
[4] The letter VAU and that only is referable to the Divine Son.

PROSOPUS is, however, " neither the Ahriman of the Persians nor the evil principle of the Manichæans, but a more exalted concept, a mediating shadow between the infinite light and the feeble eyes of humanity ; a veil made in the likeness of humanity with which God Himself deigns to cover His glory ; a shadow which contains the reason of all mysteries, explaining the terrible Deity of the prophets, who threatens and inspires fear. It is the God of the priests, the God who exacts sacrifices, the God who sleeps frequently and is awakened by the trumpets of the temple, the God who repents having made man, but, conquered by prayers and offerings, is appeased when on the point of punishing." [1]

That this interpretation has attracted a few unversed students who did not have the texts before them may be no cause for surprise. It was pleasant to make acquaintance with a supposed esoteric tradition in which all theological difficulties seem to dissolve together. While on the one hand it might be little short of incredible that the Kabbalah should conceal so reasonable and elegant a doctrine, the putative symbolism was on the other so plausibly accounted for that it encouraged an easy acceptance. When we come, however, to the analysis of text and construction we find that the one does not warrant the other and that the evolution of the God-idea in humanity had no more occurred to the authors of the ZOHAR than it would have occurred, *e.g.*, to Grant Allen to write a BOOK OF OCCULTATION. It is not a case in which it is necessary to tax space and patience by the exhaustive demonstration of a negative. The validity of the construction is seen by the text with which it is connected. We know how much was read by Fitzgerald into Omar Khayyám, but his verses are literal and line upon line compared with the high fantasy of Lévi's Zoharistic analysis. As an example of this it is sufficient to refer the student who may desire an express case for comparison to the forty third section of IDRA RABBA as it stands in the Latin version of Rosenroth and the excursus on Justice in the BOOK OF SPLENDOUR which follows, says Éliphas Lévi, the text of Rabbi Simeon. It is mere illusion and mockery.[2]

Another extreme instance is the fantastic inversion of the SEPHIROTH which gives despotism an absolute power as the dark side of the supreme power in KETHER ; blind faith as

---

[1] LE LIVRE DES SPLENDEURS, pp. 69, 70.   [2] *Ibid.*, pp. 86 *et seq.*

the shadow of eternal wisdom in CHOKMAH; so called immutable dogma, which is at the same time inevitably progressive, as the antithesis of active intelligence in BINAH; blind faith again as the inversion of spiritual beauty in TIPHERETH; divine vengeance as opposed to eternal justice in GEBURAH; willing sacrifice as the shadow of infinite mercy in CHESED; abnegation and voluntary renunciation as opposed to the eternal victory of goodness in NETZACH; eternal hell as opposed to the eternity of goodness, presumably in HOD; celibacy and sterility as opposed to the fecundity of goodness, presumably in JESOD; while MALKUTH, corresponding to the number of creation, is said to have no negative aspect, because celibacy and sterility produce nothing.[1] Without dwelling on the carelessness of the arrangement, in part sephirotic and in part transposing and abandoning the sephirotic series, or on the failing ingenuity which repeats the same contrasts, I may point out that advanced views on the transfiguration of dogmas and on vicarious atonement are not the findings of illuminated rabbins in the middle ages or earlier but belong to the excursions of modern thought, and that since arbitrary tabulations and artificial contrasts are easy exercises, and can be varied to infinity—more especially when the text itself is scouted—we may appreciate the contrasts here created by the evidence which supports them and that is simply the magisterial affirmation of the interpreter.

It remains to say that Éliphas Lévi represents the invention of a new and gratuitous phase in the study of the Kabbalah, undertaken neither as an object of research nor as a part of the history of philosophy. The students whom we have considered heretofore have been either Christian propagandists or writers by the way whose connection with the subject is unsubstantial; but the standpoint of Lévi is that there is a religion behind all religions and that it is the veiled mystery of Kabbalism, from which all have issued and into which all return. Christian doctrine, in particular, is unintelligible, apart from the light cast on it by the deliberations of the Holy Assemblies. Now it is precisely this standpoint, its derivatives and connections, that created French occultism in the generation which followed Lévi. In the past the magician was content to evoke spirits, the alchemist to produce gold when he could, the astrologer to spell the dubious

---

[1] LE LIVRE DES SPLENDEURS, pp. 74 *et seq.*

messages of the stars, the Kabbalist of sorts to be wise in anagrams and word-puzzles, but these things were regarded henceforward as parts of a greater mystery, and in a very true sense Éliphas Lévi was the magus who opened before his readers the wide field of this imaginary view. He had no antecedents in scholarship but he drew suggestions from there and here in the texts, and he wrote it all up and he coloured it. The more he wrote and the more he coloured there is no need to say that his delineations diverged the further from all likeness to his sources, and so of all claims thereon. This is illustrated in a plenary sense by his posthumous MYSTÈRES DE LA KABBALE, 1923, and by his letters to Baron Spedalieri which have been printed through the moons and the years in LE VOILE D'ISIS of Paris.

XVII.—TWO ACADEMICAL CRITICS

Having regard to the fact that, as already stated, there has been always in England a small number of persons who have been interested, mostly through sympathy with subjects called esoteric, in the study of the Kabbalah, it may appear incredible that there are no memorials of their interest between the period of Thomas Vaughan and the year 1865, a space of two centuries. There is a similar hiatus in the merely academical interest represented by Burnet. I do not say that there have been nowhere any references to Kabbalism; they may have made up in number what they wanted in learning and authority; and a few curious gleanings might be gathered from early editions of the larger encyclopædias; but as there has been no mystical student who wrote anything of moment concerning it, so there has been no scholar apart from such interests who has treated the subject seriously. The work of Dr. Ginsburg, once so well known that even now it scarcely needs description, may be said to have marked an epoch, because it was the first clear, simple and methodised account of Kabbalistic doctrine and literature. It leaves naturally much to be desired, as it arose in an informal manner out of a meeting of some literary society in Liverpool, and the nucleus of the short paper produced for the occasion in question was afterwards expanded into a slender volume. It is a meagre measure that is thus allotted to so large a subject, but it was as much as might be warranted by the existing interest, which is determined sharply by the fact that no second edition was needed until quite recent years. There is good reason to believe that it did not represent Dr. Ginsburg's knowledge at the period, yet it went much further than encyclopædic or theological notices. Dr. Ginsburg is entitled to a place among Christian students of the Kabbalah because of his conversion in 1846, and I purpose in this brief notice, which is concerned mainly with a standpoint, to connect him with the name of a writer who belonged to his period in France. Both were accomplished Hebrew scholars; both of Jewish origin. Dr. Ginsburg did much valuable work in connection with the Trinitarian Bible Society, while M. Isidore Loëb, so far as I am aware, remained in the faith of Jewry, and it is therefore only by way of contrast with his English prototype that I am warranted in referring to him in this place. There was a period of a quarter of a century between the two writers, and as their point of view is in general respects similar and indeed suggests that the French critic may have profited by the English, it is interesting to note the one matter over which they diverge, namely, the authorship of the ZOHAR.

It has been objected against Dr. Ginsburg that he draws chiefly from Continental writers, reflects their views and shews little independent research. His quotations from the ZOHAR are, it is said, derived from Franck, and are open therefore to the harsh criticisms passed on them many years ago in Germany. These matters are perhaps of slight importance to those who are in search of elementary knowledge, whose purpose is served well enough by the translations of Franck and for whom a digest of fairly informed criticism is about the best text-book possible. The fact itself made Dr. Ginsburg's little treatise the English representative of a particular school, being that of the hostile judgment which refers the Zohar to the authorship, more or less exclusive, of Moses de Leon. In England Dr. Schiller-Szinessy's article on the MIDRASHIM in the ninth edition of the ENCYCLOPÆDIA BRITANNICA, referring the nucleus of the book to Mishnic times and regarding Simeon ben Yohai as author in the same sense that R. Johanan was author of the PALESTINE TALMUD, has helped to create another and more qualified manner of regarding the ZOHAR. The critical objections of Dr. Ginsburg derived from the work itself have been disposed of in the majority of cases, and the few which still remain can establish nothing conclusively. They have been noticed briefly elsewhere in the present work. The fact that M. Isidore Loëb, who so closely reproduced Dr. Ginsburg, abandons the theory of unqualified imposture, signifies that some progress was made with the subject towards the end of the nineteenth century, and as it is one of the purposes of the present study to place the evidence of this and analogous facts before the English reader, I feel warranted in giving space to the following synopsis of M. Isidore Loëb's essay, as it may not be accessible to some who are acquainted with that of Dr. Ginsburg. There is a literary excellence in the one which is fairly precluded by the circumstance that called the other into being, and it is a matter of regret that the sole contribution of M. Loëb towards the elucidation of Kabbalistic literature occurs in LA GRANDE ENCYCLOPÉDIE. M. Loëb was, however, for some time president of the publication committee of the French Society of Jewish Studies. His other literary work comprises a monograph on Jewish chroniclers, a table of Jewish calendars, and some observations on the situation of the Israelites at his period in Turkey, Serbia and Roumania. In the essay with which we are concerned he records the opinion that the term Kabbalah may not be anterior to the tenth century and that the claim to antiquity which it signifies is supported by no written monument. It seems difficult in the nature of the case that it should be so substantiated. M. Loëb, however, makes a very proper distinction between the metaphysical or mystical Kabbalah and the gross thaumaturgy connected with the practical branch. To the original elements of the first he ascribes, like all critics, a high antiquity, but not, as it need scarcely be said, of a kind which would permit it to be regarded as the perpetuation of an indigenous, much less an uncorrupted Tradition. As we have had occasion to see, this claim is no longer made by any competent student of the subject. For M. Loëb the Kabbalah is a part of the age-old reverie which seeks to explain the disparity between an infinite God and a finite world by means of intermediate creations through which the Divine Power descends, diminishing in its spiritual qualities as it removes further from its source, and becoming more imperfect and material. The difficulty is removed by this anthropomorphic process much in the same manner as the difficulty of a *terra firma* for the elephant which supports the universe is disposed of in Indian cosmology by assuming the tortoise. In other words, it is not removed at all. At the same time the explanation of Emanationist Mysticism, which is not all Mysticism, as M. Loëb seems to assume, is not in the last analysis open to greater objection than any other speculative attempt to bridge the gulf between finite and infinite. Passing from this consideration the French critic discovers the foundation of Kabbalistic Theosophy in the Scriptural personification of Wisdom, and the chief elements of its symbolism in the prophetical books, about which points there is no question whatever, and they are matters of common knowledge. So also he refers correctly the name or catchword of the ZOHAR to Daniel xii. 3. He cites the number of the beast in the Apocalypse, as every one has cited it before him, in illustration of GEMATRIA; but he raises a less hackneyed point by suggesting, on the authority of Munk, that TEMURAH was employed by Jeremiah. He does better service by reminding us that the Essenians attached great importance to symbolical angelology, and that each individual of that obscure fraternity was required to remember accurately the names of the angels. It is, however, among the Jews of Alexandria that, following several previous authorities, he discovers the main germs of Kabbalistic Mysticism; but in this connection he cites only the Platonic doctrine of the Logos, its influence on the Greek Septuagint and on the Chaldee version of the Old Testament.

On the whole, I do not think that M. Loëb's critical faculty, or indeed his erudition, is at all comparable to his graceful synthetic talent. To cite a crucial instance, he dismisses one testimony to Kabbalistic Tradition by saying: " Despite the contrary assertions of the TALMUD, we refuse to believe that Johanan ben Zoccai (*sic*) or his contemporaries devoted themselves to mystical doctrines or secret things." It is to the second century that he refers the " ravages " of Gnosticism among the Jews of Palestine, and cites various subtleties of the doctors which arose at that period. He sketches the decline of the Palestine Schools and the rise of those of Babylon, " the traditional country of Magic." He cites from Rab, the Babylonian of the third century, that passage which I have mentioned elsewhere, and confesses that it is another germ of the mediæval Kabbalah, that is, the doctrine of the Sephiroth. With a rapid pen he runs over the great impetus given to Jewish literature under Arabian influence from the middle of the seventh century. He refers to the ninth century that all-important treatise entitled The Measures of the Stature of God, which is, in fact, as we have seen, the first form of the Zoharistic Macroprosopus, and is mentioned apparently by Agobad. He places the Alphabet of Akiba, dealing with the symbolism of the Hebrew letters, about the same period, together with a crowd of apocalyptic treatises, including Pirke of R. Eliezer, which has an elaborate doctrine of Pneumatology. Among all these he distinguishes the Sepher Yetzirah as occupying a place and deserving a rank apart. He admits its comparative antiquity, seeming to regard it as immediately posterior to the Talmud, which he affirms to have been finished A.D. 499. He describes it as a philosophy and a gnosis, and supposes it to have been written in Palestine under the direct influence of Christian and Pagan Gnosticism. The opinion is interesting, but, of course, entirely conjectural, and as the doctrine of emanation is not clear in the Sepher Yetzirah, we should not accept hastily the theory of an influence which assumes it. When he observes further that its fountain-heads must be sought in Azriel's Commentary on the Sephiroth and in the Bahir, I fail to understand the grounds on which he attributes a superior antiquity to those works. He assigns to the Zohar itself a Spanish origin, but does not press the authorship of Moses de Leon. Among the fine points of his criticism is a picture of the pure Talmudists of the period of Maimonides, especially those of the Peninsula and the South of France, living under the influence of Arabian philosophy, without philosophical doctrine, without perspective, having only the literature of the Law, and the anthropomorphic Mysticism of the Jewish Schools of Northern France, between which the Kabbalah rose up as a mediator, " completing Talmudism by philosophy, correcting philosophy by Theosophy, and anthropomorphic Mysticism by philosophic Mysticism."

XVIII.—THE MODERN SCHOOL OF FRENCH KABBALISM

Éliphas Lévi died in 1875, having founded, as it must be admitted, a new school of occult philosophy, not in its way without a certain brilliance but built on sands of dream. For the ten years which preceded his death he had made no outward sign. There are mendacious rumours of the initiations which were offered him and of the Rites which he remodelled; but all that is known certainly is that he collected around him a small group of private students who looked up to him as their master, regarded his fantastic speculations almost in the light of revelation and, following his leading, accepted the Kabbalah as a great synthesis of religious belief. It was not till another ten years, after his death, had elapsed that any visible result of his influence became manifest. During that period a marked change had come over speculative thought there and here in Paris; many of the younger generation broke away from the traditions of positivism and materialism, and, without returning to the Church, passed off in the direction of occultism, and occultism moderated by science became a characteristic of the succeeding epoch. When about the year 1884 the Theosophical Society opened a lodge in Paris and began the publication of a monthly magazine, some few of the French occultists gathered round it, and one of the most noticeable in the group was Gérard Encausse, the young *chef de laboratoire* of an eminent doctor celebrated in connection with one of the schools of hypnotism. His first contributions appeared in the pages of LE LOTUS and his first work, on the elements of occult science, so called, was published under the auspices of the Society. A rupture took place, however, and the seceding members, abandoning for the moment their interest in *la métaphysique orientale*, established, so to speak, a school of western occultism, of which Dr. Encausse became the moving spirit and Éliphas Lévi the most immediate inspiration of the past. The ostensible characteristics of this school were Neo-Martinism and Neo-Rosicrucianism, but the conceptions associated with these names suffered developments which effaced their original outlines. So also the admired masterpieces of Éliphas Lévi became a point of departure quite as much as a guide. It is, broadly speaking, nevertheless, the work of Lévi which was continued, and along with other occult interests the study of the Kabbalah was revived under the reflected impulsion of his enthusiasm. It was in no sense an exhaustive and still less a critical study; it began by taking too much for granted and its textual knowledge was negligible. There was, however, no writer of this group who had not something to tell concerning Jewish Theosophy, while its activity engendered consequences of much the same kind outside its immediate circle.

The two names which most call for notice in this connection are Dr. Gérard Encausse and Stanislas de Guaita. The literary and occult antecedents of the first writer are Saint Yves d'Alveydre, Fabre d'Olivet, Éliphas Lévi and Adolphe Franck. From the first he derived a systematic view of Jewish history, from the second his notion of esoteric mysteries concealed in the Hebrew language, from Lévi unfortunately a burden of historical suppositions, and from Franck an academic precedent for the modified antiquity of Kabbalistic literature. On the other hand, Stanislas de Guaita belonged to a literary school of occultism and as such he connects with Sar Péladan. I propose to consider the position of both these writers in short sub-sections and to connect them with a third who is governed by very different motives and principles.

A.—Papus

The word Papus signifies physician, and according to a commentary of Éliphas Lévi on the NUCTEMERON of Apollonius, it is the title of a genius belonging to the first hour of that mystical period, understood, in Lévi's words, as "the day of the night." It is also the pseudonym adopted by Gérard Encausse, head of the French Martinists and once leader of occult activity in Paris. Papus became a voluminous writer, methodical and laborious, and some of his work had value along its own lines. From the beginning of his literary life he was occupied with Kabbalistic questions, and so far back as the year 1887 he made the first French translation of the SEPHER YETZIRAH, which appeared in the theosophical review LOTUS. It is not a satisfactory version and was superseded speedily by that of Meyer Lambert, as Papus recognised himself. He appears to have depended on the Latin text in the collection of Pistorius which renders throughout the words " ineffable SEPHIROTH " as SEPHIROTH *præter ineffabile*, thus making the BOOK OF FORMATION responsible for the Theology of AIN SOPH, and it is a point of critical importance that it is not to be found therein.

In 1892 Papus published a methodical summary of the

Kabbalah, together with a bibliography, which is again open to criticism. The bibliography was constructed upon the most debatable of all principles, viz., the increase of numerical importance by adventitious elements which are not Kabbalistic at all, and again by the inclusion of works which were evidently unknown to the writer, with results that are occasionally ludicrous. Thus, in the one case, among books in the French language, we find Figuier's ALCHEMY AND THE ALCHEMISTS, which contains no reference to the Kabbalah; Saint-Martin's CROCODILE, a clumsy satire open to the same objection; Eckartshausen's CLOUD ON THE SANCTUARY, also non-Kabbalistic; and a number of esoteric romances which have as much claim to insertion as Baudelaire's translation of Poe.[1] In the other case, Dr. Papus, who was only superficially acquainted with English, classified among Kabbalistic writings Massey's translation of Du Prel's PHILOSOPHY OF MYSTICISM, my own LIVES OF ALCHEMYSTICAL PHILOSOPHERS, Dr. Hartmann's WHITE AND BLACK MAGIC, a catalogue of second-hand books issued by George Redway, and, unfortunate above all other instances, the once celebrated SUPERNATURAL RELIGION. The bibliography of works in the Latin language is better done, though it contains some useless numbers.

As regards the treatise itself, it is little more than a series of tabulated quotations from Franck, Loëb, de Guaita, Kircher and so forth, with a number of serviceable diagrams derived from similar sources. It was passable at its period as a French introduction to the subject for the use of French occultists. But it made the mistake of attributing importance to the debased Hebrew influences found in the literature of Ceremonial Magic. Having appreciated in another section the claim of the clavicles to recognition in Kabbalistic literature, it is here only necessary to say that in the work under notice there is no attempt to justify their inclusion, which is explained by the sympathies of the author, who in this connection owes something to the French version of Molitor.

Dr. Papus had also a bias common to the majority of French

---

[1] Another instance is Julien Lejay: LA SCIENCE OCCULTE APPLIQUÉE à l'économie politique, in a volume of composite authorship, entitled La Science Secrète. I may observe, however, that this volume contains a paper on the Kabbalah by Papus, subsequently embodied in his larger work. Outside this, the only reference to the subject is in an essay by F. C. Barlet, which refers the origin of the Kabbalah to the fourth century.

and English occultists of Victorian days, and by this bias he was led irresistibly to prefer the imperfect equipment of past authority to the result of modern scholarship. In Egyptology he knew no higher name than that of Court de Gebelin; in problems of Hebrew philology his great master was Fabre d'Olivet; and hence, on the one hand, we shall not be surprised to find that he regarded P. Christian as a source of serious information concerning Egyptian Mysteries of Initiation, or, on the other, that he considered the Hebrew of the Mosaic books to be identical with the idiom of ancient Egypt.[1] The position of writers who base their views on language-studies undertaken at the beginning of the last century is not more reasonable than would be that of a person who should attempt now to defend the antiquity of the Rowley poems. But it might be scarcely worth while to speak of it were it not for the consequences that it involves, at least in the case of Papus, as, for example, his views on the descent of Esoteric Tradition from Moses and its identity with the Mysteries of Egypt.

I have said sufficient to indicate that the historical aspect, so far as it exists in Papus, is altogether unsatisfactory, and there is indeed no need to reckon with it. As regards the special motive of our own inquiry, the standpoint of Papus is that the Kabbalah is the keystone of all the Western Tradition of Transcendentalism; that the alchemists were Kabbalists, and so also all mystical fraternities, whether Templars, Rosicrucians, Martinists or Freemasons; that the source of the Kabbalah was Moses and that Moses drew from Egypt, whence the Kabbalah is the most complete summary in existence of Egyptian Mysteries. Why those mysteries

---

[1] He was not alone among French writers of his day in taking a similar view. M. Edouard Schuré, in LES GRANDS INITIÉS, *Esquisse de l'Histoire Secrète des Religions*, Paris, 1889, maintains that, " owing to the education of Moses, there can be no doubt that he wrote Genesis in Egyptian hieroglyphics, having three senses, and confided their keys and oral explanations to his successors. In the time of Solomon it was rendered into Phœnician characters, and after the captivity of Babylon into Aramaic Chaldean characters by Esdras. The esoteric sense was lost more and more, and the Greek translators had a very slight acquaintance therewith." In this case it may have been the remnant of such knowledge which made the Jews so hostile to the Septuagint. M. Schuré continues: " Jerome, despite his serious intention and his great mind, penetrated only to the primitive sense when he made his Latin translation. The secret sense does, however, remain buried in the Hebrew text, which plunges by its roots into the sacred tongue of the temples," and the writer affirms that it flashes forth at times for the intuitive, that for seers it " shines forth once more in the phonetic structure of the words adopted or created by Moses," and that by the study of this phoneticism, by the keys which the Kabbalah furnishes, and by comparative esotericism, " it is permitted us at this day to reconstruct the veritable Genesis." Pp. 180, 181.

should have an absorbing claim on our respect does not appear from Papus, but the sub-surface understanding is undoubtedly that a Tradition of Absolute Religion has been perpetuated from antiquity, and with all his dissemblings and palterings, with all the hindrance of his scepticism, that also is Lévi's standpoint, as we have seen in an earlier section.

B.—Stanislas de Guaita

Associated with the literary work and much of the active propaganda of Dr. Gérard Encausse, the name of the Marquis Marie-Victor-Stanislas de Guaita, though scarcely known in England, was valued in occult circles of Paris, and his death at the early age of thirty-six years occasioned profound sorrow.

It will perhaps be unnecessary to state that he was a disciple of Éliphas Lévi, whose works he regarded as constituting "the most cohesive, absolute and unimpeachable synthesis that can be dreamed by an occultist." If we add to this that De Guaita is described by Papus as occupying beyond contradiction the first rank among the pupils of Lévi, we shall have a fair knowledge of his position. He began his literary life as a poet, and in that character connects with the school of Baudelaire. His occult preoccupations appear, however, in his verses, and he soon devoted himself exclusively to occult subjects. His works entitled THE THRESHOLD OF MYSTERY, THE SERPENT OF GENESIS and THE KEY OF BLACK MAGIC were admired for their "magisterial form," which recalls that of his master. He expounded Kabbalistic Tradition and considered that in "Neo-Mosaic Christianity, explained by the Holy Kabbalah and Alexandrian Hermeticism (under certain reserves), the absolute truth must be sought in all knowledge." [1]

At an early period of his enthusiasm Stanislas de Guaita founded a Kabbalistic Order of the Rose-Cross, comprehending three Grades, to which entrance could be obtained only after successful examination, while the possession of the three Grades of the Martinist Order—an invention of Papus—was an indispensable preliminary condition. When the numerical strength of the association had attained the limits

---

[1] From a *Lettre inédite* quoted in L'INITIATION, tom. xxxviii., No. 4, Jan., 1898, pp. 12, 13.

prescribed by its constitution, it was closed rigorously by decision of the Grand Master. De Guaita is termed an erudite orientalist by his friends, who mention also the Hebrew folios which enriched his library.[1] Finally, it is recorded that he believed himself more thoroughly possessed of the Kabbalah than all others. But if we may accept the authority of Dr. Marc Haven he seems to have distinguished two species of Kabbalah, the first a science which no one could teach and no one could learn, except with the most arduous toil and by years of sacrifice, for it is " more rugged than Wronsky, more diffuse than Spanish Mysticism, more complex than Gnostic analysis." And after all it appears to be only a pseudo-Kabbalah. The other is apparently the Kabbalah as presented by William Postel, Nicholas Flamel, Khunrath, Saint-Martin and so forth. I must confess that this distinction is a puzzle. I know well enough that Saint-Martin was not a Kabbalist, except in the most phantasmal sense and by a most remote derivation. I know that Flamel the alchemist, if he ever wrote anything, was concerned with the transmutation of metals and not with the mysteries of AIN SOPH. It is, however, the Kabbalah of such Kabbalists that is said to illuminate the pages of de Guaita and to have inspired his active works.

Despite therefore his accredited erudition, the author of the SERPENT OF GENESIS has no message for the student of Kabbalism: the ZOHAR has its difficulties, by which he was clearly intimidated and the work had not been translated. But the kind of distinction which de Guaita sought to establish offers at least one point of interest. Postel, Flamel, Khunrath, Saint-Martin, are names which stand in his mind for Kabbalistic Christianity, for that marriage of the Zohar and the Gospel to which he refers expressly.[2] He differs therefore from his fellow propagandist Papus, who exhibits few Christian sympathies and is attached more consistently to the doctrine of Éliphas Lévi. But in de Guaita, as in Lévi, it is not orthodox Christianity, as understood, on the one hand, by Mirandula and Postel or, on the other, by Rosenroth, with

---

[1] *Op. cit.*, pp. 32 *et seq.*
[2] "The ZOHAR has wedded the Gospel; the spirit has fructified the soul; and immortal works have been the fruits of this union. The Kabbalah became Catholic in the school of St. John, the master of masters, incarnate in an admirable metaphysical form . . . the absolute spirit of the science of justice and love which vivifies internally the dead letter of all the orthodoxies."—LE SERPENT DE LA GENÈSE, p. 183.

which his Kabbalah is connected, but Christianity permeated by Gnostic elements, and this is the special characteristic of modern occult students who have taken any interest in the light cast on the religion of Jesus by the post-Christian developments of Jewish Theosophy. Thus, the missionary enthusiasm of the early Christian Schools of Kabbalism, and the Messianic dream constructed by Jewry out of the elements of the ZOHAR, have been exchanged for an attempt to go back upon the path of doctrinal development and to discover in analogies between the Kabbalah and the Gnostics a practicable thoroughfare into debated regions of esoteric religion. As disappointment waited on the mistaken ardour of the first zealots, so it was equally in store for the revived zeal in Kabbalism.

C.—LÉON MEURIN, S.J.

Having to establish some points of accidental connection between the Kabbalah and Freemasonry, it seems possible to include among Kabbalistic students the most fantastic investigator of this subject, once Archbishop of Port Louis. It is true that his large treatise, FREEMASONRY THE SYNAGOGUE OF SATAN, is a product of the troubled dream of the Papacy concerning the *Liberi Muratori* and can be saved only—if saved indeed at all—by the sincerity of its intention from a place in bogus literature; it is true also that it connects with a squalid imposture long since unmasked; but it shews a considerable acquaintance of the superficial order both with Kabbalistic Doctrine and Masonic Symbolism; and it is worth noticing how the Tradition of the Jews was appreciated at the end of the nineteenth century by a Catholic critic who was also an ecclesiastic of some eminence and a member of the Society of Jesus.

It is unnecessary to say that it is an entirely hostile criticism. " In place of the orthodox synagogue and the true doctrine of Moses which God Himself inspired, modern Kabbalists represent the paganism with which certain Jewish sectarians became imbued during the captivity of Babylon. We have only to study their doctrine and to compare it with those of civilised nations in antiquity—Indians, Persians, Babylonians, Assyrians, Egyptians, Greeks and so forth—to become assured that the same pantheistic system of emanation is inculcated by all. We find everywhere an eternal principle producing a primeval triad and thereafter the entire universe, not by creation but by substantial emanation. Hence we are compelled to recognise a close connection between Kabbalistic philosophy and ancient paganism which is difficult to explain except by the inspiration of the same author, in other words, the Lying Spirit who is the enemy of mankind."

The entire treatise may be regarded as a development of this paragraph, which, it must be confessed, is the view that would be taken inevitably by the Latin Church. We have seen that under the auspices of Christian Kabbalists, with Picus de Mirandula as their mouthpiece, there was for one moment a sign of *rapprochement* between the Church and Jewish Tradition; but it was impossible in the nature of both, and the Church was saved then, as it has been saved occasionally since, as if by some happy intuition which preceded any real knowledge of the interests at stake.

The general position being thus defined, Mgr. Meurin proceeds at a later stage to develop his impeachment by exhibiting the fundamental error of all pantheism, that, namely, which concerns the transition of the Infinite to the Finite, which wears, he tells us, for any serious thinker, the aspect of a fraudulent device. Basing his argument on the well-known verse in WISDOM: "Thou hast ordered all things in measure, and number, and weight," he advances that we must seek in these the distinction between the Infinite and the Finite, for such categories do not exist in God, or rather they are "elevated above themselves and lost in a superior unity." Creation out of nothing is the only rational solution of the grand problem concerning the origin of a world which is governed by number, weight and measure, a doctrine which assumes no passage from Infinite to Finite, since it does not derive the universe from the divine substance by an emanation of any kind. "It is true that *ex nihilo nihil fit*. But in the creation there is not only the *nihilum*; there is also the *Omnipotens*, and it is untrue to say that with nothingness and the all-powerful, nothing can be made. *Ex nihilo nihil fit a Deo* would be a false axiom."

In a study like the present it would be out of place to discuss the points at issue between emanationists and creationists. We have seen that the Kabbalah is by no means utterly and only a system of emanation: it is a medley which tends occasionally in that direction; but it has also a world of creation and a creation myth. The doctrine of orthodox religion on a question of fundamental philosophy is in no danger from a certain element of confusion in such reveries. But the whole controversy concerns a *res ardua et difficilis*, as Isaac de Loria would have termed it, which fortunately cannot produce a single consequence of importance to the human mind, though it is precisely to such arid speculations that official orthodoxy has always attached an eternal consequence for the soul.

Mgr. Meurin remains, however, the consistent and correct exponent of the Church which he represented, and so far as this Church is concerned he has registered, as we must admit fully, the non-Christian nature of Kabbalistic doctrine. We may go further and allow that in other places he scores occasionally a logical point against it. We have, for example, such notions as the commencement of thought in AIN SOPH which precedes the emanation of understanding in the Three Divine Supernals, thus reversing the psychological order, as the prelate observes, besides formulating an absurdity concerning the one Being in whom there is no beginning. It may well be that in the last analysis these things are to be understood more profoundly than is suggested by their surface meaning, but they are crude and misleading enough in their outward sense.

XIX.—THE KABBALAH AND ESOTERIC CHRISTIANITY

A discussion of points of contact between Christianity and the Mystical Tradition of the Jews should not proceed without some reference to a scheme of mystical Christianity which obtained for a period a certain vogue in English esoteric circles and met with especial commendation from certain Kabbalistic students. I refer to the New Gospel of Interpretation, founded on illuminations received, or believed to have been received, by Anna Bonus Kingsford, and developed since her decease, not always well and wisely, by her collaborator and co-recipient, Edward Maitland, long since also passed away. The text-books of this movement were, firstly, a small collection containing the illuminations, and, secondly a formal treatise which, under the title of THE PERFECT WAY, constituted a philosophical development and historical verification of the doctrines received by the seeress. The late McGregor Mathers dedicated his pretentious and inexact translation of certain Zoharistic books from the Latin of Rosenroth to the authors of this treatise on the ground that it was "one of the most deeply occult works that has (*sic*) been written for centuries." The dedication described it also as an "excellent and wonderful book," touching much on the doctrines of the Kabbalah and laying great value upon its teachings. It was welcomed in terms of still higher appreciation by Baron Spedalieri, of Marseilles, the disciple of Éliphas Lévi, who regarded it as "in complete accord with all mystical traditions, and especially with the great mother of these, the Kabbalah." In connection with this appreciation the respectable French occultist observed: (*a*) That Kabbalistic Tradition as we now possess it is far from genuine, and was much purer when it first emerged from the sanctuaries. (*b*) That when William Postel and his brother Hermetists predicted that the literature containing the Secret Tradition of the Jews would become known and understood at "the end of the era," they meant that it would be made the basis of "a new illumination," reinstating that Tradition in its purity. (*c*) That this illumination and this restoration have been accomplished in THE PERFECT WAY. He adds: "In this book we find all that there is of truth in the Kabbalah, supplemented by new intuitions, such as present a body of doctrines at once complete, homogeneous, logical and inexpugnable. Since the whole tradition thus finds itself recovered or restored to its original purity, the prophecies of Postel and his fellow Hermetists are accomplished; and I consider that from henceforth the study of the Kabbalah will be but an object of curiosity and erudition, like that of Hebrew antiquities."

If this be the case, the inquiry with which we have been occupied at such considerable length is only prolegomenary to the New Gospel of Interpretation, and our concluding words should be simply to direct the student who is in search of the true meaning of Esoteric Tradition in Israel to the doctrines contained in this last word of revelation. Indeed, such a course would seem at first sight the only one which could be followed. I must add, however, that the opinion expressed by Baron Spedalieri produced no consequence, that the Kabbalistic School of occultists in England did not follow the lead thus indicated, and did not endorse the opinion, while the New Gospel of Interpretation took no permanent hold on the occult or any other prevailing thought of the time. I infer also that Baron Spedalieri's statement as to the adulteration of the genuine Tradition in the Hebrew Kabbalah was not traversed seriously, but for its recovery occultists of the period were disposed to look backward towards Egypt rather than to any form of supplementary revelation.

I do not propose to recite here even the leading aspects of the system of Esoteric Christianity developed in THE PERFECT WAY, for the work is well known and its substance has been made accessible in many forms, thanks to the untiring devotion of Edward Maitland. It does offer some points of contact with the Tradition of the Kabbalah, especially as to the dual nature of God, or the Divine-Feminine, and " the multiplicity of principles in the human system "; but it would be easy to exaggerate their extent, as also, in some less conspicuous cases, their importance. The traceable references are few and superficial. We may find, for example, the Kabbalistic doctrine of AIN SOPH and His emanations in the statement that " God unmanifest and abstract is the Primordial Mind, and the Kosmic universe is the ideation of that Mind," but it is not a far-reaching correspondence. So also the conception of Macroprosopus reflected in Microprosopus is sketched thinly by the following passage. " In ' the Lord ' the Formless assumes a form, the Nameless a name, the Infinite the Definite, and these human. But, although ' the Lord is God manifested as a man ' in and to the souls of those to whom the vision is vouchsafed, it is not as man in the exclusive sense of the term and masculine only, but as man both masculine and feminine " (MICROPROSOPUS it will be remembered is androgyne), " at once man and woman, as is Humanity itself." I should add that the " new Gospel " maintained the divinity of the Kabbalah on the ground of the purity of its doctrine of correspondences, which shews that " this famous compendium belongs to a period prior to that destruction by the priesthoods of the equilibrium of the sexes which constituted in one sense the Fall." With this statement of its Divine origin may be brought into contrast the interpretation of the claim made by the Kabbalah as to the manner of its delivery. " When it is said that these Scriptures were delivered by God first of all to Adam in Paradise, and then to Moses on Sinai, it is meant that the doctrine contained in them is that which man always discerns when he succeeds in attaining to that inner and celestial region of his nature where he is taught directly of his own Divine Spirit, and knows even as he is known." As THE PERFECT WAY and its connections assume to be the outcome of a similar quality of discernment, it follows, of course, that it is a recovery of " the doctrine commonly called the *Gnosis*, and variously entitled Hermetic and Kabbalistic."

I should add that many thoughtful persons have found in THE PERFECT WAY a "fountain of light, interpretative and reconciliatory," and that some of its interpretation indicates a suggestive quality of genius; yet it was not free at the beginning from the fantastic element, and it depends largely on philological arguments which are more than fantastic. Also at the close of Maitland's life he wrote much which must have been regretted by his friends, bringing his earlier work into discredit by exaggerated claims concerning it. Taking it as a whole, THE PERFECT WAY can be regarded only as a series of suggestions and intuitive glimpses concerning the postulated hidden sense of several sacred scriptures.

XX.—THE KABBALAH AND MODERN THEOSOPHY

The attempt which was made in the year 1875, by the foundation of the Theosophical Society, to extend and centralise the study of Oriental Occult Philosophy, has, in spite of its chequered history, succeeded to a large extent in that object. If we remove from consideration certain claims advanced by the founders, and if we regard the Society rather as it assumed once at least to regard itself, namely, as an organisation designed to promote a neglected branch of knowledge, we have only to survey its literature during the past fifty years to see how large a field it has succeeded in covering. No unbiassed student will be inclined to overlook this fact, and as the Theosophical Society possesses at least this aspect of importance, it will be useful to ascertain how far the expositions of eastern philosophy which we owe to it connect with the subject of our inquiry.

It may be said in a general manner that the correspondences

which I have established already were recognised from the beginning of the movement and, so to speak, at its fountain-head. The cosmology and metapsychics of Jewish Esoteric Tradition were regarded, roughly speaking, by Madame Blavatsky as reflections or derivatives from an older knowledge and a higher teaching which has existed from time immemorial in the farthest East.[1] Beyond or outside this broad affirmation and representative point of view one does not trace a sufficient warrant in knowledge for the expression of particular opinions. The author of Isis Unveiled and The Secret Doctrine had an enormous budget of materials, but not very carefully selected. On the one hand, she offers information which we are not able to check because we do not know her authorities; on the other she makes statements occasionally with which it is difficult to agree. Thus, she distinguishes between the ordinary, or Judaistic, and the universal, or Oriental Kabbalah. If little be known of the one, there is nothing, at least nothing that is definite, known of the other. "Its adepts are few; but these heirs elect of the sages who first discovered ' the starry truths which shone on the great Shemaïa of the Chaldæan lore ' have solved the ' absolute ' and are now resting from their grand labour."[2] That is a statement which, of course, we cannot check, and for any critical study of the Jewish Kabbalah it can therefore carry no weight. It may be taken to indicate a feeling at its value among certain occultists that the Hebrew tradition has been perverted.[3] It may be accepted also as evidence that because the term Kabbalah signifies an oral reception it has come to be used in connection with almost any unwritten knowledge. Such a course is very inexact and misleading; but the same abuse of words is found in Paracelsus and many later writers. It serves, however, a purpose not intended

---

[1] As might be expected, some of her followers did not fail to go further, *e.g.*, the late W. Q. Judge, who was able to affirm categorically that Abraham, Moses and Solomon were members of an ancient lodge of adepts from whom this high teaching has been handed down. The Ocean of Theosophy, New York, 1893, c. 1. " Echoes " of this kind " from the burnished and mysterious East," to quote Judge terminology (Echoes from the Orient, p. 5, New York, 1890), did not find response among theosophical writers in England.

[2] Isis Unveiled, i., 17.

[3] Another theosophical writer, however, maintains that "the collection of writings known as the Bible constitutes but one of a number of records which are all derived from and based upon one unifying system, known at times as the Ancient Wisdom Religion, or Secret Doctrine." W. Kingsland: The Esoteric Basis of Christianity, Part I., p. 15, London, 1891.

by those who use it: it distinguishes between scholar and sciolist. The statement which we cannot check is, however, usually accompanied by the statement that we can. In the present case we are told that the BOOK OF OCCULTATION is "the most ancient Hebrew document on occult learning,"[1] and I doubt much whether this would be countenanced by any student who was acquainted with the strong claims of the BOOK OF FORMATION, to say nothing of the literature which belongs to Talmudic times. It is added that SIPHRA DI ZENIOUTHA was compiled from another and older work which is not named, but it is stated that there is only one "original copy" in existence, and that this is "so very old that our modern antiquarians might ponder over its pages an indefinite time, and still not quite agree as to the nature of the fabric upon which it is written."[2] Till antiquaries are furnished with the opportunity they will be tempted to overlook this claim. With both these classes of statement we may contrast the affirmation that is not evident in itself and is supported by doubtful reasoning. Thus we are told of Oriental Kabbalists who assert that the traditions of their science are more than seventy thousand years old, concerning which claim it is observed that modern science cannot prove it to be false; but the question is whether Kabbalists, oriental or otherwise, can produce evidence in support of its truth. We may pass over the writer's personal pretension to a first-hand acquaintance with Kabbalistic books once indisputably in existence, but now regarded as lost. Of such is the Chaldæan Book of Numbers,[3] which, according to another authority, is a companion to the ÆSH MEZAREPH,[4] but is declared in ISIS UNVEILED to be a part of the great Oriental Kabbalah, namely, the patrimony of the persons previously described as having "solved the absolute."[5] To the lesson which is taught by observations of this kind we may add the borrowed view which rests on bad criticism, as, for example, that the TALMUD is "the darkest of enigmas even for most

---

[1] ISIS UNVEILED, i., 1.
[2] *Ibid.*
[3] This work is said to be much superior to the ZOHAR. SECRET DOCTRINE, i., 214. It is, in fact, the only real Kabbalah, *ib.*, iii., 170. It appears to be now in possession of certain Persian Sufis (*ib.*), an interesting statement which I have not, however, felt authorised to make use of in Book II., § 6, of this study.
[4] This is Westcott's opinion. Madame Blavatsky adds that the SEPHER YETZIRAH is also a portion of the Book of Numbers.
[5] *Op. cit.*, i., 579.

Jews,"¹ thus attributing a mystical sense to the commentaries on the exoteric laws of Israel, the value of which attribution has been exhibited already.²

It would serve no purpose to enumerate any further challengable assertions which rest more or less exclusively on the good authority of Madame Blavatsky. It will be sufficient to refer to her views upon the authenticity of the ZOHAR.³ On the one hand the author is said to be R. Simeon ben Yohai;⁴ again, it was "edited for the first time" between A.D. 70 and 110;⁵ and yet again, it was written, as it now stands, by R. Moses de Leon, the original being lost, though at the same time its contents were "scattered through a number of minor MSS." R. Moses had Syriac, Chaldaic, and Christian Gnostics to help him. Such opinions are without any warrant for criticism.⁶

---

¹ ISIS UNVEILED, i., 17.
² The best test of Madame Blavatsky's first-hand knowledge of the subject is the fact that she calls the LIBER DRUSHIM of Isaac de Loria a part of the TALMUD, and thence proceeds to exhibit the Sephirotic doctrine as a characteristic of that collection. SECRET DOCTRINE, i., 438. The symbolism of the Lesser Countenance is also referred to the TALMUD. Ibid., i., 350.
³ It is not perhaps surprising that she should regard the ZOHAR as not sufficiently esoteric. Ibid.
⁴ Ibid., iii., 92. She says also that it was on account of his possession of the "secret knowledge" that R. Simeon was forced to take refuge in the cave. After this version of a matter of fact we shall not be surprised to learn that St. Peter was a Kabbalist (ib., iii., 125), that the Comte de St. Germain had access to unknown Vatican MSS. on the Kabbalah, which MSS. contain information regarding the Central Sun (ib., ii., 237), or that the ZOHAR is "called also the Midrash," as if the last term were particular, and not generic (ib., iii., 167).
⁵ Ibid., iii., 167.
⁶ Ibid., i., 114, 230; iii., 167.

BOOK XI

THE KABBALAH AND OTHER CHANNEL OF SECRET TRADITION

BOOK XI

THE KABBALAH AND OTHER CHANNELS OF SECRET TRADITION

I.—THE KABBALAH AND MAGIC

It was intimated at the outset of our inquiry that certain speculations, belonging to the more immediate past, do not consider any single system as the exclusive depository of supposed hidden knowledge; a variety of channels are recognised, and by the network of communications subsisting between these channels the secret arts are methodised and their identities and analogies exhibited. There is an enormous divergence of opinion as to what may and may not constitute a path of the postulated Secret Tradition, individual predilection exercising, as will be understood, no inconsiderable influence. We may conclude in a general manner that the Tradition being ubiquitous by the hypothesis is thought to have assumed its forms everywhere and at all times. There was, for example, no exoteric religion which did not possess *ex hypothesi* an esoteric interpretation [1] and there was no esoteric interpretation which did not connect that religion with all that is signified more especially here by secret teaching. For this hypothesis an integral connection of Kabbalism with other systems belonging to remote periods would be evidence enough that it had its root in the Secret Tradition; but, without denying altogether that there may be a certain warrant for a not dissimilar view, we have found that many of the resemblances may be accounted for in a more natural and spontaneous manner. As, however, it was in the western world that Kabbalism grew up and flourished,[2] it is

---

[1] John Yarker: NOTES ON THE SCIENTIFIC AND RELIGIOUS MYSTERIES OF ANTIQUITY, p. 5.

[2] If the derivation of the ZOHAR from R. Simeon ben Yohai be admitted, Palestine was, of course, the birthplace of that work. Dr. Schiller-Szinessy, who defended this derivation, accepted also what follows therefrom.

necessary to observe its connections—real or supposed—with other channels by which an arcane knowledge is believed to have been communicated to the West. These are Magic, Alchemy, Astrology, the occult associations which culminated in Freemasonry, and, finally, an obscure sheaf of hieroglyphs known as Tarot cards. There is also a side question as to whether devotional Mysticism, apart from any formal initiation, shews any trace of Kabbalism over and above that of unconscious analogy. Like the several studies which have preceded it, the object of this eleventh book is rather to correct crude misconceptions than to establish novel views. Far too much stress has been laid upon the common basis of occult arts and reveries, while those who look for their enlightenment more especially to Kabbalistic apparatus have been predisposed unduly to discern Kabbalism at the root of all. We shall see that in most instances the connection was accidental, a matter of adornment, late in its introduction, or chiefly of the historical order. The paramount exception to this statement is the first subject with which we have to deal here. There is no doubt that Ceremonial Magic in the West [1] owes its typical processes and its peculiar complexion to Kabbalism, though it would be folly to pretend that without Kabbalism there would have been no Western Magic.[2]

I propose in the present section to restrict the use of the term Magic within the narrow limits of its common acceptation. To take it in its pretended higher sense,[3] as equivalent to Divine Wisdom, might make it seem almost superfluous to inquire whether it connects with a Tradition which lays claim to the same definition. The question as it is understood here is rather historical than metaphysical, and is concerned only with the western world. The White and Black Magic of the Middle Ages constitutes a kind of spurious practical

---

[1] "The Kabbalah is the source of all the vain imaginations which form the basis of Magic, and many Jews devoted to the Kabbalah are also addicted thereto, abusing the Names of God and the angels for the performance of things supernatural." Moreri: GRAND DICTIONNAIRE HISTORIQUE, Tom. ii., s.v. *Cabale.* Amsterdam, 1740.

[2] The strength of the connection is exhibited by the modern literature of occult *colportage* in France. LA GRANDE ET VÉRITABLE SCIENCE CABALISTIQUE is still *la Sorcellerie dévoilée*, and it is under such titles that mutilated reprints of the GREAT ALBERT, the LITTLE ALBERT and the RED DRAGON have appeared in obscure by-ways of Paris, usually without place or date. Similar productions of the eighteenth century also exhibit it: see the anonymous TÉLESCOPE DE ZOROASTRE *ou Clef de la Grande Cabale divinatoire des Mages, s.l.,* 1796.

[3] It would be unwise to deny altogether that there is such a higher sense, but such attempts to present it as Dr. Franz Hartmann's MAGIC WHITE AND BLACK are coloured too highly to possess historical value.

Kabbalah which represents Jewish esoteric doctrine debased to the purposes of the sorcerer, and it is necessary that we should estimate it at its true worth, because it has been the subject of misconception not only among uninstructed persons but even professed expositors.

A study of the Zoharistic writings, their developments and commentaries will shew that the ends proposed by the Speculative Kabbalah are very different from evocations of spirits, the raising of ghosts, discovery of concealed treasures, the bewitchments and other mummeries of Ceremonial Magic. The Kabbalah does, however, countenance, as we have seen, the doctrine of a power resident in Divine Names,[1] and it is in fact one of the burdens of its inheritance. Of the antiquity and diffusion of that doctrine there can be no doubt; in one or other of its forms it has obtained almost universally, and, like all universal beliefs, behind the insensate character which it exhibits externally there may be—by mere possibility—an inward reason which accounts for it. Without attempting an inquiry in which we are not unlikely to be baffled, it is sufficient to indicate here that at the sources to which Kabbalistic Tradition is referred, namely, Akkadia, Chaldæa and Babylonia, this doctrine prevailed: it was no doubt brought away from Babylon by the Jews, and they carried it with them into the dispersion of the third exile. It inspired a whole cycle of bizarre legends concerning Solomon and his marvels. More than this, it may be said to be connected directly with Kabbalistic symbolism concerning the divine powers and qualities attaching to the Hebrew Alphabet. The worlds were made, so to speak, by the instrument of a single letter, and four letters are the living forces which actuate them. There can be therefore no question that every Kabbalist accepted, symbolically at least, the doctrine of the power of words. It must have passed very early into unfortunate applications [2]; Sacred Names were written on amulets and talismans which were used to heal diseases, to

---

[1] See the important chapter on the Name of God in J. Leusden's PHILOLOGUS HEBRÆUS, 1672.
[2] The SEPHER RAZIEL, referred falsely to Eleazer of Worms, and posing as an angelic revelation to Adam and Noah, has been mentioned. With its long catalogues of angelic names, its talismans and philtres, its double seal of Solomon, its mystical or occult alphabetical symbols, its figures for the government of evil spirits, and its conjurations by means of Divine Names, this work constitutes one of the storehouses of Mediæval Magic, besides being broadly representative of the Practical Kabbalah at large.

avert evil chances and so forth.¹ But it was a part also of the Chaldæan doctrine that a ceremonial utterance of the Divine Name could, in some obscure way, influence the God to whom it was attributed. Above all, the demons and evil spirits became subservient to the power of such words. Here is the germ of which the last development, or rather the final corruption, is to be found in the French and Latin Grimoires of Black Magic.

It was, broadly speaking, somewhere about the fourteenth century that a Latin literature rose up in Europe, passing subsequently into the vernaculars of various countries, containing processes for compelling spirits by means of Divine Names which are corruptions of Hebrew terms.² The processes pretend to be translated from the Hebrew, but, if so, the originals are either not extant or have been altered out of all knowledge. The chief of them is known as the KEY OF SOLOMON, of which there are two recensions, more correctly regarded as distinct works under an identical title.³ Among the points which should be observed concerning them is the fact that while they are concerned with all classes of spirits, good and evil, for every variety of purpose, but mostly illicit, they contain no formulæ for dealing with the dead, and this, I think, indicates their Jewish origin, for the Jews had very strong feelings as to the sacred nature of the repose of the human soul. Out of these two works there was developed subsequently a variety of processes, more distinctly spurious, which did enter into Necromantic Mysteries. They begot also many variations adapted for the use of Christian operators, and containing Sacred Words the efficacy of which would not have been acknowledged by a Hebrew.

It is one thing to note the existence of this literature and to confess its derivation; it is another to exalt collections like

---

[1] So far as regards the early Christian centuries, the question is settled by a reference in the thirty-third Sermon of Origen by way of commentary on St. Matthew, wherein allusion is made to a book of exorcisms or adjurations of demons passing under the name of Solomon, which was no doubt the prototype of later KEYS and GRIMOIRES.

[2] Jean Wier, a demonologist of the sixteenth century, in his HISTOIRES, DISPUTES ET DISCOURS *des Illusions et Impostures des Diables*, originally in Latin, gives a list of magical works current at his period under great names of the past, and points out that their art has depraved the most secret interpretation of the Divine Law, known as Kabbalah among the Jews.—See the reprint of this work, Paris, 1885, 2 vols., i., 175.

[3] A text passing under this name was condemned in a Decree of Pope Gelasius. See Antonius van Dale: DE ORIGINE ET PROGRESSU IDOLATRIÆ, Amsterdam, 1696, p. 558. See also the Jewish Encyclopædia, Vol. XI, *s.v.* SOLOMON, concerning MAFTEAH SHELAMOH, a book of incantations, said to have been extant in Hebrew so late as 1697 and supposed to be the original of the Latin CLAVICULÆ SALOMONIS.

the KEY OF SOLOMON into embodiments of genuine Kabbalistic Tradition. It is an insult to the rabbins of the Holy Synod to suggest their connection with the puerilities and imbecility of Ceremonial Magic. This, however, has been done in England and was being done until recently in France.[1] The professed Kabbalistic occultists of the latter country have ascribed a superior importance and an additional aspect of mystery to the worthless CLAVICLES of Solomon, by representing that they are the only written memorials of a most secret oral branch of Practical Kabbalism, instead of the final debasement of a perfectly traceable, if not rationally accountable, doctrine concerning Divine Names. Papus observes: " The practical part of the Kabbalah is barely indicated in a few manuscripts scattered through our great libraries. At Paris, the *Bibliothèque Nationale* possesses one of the finest exemplars, of which the origin is attributed to Solomon. These manuscripts, generally known under the name of CLAVICLES, are the basis of all the old Grimoires which circulate in country places (the GREAT ALBERT and LITTLE ALBERT, RED DRAGON and ENCHIRIDION) and of those which once drove priests into mental alienation by sorcery." The statement does not exhibit much acquaintance with the works which it mentions; the ENCHIRIDION in its earliest forms owes little to the KEYS OF SOLOMON, and the GRIMOIRE OF HONORIUS is not more concerned with sorcery than are Rituals like the RED DRAGON. Finally, the intellectual and moral difference between the Clavicles and their derivatives is so slight that it is scarcely worth labouring. As regards their scope and intention, the Clavicles are themselves Grimoires. I have indicated the possibility that behind the ancient doctrine of the virtue resident in certain theurgic words and formulæ there may be concealed a Secret of Lower and Averse Sanctuaries; so also the apparatus of Ceremonial Magic may be a travesty and disfigurement of practices known also to Occult Sanctuaries; but no one is on the track of these mysteries who begins by mistaking *signum* for *signatum* on the one hand or the mutilated reflection for the original on the other.

---

[1] There is some ground for supposing that the first express attempts to identify Magic with Kabbalism must be referred to Germany. There are numerous earlier examples, but Welling's OPUS MAGO-CABBALISTICUM, Hamburg, 1765, is a good instance, and it is also a work of some interest.

The general fact remains that it was by a perversion of the Kabbalah that we have obtained Grimoires, and that the student of Jewish Tradition must tolerate this fact as best he can.[1]

I should prefer to ignore altogether this so-called practical part of the Kabbalah, but so much importance having been attributed to it by modern occultists, it seems necessary for the sake of completeness to say something briefly of its materials and its method in their later developments. It was concerned above all with the Names of God, firstly, as they are found in Holy Scripture, and, secondly, as their mysteries were unfolded by means of Kabbalistic processes. It attributed certain names of power to the ten SEPHIROTH, and these were regarded as analogous to the divine forces and attributes associated with these.

The Divine Name connected with KETHER was that signifying the essence of the Deity, EHEIEH (AHIH). That of CHOKMAH is JOD, JAH, or TETRAGRAMMATON, commonly rendered Jehovah (JHVH), and susceptible of twelve permutations, similar to the sealing names of IHV in the SEPHER YETZIRAH. These permutations are called Banners by Kabbalists. The title JEHOVAH ELOHIM (JHVH ALHIM) is attributed to BINAH and signifies God of Gods. EL (AL) is referred to CHESED, and its meaning, according to Rosenroth, is God of Grace and Ruler of Mercy. GEBURAH is in correspondence with ELOHIM GIBOR, the strong God Who avenges the crimes of the wicked. ELOAH VA DAATH is the Divine Title of TIPHERETH (ALVH V DATh); JEHOVAH or ADONAI TZABAOTH (ADNI TsBAVTh), the God or Lord of Hosts, is connected with NETZACH; ELOHIM TZABAOTH, of similar meaning, belongs to HOD; SHADDAI EL CHAI (ShDI AL ChI), the omnipotent living God, is referable to JESOD; ADONAI MELEKH (ADNI MLK) to MALCHUTH.

But the ten SEPHIROTH are connected with the ten numbers,

---

[1] A work belonging to this class, but more elaborate and interesting than most of them, goes to shew that a Jew in possession of the "Holy Traditions of the Kabbalah" and also of the secrets of practical Magic, bequeathed the first to his elder and the second to his younger son. What happened when there were more than two sons does not appear.—See the BOOK OF THE SACRED MAGIC, translated by S. L. MacGregor Mathers, London, 1898. The original is an MS. in the Arsénal Library, Paris, and belongs to the 18th century, but it claims to have been written in Hebrew in the year 1458, which claim, by the internal evidence, is manifestly imposture. Even its Jewish authorship is unlikely. Mathers, who had a certain erudition but was devoid of critical judgment, accepted every claim advanced by this work, as he accepted that of the KEY OF SOLOMON.

and hence there was an occult power resident in numerals analogous to that which was inherent in Hebrew letters; the Divine Names belonging to the SEPHIROTH were those also of the scale of the denary; but over and above these there were other names referred to numbers based on the number of the letters which gave expression to these names. Thus, the number one was represented by the single letter JOD, understood as a Divine Name, and not in its alphabetical order, in which it is equivalent to ten. The number two was represented by JH and AL; the number three by ShDI = Shaddai; the number four by JHVH and AHIH; five by ALHIM, to which I presume that Christian Kabbalism added JHShVH = JEHESHUAH or Jesus; six by ALVThIM and AL GBVR; seven by ARARITA and AShRAHIH; eight by ALVH V DATh and JHVH V DATh; nine by JHVH TsBAVTh, ALHIM GBVR, and JHVH TsDQNV; ten by ALHIM TsBAVTh and by the extended TETRAGRAMMATON JVD HE VAV HE. It may be added in this connection that according to Cornelius Agrippa simple numbers were used to express divine things, numbers of ten were for celestial, numbers of one hundred for earthly, and numbers of a thousand for things to come. The Divine Names and their qualifications were also tabulated in reference to the twenty-two letters.

Of these Names the greatest power and virtue were attributed to TETRAGRAMMATON, which was the root and foundation of all and the ruling force of the world; its true pronunciation, as already seen, was one of the secrets of the Sanctuary and for Kabbalistic Magic was the master key of all successful operation. With this was connected the name of 72 letters obtained by the Kabbalistic computation of the numbers of the letters of TETRAGRAMMATON after a conventional manner, as follows:—

$$\left.\begin{array}{r}\text{Jod} = 10 \\ \text{Jod He} = 15 \\ \text{Jod He Vau} = 21 \\ \text{Jod He Vau He} = 26\end{array}\right\} = 72$$

After the Divine Names come those of the Orders of Angels and chiefs of the hierarchy, concerning which something has been said already in the section on ANGELS AND DEMONS. It would serve no purpose to enumerate all the complicated apparatus developed in this connection. The ten archangels and the ten angelic orders corresponded to the ten Divine Names connected with the SEPHIROTH and the Name of 72 letters had 72 other angels attributed thereto, whose names were extracted by a conventional device from Exodus xiv. 19, 20, 21. There were angels of the cardinal points, rulers of the four elements, angels of the planets, angels of the Divine Presence, and in opposition to all these there were also evil spirits, princes of Devils, held to be "offensive in the elements," and so forth. This apparatus passed bodily over to the Ceremonial Magic of the Middle Ages, which the debased Kabbalah may be said to have constituted and ruled throughout, and it is for this reason that Western conventional Magic has so little connection with folk-lore.

It is to be understood that so far I have presented developments of later Kabbalism, the elements of which pre-existed, however, in Israel, and this laid down we have finished with one aspect of the occult subject in its relation to the Secret Tradition of Israel. Beyond this, and much more important —that is to say, from a theosophical standpoint—there is the fact that the voice of the ZOHAR testifies in no uncertain manner as to the view concerning Magic, its connections and derivations, held by all true Sons of the Doctrine and imposed by inference on those who might seek to come after them, following in their path. This notwithstanding, we may find here and there in the long sequence of debate that the same standpoint is not maintained invariably on specific details, and there are certain statements which might lend colour to an opinion that the root-matter of one and another department of occult experiment may be found therein. It is said, for example, that there is a mystery known to the holy thaumaturgists concerning the miraculous powers which inhere in the sacred celestial letters and that if these are written inversely, after a certain manner, the extinction of the guilty can be brought about thereby.[1] Now it is to be observed that the so-called celestial characters are not those which are written with the hand by human scribes, but are the Great Letters, alive and givers of life, emblems of all intelligence and therefore endowed with understanding. By the Zoharic hypothesis, they existed before the creation and—as we have seen in its

---

[1] Z., Pt. I, fol 67b ; I, 398.

place—one of them was concerned therewith. The explanation of this fable is that, for all the sages of Israel, thought must pass into expression, because that which is done in heaven must be done also on earth. The Sons of the Doctrine must reflect therefore in their hearts on the Secret Doctrine, as the Divine Thought was turned upon itself in the eternity which preceded creation; but it must pass also into expression, because at length the creation was formulated, and this expression enters into record by means of letters. These are further the elements of that Law by which the world was made, and the use of their reflections on earth was another instance of accomplishing below that which is performed on high. After what manner the holy thaumaturgists brought down the celestial letters for the purpose under consideration, or for any other, is not told in the story, and I suppose that for sane persons there can be no question that the intimation must be understood allegorically, though I am not proposing to explain after what manner—as the unexpressed meaning exceeds my purpose. For the rest, I am certain that the ZOHAR was unknown to the adepts of magical workings; it reflects there and here some practices which obtained in Jewry, and the TALMUDS are a source of sporadic information to whose who would pursue the subject.

The general thesis of the ZOHAR is that the art of Magic came from the sages of the East,[1] and as it is said by the Scriptures that the wisdom of Solomon surpassed that of the Egyptians, as well as of all the East,[2] it seems to be understood that he drew from some superior source, in respect of occult " science." The intention is not, however, either to exonerate the science or to justify the king in this branch of his learning. He seems to have pursued it when he fell away from justice, but it was otherwise during the building of the Temple[3]: then he beheld wisdom face to face and had no need of occult arts. That of the Egyptians is regarded

---

[1] Z., Pt. I, fol. 223a; II, 478.
[2] I Kings iv. 34. It is very difficult to understand the purpose of the ZOHAR in this reference. Somehow Shekinah was his teacher, but it is not certain, and the question is scarcely worth pursuing.—See Z., Pt. I, fol. 223a, b; II, 478-481.
[3] Ib., fol. 150a; II, 190. There is more on the subject which need not be quoted here. We have seen in our study of the Deluge-Myth that Magic is older than the Deluge: it existed also during the patriarchal age. Laban was the greatest magician in the world, and by the aid of his idols learned all that he wished to know.—Ib., Pt. I, fol. 164b; II, 243.

as the lowest of all,[1] presumably because the subjugation of Israel is said to have been its chief object, and it failed at the end therein. It was not, however, mere trickery; the wands which changed into serpents became actual serpents, not only in dream or vision, and those of Aaron which devoured them were actual in like manner.[2] The Egyptian masters had acquired ten degrees of Magic, corresponding to the averse or evil SEPHIROTH, the Inferior Crowns,[3] which rule in all Magic. In virtue of his communications with the abyss, Pharaoh himself was skilled more highly in occult practices than any of the magicians he employed.[4] Abraham seems to have been drawn in this direction, and when he first went into Egypt it was for the profound study of Egyptian occult art, though not as one who was seduced or one who became attached thereto.[5] He penetrated the secret of evil only to reascend towards the good. As regards the later children of the East and their wisdom, there is a sense in which Abraham was himself a fountain of knowledge, for the presents made by him to the children of his concubine seem to have been a medley of true knowledge and occult arts, which were taken eastward and deteriorated in the course of the centuries.[6] There is thus a vestige of truth in the eastern wisdom, but it is combined with impure Magic. The source of all magical power, howsoever it may be derived through individual persons, is the first serpent, who is the impure spirit, and the theory is that in order to attract this spirit the magicians must begin by defiling themselves, apparently by sex acts against Nature.[7] The workings are facilitated by the fact that the impure spirit bestows himself for nothing, so that the path to the abyss looks easier than the path to the heights. The authority for this statement is not fortunately the Secret Tradition in Israel but a Book of Magic said to have been transmitted to Solomon by the demon Asmodeus.[8] It

---

[1] Z., Pt. I, fol. 223b; II, 481. "It is designated under the name of the maid-servant seated behind the mill."

[2] Ib., Pt. II, fol. 28a; III, 134.

[3] Ib., fol. 30b; III, 145. Ib., fol. 35b; III, 171. "All the streets of Egypt were full of magicians, and in each house were to be found articles belonging to the works of Magic."

[4] Ib., Pt. II, fol. 37b; III, 179. Also, fol. 52b; III, 236.

[5] Ib., Pt. I, fol. 83a; I, 478.

[6] Eliphas Lévi makes a great point of these "presents." See my rendering of THE HISTORY OF MAGIC, p. 48. See also Z., Pt. I, fol. 133b; II, 127.

[7] Z., Pt. I, fol. 125b; II, 100.

[8] Ib., Pt. II, fol. 128a; IV, 10. The very opposite is taught in the Grimoires concerning evil spirits, of whom it is said that this kind of creature gives nothing for

THE KABBALAH AND MAGIC

affirms also that the Holy Spirit demands a price, must be bought and the cost is high. The ZOHAR explains that this price is one of effort for the purification of heart and soul, that the aspirant may be made worthy of serving in the Tabernacle of the Spirit. The present state of the art is defined at the end of the ZOHAR when it is said that Magic has been abolished by the Holy One.[1] In other words that has prevailed which is always above Magic, namely faith, this being friendship with God, whereas Magic is friendship with the demon.[2]

The term Magic is sufficiently general to answer for some other arts and practices included in the department of pseudo-occult science. Astrology stands to some extent apart, and it is perhaps for this reason that it is a subject of distinct and particular condemnation. The thesis is that it is a lying science, understood as the prediction of future events of the human order by the constellation rising at nativity, and the consequent pretension that the day, hour and minute of each man's birth exercises an influence on his future.[3] When God directed Abraham to look up to heaven, it was a counsel to forsake Astrology, this having predicted apparently that he would die without children, whereas God promised him a posterity not less numerous than those stars which in this matter seemed to have been in combination against him.[4] The point is, and it appears fully elsewhere, that Abraham had studied Astrology, presumably in Egypt; that he was wrong in fact, was told to neglect the study and have faith in the Divine Name, when a son would be given to him.[5] When it was said in the Scriptures that Abraham believed in God,[6] this means in contradistinction from the testimony of stars, and this faith was imputed to him for righteousness. At the same time it is not denied that many things are indicated

---

nothing. Whatsoever is evoked, for example, must be satisfied on its own part; if it be a question of obtaining some hidden treasure, a coin must be thrown to the fiend who assists in securing it.

[1] "The Holy One, blessed be He, has caused Magic to disappear from the world, in order to prevent men, under the seduction thereof, from forsaking the fear of God."—Z., Pt. III, fol. 299b; VI, 128. It is like a final message of the text. I observe that Parisian occultism, after all its futilities, false-seeming and ignorant ascriptions respecting Kabbalistic Magic, has preserved a discreet silence since the publication of the ZOHAR in its own language.

[2] Ib., Pt. II, fol. 52b; III, 237. It is said that Pharaoh was unacquainted with this truth and had found no confirmation of the doctrine that the Divine Name Jehovah, as formulated by Moses, had dominion over the whole earth.

[3] Ib., Pt. I, fol. 78a; I, 458.
[4] Ib., fol. 90b; I, 514.
[5] Ib.
[6] Ib.

by the course of the stars in heaven; but the Holy One changes them according to His will.[1] Here is one aspect of the admission in respect of the subject; another says that, according to an old book, there are times when the moon is hollowed, and souls born at this period will be overwhelmed with sufferings and poverty, without reference to their personal deserts.[2] On the other hand [3] those who come down into incarnate life when the moon is full will enjoy all earthly prosperity. The ZOHAR explains that in the first case the souls are those whom the Holy One loves the most and allows to suffer in this world, so that they may be purified from stain.[4] ... This notwithstanding, the lunar intimation remains correct and Astrology is justified by the hypothesis.

The subject of occult reverie suggests that of demonology, as to which there is much information scattered throughout the text, and it may be well to summarise the Zoharic doctrine of evil spirits—apart from the Fall of the angels, already dealt with, and outside the methodical developments of later Kabbalism. Speaking generally, the evil spirit is a serpent, and he who rides on the serpent is Samael.[5] The wife of Samael is that adulterous woman who seduces humanity at large.[6] It is suggested that demons existed prior to the creation, but there came a time when in company with all other maleficent and impure spirits, they were authorised to go about the world and ravage therein.[7] Their abodes are in ruins, in great forests and in deserts.[8] They are all emanations from the serpent, and this is why the evil spirit reigns in the world.[9] These are apparently one class, and another are the scourges which Adam engendered during those years when he was in separation from his wife.[10] A third class

---

[1] Z., fol. 90b; I, 514.

[2] Ib., fol. 180b, 181a; II, 313, 314. When it is said that the moon is hollowed, the meaning is that it is sometimes waxing and sometimes waning, through the wiles of the old serpent.—Ib.

[3] There is another point: the ancient and prevailing connection of angels and certain stars is admitted by the ZOHAR, which holds also that angel succeeds angel, and in some manner that does not transpire this putative fact places human temperaments under the ascendant of that constellation which happens to preside at birth. It will be seen that the principles on which Astrology rests do not seem to be denied, and that the "lying science" is the attempt to calculate the influences and predict thereby. The authority in the present instance is THE FAITHFUL SHEPHERD.—Z., Pt. II, fol. 42a; III, 191, 192.

[4] Ib.

[5] Ib., fol. 35b; I, 221.

[6] See Book VII, § 3.

[7] Ib., fol. 169b; II, 265, 266.

[8] Ib.

[9] Ib.

[10] See Book VII., § 3.

arises from the fact that when the soul is apart from the body during sleep the impure spirit may attach itself to the latter, or in other words, that female demons may cohabit therewith.[1] They conceive and bring forth children as a result of the union. Such demons are in the likeness of man but without hair on their heads.[2] It would appear that holy men, or people having holy souls, are not less liable than others to be thus defiled in the body. I do not know whether these three categories correspond to those of the MISHNA, some of whom resemble angels while some are like men and others are comparable to beasts.[3] They are versed occasionally in the oral law for the better misdirection of mankind.[4] Another account says that there are many hierarchic degrees in the kingdom of the demons. Every three groups have at their head a chief placed in charge of one or other nation of the earth.[5] These chiefs in their turn are overruled by superiors entrusted with the direction of the stars, so that each nation is indirectly under the influence of a certain star, which, it will be seen, is another astrological intimation. Hence the destiny of one nation is never like that of another.[6] The reign of these chiefs will continue till the Holy One shall Himself come down and govern here below.[7] Most curious of all is the intimation that if these degrees or groups are disintegrated there will be found at the centre a sacred kernel which draws all, even the impure side.[8]

Having regard to the consideration allotted to the interpretation of dreams by the Old Testament, it would surpass expectation if the ZOHAR rejected the possibility, more especially with the authority of the TALMUD to support the affirmative view. It does something, however, to reduce the rank of dreams. They are the gross form of that which the soul sees when it is separated from the body. The soul then discerns things as they actually are, while the body perceives

---

[1] Z., Pt. I, fol. 169b ; II, 266, 267.
[2] Ib.
[3] An exact description of the Infernal Hierarchies according to the Grimoires—not that they are borrowing from the ZOHAR but because the province of images is restricted.
[4] So also one of the demons in Goëtic Theurgy is supposed to give true answers respecting things human and divine.
[5] Z., Pt. I, fol. 177a ; II, 296.
[6] Ib., fol. 177b ; II, 297.
[7] Ib. This has been mentioned previously in other terms. It does not seem to differ from the doctrine of Latin Theology.
[8] The logical consequence is realised in another place, where it is said that this vestige or kernel can never be lost utterly.

them only in a form corresponding to its own degree.[1] Every dream is regarded as an admixture of truth and falsehood[2]; but the most curious thesis of all is that a dream is realised according to the interpretation placed upon it: should this be favourable,[3] favours will overwhelm the man, but in the contrary case he will be weighed down by adversity. The reason is that the word governs,[4] and it follows that no dream must be disclosed to any one by whom the dreamer is not loved. There are in all three degrees—dream, vision and prophecy: the greatest of these is prophecy.[5]

Now it so happens that the Doctrine of Signatures, of which we seem to hear first in Paracelsus—so far as Latin-writing Europe is concerned—and which was derived from him into the theosophical system of Jacob Böhme, is a doctrine of Kabbalism, and though the Zoharic allusions are few and far between in respect of actual definition, they enable us—with the aid of their developments—to conclude that the mental environment of Paracelsus included some reflections from Zoharic sources. According to the sage of Hohenheim, there are elements and signatures of elements[6]; a science of the signatures exists, and it teaches how heaven produces man at his conception, how also he is constellated thereby.[7] Stones, herbs, seeds, roots and all things whatsoever are known by their signatures, that which lies within them being discovered thereby.[8] In respect of man, signature has three species, which are chiromancy, physiognomy and proportion.[9] The ZOHAR has a good deal to tell us on the first two, while

---

[1] Z., Pt. I, fol. 194a; II, 367.
[2] *Ib.*, fol. 183a; II, 322.
[3] *Ib.*, fol. 183a; II, 323.
[4] *Ib.* I think that this is the only place in which a definite, over-ruling power is attributed to the formulation of thought in speech, apart from those words which—like Divine Names—are supposed to be essentially potent. The explanation is probably that the dream-interpreter was in a kind of prophetic state; but this is to be distinguished from the ceremonial and magical use of words, as—for example—when it is said of the pre-diluvian sorcerers that, with the aid of the mysteries contained in their secret book, it was enough for them to utter words and the desired things were accomplished.—*Ib.*, fol. 76a, b; I, 449.
[5] *Ib.*, fol. 183a; II, 323, 324.
[6] PHILOSOPHIÆ AD ATHENIENSES LIBER II, *Textus* x, p. 247.
[7] EXPLICATIO TOTIUS ASTRONOMIÆ: *Interpretatio Alia*, p. 666.
[8] *Ib.*, IN SCIENTIAM SIGNATAM PROBATIO, p. 669.
[9] *Ib.*, s.v. DE MASSA ET MATERIA *ex qua Homo factus est*, p. 666.—See OPERA OMNIA, Vol. II, Geneva edition, 1658. See also my HERMETIC AND ALCHEMICAL WRITINGS OF PARACELSUS, Vol. II, pp. 268, 294, 295, 305. The 9th book DE NATURA RERUM treats at considerable length *de signatura rerum naturalium*.

it has a supplement, so to speak, concerning character and hair.¹ I do not know how the findings would appeal to those artists of our own day who deal in such subjects; but it is desirable to point out that—within the consciousness of Kabbalistic doctors—such things were no part of the decried occult sciences; they were matters of observation arising from that doctrine of correspondences which obtained in all directions. I append the following particulars, gleaned from there and here, without pretending to know whether they have points of concurrence with later readings of character on the same bases, or whether they differ therefrom. I should expect that the ZOHAR would be found peculiar to itself— here, as in more important matters.

There are seven considerations regarding hair and the dispositions indicated thereby: (1) Hair which is crisp or frizzy and inclined to stand up signifies a choleric temper; the heart is tortuous like the hair, and such a person should be shunned. (2) Straight and silky hair is usually that of a good companion, one who succeeds in business—if not undertaken alone. He is prudent respecting Supreme Mysteries, but cannot hold his tongue about matters of daily life. (3) Hair that is coarse and straight signifies one who does not fear God, but works evil knowingly. He will become better, however, if he reaches an advanced age. (4) A man having black and glossy hair will succeed in material things, but he must work alone. (5) The success of a black and dull-haired man is rather of an intermittent kind, and he may quarrel with his business associates; should he take to the study of the Holy Law, he will make progress therein. (6) A prematurely bald man will do well in business; but he will be crafty, avaricious, hypocritical and one who makes a pretence of religion. (7) A man who grows bald in the natural course of years will undergo great changes otherwise; if he has been of good conduct previously, he will now be bad, but he will turn into paths of virtue if he has been so far an evil liver. I dare not furnish particulars, but these ascriptions are referable to mysteries belonging to certain Hebrew letters. Since some of the conclusions are a little hard and arbitrary—under the reserve of sacred letters—it shall be added that certain alternative readings at a later stage do not

---

¹ The general references are to Z., Pt. II, fol. 70b to 78a; III, 311–328, and *ib.*, fol. 284b to 288b; IV, 312–315.

endorse them entirely; but from this secondary account it will be sufficient to cite a ruling in respect of auburn hair. On the understanding that it is curly, the head which wears it will fear sin, will feel compassion for all in misfortune and will have the welfare of others as much at heart as his own.

Physiognomy is a larger subject, and being treated at some length, I shall be content with a few typical examples. The man whose forehead is low and flat acts without thinking, is fickle in notions, believes himself wise and understands nothing. His tongue is like a biting serpent. The man who has deep wrinkles on his forehead which are not in parallel lines, and which are replaced when he speaks by parallel and less deep wrinkles, is to be shunned under most circumstances, as he seeks nothing but personal interests and will keep no secrets. A large and full forehead denotes the best kind of personality, capable of acquiring knowledge with the least pains and successful in all search after spiritual felicity. In money questions he may succeed at one time and fail at another, but he is not solicitous regarding material things. The man with blue eyes has a tender heart and one that is free from wickedness, but he follows his own ends and is careless proportionally about wrong done to others. He seeks pleasure but not of an unlawful kind, yet if he should fall into evil ways, he would remain therein. A man with green, shining eyes is touched with madness, believes himself superior to others and lets them know it; he will not prevail against enemies, and he is inapt for the Mysteries of the Law. A man with clear but yellowish eyes is passionate, though often sympathetic towards the sufferings of others; yet is he cruel in his anger, and he also cannot keep secrets. A man with dark grey eyes will succeed in the Mysteries of the Law, and if he perseveres in its study he will make steady progress therein: he will also prevail over enemies.

The distinctive marks of the countenance are modified by conduct, and differ from general inherited types, which correspond broadly to the four living creatures of Ezekiel's vision. There are those which are distinctively human, those which are leonine, bovine and in aspect like that of the eagle. There are also four types which are said to be imprinted by the soul, being: (1) That of the virtuous man, who is distinguished by a small horizontal vein on either temple, the one on the left being bifurcated and crossed by another small, vertical vein. (2) That of a man who returns to his Master after leading a bad life. He is repulsive at first, but others are finally drawn towards him; he does not care to be looked straight in the face, because he thinks that his past may be legible: he is alternately pale and yellow. He has one vein descending from right temple to cheek, another under the nose and this joins with two veins on the left cheek. These last are united by another vein, but the last will disappear when the man is habituated to a virtuous life. (3) That of a person who has fallen off completely from the good way. He has three red pimples on either cheek and some faint red veins beneath them: should he be converted the pimples would remain but the veinlets vanish. (4) That of a man who has been incarnated a second time, to repair the imperfections of his first sojourn on earth. He has a vertical line on the right cheek, near the mouth, and two deep lines on the left cheek, also vertical. His eyes are never bright, his health is poor, and the cutting of his hair and beard changes his appearance completely. Thick lips are those of the evil speaking. If a medium lower lip is cleft the person will be of violent temper, but he will succeed in business. Unusually large ears are a sign of stupidity and even of tendencies to mania; persons with very small and well-shaped ears are awakened in mind and yearn for knowledge.

I need some indulgence for bringing in these details, and I will forbear from dwelling on chiromancy, except to say that the lines of the hand are believed to shew forth great mysteries, including those of the fingers. On the contrary I might not be forgiven by the few who know if I omitted to certify that a man with two great hairs between the shoulders is one who swears without ceasing and to no purpose. The presence of three such hairs is the sign of a happy nature. To make an end of these fantasies, he who has been guilty of adultery and has not done penance is identifiable by an excrescence with two hairs, below the navel. If he repents, the swelling will remain but the hairs will fall off.

Hereof is the ZOHAR when it makes an excursion into by-ways beyond its province, and it is likely enough that those who take palmistry and physiognomy seriously will regard the indications as worthless, even from their standpoint. It is none of my own concern. The lesson in general concerning the occult arts is another matter, and it counts to the text for righteousness; it stands also much better in its own context than can be made to appear herein. For the rest, even when it says that they are lying, the ZOHAR does not deny the arts; they come from the pit and are deceptions belonging to the pit, but they are not vagrant trickeries. There is the greater reason to eschew them, and the work of condemnation has more than prudence or scriptural ordinance behind it: there is the sense mystical of the essence and truth of things. The Book of the Secret Law in Israel puts forth its arms to draw those for whom it was written, among the Academies and Synagogues of the past, from the world of pictures, wherein the images of mind are multiplied and superposed one upon another, into the inward ways of thought, into a true refuge, where—in processes of silent prayer and contemplation—the mind is released from images and the Glory of the Indwelling Presence is seen and understood in the heart.

II.—THE KABBALAH AND ALCHEMY

Some reference has been made to the subject of Hermetic Tradition when considering the Kabbalistic treatise entitled PURIFYING FIRE. We have seen that Hermetic and Kabbalistic Philosophies are ascribed frequently to a common source, and this has been the case with sympathetic as well as hostile critics. The question, however, is complicated, and though I should hesitate to differ from a consensus of informed authorities,[1] I am not less sure that as regards the branch of Hermetic Philosophy which is known under the name of Alchemy, we should be exceedingly careful about making and accepting statements. We must begin first of all by distinguishing the earlier books ascribed to Hermes Trismegistus, and not concerned with the transmutation of metals,[2] from such late compositions, to make use of no

---

[1] In a pamphlet entitled THE SCIENCE OF ALCHYMY, by "Sapere Aude," Fra. R.R. et A.C., the "sages of mediæval Europe" are said to have derived their knowledge of this subject, (1) from the Arabs, (2) from the heirs of the traditional lore now identified by the name "Kabbalah," (3) from ancient Egypt. Of these alleged sources, the first only is historically true in the sense that the Arabian alchemists derived from Byzantium: the other notions belong to the slush of occult reverie.

[2] Compare, however, the anonymous preface to the first English translation of the DIVINE POIMANDER, that of Dr. John Everard, 1650. Here the possession of "the great Elixir of the Philosophers" is ascribed to Hermes Termaximus. See also

stronger term, as the EMERALD TABLE and the GOLDEN TREATISE. When Isaac Myer affirms that many of the doctrines of the Kabbalah, more or less veiled, may be found in the books attributed to Hermes Trismegistus,[1] the reference obtains only, and can be intended only, to the DIVINE POIMANDER, the ASCLEPIOS and other tracts, the existence of which can be traced about or prior to the fourth century, A.D. We may search the Greek alchemists in vain for any doctrinal connection with these works, though Hermes is included among great names of antiquity which are associated with the making of gold, and there are also other references to this mystical personage. While we must discount altogether such extreme opinions as that of Isaac Casaubon, who represents the earlier Hermetic treatises as the work of a Kabbalistic adept who was probably a Jew of Alexandria,[2] we have general reasons for admitting that there were points of contact between Neo-Platonism and the Kabbalah,[3] as seen in an earlier section. The connection of Alchemy with Hermes is not through the Hermetic books of the Neo-Platonic period, and its Kabbalistic correspondences must also be sought elsewhere. Among the writings of Zosimus the Panopolite, which belong to the third century,[4] there is a quotation from the TRUE BOOK OF SOPHE THE EGYPTIAN concerning the Divine Lord of the Hebrews and the powers of Sabaoth, which affirms that there are two sciences and two

---

Westcott's observations prefixed to his verbatim reprint of Everard, COLLECTANEA HERMETICA, vol. 2, London, 1894.

[1] THE PHILOSOPHY OF IBN GEBIROL, pp. 166, 167.

[2] M. Berthelot observes, however, that "the *rôle* attributed to the Jews in the propagation of alchemical ideas recalls that which they enjoyed at Alexandria during the contact of Greek culture with the culture of Egypt and Chaldea. It is known that the Jews exercised an influence of the first importance in this fusion of the religious and scientific doctrines of the East and of Greece, which presided at the birth of Christianity. The Alexandrian Jews were for one moment at the head of science and philosophy."—LES ORIGINES DE L'ALCHIMIE, Paris, 1885.

[3] Le Chevalier I. A. de Goulianov in his ESSAI SUR LES HIÉROGLYPHES D'HORAPOLLON, &c., Paris, 1827, connects Hermetic and Kabbalistic Tradition on the fantastic ground that Enoch, who plays such an important part in the revelation, of the Kabbalah, is identical with the Edris of the Orientals and with Hermes (p. 48).

[4] As Louis Figuier's popular work, entitled L'ALCHIMIE ET LES ALCHIMISTES, was once quoted freely by occultists, and is still presumably in the hands of some of them, it will be well to point out that he classes all Byzantine literature of Alchemy as apocryphal, and the work of monks belonging to the 8th, 9th, and 10th centuries. There was never much excuse for this opinion, and it is only necessary to add that since the researches of Berthelot it has become impossible. I may add that, throughout, Figuier's work is most inaccurate as regards its facts, and of no consequence as to its opinions and inferences. Consult, on the point involved, the third edition, p. 6, Paris, 1860.

wisdoms, that of the Egyptians and that of the Hebrews, the second being rendered "more solid by Divine Justice."[1] Both come from remote ages; they do not investigate material and corruptible bodies; their generation operates independently of any foreign action, sustained by prayer and Divine Grace. Then comes the following significant passage, which accounts for the philosophical work of Alchemy being likened to that of God in the creation. "The symbol of chemistry is drawn from creation (in the eyes of its adepts) who save and purify the divine soul enchained in the elements, and, above all, who separate the divine spirit confounded with the flesh. As there is a sun, the flower of fire, a celestial sun, the right eye of the world, so copper, if it become flower (that is, if it assume the colour of gold) by purification, becomes then a terrestrial sun, which is king on earth, as the sun is king in the sky."[2] There is no doubt that this is a very important citation.[3] It shews why early Hermetic books came to be regarded as alchemical in later times, and it institutes a striking parallel between Egyptian and Jewish science. But that the latter is the science of the Kabbalah there is no evidence to cite. So also a reference to the LABYRINTH OF SOLOMON which occurs among the remains of still earlier Greek alchemists is a mediæval interpolation.[4] In short, the celebrated Byzantine collection, which is so far the source of all Alchemy, shews no traces of acquaintance with any Jewish Secret Tradition. The same observation applies to the early Arabian and Syriac alchemists who drew from Greek sources, though some extracts from Zosimus, with analyses, in a Syriac MS. possessed by the University of Cambridge, mention the talismans of Solomon, referred to the seven planets, and the power which they exercise over demons. When we add to this that in spite of such evidence for the connection between Alchemy and the Kabbalah as is offered by the late ÆSH MEZAREPH there is nothing, as already seen, to support it in the ZOHAR,[5] it must be inferred

---

[1] COLLECTION DES ANCIENS ALCHIMISTES GRECS, *livraison* ii., p. 206.
[2] *Ibid.*
[3] See, however, my SECRET TRADITION IN ALCHEMY, pp. 80, 81.
[4] COLLECTION DES ANCIENS ALCHIMISTES GRECS, *livraison* ii., p. 206.
[5] Dr. Gerhard Scholem, who has been cited in a previous note, gives an extract from SEPHER HA BAHIR, adding that it is used in the ZOHAR, but is garbled therein. The extract says that gold is called זהב because it contains the three principles. They are not, however, those of Alchemy, the letter ZAIN corresponding to a principle called human, HE to the soul and BETH to the balance between them. So also Dr.

that these two Esoteric Traditions grew up for a long period in independence of one another.[1] Furthermore, there is no trace of any science of transmutation in ancient Egypt, and it is worth noting that the claim of Alchemy rose into prominence precisely at that period when certain Chinese ports were first thrown open to western commerce. If it be true, as it has been affirmed, that Alchemy flourished in China from a remote period, that it possesses a literature, and that the terminology of this literature offers analogies with that which prevailed afterwards in the West, it may well be that we must look to the furthest East for the cradle of what is usually understood by Hermetic Science, namely, that of transmutation.[2] The subject is far too large to enter on in this place, but we shall do well to remember that the doctrine of the Macrocosm and the Microcosm, the analogy between spiritual and material, the Zoharistic symbolism of the balance, have all been traced to the oldest sacred books of the Chinese.[3] The analogies may not be so striking as the persons who have discovered them have thought; as to this, we have no real means of deciding; but they indicate at least the possibility of a common source for both Esoteric Traditions at a centre not as yet acknowledged and at a very far epoch of the past.

Of course, as time went on, and as alchemical literature

Scholem cites ZOHAR I, 249b-250a; II, 23b-24b; II, 147a, 148a; and II, 171. But again they are not alchemical in the sense of alchemical symbolism, as this is known among us by the witness of its western literature. We hear of the solar rays shining straight on mountain summits in the days of Solomon and turning earth to gold; of gold, silver, copper and iron being made of the four elements; of gold under the presidency of Gabriel and silver under that of Michael; of silver corresponding to mercy and gold to severity; of gold representing joy; and of seven kinds of gold, the seventh of which is celestial, illumines all and cannot be contemplated by the eye. All this is not Alchemy, and I agree with Dr. Scholem when he says otherwise that the Hermetic Quest was one thing and that of Kabbalism another.

[1] It is fair, however, to state that the Leyden papyrus which contains the earliest known process of alchemical sophistication forms part of a Gnostic and Theurgic collection. On this point, see Berthelot's COLLECTION DES ANCIENS ALCHIMISTES GRECS, livraison Ie., pp. 6 et seq. Albert Poisson, whose THÉORIES ET SYMBOLES DES ALCHIMISTES is a contribution of consequence to the elucidation of Hermetic Art, observes that " Alchemy among the Greeks was, by reason of its very origin, mixed up with Magic and Theurgy. Later on, thanks to the philosophic Arabs, this science became purified, and it was not till the fifteenth or sixteenth century that it allied itself afresh with the occult sciences properly so called. Thenceforth a considerable number of alchemists demanded the Key of the Great Work from the Kabbalah, Magic and Alchemy."—Op. cit., p. 27. Paris, 1891.

[2] See THE CHINESE, by Dr. W. A. P. Martin, New York, 1881.

[3] The most accessible work of reference is Isaac Myer's PHILOSOPHY OF IBN GEBIROL, Appendix B. I mention this hypothesis so that it may be taken for what it is worth. See Book II, § 5. But see also my SECRET TRADITION IN ALCHEMY, cap. v.

developed in Europe, a connection undoubtedly arose with the Kabbalah.[1] The ÆSH MEZAREPH is one of its evidences; some Kabbalists became alchemists; a few alchemists studied the Kabbalah. But it is still a slight and occasional connection, which we must be careful not to exaggerate: there is also very little trace of it prior to the seventeenth century,[2] when writers like Fludd concerned themselves with both subjects, and Khunrath[3] introduced Kabbalistic symbolism into the pictorial emblems of transmutation.[4]

The best proof of these statements is the literary history of the ÆSH MEZAREPH itself. Mathers in his pretentious manner observes that it is "known to few, and when known is understood by still fewer."[5] If this were its position in the year 1887, it may be added that when Alchemy most flourished in the West, the treatise had never been heard of, being first mentioned by Rosenroth at the end of the seventeenth century. Prior to that date there is no case within my knowledge of its quotation by any alchemist, and although KABBALA DENUDATA was described on its title-page as *Scriptum omnibus philologis, philosophis, theologis omnium religionum*, atque PHILOCHYMICIS *quam utilissimum*, I believe that only one alchemical writer concerned himself with it after the appearance of its fragments among the *Apparatus in Librum Sohar*. This was the "Lover of Philalethes," already cited, who collected and translated the fragments in 1714 and also published in the same year A SHORT ENQUIRY CONCERNING THE HERMETIC ART,[6] which introduces certain citations from ÆSH

---

[1] "Alchemy, a science of observation, could not profit in any way by its alliance with the Kabbalah, which was purely a speculative science."—Poisson, THÉORIES ET SYMBOLES DES ALCHIMISTES, p. 28.

[2] Poisson refers this confusion of one occult science with another mainly to Paracelsus, but I have given proof already of the very slender connection between this adept and the Esoteric Tradition of the Jews.

[3] AMPHITHEATRUM SAPIENTIÆ ÆTERNÆ, with which compare the second tract of the TRINUM CHEMICUM, Strasbourg, 1700.

[4] There is a treatise entitled THE AZOTH OF THE PHILOSOPHERS which passes under the name of Basil Valentine, and has suggested a connection with Kabbalism to a few, because the term AZOTH is composed of the first and final letters of the Greek, Latin and Hebrew alphabets. It has been called into requisition accordingly, but the foundation is exceedingly slight. Moreover, the term is at least as old as pseudo-Geber, while the treatise attributed to Basil Valentine is of doubtful authenticity, and was excluded from the collection of Mangetus.

[5] THE KABBALAH UNVEILED, Introduction, p. 15. He belonged to the second class.

[6] Reprinted in Wynn Westcott's COLLECTANEA HERMETICA, vol. 3, London, 1894; the preface, which is not by the editor, states that the SHORT ENQUIRY was "written with special reference" to ÆSH MEZAREPH, but there seems no foundation for this view. The little tract is largely a collection of opinions and quotations, not always

MEZAREPH and connects them with the symbolism of the Doves of Diana first introduced into Alchemy by Eirenæus Philalethes.

It follows, however, from what has been stated previously that the literary connection between the Kabbalah and Alchemy does not begin so late as the first quarter of the eighteenth century [1]; and though ÆSH MEZAREPH seems to have been cited methodically by only one writer, the influence of KABBALA DENUDATA may be traced in Germany soon after its publication by means of an anonymous tract which pretends to treat of the Chemical Kabbalah [2] (*cabala chymica*) and has these words on its headline. This little work is incidentally of importance in more than one respect. On p. 16 there is a curious *Figura Cabalæ*, where the light from *Ens Entium* falls on a bearded figure holding the compass in the right and the square in the left hand, thus giving two characteristic symbols of Emblematic Masonry in connection with the secret arts at a date when such a connection would scarcely be expected on the Continent by modern scholarship. There are also some observations worth noting on the subject of regeneration which are useful for the mystical aspects of Alchemy.[3] Unfortunately the correspondences between the Kabbalah and transmutation seem to be confined to the title which I have quoted.

Some information on the subject might be expected—among works of the past—in Hoefer's HISTORY OF CHEMISTRY,[4] which claims to include an exposition of Kabbalistic doctrines concerning the Philosophical Stone;

---

derived from the best sources, for its author appears to regard Edward Kelley and Elias Ashmole as of equal authority with the acknowledged adepts of Alchemy.

[1] I except such slender analogies as the correspondence traced by *Sapere Aude* between the three worlds of Jean D'Espagnet and the four worlds of the Kabbalists. See HERMETIC ARCANUM, Collectanea Chemica, vol. 1 (Westcott's Edition), London, 1893.

[2] CABALÆ VERIOR DESCRIPTIO: *das ift, Brundliche Beschriebungund Enveisung aller naturaliscben und uber naturaliscben Dingen boiedurch das Verbum Fiat das alles erschasun* . . . Hamburg, 1680. There was a later edition, Frankfort, 1761.

[3] A work of similar pretensions is F. Kiern's CABALA CHYMICA: *concordantia chymica, Azoth Philosophicum Solificatum*, Mülhausen, 1606. Here the term Cabala is simply a catchword derived from Paracelsus, and is used in this sense by a compiler belonging to the group of Paracelsian exponents, of whom Benedictus Figulus and Alexander von Suchten are the names now most remembered or least forgotten.

[4] Ferdinand Hoefer: HISTOIRE DE LA CHIMIE *depuis les temps les plus reculés jusqu'à notre époque ; comprenant une analyse detaillée des MSS. alchimiques de la Bibliothèque Royale de Paris ; un exposé des doctrines cabalistiques sur la Pierre Philosophale*, etc., 2 vols., Paris, 1842, 1843. Mr. H. C. Bolton observes that this work is superseded so far as MSS. are concerned by the researches of Berthelot. See A SELECT BIBLIOGRAPHY OF CHEMISTRY, Smithsonian Miscellaneous Collections, Washington, 1893, p. 119.

but the term proves on examination to be used in the loose sense of the period, and out of two very large volumes there are only two pages devoted to the subject of the Kabbalah.[1] The authorship of the SEPHER YETZIRAH is attributed to R. Akiba and that of the ZOHAR to R. Simeon. It is affirmed also that Jewish and Arabian alchemists possessed an old knowledge of Kabbalistic books, and that they were held by adepts in as much honour as those of Hermes Trismegistus. The evidence is unfortunately wanting, and as M. Hoefer maintains also that the science of transmutation was pursued in ancient Egypt, it would be unsafe to accept his opinion unsupported by other authority.[2]

Before dismissing the Kabbalistic connections of Alchemy, a word must be said concerning two works which have been supposed to be examples of that connection, and to which some importance has been attached.[3] Both have the advantage, which they share in common with Khunrath and his AMPHITHEATRUM, of precedence over the publication of Rosenroth's KABBALA DENUDATA, and one is prior to any printed edition of the ZOHAR. It will be needless to say that neither shews an acquaintance with ÆSH MEZAREPH, nor do I observe in their contents anything to connect them with the Sephirotic attribution of metals which is characteristic of that work. One is a treatise by Joannes Augustinus Pantheus, a Venetian priest, entitled ARS ET THEORIA TRANSMUTATIONIS METALLICÆ, *cum Voarchadumia Proportionibus, muneris et iconibus rei accomodis illustrata*. It was published at Venice in April, 1530.[4] Following the author himself, the Hermetic Lexicons interpret Voarchadumia, (*a*) as "a liberal art gifted with the virtues of occult science," a definition which leaves something to be desired; (*b*) as the Kabbalistic science of metals. It is further a species of alchemical metallurgy,

---

[1] T. i., pp. 242–244.
[2] There is indeed one authority cited, namely, the APPARATUS of Rosenroth, KAB. DEN., i., 441–443, and this is a quotation from the ÆSH MEZAREPH, c. 7.
[3] There are others naturally in the large literature of Alchemy, but they are not of Hermetic value, and, as in all cases, the Kabbalistic connection is thin and elusive. Such is the PHILOSOPHIA SALOMONIS, *or Secret Cabinet of Nature*, a German anonymous treatise published at Augsburg in 1753. Here the Royal Stone of Alchemy is connected with the art of King Solomon, but there is no Kabbalistic knowledge, and the work is quite worthless. See also : Cabala : SPIEGEL DER KUNST UND NATUR IN ALCHYMIA, Augsburg, 1690, remarkable for its curious folding plates.
[4] Rare in the original edition, but rendered accessible by the reprint in Lazarus Zetner's THEATRUM CHEMICUM, Argentorati, 1613, etc., second edition, 1659. See vol. ii., pp. 459 *et seq.* A Paris edition of the tract is mentioned also, date 1550.

concerning "auriferous metallic veins"; it explains "the intrinsic fixed form and the natural yellow colour of gold"; it distinguishes the heterogeneous, combustible, volatile parts, and exhibits how the same may be conducted to the grade of perfection. It defines, lastly, the Matter of the work as "a heavy, corporeal, fixed, fusible, ductile, tinged, rarefied and arcane substance of Quicksilver or Mercury, and of an incombustible Metallic Sulphur, educed and transmuted into true gold by means of cementation."[1] It will be seen from this specimen of style that the work is very nearly unreadable, even for an alchemical treatise, and it will be enough for the present purpose to note the fact of its existence and to observe that it seeks to throw light on the mysteries of transmutation by calculations of GEMATRIA. It exercised no influence, and no importance can be ascribed to it.

The other work is much better known to fame and it offers several interesting, and so far unsolved, problems to the student. This is the MONAS HIEROGLYPHICA of Dr. John Dee, first published in 1564, and containing an analysis of the planetary symbols attributed to the metals.[2] Thus, the symbol of Mercury ☿ is composed of the crescent ☽, which is the sign of silver, the circle ☉, which is that of gold, and the cross representing the four elements. Special alchemical importance is attributed to their union in the sign which represents the fundamental matter of the philosophers as well as metallic quicksilver. It will be seen that this is not in any sense information which helps to connect Alchemy with Kabbalism, though it is important for the obscure question of the symbolism and history of astronomical signs.[3]

I may observe in conclusion that there is one possible connection between Alchemy and Kabbalism which would appear to be overlooked by all those who have instituted a comparison between them. It is supplied by the obscure but subsisting analogies between the ancient document of Latin

---

[1] See the anonymous English translation of Martinus Rulandus: LEXICON ALCHEMIÆ, *sive Dictionarium Alchemisticum*, the edition of 1612. This translation, without date or place, was restricted to six copies, and includes a large SUPPLEMENT to the Alchemical Lexicon of Martinus Rulandus. The explanation of *Voarchadumia* occurs on p. 438.

[2] For the astrological aspect of this analysis, see some curious speculations in Alan Leo's PRACTICAL ASTROLOGY, second edition, *n.d.*

[3] For information and references see § xliv. of the ECLAIRCISSEMENT ASTRONOMIQUE appended to M. Bailly's HISTOIRE DE L'ASTRONOMIE ANCIENNE, 2nd edition, Paris, 1781.

Alchemy known as TURBA PHILOSOPHORUM [1] and the two Synods of the ZOHAR. I am not, of course, referring to the accidental similarity of form, though, having regard to the history of the TURBA, this accident is certainly a feature of interest. There are statements and allusions in this obscure colloquy, more especially regarding the four elements of ancient chemistry, which offer curious points of contact with Kabbalism. When we add to this that some scholars—including Berthelot—have referred the TURBA in the guise that we at present possess it to a Hebrew original, now lost, and that its date, so far as it can be assigned, is somewhere between the promulgation of the BOOK OF FORMATION and the ZOHAR, enough has been said in indication of a possibility upon which there is no need, as indeed there are few materials, to insist further.[2]

III.—THE KABBALAH AND ASTROLOGY

The Victorian schools of French and English Kabbalism were inclined, as remarked already, to claim that all " occult sciences " are rooted in the Secret Tradition of Israel ; but it seems more correct to infer that the Kabbalah has been engrafted on some of them, and in this manner we have

---

[1] See TURBA PHILOSOPHORUM, or Assembly of the Sages, called also the Book of Truth in the Art, and the third Pythagorical Synod . . . Translated from the Latin . . . By A. E. Waite, London, 1896. I must confess that I have no theory as to the two previous Synods.

[2] It is due to my readers, and to the subject, to confess that I have not made an exhaustive examination of alchemical literature in reference to its connections with Kabbalism. I have made myself acquainted with all sources which have been cited by those who affirm them, but as their observations have not been based upon a wide study of the alchemists, it is possible that future researches may discover something which has, so far, been overlooked on both sides. I should note also that, according to M. Berthelot, " the Kabbalah was bound up during the middle ages with Alchemy, and the connection goes far back," that is, to the Leyden Papyrus as well as to the Greek alchemists. But I infer that this great authority has, so far as the mediæval period is concerned, received only a derived impression, or that at least his notion of the Kabbalah has been obtained as such notions most commonly are. All his instances as to the earlier connections must be rejected decisively. Some of them, such as the LABYRINTH OF SOLOMON, have been dealt with already ; others are mere names—Abraham, Isaac, Jacob and the word Tsabaoth " in papyri of the same family as No. 75 of Reuvens." It is further obvious that a reference by Zosimus to Solomon and his wisdom establishes no Kabbalistic analogy. Finally, when the Greek alchemist traces the revelation of the Sacred Art from the Egyptians to the Jews, " who published it to the rest of the world," we must remember that this view belongs to a period which referred all science and philosophy to the chosen people on the principle of Aristobulus and Philo, so that this also proves nothing. *Les Origines de l'Alchimie* . . . Observe that Watt's BIBLIOTHECA BRITANNICA, ii., 179 *n*, gives a reference to a work by H. C. van Byler, entitled, TRACTATUS CABBALISTICO—CHYMICO—PHILOSOPHICO—MAGICUS. Cologne, 1729, but I am not acquainted with its contents.

Kabbalistic Astrology, as we have also Kabbalistic Alchemy. To determine the superior accuracy of either view we must have recourse exclusively to history and literature. It is only in the instance of Ceremonial Magic that the voice of both is unanimously in favour of a Kabbalistic origin as regards the western world. From *a priori* considerations we shall be disposed to believe that the case of Astrology will prove something like that of Alchemy, namely, that its history and literature contain little to connect it essentially with Jewry, outside the casual traditions and express condemnation of the ZOHAR. It has the air of an exact science and seems to suggest few possible analogies with the speculations of a theosophical system. There are two facts, however, which are above challenge, firstly, that the Jews were much addicted to Astrology,[1] and, secondly, that the prophetic science of the stars, as it is known in the West, has derived something from later Hebrews. Against these must be placed two other facts, not of less significance, namely, that ancient Israel contributed very little to the science of astronomy, that Jewish astronomical writings belonging to the Christian centuries draw chiefly from Arabia, and that as regards Astrology in Jewry, during the Kabbalistic period, it was imbedded in fantastic notions and puerile processes. We are not called to deal here with the history of the art: we know that Josephus traces it to Seth and assures us that he himself had visited the two famous Pillars reported to have survived the deluge, and on which all the rules of Astrology are said to have been engraved. Josephus may have been deceived easily, or he may have been tempted to claim for his nation on the warrant of a fable the precedence in a study to which the notion of learning was attached. Seth and the Pillars set apart, we know also that antique Chaldea was a great centre of Astrology, that it flourished among the Babylonians, that it was practised in Egypt; and it is natural to suppose that the Jews must have had their share in the knowledge of each of these peoples. There may have been even a Kabbalah

---

[1] The question whether the art was condemned by the Law of Israel has been a subject of some debate, and we have made acquaintance with Zoharic intimations on the theosophical side of the subject. Perhaps the best opinion considered that it was. See on this point the CONCILIATOR of Menasseh ben Israel *sive de conventia locorum S. Scripturæ quæ pugnare inter se videntur*, Frankfort, 1633, p. 142. It was debated also by Gaffarel, writing from the Christian standpoint. He contrived to defend the art by distinguishing it into two branches.

of astrological procedure communicated to Christian times.[1] All this, however, is beside the real question; we are not justified in looking for the ZOHAR or its influence in Jewish writings on mathematics or natural philosophy, for the simple reason that the ZOHAR does not connect seriously with these subjects. We are at liberty, however, to ask ourselves one question. Astrology works upon data which are very obscure in their history,[2] and there are doctrines connected with it which even to the "occult student" may seem insufficiently grounded. It would be interesting to ascertain whether they have any Kabbalistic correspondences, notwithstanding the condemnation of the ZOHAR. As to the data, I suppose that no one has attempted to institute a parallel, but it has been thought that some astrological theorems may have a connection with Kabbalistic apparatus. Let us see therefore what is said upon this subject by its students.

The attribution of metals to the SEPHIROTH in ÆSH MEZAREPH suggests planetary attribution, and a tabulation has been constructed by Papus,[3] following the authority of Kircher:—

1. KETHER corresponds to the Empyrean.
2. CHOKMAH   „   „ Primum Mobile.
3. BINAH   „   „ Firmament.
4. CHESED   „   „ Saturn.
5. GEBURAH   „   „ Jupiter.
6. TIPHERETH   „   „ Mars.
7. NETZACH   „   „ Sun.
8. HOD   „   „ Venus.
9. JESOD   „   „ Mercury.
10. MALKUTH   „   „ Moon.

It is possible, as ÆSH MEZAREPH affirms, that "all systems tend to the one truth," but this scheme is not in accordance with either of its own attributions. These are followed by

---

[1] P. Christian affirms that there was, but he offers no evidence in support of his assertion that the SPECULUM ASTROLOGIÆ of Junctin was a kind of synthesis of the astrological labours of the "Arabian and Hebrew Kabbalists."—HISTOIRE DE LA MAGIE, l. vii., Clefs générales de L'Astrologie, p. 579.

[2] The history, moreover, has never been elucidated by any writer on the subject. Mr. W. Gorn Old's NEW MANUAL, 1898, does not attempt to account for the grounds on which the old judgments are based.

[3] For Papus consult LA KABBALE, already cited frequently; for Kircher ŒDIPUS ŒGYPTIACUS. The synopsis of the Kabbalah in this rare work has been translated recently into French.

Rosenroth; but R. P. Esprit Sabathier, in that strange little treatise on Kabbalism which once exercised so much fascination on French students of the subject, refers Mars to GEBURAH and Mercury to HOD.[1] When there is no unanimity we must infer that there is no point of importance involved and that attributions and tabulations of this kind are less or more conventional and can have little application to Astrology itself. In modern times, however, all divinatory practices, which in every case possess or suggest astrological connections,[2] have received some kind of Kabbalistic attribution. Thus, the planetary correspondences of the figures used in geomancy have been adjusted to the SEPHIROTH; Kabbalistic principles have been applied to chiromancy; physiognomy alone, possibly because it has never had much attention at the hands of professed occultists, seems an exception to this rule, although, as we have seen previously, there is direct warrant for it in the ZOHAR.[3]

The most accessible information on Astrology among the Jews is in the CURIOSITIES of James Gaffarel, who based his observations on a direct knowledge of its chief rabbinical exponents during the Christian centuries.[4] To reduce what he says to a sentence, the Jewish astrologers read the heavens like a book, they regarded it as a book, and, for the purposes of methodising its contents with a view to its interpretation, they collected the stars into hieroglyphic characters, which were, in fact, the Hebrew alphabet. Their process was therefore not an astrological process, but more correctly one of divination, and as to its value, we have only to glance at the Hebrew planisphere furnished by Gaffarel to see how arbitrary was the nature of the arrangement. At the same time it suggests a correspondence with the fundamental

---

[1] See L'OMBRE IDÉALE DE LA SAGESSE UNIVERSELLE, 1679. A reprint of this work has appeared in Paris. The original is rare, and there is no copy in the British Museum; but the reader may consult the Table given by Papus at pp. 80, 81 of his treatise on the Kabbalah, where the attribution in question will be found.

[2] Thus, the PRINCIPLES OF ASTROLOGICAL GEOMANCY became the subject of a special treatise by Franz Hartmann, M.D. (London, 1899), while Rosa Baughan compiled a curious medley of Chiromancy and Astrology under the title of THE INFLUENCE OF THE STARS.

[3] Physiognomy has been, of course, connected with Astrology, and an old work published about the beginning of the seventeenth century under the title of BOOK OF PALMISTRY, PHYSIOGNOMY AND NATURAL ASTROLOGY illustrates this connection. See also A TREATISE ON ZODIACAL PHYSIOGNOMY, by John Varley, London, 1828.

[4] A summary of Gaffarel's information, with some pertinent criticisms, will be found in Éliphas Lévi's RITUEL DE LA HAUTE MAGIE. See also TRANSCENDENTAL MAGIC, part ii., and MYSTERIES OF MAGIC, pp. 248, 252, 253, 254. Second edition, 1897.

notion of SEPHER YETZIRAH, though the fact has not been observed by any previous writer. There could be nothing more natural for those who believed that the heavens and the earth were made by the inscription of letters in the air than to discover these letters in the configurations, apparently fortuitous, of the starry heavens.[1] In place therefore of the unmeaning mythological figures of pagan antiquity they imagined the twenty-two elements of the divine word manifested to the chosen people, and the imagination once justified by the apparent delineation of the characters, it became part of the scheme of the universe.[2] To read the sense of the heavens so that they could give the meaning thereof was an operation no less sacred in its intention, mysterious in its methods, and strange in its results[3] than the application of Zoharistic processes to the disentangling of the mystical meaning beneath the letter of the Scriptures. This is the true Kabbalistic Astrology,[4] based on a Kabbalistic Doctrine which is its justification and of which it is in turn the logical development. Outside the SEPHER YETZIRAH, it has the countenance of the ZOHAR itself. But it has little in common with the science of the stars, as this has been pursued in the western world; it can offer nothing in evidence of its considerations, even as Astrology in the West has nothing to tell us concerning the Kabbalistic Mystery of AIN SOPH. It is better therefore not to confuse further the complicated issues of occult arts by the suggestion of fantastic influences and unrealisable communications.[5]

It will be anticipated of course that a literature so large as

---

[1] These are the Celestial Letters mentioned previously, or at least their cosmic counterparts.

[2] This is the Zoharic notion, and it was claimed that by means of the signs and figures in the heavens most profound secrets and mysteries could be discovered. So regarded, the stars and constellations are a subject of contemplation and a source of mysterious delight for the sage.—Zohar, ii., 76a, Mantua.

[3] Compare those other strange results in Symbolical Astrology of which Ruysbroeck the Mystic speaks in the BOOK OF THE TWELVE BEGUINES, Latinised by Surius under the title *De Vera Contemplations*. Needless to say this Astrology is not judicial. The late Mr. Hargrave Jennings has also some pleasing fantasies on the "astronomy of the mind" in THE INDIAN RELIGIONS, pp. 207 *et seq.*, London, 1890.

[4] Which Astrology, as Lévi observes rightly, must be distinguished from what is commonly understood by Judicial Astrology. See MYSTERIES OF MAGIC, p. 247.

[5] As an instance of the extraordinary lengths to which speculations of this kind have been carried, outside astronomical connections, see Dr. J. Lamb's HEBREW CHARACTERS DERIVED FROM HIEROGLYPHS, London, 1835. The hieroglyphics in question are "re-constituted," and various doctrines, passages and words of the sacred writings are interpreted by recourse to them. But it happens unfortunately that scholarship had yet to do its work in the light of the Rosetta Stone.

that of the Jews and embracing, as we said at the inception of our inquiry, so wide a range of subjects could not have grown up without contributing anything to the knowledge of the heavens. In the third century the Jews of Babylon have been called famous as doctors and astronomers and, partly for this reason, are said to have been in high credit at the Persian Court during the reign of the usurper Artaxerxes. Samuel Lunaticus, to whom astronomical tables are attributed, the head of the Academy of Naharden, is an instance in point, and R. Ada, also of Naharden, is another. Abba Aricha, better known as the Babylonian Rav, founder of the Academy of Sora, was an early student of astronomy, and names might be multiplied easily. Side by side with medicine and the interpretation of dreams, Astrology was pursued by eastern Jews of the tenth and eleventh centuries. In 1150, or thereabouts, R Avi Joseph wrote a treatise on the intelligences which move the heavens and concerning the judgment of the stars. Aben Ezra, about the same period, is a considerable name among astronomers of Jewry as well as in doctrine and philosophy. Abraham Chiia and Abraham Nasi are also contemporary students of the same art. In the second half of the thirteenth century, during the reign of Alphonso X., King of Castile, himself called the astrologer, the rabbins were in estimation for their knowledge of the heavens, and the Tables attributed to Alphonso were the work of a Jew whom he employed. In the fifteenth century the family of Alcadet produced two astronomers, and Abraham Zacut, author of the SEPHER YUHASIN, was another student of the subject in the days of Ferdinand and Isabella.

Meagre as are these indications, having regard to the fact that astronomy was pursued usually in connection with the judgment of the stars, *i.e.*, with Judicial Astrology, they are sufficient to establish that this occult practice is to be found in Jewry during most of the Christian centuries.

The reader who desires to become acquainted with the first principles and procedure of Jewish Astrology may consult the CURIOSITIES of Gaffarel, whose information is drawn from R. Moses, R. Aben Ezra, R. Jacob Kapol ben Samuel, &c. This learned but pedantic writer rejected what is called Kabbalistic Astrology, with its Sephirotic attributions [1]; but

---

[1] So far as I am aware, no astrological work developing these connections has ever been printed in any European language, but books like John Bishop's MARROW OF

the system which he develops is not less fantastic, and is that indeed which I have described briefly in an earlier part of the present section. It would be out of place to extend references, for, as on the one hand Sephirotic Astrology is set aside even by so determined a Kabbalist as Gaffarel, so, on the other, the secrets of the Hebrew planisphere and the mysteries of stellar writing do not connect with the practice of the art in the West.

It may be added that a contemporary writer, Mr. W. Gorn Old, has published a Kabbalistic Astrology [1]; but it is merely a process of divination, like that attributed to Cagliostro, which was developed at great length and applied to the science of the stars by P. Christian.[2] It is obvious that the use of the term Kabbalistic in such a connection is merely a *façon de parler*, unfortunately in very common use. This is made further evident by the parallel application of the term Hermetic, not only as an analogue, but an actual equivalent. Mr. Old's process is affirmed to have been "in use among the ancient Kabbalists," but this is merely speculative and an inference from certain alleged Tarot connections.

IV.—THE KABBALAH AND FREEMASONRY

The researches and findings of Masonic scholarship notwithstanding, occult reverie has not emerged altogether from the old maze of fables concerning the origin of Speculative Freemasonry. Even now, in France and England, it is thought by uncritical writers to have a past extending behind it into remote ages. In one or another sense it is still a survival of the Ancient Mysteries; but this term is used in a general sense, not as signifying only the initiations of Egypt, of Greece, or of Rome, but rather the secret power and intelligence which is thought to have been present behind the philosophical associations of all ages and most civilised countries. During the Christian period the knowledge which would otherwise have perished was preserved *ex*

ASTROLOGY, London, 1688, with its list of the governing angels of the signs and the planets, suggest Kabbalistic connections through the vehicle of Ceremonial Magic.

[1] KABALISTIC ASTROLOGY, *or Your Fortune in your Name*, by Sepharial, London, n.d. (? 1892). It has been mentioned in a previous note.

[2] In his HISTOIRE DE LA MAGIE, books ii., iii., and vi. Also in L'HOMME ROUGE DES TUILERIES. Some account of Cagliostro's Method will be found in Grand Orient's MANUAL OF CARTOMANCY, &c., of which several editions have appeared.

hypothesi among successive occult fraternities, some known to history, such as Templars and Rosicrucians, the rest working in complete silence. Corporately or otherwise, they were all affiliated with each other, and Symbolical Freemasonry forms the last link in the western chain of transmission.

As there is little need to say, no presentation of this hypothesis has been able to survive analysis, and it is left at most with a possible connection between Masonry and Rosicrucianism, a little before and after the Grand Lodge epoch of 1717. The evidence is, however, inconclusive, or at least unextricated.[1] This being the state of the case, and the claim on antiquity which is made for Freemasonry by some of its unwise votaries not having been urged by the institution on its own behalf outside the Rituals, there is nothing *prima facie* to accredit the idea that it has been ever a channel of any Secret Tradition except its own, or to warrant us in supposing *a priori* that it should have any distinct analogies with Kabbalism. And as a fact its position in this respect is much like that of Alchemy, seemingly fortuitous, a question of subsequent introduction, as much imputation as reality, a varnish rather than a permeating tincture, and yet, like all such positions, interesting. To establish my point, I must refer to the fact that since Masonry appeared on the historical plane, occultists and even mystics have tended towards it, that it has received them all amiably, and that—now, of course, in the past—all have elaborated the system in accordance with their particular notions. During the prevalence of the passion for Rites we know that alchemists, Swedenborgians,[2] Martinists, theurgists, astrologers, all invented new Grades and new Orders, and as at this period there were also Kabbalists, so in one or two instances we hear of Kabbalistic Rites, especially of Rites and Grades which exhibit Kabbalistic influences. As Freemasonry is not Swedenborgianism, as it is not Alchemy, as in spite of Elect Cohenim, the Evocations and Rituals of Pasqually, and the pretended marvels of Schrœpfer, it is not

---

[1] See, however, my BROTHERHOOD OF THE ROSY CROSS, *cap.* xvi, pp. 443–446; also my EMBLEMATIC FREEMASONRY, II, pp. 21–45.
[2] The history of the Swedenborgian Rite being exceedingly obscure, and yet possessing considerable occult interest, it may be observed that some account of it was published at New York in 1870 by Samuel Beswick. It is not to be trusted, however, on the score of accuracy.

Theurgy or Magic, nor—unless at its root—the Mysticism of any of the true Mystics, so it is not Kabbalism, but it has been put to use in Kabbalistic as in other interests.

It must be added that the few Kabbalistic Degrees which have left any record behind them beyond their name, and the uncommon swiftness with which they passed into extinction, give no evidence of acquaintance with Jewish Esoteric Tradition. They represent the Kabbalism of the period. There is no need to speculate as to its quality in most cases; it has bequeathed its literary remains in Grimoires and Grand Clavicles, in the spurious thaumaturgic processes of Abramelin, and in amusing Kabbalistic correspondence with the Seigneur Astaroth,[1] the lees and lavations of rabbinical conduits. As it will be well to enforce these statements by means of documentary evidence, I will add an account of one Kabbalistic Grade which may be taken to represent the whole. It is otherwise among the best of its kind.

A degree of Knight of the Kabbalah once existed among those innumerable developments of the Fraternity which were termed high by their disciples and spurious by some who resented innovations, and especially those which led to nothing. It has long since fallen into disuse. The object of the Candidate, according to the Catechism of the Degree, was "to know, by means of numbers, the admirable harmony which subsists between Nature and Religion." It defines the Kabbalist as a man who has acquired the Sacerdotal Art and the Royal Art by the communication of Tradition. The device was *Omnia in numeris sita sunt*. The Master of the Lodge in which the Degree was communicated seems to have been called President of the Sanhedrim and Rabbi. The mystical significance of numbers [2] was developed by the Catechism in a somewhat curious manner, which it may be worth while to summarise.

I = in the moral order, a Word incarnate in the bosom of a virgin, otherwise, Religion; in the physical order, a spirit embodied in the virgin earth, or Nature. It is the

---

[1] See D'Argens: LETTRES CABALISTIQUES, *ou Correspondance Philosophique ... entre deux Cabalistes*, &c., 7 vols., La Haye, 1754.
[2] The numerical mysticism of the Kabbalah is based, of course, on the SEPHIROTH; most of its developments are very late, and possess a magical complexion, for which reasons they do not enter into the scheme of this study. Those who are concerned may consult an attempt to simplify chronology by Kabbalistic figures in Michael Aitsinger's PENTAPLUS REGNORUM MUNDI, Antwerp, 1579. On the general subject, see Petrus Bargus: MYSTICÆ NUMERORUM SIGNIFICATIONIS LIBER, Bergomi, 1585.

generative number in the order of Divinity—apparently a false symbolism, because the monad neither generates nor is generated, whence Éliphas Lévi says more correctly that the monad supposes the duad, and thence, through the triad, all numbers are evolved.

II = in the moral order, man and woman; in the physical, active and passive. It is the generative number in created things.

III = in the moral order, the three theological virtues; in the physical, the three principles of bodies. The reference here is to Salt, Sulphur and Mercury, thus indicating the Hermetic connections of this Grade. Three also denotes the triple Divine Essence.

IV = the four cardinal virtues, the four elementary qualities—another Hermetic reference—and it is, moreover, the most mysterious of numbers, because it contains all the Mysteries of Nature.

V = the quintessence of religion, and the quintessence of matter—which again is alchemical. It is also the most occult number, " because it is enclosed in the centre of the series." The precise meaning of this last statement does not appear, but it may possibly refer to the pentagram as one of the emblems of the Grade.

VI = the theological cube and the physical cube. It is the most salutary number, " because it contains the source of our spiritual and corporeal happiness." Is this a reference to the symbolical adultery of the first man whereby the coming of the Liberator was necessitated?

VII = the seven sacraments and the seven planets. It is the most fortunate number, " because it leads us to the decade, the perfect number."

VIII = the small number of the elect, or the wise. It is the most desirable number, " because he who possesses it is of the cohort of the Sages."

IX = the exaltation of religion and the exaltation of matter. It is the most sublime number, because Religion and Nature are both exalted thereby.

X = the ten commandments and the ten precepts of Nature. It is the most perfect number, " because it includes unity, which created everything, and zero, symbol of matter and chaos, whence everything emerged. In its figures it comprehends the created and uncreated, the beginning and end, power and force, life and annihilation. By the study of this number we find the relations of all things, the power of the Creator, the faculties of the creature, the Alpha and Omega of Divine Knowledge.

XI = the multiplication of Religion and the multiplication of Nature. It is the most multiplying number, "because with the possession of two units, we arrive at the multiplication of things."

XII = the twelve articles of faith; the twelve apostles, foundation of the Holy City, who preached throughout the whole world for our happiness and spiritual joy; the twelve operations of Nature; the twelve Signs of the Zodiac, foundation of the *Primum Mobile*, extending it throughout the universe for our temporal felicity. It is thus the most solid number, being the basis of our spiritual and corporeal happiness.

The numbers after twelve were left to the discernment of the Candidate. The Catechism shews also that this putative chivalry concerned itself with the Universal Spirit of Alchemy and even with the quadrature of the circle. The history of the Knights of the Kabbalah is unfortunately involved in obscurity; but it will be seen that it was Christian and Catholic, which furnishes a resemblance to other and later institutions professing similar purposes and having similar religious sympathies.[1]

Had the BOOK OF OCCULTATION been made in the eighteenth century the theme of a Masonic Grade, had the Lodge represented the Tree, the Master in the East KETHER, and the officers the remaining SEPHIROTH; had the Ritual been constructed from the ZOHAR and the Catechism from the Apparatus of Rosenroth, all this would have proved nothing as to the Kabbalistc connections of Masonry. Within comparatively recent years a powerful Masonic Order underwent a species of development in this direction through the labours of Albert Pike, and it would almost seem that he had a mind to transform the Ancient and Accepted Scottish Rite into a seminary of occult study. There may be many of its own brethren at the present time in whom this statement will excite only incredulity; but it is not the less certain that

---

[1] Among the degrees collected by the French Mason Peuvret, there was that of MAÇON CABBALISTIQUE. The Metropolitan Chapter of France specified the 80th Grade of its mammoth collection on paper by the title of CHEVALIER DE CABALE.

Albert Pike was more than an ardent admirer of occult philosophies, or that he pursued the subject into regions of which Masonry has no conception. He was seconded also by numerous like-minded persons who occupied high dignities in the United States' Southern Jurisdiction.

The evidence of all these things is to be found (*a*) in his transformation of the Rituals, (*b*) in the vast body of instruction which he compiled, chiefly from sources in occult literature, for all Grades of the Order. No person who is acquainted with MORALS AND DOGMA can fail to trace the hand of the occultist therein, and it is to be observed that, passing from Grade to Grade in the direction of the highest, this instruction becomes more and more Kabbalistic. It matters little that the sources from which Pike drew were of the worst rather than the best, or that, though a man of wide reading, he was not a critic; for we are concerned only with a tendency and its development. He accepted *en bloc*, for example, the construction placed on Kabbalism by the most unsafe of all its expounders, Éliphas Lévi, from whom he translated verbatim at great length, and, following his professed habit, with no specific acknowledgment, while for the rest his only source of further information was KABBALA DENUDATA, of which, however, he shews no analytical knowledge, seeming to regard LIBER DRUSHIM as entitled to rank in authority with SIPHRA DI ZENIOUTHA. In spite of these limitations he made available an amount of information on occult subjects with which no previous scheme had ever provided Masonry. Yet with all his strenuous efforts the seal of occultism was not impressed effectually on the Ancient and Accepted Scottish Rite, and it remains therefore that the Oriental Rite of Memphis, Ancient and Primitive,[1] and that of Misraïm,[2] with its long Kabbalistic Class or Series of Degrees, are the only sections of high-grade Masonry which claim a distinct purpose of an occult kind: it is not necessary to say that in England, at least, they have failed in obtaining recognition

---

[1] See Marconis et Moultet: L'HIÉROPHANTE, *développement complet des Mystères Maçonniques*, Paris, 1839. LE RAMEAU D'OR D'ELEUSIS, another work by Marconis, is also interesting as the views of an amiable but somewhat moonstruck student upon the Mysteries in connection with Masonry.

[2] A history of this institution, with all the fabulous and indeed mendacious elements which might be expected, was written by Marc Bédarride and published in two volumes at Paris, 1845, under the title, DE L'ORDRE MAÇONNIQUE DE MISRAÏM, *depuis sa creation jusqu'à nos jours*, &c.

as acceptable developments of Masonry, and both have passed into abeyance.[1]

We see therefore that Kabbalistic influence is confined to so-called High Grades. It would be absurd to discuss the possibility of its presence in the Blue Lodges or seek to interpret the Legend of the Master Grade in connection with Jewish Tradition, outside at least the allegory of the Lost Word. The symbols, however, which are familiar to the initiates of these Lodges do connect with Kabbalism, if not with other forms of occult philosophy; but the presence of the Seal of Solomon among the heirlooms of the Brotherhood being, so far, unaccountable, it is useless to insist on the connection, because nothing logically follows from it. So far as history is concerned, Kabbalism and Masonry once joined hands in the sphere of the Higher Grades, and as a historical fact this is interesting, but that it is otherwise significant must be left to those who affirm it.

V.—THE KABBALAH AND THE TAROT

It is known to innumerable persons who are not occult students at the present day that the Tarot is a method of divination by means of seventy-eight symbolical picture-cards, to which great antiquity and high importance have been attributed by several expositors. Their literary history is also fairly well known. They were mentioned first by the French archæologist Court de Gebelin at the close of the eighteenth century, and were attributed by him to an Egyptian origin. Much about the same time the subject was taken up by a professed cartomancer, named Alliette, who wrote a great deal about them in several illiterate tracts, and endeavoured to trace their connection with Egypt through the Jewish Kabbalah. The inquiry then fell into neglect, except in so far as Continental fortune-tellers were concerned, until the year 1855, when Éliphas Lévi made his first contribution to occult subjects.

In 1857, J. A. Vaillant[2] endeavoured to prove their Chinese

---

[1] The fourth Series of the Rite of Misraïm is designated Kabbalistic.
[2] Histoire Vraie des Vrais Bohémiens. As a notice of the gipsies this work is exceedingly good for its period; its Tarot speculations are worthless, and its philological arguments absurd. M. Vaillant described the Tarot as "the synthesis of ancient faith, a deduction from the sidereal Book of Enoch" (412). Its origin he affirms to be lost in the night of time (413). He mentions the Kabbalah only to establish its connection with Cabul! (p. 54).

origin [1] and transmission by means of the gipsies; their connection with these nomads was adopted subsequently by Lévi, who gave great prominence to the Tarot in all his writings up to the year 1865. The subject was taken in hand also by P. Christian, who published a large HISTORY OF MAGIC in 1870. He developed still further the Egyptian hypothesis, but no statement which he makes can be accepted with the least confidence. In the year 1887 I was the first who introduced the claims of the Tarot to English readers in a digest of the chief works of Éliphas Lévi. A contribution to the inquiry was made shortly after by the French occultist Papus, whose volume entitled the TAROT OF THE BOHEMIANS, though of no critical value on the historical side, remains an elaborate summary of all the arguments which have been produced from the standpoint of occult reverie and invention in France.

The point which concerns us here is, of course, the alleged Kabbalistic connections. Éliphas Lévi says that the Tarot cards are a key to the Esoteric Tradition of the Jews, and "the primitive source of Divine and human Tradition"; he institutes an analogy between the symbols of its four suits and the four letters of the Divine Name TETRAGRAMMATON, and between the ten SEPHIROTH and the ten small cards belonging to each sequence. He gives also the correspondences between the twenty-two Trump Cards and the letters of the Hebrew Alphabet, for which he quotes the authority of "divers Kabbalistic Jews," the fact notwithstanding that there is no trace of any reference to the Tarot by Kabbalistic writers of the past. It must be admitted, on the other hand, although the historical evidences cannot be said to exist, and have been supplied from treasures of imagination, that the Tarot is actually, as it is claimed to be, of considerable importance symbolically. I may be permitted to register also my feeling that it has Kabbalistic connections, some of which were broadly outlined by Éliphas Lévi.

---

[1] Occult writers mostly favour Egypt as the birthplace of the Tarot, and this is consistent with their views on the origin of the Kabbalah. So Mons. Z. Lismon has published a version of the cards under the title of LIVRE DE THOT, *Jeu des 78 Tarots Egyptiens*, with explanatory booklet. Compare R. Falconnier: LES XXII. LAMES HERMÉTIQUES DU TAROT DIVINATOIRE, which pretend to be re-constituted exactly according to "the sacred texts and translation" of the Magic of old Egypt! Of more recent times the Masonic littérateur Oswald Wirth has produced two versions of the Trumps Major, while in England a complete set, of symbolical and artistic value, has appeared under my own auspices.

There is, moreover, a Jewish Tarot of great rarity which has never been published; but it belongs to the worst side of so-called Practical Magic.

Unfortunately, the interpretations of Tarot symbolism which have been attempted by various writers are worthless, in the first place because they have proved themselves incapable of conducting an historical inquiry; they have allowed affirmation to take the place of evidence; they have regarded a hint as a sufficient ground of conviction; they have made conjecture certitude. Setting aside Court de Gebelin, who was merely an inquirer hampered by the limitations of his period; setting aside Lévi, who seldom made an accurate statement about any matter of fact; observe how Papus pursues his inquiry into the origin of the Tarot. It is by an appeal to writers who preceded him, as if their authority were final; to Court de Gebelin, who was a groper in the dark during the childhood of archæological research; to Vaillant, with his fascinating theory of gipsy transmission which is about as conclusive as Godfrey Higgins on the CELTIC DRUIDS; to Lévi, whose "marvellous learning" is so much and so unsafely insisted on by the whole French school. Papus contributes nothing himself to the problem on its historical side except an affirmation that "the game called the Tarot, which the Gypsies possess, is the Bible of Bibles."

In the second place, the supposed Hebrew symbolism of the Tarot, which, in justice to Papus, is laboriously elaborated —though apart from all inspiration—becomes disorganised if there is any doubt as to the attribution of its Trump Cards to the Hebrew Alphabet. Now there is one card which bears no number and is allocated therefore according to the discretion of the interpreter. It has been placed in all cases wrongly, by the uninstructed because they had nothing but their private judgment to guide them, and by some who claimed to know better because they desired to mislead. It happens, however, that they also were at sea. I may go further and say that the true nature of Tarot symbolism is perhaps a secret in the hands of a very few persons, and outside that circle operators and writers may combine the cards as they like and attribute them as they like, but they will never find the right way. The symbolism is, however, so rich that it will give meanings of a kind in whatever manner it may be disposed, and some of these may be suggestive, though illusory none the less. The purpose of this short paper is therefore to shew that published Tarots and the methods of using them may be serviceable for divination, fortune-telling and other trifles; but they are not the key of the Kabbalah, and that the Royal Game of Goose may be recommended with almost as much reason for the same purpose. Papus was therefore misdirecting his many followers when he advertised his involved readings as the " Absolute Key to Occult Science."

VI.—THE KABBALAH AND MYSTICISM

On the one hand the history of Kabbalism is so imbedded in that of mere occultism, that it is scarcely known or admitted in any distinct connection. On the other hand, to the pure mystic, there is so much in the Kabbalistic system which is extrinsic to the subject of Mysticism, that there is a temptation to underrate its influence, though herein is its test of value, and it is a palmary purpose of the present long research to produce the materials and in fine pronounce upon them. I am offering at this point a few preliminary considerations only, based on the fact that Western Mysticism was the channel of a great Tradition in Christian Times.

It is to be observed here and now that the correspondence and difference may perhaps be brought into harmony if it be permissible to regard Mysticism in two ways—as a philosophical doctrine, or rather body of doctrine, that is to say, an ordered metaphysics, held intellectually,[1] but also as a mode of conduct practised with a defined purpose, in a word, as mystical doctrine and mystical life, it being understood that the doctrine is rooted in first-hand experience derived from the course of life. The practical mystic is the saint on the path of his ascent into the mystery of Eternal Union, concerning whom it is consonant with the purpose of our present inquiry to speak at the moment only with great reservation, seeing that the Mysteries of Divine Life do not fall within the limits of historical research. I conceive that the sum of Kabbalistic instruction is not without service to the disciple

---

[1] And this would be the correspondence of the ZOHAR with Mysticism. For example, the doctrine of ecstasy is assuredly found therein, but not in the same way that we find it in Ruysbroeck or St. John of the Cross. It is more especially a rationalised system of mystical thought.

of this secret path, because of the Zoharic doctrine that a science of Holy Unity, into which all things return as all come forth therefrom, can be attained by man.[1] *Invenit sanctum*. Like all other studies, and perhaps not more so than any other methodised Theosophy, it has, moreover, a certain office in the *sanctum facit*. For that far larger class to whom the possibility of great sanctity is denied, who are in search rather of a guide for thought upon questions of fundamental philosophy, I conceive that the Kabbalah—but obviously, like other metaphysics—has useful and reassuring lights. It is a source of intellectual consolation that one of the most barren of all the ways pursued by the human mind has its own strange flowers and fruit. It is also, as I have sought to shew, something more than an inheritance from the past, even an inheritance that has been transmitted from a period far back in human history. The ZOHAR at least has the power of stirring those depths in the human heart which are beyond the "plummet of the sense"; it seems occasionally to "strike beyond all time, and backward sweep through all intelligence," and to say this, is to confess that it is of the eternal soul speaking, here under the common influence of right reason, there in ecstasy and vision, and again, as it would seem in somnambulism or even in frenzy. Now, the speech of the human soul, in what state soever, is not without a message to the mystic, be it even in certain cases a word of warning only. There is no need to add that on its Theosophical side the Kabbalah connects assuredly with Mysticism.[2]

With occultism, of course, it is not without connection on the theurgic side throughout all its history, as the doctrine of Names and their power exhibits but too well. The difference between occultism and Mysticism is much more than that of a Latin equivalent for a Greek term, as might appear at first sight. We are all acquainted with the distinction which is made between the magnetic and hypnotic sleep. They have

---

[1] Zohar, I., 51a, Mantua.
[2] M. Anatole Leroy Beaulieu says that the Jew is not inclined to Mysticism, and seems never to have been so. "Judaism has always been a law, a religion of the mind, an intellectual creed, not favourable to mystic transports or divine languors." He denies also that Kabbalism was indigenous in Jewry. "The mysteries of the Kabbalah, and those of the Hassidim, the neo-Kabbalists, seem to have been a foreign importation; according to the best judges, the Kabbalah itself is not rooted in Judaism."—ISRAEL AMONG THE NATIONS, translated by Francis Hillman, London, 1895, p. 292. This view shews little first-hand acquaintance with the subject.

much in common, but they are pathologically separate, having diverse characteristics and a divergent mode of induction. Sleep, however, is obtained in both, and this is their superficial and obvious point of union—so superficial and so obvious that the ordinary observer would scarcely fail to identify them, while they have been identified also on grounds which are not precisely those of ordinary observation. Between occult arts and mystical science there is the common and rather banal point of union which is created by the inherent notion of secrecy. Beneath this fantastic resemblance there is the more important fact that they both profess to deal with inner and otherwise uninvestigated capacities of the human soul. In the case of occultism it is, however, for the kind of end which we connect with the notions of Magic. For example, Talismanic Magic, so called, is ostensibly the art of infusing a supposed recondite spiritual power into some object composed artificially. This is an operation of occult art because it deals with a power which is, by the hypothesis, of a secret or generally unknown nature and applies it in accordance with the formulæ of a concealed instruction. A knowledge of the capacities which are latent in human nature may suggest Mysticism, which is the development of such capacities in the direction of Divine Union. There is usually, however, no person less really mystic than the occultist conventionally understood, while the mystic on the path of attainment in the life of sanctity is exploring the world of grace, not that of psychic power.

The end of Mysticism is the recovery or attainment of consciousness in God, and there are two exotic Kabbalistic doctrines which not only connect therewith but belong thereto. The first is found—but once only—in the ZOHAR and has been referred to in these pages: it is the doctrine of TSURE, of the supernal part of the soul, which does not leave the Supernals, but from beginning without beginning to endless end is rooted in God for ever. The second is in later Kabbalism and is expressed tersely by Rosenroth in one pregnant Latin sentence: *Linea autem media ascendit usque ad* AYIN SOPH. The ascent of the soul to God is by the Middle Path in the Tree of Life, and the soul is led thereby not only to the World of the Supernals but to the deep beyond the deep and the height beyond the height, which is the abyss and height of Deity. So does the Holy Kabbalah join hands with the Mysticism of all the ages, and so is it part of our inheritance.

[It should be added that TSURE, which signifies Prototype and corresponds to ATZILUTH, is said to be connected with NESHAMAH by "an invisible thread," constituting a bond of union which is also a path of ecstasy. NESHAMAH ascends thereby and attains therein—namely, union with the supernal part.]

BOOK XII
FINAL CONSIDERATIONS

BOOK XII

FINAL CONSIDERATIONS

I.—DEVELOPMENTS OF LATER KABBALISM

The circulation of the ZOHAR by Rabbi Moses de Leon at the end of the thirteenth century—he being its concealed author, according to one section of opinion—proved unquestionably as great a surprise to the community of Israel as it was to the Christian scholars when they came to know of it later. I speak here with a qualification because our first information concerning Zoharic MSS. comes to us from Picus de Mirandula towards the end of the fifteenth century, and we have seen that his was the first voice which testified to the presence of Christian elements therein. On the other hand, the Jewish expositors belong to the sixteenth century and later; but I speak of those who are of repute, and if any one wishes to go farther into the matter there are the great rabbinical bibliographers to tell of things unprinted which are among the treasures of the Vatican and other libraries of Europe.[1] Speaking generally—as I have mentioned elsewhere—the impetus of studies in both directions must be sought in the Cremona and Mantua editions of the ZOHAR. So far as the records are concerned, it must not be said that there is a very large literature on either side; but a few sons of Israel had recourse to the wonderful memorial with as much zeal as Mirandula and his successors. To the better Kabbalistic Jew it offered an illimitable field of development and the indulgence of that particular sort of metaphysical speculation which was dear to his heart at the period. There

---

[1] The most important of the older bibliographies are (1) Johannes Buxtorf: BIBLIOTHECA RABBINICA *novo ordine alphabetico disposita*, 8vo, Basle, 1613. (2) Bartolocci: BIBLIOTHECA MAGNA RABBINICA: *De Scriptoribus et Scriptis Rabbinicis*, 4 vols., Folio, Rome, 1678-92. (3) Imbonatus: BIBLIOTHECA LATINA-HEBRAICA (a sequel to No. 2, by the editor of Bartolocci's work, most of which was published posthumously), Folio, Rome, 1694. (4) O. Christoph. Wolf: BIBLIOTHECA HEBRÆA, 4 vols., 4to, Leipzic, 1715.

could be no greater opportunity, for I have indicated that the ZOHAR assumes throughout a more or less perfect familiarity with the chief heads of its subject, and it is not therefore concerned with presenting a formal system of the Secret Doctrine. The later Kabbalists provided that which was wanted there and here out of their own heads, with the help of any *flotsam* and *jetsam* of theosophical reverie which was passing from mouth to mouth in and about the Academies from Sapeth to Beaucaire. We know that about the middle of the eighteenth century two sects arose in Jewry, claiming the ZOHAR as their authority in chief. One was the sect of Pietists or New HASIDIM, which rejected the TALMUD, together with external forms, and was zealous in the practice of Contemplative Prayer, as recommended by the ZOHAR to those who are in search of inward knowledge concerning Divine Mysteries. It was incorporated for the quest of perfection along these lines.[1] Solomon Maimon has left some particulars concerning the vagaries of these enthusiasts, who were followers of Israel Baal Shem[2]: it survived bitter persecution on the part of orthodox Jewry and was still active in Poland at the middle of the nineteenth century. It is now, I believe, in dissolution rather than decline. The second was the sect of Zoharists who belonged to the same country and were also anti-Talmudic. It was established by Jacob Frank, and it embraced Christianity.[3] I mention these matters, because they shew the kind of influence exercised by the ZOHAR at one period in a particular locality. Of its secret influence on remote continental Jewry, in places like Galicia above all, we shall probably never know, so that the later developments of Kabbalism are without adequate records.

---

[1] I am reflecting current opinion of the eighteenth and nineteenth centuries, but assuring my readers that there is no call for inquiry either as to the kind of perfection or the particular practice of prayer. While it is true that the end of both was spiritual communion with God, the anticipated fruits of this were the gift of prophecy and power to work miracles. Moreover, those who had attained the height of Hasidism acted as mediators between God and the rest of humanity.

[2] Israel ben Eliezer Ba'al Shem Tob, who acquired extraordinary repute as a teacher and yet more as a healer in Podolia, *circa* 1740 and onward.

[3] There is an excellent account of Frank in THE JEWISH ENCYCLOPÆDIA, V, 475–478, to which readers may be referred. He was born in Podolia about 1726 and died in 1791, the work being carried on by his beautiful daughter Eve, who became "the holy mistress" and "the leader of the Sect." At the beginning its conversion to Christianity was in view of a coming Messianic religion. After the death of Eve in 1816, the Frankists of Poland and Bohemia are said to have been transformed gradually "from feigned to real Catholics, and their descendants merged into the surrounding Christian population."

It would serve little purpose to extend this study by additional summaries of contributions made in the sixteenth and seventeenth centuries to the understanding of the ZOHAR. There were scholiasts and expositors outside those who have been considered in the ninth book: some of them produced lexicons dealing with obscure and "foreign" words found in the text; some wrote commentaries on particular sections; some analysed the Kabbalistic system presented in the ZOHAR. In respect of one and all it may be said that for those—if any should remain—who believe in a floating Tradition transmitted from mouth to mouth among the later doctors of Israel, it would be advisable that they should not regard the memorials to which I refer as its representatives in written form. As indicated already in respect of a few examples, that which they did was to reproduce current speculation, to which they added their own. Had the debates at Salamanca been reduced into what FAMA FRATERNITATIS R. C. calls "a true memorial," the later Kabbalists—supposing their admission to the conclave—might have added their quota, and it might have been according to the law and order respecting the rule of debate; but it would have remained within these measures, a sequence of excursions in theses, with an open field in regard to counter-theses. All the contentious voice of certitude notwithstanding, I have not found that the additional literature of Zoharic Kabbalism possesses a higher claim. It seems above all other things certain that on the higher doctrines of the ZOHAR, on Shekinah and the Mystery of Sex, it offers nothing at all.

In comparatively recent days, we have been told by responsible writers that the ZOHAR itself made its own way among the Jews rapidly; that "even representatives of Talmudic Judaism began to regard it as a sacred book"; and that "Zoharic elements . . . crept into the liturgy of the sixteenth and seventeenth centuries."[1] But again the higher teaching did not unfold, or I at least have failed to trace its development. There were poets who arose in Jewry and adopted there and here some elements of Zoharic symbolism; but it was that part which is called by the unhappy name of erotic symbolism, the notion of the Lover and Beloved brought down into terms of sense. Of the soul's supernal

---

[1] JEWISH ENCYCLOPÆDIA, xii, *s.v. Zohar.*

part, which does not leave the Supernals, the poets do not speak, nor do those who were doctors in their day and called Masters in Israel. Of AIN SOPH as a mental proposition or a doctrine of Transcendental Theology we hear from time to time, and may become fairly well acquainted with it on the historicity side; but of experience of the soul in God beyond the forms and images, beyond the names and attributes, there is again nothing. The considerations belong to debate and the expositions have their place in systems, unlike the brief and pregnant sentences in some of the early texts, which speak in comparison from the centre and the great vistas open. They open, that is to say, for some of us, and for one at least of these, confessing in humility, there is new realisation of his own formulary, far in the past years, that the soul comes forth from that centre, and the centre draws it back.

A word may be said in concluding this section on some works of modern scholarship which are considerable and important in their way. When my first study on the Secret Tradition in Jewry was passing through the press, Dr. S. Karppe published at Paris in 1901 his own elaborate ÉTUDE SUR LES ORIGINES ET LA NATURE DU ZOHAR, which approached the subject from a standpoint very different to my own, but was at the same time a valuable contribution to our knowledge of Jewish Theosophy, and I noted with satisfaction that there were various debated points on which, working thus independently, we had reached the same conclusion. Dr. Karppe's study was designed for the scholar and the philosopher, while my own, as explained, was intended, primarily at least, for the theosophical student. The Jewish Mysticism which led up to and preceded the ZOHAR was very fully presented by him, but of the influence exercised by that work and of its after history he had nothing to tell us. On the other hand, the scheme of my own treatise led me of necessity to pass somewhat lightly over pre-Zoharic Theosophy, over Saadyah, Ibn Gebirol, Judah Ha Levi, Aben Ezra, Maimonides, &c., because they did not affect materially the mystical thought of Europe, and give prominence to Kabbalistic literature in its later phases, to the Christian students of the subject, and to its influence upon other proposed channels of Secret Tradition in Europe. Among the points of agreement between Dr. Karppe and myself may be mentioned the common recognition of the heterogeneous nature of the ZOHAR, which justified me in terming it a medley; of the specifically Jewish character of Zoharic Mysticism, which justified me in denying that it is referable exclusively to any one school of thought outside Jewry; of the rapid deterioration of the Kabbalah, subsequent to the appearance of the ZOHAR, into a thaumaturgic system; of the undue prominence which has been given to the commentaries on the ZOHAR and the false impressions which have been the result; of the preconception which governed the mind of most Christian students of the literature, by which they were led to regard it as an unacknowledged depository of Christian doctrine; of the absence in the SEPHER YETZIRAH of any distinctive pantheism or emanationism. There was also considerable similarity, both of thought and treatment, in the development of the Kabbalistic and typically Zoharic doctrines concerning God and the universe, more especially concerning AIN SOPH and creation *ex nihilo*. It would be easy to multiply these instances, nor less easy to furnish numerous points of divergence; for, on the other hand, Dr. Karppe laid too much stress, as I think, on his distinction between the early Jewish Mysticism and that of the Zoharic period, not because such a distinction is either non-existent or unimportant in itself, but because I cannot find that it has been challenged by any qualified writer. And I must, of course, as a mystic, take exception to the conception of Mysticism expressed or implied throughout the whole work. Mysticism is not a double doctrine, whether of monotheism for the initiate and of many deities for the vulgar, or of any other such antithesis as priestcrafts may have devised in the past; but it is outside possibility to do more in the present place than refer to this point and register the bare fact that the students to whom personally I appeal would join issue with Dr. Karppe now, as they must have done then, respecting all that follows from his conception, whether it be a matter of simple definition, such as that Mysticism is a reprisal of faith against science, or of historical criticism, as for example when he observes that the Doctrine of Ecstasy is almost unknown to Jewish Theosophy, a statement, however, which the author himself abundantly, though not explicitly, modifies at a later stage of his study. The student will notice also a tendency in certain instances to pass over questions of criticism as if there had never been a dispute regarding them: on the one hand the commentary of Hay

Gaon is made use of as if no scholar had challenged its authenticity; and, on the other, the late date of the BAHIR is taken for granted. Criticism may not have said its last word on either subject, but Dr. Karppe ignores the criticism.

The work has been long out of print and was tabooed matter from the beginning for the occult circles of Paris, which had eyes only for visions evoked on the subject by the wand of Éliphas Lévi. It was not until after two and twenty years that the next exposition of importance appeared in France, entitled LA KABBALE JUIVE,[1] by M. Paul Vuillaud, and was in a plenary sense of appeal and interest. I had published my second work on Israel and its Secret Doctrine so far back as 1914 and had turned from research thereon into higher fields of Mysticism, when M. Vuillaud brought me back for a season into the old paths of speculation, reminding me of things innumerable and casting new lights as I travelled. It must be said that he brought me also not a little satisfaction which might be called malicious, as I thought of *les écoles esotériques* of Paris ; of their devotion to Éliphas Lévi, the *grand Kabbaliste :* of his egregious MYSTÈRES DE LA KABBALE ; of the excellent Dr. Papus, who had brushed those Mysteries also with the " extreme flounce " of Mrs. Browning and her AURORA LEIGH ; but last of all, Chateau, who took off the Latin vesture of Rosenroth's extracts and having clothed them in French was held to have " translated " the whole ZOHAR. To the confusion of all there was one knocking now at their gates who carried titles of knowledge and had a mind to cast out traffickers in spurious wares from the precincts of the Kabbalistic Temple. *Les écoles* sent Karppe to Coventry, and I suppose that M. Vuillaud will have watched with diversion that conspiracy of silence which awaited him also in those directions.

It is impossible in a short notice to say anything adequate or that can rank even as descriptive of so large a work : I can note only here and there, but with difficulty even then, for one tends to be drawn into side issues through predilection arising from old familiarity with the same paths. An early chapter on Generalities of Jewish Mysticism is full of such temptations, while another is the question of so-called Kabbalistic precursors and the position among them, for

---

[1] The sub-title is *Histoire et Doctrine*, 2 vols., 1923.

example, of Ibn Gebirol. I should like to compare at some length what is said of him from this point of view with the study of Isaac Myer, long ago now in America. But my readers must be at the pains for themselves, because Vuillaud's chapter on SEPHER YETZIRAH must set all these aside: it proves representative enough, though there is little that can be called new. Those who are acquainted with Mr. Knut Stenring's version, introduced some time since by myself, will find it very much to their purpose. M. Vuillaud's conclusion is that SEPHER YETZIRAH is not a "preface" to SEPHER HA ZOHAR, but that the two works belong to one and the same tradition, the first being more explicit than the second and a summary of certain Kabbalistic themes, "notably that of Divine Revelation considered under the form of symbolical writing, and of emanation and cosmic evolution, contemplated from the mystical as well as the natural standpoint and developed in the order of harmonious analogy." The possible authorship of Elisha ben Abuyah is passed over—*pace* Dr. Robert Eisler—with a mocking reference, in dismissing a hypothesis of Epstein which regards the tract as designed for the instruction of youth.

The antiquity of the ZOHAR is considered in a long excursus which embodies an acute analysis of salient points in hostile criticism and seems to dispose of them effectually. They are taken in succession and examined in their different aspects, variously put forward as their champions followed one another, from the date of the vowel-points—which are mentioned, as we have seen, in the ZOHAR—to the antiquity of the first intimations on AYIN SOPH and the SEPHIROTH. Thereafter follows the story of Isaac de Acco and the quest which he attempted concerning the great text—as it has been given on my own part, and with much the same results. M. Vuillaud concludes, like some others, including Professor Schiller-Szinessy, that the ZOHAR is not a forgery by R. Moses de Leon; that it is a collection of many texts referable to various dates; that the arguments against it are of anything but irresistible force; that it represents an ancient Tradition, a school, and is the "authentic expression" of old Jewish wisdom, notwithstanding "interpolations, suppressions and changes" in the actual form, which things are an outcome of successive developments. M. Vuillaud goes further, citing unquestioned writings under the name of R. Moses, to the confusion of hostile critics. As regards De Pauly's French version of the ZOHAR, he is aware of its omissions and mentions one of them at least. This notwithstanding, his "critical essay" is dedicated with lively affection and gratitude to Émile Lafuma-Giraud, whose editorial labours gave us the French ZOHAR, after the death of its translator. Moreover, one of his longest extracts [1] from the text follows the De Pauly version, though elsewhere he appears to translate on his own part.

I have dealt with matters about which my readers are most likely to desire the views of a recent expositor in the field. For the rest, M. Vuillaud gives studies on Sephirotic Doctrine ; on the relation of Kabbalah to Pantheism ; on Shekinah the Indwelling Glory and Metatron the Angel of the Presence ; on Messianic Theosophy, more especially in the Zoharic School, the sects which have arisen therefrom, the Sabbataï Zevi movement and the excesses of later 'Hassidim. A chapter on the influence exercised by the Kabbalah on its earlier Christian students recalls my own monographs, though I miss a few names which are not without consequence to myself : the folios which they brought into being are still on my shelves. One of the most curious considerations, developed at some length, deals with the Kabbalah and Freemasonry. For Banamozaga and some few others, "Masonic Theology"—so dignified—is identical, we are assured, with the Secret Tradition in Israel. Certain authors of note and all the posse of zanies are quoted in this connection, not without rudimentary realisation at least of a distinction between the two classes and of the more important, if obvious, fact that the said Theology is after all *peu de chose*. M. Vuillaud has a good time, and offers as much to his readers among all the follies and nonsense ; but he is apparently not a Mason, has not been at work seriously and misses the rootmatter of the whole correspondence, such as it is, and such as I have sought to develop it, here and elsewhere, in my own case. He misses, moreover, a wider occasion for distraction, being unacquainted with High Grades, their Rites and their Orders, which claim derivation from Kabbalism.

The volumes are written in a curiously discursive style, which does not mean that the author is diverging continually

---

[1] *Op. cit.*, Vol. I, pp. 272–274.

from his main issues, but he is very much at ease about them, is never in haste to proceed and finds an opportunity always to look at the various aspects. It may be said that the theme throughout is one of Zoharic Kabbalism, while the impression left on the reader is that which it is designed unquestionably to convey, namely, that the best evidence for the age of the Secret Tradition for which the word Kabbalism stands in the language of Jewry is the *milieu*, the environment, the atmosphere amidst which Christianity itself happened to be born and in which it grew at the beginning. The cosmic matter and nebulæ—so to speak—that are crystallised in the main Kabbalistic text is the age-long story of the theosophical mind of Israel, in Palestine, in Babylon, and at that great meeting-place of life and thought, Alexandria.

It does not appear that M. Vuillaud is himself a Son of Israel, and though he is well and sympathetically acquainted, he is not exactly a Son of the Doctrine. He has described his work exactly in the parenthesis beneath its title: it is a critical essay, having apprehension as such; but I do not find evidence that he is aware anywise of a life and reality deep in the heart of the Doctrine. His contemplation of Shekinah—as Our Lady of Israel comes before us in the ZOHAR—offers proof of this: it is well enough done and is not apart from sympathy; but as it begins so also it remains, an enlightened critical appreciation. Of Zoharic Sex-Doctrine he says little, and that there is anything pregnant in its intimations he does not dream. The work taken as a whole is a study of that which environed the central thing rather than of the thing itself. This is why it is so informing externally, but why also—as it seems to me—there is something deficient, and that something belongs to the secret life of the subject.

As regards Germany it has been stated that there are schemes in the making, including translations of the BAHIR and SEPHER YETZIRAH, but I have not heard of any considerable critical work on the literature at large or its chief representative text. It remains to add that Jewish scholarship in England has not been drawn especially towards the subject of Kabbalism: so far back as fifteen years ago, Dr. J. Abelson said that "works in English are unfortunately very few," and the statement obtains to-day as it did at that time. There is, however, his own extended study on the IMMANENCE OF GOD IN RABBINICAL LITERATURE, which appeared in 1912 and should be consulted for the doctrine of Shekinah, the significance of MEMRA and the Rabbinical Theosophy of the Word. It was followed some twelve months later by a small volume on JEWISH MYSTICISM, which has chapters on SEPHER YETZIRAH —referred in all likelihood to the sixth century—the ZOHAR, Ten SEPHIROTH and the soul in man. It is held incontestable that the ZOHAR is considerably later than the second century and that much of it is a development of doctrine " embodied in the TALMUD and MIDRASHIM "; but "it could not possibly be the production of a single author or a single period of history."

I am brought in this manner to include among those final considerations which mark the term of our research a summary note on the present position of scholarship respecting its broad subject: there will be drawn thus into a focus the occasional lights and beacons which have shone upon our path in its travelling. They belong, however, only to the external side. As regards the documents of Kabbalism, that which was foretold by Dr. Schiller-Szinessy has substantially come to pass, and all that was said once about MIDRASHIM which embody the Secret Tradition is in course of re-expression from another and very different standpoint. The German school of Dr. Graetz, whose English exponent was Ginsburg, has passed utterly away, and the Zoharic writings are regarded now as a growth of several centuries, not apart from a certain root in Talmudic times. Their connection with R. Simeon ben Yohai remains where we should have expected, in the realm of legend and unlikely to emerge therefrom: it is not flouted, but no hypothesis is pledged thereto. The final shape assumed by the ZOHAR—in a word, its reduction according to the extant and only form—may not be much anterior to the first reports concerning it. Some of the increment and some or all of the redaction may be attributable by a bare possibility to Moses de Leon; but I conclude that every statement concerning this personality must be taken under all reservation, the account in SEPHER YUHASIN having little, if any, evidential value.

The period of R. Akiba is not unwarrantable or repugnant as a date of the SEPHER YETZIRAH, or some earlier form of that document; but the extent to which it anteceded the ninth century remains at present conjectural. And now in respect of content, the SEPHER YETZIRAH and ZOHAR incorporate beliefs which in some form or other belong to all occultism: they are part of the burden of Kabbalism, but they go back through the ages and would or might have been acquired by the Jew in his early settlements and successive captivities. Outside these, the *corpus doctrinale* of the ZOHAR, in so far as it is fantastic commentary on Scripture has—within my knowledge—invoked no special research and may be in its procedure of no assignable date. Having no concern in arbitrary systems or artifices apart from system, the inquiry has not been pursued on my own part. In so far as the *corpus doctrinale* consists of metaphysical subtleties, theosophical reveries or great spiritual lights, they are regarded, generally speaking, as post-Talmudic, but sometimes with occasional roots in a further past. If I speak for myself and look upon the Kabbalistic writings broadly, they appeal to me in the first place as documents of humanity, but among such as memorials of Israel and its peculiar genius, possessing their connections with other systems and other modes of thought, but by correspondence, by affiliation, by filtration, by causal identity, rather than by historical descent. The ZOHAR in particular is one of the chief Theosophical Manuals of the human mind, full of greatness and littleness, of sublimity and folly, but testifying continually in its higher intimations to a doctrine of certitude, attained at first hand by inward experience and not merely by a path of debate. The interest which it aroused on its appearance has in some measure survived all criticism, and the work itself has lived down even the admiration of its believers. It is to be accounted for naturally and historically as a genuine growth of its age; but while it is not an " imposture " or a " forgery "—as it used to be called crassly in days that are fortunately dead as well as beyond recall—so also it is not *a clavis absconditorum a constitutione mundi* or the key of all veridic secret knowledge, as old follies have termed it. In particular it contains no vestiges of that Doctrine of Secret Religion, belonging to time immemorial and behind all Religion, which some of its expositors claimed once to find therein. It is secret in the sense of Theosophical Doctrine in Jewry, appealing to an elect school among that elect people and no further; it supposes and involves the whole claim of Jewry. The existence of a Hidden Doctrine of Religion perpetuated from antiquity lies plainly upon the surface of the ZOHAR, but it happens to be that of the immortal medley and not that of the expositors to whom I refer and all or sundry of their so-called esoteric schools. Nor is it the Religion behind Religion of the late Professor Max Müller, or a highway or byway of Secret Doctrine according to Madame Blavatsky. It is none of these things and none of their shadows and reflections in the modern varieties of occult belief. It belonged to the Sons of the Doctrine who kept the Written Law that they might come to know of the Oral; and as to those who were denied for ever an entrance to its Holy Temple, they were all the nations of the world, the Gentiles outside the Covenant. The Doctrine stood, in other words, behind one Religion, one and no other. That which by the hypothesis lies therefore at the back of all Religions cannot be proved by recourse to Kabbalistic literature; and had this notion been rested thereupon it would be to that extent discounted. The question, however, does not stand or fall by the Kabbalah.

There is reached here and now one term of our research, but another remains over and belongs to the last section of this book, that is to say, whether—the Sons of Doctrine notwithstanding and all their dream of special and exclusive election—there is not something in the Secret Doctrine of Israel at its highest which belongs to all Religion, at the highest of that, and is therefore as much of our concern in this day as it was of the Holy Assemblies in that of R. Simeon, according to the Sacred Tradition.

II.—THE ALLEGED CHRISTIAN ELEMENTS

I have made some occasional allusions, as required by the matter of the moment, to those particular interests, circumstances and dedications in religion under which the ZOHAR assumed the vesture of the French language.[1] It has been

---

[1] We have seen that the French translation was the work of Jean de Pauly, leaving over the question whether this was an assumed name, as alleged by hostile criticism in certain Jewish quarters. It was published posthumously by M. Emile Lafuma-Giraud, who completed and corrected it, with the help of other Rabbinical scholars. As an example of personal views, their titles and their warrants, it may be noted that in De Pauly's judgment the three IDRAS—being the ASSEMBLY OF THE SANCTUARY and the GREATER and LESSER HOLY ASSEMBLY or SYNOD—are referable to the second or third century before Christ. M. Lafuma-Giraud says justly that this is rejected by all critical learning. His own conclusion is that the ZOHAR as a whole embodies very old materials, combined with much that is of comparatively modern authorship.

owing to a group of *literati*, incorporated—so to speak—for the purpose and actuated by an old and time-honoured zeal for its interpretation in a Christian sense [1] —at least as regards the chief elements of the text. I have indicated also at need the personal gratitude with which I should welcome a proof in this direction. I believe in my heart that the mystery of the Christ in Palestine is the Mystery of a Holy Sanctuary, hidden in the heart of the Providence which moves humanity forward; but it is not my intention to say anything on this subject unless and until I shall have opened another path in the mystic quest. It is one thing, however, to confess, under every prudent qualification, to such a view, but it is another to affirm that the ZOHAR, written long after the advent of Christ, is a secret storehouse of Christian Doctrine, confessing under veils to the Divine Mission of the Master of Nazareth. The bias of the translator in this direction was in several cases so strong that some paraphrasings, in which Christian predilections obscured the true sense, have been excised and redone by revisers. The supplementary task of annotation, which is partly the work of De Pauly but in the main that of his editor, is a storehouse of debate on the whole subject, and it goes even so far as to suggest that a considerable portion of the text, or of its codification at a given period, was the production of a Christian school which, in some undemonstrable manner, lay hidden in Jewry. Under these circumstances it is not surprising that the translation has been challenged in Jewry.

It is not worth while to follow out a speculation of this kind unless the canon of criticism on which it rests should be found to speak with authority, and this is by no means the case. But seeing that the ZOHAR does not correspond internally to that which it would appear on the surface, namely, verbatim reports of debates held in the first century of the Christian era,[2] but is—on the contrary—a work of

---

[1] The claim is not only the old claim but the expression is almost identical when it is said that Christian Teaching is neither more nor less than a continuation of Jewish Tradition, and that the ZOHAR—as the reflection of that Tradition within certain measures—formulates plainly, amidst all its obscurities, the doctrine of the Trinity and of the Man-God, Who came upon earth 2000 years ago. See EPILOGUE to the French translation, fol. 6.

[2] An occasional *lapsus memoriæ* determines the value of the implied claim in the negative, as we should expect antecedently, when the unknown editor is found reminding readers of that which has been written or said previously. The ZOHAR is a literary document and bears the marks of its making.

various periods and multifarious authorships, having further a certain rough method and sequence preserved moderately throughout, a certain unity of purpose, there is nothing improbable in the idea that it was the work of an exegetical school—if only for the very innocent and candid reason that Kabbalism supposes Kabbalists. My reference is here to the text itself, apart from the additional documents which are brought in at various points. Speaking rather in a tentative and fluidic sense than in one that is dogmatic and formal, I believe personally that some of these [1] have their roots in a further past than can be claimed for Commentaries on the Pentateuch, at least in their extant form. It is, however, no part of my concern to insist on the question of antiquity, either in respect of the fact or its importance. The existence of a Secret Tradition in pre-Christian times is beyond my province of research, [2] as I do not happen to have taken all knowledge for my subject. Herein, as in my other writings, I am dealing only with an epoch of Christendom. If it could be shewn that the ZOHAR did not antecede the twelfth or thirteenth century in any part of the collection, even this substituted antiquity would be adequate for my purpose, if I found that its intimations offered aspects of importance within the measures of Secret Tradition.

There was assuredly a Secret School of Kabbalism, and it is a subject of incessant reference in the ZOHAR under the general title of Sons of the Doctrine. Whether it was an incorporated school—as we should understand the expression at this day—is another question. It is said in one place that man is renewed or reborn by every new idea respecting the Secret Doctrine [3]—almost as if the latter constitutes a sequence of principles, presupposed and wholly understood, out of which many developments might issue. It was not consequently always a matter of Tradition. Granting that there was this common or general root, not only were fresh lights

---

[1] On the other hand it is thought that some are later still, and one has been even ascribed to the fourteenth century. If this be correct, it follows of course that they were added by the editors of the first printed editions, and it is of common knowledge that these varied in respect of their contents.

[2] Having stated this fact on the score of sincerity, it may be well to add that an exhaustive study of the Kabbalah itself, whether or not as a branch of Secret Tradition, would have to be made in connection with that of comparative religion, again demanding qualifications on which I can make no claim, not to speak of space for its development which would be impossible, here at least.

[3] Z., Pt. I, fol. 5a; I, 25.

possible but their discovery became a source of joy—where and whensoever it arose, with whomsoever it might be for a mouthpiece.[1] The disciples of the ZOHAR held open minds, giving ready—even rapturous—welcome to any new idea, if it carried the proper warrants. But it is said further, and not in full consonance with what I have just intimated, that the message must be one of a master—meaning presumably that he must either be known as such or must prove himself.[2] It was a case, however, that by his own words ye shall know him. A stranger in the course of some journey, a poor and outwardly despised person, might so exhibit his titles, when he was recognised and acclaimed on the spot.[3] It follows that the masters, as such or otherwise, were not always known to one another, so that if the Society of the Secret Doctrine was after any manner incorporated, it must have been scattered widely and propagated by a process of segregation—if I may so call it—by instruction or communication from master to disciple, from father also to son. As to the latter classes the counsel was one of silence, because he who pronounces sentences without having attained the grade of a master of sentences would produce only misfortunes.[4] Under the guide of ordinary reason, one would say that this must be interpreted intellectually, as of the misfortunes of ignorance, mistakes and mental mischances, or confusions arising therefrom. However, Rabbi Simeon ben Yohai cautioned his auditors on one occasion never to pronounce a word touching the Secret Doctrine without being entirely certain as to its exactness.[5] To do otherwise might cause the death of legions. This is an alleged consequence which calls to be understood literally, and I mention it because—although it can be nothing but a grotesque hyperbole of speech [6]—it

---

[1] For example, in the section MISHPATIM, which contains the discourse of Rabbi Yebba the Ancient, as we have seen, that master of Theosophy is treated at first with derision, for he is unknown and appears anonymously, with some crooked questions in his mouth; but before he has finished the colleagues have thrown themselves more than once at his feet, with tears in their eyes, protesting that had they come into the world for no other purpose than to hear his words, their existence would not have been useless.—Z., Pt. II, fol. 99a; III, 398. They were hearing new things.

[2] *Ib.*, Pt. I, fol. 5a; I, 27.

[3] *Ib.*

[4] Some of the incidents to which allusion is made here are quite in the dramatic manner; perhaps it is only to our modern minds that they betray the literary hand, but this is how they impress at least one sympathetic mind. The section MISHPATIM is again a case in point, but there are several instances.

[5] Z., Pt. I, fol. 5b; I, 27.

[6] There are analogies on the other side of the scale, as, for example, when it is said

looks for a moment as if the great teacher of Kabbalism were quoting the penal clause of a pledge by which the Sons of the Doctrine were bound together. It reads like the vengeance threatened in the obligations of secret societies—if their mysteries are betrayed by recipients. Another counsel was to examine the Secret Doctrine attentively before it was given out or taught, so that all error might be avoided.[1]

Being, *ex hypothesi*, originally oral doctrine which passed—in so far as it did pass—at a much later period into writing, it was obviously stored in memory, by the implicit of the claim; and the glaring inconsistencies which are met with ever and continually throughout the text of the ZOHAR are really a rather strong presumptive testimony to this kind of transmission. If Rabbi Moses de Leon had, as it used to be suggested, conceived and begotten the whole colossus of words out of his own head, he would not have fallen out with himself in quite such an obvious manner—even if we grant that forgeries have an ill-starred manner of betraying themselves there and here, so that they are for the most part a miscarriage rather than a making. But while accepting under all necessary reserves the general idea that the ZOHAR embodies some ancient MIDRASHIM [2] which are less or more complete and is, for the rest, a late compilation made up from similar sources, it must be recognised that it bears in an extraordinary degree the marks of compilation—as I have said. In connection with my present point it would be possible to quote several cases in which the imaginary *turba philosophorum* seem to have been making up the Secret Doctrine as they went along at the moment. It is better to face these facts, but it may be added that they and the late editing—otherwise so transparent—leave untouched that which is necessary to my purpose, being the existence of old material belonging to the

---

that the Holy One, blessed be He, comes down into three of the Heavenly Schools—one of them being that of Rabbi Simeon—and listens to the expositions of the Secret Law. Moreover, a new idea produced with authority concerning the Doctrine ascends to the Ancient of Days and is ornamented with 370,000 crowns, after which it becomes a heaven. Others are metamorphosed into lands of the living.—Z., Pt. I, fol. 4b, 5a; I, 22, 23, 25.

[1] *Ib.*, Pt. I, fol. 5a; DE PAULY, I, 28.

[2] This was the opinion of S. Munk in MÉLANGES DE PHILOSOPHIE JUIVE ET ARABE, as far back as 1859, but the work as a whole, " in the form under which it has been transmitted," is not older than the thirteenth century, and its authors lived in Spain. The last point seems to rest on the evidence of a single word, and, according to the French edition of the Zohar, it fails thereon. Munk, however, recognised that certain doctrines—as, for example, that of the microcosm—go back to the ninth century.

Secret Doctrine. It may be of the tenth century and it may be earlier; some vestiges may even go back to pre-Christian times, but this does not signify.[1]

The literature of Alchemy made a great and new beginning, somewhere about that period, or when it assumed a Latin garb: the literature of the Holy Graal was posterior by some two centuries; the other written testimonies to a Secret Doctrine under the ægis of Christendom were products of a still later period. What was the message of Theosophical Jewry in comparison with the alternative messages? As a purpose in literature, does it connect with the other and the later purposes, as a school with some other schools in respect of the end proposed—or is it of itself and no other? The Mystery of the Graal is of the mystical body of Christ; the Mystery of Alchemy is many-sided, but on one very late side it is of the body of man in its transmutation; the Mystery of Rosicrucianism—at the highest—is one of Divine Union, but here again there is more than a single aspect and one is the body of resurrection; the Mystery of Speculative Masonry is of the building up of man into a spiritual house, meet for the inhabitation of God. And the Secret Doctrine of Israel concerns a Mystery of Sex summarised as the mystical body of Shekinah, while it includes the shadows and outlines of a science of perfection, of union also therein, so that amidst all variations of process, distinction in symbolism and diversity as to root-ideas in doctrine, the question is answered by saying that it is not only in analogy but in living concurrence with other witnesses.

As such, it is to my own mind a matter of considerable consequence that it is not a Christian witness, while acknowledging that if it were it would be of consequence even greater, though of another kind; and my task in the present chapter is to shew that the case on the contrary side presented by those who have put forward the French version of the ZOHAR—whatever its value otherwise—is a case unproved.

Now, the points at issue between Israel and Christendom on the subject of Messiah are obviously of a very simple

---

[1] I mean that it does not matter so far as my purpose is concerned. As explained in my preface, I have been trying for some years past to hold up a certain glass of vision which tends to shew that the same term of research was sought everywhere in the secret literary schools and in two Instituted Mysteries belonging to the Christian centuries. It is not essential that Kabbalism, being a non-Christian system, should be linked into the chain, but it is important if it does enter therein, whether late or early in its origin.

kind, so far as the ground is concerned, for unless the Christ of Nazareth—as His story appears in the records—had (1) offered, or (2) had been represented as offering, at least some considerable proportion of the marks and seals by which He might be entitled to acknowledgment, the claim could not have been (1) proffered on His own part, or (2) sustained on that of His believers. Otherwise, the expectation of Jewry was one thing and the event another, or there would have been no colourable basis for His rejection in the natural reason of things. I suppose that the time has gone past when it was thought possible to affirm that Jesus, Son of Mary and putative Son of the carpenter Joseph, was antecedently likely or tolerable as the Deliverer to come and that it was owing to wilfully hardened hearts, to eyes that were blinded wilfully, that He was not recognised as such. It is not less true that any claimant was, in a sense, antecedently improbable, because of the complete vagueness characterising every intimation by which He is supposed to be foreshadowed. As it so happens—justly or unjustly—Israel expected a Deliverer who would be a mighty warrior before the face of the Lord Who sent him and before the faces of the nations whom he was to scatter, who was to deliver the Gentiles into the hands of Jews, that the one might be sacrificed by the other to that Samael who is the master of the Gentiles. In other words, they expected a personality as much and as little promised in prophetic literature as it was foretold that He who was to come would be crucified between two thieves who are the Written and Oral Laws, would rise up on the third day and would ascend into Heaven. Jewry was entitled to its dream in proportion to the sincerity of its expectation, whether this was warranted or not; the little company of disciples, whom the events of the crucifixion had scandalised, were entitled no less to theirs, when after the resurrection they received their Christ as the Lord of Glory, and so far as the present consideration is concerned, the question on either side is not of our business further.

The speculative thesis before us is that by the evidence, expressed or implied, of SEPHER HA ZOHAR the Messiah has come. So far as expression is concerned this thesis is manifestly untrue, while so far as implication goes I am very certain that the text is on the opposite side. It contains no particle of real evidence concerning that imputed sect in

Jewry which—under the title of Sons of the Doctrine—had confessed to the Christ of Nazareth and were putting forward their views under veils. It is clear, in the first place, that if such evidence exists it lies within the veils, as it is not suggested that it is part of the surface sense, and hence the question is reduced to its minimum so far as circumstances will permit. In the second place, I have to shew that it is not contained in the hidden sense.

Let me solicit my readers at the outset to recall and recur at need to all that which has been ingarnered and to the conclusions reached in preceding chapters: (1) On the Sephirotic allocations of the consonants comprised in the Divine Name, but especially those of the VAU and final HE; (2) On the feminine nature and offices, the betrothals and espousals of Shekinah above and below, but on those in particular which concern our Lady of Providence in her manifestation here on earth, the companion and guide of our exile; (3) on the relation of Shekinah to the Holy Spirit; and (4) on the coming of Messiah. We found that the VAU is the begotten Son of the YOD and HE, being ABBA and AIMA abiding in CHOKMAH and BINAH; that He is extended through three Kabbalistic Worlds below the Supernals in ATZILUTH; that He came into the world with a twin-sister, namely, the HE final, who was also his predestined spouse; that she was at first latent within Him but was afterwards drawn forth and put with Him in the nuptial state, that is to say, face to face, like Adam and Eve; that she descended or fell to earth, as Eve also fell, and is to be raised up by the VAU hereafter; that the Shekinah and Holy Spirit are in a condition of superincession; and that the Messiah is he who has been expected always, a warrior and king to come.

The counter-thesis requires very careful tabulation, for it is scattered through a great many notes and is not presented formally. I shall connect it with two subsidiary points, which will illustrate further the uncritical bias with which we are called to deal.

In respect of Shekinah and Messiah it is maintained that the former designates the Second Degree of the Divine Essence, otherwise the Second Person, in CHOKMAH—and is also the Word. The Shekinah in transcendence is the Word before incarnation and below is the Word made flesh. It is stated in the ZOHAR that Shekinah does become incarnate, and in so doing assumes the form of man. The incarnation of Messiah is by operation of the VAU, and the ZOHAR indicates that there is unity between God and the Redeemer. This incarnation of the HE, or Word, is recognised by Rabbi Simeon. The Messiah is METATRON, or the body of Shekinah —which is said to be the same thing. The Lesser Countenance of the IDRAS designates the Word incarnate on earth, and the Greater Countenance is the Word prior to manifestation in created things. One passage of the ZOHAR is declared to have no meaning unless the incarnation is admitted, while it is held that another announces the mystery in formal words. Finally, it is believed that there is an allusion to Mary the Mother of Messiah and to her son Jesus Christ when it is affirmed—as we have seen otherwise—that " the world will remain under the domination of the serpent until the coming of a woman like unto Eve and of a man like unto Adam, who shall vanquish the evil serpent and him who rides thereon." [1]

As I have presented and collated these points, so that they may carry their own message with all the force that is possible, they would look rather plausible on the surface, if we knew nothing of the state of things as the result of our research. I feel that the whole question is determined already in a negative sense by my readers as well as myself, but I will analyse the various clauses, so that no false impression may be possible.

(1) We have seen that the Shekinah is on both sides of the Tree; that it is in CHOKMAH as well as BINAH, because the Supernals are in unity; that it is in KETHER for the same reason. (2) We have seen that the Holy One uttered forth the Word and that the Builder—who is Shekinah—acted thereon: there is thus a distinction between God, His Word and the Architect, but again the Three are One, because all is one in ATZILUTH. The affirmation that Shekinah in transcendence is the Word before manifestation and below is the incarnate Word is made on several occasions, but unfortunately in respect of extracts which carry no conviction because they do not convey the intended message. It is said, for example, in the ZOHAR that the daily morning sacrifice [2] is signified in the words of Isaiah which it renders: " And the Lord shall keep thee always in repose "; [3] but this

---
[1] Z., Pt. I, fol. 145b, 146a; II, 174.
[2] Ib., Pt. I, fol. 141a; II, 151.
[3] The Authorised Version reads: " And the Lord shall guide thee continually."—Is. lviii, 11. Compare the Vulgate: *Et requiem tibi dabit Dominus semper*.

THE ALLEGED CHRISTIAN ELEMENTS

sacrifice of the morning-tide is held by the French editors to mean the Shekinah above, while the afternoon sacrifice signifies the Shekinah in manifestation. Now, if this is correct—as it may be—there is no reference to the Word and much less to the Word made flesh. We find further in the ZOHAR a fantastic etymology of the word Sabbath,[1] according to which it is identified with that only begotten Daughter who is Shekinah below. This is for our delectation; but as an instance of their canon of criticism the editors have recourse to the TALMUD, where they find that the Sabbath came secretly into the world, unlike other gifts of God to Israel, and thence they conclude that the only Daughter is the only Son and was born secretly in flesh. (3) It is never said in the ZOHAR that the Shekinah becomes incarnate and much less that then it assumes the form of man. The passage referred to specifies that the letter VAU is a symbol of the body of man in an erect position, and adds cryptically:[2] " Hence God willed that Shekinah should be present at the building of the Tabernacle " by Moses. The editors argue that if this does not mean what they postulate there is no sense in the passage. The second alternative is preferable to the arbitrary construction. (4) The ZOHAR does not say that the incarnation of Messiah is operated by the VAU. The passage in question is dealing with Gen. xix. 33, concerning the first-born daughter of Lot: " And he perceived not when she lay down, nor when she arose." The word which corresponds to " arose " in Hebrew " is augmented by a VAU," to shew that the child whom she conceived was to constitute the stem of Messiah.[3] (5) The incarnation of the HE or Word is not recognised by Rabbi Simeon, who is referring only to the descent of Shekinah into Egypt,[4] accompanying Israel and guarded by 42 angels, as we have seen elsewhere. (6) METATRON is not identified with Messiah.[5] It is said in the place referred to that the " eldest servant "[6] of Abraham is the image of METATRON, who is the servant sent by his Master. (7) The reference to the Lesser and Greater Countenances is purely arbitrary. The passage out of which it arises says (a) that the Little VAU shall awaken to unite and renew the souls in migration, and

---

[1] Z., Pt. I, fol. 23b; I, 146, 147.
[2] Ib., Pt. II, fol. 181a; IV, 152, 153.
[3] Ib., Pt. I, fol. 110b; II, 48.
[4] Ib., Pt. II, fol. 4b; III, 15.
[5] Ib., Pt. I, fol. 181b; II, 316.
[6] Gen. xxiv. 2.

(*b*) that at the period in question God shall send down new souls to earth.¹ The editors add that the Great VAU is the Holy Spirit above and the Little VAU the Holy Spirit below—after descent to earth—but I know of no place in which the VAU is said to descend except in connection with the HE final and then what is stated is not in consonance with the prevailing symbolism. The VAU must descend also to raise up the HE final. (8) Another passage which is affirmed to have no meaning unless it relates to the incarnation of Shekinah is as follows: "A tradition tells us that when the Holy One, blessed be He, regards the world and finds that the works of men are good here below, the Sacred Ancient is revealed to the world in the form of the Lesser Countenance, so that all men may see God and be blessed thereby." ² Whatever the meaning may be, the construction offered by the editors is impossible, as the Lesser Countenance is the VAU in its extension through the worlds, and this is not the Shekinah. (9) Here also is the passage which is held to announce the said incarnation formally: "I have found in the book of King Solomon that אשר = ASHER was born in the Heavenly Palace of Delight from the embrace of two other Supreme Degrees.... It is a prediction that אהיה = EHEIH will engender ASHER." ³ The reference is to the words: אהיה אשר אהיה = I am that I am, and the text itself explains that it is dealing with the revelation of the Sacred Name in successive degrees: (1) EHEIEH, (2) ASHER EHEIEH, (3) JEHOVAH. The revelation was to Moses. (10) The alleged allusion to Mary and her Son Jesus in the words quoted above is negatived by the fact that the Blessed Virgin was the mother of Christ, whereas Eve happens to have been the wife of Adam.⁴ It is a pity to create analogies over things which have no similitude.

I will mention only one thing more on this part of the subject. The HE final comes down to earth and has done so from the beginning of things, according to the ZOHAR. If we could suppose for a moment that there is authority in the

---

¹ Z., Pt. I, fol. 119a; II, 77. The period is that of Messiah the King in his triumph, when the VAU shall be united to the HE, when the sons of Ishmael shall make war on all other nations about the precincts of Jerusalem. The reference to new souls shews also that it is just before the great resurrection. As regards the Greater and Lesser VAU, the ground and nature of the distinction do not appear.
² *Ib.*, Pt. III, fol. 15a; V, 44.
³ *Ib.*, 116, fol. 65b; V, 179.
⁴ *Ib.*, Pt. I, fol. 145, 146a; II, 174.

THE ALLEGED CHRISTIAN ELEMENTS

text for an actual incarnation of the HE—that is, of Shekinah—she could appear only as a woman, or the whole symbolism would be falsified. There is indeed one passage in which the Daughter of the King is said to have taken flesh [1] but Metatron was her body, even as Shekinah herself is said in another place to be the body of the Holy One. It is flesh of the Land of Life and not of earth. If any personality symbolised by any consonant of the Sacred Name is really expected by Kabbalism to assume the limitations of mortality in the bonds of the body of earth, that consonant is VAU, and what is meant can be only the incarnation of the Begotten Son, who is assuredly the Lesser Countenance of the IDRAS. At this point I will remind my readers of that which was stated at the end of Book VII, § 8, concerning the coming of Messiah.[2] There on the authority of the ZOHAR we have seen that the creation of man was designed to prepare a way for the advent of that Divine Personality.[3] The memorable passage is passed over by the French editors without a word of comment, owing no doubt to their unfortunate and impossible predilection for Shekinah as Christ. They could have done much better with the alternative materials, so far as the logic of symbolism is concerned. They would not of course have made out a case in favour of Jesus of Nazareth as Messiah of the ZOHAR, because it is obviously the intention of the text to shew that its New Adam, the Deliverer to come, is not without an Eve who is at once his sister and spouse, who has had an office in creation through all ages. For this feminine personality there is no room in the Christian scheme, because, although I regard Shekinah as practically identical with the Blessed and Holy Spirit, the suggestion that this latter is in the relation of wife to Messiah or belongs to the side of womanhood means that Latin Trinitarian doctrine calls to be revised and the French editors seem evidently under the obedience of Rome in respect of official religion.

Having reached this point, we can deal shortly with their views on the subject of the Holy Spirit, Which is identified with the VAU of the Sacred Name and is located in BINAH. There is one passage in the ZOHAR where, in consonance

---

[1] Z., Pt. II, fol. 94b; III, 378, 379.
[2] See p. 324.
[3] Z., Pt. I, fol. 19b; I, 119. I am sorry to add that the subject is connected with the notion of an infernal "shell" or "mark"—Lilith, or one of her type—said to be the cause of epilepsy in children.

with much that precedes and comes after, the VAU is said to issue from the HE in transcendence, while the second HE issues from the VAU.¹ The first clause of this statement is understood as the Holy Spirit proceeding from the Word and the second as intimating that the Messiah or Christ takes flesh by the operation of the Holy Spirit. The real intention is that which recurs everywhere—namely, to indicate that the union of YOD and HE primal causes the HE as Mother to conceive and beget of YOD, the Father and Spouse, that which is Son of both, namely, the VAU, who comes into being carrying the second HE latent within him; but this is subsequently removed from him in a profound Adamic sleep and they dwell as spouses in unity. As there is no need to say, it would be difficult to find symbolism in more complete opposition to Christian Trinitarian doctrine or to the Christian scheme of the Incarnation. By an accident of things, we are reminded in another note that the Holy Spirit is compared to the light of the moon; but we know that the moon is Shekinah, and the Holy Spirit is therefore the light of Shekinah which seems to correspond with its office—otherwise but analogically indicated when it is implied that the Spirit is the breath of Shekinah. As regards that place in the ZOHAR where the Indwelling Glory is plainly identified with the Holy Spirit,² the difficulty is disposed of by saying that it is a transcriber's mistake; but to justify this, even in a preliminary sense, the error would have to be characteristic of one codex only, *plus* any edition or manuscript which may have derived indubitably therefrom. Now we have seen that the trend of all collated extracts seems towards identification rather than distinction, or to something so like it that the two principles pass one into another and are interchanged continually, while in respect of the single extract which makes distinction absolute, I should be not less or more in order—perhaps even more—if I suggested, on the contrary, that the copyist's mistake is there. I do not adopt such devices; the ZOHAR is a contradictory collection; but I abide by the consensus of intimations.

If, however, we wish for even more typical specimens of the true value attaching to the annotations on their polemical side, we must have recourse to what is said about the Eucharist.

---

¹ Z., Pt. I, fol. 193b; II, 365.
² See Book VIII, § 1, p. 366.

According to the ZOHAR, there is a wine which is the synthesis of all joys,[1] an ancient and sacred wine which was known to Jacob,[2] Joseph and David.[3] METATRON in the personality of Enoch is said to have administered it to the patriarchs.[4] It is not connected with the wine carried by Melchizedek, but—according to the French editors—we have here an allusion to the mystery of transubstantiation. So also the unleavened bread, which is called bread of affliction in the Old Testament, and is therefore the very antithesis of Eucharistic Bread, is declared in the ZOHAR to represent the female in separation from the male,[5] who would be presumably represented by the yeast. Such separation means of course affliction for Kabbalism. There is, however, some undemonstrable way in which this understanding of unleavened bread is held to mean the Eucharist—in which case it can be only that of the Latin Rite, where the bread is in separation from the wine. There is also a Zoharic reference to the offering of bread and wine, the one representing joy and the right side, while the other is the left and is therefore affliction, though it is not specified in the text.[6] This, say the editors, exposes clearly the Mystery of the Blessed Sacrament. We are prepared in such manner for the last suggestion which I feel called to mention here. At the death of Rabbi Simeon, his son, Rabbi Eleazar, overcome with grief, exclaims that " all the colleagues should drink blood." [7] This indicates the " offering of the Holy Sacrifice and proceeding to transubstantiation."

Under all these considerations, not to speak of many others of similar purport and intention, we can understand that the Kabbalistic Community of Israel is identified with the Church of God, in the sense of the Christian Church. When it is said to be above, it is the Church Triumphant and Glorious in Heaven; below it is the Church militant on earth; but it is left to the reader's discrimination whether it is centred at Rome.

---

[1] Z., Pt. I, fol. 142b; II, 157.
[2] Gen. xxvii. 25.
[3] Z., Pt. III, fol. 189a; V, 496.
[4] Ib. Seven firmaments, seven palaces, six directions, and five pathways issue from this wine.
[5] Ib., Pt. I, fol. 157a; II, 216, 217.
[6] Ib., Pt. II, fol. 29a; III, 139. I suppose that when any sacred text speaks of bread and wine, our Christian pre-occupations on the subject will look inevitably for Eucharistic analogies. I was on the watch myself anxiously at the beginning of my Zoharic studies, but I suffered disappointment only.
[7] Ib., Pt. III, fol. 296b; IDRA ZOUTA, VI, 120.

I am sure that the work of annotation has been done by the French editors with sincerity and even with zeal, but on the side of their palmary concern it has not been done with insight. There seems to me nothing more unfortunate in the long story of attempts to construe the Kabbalah in a Christian sense than the presentation of Shekinah as Christ and, as I have indicated, without dwelling thereon, another way was possible—by no means satisfactory, but not at least ridiculous. Our Blessed Saviour has been placed in many anomalous positions by those who seek to glorify Him and desire that His cause should prevail, but in none surely which is quite so curious as this.

III.—CONCLUSION ON JEWISH THEOSOPHY

As regards the message of the Secret Doctrine in Israel, apart from the body of texts, those who seek in the ZOHAR for a deeper knowledge—outside dogmatic affirmations, already cited—concerning the term of mystical experience, as it has reached expression in the great texts of mystical literature, will not find what they need in the plain and simple way that they are likely to need it, though I believe that the experience is there. It follows, however, a perilous path of symbolism; but there is this further to be said—that, perhaps more than most others in the great schools, the Doctors of the Hidden Law realised that it has not entered into the heart of man to conceive what God has prepared for those who love Him. They must have known at least how the experience transcends expression, as the mournful failures of mystical literature bear witness on every side. I take it that this is why the union of male and female—which is their adopted form of symbolism—the more it is raised into transcendence is the deeper covered with veils. On the sanctification of the natural act and the path therein, they speak with reasonable fullness, all things perhaps considered. They are explicit also on the correspondence between things above and below therein, but without a word or part of a word which tells of the end attained. This is not to say that the term of Divine Union is never indicated; but we shall see by collating the allusions that if they are spoken from the centre, at least in the wording itself, the centre seems very far away. In the first place, as to that path which may lead to the Mystery of Union : the thesis is that the just aspire to contemplate the delights of the Lord and in Him their delights are found:[1] it is in the Lord Himself, and so only, that they desire to rejoice. The counsel in symbolism is that those who seek to contemplate the Mystery of Sacred Union shall consider the flame which springs from a lighted candle. Two colours will be perceived, one being white and the other a kind of blue. The one is above and the other is the pedestal of the first: they are united and yet distinct.[2] Here is an analogy borrowed from a material object and indicating something which is postulated concerning the state of integration in God. The path is one of holiness,[3] for it is by the ascent of this as by a ladder that man is able to be joined with the Holy One. Hence God said to Abraham: "Get thee out of thy country."[4] Here was a call from earthly into spiritual life. The necessity of this call and the departure which follows thereon resides in the fact that whatsoever is produced in this world is in a state of separation; union exists only in the world above, according to the words: "From thence it was parted and became into four heads."[5] This is held to be the doctrine of distinction, diversity and inevitable separateness in the way of manifestation. The path is followed in the faith which precedes experience, and the postulate of this faith abides in the recognition of unity in heaven, on earth and in all the worlds. Those who can realise along this line are counted among the just whose will is done by the Holy One.[6] The ZOHAR in this place is either written more wisely than its makers knew or we have a hint of Secret Doctrine and even of experience which never passed fully into expression. The essential of progress in the path is that man shall apply himself to the study of the Law and shall cleave thereto, so that he may be judged worthy of being united to the Tree of Life.[7] This is another symbol of the union, for as a tree is composed of leaves, branches and trunk, so are the souls which emanate from the Tree of Life grafted in the Holy One.[8] But there are distinctions, states and stages, and for this reason some souls may be compared to the leaves and some to the branches; yet a common faith unites them and makes of them one tree.

---

[1] Z., Pt. I, fol. 219a; II, 465.
[2] Ib., fol. 51a; I, 296.
[3] Ib., fol. 79b; I, 465.
[4] Gen. xii. 1.
[5] Gen. ii. 10.
[6] Z., Pt. I, fol. 191b; II, 355.
[7] Ib., fol. 193a, b; II, 364.
[8] Ib.

Prayer is an aid on the path, and there are two kinds of prayer held to be indicated by David when he speaks of the words of his mouth and the secret meditation of his heart.[1] The one is the prayer of words and the other is the prayer of silence, the state of the latter being very deep, according to the ZOHAR. It is foretold that " I will multiply thy race as the sands of the sea, the multitude of which is innumerable," [2] and this refers to the state of silent, unexpressed and inexpressible prayer, for which reason it is said to conceal the Mystery of Perfect Union in the Divine Essence.[3]

While the intellectual idea of a final union between the soul and God emerges with tolerable clearness in the sense that a state is suggested which seems to exceed that understood by the Blessed Vision of Theology, the evidence is as usual rather out of harmony with itself and does not correspond always with the two primary dogmas which belong to the root-matter of the whole subject. It is said in the first place that in their intercourse the Holy One and the Community of Israel are called one,[4] as also that there is no separation in the joy of heaven,[5] yet there are other modes of expression which are less clear in their nature. That of integration in the body of the heavenly King must be counted in this class,[6] and again it is said that the Master is in the midst of those who love Him,[7] which corresponds more probably to the state of eye to eye than to that of oneness.[8] Perhaps the clearest intimation is in a short commentary on the words, " Let him kiss me with the kisses of his mouth," [9] which are held as referring to the union of all spirits with the Supreme Spirit, called otherwise the condition of grand, perfect and eternal joy.[10] Imperfect spirits will enter into perfection by its means,

---

[1] Z., Pt. I, fol. 169a; II, 264, 265.—Ps. xix. 14.
[2] Gen. xxxii. 12.
[3] Z., Pt. I, fol. 169a; II, 265. It is said in another place that man must not raise his voice in prayer higher than is necessary, or he is not likely to be heard. The reason is that true prayer is made in silence. There is an obscure suggestion also that the prayer of silence is spoken by the Divine Voice within us. So also the later mystics say that Christ prays in us.—Ib., fol. 209b, 210a; II, 440.
[4] Ib., Pt. III, fol. 93b; V, 248.
[5] Ib., fol. 4a; V, 7.
[6] Ib., Pt. II, fol. 87a; III, 358.
[7] Ib., Pt. II, fol. 211a; IV, 220.
[8] The words, " to behold the beauty of the Lord, and to inquire in His Temple " (Ps. xxvii. 4) are contrasted with, " Then shalt thou delight thyself in the Lord " (Is. lviii. 14), to shew that the latter signifies a deeper state of union; but those who attain hereto are very few in number.—Ib., Pt. I, fol. 219a; II, 465.
[9] Song of Solomon, i. 2.
[10] Z., Pt. I, fol. 44b; I, 262.

and spirits that would be otherwise apart from life will diffuse a great brilliance by its aid.[1] This mystery is expressed also in those other words of Scripture: "And Jacob kissed Rachel."[2] It is obvious therefore that the analogy is one of human union, and it is said cryptically that the perfect union above is accomplished only in so far as seed shall be communicated by the Seventh Palace above to the Seventh Palace below.[3] It is then perfect, and blessed is he who knows how to effect it, for he is loved above and below:[4] he is the just man who is the foundation of the world.[5] In the state of perfect union all is concentrated in the Supreme Thought, the forms and images disappear, and this Thought animates and enlightens all.[6]

I have left until the present concluding section the suggestions which it is my intention to offer on the Mystery of Sex in Kabbalism, as it seemed desirable to isolate my own views from the evidence or intimations of the text. It will be observed that the Mystery in its unfolding comprises (1) the doctrine concerning an union between male and female principles postulated as inherent in Deity and illustrated as to its nature by analogies in physical humanity, which analogies have to be checked by (2) the doctrine of the essential unity between Jehovah and Elohim, Who are the male and female principles in question. The analogy breaks at this point and is not restored by (3) the hypothesis that Adam and Eve were

---

[1] Z., Pt. I, fol. 44b; I, 262. This union is said to depend entirely on the prayer of man.
[2] Gen. xxix. 11.
[3] Z., Pt. I, fol. 45a, b; I, 263.
[4] Ib., fol. 45b; I, 263, 264.
[5] Prov. x. 25.
[6] Z., Pt. I, fol. 45b; I, 264, 265. There are the following additional allusions on the subject of union and its correlatives: (a) By following the ascending path of the SEPHIROTH, there is reached that supreme place where all is united and all henceforth is one.—Ib., fol. 18a; I, 111. (b) So long as severity rules this world there is no union, the reason being that union is mercy, peace and the covenant. It is thought to be proved by the words: "And God remembered Noah" (Gen. viii. 1).—Z., Pt. I, fol. 69b; I, 409, 410. (c) True unity depends on attachment to the Supreme King. When the river which went forth out of Eden was divided into four heads, this signified separation in manifest things; but it was in union at the source itself.—Ib., fol. 74b; I, 440, 441. (d) A sacred union is attained at times in prayer.—Ib., Pt. II, fol. 57a; III, 254. (e) Those who dwell in the higher region are united in joy and never separated.—Ib., Pt. III, fol. 4a; V, 7. (f) Lastly, the union of God in Himself—which is the ground of all other unions—is believed to be exhibited perfectly in the words—JEHOVAH ELOHENOV JEHOVAH (Deut. vi. 4). ELOHENOV is the root mentioned in Is. xi. 1: "And there shall come forth a rod out of the stem of Jesse, and a branch shall grow out of his roots." The final JEHOVAH is the pathway here below; in order to know the Mystery of Union it is indispensable to follow the pathway.—Z., Pt. III, fol. 7a; V, 20.

originally side by side, which hypothesis is grounded on certain monstrous births that occur from time to time in humanity and are a yoking but not an unity. Nor is it restored by a literal understanding of Genesis, according to which Eve was dormant in Adam, not active and conscious within him, for in the latter case he could not have been said to be alone. There is finally no intention of maintaining the correspondence, because (4) the original generation of souls was in separation as male and female, and (5) this distinction will continue to be maintained in the eternal world by the mode of simple reunion in companionship, *plus* a transcendental intercourse the rapture of which is increased by a visual contemplation therein of God and His Shekinah, Who is also God. (6) But an important content of the Mystery is the generation of souls as a result of Divine Intercourse, and this is imitated on earth by incarnate man, as it (7) will continue to be imitated in heaven, where the union of created souls will produce fruit after their own kind.

We are not concerned with applying tests of value to the metaphysical part of the doctrine, for its collation with other doctrines leads to insuperable difficulties, some of which have been illustrated by the lights of later Kabbalism. There is, however, the doctrine of experience, and I wish to say that if we accept Zoharic teaching on its own warrants, then the imitation on earth of that which is operated in the transcendence, being done—if I may so express it—in the sense of God's ineffable union, did not unreasonably become, in the eyes of those who not only held the doctrine but performed the practice, a work of sanctification. Now, the question is where it may have brought them. The ZOHAR is silent hereon, except in so far as it testifies with no uncertain voice to the presence of Shekinah in the houses of the Holy Doctors of the Law. But this presence followed them in their travels abroad, and there is one allusion at least to a state in which it was realised invariably as indwelling in the soul.[1] It seems to me that these are three qualities of intimation as to a Divine Realisation in consciousness resulting from the manner of life laid down as indispensable thereto. In this case the Sons of the Doctrine walked not only by faith but by experience, and it follows that the mystery in its practice had a consequence within themselves as well as in their children.

---

[1] Z., Pt. I, fol. 166a; II, 250.

More than this cannot be said on the evidence which lies before us, and of the issue which came of the unions thus adumbrated it is obvious that we can say nothing. One of the Instituted Mysteries tells us in its moving ritual that the children of philosophers belong to philosophy, and we may believe—if we can and will—that in the case under notice they were worthy of their high calling and birthright.

In what manner does this Secret Doctrine of Israel affect us as mystics in the twentieth century? There is firstly the doctrinal side, and it will be seen that those among us who belong to the Christian Tradition, more especially on the orthodox side, must be conscious that they are moving through the great text as through a strange world of images—vestiges of many pantheons, many systems of the past, and legends of the soul in man. I have mentioned already that the Theological Doctrine of the Trinity must complete its own symbolism, if it is to be held as a product of the logical mind, and that therefore the Eternal Father is *ex hypothesi* the Eternal Mother, or in the sense and reason of things there could be no generation of an Eternal Son. The Zoharic male and female in the Deity cannot be therefore repugnant to the Trinitarian. Beyond this point the Kabbalistic system moves farther and farther, as it proceeds, from the field of Christian Theology. If it were not complicated by irreconcilable elements in the medley of texts and testimonies, so that on the one hand we have the creation of souls *en masse*, as if by the conventional *Fiat*, and on the other their unceasing generation as the result of Divine Communion, to say nothing of minor alternatives, there is much that is suggestive in the second dream, and for those who feel able to accept any definite hypothesis on the subject it may have an appealing aspect. We know also that the tradition of souls being created, generated or otherwise evolved in pairs is old and far diffused. I am not sure that it does not belong to " the hunger and thirst of the heart " after something like a timeless sanction of human relations; but it is difficult to regard it either as part of a secret doctrine or as convincing *per se* if it were.[1] The kind of reunion which constitutes the beatitude

---

[1] A distinction on Secret Doctrine is desirable in this connection, it being understood that I am speaking *ex hypothesi* on both sides of the subject. There is that which is based on experience and is kept secret because the nature of the experience is regarded as a thing to conceal from public knowledge. If an Order of Alchemists discovered a very simple process of transmuting metals, they might keep it secret presumably for

of the Elect who experience the rapture of intercourse—one with another—in the sight of God is rather like an houri's paradise conducted on monogamic lines, and it looks a little strange, moreover, in the face of its contrasts at other points in the text.[1] I refer to the continued study of the doctrine by the Elect in the Lower Paradise and by the Community of Israel gathered into the transcendence of BINAH.[2] I do not say that these ideas of a Paradise of espousals and a College of transfigured adepts are absolutely exclusive, but I am equally certain that they were never meant to dwell together in unity. The nuptials of Rabbi Simeon at the close of the Lesser Holy Assembly were, one feels, of another order[3] than most of the psychic marriages proclaimed in the ZOHAR. When, however, the scheme is detached to some extent from its setting, it is worth while formulating its irreducible minimum as follows : (1) The Communion of the Divine Duality, Ineffable Male and Female, in the Supernal World, generates human souls, male and female, in Its own likeness, who assume flesh—according to a law of succession. (2) They are intended to find one another in earthly life and to enter into marriage therein ; but there are various interventions which postpone and even seem to frustrate the general design : yet it is accomplished unfailingly in the case of those who keep the Law. (3) The souls return into the spiritual world and are reunited for ever therein. (4) The keeping of the Sex Law, which is part of the Secret Doctrine, insures the procreation of those who may be called the Children of the Doctrine, assuredly a " peculiar people."

It would not be worth while to place on record a personal opinion if it were not one which I feel is likely to be shared— in the detached manner that I design to put it forward. If we draw together from all sources whatever the soul's

---

their own benefit. If they discovered a simple way to compose an elixir of life which would confer physical immortality, they might keep it secret out of mercy to mankind. This is one side of the question, and the other is speculative doctrine, which there is no true reason to reserve from others, more especially as it seldom differs essentially from independent analogous forms and is usually not new at all.

[1] It is beautiful and moving, however, within its own measures, and the heart goes out to greet it.

[2] This is a subject of continual reference and is a clear issue in respect of departed souls gathered into the Lower Paradise. Israel in the Supernal World offers points of difficulty in most allusions. It is even described as a Degree of the Divine Essence uniting all legions above.—Z., Pt. III, fol. 197a ; V, 507. Presumably it is the history of souls in perfect union, almost in the state of absorption.

[3] See IDRA ZOUTA, ib., fol. 296b ; VI, 121, and Pt. I, fol. 218a ; II, 461.

legends, her travels and metamorphoses, into a single storehouse of memorials, I question very much whether we should find in our collection a more tolerable proposition at its value, and I make this qualification because I am not suggesting that either one or another is convincing. I do not know of any light on the mystery of man's beginning in his inward state which carries the seals of mastery, for the literature of mystical attainment, the records of our precursors on the path which leads to God, have nothing to testify thereon, as it is not the concern of their experience. Each school reproduces therefore the accepted teaching of its time and place.[1] The ZOHAR shews in its own manner that the end is like the beginning, and if it be only a tale of faërie, it is one of grace as such.

Having said what is possible on this part of the subject, there arises in the next place that which must be called indubitably the most important question of all, and though it is one that is difficult to approach it would be quite impossible to pass over and not miss the whole point of the present study. I have said at the beginning of this chapter that the form of symbolism adopted in respect of Divine attainment by the doctors of the Hidden Law is that of male and female in their union; it begins here on earth and it is raised into all the heavens; *mutatis mutandis*, it is the same kind of intercourse on all the planes,[2] and all planes or worlds are in communication one with another, not merely by the analogy which obtains but in a manner which is represented by the recurring image of the world above being married to the world below. We have seen that he is called perfect and blessed who knows how to effect such an union, and this so far as the individual is concerned can be only by fulfilling

---

[1] The inference is obvious and is, I think, utterly true. If we take the Christian records, that part of them which deserves to be called mystical is either a study of conditions, processes, practices leading to the term in God or it is concerned with experience attained in the term. The first may depend from dogma—*e.g.* the idea that an ascetic path is of Divine counsel—but it does not explain the counsel or ordinance; the second is a realisation of the Divine in consciousness and has nothing to do with vision, as when Dr. John Pordage seems to have seen the Trinity manifest in arbitrary forms. The deep mystical state is imageless and is not a light on theological teaching.

[2] I hope that the qualification will be quite clear to my readers. The body of man was the most sacred thing for Kabbalists and there is absolutely no question that it was in perfect analogy with the body of heaven in its clearness: they were not afraid of their symbolism and they accepted all its consequences. The result was what on the surface is called gross physicalism; but there is sufficient evidence that when they happened to drop their symbolism, or to adopt another form, they realised that the things of the spirit are understood spiritually.

that which he is appointed to do under the provisions of the Secret Law. My hypothesis is that in so doing he became conscious of what—for want of a better expression—I must term the cosmic union, in which the personal act would be merged, so that he shared in the loving intercourse which obtains, according to Kabbalism, above and below. By this also the worlds are bound together, God is united to creation and the soul of man partakes within its proper measures—and under the reserves of all the veils by which he is covered during the life of earth—of that universal and divine communion.

I have said that there are intimations of this state in eastern teaching, by which I mean India, but that—so far as I am aware—they have not passed into writing. It was testified also in the past—once at least—by a spiritual alchemist that he was acquainted with the mystery of his art but had never proceeded to the practice because he had not found a woman who could help him in the work.[1] So also when Thomas Vaughan speaks of " the conjugal mystery of heaven and earth " I believe that he had some notion of these workings, whether as the result of experience or merely in an intellectual way, by the study of concealed literatures.

It would be possible to carry these considerations much further, but I do not feel that they are meant for presentation at length in this place. The suggestion is that, expressed in very plain language, there is something to be fulfilled between man and woman by a marriage of Nature and Grace of which the sacramental aspect sometimes attributed to earthly marriage is the merest shadow and vestige. We have seen what Zoharic Theosophy adumbrates on this work; I have found vestiges of the same testimony in the allegories of some alchemical books,[2] and there are other traces of the experience or of notions concerning the experience in the Philadelphian

---

[1] The question is whether this is the open door of the Hermetic Mystery—*introitum apertus ad occlusum regis palatium*—in so far as the literature is apart from experiments in the mineral kingdom. It was once suggested that the key was to be sought in something done between operator and subject, after the manner of the trance-state induced by mesmerism. In *The Hidden Church of the Holy Graal* I have sought to establish certain crude analogies between the spiritual work in Alchemy and that in the Eucharist; it obtains within its own measures, but everything depends on the true meaning of the breaking of the Host into the Chalice.

[2] The LIBER MUTUS, first published at Rupella in 1677, and reprinted in Mangetus, BIBLIOTHECA CHEMICA CURIOSA, is of some importance as a case in point, but the allegories are in pictures only. I have called it elsewhere THE BOOK OF THE SILENCE OF HERMES.

mystical school of the late seventeenth century in England.[1] It is better—for the moment at least—that those who feel drawn in this direction, with clean hearts and minds turned towards God, should follow out the needful researches for themselves in the literatures to which I have alluded. They may come to see that the analogy instituted by the Latin Church between those who are joined in wedlock and the union of Christ with His Church has a deeper meaning than has been discerned in the public ways; that in certain grades of consecration the spouse and the beloved on earth do stand for Christ the Lover of the soul and for the soul in that nuptial union which is called the mystical marriage in great and holy texts; the *absconditus sponsus* may be under veils of the living man, and the *sponsa* may realise in the person of her own consciousness that the soul is indeed the bride.

I am the last person in the world to enforce practical conclusions, but if those who are prepared thereto within and without—and this not too late in life—were to enter the nuptial state and fulfil it consistently, as also with high reverence, in the sense of the ZOHAR, I think that the world might be changed and that a generation to come born of such unions might be children of a risen life.

For the rest, in conclusion, it will be seen that I have not put forward the Secret Doctrine in Israel as one who regards its part major as of great Theosophical and high mystical importance, though I hold its memorials not merely as of living interest but as belonging to that kind which does not die; for at the back of all its reverie, the strange fantasia of symbols and images, there is the pulsating heart of a dedicated humanity, set in and out of season to justify the ways of God to those who could see through its particular glass of vision. I speak as one who has found God in many strange ways of thought, and—what is perhaps more unusual—in very simple and homely ways. I look to go further, for much that has never been spoken or said, and so remains for expression, is not indeed beyond it. But the Kabbalistic Jew, dreaming of liberation and of union under the grievous yoke of his law, giving it the wings of interpretation and rising himself thereon,

---

[1] From this point of view and otherwise, all the writings belonging to the Philadelphian school demand consideration anew, including Robert Roach's IMPERIAL STANDARD OF MESSIAH TRIUMPHANT, THEOLOGIA MYSTICA of John Pordage, the works of Jane Lead, and the rare PHILADELPHIAN TRANSACTIONS.

is of my own lineage in the spirit, of my kinship in the heart of quest. His Fall of man is no mere dream, because it is highest symbolism. His myth of Paradise has a voice speaking within it from a far home of the consciousness: though the eyes of flesh may be dazzled and the longing of sense may sink when the glories of our end are published, I know that, be it ever so splendid, there is no place like home. The Jew's Covenant in the flesh is assuredly, in Zoharic understanding, one of God's most true Covenants; the Master Who seals us within does often seal us without, whence peers and co-heirs have always known one another in every place of the world, and every sign-manual of heaven is honourable and worshipful, since it sets apart to His service. The outward and inward Law is like the book of our life itself, *intus et foris scriptus;* there is nothing so allusive in the whole world of images; it is illustrated in all our ways—without in the rule of our conventions, without in the external veneer of our too imperfect conformities, without in the age-long tale of our schooling and self-schooling; but within in our hungers and raptures after the " good things of the Lord in the Land of the Living," in the thirst after righteousness which we cannot attain ourselves and can scarcely formulate, in the ineradicable covetousness with which we would grasp at what God has prepared for those who love Him. The beauty of the courts of the Temple—Temple of Solomon and Zerubbabel—its Holy Place and the Holy of Holies beyond, has eaten up our hearts with desire. Do we not also expect the coming of Messiah, while confessing to the Messiah Which has come, Whose star we have seen in the East, nor yet in the East alone but all the quarters of Heaven, through the ages and nations? Son of Issachar, Son of David, Son of Joseph, true legitimate and true King for ever, do we not know that for us He has never come without until He has come within? *Domine, non sum dignus ut intres sub tectum meum:* yet are we His stable in Bethlehem, yet is He born in us. *Sed tantum dic verbo*—O Word of Words, speak it in the inward silence—*et sanabitur anima mea.* And the legend of the soul in Kabbalism, at however far a distance, flashes and reflects within us its changing aspects of that long, strange journey of old taken by those who came forth, and perchance are still coming, taken by those who go back; God-speed them in both respects, and give to those who seek it safe conduct and the blessed end. Yes, there is truth in Kabbalism, all its contradictory messages notwithstanding; the contradictions themselves are but turnings of the glass of mind, hither and thither, to encompass all directions—opposites included, and included the pairs of these. But the great message of all is the message of the Indwelling Presence, though it comes to us who are mystics under unwonted forms and in a peculiar radiance of vesture. The Divine Fatherhood is one side of the shield of faith and the other is Divine Motherhood. Whether we regard it as doctrine handed down from an immemorial past—few of us can so regard it—or whether we decide in our excess that it was conceived by Moses de Leon and born of his brain and pen, it is a wonderful heritage of mind which has come into our hands, and perhaps at this day it has a greater message for us than it had ever for our brothers in Jewry. I could almost wish that this Moses were the one and very man, for I do not think that in the wide world there would be the same kind of greatness as his. But taking things as they are, and by what we know of his writings, there is nothing so unlikely.

It follows that I have not put forward the Secret Doctrine in Israel as one who believes that it is literally what it claims to be in respect of antiquity, though I have made evident that in my opinion the ZOHAR incorporates old MIDRASHIM. It makes no claim except as to Oral Tradition, and about this I have no opinion. It follows also that I have not put it forward as a sum total of wisdom, written or unwritten; but I do believe that in the expounded Mystery of Sex—so far as it is indeed expounded—it suggests a great experiment which—" once in time and somewhere in the world "—may have been practised in hidden sanctuaries that were homes of man and woman. The doctrine of sex in the ZOHAR is that *desideratum* which I mentioned at the beginning, a Key general to the House of Doctrine: all other teaching in the great Theosophical Miscellany may be said to encompass it, as the Divine Names and SEPHIROTH stand about the figure of the Cosmic Christ in the eloquent diagram of Khunrath. It is the central root which I have mentioned, and from this root the Tree of Knowledge grows. As the ZOHAR intimates, it becomes the Tree of Life. At this end of our travelling, we have reached what was set before us when our quest was undertaken first, namely, a *terminus ad quem*, from which we can look over the strange path that we have followed, surveying it under one light. Shekinah is the high light which shines thereon. We have seen that this Lady of Mediation is the President over that nuptial intercourse which I have described as begun on earth and completed in the World of the Supernals. The return journey of the soul is performed therefore under her light, in and by her grace, with the sustenance of her mysterious power. For us at this day she can be a Principle only, but it is Divine as such; and after what manner—if indeed other than this—she was understood by Sons of the Doctrine during earlier days of their exile through the long centuries of Christendom, we must be content to leave. It would be a satisfaction to find the answer, but it is not of our vital concern: enough if we have convinced ourselves—and this, I think, we have done—that the central testimony signifies as authentic and true of voice. It follows in fine therefore that SEPHER HA ZOHAR, the BOOK OF SPLENDOUR, has something to tell us at this day which calls to be heard by those who have ears. God preventing, I do not affirm that it offers an only way, since ways are many to the height. From the beginning of things He has called man and woman in all the states of life, in childhood and virginity, in espousals and widowhood; and He Who makes all things one has called the Lover and Beloved, that they may go up hand in hand and become one in Him. Hereunto is that which can be said in the public places, and for all that remains over—*Sacramentum Regis abscondere bonum est*.

There are things, however, which also remain over outside the Mystery of Sex, and they recall me to that question which has been mentioned and left open, whether, namely, there is something in the Secret Doctrine of Israel which belongs to all Religion and is no man's patrimony by virtue of official belief or election as a peculiar people. The doctrine that we come forth from the Centre and that the Centre draws us back is formulated rarely in Kabbalism and never in clear terms; but it is implied or adumbrated continually, and it belongs to the higher understanding of all Religion. That Centre is AYIN SOPH according to the ZOHAR, and it is the Font and Source of all. Whether it indicates that the soul returns thereto arises for determination in the next place: if so it can be only by virtue of something inherent and essential in the soul's nature. The nature of that something is defined in affirming that God is within and His Kingdom. But this is common to all Religions understood at their highest. It is formulated by the ZOHAR in the Doctrine of TSURE, that most pregnant intimation concerning the prototypical soul in ATZILUTH, the supernal part of soul which does not leave the Supernals. This is the inward Kingdom of God and this the God Who is within. There is also a very eloquent shewing forth of the return journey in the figurative language of the Tree. We know that AIN SOPH is situated in the Symbolism above the Tree, the head of which is the Supernal SEPHIROTH. We have found also that the Central Pillar in the Tree of Life is the line of the soul's ascent, that the Sons of the Doctrine go up thereby on the way of return to God. This means and can mean only the realisation of TSURE, or the soul's union with the soul's Divine Part which itself is in union always with the Divine in the universe. The God Who is within is God. There is one thing more : the Atziluthic state of the soul is not the end of its progression, and an ineffable horizon expands from one dogmatic affirmation which is formulated once and once only. On my own part, I cite it for the second time, as it was met with in the Latin of Rosenroth : *Linea autem media ascendit usque ad* AIN SOPH. It follows that the soul goes on, an eternal " travelling in the subject," as I have called it elsewhere.

If it be said that these high things were conceived only in the mind by Sons of the Doctrine, my appeal is to all records of Mysticism, on the faith of which it is to be affirmed that the proper part of man is to conceive in the mind if he seeks to conceive in experience. The mode, moreover, is not defined by the evidence : in other words, the records may connote experience, as well as debate about it. However this may be, that which confronts us in Kabbalistic *Theosophia Magna* is a modality of soul in attainment which is second to none in the whole of mystical testimony, and *per contra* it exceeds all. It is the state beyond the summit of the Mount of God, an ascension into the great silence beyond all modes and forms.

After the rapture of Metatron, that great Angel of the Presence, vibrating on the threshold of Godhood; after KETHER, where Jehovah is united with Elohim; after *Mysterium* Shekinah, presiding over Sacred Births and Divine Marriages, there is set before us as the last estate of man and the last word concerning it, AIN SOPH, that which is conceived in the mind and realised from far away in the heart respecting unknowable darkness at the *centrum concentratum* of light unknown, a state beyond all being, the soul at that centre, and after all the warfare in manifold lives of quest, the soul at rest therein. We have made a long journey, and there is nothing now to follow: there is to be said only, in the humility of certitude, that it has been worth all the toil. I testify that the mind which conceives this end of being, beyond all being, in the eternal nowhere and the ineffable nought of nought is already there, in that unsearchable inward part which does not leave the Supernals, even where *linea media contemplationis suae ascendit usque ad* AIN SOPH.

APPENDICES

APPENDIX I

SEPHIROTIC DEVELOPMENTS

It has been said that later Kabbalism complicated almost inextricably the Four Worlds of the ZOHAR, one and the chief reason being that it attempted to methodise the inchoate and contradictory elements which are drawn into the fountain text. It is not unlikely that a lively apprehension on the subject may have been communicated to the general reader by an exceedingly simplified summary of the Worlds and their SEPHIROTH in the third section of my Fifth Book. For the benefit of those who may feel concerned about subsequent developments according to the mind of Kabbalism, I shall be justified perhaps in devoting a few pages to the following sketch, derived from various sources. We have seen that AIN SOPH passed, by the hypothesis, from latency into activity, still subsisting, however, in a state which is inconceivable humanly, being that of pure abstract thought. The concentration of this thought is depicted in KETHER, which is also Divine Will in primordial manifestation. The Supreme Crown [1] is, symbolically speaking, the base or sphere of the Divine Consciousness from which it would follow that self-knowledge cannot be postulated in respect of AIN SOPH itself. But this is contradicted explicitly in another text. By the second manifestation abstract thought entered into or developed the relationship of time, so that it could be regarded as that which was, which is and is to come. Lastly, it established a relation with Nature—that is to say, its development produced the universe.

By a slight extension of the symbolism KETHER is regarded also as the Throne of the Ancient of Days,[2] and as the Divine

---

[1] In the treatise entitled GATES OF LIGHT it is said that the name of KETHER is applied to the first SEPHIRA because even as a crown encircles the head so does KETHER encircle every SEPHIRA. It is the world of "Direction," which encompasses all things. This statement involves the view that the SEPHIROTH were emanated as a series of concentric circles.

[2] The term Throne is applied to several of the SEPHIROTH. Thus MALKUTH is the Throne of Judgment, TIPHERETH that of Mercy. Sometimes, however, BINAH is

Consciousness is the veil of the subsistent state, AIN SOPH is represented further as the central point of KETHER, regarded as a sphere, while the circumference is infinity, which is, as it were, the Divine Vestment. The later Kabbalists explain further that this is because KETHER has no vessel or receptacle wherein it may be contained.[1] Hence also it is beyond all cognition. The BOOK OF FORMATION affirms, however,—as we have seen—that the properties of all the SEPHIROTH are infinite.[2] As the vessel of the Divine Consciousness, which itself is contained by nothing,[3] KETHER comprehends all things:[4] it is the egg in which reposes the germ of the universe, to borrow the symbolism of another system. In particular it encompasses the remaining SEPHIROTH, which are the sum of all things. The Word of God circulates in all, and KETHER is, in a special sense, the Spirit of the Living God.

The second SEPHIRA is Wisdom, which, however, is held to be of a middle quality, for the highest of all, the truly celestial Wisdom, can be referred only to KETHER. That of CHOKMAH is, notwithstanding, so transcendent that no creature can attain it. It was concealed from Moses, and the Wisdom for which Solomon was magnified belongs to an inferior order, which connects with the lowest of the SEPHIROTH. The SEPHIRA CHOKMAH is described by the BOOK OF FORMATION as the Breath of the Spirit of God.

---

termed the Throne of Mercy, because it is as a seat under the supernal dilections. TIPHERETH is called also the Throne of Glory when it receives the influence of the Thirty-Two Paths of Wisdom. See Bk. V, § 4. The same name is applied to MALKUTH, because it is the seat of TIPHERETH. The term Throne taken simply signifies MALKUTH, and BRIAH, which is the seat of MALKUTH.—KABBALA DENUDATA, *Apparatus in Librum Sohar*, s.v. *Thronus*, vol. i. p. 483, citing the GARDEN OF POMEGRANATES, by R. Moses of Cordova. These points are cited only to shew the chameleon character of the symbolism, at issue too often with the Tree of Life itself.

[1] See *Morals and Dogma of the Ancient and Accepted Scottish Rite*, compiled by Albert Pike, Grand Commander of the Southern Jurisdiction, U.S.A. The authority is not stated, but it is derived from THE ROYAL VALLEY, by R. Napthali Hirtz.

[2] SEPHER YETZIRAH, c. I, par. 4.

[3] This appears paradoxical, but just as Fichte and Carl du Prel have maintained that the human ego is not wholly embraced in self-consciousness, so KETHER is presumably the vessel of the Divine Consciousness in the sense that it receives an influx therefrom, by a reflection from AIN SOPH to its centre. Readers may remember the Universal Solvent which yet could be contained in a phial, a diverting incident in one of the TALES OF THE GENII. According to THE ROYAL VALLEY, AIN SOPH had full consciousness and appeciation, prior to their actual existence, of all the grades and impersonations contained unmanifested within Itself.

[4] There is hence, as Isaac de Acco observes in his treatise on THE ENLIGHTENMENT OF THE EYES, an unity of the ten SEPHIROTH in themselves, which unity is concentrated always in AIN SOPH. It must be admitted, perhaps, that this idea is contained implicitly in the Zoharic statement that AIN SOPH is the beginning and end of all degrees in the creation.

APPENDIX I

BINAH, Intelligence or Understanding, is represented symbolically by the same fundamental authority as the moisture of the Breath of the Spirit. It is the highest SEPHIRA with which man can establish correspondence, but it contains at the same time one mystery which was also concealed from Moses. The root of all roots and the foundation of all foundations is communicated thereby to man, who could otherwise have no knowledge of the antecedent states of the Divine Nature.[1]

Magnificence or Mercy, GEDULAH or CHESED, the fourth emanation, is the warmth or fire contained within the moisture breathed forth by the Spirit of God. It expresses the Eternal Love and Compassion, connecting with life and vitality. It is the base of that *beneplacitum termino carens* which is ascribed to CHOKMAH and supposes implicitly the free will of the Divine Agent. It follows from this as a consequence that the universe was made or emanated, not because anything was wanting to the Divine completeness, but out of the fullness of goodwill, though some of the later Kabbalists, especially Isaac de Loria,[2] are not of one mind as regards the last point. Symbolically speaking, CHESED is therefore the SEPHIRA by which God constituted the world, operating through the Holy Shekinah.

The fifth SEPHIRA is GEBURAH, signifying Judgment, Justice, Judicial Power, known also as PACHAD, or Fear. It is the Supernal Tribunal, before which no creature can subsist. The treatise entitled SCHAARE ZEDEK excepts, however, those valiant heroes of the Lord who have overcome their concupiscence.

TIPHERETH, or Beauty, the sixth SEPHIRA, is, in a sense, the conjunction of Mercy and Judgment and summarises the Divine goodness: it is the heart of the Pillar of Benignity. It is to be noted that VAU, the letter which symbolises the Divine Son extended on the Tree of Life as on a Great Cross

---

[1] All things, according to the commentary of Isaac de Loria, in a certain and most abstruse manner, consist and reside and are contained in BINAH, which projects them and sends them downwards, species by species, into the several worlds of Creation, Formation and Fabrication. BINAH is hence represented as a great reservoir or ocean; it is the source of prophetic inspiration, as CHOKMAH is that of revelation. We have seen that it is more especially the Shekinah in transcendence, at once her essence and abode. We have seen also that the world was made by Shekinah, and she made it in the spirit of CHESED, the fact notwithstanding that she belongs more especially to the Severity side in the Tree of Life.

[2] See LIBER DRUSHIM, a metaphysical introduction to the Kabbalah, KABBALA DENUDATA, vol. i. pt. 2.

of Manifestation, is denominated TIPHERETH, because it contains all things, exercises dominion in all and is invested with all Sacred Names.¹

But the Divine Benignity is manifested by the Victory signified in NETZACH, the seventh SEPHIRA. There are three rays diffused from the splendour of Providence—Benignity, Beauty and Victory. When they shine and are diffused over the SEPHIROTH the whole world is filled with joy and perfection, for the Divine goodness itself looks forth upon all creatures, and all the worlds are in fullness and completeness.² This SEPHIRA is also termed Eternity.

The eighth SEPHIRA, HOD, signifies Glory, Adornment, Splendour. In combination with NETZACH it is called the armies of Jehovah, and these two SEPHIROTH signify two hills of Zion, on which the dew of Hermon falls. All the salutations and praises contained in the Psalter of David belong to this emanation. It is the place of praise, the place of wars and victories, and of the treasury of benefits.³

JESOD, the Basis or Foundation, the ninth SEPHIRA, is the storehouse of all forces, the seat of life and vitality, and the nourishment of all the world.⁴

MALKUTH is the tenth SEPHIRA, signifying Dominion, Royalty, Kingdom. In the LESSER HOLY SYNOD it is termed "the Mother of all the Living." According to later Kabbalism, it is the final manifestation, emanation or development of the Divine Nature taking place in the Divine World, and is therefore that point at which the more external orders make contact with the supernal.⁵ This is unintelligible as it stands, but it should be understood that the commentators and interpreters represent the Sephirotic Decade as repeated

---

¹ The authority is SCHAARE ORAH, § V.
² APPARATUS *in Librum Sohar.* KABBALA DENUDATA, s.v. *Superatio,* i.e. *Netzach,* pp. 589 *et seq.,* citing SCHAARE ORAH.
³ *Ibid.* s.v. *Decus, Gloria,* i.e. HOD, pp. 268 *et seq.,* deriving from the same work. According to the ZOHAR, NETZACH and HOD correspond to extension, multiplication and force, and thence issue all the forces of the universe, for which reason these SEPHIROTH are also termed the Armies of the Eternal. *Zohar,* iii., 296a, Mantua.
⁴ KABBALA DENUDATA, *Apparatus,* s.v. *Fundamentum,* i.e., JESOD, pp. 439 *et seq.* The authority is PARDES RIMMONIM. The key of the symbolism is given by Rosenroth as follows, but without comment, as if it lay beyond his measures : *In personis* FUNDAMENTUM *denotat membrum genitale utriusque sexus.*
⁵ Hence it is said that the tenth SEPHIRA is the SHEKINAH, that is, the place of the manifestation of Deity. But this is the Lower Shekinah, represented by the final HE of the Divine Name. It should be added that when the text describes MALKUTH as a final manifestation in the Divine World it follows that ATZILUTH, the World of Deity, contains the whole Sephirotic Decade. It is the prototype and the witness above of that which abides below.

through each of the Four Worlds, and the reference in this place is therefore to MALKUTH in ATZILUTH, the World of Deity. To increase complications and confusions there is the Decade in each SEPHIRA.

To this brief general description, which rests on the authority and reproduces the words of the Kabbalists, I will now add the heads of a modern interpretation, which is, of course, conjectural and a personal point of view, but has a reasonable aspect and illustrates, perhaps unawares, the office of Divine Thought in the Zoharic evolution of the universe, as well as embodying later intimations.

AIN SOPH, the Unknowable and Absolute, manifests through the efflux of the spiritual and material universe, using the SEPHIROTH as its media. The first emanation symbolises Abstract Thought, the Absolute assuming consciousness to manifest outwardly. The second emanation represents the association of abstract ideas in the intellect, which association is Wisdom. The third emanation is Mind receiving the impression of the abstract ideas. These three constitute the Spirit of the World. The second triad of SEPHIROTH, Mercy, Judgment and Beauty, includes the principles of construction and symbolises the abstract dimensions of matter, length, breadth, depth and their double polarity. CHESED and GEBURAH are the centripetal and centrifugal energies between the poles of the dimensions. In their junction with TIPHERETH they represent all ethical life and perfection. They correspond to the Soul of the World. The third triad is dynamic; its SEPHIROTH signify the Deity as universal potentiality, energy and productive principle. They answer to the idea of Nature, the *natura naturans*, however, and not the *natura naturata*. The tenth SEPHIRA, or MALKUTH, represents the Concrete, and is the energy and executive power of the Abstract Intellect.[1]

---

[1] Summarised from Isaac Myer's PHILOSOPHY OF IBN GEBIROL, § xiii.

APPENDIX II

THE FOUR WORLDS IN LATER KABBALISM

IF scholiasts and commentators have complicated the Worlds of the ZOHAR, it must be granted that they had at least the will to methodise, and it is possible therefore to present a summary of their views in a brief conspectus. The visible world was for them the last consequence in the development of the attributes of God, while the SEPHIROTH were symbols of those attributes, and the manner of their unfoldment is like a history of Divine Evolution. It is affirmed, for example, that God called Himself Wisdom in CHOKMAH and Intelligence in BINAH; that in CHESED He assumed the character of Greatness and Benignity, in GEBURAH of Severity, in TIPHERETH of Beauty, in NETZACH of Victory, in HOD of our Glorious Author, and in JESOD of our Support, all worlds and vessels being maintained thereby; while in MALKUTH He adopted the title of King. We must recall again, however, in this connection that the Sephirotic Decade is in each of the Four Worlds, according to later Kabbalists, and therefore that this enumeration belongs to ATZILUTH in a primary sense, whereas in the realms below it obtains by derivation only. From the World of Deity, the Archetypal World and World of Emanation, the Divine Virtues were projected downward and there was produced a Second World, that of BRIAH or Creation, regarded as the World of highest finite intelligence, technically that of the archangels. Thereafter the prolongation was continued into a Third World, that of YETZIRAH, or Formation, the abode of angelic choirs. Though further removed from Supreme Perfection, there is not a taint of the material in this place of incorporeal beings. It is otherwise with ASSIAH, the World of Action, the fourth product of the tenfold emanation, for this is the region of matter, the earth of man in particular, and also the dwelling of those demons which are called shells or *Cortices* by the later Kabbalists. In common with many other systems of unqualified or qualified emanation this material world is regarded as the gross purgations of the upper regions. It should be observed in such connection that the SEPHIROTH or Virtues which permeate the four systems deteriorate as they proceed further, and that the corruption of the infernal world, the formless region and the seven hells of Kabbalism are apparently the extreme limits of the outpouring which begins in KETHER. Thus, in order to explain the imperfections found in the world-craft of a perfect Author the degeneration of His infinite energy is not disdained as a resource. It is easy to criticise such a system, or to set it down as beneath criticism; but, again, the disability is common to the dreams of all emanationists, even when they invoke creation at one point or other of their reverie. It remains to say that we have the authority of the ZOHAR for regarding the demons as products of the will of God and designed for a specific purpose.[1]

Broadly speaking, the Four Worlds of the later Kabbalah may be regarded as corresponding in the physical order:

(a) ATZILUTH, to the Primum Mobile.
(b) BRIAH, to the sphere of the Zodiac.
(c) YETZIRAH, to the planetary chain.
(d) ASSIAH, to the world of the four elements.

Thus, astronomy is at the basis of the conception—or is at least incorporated therein.

The doctrine of the Four Worlds originated between the period of the SEPHER YETZIRAH and that of the promulgation of the ZOHAR, and it received many increments from commentators on the latter work. It is first met with in the BOOK OF EMANATION, which is a product of the school of Isaac the Blind. This treatise is ascribed, doubtfully enough, to R. Jacob Nazir, who belonged to the second half of the twelfth century. Its distribution of the Four Worlds differs from the above tabulation, as, for example, by referring the souls of the just to BRIAH, the archangelic world. It should be added that the ZOHAR recognises also a distribution of the SEPHIROTH into Three Worlds—(1) Intelligible, (2) Moral, (3) Natural.

---

[1] We have already seen that, according to the BOOK OF FORMATION, the ten SEPHIROTH are the infinite of evil as well as of good.

APPENDIX III

THE INSTRUMENTS OF CREATION

The doctrine of AIN SOPH may be assigned a high place among old theosophical dreams; the Sephirotic system may not suffer by comparison with other emanation reveries and may even challenge all; the metaphysics of the Two Countenances is crude on the surface and in the texts from which it depends is perhaps the most barbaric and unintelligible of all symbolism; but a considerable profundity of meaning may be discerned within it: there have been attempts in this direction. The cosmology of SEPHER YETZIRAH, with its development in the ZOHAR, belongs, however, to more purely fantastic aspects of Kabbalistic dream, and yet in its later form there lies something behind it which suggests—in the language of Jacob Böhme—" a deep searching " of the Divine Mind. I do not propose to add anything on this part of the mythos; but the very curious and indeed bizarre scheme of the SEPHER YETZIRAH in respect of the Hebrew Letters may be tabulated by way of supplement to what has been set forth previously.

We have seen that the World of BRIAH is that of Creation, but whatever reservations may be inferred from later Kabbalistic writers on the axiom *ex nihilo nihil fit*,[1] we have seen also that their use of the term Creation does not at all correspond to the sense of Christian cosmology, because that which they called Nothing evasively was the plenitude in which the All lay latent. Further, the World of BRIAH was not that in which anything material was formed, emanated, or otherwise brought into actual being; it was rather the Elohistic World, that of Panurgic force and intelligence, which became formative in YETZIRAH, but did not produce matter except in the Fourth World. Now the materials used and shaped, or, perhaps, more properly speaking, the instruments, the matrices of the material world, were in all simplicity the letters of the Hebrew alphabet, as explained previously.

---

[1] According to Myer, the speculative or metaphysical Kabbalah is an attempt to harmonise Hebrew monotheism with the "fundamental principle of ancient philosophy," namely, the axiom quoted above. PHILOSOPHY OF IBN GEBIROL, p. 230. This was also the design of Maimonides in his GUIDE OF THE PERPLEXED.

APPENDIX III

According to SEPHER YETZIRAH, God imparted to them form and weight by combining and transforming them in divers manners, ALEPH with all the rest and all the rest with ALEPH; BETH with all and all with BETH; and so of the rest.[1] Some hundreds of permutations were obtained in this manner, which *ex hypothesi* are the origin not only of all languages but of all creatures. As these permutations can also, by a later hypothesis, be reduced to a single Name, that of TETRAGRAMMATON, otherwise JOD, HE, VAU, HE = Jehovah or Yahwe, it is said that the entire universe proceeds from this Name.[2] The reader will discern at once the nature of the device, which may be methodised by a simple process:

The world came forth from God:
But the name of God is יהוה;
Therefore the world came forth from יהוה.[3]

The fundamental letters of the BOOK OF FORMATION are not, however, those which compose the Divine Name: they are *Aleph* (א), *Mem* (מ) and *Shin* (ש), distinguished as the Three Mothers and corresponding to Air, Water and Fire. The heavens are formed of Fire, the Earth is of Water, and the Air of the Mediate Spirit.

Their correspondences are: in the year, the torrid, frigid and temperate seasons; in man, the head, belly and breast.

Besides the Three Mothers there are seven double letters— *Beth* (ב = B), *Ghimel* (ג = G), *Daleth* (ד = D), *Kaph* (כ = K), *Pe* (פ = P), *Resh* (ר = R) and *Tau* (ת = T, Th). These seven signs stand in the Book of Formation for:—

Life		Death
Peace		Strife
Knowledge		Ignorance
Wealth	and their opposites	Poverty
Grace		Sin
Fruitfulness		Sterility
Dominion		Slavery

---

[1] SEPHER YETZIRAH, c. ii. par. 4. Cf. the Talmudic teaching that the present world was created by God with the letter HE and the world to come with the letter JOD.

[2] And thus the Name in its realisation—understood in the heart and mind—gives all knowledge according to the Kabbalists. Compare Éliphas Lévi, who reduces the doctrine to an axiom: "All knowledge is in a word, all power in a name; the intelligence of this name is the Science of Abraham and Solomon." CLEFS MAJEURES, Paris, 1895.

[3] It will be unnecessary to point out that this is a logical *non sequitur*, but it must be added that for the Kabbalistic Jew the True Name of God, as indeed of any existence, was a manifestation of its essence and, as such, inseparable therefrom.

Their correspondences in the universe are:—

East	Depth
West	North
Height	South

and the Holy Palace, fixed in the centre and sustaining all things. When the seven double letters had been shaped by the Deity, He combined and created therewith the planets in the heaven; the days in the year—*i.e.*, the seven days of creation; and the gates in man—*i.e.*, eyes, ears, nostrils and mouth.

There are, finally, twelve simple letters, having the following correspondences in man and the world:—

He	= ה, E	= Sight	= N.E.
Vau	= ו, V	= Hearing	= S.E.
Dzain	= ז, Z	= Smell	= E. Height
Cheth	= ח, Ch	= Speech	= E. Depth
Teth	= ט, T	= Digestion	= N.W.
Yod	= י, I	= Coition	= S.W.
Lamed	= ל, L	= Action	= W. Height
Nun	= נ, N	= Motion	= W. Depth
Samek	= ס, S	= Wrath	= S. Height
Ain	= ע,	= Mirth	= S. Depth
Tsade	= צ, Ts	= Meditation	= N. Height
Quoph	= ק, Q	= Sleep	= N. Depth

By means of the twelve simples there were created the Signs of the Zodiac, the twelve months and the twelve directors of man—*i.e.*, the two hands, the feet, the two kidneys, the liver, the gall, the spleen, the colon, the bladder and the arteries.

I must leave my readers to decide how this bizarre system is to be interpreted. It has been regarded by one or two critics who have neither mystical nor occult leanings as a serious attempt to devise a philosophical cosmology;[1] but for myself I must confess that I do not see in what manner it is superior to the familiar fable of the elephant and the tortoise. There are those, of course, who discern in it a secret meaning, who remember, for example, that the letters of the Hebrew Alphabet stand also for numerals, and do not fail to cite the

---

[1] Dr. Alfred Edersheim seems to speak in this sense in his HISTORY OF THE JEWISH NATION *after the Destruction of Jerusalem*. I have used the third, posthumous edition, revised by the Rev. H. A. White, M.A. London. 1896. See p. 408.

scriptural statement that God made everything by weight, number and measure.

Indeed, the SEPHER YETZIRAH may be regarded as a commentary on this declaration. As a rule, however, I think that the Kabbalists, like other makers of systems, arcane and otherwise, meant that which they said, and if they did not say all that they meant the unexpressed residuum was along the lines of the sense expressed. When they affirmed therefore that the world was made by means of the letters of the alphabet, they really meant what they stated; but if it be asked whether they understood by those letters the symbols of hidden powers, it may be inferred that they did, perhaps beyond question, having regard to the reason of things. The letters are, in this case, more than mere symbols: they are vessels or manifestations of concealed virtues. The sense is therefore true *ex hypothesi* in a literal and transliteral manner.

The warrant of the hypothesis must be sought in the Talmudic system, which believed that the body of the sacred text was divine like the sense which was its soul, which soul had, even as man himself, an inner spirit, the highest of all, namely, the concealed meaning. Now, the letters of the alphabet were the materials of the textual body, to the care and preservation of which the traditional science of the Massorah was devoted.[1] For the mystical Jew, who discerned strange abysses of mystery in the smallest peculiarities of the THORAH, there was a weird fascination in the fact that all the wonders and sanctities of the Law and the Prophets resulted from the diverse combinations of twenty-two letters, and he came to regard this handful of conventional hieroglyphs as so many sacraments or instruments by which Divine Wisdom was communicated to man. In a word, for

---

[1] The MASSORAH was concerned with the body of the text, the rules as to reading and writing the THORAH, and special considerations on the mystical sense of the sacred characters. It belongs therefore to the criticism of the Hebrew text. It was also, as already seen, that which was delivered openly by the rabbins in contradiction to that which was supposed to have been communicated secretly. Thus it taught the true reading of doubtful passages, the true pronunciation of uncertain words, the correct subdivisions of the books, and so forth. Buxtorf's work entitled TIBERIAS (Basiliæ, 1620, 4to) deals with the MASSORAH. Compare Molitor's PHILOSOPHY OF TRADITION. Some French writers belonging to the occult school pretend that its exoteric formulæ were designed to conceal every trace of a secret sense in the THORAH. See MISSION DES JUIFS, p. 646, by Saint-Yves d'Alveydre, who follows Fabre d'Olivet in LA LANGUE HÉBRAÏQUE RESTITUÉE. The MASSORAH compiled from MSS., alphabetically and lexically arranged, has been published by C. D. Ginsburg. 3 vols. London. 1880-85.

him they ceased to be conventions; a Divine Revelation required a Divine Language to express it, and the alphabet of that language was a derivation from the noumenal world, vessels of singular election, instruments of Deity, from which it was an easy transition to suppose that such channels of spiritual grace and life must have fulfilled some exalted office in the shaping of the universe itself.

APPENDIX IV

DIVINE NAMES

It is not my intention to produce a monograph on the Names and Titles of God in Kabbalistic and Rabbinical literature: it would be unlikely to serve any purpose of those whom I address. There is a sufficient study of the subject in the JEWISH ENCYCLOPÆDIA, Vol. IX, pp. 160–165, with the necessary references to other places in the collection. The following bare indications are added to elucidate allusions in my text. TETRAGRAMMATON, the so-called Ineffable or Unpronounceable Name, is the Name of Four Letters, יהוה = YHWH = YAHWEH or YAHAWEH, the Jehovah of our incorrect rendering, which Hebrew scholarship has characterised as philologically impossible. It is *Nomen Ineffabile*, that is to say, inexpressible, because the vowels thereto belonging are now unknown, having passed out of memory after the destruction of the Temple in the year 70 A.D. There is an explanatory Talmudic tradition that the utterance of the Sacred Name was prohibited at the death of the High Priest Simeon the Righteous. When it is said that the pointing of Adonai or Elohim is substituted by Massoretic practice for the lost vowels, this does not mean that there was an attempt to pronounce the Name with their aid but that one of the alternatives was to be used instead. It will be remembered that God is made to say in the ZOHAR: My Name is written YHVH but is read Adonai.

As regards the Sacred Name of Twelve Letters, which has been mentioned once in my text, according to one explanation it is formed as follows: הקדוש ברוך הוא = *Sanctus Benedictus Ille*; but another derives from the word אמן = Amen, in Isaiah, lxv, the letters of which represent *ex hypothesi* אדני המלך נאמן = *Dominus Rex Fidelis*. There has been reference also to a Name of Forty-two Letters, which is accounted for in various ways: (1) by inscribing other Divine Names letter by letter at full length; (2) by the fact that the first eight words in Genesis total forty-two letters; (3) by tabulating forty-two Divine Titles which do not rank as Names, but are held to represent all the attributes of God, and regarding their initials as composing the Extended Name. I have made a selection only as it is obvious that there is no end to devices of this kind. Finally, the ZOHAR refers on more than one occasion to SHEM HA MEPHORASH, and this is the Sacred Name of Seventy-two Letters. It happens that Exodus xiv. 19–21, has this number of alphabetical symbols in each of the three verses and thus can provide not only a triple illustration of the Super-extended Name but the three can produce when combined no less than seventy-two other distinct Names. It need not be said that there are other methods of extraction, and Athanasius Kircher offers us the benefit of all which he has met with or selected to throw light on ŒDIPUS ÆGYPTIACUS. There are printed works and manuscripts which deal yet more fully with the subject. All the Hierarchies of pseudo-Dionysius and all the pan-Dæmonium of Magical Black Grimoires are taxed to extend their tabulations. I leave it therefore at this point and with it the whole subject, to those who are concerned.

APPENDIX V

PHASES OF THE SOUL

THE Kabbalistic division of the soul into five parts has been given in Book VI, with the necessary elucidations. The following variant occurs in the DISCOURSE OF THE ANCIENT ONE, and it is given here because of its importance as a point of junction between Zoharic formulations on the subject and those of subsequent expositors. The soul in its various phases was distributed through all the worlds of Kabbalism, and every phase was held to contain all the others. It will be seen that this unmanageable complexity is justified by a text imbedded in the ZOHAR itself.

"When the child of man is born into this world there is appointed to him natural life (NEPHESH) from the side of the animals, the clean side, from the side of the Holy Wheels (the AUPHANIM, a Kabbalistic order of angels, assigned by some attributions to CHOKMAH). Should he deserve more there is appointed to him a rational spirit (RUAH) from the side of the Holy Living Creatures (HAYYOTH HA KADOSH, another order of angels, commonly attributed to KETHER by later Kabbalism, which seems, however, inconsistent with this tabulation). Should he deserve even more there is appointed to him a higher spirit, NESHAMAH, from the side of the Thrones (*i.e.*, ARALIM, the order of angels ascribed to BINAH, whence come the higher souls, according to the BERESHITH section of the ZOHAR proper). These three are the mother, the male servant and the handmaid, even the Daughter of the King. Should he deserve yet more there is appointed to him an animal soul (NEPHESH) in the way of ATZILUTH (that is, the lowest essence of the supernal portions of the soul, again in late Kabbalism), from the side of the Daughter, YEHIDAH, the only one (YEHIDAH is the quintessence, the highest nature of the soul, under TSURE), and the same is called Daughter of the King. If he still deserve more, there is appointed to him the rational spirit (RUAH) of ATZILUTH, from the side of the

Central Pillar (that is, Benignity, the middle Pillar of the Sephirotic Tree), and he is called the Son of the Holy Blessed One, whence it is written: ' Ye are the children of the Lord your God (Deut. xiv. 1). And if he deserve even more there is appointed to him a higher spirit (NESHAMAH) from the side of ABBA (the Supernal Father, attributed to CHOKMAH in the Atzilutic world) and of the Supernal Mother (AIMA, attributed to BINAH in the same world), whence it is also written: ' And He breathed into his nostrils the breath of life ' (literally, souls of life, Gen. ii. 7). What is life? It is JAH (the Divine Name attributed to KETHER by another Zoharic text), whence we have heard: ' Let everything that hath breath *(i.e., life, i.e.,* all souls) praise the Lord' *(i.e.,* JAH), Ps. cl. 6). And in it is TETRAGRAMMATON *(i.e.,* J.D.V.D., *i.e.,* JHVH) perfected. But if he deserve still more there is appointed to him JDVD, in its plenary fullness, the letters of which are JOD, HE, VAU, HE: HEH, VAU, HEH, JOD, which is man in the path of ATZILUTH, and he is then said to be in the likeness (*simulacrum*) of his Lord, whence also it is said: ' And have dominion over the fish of the sea ' (Gen. i. 28)); that is, he shall rule over all the heavens and over all the AUPHANIM and SERAPHIM, over all the Hosts and Powers, above and below. When therefore the child of man deserves the NEPHESH from the side of the Daughter YEHIDAH, this is to say: ' She shall not go out as the men-servants do ' " (meaning probably that he shall serve God in His house for ever, Exod. xxi. 7).[1]

---

[1] Zohar, ii. 94*b*, Brody ed.

INDEX

AARON, Rod of, 334, 526.
Aaron the Great, his commentary on the SEPHER YETZIRAH, 111.
Abaddon, 329.
ABBA and AIMA, the Father in CHOKMAH, 137, 146, 204, 206; Supreme Mother, allocated to BINAH, 137, 204; Mother below, 342, 345; Father, 206; the Supernal Father and Mother, 201, 211. *See also* 69, 137, 241, 362, 363, 416, 581.
Abbah, R., the traditional scribe of R. Simeon, 57, 141; eulogy of R. Simeon, 147.
Abel, 251, 287.
Abelson, Dr., on Sufism in the ZOHAR, 80, 571–572.
Abraham, his call and its symbolism, 297; Garden of the Lord, 298; meeting with Melchizedek, 299; the Sacred Covenant, 300; its Mystery of Sex, 302.
Abraham, R., his commentary on the SEPHER YETZIRAH, 56, 106; its Zoharic elements, 107; on AIN SOPH, 107; alleged identity with the instructor of Flamel, 108, 109. *See also* Flamel.
Abraham Abulafia, suggested author of the ZOHAR, 60, 81; his writings, 92; his Messianic enthusiasm, 92, 93, 98.
Abraham ben David Ha Levi, his Aristotelian tendency, 46; a great orthodox apologist, 92; his ORDER OF THE TRADITION, 93, 107; Abraham b. David the younger, 92, 106, 108, 109.
Abraham de Seba, R., 286.
Abraham of Posquière, suggested author of the ZOHAR, 60, 94.
Abraham ben Samuel Zakut, his BOOK OF GENEALOGIES, 52; his estimate of the ZOHAR, *ib.*; his narrative concerning Isaac de Acco, 53–55.
Abraham ben Meïr ibn Ezra, 46.
Abraham ibn Wakhar, 94.
Abramelin, spurious work attributed to, 49, 522.
Abravanel, *i.e.*, Leo the Hebrew, his DIALOGUES ON LOVE, 428; sketch of the author, 429; singular mistakes in regard to his work, 429, 430; summary account of, 430–432.
Absolute, beginning of Kabbalistic philosophy, 185; the essence of all, 189; postulation of its existence by the Kabbalah, 191.
Abu Alphrag on the alleged True Synagogue, 93.

Academy of Sura, 90.
Adam, his Gift of Wisdom in Paradise, 16; its restoration after the Fall, 17; Adam and the Glory of God, 263; made male and female, 265; his mystic sleep, 266; his gradual degeneration, 279; his nakedness, 281; fleshly vestments, 283; the expulsion, 289; the wives of Adam, 287.
Adam Kadmon, archetypal and primordial man, x; abode in ATZILUTH, 266; a second Adam in BRIAH and YETZIRAH, *ib.*; an Averse Adam, 419.
Adam Microprosopus, 256.
Adam Protoplastes, 211, 238, 418; Adam of the Earthly Paradise: see Book VII., sections 1, 3.
ADONAI, substituted for the TETRAGRAM, 162, 163, 342, 343. *See also* 351, and, generally, under Divine Names.
ÆSH MEZAREPH, an application of Kabbalism to Alchemy, 424; language of, *ib.*; probable period, 425; Lévi's alleged reconstitution, 426; difficulties of the treatise, 427; Sephirotic attribution of the metals, 427, 428: for minor references see 440, 534, 536, 538–540.
AGLA and ARARITA, 83, 84.
Agobad, St., probable reference to the SEPHER YETZIRAH, 43, 44, 74.
Agrippa, Cornelius, sketch of, 452–455; gives earliest methodical description of the Kabbalah, 452; probable source of his acquaintance, 453; summary of his instruction, 453, 454; his subsequent retractation, 454, 455; influence of Agrippa on Vaughan, 473, 474. *See also* x, 441, 476.
Ahasuerus, 368.
AIMA ELOHIM, 551.
AIN SOPH, the Kabbalistic name of the unmanifest Deity, 187; its meaning, *ib.*; the subsistent state of Deity, 189; transcendency of, 189–191; problems created for the Jew, 191; the decade and AIN SOPH, 194; passage from latency to activity, 605; AIN SOPH as the central point of KETHER, 209, 606; the SEPHIROTH in union with AIN SOPH, 411; manifestation, 220, 609; philosophical claims of the doctrine, 612; doctrine of, fundamental in the Kabbalah, 66; an ultimate concept of metaphysics, 66; not described by Saadya Gaon, 104; according to Azriel, 110; the Supernal SEPHIROTH an emanation from AIN SOPH, 197; the inaccessible

God, 351; ascent of Shekinah, 347; a World of Hiddenness, 197; Font and Source of all, 600; Ain-Soph Aour, 20, 208. *See also* 566, 601, 602.
Aitsinger, M., 550.
Akiba, R., traditional author of the SEPHER YETZIRAH, 42; claims of the attribution, 43; his mystical tendencies, 64; his death, 42. *See also* 81, 540, 572.
Al (El). *See* Divine Names.
Albelda, M., 481.
Albo, J., 481.
Alchemy, rabbinical influence on, 424; the Flamel legend, 108, 109, 424, 426; alchemical allusions in the ZOHAR, 536; Alchemy and the SEPHIROTH, 427, 428; Alchemy and Paracelsus, 456; general connection with Kabbalism, 534-542. *See also* v, 22, 579.
Alliance, Eternal. *See* Covenant.
Alphabet, Mysteries of, 16. *See also* SEPHER YETZIRAH and Instruments of Creation.
Alphabet of Akiba, 42, 45, 88.
Altar, 264, 293, 294, 389.
Al Tufail, 78, 79.
Amalek, 274, 275, 276.
Amelineau, M. E., on the coincident development of Gnosticism and Kabbalism, 69.
Ancient, Ancient of Days, Ancient of Ancients. *See* Vast Countenance.
Angels, the Hierarchies according to Mirandula, 445; according to pseudo-Dionysius, 271; according to later Kabbalism, 254-256. *See also* 263, 269-277, and s.v. Pneumatology.
Angus, Joseph, on exegetical methods, 36.
Apple, 279-283; Garden of Apples, 307.
Apron. *See* Vestures.
Aquinas, St. Thomas, 95, 330, 362.
Arabian Philosophy, 76.
Archangelus de Burgo Nuovo, Commentary on Mirandula, 443; excerpts from, 446, 448; his apparent view of the Kabbalah, 460.
Architect, under God, Shekinah as, 342, 582.
ARIK ANPIN. *See* Vast Countenance.
Aristobulus, 71.
Aristotle, yoke of, in Jewry, 46; influence on Abraham b. David Ha Levi, 93; alleged influence on Avicebron, 94, 97; Saadya Gaon, an Aristotelian philosopher, 106; Azriel opposed by the Aristotelian party, 109.
Ark of the Covenant, 172, 292, 313, 356, 368.
Arnold, Matthew, 227, 277.
Asher, 584.
Asmodeus, 526.
ASSIAH. *See* Four Worlds.

Astral Light, 32, 217.
Astrology, not essentially connected with the Kabbalah, 542, 543; much studied by the Jews, 543; Astronomy and the SEPHIROTH, 544, 545; summary of Jewish Astrology, 545-548; Jewish Astronomy, 547; Sephirotic Astrology according to Gaffarel and modern occultists, 547, 548; Astrology condemned by Picus, vii; its condemnation by the ZOHAR, 9, 527, 528.
Atonement, 158.
ATZILUTH, xv, 197, 206.
Augustine, St., 278.
Averroes, 96, 441.
Avicebron. *See* Gebirol.
Aza and Azael, 273, 274.
Azriel, R., on the SEPHIROTH, 98; on the SEPHER YETZIRAH, 103, 109, 110. *See also* 498.

BAAL-SHEM, Order of, 81, 564.
Babel, 295, 296.
Bailly on the Astronomical Signs, 541.
Bakoda, R. Behai ben Joseph ibn, his treatise on the DUTIES OF THE HEART, 55, 56.
Balaam, 274, 368.
Balance, 136.
Bar Cochba, his Messianic mission, 42, 81.
Barth, F., on Kabbalism in Cornelius Agrippa, 453.
Bartolocci, Julius, his rabbinical bibliography, 3, 26; his prejudgment of the Kabbalah, 48; on Abraham ben David Ha Levi, 93; on the Commentary of R. Saadya Gaon, 103; on other commentators of the SEPHER YETZIRAH, 111; on the commentators of the Canticle of Canticles, 178; on Abravanel, 429; on the minor literature of Kabbalism, 178. *See also* 91, 103, 412, 432.
Barzillai, Judah ben, on the SEPHER YETZIRAH, 111.
Basnage, on the date of the original ZOHAR, 59; importance of the tenth century for Israel, 89; on R. Eliezer's Commentary on the SEPHER YETZIRAH, 111; his slight knowledge of the ZOHAR, 115; on Talmudic references to former creations, 141, 142; on the date of Moses of Cordova, 410; on that of Isaac de Loria, 412; on Henry More, 470. *See also* 43, 55, 67, 92, 142, 410, 411, 429.
Ben Dior Ha Levi, 92.
Benjamin, 251.
BERESHITH RABBA, 136.
BERESHITH, Mystery of, 15; Zoharic explanations of, 211, 221, 227; according to Mirandula, 449; according to Henry More, 471.

Bertet, Adolphe, on Kabbalism in the Pentateuch, 24.
Berthelot, on the spurious books of Geber, 49; on Jewish influence upon Alchemy, 535; on the Leyden papyrus, 537; on the Kabbalah and Alchemy, 542, 549.
Beswick, Samuel, on the Swedenborgian Rite, 549.
BETH-EL, 299.
BETH ELOHIM, 190, 258.
Betrothed, 209, 358.
Beyers, on the Christian aspects of the Kabbalah, 477.
BINAH. *See* SEPHIROTH.
BINAH IMRI, 121, 409.
Blavatsky, H. P., on the Kabbalah and its literature, 511, 512, 513, 574.
Blunt's DICTIONARY OF DOCTRINAL AND HISTORICAL THEOLOGY, its worthless article on the Kabbalah, 5; on the language of the ZOHAR, 63; absurd mistake as to the GREATER and LESSER ZOHAR, 120.
Body of God, description of, 44, 88.
Böhme, Jacob, 225, 278, 279, 376, 530.
BOHU, 198.
Bois, Jules, on Raymond Lully, 439.
Boismont, Brierre de, on Vampires, 258.
Bono-Homo, Alphonsus, 317.
BOOK, SECRET, 16, 17; BOOK OF CONCEALMENT OR MODESTY, 119 *et seq.*; BOOK OF GOD, 301; Book of Enoch, 17; BOOK OF MYSTERIES, 295; BOOK OF MAGIC, 526; BOOK OF BRIGHTNESS, 150 *et seq.*; BOOK OF SOPHE, 535; BOOK OF THE GENERATIONS OF ADAM, 16, 17.
Bread and Wine, 175, 299, 586, 587. *See* Eucharist.
BRIAH. *See* Four Worlds.
Bride and Bridegroom, 209, 211, 342, 352; Bride of Heaven, 19; Bride of God, 344; Divine Bride, 357, 363.
Bride of MICROPROSOPUS, 146, 147, 209, 210, 211.
Brière, M. de, on the transmission of Secret Knowledge, 24.
Browne, E. G., on Islamic Mysticism, 80.
Bryant, Jacob, on the Mysteries, 295. *See also* 68.
Buddæus on the BAHIR, 152.
Burnet, Thomas, his criticism of the Kabbalah, 483; on the transmission of the secret wisdom of Moses, 483; on the Nominal and Real Kabbalah, 484; errors and speculations, 484, 485; on Oriental Allegories, 485.
Buxtorf on the BAHIR, 152.
Byler, H. C. van, on Kabbalistic Alchemy, 542.

CAHEN, Samuel, on the origin of the ZOHAR, 59.

Cain, 273, 286, 287.
Calmet, 33.
Canaan, 299, 329, 332.
Casaubon, I., 535.
Celestial Chiefs, 297.
Chamai R., on the Kabbalistic Art, 432, 433.
Chasdai, R., connection with Hay Gaon and Gebirol, 90.
Chateau, M. H., his alleged French version of the ZOHAR, 116.
CHESED. *See* SEPHIROTH.
Chinese Kabbalah, 68.
Chiromancy, 530, 533.
CHOKMAH. *See* SEPHIROTH.
Christ, 286, 317, 321.
Christian, P., alleged Astrological Kabbalah, 548; on Cagliostro's process of divination, *ib.*
Christian Elements in the ZOHAR, 574-588.
Christian Trinitarian Doctrine, 586.
Cimara, Comtesse de, 213, 214, 215, 216.
Circumcision, 212, 232, 299-302. *See* Covenant.
Claverus, on the ÆSH MEZAREPH, 425.
Closed Eye, The, 143.
Commentary on Ruth, fragments in the ZOHAR and possible authorship, 177-179.
Community of Israel, 222, 229, 303, 313, 358, 382, 587, 590, 594.
Confucianism, 68.
Converts from Kabbalism, 21, 433.
Correspondences, 72, 135, 225, 227, 397.
Cortices, the demons of Kabbalism, 256; attributed to ASSIAH, *ib.*; as recrements of the Edomite Kings, 418.
Countenances. *See* Lesser and Vast Countenances.
Court de Gebelin, as an authority on Egyptology and the Tarot, 554, 555.
Cousin, Victor, his confusion on the subject of the Kabbalah, 488.
Covenant, 15, 19, 299-302; Sign of, 300, 301, 302, 303, 378, 394, 395; Inward Covenant, 232.
Creation of man according to the ZOHAR, 232, 262, 265; creation *ex-nihilo*, 193, 194, 506; instruments of creation, 612-616; creation the Garment of God, 225. *See* Doctrine of Cosmology.
Cremer, Abbot, forged alchemical testament attributed to, 439.
CROWN OF THE KINGDOM, Sephirotic poem of Avicebron, 96.
Cryptography and symbolism, 22, 23.
Cudworth, Ralph, a great theosophist, 480; his INTELLECTUAL SYSTEM, 480, 481; connection with Kabbalism, *ib.*; his appeal to rabbinical authorities, 481, 482.

Cuirass. *See* Vestures.
Cybele, 4.

DAATH. *See* SEPHIROTH.
Dale, Antonio van, his reference to the KEY OF SOLOMON, 520.
DALETH, Path of, 304.
D'Alvedre, St. Yves, influence on French occultism, 500; on the MASSORAH, 615.
D'Argens, his so-called Kabbalistic correspondence, 550.
Daughter, 207, 208, 209, 210, 342, 350, 363, 369; Daughter of the King, 19, 211, 245, 322, 585.
Daughters of Men, 273.
David, 17, 18, 228, 313, 590.
Davis, Edward, 295.
De Brière on Ancient Eastern Symbolism, 24.
Dee, Dr. John, his MONAS HIEROGLYPHICA, 541.
Delanne, Gabriel, his reference to Mirandula, 442.
DELINEATION OF THE HEAVENLY TEMPLES, important pre-Kabbalistic treatise, 88, 90.
Deluge, 291, 292, 294, 312. *See* Book VII., § 4 *passim*.
Demonology, 256, 258, 528, 530. *See* Infernal Hierarchy.
De Pauly, 574, 575; his translation of the ZOHAR, 7, 8, 574, 575. *See also* 15.
DESATIR, CELESTIAL, its analogies with Kabbalism, 78.
Dionysius, analogies with Kabbalism, 208, 271.
DISCOURSE OF THE AGED MAN, tract of the ZOHAR, 120; excerpts from, 147–150.
DISCOURSE OF THE YOUNG MAN, 120; summary, 174, 175.
Doctrine, Secret, xiii, 7, 8, 9, 10, 11, 14, 17, 19, 20, 21, 22, 220, 229, 261, 265, 310, 332, 341, 371, 386.
Donolo, Sabbatai, his commentary on the SEPHER YETZIRAH, 111.
Douma, Angel of Vindication, 328.
Drach, Chevalier, on the uses of the term Kabbalah, 37; its authority, 94; on Abravanel, 429; on Talmudic Messiahs, 320.
Dreams, 529, 530.
DUTIES OF THE HEART, treatise quoted by the ZOHAR, 55, 56.

EARTHLY PARADISE, 15, 17, 261–269, 294, 343, 383, 485. *See* Eden.
East, Wisdom of, 525, 526.
Eckartshausen, on a more advanced School, 25.
Eden, Higher and Lower, 237, 238, 240, 245, 264, 279, 283, 285, 289, 290, 298, 312, 319, 325, 326, 342, 343, 351, 352,
353, 374, 382, 392, 393, 394, 395, 401;
Rivers of Eden, 201, 264, 302, 342, 343.
Edersheim on emanationism and the TALMUD, 29; Talmudic traditionalism, 29; cosmology of the SEPHER YETZIRAH, 614; description of, 42; on Akiba, 42; on the Hasidim, 86; on the Kabbalah, 61. *See also* 43.
Edom, Kings of, in Zoharic symbolism, 141, 142, 416, 417, 418, 421.
Egypt, 67, 298, 311, 525, 526.
Egyptian Wisdom, 67, 298, 299, 525, 526.
EHEIEH, 584.
Eirenæus Philalethes, eminence in Alchemy, 473.
Eisler, Robert, 8.
El, 323.
Eleazar, R., 168; Eleazar the Great, 400.
Eleazar of Worms, his Kabbalistic school, 16, 98; his commentary on the SEPHER YETZIRAH, 111.
Elias del Medigo, vii.
Eliezer Hagabite, Kabbalistic doctor, 89.
Eliezer, R., his mystic system, 90.
Elijah, 199, 220, 226.
Elohim, a title of Shekinah, 342. *See* Book VIII., § 1, for recurring affirmations and developments.
Emanation and the Kabbalah, 193; emanation and Divine Immanence, 194; as the manifestation of the Absolute, *ib.*; the World of Emanation, *ib.*; emanationism and pantheism, 193. *See also* 197, 199.
Embryonic Return, 249, 419, 420.
EMERALD TABLE, 133, 535.
Encausse, Gérard. *See* PAPUS.
ENOCH, BOOK OF, 17.
Enos, 295.
Eschatology, Book VII., § 9. *See also* 247, 248, 249, 336, 337, 377.
Essence, Divine, 186, 187, 189, 190.
Esther, 368.
Eucharist, 130, 131, 161, 169, 587.
Evangelical Design of Christian Kabbalism, ix, 444, 458, 478.
Eve, her formation from the side of Adam, 264–267; her original union with Adam, 279; her seduction, 280 *et seq.*; Eve as the Forbidden Fruit, 283; sin of Eve, 284; Eve and Samuel, 286, 287.
Evil, 201, 202, 203, 270, 274, 282, 283.
Evolution, 249, 313.
Ezekiel, 305, 306.
Ezra, 314.
Ezra, Moses ibn Jacob Ben, his Kabbalistic connections, 92; alleged invention of the Kabbalah, 94.

FABER, G. S., Rev., 295.
FAITHFUL SHEPHERD, fragments in ZOHAR, on vicarious atonement, 158, 159; on

Job and the Accuser, 159, 160; on the Holy Shekinah, 161, 162; on METATRON, 163; analysis and excerpts, 157-163, 187, 190, 213, 253, 314, 320, 343, 346, 348, 350, 399, 401.
Falaquera, disciple of Maimonides, 92.
Fall of Man, as expounded in the ZOHAR proper, Book VII., § 3; according to the BAHIR, 156; according to ZOHAR HADASH, 287; according to the CONCLUSIONS of Mirandula, 598.
FAMA FRATERNITATIS, 565.
Farrar, F. W., description of the TALMUD, 29.
Fichte, J. G., 430.
Figuier, Louis, as cited by Papus, 501; on Byzantine alchemical literature, 535; on the alchemists, ib.
FILIOQUE clause, 362.
Finn's SEPHARDIM, 53, 76.
Flamel, Nicholas, his instructor in Alchemy, 82; alleged evangelical zeal, 82; misstatements of Éliphas Lévi, 426; opinion of Stanislas de Guaita, 504.
Flaming Sword, 289, 319, 399.
Fludd, Robert, place among English occultists, 467; mystery of his life, 467, 468; his Kabbalistic studies, ib.; on the practical Kabbalah, 468, 469; not acquainted with the ZOHAR, ib.; his use of the term Kabbalah, 469.
Fount of Wisdom, 409.
Fountain of Life, treatise of Avicebron, 95.
Four Worlds of Kabbalism, World of Deity or ATZILUTH, 199; its sole occupant, ib.; World of Creation or BRIAH, ib.; World of Formation or YETZIRAH, ib.; World of Action or ASSIAH, ib.; astronomical correspondences, 611; earliest traces of the doctrine, 196: as regards ATZILUTH, see xv, 197, 206; as regards BRIAH, 198, 253; as regards YETZIRAH, 200, 255, 256; as regards ASSIAH, 200, 258.
Franck, Adolphe, on the SEPHER YETZIRAH, 44; his defence of the Kabbalah, 145; on the language of the ZOHAR, 57, 58; on the connection between the SEPHER YETZIRAH and the ZOHAR, 134; on Kabbalistic eschatology, 145; on the BAHIR, 154; on Raymond Lully, 441; on William Postel, 462; on the Kabbalism of Henry More, 470; on Isaac de Loria, 418.
Frank, Jacob, 81, 564.
Freemasonry, its alleged mystic origin, 548; historical origin, 549; connection with occultism, ib.; Kabbalistic Degrees, 549-553; occultism and the Scottish Rite, 553; Masonic Rosicrucianism, 549; the Higher Grades and Kabbalism, 552-554.
Freidlander, M., 236.
Frinellan, his VOCABULAIRE INFERNAL, 33.

GABRIEL, 303.
Gaffarel, his astrological processes, 83; on the Kabbalistic MSS. of Mirandula, viii; on Astrology and the Law of Israel, 545.
Galatinus, Petrus, on the evangelical value of the Kabbalah, 48; his study of Messianic Doctrine, xi. *See also* 31.
Galicia, 564.
Galilee, 336.
Gamaliel, R., 42.
Ganz, David, on the compilation of the MISHNA, 27; his treatise on Sacred and Profane History, 93.
GARDEN OF POMEGRANATES, on the name AIN SOPH, 188; authority of this treatise among Kabbalists, ib.; its obscurities and difficulties, 411; on Pneumatology, ib.; on good works, 412; quoted by ÆSH MEZAREPH, 425.
GATE OF THE HEAVENS, 422.
GATES OF LIGHT, on the Divine Will, 193; on the Gates of Understanding, 219.
Gates of Understanding, a sketch of universal science, 218; late origin 219. *See* 390.
Geber, Latin writings attributed to, 49; quoted by ÆSH MEZAREPH, 425.
Gebirol, included among early Kabbalists, 91, 94; his writings and their evidence on the antiquity of the ZOHAR, 96; the school with he connects, 94; his chief doctrines, 97; his FOUNTAIN OF LIFE, 95; sketch of his life, ib.; reference to the SEPHER YETZIRAH, 96, 97; his alleged pantheism, 97; Greek complexion of his philosophy, ib.
GEBURAH. *See* SEPHIROTH.
GEMARA, 28, 29.
GEMATRIA, exegetical method of, 36; example of, 219; in ÆSH MEZAREPH, 427, 428.
Gentiles, 333, 396, 401, 580.
Gikatilla, Joseph, 410, 433. *See* GATES OF LIGHT.
Ginsburg, C. D., on early Kabbalistic literature, vi, xii; on pre-Kabbalistic literature, 88; on the SEPHER YETZIRAH, 89; on the origin of the ZOHAR, 94; analysis of his work on the Kabbalah, 495, 496. *See also* 25, 89, 117.
Gnosticism, 69, 497.
God and His attributes, 181, 182; correspondences between God, Man and

Nature, 185; Mystery of God, 186; Unknown and Unknowable God, 186, 187; Majesty of God in Kabbalism, 185-191; God and the SEPHIROTH, 202. *See* s.v. Absolute.
GOLDEN TREATISE, ascribed to Hermes, 535.
Goldschmidt, L., his translation of the SEPHER YETZIRAH, 102.
Good Works, Zoharic Doctrine of, 185.
Gould, R. F., on Aristotelian Influence among the Jews, 46; on Paracelsus, 456.
Goulianov, Chevalier de, on Hermetic and Kabbalistic Tradition, 535.
Graal, Holy, 579.
Graetz, Dr., indiscriminate hostility of his criticism, 61; on the origin of the ZOHAR, 94; his estimate of Moses de Leon, 61; on the Mysteries of Simeon ben Yohai, 63; on the SEPHER YETZIRAH, 65; on the writings of Abulafia, 92; followed by Ginsburg, 89; on Gebirol, 97; definite rejection of his views, 572.
Grapes, 279, 281, 294.
Great Adam, 446.
GREATER HOLY SYNOD, 119; its literary aspect, 139; on the authorship of the BOOK OF CONCEALMENT, 139, 140; content of the SYNOD, 141; the recorder of its discourses, 141; summary account of its symbolism, 141-145, 208, 209.
Greek Church, 362.
Greene, W. B., on the MASSORAH, 33; on the Worlds of the Kabbalah, 34; on the Kabbalistic Balance, 217.
Grimoires of Magic, alleged place in the scheme of Kabbalism, 84; close connection with the Magical Clavicles, 521.
Guaita, Stanislas de, on Christian Kabbalism, 503; on the Egyptian origin of Kabbalism, 65; his literary work, 503; his Rosicrucian Order, 503, 504; his views on Kabbalism, 504, 505.
Gui de Viterbi, x.

HAÏÂ, higher or fourth principle of the soul, 105; according to Saadya Gaon, *ib.*; the Heavenly HAÏÂ, 418; also a name of RUAH, 241; higher life in man, 244; in correspondence with ABBA, 418.
HAIKLUTH, Palaces, Abodes, 120.
Hair, character by, 531, 532.
HALAKHA, arrangement of, attributed to R. Akiba, 42; distinction between HALAKHA and HAGGADA, 30.
Ha Levi, Judah, R., on the SEPHER YETZIRAH, 42, 200.
HALICHOT OLAM, 29.

Hareau, B., on the Scholastic Philosophy, 414.
Harrison, Clifford, on Bacon as a Rosicrucian, 466.
Harrison, C. G., on the Pantheism of the Sephirotic System, 99.
Hartmann, Franz, on the higher sense of Magic, 518; on Astrological Geomancy, 545.
HASHMALOTH, or Omissions, 118, 170.
HASIDIM, New, or Pietists, 564.
Haven, Marc, on the Kabbalism of Stanislas de Guaita, 504.
Hay Gaon, and the Secret Tradition, 90, 91; on the interpretation of dreams, 91; alleged Commentary on the SEPHER YETZIRAH, 106.
Hayyim, R., 413, 420.
HE. *See* Sacred Name.
Hebrew literature, its extent and development, 3; characteristics, 4.
Heckethorn, C. W., absurd explanation of the term Kabbalah, 4; error as to the literal Kabbalah, 32.
Hellenism, 255.
Helmont, Mercurius and J. B. van, their alchemical researches, 477.
Hermetic Books, antiquity of their occult traditions, 50; earlier and later series, 535.
Hermetic Maxim, Kabbalistic parallel, 133.
Hershon, P. J., on the divisions of the Kabbalah, 35.
HIBBOORAH KADMAÁ, Primary Assembly in the ZOHAR, 120.
HIDDEN CHURCH OF THE HOLY GRAAL, 596.
HIDDEN THINGS OF THE LAW, extracts in ZOHAR, 163, 164; value of its exegesis, 164; on the stages of mystic vision, 164, 165; on the vision at Mamre, 165; condemnation of Magic, 166, 167.
Hierarchy, Angelic, 254-256; Infernal, 257-259. *See also* 396, 397, concerning the Evil Tree.
Higgins, Godfrey, 295.
Hillel the Great, 43.
Hirtz, R. Napthali, on the Divine Will, 193; analysis of his ROYAL VALLEY, 420-422.
HOD. *See* SEPHIROTH.
Hoefer, F., on Kabbalism and Alchemy, 539, 540.
Hogostratus, xi.
Holy of Holies, 372.
Holy Spirit, 362-369.
Hook, Dean, on Kabbalism and the early heretics, 62.
Hosmer, T. K., on the Kabbalah and Demonology, 34.
HOUSE OF GOD, 422, 423.
Hulsius, Antonius, 317.
Hypostases, Divine, 16.

IDRA DE MASCHCANA, Assembly of the Sanctuary, 119, 208, 349.
Idras, i.e., Texts of the Holy Assemblies, 119, 120. See GREATER AND LESSER HOLY SYNOD.
Imbonatus, Jos., 563.
Immanence, Divine, 226; a foundation of the Kabbalah, 192; in contrast to pantheism, 194. See EMANATION.
Incarnation, 586.
Instruments of Creation, scheme of, 612-616.
Intermediaries, between Deity and matter, 191, 196.
Intruders, 321.
Irira, Abraham Cohen, his PORTA CŒLORUM, 71, 422; notice of his other Zoharic Commentary, 423; his Platonic leanings, 422.
Isaac ben Abraham, 60.
Isaac ben Moses, his forged ZOHAR, 182.
Isaac de Acco, his search for the MSS. of the ZOHAR, 53; meeting with Moses de Leon, ib.; failure of his quest, 54; abrupt termination of his narrative, ib.; on the language of the ZOHAR, 57, 115.
Isaac the Blind, an alleged author of the ZOHAR, 60; connection with Avicebron, 94; his school a precursor of Kabbalism, 98; alleged teacher of Azriel, 109; his supposed Commentary on the SEPHER YETZIRAH, 111.
Isaiah, 226, 317, 318.
Ishmael, R., suggested author of the DELINEATION OF THE HEAVENLY TEMPLES, 91.
Isis, 372.
Israel of Podolia, 81.
Issachar ben Napthali, his synopsis of the ZOHAR, 423, 424.

JACOB, 228, 353, 354, 355, 383, 401, 591.
Jah (Yah), 105, 137, 207, 208, 232, 393, 620.
Jami of Herat, his SEVEN THRONES, 77, 78.
Jeheshuah, connection with the TETRAGRAM, xi.
Jehovah, symbolised by the Written Law, 343.
Jehovah and Elohim, 225, 230, 352.
Jehovah Elohenou, 353.
Jehovah is Elohim, 342, 359.
Jellinek, on the term SEPHIRA, 195; on the names of the ZOHAR, 56; his citations from Moses de Leon, 58.
Jerusalem, 263.
JESOD. See SEPHIROTH.
Jesse, Root of, 318.
Jesus of Nazareth, 320, 584, 585.
Job, sufferings of, 159, 160, 328.
Joel, on emanationism and the Kabbalah, 194.

Joseph Gikatilla ben Abraham, 219.
Joseph, R., his Arabic translation of the TALMUD, 76.
Joshua, 312.
Joshua ben Hananiah, the master of Akiba, 42.
Judah ben Barzilli, iii.
Judah Hadessi, 58.
Judah Ha Levi, 111, 200.
Judah the Prince, 27.
Judas Azael, 438.
Judge, W. Q., on a Secret Lodge of Adepts, 511.
Judgment, Last, 325.

KABBALAH, suggested derivations, 4; true derivation of the term, 5; a secret traditional knowledge, xii, xiii, 5; the hidden thought of Israel, 6; difficulty of its literary methods, 8, 21, 22; two ways of regarding its importance, 23, 24; its real interest not exegetical or historical, 25; failure of occult expositions, ib.; whether a channel of the Secret Tradition, ib.; popular identification with Magic, 33; four groups of Hebrew Tradition, 35, 36; mystery infused by the Kabbalah into the Bible, 186; Theoretical and Practical Kabbalah, 36, 37; Higher Secret Doctrine, 341-405; conclusion thereupon, 588-602.
KABBALAH DENUDATA of Rosenroth, 6; motives which led to it, 478; considerations of the preface, ib.; sacrifices involved by the work, 479; its critical standpoint, 480; its ambitious design, 115, 116; excerpts and references, 136, 186, 189, 409, 411, 413, 421, 422, 538.
Kabbalah, Practical, 36.
Kabbalism, Secret School of, 576.
Kairites, 79.
Kapila, 4.
Karppe, Dr. S., 42, 44, 58, 182, 566-568.
Kenealy, E. V., on the term Kabbalah, 4; on the wisdom of Adam, 16.
Kennedy, H. A., his Study of Philo, 70.
Kerubim, 319, 356, 357, 369, 399.
KETHER. See SEPHIROTH.
KEY OF SOLOMON, a transparent forgery, 49; nonsensical processes, 84; in two recensions, 520; as an embodiment of Kabbalistic Tradition, 521.
Khunrath, reference by Éliphas Lévi, 478; by Stanislas de Guaita, 504; his connection with Kabbalism, 538. See also 341.
Kiern, F., his Kabbalah of Alchemy, 539.
King, Supreme, 314; Sacred King, 359, 590; King and Queen, 211, 313, 350.

King, C. W., on the Ancient Traditions of the ZOHAR, 69; on the analogies between Gnosticism and the Kabbalah, *ib.*
Kingsford, Anna, 507.
Kingsland, W., on the Ancient Wisdom Religion, 511.
Kircher, Athanasius, on the Gates of Understanding, 218; on Kabbalistic correspondences, 72.
Konitz, a defendant of the Kabbalah, 46.
KUSARI: its references to the SEPHER YETZIRAH, 92.

LABAN, 274, 525.
LABYRINTH OF SOLOMON, 536.
Lafuma-Giraud, Emile, 15.
Lamb, Dr. J., on the Hebrew characters, 546.
Lamb, Paschal, 271, 391.
Lamb of God, 354.
Lambert, Mayer, on the date and character of SEPHER YETZIRAH, 45; on the Commentary of Saadya Geon, 104.
Land of the Living, 395, 476.
Land, Holy, 238, 297, 298, 310, 324, 335, 360, 366, 374.
Landauer, M. H., on the authorship of the ZOHAR, 60.
Latin Church, 278, 291, 317, 325, 336, 362, 587, 597.
Lead, Jane, 597.
Leah, 354, 367, 401.
Leiningen, Carl, on Pneumatology, 237.
Lejay, Julien, 501.
Lelièvre, A., on the divinatory sciences, 83.
Leroy-Beaulieu, A., on the HALAKHA and HAGGADA, 30; on the Jew and Mysticism, 558; on immortality and resurrection in the TALMUD, 236.
Lesser Countenance, symbolism of, 137, 138, 141, 143-145, 146, 147, 209, 210, 211, 582, 583, 584.
LESSER HOLY SYNOD, 119, 120; as described by Rosenroth, 146; design of its revelations, *ib.*; nature of the discourse, *ib.*; Kabbalistic doctrine of the sexes, 146, 147; account of R. Simeon's death, 147.
LETTERS FROM A MYSTIC, Mysticism of the Divine Name, 45.
Letters, Hebrew, their pre-existence and emanation, 221, 231; Great Letters, *ib.*; BETH as the instrument of creation, 222, 231, 232; its matrices, 223.
Leusden, J., on the name of God, 519.
Levi, David, on the antiquity of the Vowel-Points, 56.
Lévi, Éliphas, his misconstruction of the TALMUD, 30, 31; on the Divine Name, 613; on the thirty-first Path of Wisdom, 217; on the BOOK OF CONCEALMENT, 135; on MICROPROSOPUS, 491; its symbolism, 492; on the ÆSH MEZAREPH, 426; on Raymond Lully, 439; translation of Mirandula's CONCLUSIONS, 445; variants from same, 445 *et seq.*; on the Collection of Pistorius, 459, 460; on William Postel, 461, 462, 463, 464; sketch of Lévi's position as a Kabbalist, 487-494; as judged by De Guaita, 503.
Leviathan, 288, 336.
Levirate, 205.
Levita, Elias, on the Vowel-Points, 55.
Libavius, Andrew, 468.
LIBER DRUSHIM, excerpts in the collection of Rosenroth, 415; analysis of, 414-416; influence on Henry More, 413.
Liberating Angel, 344.
LIBER MUTUS, 596.
Lilith, Kabbalistic bride of Samuel, 258, 288, 289, 419.
Lillie, A., 71.
LINEA MEDIA, 601, 602.
Lismon, Z., on the Tarot, 555.
Loëb, Isidore de, on French and Spanish Jews in the thirteenth century, 29; on METATRON, 254; Loeb's study of the Kabbalah, 496.
Longelus, Ranutius, 83.
Loria (Luria), Isaac de, on BINAH as source, 607; on the BOOK OF CONCEALMENT, 136; his developments of Zoharic Pneumatology, 418; his teaching recommended by Rosenroth, 121, 122; his position and period, 412, 413; his works, 412-420; summary of same, *ib.*
Lot, 277, 299, 336.
Lover of Philalathes, 236.
Lover and Beloved, 232, 267, 322, 379.
Löwy, Rev. A., 3.
Lucifer, 229, 276.
Lully, Raymond, his true work, 82; his connection with Kabbalism, 438; his date and legend, 439; the Lully of Alchemy, 228, 439, 440; errors of Franck, 441; his scholastic system, 440.
LUMINOUS BOOK. *See* SEPHER HA BAHIR.
Luria, David, 46.
Lütkens, M. Nicolai, 480.
LUX IN TENEBRIS, its observations on the ZOHAR, 400.

MAAMAR TO HAZEE, Come and See Discourse in the ZOHAR, 120.
MACROPROSOPUS, longanimity of, 143; relation with MICROPROSOPUS, 137; doctrine of, fundamental to the Kabbalah, 66; late in the history of speculation, *ib.*; symbolical develop-

ment of, 136-145; ever hidden and concealed, 137; Soul of the Greater World, 211; according to Isaac de Loria, 417.
MacKenzie, Kenneth, on the unknown writings of Pasqually, 486.
Magic, Ceremonial and Philosophical, v; popular connection with Kabbalism, v; general considerations on the connection, 437; influence of Kabbalism on Western Magic, 521; White and Black Magic, 518; power of Divine Names, 519, 520; processes of debased Kabbalism, 520; the Keys of Solomon, 521; the Grimoires, 522; summary of the Doctrine of Names, 522-524; ZOHAR on Magic, 517-527.
Maier, Michael, his TRIPUS AUREUS, 439; connection with Fludd, 468.
Maimonides, his Aristotelian tendency, 46; said to have turned a Kabbalist, 92; eulogy of, 93; unacquainted with Avicebron, 94.
Maitland, Edward, 507.
Male and Female Principles, a Keynote, 357.
MALKUTH. See SEPHIROTH.
Mangetus, 439.
Manning, Cardinal, on the Daimon of Socrates, 442.
MANSIONS OR ABODES, excerpts in ZOHAR, 175; symbolism of, 175-177.
MARAH KOHEN, Vision of the Priest, 121, 409.
Marconis on Masonic Mysteries, 553.
Marcus, what he brought into Gnosticism, 69.
Marriage. See Mystery of Sex.
Mary the Virgin. See Queen of Heaven.
Masonry, 579. See Book XI., § 4.
Massey, Gerald, 144.
MASSORAH, 33, 615.
MATHERS, S. L. MacGregor, his gratuitous assumption, 22; false impression created by, 25; his translation of the occultation series, vi; the importance which he attributes to same, 135; blunder concerning the treatise BETH ELOHIM, 26; on the PERFECT WAY, 508; devoid of critical judgment, 522; assertion concerning ÆSH MEZAREPH, 538.
MATHNITIN, Repetitions, 119, 120, 172, 173, 335, 336, 398, 399.
MATRONA, 202, 209, 210, 266, 313, 314, 335, 345, 352, 357, 361, 381, 400.
Matter, on Gnosticism and the Kabbalah, 62.
Mead, G. R. S., 69.
MEASURE OF THE HEIGHT, pre-Kabbalistic treatise, 88.
Mediatrix, 399.
MEIMRA, 211.

Melchizedek, 299.
Memphis and Misraïm, Rites of, 553.
MEQUR CHOKMAH, 121, 409.
MERCAVAH. See WORK OF THE CHARIOT.
Mercy-Seat, 356, 357.
Messiah, according to the ZOHAR, 316-324.
METATHESIS, 83.
METATRON, the Angel of the Presence, 254, 313, 319, 333, 335, 344, 351, 353, 360, 366, 399, 469.
Metempsychosis, rejected by Saadya Gaon, 105; taught by Isaac the Blind, 109; and by Manasses, 434.
Meurin, Léon, on the Synagogue of Satan, 67, 505; a troubled dream of the Papacy, 503; on Freemasonry, the Kabbalah and Pantheism, 505-507.
Mevi, R., 432.
MEYER, his edition of the SEPHER YETZIRAH, 101, 102.
Michael, as High Priest, 130, 131, 244.
MICROPROSOPUS, emanation of, 137; relation to MACROPROSOPUS, 137; a fundamental doctrine of the Kabbalah, 66; late character of its speculation, ib.; Sephirotic attribution, 211; manifestation of, 137, 211; Soul of the Lesser World, 211; androgyne nature, 144, 146, 211; symbolical development, 137-146; according to De Loria, 417.
MIDRASH CONEN, 90, 136.
MIDRASH HA NEELAM, SECRET MIDRASH, 118, 120. See SECRET COMMENTARY.
MIDRASH HAZEETH, 120.
MIDRASH RABBA, 311.
MIDRASH RUTH, 120, 177-179, 277.
MIDRASH TALPIGOTH, 318.
MIDRASH of R. Simeon, an alleged name of the ZOHAR, 56, 63.
MIDRASHIM, Ancient, 578, 599.
MIDRASHIM and TARGUMIM, 51, 56.
Mirandula, Picus de, his evangelical zeal, ix; not a partisan of magic, 443, 444; not acquainted with Avicebron, 96; conversion effected by, 433; Lully and Mirandula, 441; his Kabbalistic MSS. vii, viii, 442; sketch of Mirandula, 443; his KABBALISTIC CONCLUSIONS, ix, 445-452; his treatise on Astrology, 444; Agrippa and Mirandula, 444, 452.
MISHNA, compiled by R. Judah, 27; MISHNA as part of the TALMUD, 28; date according to Morinus, 29; sections of, 31, 32; error of Heckethorn, 32. See also 343, 360, 361.
MISHNAYOTH, 27.
Moab, Plains of, 310.
Modesty, 378.
Molitor, as interpreted by Papus, 84, 151.
Moon, and Oral Law, 17, 18.
Mordechai, R., 425.

Mordell, Phineas, 45, 102.
More, Henry, his contributions to the KABBALAH DENUDATA, 116, 470; object of his Kabbalistic studies, 470; remarks on Isaac de Loria, 470, 471; exposition of Ezekiel, 471; his CONJECTURA CABALISTICA, 472, 473.
Morerus on Magic, 518.
Morinus, 29.
Moses, 17, 303–312.
Moses Abraham ben Samuel Zakut, 52.
Moses de Leon, R., his alleged authorship of the ZOHAR, vii, 46; an almost impossible theory, 50, 51; evidence adduced for it, 51, 52; narrative in the SEPHER YUHASIN, 53, 54; does not prove the authorship of R. Moses, 54; sketch of the internal evidence, 55; how met by the defenders of the ZOHAR, 55–57; points of weakness in the defence, 58; further speculation concerning R. Moses, 59.
Moses ibn Jacob ben Ezra, 92.
Moses of Cordova, his PARADISE OF POMEGRANATES, 121, 409, 410; on the simplicity of AIN SOPH, ib.; his pneumatology, 411, 412; date of R. Moses, 410; high authority of his treatise, 410; summary account of it, 410–412.
Mother of God. See Queen of Heaven.
Munk, Solomon, on the pantheism of the Kabbalah, 193; on the TALMUD and Kabbalah, 29, 30; on the authorship of SEPHER YETZIRAH, 43; on the language of the ZOHAR, 57; on certain similarities between Maimonides and the ZOHAR, 94; on the fusion of the Kairites and Motozales, 79; on Avicebron, 95; his classification of the Kabbalah, 41. See also 46, 50.
Myer, Isaac, his erudition and his assumptions, 26; distinction between the Kabbalah and the TALMUD, 32; on the Kabbalah and the New Testament, 6; on the Speculative Kabbalah, 612; on the Aristotelian and Kabbalistic systems, 46; on the acquaintance of Maimonides with the ZOHAR, 94; on the Kabbalistic connections of Avicebron, 95; on Hay Gaon's alleged Commentary on the SEPHER YETZIRAH, 106; on the higher soul of the THORAH, 123; on Hay Gaon and the ZOHAR, 182; on Paracelsus and the Kabbalah, 455; on the Hermetic Books and the Kabbalah, 535; on a Chinese Kabbalah, 537.
Mysteries, Instituted, 593.
MYSTERIES OF LOVE. See Abravanel.
Mystery of Faith, 220, 222, 231, 237, 247, 261, 269, 292, 304, 306, 378, 389, 390, 391, 392, 394, 397.
Mystery of Sex, Book VIII., § 2 passim. Supplementary and minor references, 19, 261, 263, 276, 293, 314, 347, 370, 371, 377–405, 591–597, 599.
Mysticism and the Kabbalah, Kabbalistic history imbedded in that of occultism, 557; old Jewish doctrine concerning the mystic communication between Divine and human, 186; analogies between the Mystic Marriage and the Kabbalistic doctrine of the Prototype, 559, 560; the Kabbalah of service to the practical mystic, 557; a certain message, 558; the points of contact, 558, 559.

NAAMAH, 288, 289.
Nagrela, Joseph ibn, 96.
Nahmanides, 52; alleged transmission of the ZOHAR from Palestine, 53; a pupil of Azriel, 109; his Kabbalistic writings, 110, 111; opposed by R. Mevi, 432.
Name, Divine (including its separate consonants), its division, 18; loss of its proper vowels, 18; creation hidden in the Divine Name, 221; Immanence of the Name in the universe, 222; the Name as the Mystery of Faith, 223, the Law comprised in the Name, 224; partition of the Divine Name, 315, 322; its restoration, 335. See also 345, 346, 349, 378, 379.
Name, Sacred, of 12 letters, 617.
Name, Sacred, of 42 letters, 223, 275, 617, 618.
Name, Sacred, of 72 letters, 16, 618.
Name of Shekinah, True, 311.
Names, Power of Divine, 44, 45, 105.
Napthali Hirtz, R., 193, 420–422.
Nazir, Jacob, his BOOK OF EMANATION, 611.
Nebo, Mount, 303.
Nehunya, R., alleged author of the BAHIR, 152; other attributed writings, ib.
Neoplatonism, 124.
NEPHESH, 105, 129, 241, 242, 243, 244, 246, 325, 327, 418, 421, 619, 620.
NEPHILIM, 274.
NESHAMAH, 105, 129, 241, 242, 243, 244, 246, 325, 418, 421, 619, 620.
NETZACH. See SEPHIROTH.
Nicholson, Reynold A., 79.
Nicolas, M., on the authorship of the SEPHER YETZIRAH, 43; on the antiquity of the Kabbalah, 63.
Noah, 292, 293, 294, 295, 359, 591.
Norrelius, Andreas, on the Christian aspects of the ZOHAR, 479.
Norse Mythology, suggested analogies with the Kabbalah, 69.
NOTARIKON, a Kabbalistic method of exegesis, 9, 37, 41, 83.
Notary Art, its connection with Kabbalism and with Lully, 440.

Nuctemeron, 500.
Numbers, Mysticism concerning, the decade as an emanation of Deity, 194; numbers and the SEPHIROTH, 195; in the SEPHER YETZIRAH, 196; Hebrew letters and numerals, 614; numbers in Kabbalistic Freemasonry, 550 et seq.
Nuptials, Divine, 393.
Nus, Eugène, on the YI-KING, 68.

OCCULT PSEUDO-SCIENCES, 9, 10, 24, 83, 84, 171, 173, 174, 297, 517–534.
Ockley, Simon, his translation of the IMPROVEMENT OF HUMAN REASON, 79.
Old, W. G., his MANUAL OF ASTROLOGY, 544; on Kabbalistic Astrology, 548.
Oliver, Rev. George, on the diffusion of the Mysteries, 68.
Onan, sin of, 291, 292, 333.
Onkelos, quoted by Mirandula, 449; his Aramaic dialect not identical with that of the ZOHAR, 57. *See also* 210, 226.
Oral Law, 10, 12, 13; image of Shekinah, 343, 360, 361.
Origen on Exorcisms, 520.
Osiris, 222.

PALACES, 119, 175–177, 247, 248, 333; Palace of Delight, 247. *See* Mansions.
Palladius, PARADISE of, 403, 404.
Palmer, E. H., on R. Judah the Prince, 27.
Pantheism, 185, 193.
Pantheus, J. A., 540, 541.
Papus, *i.e.*, G. Encausse, his assumptions concerning the Kabbalah, 26, 37, 38; on the Paths of Wisdom, 218; translation of the SEPHER YETZIRAH, 102, 500; on an alleged French translation of the ZOHAR, 116; his connection with the French occult movement, 499, 500; his occult antecedents, 500; his summary of the Kabbalah, 36, 37, 38, 500–503; on the Practical Kabbalah, 82; on ÆSH MEZAREPH, 544; on the Tarot, 556.
Paracelsus, alleged traces of the Kabbalah in his system, 455–458; value of his references, 457; not a student of the Kabbalah, 458.
PARADISE of Palladius, 403.
PARDES RIMMONIM, 121. *See* GARDEN OF POMEGRANATES. *See also* 198, 409.
Pasqually, Martines de, 486.
PATHACH AINIM, Gate of the Eyes, 121, 409.
Paths, 190, 203, 335.
Paths of Wisdom, doctrine concerning, 213; special nature of their interest, *ib.*; translation of the document which embodies them, 213–217; their modern accent, 217; according to Papus, 218; Avicebron's poem on the Paths, 97.

Patmore, Coventry, 380.
Paul, St., 250, 270.
PEKOODAH section of the ZOHAR, 120.
Pelling, Edward, 482.
PERFECT WAY, its Kabbalistic allusions, 509; opinion of Baron Spedalieri, 508, 509; value of same, 509; statement of the allusions, 509, 510; general inference, 510.
Pharaoh, 526.
Pherruts Schibbur, Jewish academy of, 91.
Philadelphian School, 596, 597.
Philo, his Pneumatology, 237; his analogies with Kabbalism, 70–72; Jewish tendencies represented by Philo, 365.
Phylacteries, difficulty in the ZOHAR concerning, 55; how met by its defenders, 56.
Physiognomy, as understood by the ZOHAR, 173, 174, 532–534.
Pike, Albert, on the true name of Satan, 258; on Kabbalism and the religion of Zoroaster, 67; on Kabbalism and Northern Mythology, 69; his transformation of the Scottish Rite, 552–554; *See also* 606.
Pillar of Benignity, Middle, 201, 202, 203, 272, 280, 347, 350, 373, 400; the image of Shekinah as Elohim, 343.
Pillar of Mercy, 201. *See also* SEPHIROTH.
Pillar of Severity, 201. *See also* SEPHIROTH.
PIRKE of R. Eliezer, 90, 498.
Pisgah, 310.
PISTIS SOPHIA, 69.
Pistorius, his collection of Kabbalistic writers, xi, 459, 460; object of same, 461. *See also* 101, 213, 428.
Pneumatology, the Doctrine of the Soul in Kabbalism, 235–253; according to Saadya Gaon, 104, 105; a recurring subject in the ZOHAR, 235; according to Moses de Cordova, 411, 412; according to Isaac de Loria, 417–420; according to A. Cohen Irira, 423.
POIMANDER, DIVINE, 534, 535.
Poisson, A., on Alchemy, 537, 538.
Pordage, Dr. John, 595, 597.
Porter, Noah, 189.
Poscantius, Benedictus, 317.
Postel, William, on the SEPHIROTH, 196; his alleged translation of the BAHIR, 157; his legend, 461; notice of his life, 461, 462; his connection with Kabbalism, 462, 463; extravagance of his views, 463, 464; his translation of the SEPHER YETZIRAH, ix, 464, 465; other writings, 465; according to Stanislas de Gua a, 504. *See also* 508.
Pott, Mrs. Henry on the Rosicrucians, 466.

Prayer, 248, 361, 370; Prayer of Contemplation, 564; House of Prayer, 359; Prayer of Silence, 590.
Prayer of Elijah, 180, 181.
Pre-existence, found in the TALMUD, 235; taught in the ZOHAR, 237-241; accepted by Saadya Gaon, 105; pre-existence of the soul of the Messiah, 323, 324.
Princes of the Exile, 3.
Principle, Supreme, 212.
Procreation, 280.
Propitiatory, 313, 393.
Pumbaditha, Jewish academy of, 91.
Punishment, everlasting, 328; not everlasting, 328, 329.

QUEEN of Heaven, 353, 369, 370, 376.

RAAIAH MEHEMNAH. *See* Faithful Shepherd, *also* 119, 120.
RABANUS, quoted by Agrippa, 454.
Rachel, 251, 354, 401, 591.
RAZA DE RAZIN. *See* Secret of Secrets, 120, 173, 174.
Raziel, 16, 134, 519.
Reggio, Isaac, vii.
Reincarnation, the idea in Kabbalism, 249-253; differs from Kabbalistic Revolution, 250; rejected by Saadya Gaon, 105. *See* METEMPSYCHOSIS and REVOLUTION.
Relandus, Adrianus, on a second sense in the TALMUD, 31.
Renan, Ernest, 97.
Resurrection, a tenet of TALMUD and Synagogue, 236; in the profession of faith of Maimonides, *ib.*; as taught in the ZOHAR, 332-337; office of METATRON, 333; treatise of Manasses, 433, 434.
Reuchlinus, his translation of the SEPHER YETZIRAH, 101; his group, 458, 459; his Lutheran tendencies, 460; his Kabbalistic writings, x, xi.
Revolution of Souls, as a root in the ZOHAR 148; the treatise of Isaac de Loria, 148, 252, 417-420.
Riccius, Paulus, his translation of the SEPHER YETZIRAH, 101; his conversion to Christianity, 459; his CELESTIAL AGRICULTURE, xi.
Rittangelius, his edition of SEPHER YETZIRAH, 101, 106, 107.
Ritual of the Dead, 60.
Roach, Robert, 597.
Robe of Glory. *See* Vesture.
Rodkinson, Michael, his translation of the BABYLONIAN TALMUD, 18, 27; excerpt from, 140.

Rome, 320, 323.
Rose Cross, Kabbalistic Order of, 503.
Rose of Sharon, 126, 131, 132, 310; Roses, 264.
Rosenroth, C. Knorr von, his importance to occultists, 476; his occult connections, 477; characteristics, 477; religion, 482; views on the conversion of the Jews, 409, 413; his sacrifices and labours, 483; his critical standpoint, 479. *See also* 6, 135, 409.
Rosicrucians, historical evidences of the Order, 466; as students of the Kabbalah, 465; Masonry and Rosicrucianism, 466; Mystery of the Rosy Cross, 579.
Rossi, Abbé de, his analysis of the ZOHAR, 115.
Ruah, 105, 129, 241, 242, 243, 244, 246, 325, 418, 421, 619.
Rulandus, Martinus, on the terms of Alchemy, 541.
Ruysbroeck on Symbolical Astrology, 546, 557.

SAADYA Gaon, his Commentary on SEPHER YETZIRAH, 90, 104; written in Arabic, 104; summary of, 104—106; scarcely a Kabbalistic Commentary, 107.
Sabathier, R. P. Esprit, 545.
Sabbaoth (Tsabaoth), 198.
Sabbatai Zevi, his Messianic Mission, 81.
Sabbath, 268, 387.
Saint-Martin, his Esoteric Tradition, 486; not a student of the Kabbalah, *ib.*; Kabbalistic complexion of his lesser doctrines, *ib.*; error of French occultists, 487.
SALOMON AND ABSAL, 77.
Samaël, averse correspondence of HOD, 257; according to the ZOHAR, 280-286, 287.
Sapere Aude on the ÆSH MEZAREPH and Alchemy, 425, 426, 427; on the Kabbalah and Chaldean philosophy, 67; on the derivation of alchemical knowledge to the West, 534. *See* Westrott.
Sarah, 298, 300, 354, 357.
Satan, 275, 286, 331, 336.
Scaliger and the Knights of the Temple, 81.
SCHETHIYA. *See* Mystic Stone.
Schiller-Szinessy, on the authorship of the SEPHER YETZIRAH, 43; on modern criticism of the TARGUMIM and MIDRASHIM, 51; on the original writings of Moses de Leon, 58; on the latest date which can be ascribed to the ZOHAR, 557; on the Mishnic period of its nucleus, 27, 62.
Scholem, G., 8, 426, 536.

INDEX 633

Schœtgenius, Christianus, on the Christianity of R. Simeon ben Yohai, 60.
Schuré, Edouard, on a triple sense in Genesis, 502.
Science of the Soul in God, xiv.
Sealing Names, permutations of the Tetragram in the SEPHER YETZIRAH, 101.
SECRET COMMENTARY, fragments extant in the ZOHAR, 167; ascent of the Soul, 167, 168; the Blessed Vision, 167, 168; Shekinah and Food of Light, 168, 169; Resurrection, 335, 336, 337, 349. *See also* 380, 401.
Secret Learning, an alleged early name of the ZOHAR, 58.
Secret of Secrets, fragment quoted in ZOHAR, 173; concerns Kabbalistic physiognomy, 173, 174. *See also* 120.
Secret School, 10, 576.
SECRET SOCIETIES IN THE MIDDLE AGES—Ghoolat Sect, 76.
Secret Tradition in Christian Times, xiii, xiv.
SEDER HA KABBALAH, an important orthodox apology, 93.
Seed, Divine, 230.
Seed of Solomon, 393.
SEPHER DEREK EMETH, Way of Truth, 121, 409.
SEPHER HA BAHIR, or Luminous Book, 119, 120; its critical position, 150, 151; imputed authorship, 151, 152; further views on its authenticity, 152-156; analysis and excerpts, 156, 157, 341.
SEPHER RAZIEL, not the earliest form of occultism in Israel, 134; debased apparatus of, 469; a storehouse of mediæval magic, 519.
SEPHER YETZIRAH, as a vehicle of the Philosophic Tradition of Kabbalism, ix; part of a large mystical literature, 38; contains the germ of the Sephirotic scheme, 99; its description of the SEPHIROTH, *ib.*; does not mention the Four Worlds of later Kabbalism, 101; nor yet the doctrine of AIN SOPH, 110; on the letters of the Hebrew alphabet, 99, 102; on the instruments of creation, 99; the Paths of Wisdom as a dependency of the SEPHER YETZIRAH, 213; contains no reference to Kabbalistic Pneumatology, 104, 235; traditional authorship, 42, 98; ascribed to Akiba, 42, 43; the reference to a SEPHER YETZIRAH in the Talmuds, 44, 98; its different influence on Christian minds as compared with the ZOHAR, 47; Commentary of R. Abraham, 103, 107-109; latest possible date, 109; Commentary of Saadya Gaon, 104-106; Commentary attributed to Hay Gaon, 106, 107; Commentary of Azriel, 109; general analysis, 110; its connections and dependencies, 103-111; Commentary of Nahmanides, 103; other commentaries, 111; the SEPHER YETZIRAH said to end where the ZOHAR begins, 134; not a magical work, 437; speculative date, 65; high traditional authority, 88.
SEPHER YUHASIN, *i.e.*, Book of Genealogies, 51; view of the ZOHAR, 52; narrative of Isaac de Acco, 53, 54.
SEPHIROTH, as emanations of the Deity, 192, 194; their names, 195, 200; initial purpose of the system, 196; first met with in the SEPHER YETZIRAH, *ib.*, 200; tabulation of their qualities and symbolism, 199, 204-206; an occult explanation concerning them, 609; the SEPHIROTH in the Four Worlds, 199, 200; the SEPHIROTH and the Two Countenances, 208, 209; the SEPHIROTH and the Paths of Wisdom, 213-217; archangelic correspondences, 254, 255; angelic correspondences, 255, 256; averse correspondences, 256-258; value of the doctrine, 258; Sufic analogies, 77; Persian analogies, 78; analogies in Avicebron, 95; according to the SEPHER YETZIRAH, 99, 100, 101; how understood by Saadya Gaon, 104, 106; Azriel on the colours of the SEPHIROTH, 110; according to the Supplements of the ZOHAR, 181; according to Isaac de Loria, 415, 416; Synopsis of later Speculations, 605-609; the SEPHIROTH and Alchemy, 427, 428; concerning Daath, 195, 210, 347. *See* Appendix I.
Seraphim, 271.
Serpent, *see* Book VII., §§ 1, 2; minor references, 202, 286, 287, 292, 307, 312, 528.
Seth, 251.
SHADDAI, 198, 323, 351.
Shekinah, Book VIII., § 1 *passim.* Supplementary and minor references, xiv, 15, 165, 201, 202, 241, 254, 262, 271, 273, 298, 303, 304, 305, 306, 311, 313, 336, 384, 386, 392, 399, 411.
SHEOL, 324-332.
Shereera, Gaon R., 90, 91, 174.
SHILOH, 348.
SHIUR KOMAH, 88.
Signatures, Doctrine of, 31, 530, 531.
Simeon ben Yohai, R., his alleged authorship of the ZOHAR, 52, 54; his scribe, 57; his MIDRASH according to the TALMUDS, 63; the authorship merely traditional, 74; his traditional authorship of the BOOK OF CONCEALMENT, 139; Talmudic account of R. Simeon,

140, 141; his Discourse in the GREATER SYNOD, 141-145; in the LESSER SYNOD, 146, 147; account of his death, 147; conversations with R. Yebba, 148-150; in the BAHIR, 156; in the FAITHFUL SHPEHERD, 157. *See also* 18, 28, 261.
Simon, Richard, on an error of Walton, 32; on superstitious sciences brought by the Jews from Chaldea, 34; on Magic and Kabbalism, 35, 36; on the Christian aspect of the Kabbalistic books, 47.
Simon, R. Meir ben, 151.
Simulacrum, curious fantasy of the ZOHAR and later Kabbalism, 412.
Sinai, Mount, 304, 306.
SIPHRA DI ZENIOUTHA. *i.e.*, Book of Concealment, on AIN SOPH, 188, 208; on a holy intelligence and an animal soul in man, 235; probably the oldest part of the ZOHAR, 63, 236; its antecedent, 88; place in the ZOHAR, 135; summary of its contents, 134-139. *See also* 119, 235, 378.
SITHRA THORAH, Secrets of the Law, 118, 120. *See* SECRET COMMENTARY.
Solomon, 229, 314, 374, 525.
Sommer, G. C., viii.
Son, Begotten, 207, 209, 323, 324, 350, 362, 363, 585.
Sons of God, 272, 273.
Sons of the Doctrine, xiv, 13, 14, 169, 198, 295, 358, 376, 383, 388, 600.
Sophia, Gnostic, 376.
Sophia, Virgin, 376.
Sophonias, Prophecy of, 296.
Soul and Death, 245, 246, 325, 326, 327; phases of the soul, 14, 619, 620; creation of souls, 394-396; beatified souls, 256.
Spain and Jewry, 75, 76.
Spedalieri, Baron, on the Kabbalah and the PERFECT WAY, 508, 509.
Spencer, Herbert, on the positive representation of the Unconditioned, 189.
Spirit of God, Holy Spirit, 581, 585, 586.
Steiger, Isabel de, 25.
Steinschneider, 4, 94.
Stenring, Knut, 42, 100, 200, 213, 215.
Stone, Mystic, 228, 229.
Sufic Doctrine, hypothesis of Tholuck, 77; Kabbalistic analogies in Sufic poetry, 77-79; the Doctrine of Divine Absorption, 79; Sufism and Jewish Tradition, 80.
Sun and Written Law, 17, 18.
Supplements of the ZOHAR, two series of, 179; notice of the Ancient Supplements, 179-182; the Later Supplements, 182.
Supplementary Soul, 14.
Supreme Mysteries, 171, 265, 292.
Swedenborg, 225.

TABERNACLE, 302, 356, 363, 366, 369, 371, 393.
Tables of the Law, 307, 308, 309, 311.
Talismanic Magic, 133.
TALMUD, starting-point of, 26; its sources, *ib.*; materials embodied therein, 27; by whom methodised, *ib.*; MISHNAYOTH and rival MISHNAYOTH, 27, 28; TOSEPHTOTH, 28; the GEMARA. *ib.*; TALMUDS of Jerusalem and Babylon, *ib.*; connections of the TALMUD and Kabbalah, *ib.*, 87; errors of comparison, 28, 29; the TALMUD not Kabbalistic, 29; differences between the Traditions, 29, 30; results of their confusion, 30; errors of Éliphas Lévi, 30-32; TALMUD and Pneumatology, 105, 235, 236; TALMUD and SEPHER YETZIRAH, 34, 35; TALMUD and Tradition, 45; TALMUD and Mystic Tradition, 29; TALMUD and Mysticism, 29; closing of the Talmudic canons, 27; reference to Simeon Ben Yohai, 140.
TALPIGOTH, MIDRASH, 318.
TARGUM of Uzziel, 37.
TARGUM to the Prophets, 37.
TARGUMS, language of, 57.
Tarot, its antiquity and importance, 554; first mentioned by Court de Gebelin, *ib.*; views of Lévi and Vaillant, 554-556; analogies with the Kabbalah, 555; its history according to Papus, 556; true attribution of its trump cards, 556, 557; wealth of its symbolism, *ib.*
TELESCOPE OF ZOROASTER, 518.
Temples, First and Second, Book VII., § 7 *passim*. Minor references, 267, 274, 302, 357, 358, 525.
TEPHILIM. *See* Phylacteries.
TETRAGRAMMATON, in what manner the universe proceeds from this name, 613; its permutations in the SEPHER YETZIRAH, 101; transposition of, 447; mentioned by Fludd, 469; its attribution to the Lesser Countenance, 491; TETRAGRAMMATON and the Tarot, 555.
THEMURAH, 9, 36, 41.
Theory of Ecstasy, 80.
Theosophy, Modern, object of this movement, 510; its success, *ib.*; views on the Kabbalah, 511; various statements of H. P. Blavatsky, 511-513; the movement in Paris, 499.
Tholuck, on the connection between the Kabbalah and Sufism, 77.
THORAH, its abysses of mystery, 615; its pre-existence, 90, 616; its symbolism according to the ZOHAR, 123, 124; as the archetype of the worlds, 134; concealment of God in the THORAH, 162; the Law and the World to Come, 169.

TIKKUNIM HADASHIM, New Zoharic Supplements, 121. *See* Supplements.
TIKKUNIM HA ZOHAR, Ancient Supplements, 120, 121. *See* Supplements.
TIPHERETH. *See* SEPHIROTH.
TOHU, 198.
TOSEPHFTOTH, additional fragments in ZOHAR, 118, 120, 409; where found, 170; excerpts from, 170–172; in the TALMUD, 28.
Transcendence, 230.
Transmigration, 148.
Transubstantiation, 587.
Tree of Knowledge, 267, 268, 269, 279, 283, 284, 294, 309, 599.
Tree of Life, 20, 201, 203, 267, 268, 269, 283, 306, 589, 599.
Tree of the SEPHIROTH, 179, 200, 203, 210, 272, 290, 347, 348, 394, 396, 397, 399, 400, 401.
Triad, Infernal, 271, 397.
Triad, Sacred, 271, 368.
Trithemius, as mispresented by Lévi, 489, 490.
TSURE, spiritual principle of man in the archetypal world, xiv, 1, 188, 559, 560, 601, 619.
Tubal Cain, 274.
TURBA PHILOSOPHORUM, analogy with the Zoharic synods, 542.

UNION, Divine, 398, 579, 588.
Unity, 359.
UNIVERSE, TRUE INTELLECTUAL SYSTEM OF, 480.
Unknown God, 363.
Unmanifest Deity. *See* AIN SOPH.
Uzziel, Yosef ben, 111.
Uzziel, Jonathan ben, his CHALDAIC PARAPHRASE, 37.

VAILLANT, J. A., on the Bohemian Tarot, 554.
Valentine, Basil, alleged treatise on AZOTH, 538.
VALLEY, ROYAL, Valley of the King, late Kabbalistic treatise, 420–422, 606.
Van Dale, Antonio, 269, 520.
Vast Countenance, Symbolism of, 136, 137, 141, 142, 143, 146, 208, 209, 210, 211, 582, 583.
VAU, 137, 206, 232, 300, 314, 320, 322, 323, 324, 346, 347, 357, 363; male child or Son, 346; Quest of VAU, 315.
Vaughan, Thomas, his controversy with More, 473; a disciple of Agrippa, 473, 474; his Kabbalistic reading, *ib.*; points of contact with the ZOHAR, 474; on the true and false Kabbalah, 475; on the SEPHIROTH, *ib.*; Christian aspects of his Kabbalism, 475, 476; not a real Kabbalistic expositor, *ib.* See also 424, 466.

Vestures of the Soul, 331; Mantle of the Master, 327; clothing of unfallen man, 282; vestments of good deeds, 285, 290, 412; vesture of holy days, 333; robe of glory, 334.
Vision, Blessed, 263, 399, 590.
Vision, Mystic, 242.
VISION OF THE PRIEST, 409.
Vital, R. Hayyim (or Chaim), editor of Isaac de Loria, 121, 122, 413.
Viterbi, Gui de, alleged translator of the ZOHAR, x.
Voice, 281; Great Voice, 212; Divine Voice, 590.
VOICE OF GOD IN ITS POWER, treatise of Hay Gaon, 91.
Vowel Points, question of their antiquity, 55, 56.
Vulliaud, Paul, 8, 568–571.

WAITE, A. E., 30, 33, 48, 249, 424, 439, 459, 467, 474, 477, 486, 489, 491, 537, 542.
Walton, on the terms Kabbalah and Massorah, 32.
Way of Union, 25, 557.
Weill, Alexander, on Christianity and the TALMUD, 83; on Moses, 99; on Pantheism and the Kabbalah, *ib.*
Welling on Kabbalistic Magic, 521.
Westcott, Dr. Wynn, on the word Kabbalah, 35; his translation of the SEPHER YETZIRAH, 214 *et seq.*; antiquity of Zoharic doctrine, 65; his COLLECTANEA HERMETICA, 65, 539; on ÆSH MEZAREPH, 425, 538; on the Rosicrucians, 466, 467; on the Chaldæan BOOK OF NUMBERS, 512; on the ORACLES of Zoroaster, 67.
White Head, 170, 208, 209. Compare the BOOK OF CONCEALMENT and IDRAS.
Widmanstadt, J. A., his collection of Kabbalistic MSS., 461.
Wier, Jean, on magical books, 520.
Wigston, W. F. C., on the Rosicrucian Kabbalah, 466.
Will of God, prior to the Creation, 192, 220; operating in creation, in the production of the emanations, 193; according to Avicebron, 97. *See also* 20, 224, 248, 402, 528.
Wisdom, 189, 204, 244, 263, 296, 299, 349.
Wisdom Religion, 68.
Witchcraft, Kabbalistic sources of, 437.
Wolf, purpose of his rabbinical bibliography, 26; on the ÆSH MEZAREPH, 426; Kabbalistic MSS. of Mirandula, 443. *See also* 151.
Womanhood, 283, 345, 350, 387, 393.
Word, 198, 201, 211, 212, 219, 221, 230, 231, 281, 351, 581, 582.

Work of the Chariot, 37, 42, 87, 92, 306, 410. *See* ZOHAR.
Work of Creation, 37, 42, 87, 92. *See* SEPHER YETZIRAH.
Worlds, Four, 196–213, 219, 253, 254, 255, 256, 261, 345, 418; Worlds made and destroyed, 141, 142, 232, 416; the Worlds in later Kabbalism, 610, 611.
Writing Name, 54.
Written Law, 10, 12, 309, 343, 360.
Wronski, Hœne, on the Absolute, 189.

YARKER, John, on the Mysteries of Antiquity, 517.
Yebba, R., 148–150, 577.
YEHIDAH, fifth principle of the Soul, 105, 129, 244, 620.
YENOOKAH section of the ZOHAR, 120.
YESOD (Jesod), 195, 199, 200, 205, 206, 210, 300, 363.
YETZIRAH, the third world of Kabbalism, 197, 255, 256, 261, 354, 363, 610, 611, 612.
YI-KING, alleged connections with Kabbalism, 68.
YOD, 202, 206, 207, 300, 302, 335.

ZANGWILL, Israel, on the ZOHAR, as a forgery, 63, 81.
Zechariah, 364.
ZER ZAHAB, 112, 121, 409.
Zettner, Lazarus, his THEATRUM CHEMICUM, 540.
Zion, 210, 228, 248, 252, 262, 358, 371, 387, 390.
Zipporah, 304, 305, 356.
ZOHAR, its chief editions, viii; alleged Christian elements and complexion, ix; alleged Latin versions, x; its gift to Israel, 30; ZOHAR as the WORK OF THE CHARIOT, 41; welcome accorded to the work, 46; impression on Christian students, 47, 48; the alleged authorship of Moses de Leon, 46–54; hostile criticism considered, 55–58; other suggested authors, 59–61; antiquity of content apart from form, 61–64; language of the ZOHAR, 115; a Commentary on the Pentateuch, 117, 118; the text and accretions thereof, 118–121; texts of later development, 121, 122; notes on the text proper, 122–134; supplements and additions, 134–182.
ZOHAR AIKE, 121.
ZOHAR CHAMAH, 121, 409.
ZOHAR HADASH, 121, 182, 287.
ZOHAR SHIR HA SHIRIM, 121.
ZOHARISTS, 564.
Zoroaster, religion of, 67.
Zosimus, Greek alchemist, 133, 535.
ZOTH, *i.e.*, Sign of Covenant, 367.

www.ingramcontent.com/pod-product-compliance
Lightning Source LLC
Chambersburg PA
CBHW071711300426
44115CB00010B/1380